CCNP Security SECURE 642-637

Official Cert Guide

Sean Wilkins

Franklin H. Smith III

Cisco Press

800 East 96th Street

Indianapolis, IN 46240

CCNP Security SECURE 642-637 Official Cert Guide

Sean Wilkins, Franklin H. Smith III

Published by:
Cisco Press
800 East 96th Street
Indianapolis, IN 46240 USA

Printed in the United States of America

First Printing June 2011

The Library of Congress Cataloging-in-Publication Data is on file.

ISBN-13: 978-1-58714-280-2

ISBN-10: 1-58714-280-5

Warning and Disclaimer

This book is designed to provide information for the Cisco CCNP Security 642-637 SECURE exam. Every effort has been made to make this book as complete and as accurate as possible, but no warranty or fitness is implied.

The information is provided on an "as is" basis. The authors, Cisco Press, and Cisco Systems, Inc. shall have neither liability nor responsibility to any person or entity with respect to any loss or damages arising from the information contained in this book or from the use of the discs or programs that may accompany it.

The opinions expressed in this book belong to the author and are not necessarily those of Cisco Systems, Inc.

Trademark Acknowledgments

All terms mentioned in this book that are known to be trademarks or service marks have been appropriately capitalized. Cisco Press or Cisco Systems, Inc., cannot attest to the accuracy of this information. Use of a term in this book should not be regarded as affecting the validity of any trademark or service mark.

Corporate and Government Sales

The publisher offers excellent discounts on this book when ordered in quantity for bulk purchases or special sales, which may include electronic versions and/or custom covers and content particular to your business, training goals, marketing focus, and branding interests. For more information, please contact: U.S. Corporate and Government Sales   1-800-382-3419   corpsales@pearsontechgroup.com

For sales outside the United States, please contact: International Sales   international@pearsoned.com

Feedback Information

At Cisco Press, our goal is to create in-depth technical books of the highest quality and value. Each book is crafted with care and precision, undergoing rigorous development that involves the unique expertise of members from the professional technical community.

Readers' feedback is a natural continuation of this process. If you have any comments regarding how we could improve the quality of this book, or otherwise alter it to better suit your needs, you can contact us through email at feedback@ciscopress.com. Please make sure to include the book title and ISBN in your message.

We greatly appreciate your assistance.

Publisher: Paul Boger	**Cisco Press Program Manager:** Anand Sundaram
Associate Publisher: Dave Dusthimer	**Technical Editors:** Sean Connelly and Robert Woods
Executive Editor: Brett Bartow	**Copy Editor:** John Edwards
Managing Editor: Sandra Schroeder	**Editorial Assistant:** Vanessa Evans
Senior Development Editor: Christopher Cleveland	**Proofreader:** Sheri Cain
Project Editor: Mandie Frank	**Composition:** Mark Shirar
Designer: Gary Adair	**Indexer:** Tim Wright
Cisco Representative: Erik Ullanderson	

Americas Headquarters
Cisco Systems, Inc.
170 West Tasman Drive
San Jose, CA 95134-1706
USA
www.cisco.com
Tel: 408 526-4000
800 553-NETS (6387)
Fax: 408 527-0883

Asia Pacific Headquarters
Cisco Systems, Inc.
168 Robinson Road
#28-01 Capital Tower
Singapore 068912
www.cisco.com
Tel: +65 6317 7777
Fax: +65 6317 7799

Europe Headquarters
Cisco Systems International BV
Haarlerbergpark
Haarlerbergweg 13-19
1101 CH Amsterdam
The Netherlands
www-europe.cisco.com
Tel: +31 0 800 020 0791
Fax: +31 0 20 357 1100

Cisco has more than 200 offices worldwide. Addresses, phone numbers, and fax numbers are listed on the Cisco Website at **www.cisco.com/go/offices.**

About the Authors

Sean Wilkins is an accomplished networking consultant for SR-W Consulting (www.sr-wconsulting.com) and has been in the field of IT since the mid 1990s working with companies like Cisco, Lucent, Verizon, and AT&T, as well as several other private companies. Sean currently holds certifications with Cisco (CCNP/CCDP), Microsoft (MCSE), and CompTIA (A+ and Network+). He also has a Master of Science degree in information technology with a focus in network architecture and design, a Master of Science in organizational management, a Master's Certificate in network security, a Bachelor of Science degree in computer networking, and an Associate of Applied Science degree in computer information systems. In addition to working as a consultant, Sean spends a lot of his time as a technical writer and editor for various companies.

Franklin H. Smith III (Trey) is a senior network security architect with more than 15 years of experience in designing, deploying, and securing large enterprise and service provider networks. His background includes architect-level delivery for many enterprise, data center, and SMB networks. He holds a Bachelor of Business Administration degree in management information systems. Trey's certifications include CCSP, CCNP, CCDP, Microsoft (MCSE), and ISC2 (CISSP). His current focus is on strategic and tactical efforts related to Payment Card Industry (PCI) Data Security Standard (DSS) compliance for a Fortune 50 company.

About the Technical Reviewers

Sean Connelly, CCIE #17085 (R/S & Security), is a senior network design engineer for TASC, based in Washington, D.C. He has worked for two federal agencies over the last decade. Recent projects have included architecting a global 802.1X solution and the design and implementation of a large data center, along with active involvement in other federal cyber security initiatives. Before joining TASC, Sean was director of IT Services at ADCom, which included the design of many global WAN solutions. Aside from the two CCIEs, Sean holds a CISSP and a bachelor's degree in business administration, with a total of 14 years of IT experience.

Robert Woods is a seasoned information assurance professional with 21 years of experience in information and network security, compliance, and leadership. Recently most of his efforts have focused on securing enterprise networks for financial services organizations to satisfy regulatory and industry requirements. Specific areas of focus have included strategic and tactical efforts for the Payment Card Industry Data Security Standards (PCI DSS). Robert worked as a qualified security assessor (QSA) in a strategic role at the world's largest retailer and as a senior-level technical advisor at the largest automobile insurer in the United States. Professional certifications include CISSP, MCSE, and GSEC Gold. Robert holds a bachelor's degree in electronic systems technology (EST) from Southern Illinois University and a Master of Science degree in information assurance (MSIA) from Norwich University.

Dedications

I dedicate this book to my girls (Stacy, Anij, and Saliah), one of which was born during the development of this book. Without all of you, none of this would be possible.

—Sean Wilkins

To my wife and daughters (Jackie, Olivia, and Victoria): It is from you that I draw my strength, for you that I have the ambition to try to "do better," and to you that I dedicate this book. Thank you for the support and understanding throughout this project.

—Franklin H. Smith III

Acknowledgments

We want to take this opportunity to thank all the people who took our words and transformed them into a readable, organized, and formatted text for all of you to read and learn from. Without their efforts, this book would not have been possible. Because we only work directly with a few of these people, there are many people we will be unable to directly thank. For these people, we take this opportunity to thank you for your work in developing this project and look forward to working with you in the future.

Contents at a Glance

Elements Available on CD

Contents

Icons Used in This Book

Wireless
Router

Router

ATM/FastGb
Eitherswitch

Access
Point

Switch

Secure
Switch

Cisco IOS
Firewall

CS-MARS

IPS

SSL VPN
Gateway

IP Phone

AAA Server

Web Server

Secure
Endpoint

Database

PC

File/
Application
Server

Laptop

Wireless
Connection

Network
Cloud

Ethernet
Connection

Introduction

This book helps you prepare for the Cisco SECURE certification exam. The SECURE exam is one in a series of exams required for the Cisco Certified Network Professional - Security (CCNP - Security) certification. This exam focuses on the application of security principles with regard to Cisco IOS routers, switches, and Virtual Private Network (VPN) devices.

Who Should Read This Book

Network security is a complex business. It is important that you have extensive experience in and an in-depth understanding of computer networking before you can begin to apply security principles. The Cisco SECURE program was developed to introduce the security products associated with or integrated into Cisco IOS Software, explain how each product is applied, and explain how it can increase the security of your network. The SECURE program is for network administrators, network security administrators, network architects, and experienced networking professionals who are interested in applying security principles to their networks.

How to Use This Book

This book consists of 22 chapters. Each chapter tends to build upon the chapter that precedes it. The chapters that cover specific commands and configurations include case studies or practice configurations.

The chapters cover the following topics:

- **Chapter 1, "Network Security Fundamentals":** This chapter reviews the basic network security concepts and elements along with a review of the Cisco SAFE approach. It is this core of understanding that provides a good base for the other chapters.

- **Chapter 2, "Network Security Threats":** This chapter reviews the different methods used to exploit a network and the elements on it. With a better understanding of the methods used, network security personnel are better equipped to face these security challenges as they are found.

- **Chapter 3, "Network Foundation Protection (NFP) Overview":** NFP details a layered approach to protecting Cisco IOS Software–based devices. Attacks against the control, data, and management planes and the appropriate mitigation techniques are covered.

- **Chapter 4, "Configuring and Implementing Switched Data Plane Security Solutions":** This chapter reviews the different types of attacks that are focused at the data plane of the switches in the network. It then goes on to review the technologies that can be used to mitigate them and shows how to configure them to best protect the switched data plane.

- **Chapter 5, "802.1X and Cisco Identity-Based Networking Services (IBNS)":** This chapter reviews IEEE 802.1X and the Cisco IBNS framework that are both used to protect the network from unauthorized users. It goes into the basics of 802.1X, including the various Extensible Authentication Protocol (EAP) methods that can be used as well as the different IBNS features that can be used to secure the network.

- **Chapter 6, "Implementing and Configuring Basic 802.1X":** This chapter describes how to configure basic 802.1X authentication on a Cisco IOS Software–based device to prevent unauthorized clients (supplicants) from gaining access to the network.

- **Chapter 7, "Implementing and Configuring Advanced 802.1X":** This chapter describes how to configure advanced 802.1X authentication features on a Cisco IOS Software–based device to prevent unauthorized clients (supplicants) from gaining access to the network.

- **Chapter 8, "Implementing and Configuring Cisco IOS Routed Data Plane Security":** This chapter reviews the different types of attack that are focused at the data plane of the routers (or Layer 3 switches) in the network. It then reviews the different features that can be used to mitigate these threats and how to configure them.

- **Chapter 9, "Implementing and Configuring Cisco IOS Control Plane Security":** This chapter reviews the different types of attack that are focused at the control plane of the devices in the network. It then reviews the different features that can be used to mitigate these threats and how to configure them.

- **Chapter 10, "Implementing and Configuring Cisco IOS Management Plane Security":** This chapter reviews the different types of attack that are focused at the management plane of the devices in the network. It then reviews the different features that can be used to mitigate these threats and how to configure them.

- **Chapter 11, "Implementing and Configuring Network Address Translation (NAT) ":** This chapter reviews the Network Address Translation (NAT) feature and how it can be used in various ways on the network. NAT is an important feature that is used by almost everyone on a daily basis; a through understanding of it is vital now that the majority of the IPv4 address space has been depleted.

- **Chapter 12, "Implementing and Configuring Zone-Based Policy Firewalls":** This chapter reviews the Zone-Based Policy Firewall (ZBPFW) feature and how it can be used to secure the different parts of the network. In the modern network environment, there are a number of threats that exist that are focused on the network and the devices on it. The ZBPFW feature has a number of different capabilities that can be used to mitigate these threats and keep the network and the devices on it secure.

- **Chapter 13, "Implementing and Configuring IOS Intrusion Prevention System (IPS)":** The Cisco IOS Intrusion Prevention System (IPS) feature set is the evolution of the Cisco IOS Intrusion Detection System (IDS). Cisco IPS products go beyond the IDS signature matching by incorporating features such as stateful pattern recognition, protocol analysis, traffic anomaly detection, and protocol anomaly detection. This chapter discusses the security features of the Cisco IOS IPS.

- **Chapter 14, "Introduction to Cisco IOS Site-to-Site Security Solutions"**: This chapter introduces site-to-site VPN technologies and an overview of the many topologies and technologies that are possible with IPsec VPNs.

- **Chapter 15, "Deploying VTI-Based Site-to-Site IPsec VPNs"**: This chapter covers deployment of static and dynamic point-to-point VTI tunnels using Cisco IOS Software. IP Security (IPsec) Virtual Tunnel Interfaces (VTI) greatly simplify the configuration process that is required to create site-to-site VPN tunnels.

- **Chapter 16, "Deploying Scalable Authentication in Site-to-Site IPsec VPNs"**: Cisco IOS devices are designed with a feature called CA interoperability support, which allows them to interact with a certificate authority (CA) when deploying IPsec. This functionality allows a scalable and manageable enterprise VPN solution.

- **Chapter 17, "Deploying DMVPNs"**: Dynamic Multipoint Virtual Private Networks (DMVPN) are a feature of Cisco IOS Software that makes the deployment of large hub-and-spoke, partial mesh, and full mesh VPN topologies much easier. This chapter covers implementing DMVPN on Cisco IOS Software–based devices.

- **Chapter 18, "Deploying High Availability in Tunnel-Based IPsec VPNs"**: This chapter describes the mechanisms that can be put in place to provide a high-availability solution that will protect an organization from outages.

- **Chapter 19, "Deploying GET VPNs"**: This chapter covers the deployment of the Cisco Group Encrypted Transport Virtual Private Network (GET VPN) technology. It provides a solution that allows easy deployment of a complex, redundant, fully meshed VPN network.

- **Chapter 20, "Deploying Remote Access Solutions Using SSL VPNs"**: Remote access VPN technologies allow mobile workers to access internal resources over untrusted networks. This chapter will discuss a comparison of remote access VPN technologies and then cover configuring, verifying, and troubleshooting a basic client-based and clientless SSL VPN solution on a Cisco ISR.

- **Chapter 21, " Deploying Remote Access Solutions Using EZVPNs"**: Cisco Easy VPN is a client/server application that allows VPN security parameters to be "pushed out" to the remote locations that connect using a growing array of Cisco products.

- **Chapter 22, "Final Preparation"**: This short chapter lists the exam preparation tools useful at this point in the study process and provides a suggested study plan now that you have completed all the earlier chapters in this book.

- **Appendix A, "Answers to Chapter DIKTA Quizzes and Fill in the Blanks Questions"**: This appendix provides the answers to the Do I Know This Already? quizzes that you will find at the beginning of each chapter as well as the answers to the Fill in the Blanks questions that you will find at the end of each chapter.

- **Appendix B, "CCNP Security 642-637 SECURE Exam Updates, Version 1.0"**: This appendix provides you with updated information if Cisco makes minor modifications to the exam upon which this book is based. When Cisco releases an entirely new exam, the changes are usually too extensive to provide in a simple update appendix. In those cases, you need to consult the new edition of the book for the updated content. This additional content about the exam will be posted as a PDF document on this book's companion website (www.ciscopress.com/title/9781587142802).

■ **Appendix C, "Memory Tables" (CD only):** This appendix, which you will find in PDF form on the CD accompanying this book, provides a series of tables that highlight some of the key topics in each chapter. Each table provides some cues and clues that will enable you to complete the table and test your knowledge on the table topics.

■ **Appendix D, "Memory Table Answers" (CD only):** This appendix, which you will find in PDF form on the CD accompanying this book, provides the completed memory tables from Appendix C so that you can check your answers. In addition, you can use this appendix as a standalone study tool to help you prepare for the exam.

■ **Glossary:** This glossary defines the key terms that appear at the end of each chapter, for which you should be able to provide definitions on your own in preparation for the exam.

Each chapter follows the same format and incorporates the following tools to assist you by assessing your current knowledge and emphasizing specific areas of interest within the chapter:

■ **Do I Know This Already? quiz:** Each chapter begins with a quiz to help you assess your current knowledge of the subject. The quiz is divided into specific areas of emphasis that enable you to best determine where to focus your efforts when working through the chapter.

■ **Foundation Topics:** The foundation topics are the core sections of each chapter. They focus on the specific protocols, concepts, or skills that you must master to successfully prepare for the examination.

■ **Exam Preparation:** Near the end of each chapter, the Exam Preparation section highlights the key topics from the chapter and the pages where you can find them for quick review. This section also refers you to the Memory Tables appendixes and provides a list of key terms that you should be able to define in preparation for the exam. It is unlikely that you will be able to successfully complete the certification exam by just studying the key topics, memory tables, and key terms, although they are a good tool for last-minute preparation just before taking the exam.

■ **Fill in the Blanks:** Each chapter ends with a series of review questions to test your understanding of the material covered. These questions are a great way to ensure that you not only understand the material, but that you also exercise your ability to recall facts.

■ **CD-ROM-based practice exam:** This book includes a CD-ROM containing a free, complete practice exam. It is recommended that you continue to test your knowledge and test-taking skills by using this exam. You will find that your test-taking skills will improve by continued exposure to the test format. Remember that the potential range of exam questions is limitless. Therefore, your goal should not be to "know" every possible answer but to have a sufficient understanding of the subject matter so that you can figure out the correct answer with the information provided.

Premium Edition

In addition to the free practice exam provided on the CD-ROM, you can purchase additional exams with expanded functionality directly from Pearson IT Certification. The Premium Edition of this title contains an additional two full practice exams as well as an eBook (in both PDF and ePub format). In addition, the Premium Edition title also has remediation for each question to the specific part of the eBook that relates to that question.

Because you have purchased the print version of this title, you can purchase the Premium Edition at a deep discount. A coupon code in the CD sleeve contains a one-time-use code as well as instructions for where you can purchase the Premium Edition.

To view the Premium Edition product page, go to
http://www.pearsonitcertification.com/store/product.aspx?isbn=1587142805.

Certification Exam and This Preparation Guide

The questions for each certification exam are a closely guarded secret. The truth is that if you had the questions and could only pass the exam, you would be in for quite an embarrassment as soon as you arrived at your first job that required these skills. The point is to know the material, not just to successfully pass the exam. We do know which topics you must know to successfully complete this exam because they are published by Cisco. Coincidentally, these are the same topics required for you to be proficient when configuring Cisco security devices. It is also important to understand that this book is a "static" reference, whereas the exam topics are dynamic. Cisco can and does often change the topics covered on certification exams. This exam guide should not be your only reference when preparing for the certification exam. You can find a wealth of information available at Cisco.com that covers each topic in painful detail. The goal of this book is to prepare you as well as possible for the SECURE exam. Some of this is completed by breaking a 600-page (average) implementation guide into 30-page chapters that are easier to digest. If you think that you need more detailed information on a specific topic, feel free to surf. Table I-1 lists each exam topic along with a reference to the chapter that covers the topic.

Table I-1 *SECURE Exam Topics and Chapter References*

Exam Topic	Chapter Where Topic Is Covered
Preproduction Design	
Choose Cisco IOS technologies to implement HLD (High Level Design)	Chapters 3, 4, 8, 9, 10, 11, 12
Choose Cisco products to implement HLD	Chapters 3, 4, 8, 9, 10, 11, 12
Choose Cisco IOS features to implement HLD 2	Chapters 3, 4, 5, 8, 9, 10, 11, 12

Table I-1 *SECURE Exam Topics and Chapter References*

Exam Topic	Chapter Where Topic Is Covered
Integrate Cisco network security solutions with other security technologies	Chapters 1, 3, 4, 5, 8, 9, 10, 11, 12
Create and test initial Cisco IOS configurations for new devices/services	Chapters 4, 5, 8, 9, 10, 11, 12
Configure and verify ASA VPN feature configurations	Chapters 20, 21
Complex Operations Support	
Optimize Cisco IOS security infrastructure device performance	Chapters 3, 4, 5, 8, 9, 10, 11, 12
Create complex network security rules to meet the security policy requirements	Chapters 1, 2
Optimize security functions, rules, and configuration	Chapters 3, 4, 5, 8, 9, 10, 11, 12
Configure and verify classic IOS firewall and NAT to dynamically mitigate identified threats to the network	Chapters 11, 12
Configure and verify IOS Zone-Based Firewalls including advanced application inspections and URL filtering	Chapter 12
Configure and verify the IPS features to identify threats and dynamically block them from entering the network	Chapters 2, 13
Maintain, update, and tune IPS signatures	Chapters 2, 13
Configure and verify IOS VPN features	Chapters 14–19
Configure and verify Layer 2 and Layer 3 security features	Chapters 4, 5, 8, 9, 10, 11, 12
Advanced Troubleshooting	
Advanced Cisco IOS security software configuration fault finding and repairing	Chapters 4, 8, 9, 10, 11, 12
Advanced Cisco routers and switches hardware fault finding and repairing	Chapters 4, 8, 9, 10, 11, 12

You will notice that not all the chapters map to a specific exam topic. This is because of the selection of evaluation topics for each version of the certification exam. Our goal is to provide the most comprehensive coverage to ensure that you are well prepared for the exam. To do this, we cover all the topics that have been addressed in different versions of this exam (past and present). Network security can (and should) be extremely complex and usually results in a series of interdependencies between systems operating in concert.

This book will show you how one system (or function) relies on another, and each chapter of the book provides insight into topics in other chapters. Many of the chapters that do not specifically address exam topics provide a foundation that is necessary for a clear understanding of network security. Your short-term goal might be to pass this exam, but your overall goal is to become a qualified network security professional.

Note that because security vulnerabilities and preventive measures continue apace, Cisco Systems reserves the right to change the exam topics without notice. Although you can refer to the list of exam topics listed in Table I-1, always check the Cisco Systems website to verify the actual list of topics to ensure that you are prepared before taking an exam. You can view the current exam topics on any current Cisco certification exam by visiting its website at Cisco.com, hovering over Training & Events, and selecting from the Certifications list. Note also that, if needed, Cisco Press might post additional preparatory content on the web page associated with this book at www.ciscopress.com/title/9781587142802. It's a good idea to check the website a couple of weeks before taking your exam to be sure that you have up-to-date content.

Overview of the Cisco Certification Process

The network security market is currently in a position where the demand for qualified engineers vastly surpasses the supply. For this reason, many engineers consider migrating from routing/networking to network security. Remember that "network security" is just "security" applied to "networks." This sounds like an obvious concept, but it is actually an important one if you are pursuing your security certification. You must be familiar with networking before you can begin to apply the security concepts. For example, the skills required to complete the CCNA exam will give you a solid foundation that you can expand into the network security field.

The requirements for and explanation of the CCNP certification are outlined at the Cisco Systems website. Go to Cisco.com, hover over Training & Events, and select CCNP from the Certifications list.

Taking the SECURE Certification Exam

As with any Cisco certification exam, it is best to be thoroughly prepared before taking the exam. There is no way to determine exactly what questions are on the exam, so the best way to prepare is to have a good working knowledge of all subjects covered on the exam. Schedule yourself for the exam and be sure to be rested and ready to focus when taking the exam.

The best place to find out the latest available Cisco training and certifications is under the Training & Events section at Cisco.com.

Tracking CCNP Status

You can track your certification progress by checking www.cisco.com/go/certifications/login. You must create an account the first time you log on to the site.

How to Prepare for an Exam

The best way to prepare for any certification exam is to use a combination of the preparation resources, labs, and practice tests. This guide has integrated some practice questions and labs to help you better prepare. If possible, you want to get some hands-on time with the Cisco IOS devices. There is no substitute for experience, and it is much easier to understand the commands and concepts when you can actually work with Cisco IOS devices. If you do not have access to Cisco IOS devices, you can choose from among a variety of simulation packages available for a reasonable price. Last, but certainly not least, Cisco.com provides a wealth of information about the Cisco IOS Software, all the products that operate using Cisco IOS Software, and the products that interact with Cisco devices. No single source can adequately prepare you for the SECURE exam unless you already have extensive experience with Cisco products and a background in networking or network security. At a minimum, you will want to use this book combined with the Technical Support and Documentation site resources (www.cisco.com/cisco/web/support/index.html) to prepare for this exam.

Assessing Exam Readiness

After completing a number of certification exams, we have found that you do not actually know whether you are adequately prepared for the exam until you have completed about 30 percent of the questions. At this point, if you are not prepared, it is too late. The best way to determine your readiness is to work through the "Do I Know This Already?" quizzes at the beginning of each chapter and the review questions in the "Fill in the Blanks" sections at the end of each chapter. It is best to work your way through the entire book unless you can complete each subject without having to do any research or look up any answers.

Cisco Security Specialist in the Real World

Cisco has one of the most recognized names on the Internet. You cannot go into a data center or server room without seeing some Cisco equipment. Cisco-certified security specialists can bring quite a bit of knowledge to the table because of their deep understanding of the relationship between networking and network security. This is why the Cisco certification carries such clout. Cisco certifications demonstrate to potential employers and contract holders a certain professionalism and the dedication required to complete a goal. Face it, if these certifications were easy to acquire, everyone would have them.

Cisco IOS Software Commands

A firewall or router is not normally something to play with. That is to say that after you have it properly configured, you will tend to leave it alone until there is a problem or you need to make some other configuration change. This is the reason that the question mark (?) is probably the most widely used Cisco IOS Software command. Unless you have constant exposure to this equipment, it can be difficult to remember the numerous commands required to configure devices and troubleshoot problems. Most engineers remember enough to go in the right direction but will use the ? to help them use the correct syntax. This is life in the real world. Unfortunately, the question mark is not always available in the testing environment. Many questions on this exam require you to select the best command to perform a certain function. It is extremely important that you familiarize yourself with the different commands and their respective functions.

Rules of the Road

We have always found it confusing when different addresses are used in the examples throughout a technical publication. For this reason, we use the address space defined in RFC 1918. We understand that these addresses are not routable across the Internet and are not normally used on outside interfaces. Even with the millions of IP addresses available on the Internet, there is a slight chance that we could have chosen to use an address that the owner did not want to have published in this book.

It is our hope that this will assist you in understanding the examples and the syntax of the many commands required to configure and administer Cisco IOS routers.

Exam Registration

The SECURE exam is a computer-based exam, with multiple-choice, fill-in-the-blank, list-in-order, and simulation-based questions. You can take the exam at any Pearson VUE (www.pearsonvue.com) testing center. Your testing center can tell you the exact length of the exam. Be aware that when you register for the exam, you might be told to allow a certain amount of time to take the exam that is longer than the testing time indicated by the testing software when you begin. This discrepancy is because the testing center will want you to allow some time to get settled and take the tutorial about the test engine.

Book Content Updates

Because Cisco Systems occasionally updates exam topics without notice, Cisco Press might post additional preparatory content on the web page associated with this book at www.ciscopress.com/title/9781587142802. It is a good idea to check the website a couple of weeks before taking your exam, to review any updated content that might be posted online. We also recommend that you periodically check back to this page on the Cisco Press website to view any errata or supporting book files that may be available.

This chapter covers the following subjects:

- **Defining network security:** Simply defines network security as it relates to this book.

- **Building secure networks:** Covers the fundamental network objects and concepts that provide a secure network.

- **Cisco SAFE:** Details the Cisco SAFE methodology and describes how it can provide an easier design experience and a more secure network architecture.

CHAPTER 1

Network Security Fundamentals

Many believe that network security is actually two words that are mutually exclusive and that the only way to secure a computer is to segregate it completely. It is true that, by restricting all physical and logical access to a computer system, you can ensure complete security. In most cases, complete security of a computer system by this method will render the "secure system" completely useless.

Maintaining even a small computer network sometimes requires a delicate balancing act to ensure that all components (hardware, software, and so on) work and play well together, and that no single system or group of systems adversely affects the operations of the entire network. This "balancing act" only increases in difficulty as networks become bigger and more complex. Implementing security measures on a network can help ensure that systems perform as designed and, in many cases, provide the capability to logically separate systems that cause problems on the network until those systems can be dealt with.

First and foremost, network security is implemented to protect the network and the systems connected to the network. In this "information age," the commodity of our time is information in many forms. This "data" is considered property by most organizations and can be extremely valuable, or to a certain extent, the release of such information can be costly. For this reason, network security has become a priority within most organizations. These issues continue to become more and more complex as technologies evolve. Newer technologies, such as those defined by Web 2.0, further complicate the ability to truly secure "data."

This chapter covers the basics of network security including best practices, policy development, and implementation as well as covers some of the newer frameworks that have been laid out by Cisco to make network security planning, designing, implementation, and operation as easy as possible.

"Do I Know This Already?" Quiz

The "Do I Know This Already?" quiz helps you determine whether you really need to read the entire chapter from beginning to end or just read sections of the chapter. If you intend to read the chapter in its entirety, you do not necessarily need to answer these questions now.

The ten-question quiz, derived from the major sections in the "Foundation Topics" portion of this chapter, helps you determine how to spend your study time.

Table 1-1 outlines the major topics discussed in this chapter and the "Do I Know This Already?" quiz questions that correspond to those topics.

Table 1-1 *"Do I Know This Already?" Foundation Topics Section-to-Question Mapping*

Foundation Topics Section	Questions Covered in This Section
Building Secure Networks	1–3
Cisco SAFE	4–10

Caution: The goal of self-assessment is to gauge your mastery of the topics in this chapter. If you do not know the answer to a question or are only partially sure of the answer, you should mark this question wrong for purposes of the self-assessment. Giving yourself credit for an answer that you incorrectly guess skews your self-assessment results and might provide you with a false sense of security.

1. Which network security element, if attacked, could directly affect traffic flows going across a segment?

   a. Routers

   b. Switches

   c. Servers

   d. Firewalls

   e. Bridges

2. Which of the following are main aspects that must be considered when securing a network?

   a. Availability

   b. Stability

   c. Confidentiality

   d. Integrity

   e. Redundancy

   f. Defensibility

3. Which of the following describes a technique that provides security to a network through the use of a multilayer approach?

   a. Hierarchical security

   b. Nested technique

   c. Security-in-Depth

   d. Defense-in-Depth

   e. Zoned security

   f. Vested technique

4. Which of the following are the main sections of the Security Control Framework?

    a. Complete control

    b. Controllable security

    c. Security management

    d. Total visibility

    e. Hieratical design

5. Which of the following actions are defined by the Security Control Framework?

    a. Harden

    b. Identify

    c. Secure

    d. Document

    e. Isolate

    f. All of these answers are correct.

6. Which of the following technologies are used by the monitor action defined by the Security Control Framework?

    a. Anomaly detection systems

    b. Control plane policing

    c. System log (syslog)

    d. QoS enforcement

    e. AAA/accounting

    f. Management traffic encryption

7. Which of the following technologies are used by the enforce action defined by the Security Control Framework?

    a. Content filtering

    b. AAA/accounting

    c. Simple Network Management Protocol (SNMP)

    d. Policy based routing (PBR)

    e. AAA/authorization

    f. Digital certificates

8. Which of the following parts of SAFE defines security mechanisms that secure the network infrastructure itself?

   a. Security Control Framework (SCF)

   b. Network Foundation Protection (NFP)

   c. Network core blueprint

   d. Integrated Security Protection (ISP)

   e. Infrastructure Foundation Protection (IFP)

9. Which of the following are valid design blueprints defined in SAFE?

   a. Enterprise Internet edge

   b. External WAN edge

   c. Intranet data center

   d. Enterprise core

   e. Internet branch

   f. ISP connection

10. Which of the following are valid steps in the SAFE architectural lifecycle?

   a. Design

   b. Optimize

   c. Operate

   d. Implement

   e. All of these answers are correct.

The answers to the "Do I Know This Already?" quiz are found in Appendix A. The suggested choices for your next step are as follows:

■   **8 or less overall score:** Read the entire chapter. This includes the "Foundation Topics" and "Exam Preparation" sections.

■   **9 or 10 overall score:** If you want more review on these topics, skip to the "Exam Preparation" section. Otherwise, move on to Chapter 2, "Network Security Threats."

Foundation Topics

Defining Network Security

People perceive and define network security in a number of different ways. For the purposes of this book, network security includes the detection and prevention of unauthorized access to both the network elements and those devices attached to the network. This includes everything from preventing unauthorized switch port access to detecting and preventing unauthorized network traffic from both inside and outside the corporate network.

Building Secure Networks

Of the various components that go into making a network secure, one of the first things to establish is what exactly needs to be protected. A number of different network element types exist on a network, and all of these must be considered throughout the design process. Table 1-2 shows a number of these different elements that must be considered when building a secure network.

Table 1-2   *Network Security Elements*

Key
Topic

Target	Potential Attacks
Routers	The types of attack used against a router depend on the attacker's intent. An access attack is used if the intent is to gain access to the router or network. A denial of service (DoS) or distributed DoS (DDoS) attack brings down the router or to introduce routing changes to redirect traffic and deny access to the network.
Firewalls	Attacks against firewalls are virtually the same as routers; however, the techniques might differ depending on the size and type of firewall being attacked.
Switches	Any attack on a specific network switch will affect how traffic flows across that segment. Because network traffic concentrates at the switches, it is important to ensure that all switches are secure. This issue has become even more important with the deployment of Layer 3 switches in place of routers.
Servers	Servers can be a large target for attackers because they are used for data storage as well as computer and network access. If an attacker was able to exploit a server, many of the devices in the network will be instantly vulnerable as data from the server can be used to access them.

The next thing to determine is what exactly needs to be done for the network and elements on the network to stay secure. Three of the main aspects of network data that need to be secured include confidentiality, integrity, and availability, as outlined in Table 1-3.

Table 1-3   *Security Aspects*

Confidentiality	The ability to maintain the confidentiality of the data on a company's network could make or break a company. If any amount of data is able to be harvested and distributed without authorization, a number of things could happen. This includes everything from identity theft and sabotage to espionage.
Integrity	The integrity of data is one thing that many take for granted. Has any data that has been received been altered in transit? If the answer to this question is ever unknown, nothing that we rely on through this data can be trusted. For example, what would happen if someone was able to hack into the database of a credit-reporting agency and alter late payments or delinquencies on your accounts? The information that is received by creditors would be incorrect, and thus decisions made based on this information would be incorrect.
Availability	The availability of the devices and data on networks is one of the most obvious and most noticed problems. Is the network available? Are the servers up and running as they should be? Many attacks that are launched on companies are not looking to exploit the data on their networks but to just interfere with their business operations. These types of attacks also require less technical skill and are thus easier to carry out.

So, the real question that needs to be answered is how to protect the network elements mentioned to provide the capability to maintain data confidentiality, integrity, and availability. The approach that is utilized to provide this by most professionals is commonly referred to as *Defense-In-Depth*.

Internetworking refers to connecting different networks so that they can communicate, share resources, and so on. Many organizations consider their perimeter to be the Internet connection; however, with the liberal use of intranet, extranet, and remote user connections, the true perimeter has faded and is now difficult to determine. This issue is further complicated by the security posture of the organizations on the far end of your intranet, extranet, and remote user connections. It is no longer possible to secure your network just by placing security devices (such as firewalls) at the Internet gateway.

Think of a network as a fortress that is under siege. You need to implement multiple layers of defense and try to use different types of defenses at each layer; this is the fundamental concept behind Defense-in-Depth. Doing so enables the network to handle a diverse range of attacks. A common example of this is an attack that successfully penetrates the firewalls and gets to the targeted server but is terminated by host-based intrusion detection/prevention systems (IDS/IPS) installed on the server. Network attacks have become more complex and can now target multiple areas of the network simultaneously.

Now, Cisco deals with these issues through multitiered security offerings. This book and exam specifically focus on how to secure the routers and switches in the network. This is done through a combination of security framework and IOS security technologies. The various IOS security technologies are covered in the other chapters of this book. An overview of the security approach and framework is covered within this chapter and in more detail in later chapters.

Cisco SAFE

In an effort to make securing a network easier, Cisco developed the SAFE approach, which focuses on the development of good network security designs; specifically, it provides design and implementation guidelines as well as best practices for security engineers to follow.

SAFE provides this through the utilization of the Cisco Security Control Framework (SCF). The SCF aims to ensure network and service availability as well as business continuity. SCF is utilized by helping to enforce the existing security policies that exist as well as to improve their visibility and control.

SCF Basics

As Figure 1-1 illustrates, SCF defines numerous actions that help improve the visibility and control of network security policies.

Key Topic

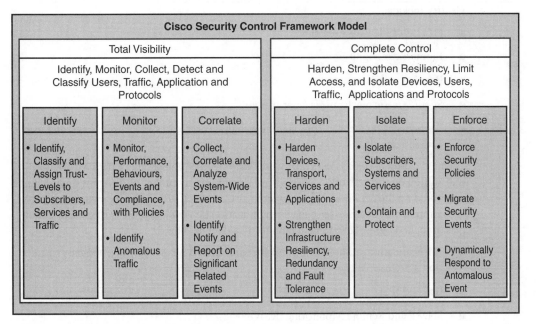

Figure 1-1 *Cisco Security Control Framework*

These two main sections of the SCF, as illustrated in Figure 1-1, are split into six actions that improve the total visibility and complete control of the data on the network:

- Identify
- Monitor

- Correlate

- Harden

- Isolate

- Enforce

For a network to be truly secure, the information passing over it must be easily visible, which when done well, makes it easier to find and root out issues before or while they are happening. The second part of this is to maintain complete control over this data; to make this happen, different things must be taken into account to ensure that this is possible.

The SCF defines the *identify*, *monitor*, and *correlate* actions that help to create total visibility of data access on a network.

If you think about it, one of the most important things that needs to be established when dealing with data on a network is whether it can be trusted, and this determination can be hard to do if the data is sourced from outside the company. This is where the *identify* action comes in. Its purpose is to define a process that helps in determining the trust level of the data on the network and also extends to define trust levels of those users and devices accessing data on the network as well. Examples of technologies that are used to help identify include

- 802.1x for identity solutions

- Biometric recognition

- Routing authentication

- Secure traffic mechanisms (encryption)

- Authentication mechanisms, including digital certificates, pre-shared keys, and user authentication

The next action defined is *monitor*, which involves the monitoring of data within and transmitted on the network. Under normal operations, a number of different things can be monitored on the network, including network elements (that is, routers, switches, servers, and computers), specific user behavior, application behavior, and the traffic itself. Examples of technologies that can help monitor this data include

- Authentication, authorization and accounting (AAA): Accounting, anomaly detection systems

- IDS and IPS

- SNMP and Remote Monitoring (RMON)

- System log (syslog)

The next action could be considered one of the most important. This is because, although the identification of resources and data is important, as well as the abundance of monitoring data that is available, all this means very little without *correlation*. Cisco defines the correlation action as "the interpretation, dissemination, analysis and classification of visibility data into meaningful operation information".[1] Examples of technologies that can help correlate this data include the following:

- Network flow analysis (Cisco Security Monitoring, Analysis and Response System [CS-MARS])

- Host intrusion event correlation

- Network Time Protocol (NTP) synchronization

The second set of actions that the SCF defines is the *harden*, *isolate*, and *enforce* actions, which help maintain complete control.

Many people are already familiar with the concept of device hardening, but for those who are not, it is essentially the configuration of a device so that it is able to withstand, adjust, and/or recover from a number of controlled or uncontrolled events. The *harden* event defined within SCF utilizes this definition and recommends a range of hardening measures to cover everything from individual devices to the entire network infrastructure. Examples of technologies that can help harden network elements include

- Control plane policing

- Component redundancy

- Device/interface redundancy

- Topology redundancy

- Simple device hardening, including patch management and device accessibility

The second action proposed to maintain complete control is the *isolate* action. This action is simple in its concept, which is to isolate the ability of an unauthorized or breached system to affect the other systems on the network. This would include both physical and logical blocks that can be used to enforce the isolation action. Examples of technologies that can isolate specific devices or data include

- Access control lists (ACL)

- Out-of-band management

- Virtual Private Network (VPN) encryption

- Management traffic encryption

- Virtual local-area networks (VLAN)

The last of the actions defined for complete control is the *enforce* action. This action is what is defined within a network to deliver results based on policy. These policies can be static in nature, including, for example, specific bottom-line-allowed use policies. They can also be dynamic in nature, which can include specific policies that are created and used to control network events as they occur. Examples of technologies that can enforce specific policies include

- Content filtering

- DDoS protection mechanisms

- IDS and IPS

- Port security

- QoS enforcement

- ACLs

- Unicast Reverse Path Forwarding (uRFP)

- PBR

- AAA - authorization

All these actions are then used to develop numerous different design blueprints. These blueprints have been based on what Cisco defines as Places in the Network (PIN). Figure 1-2 shows how all these different elements come together.

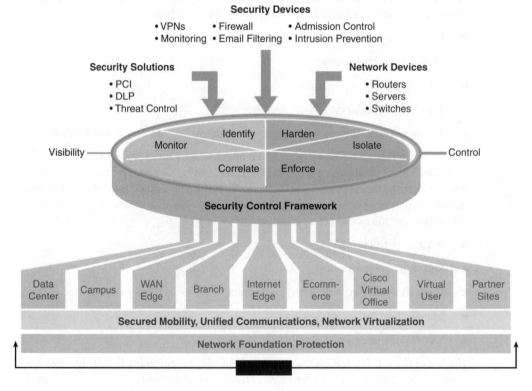

Figure 1-2   *Cisco SAFE*

Figure 1-2 shows that a number of PINs have been defined that can then be used to help plan and design different parts (or places) within the network.

SAFE/SCF Architecture Principles

Before describing the specific design blueprints that were shown in Figure 1-2, take a second to review the architecture principles that were used when developing them.

Other than the general principles that are used when using the Defense-in-Depth approach, SAFE/SCF also uses additional principles that form a basis for their design blueprints, as shown in Table 1-4.

Table 1-4 *SAFE Principles*

Key Topic

Principle	Description
Service Availability and Resiliency	One of the most basic things that must be provided by a network is availability. To ensure that the network is available, numerous measures can be taken that provide higher availability, including the implementation of multiple layers of redundancy. This redundancy can be implemented in everything from individual devices to redundant system-wide paths.
Modularity and Flexibility	One of the things that must be realized with modern systems is that point solutions (a firewall at the edge) are no longer able to fully protect the devices on the inside of the network. Part of the defined framework is the layout of specific design blueprints that provide modular modules within the network. This modularity increases the flexibility that a company has when trying to improve its network security.
Regulatory Compliance and Industry Standards	In today's modern environment, a number of different regulatory requirements must be met by different companies in different industries. The implementation of a networking system using SAFE/SCF design blueprints will have many of these requirements built in as part of the approach.
Operational Efficiency	One of the things that all companies try to achieve is higher operational efficiency. The SAFE/SCF design blueprints provide network designs that allow accelerated provisioning and easier troubleshooting and maintenance.
Auditable and Measurable Controls	On modern networks, it is important that both the network elements and the network itself are able to be thoroughly audited to improve not only network visibility but also to improve the ability to maintain policy, standards, and regulatory compliance.
System-Wide Collaboration and Correlation	It is also vital that the network elements have the ability to share the information they gather with a centralized system for data to not only be secured, but for it to be easily combined and correlated.

SAFE/SCF Network Foundation Protection (NFP)

One of the most important parts of the network to protect is the infrastructure itself. If the infrastructure of a network is able to be exploited, all the other security measures taken will be for naught. The specific parts of the infrastructure that need to be secured include the protection of the control and management planes. Because the subjects focused on in this book involve network elements, which are part of the network infrastructure, Chapter 3, "Network Foundation Protection (NFP) Overview," specifically covers the details of NFP.

SAFE/SCF Design Blueprints

As stated, the SAFE/SCF process includes blueprints that can and should be followed to achieve the best possible design. Although the specifics of each design blueprint are outside the scope of this book, Table 1-5 reviews the basics of each.

Key
Topic

Table 1-5 *SAFE Design Blueprints*

Name	Description	Security Focus
Enterprise core	The core of the network is the most important part of any network; it's what connects all the component parts of the network. Without a stable high-speed core, is there really a network? Although the core does not provide any end-user services, it does provide the central connectivity building block for all other design blueprints.	None; this is typically left to the other modules.
Intranet data center	The data center is where the majority of critical applications and data are stored. The most important part of most enterprise data operations is the availability of services and data, with security being a secondary (add-on) consideration. This blueprint, however, integrates security into the core requirements along with availability. When implemented in this way, the security of the data is ensured as it is built in, instead of being added on.	Service availability, DoS/DDoS protection, data confidentiality and integrity, and server protection.

Table 1-5   *SAFE Design Blueprints*

Name	Description	Security Focus
Enterprise campus	A campus of a network is typically the part of the network that connects to end users that all exist within a similar geographic area. This includes everything from the floor-to-floor building networks to interbuilding local connectivity.	Service availability, Network Access Control (NAC), data confidentiality and integrity, user/department segmentation, access control, and endpoint protection.
Enterprise Internet edge	The Internet edge is the part of the network that connects the company network to the Internet (as if that wasn't obvious). This includes access for the entirety of the company's network, including several functional elements, such as Service Provider (SP) edge, corporate access and DMZ, remote access, edge distribution, and branch backup.	Service availability, intrusion prevention/detection, server and application protection, and content control and protection.
Enterprise WAN edge	The WAN edge is where the corporate network provides connectivity between remote company sites.	Service availability, intrusion protection/detection, and data confidentiality and integrity.
Enterprise branch	The branch is on the other side of the WAN edge and provides connectivity to remote branch sites.	Service availability, NAC, data confidentiality and integrity, and endpoint protection.
Management	The management module provides secure management and communications between devices and central management systems.	NAC and data confidentiality and integrity.

SAFE Usage

The final piece of the framework is a methodology that is laid out to help use the different design blueprints in the best way possible. This is done through the development of a lifecycle model, as shown in the Figure 1-3.

Each of the different parts of the lifecycle has been designed to ensure a consistent process, from the initial planning of a network through the optimization of the network. According to the "SAFE Reference Guide,"[2] each of the steps are as follows:

Step 1.   During the initial planning, a threat and risk assessment is completed to determine the current security posture.

Step 2.   The cycle continues with the design and selection of the platforms, capabilities, and best practices needed to close the gap and satisfy future requirements. This results in a detailed design to address the business and technical requirements.

Step 3.   The implementation follows the design. This includes the deployment and provisioning of platforms and capabilities. Deployment is typically executed in separate phases, which requires plan sequencing.

Step 4.   After the new implementation is in place, it needs to be maintained and operated. This includes the management and monitoring of the infrastructure as well as security intelligence for threat mitigation.

Step 5.   Finally, as business and security requirements are continuously changing, regular assessments need to be conducted to identify and address possible gaps. The information obtained from day-to-day operations and ad-hoc assessments can be used for these purposes.

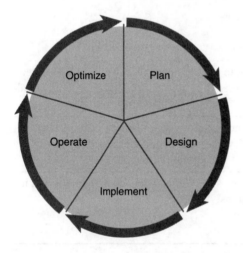

Figure 1-3   *SAFE Architectural Lifecycle*

Exam Preparation

As mentioned in the section, "How to Use This Book," in the Introduction, you have several choices for exam preparation: the exercises here, the memory tables in Appendix D, the final exam preparation chapter, and the exam simulation questions on the CD-ROM. The following questions present a bigger challenge than the exam itself because they use an open-ended question format. By using this more difficult format, you exercise your memory better and prove your conceptual and factual knowledge of this chapter. You can find the answers to these questions in Appendix A, "Answers to the 'DIKTA' Quizzes and Fill in the Blanks Questions."

Review All Key Topics

Review the most important topics in this chapter, noted with the Key Topics icon in the margin. Table 1-6 lists a reference of these key topics and the page numbers on which each is found.

Table 1-6 *Key Topics*

Key Topic Element	Description	Page
Table 1-2	Network security elements	7
Table 1-3	Security aspects	8
SCF sections	Covers the two main sections that are used in the SCF	9
Table 1-4	SAFE principles	13
Table 1-5	SAFE design blueprints	14

Complete Tables and Lists from Memory

Print a copy of Appendix C, "Memory Tables" (found on the CD), or at least the section for this chapter, and complete the tables and lists from memory. Appendix D, "Memory Table Answers," also on the CD, includes completed tables and lists to check your work.

Define Key Terms

Define the following key terms from this chapter, and check your answers in the Glossary:

router, switch, firewall, server, intrusion detection system (IDS), intrusion prevention system (IPS), Virtual Private Network (VPN), VLAN

Fill in the Blanks

1. The _____ security aspect protects network data from being altered in transit.

2. The _____ ensures network and service availability.

3. The SCF model defines the harden, isolate, and _____ actions to obtain complete control.

4. To provide _____, the SCF defines the identify, monitor, and correlate actions.

5. The Network Time Protocol (NTP) is typically used with the _____ SCF action.

6. The design blueprints have been designed around various PINs in a network; PIN stands for _____.

7. The SAFE design principle _____ was developed to make sure that designs were easily capable of meeting industry benchmarks.

8. The security focuses of service availability, DoS/DDoS protection, data confidentiality/integrity, and server protection are used most in the _____ design blueprint.

9. The part of the network that typically connects to end users that all exist within similar geographic areas is defined in the _____ design blueprint.

10. The management design blueprint is defined to increase security through the use of the _____ security focuses.

References

Cisco SAFE Reference Guide, www.cisco.com/en/US/docs/solutions/Enterprise/Security/SAFE_RG/SAFE_rg.pdf.

Cisco SAFE Solution Overview, www.cisco.com/en/US/docs/solutions/Enterprise/Security/SAFESolOver.pdf.

Cisco Security Control Framework (SCF) Model, www.cisco.com/en/US/docs/solutions/Enterprise/Security/CiscoSCF.pdf.

End Notes

[1] Cisco Security Control Framework (SCF) Model, www.cisco.com/en/US/docs/solutions/Enterprise/Security/CiscoSCF.pdf.

[2] Cisco SAFE Reference Guide, www.cisco.com/en/US/docs/solutions/Enterprise/Security/SAFE_RG/SAFE_rg.pdf.

This chapter covers the following subjects:

- **Vulnerabilities:** This section reviews the various number of vulnerabilities that must be reviewed when analyzing a network.

- **Intruder motivations:** This section reviews the possible motivating factors that are used by the attacking parties.

- **Types of network attacks:** This section reviews a list of the current network attacks and describes how they are used.

CHAPTER 2

Network Security Threats

This chapter discusses the potential network vulnerabilities and attacks that pose a threat to networks. In today's open environment, it has become obvious that security must be a key part of everything up front in order to maintain a truly secured network. In the past, network security was able to be managed through the use of a single device (point solutions) or group of devices that existed at the main network entrance. Although this placement must be part of the security design, it is only one of many pieces. The threats that exist today have evolved in such a way that threat detection must be part of not only the main entrance of the network but also part of each networking element. This integration allows several different protection technologies to be deployed throughout the network; the use of these different technologies provides technology redundancy and better security.

"Do I Know This Already?" Quiz

The "Do I Know This Already?" quiz helps you decide whether you really need to read the entire chapter. If you already intend to read the entire chapter, you do not necessarily need to answer these questions now.

The eight-question quiz, derived from the major sections in the "Foundation Topics" portion of this chapter, helps you determine how to spend your limited study time.

Table 2-1 outlines the major topics discussed in this chapter and the "Do I Know This Already?" quiz questions that correspond to those topics.

Table 2-1 *"Do I Know This Already?" Foundation Topics Section-to-Question Mapping*

Foundation Topics Section	Questions Covered in This Section
Vulnerabilities	1, 2, 7
Threats	3
Intruder Motivations	5, 6
Types of Network Attacks	4, 8

Caution: The goal of self-assessment is to gauge your mastery of the topics in this chapter. If you do not know the answer to a question or are only partially sure of the answer, you should mark this question wrong for purposes of the self-assessment. Giving yourself credit for an answer that you correctly guess skews your self-assessment results and might provide you with a false sense of security.

1. A good rule of thumb for "strong" passwords is that they follow which of the following guidelines?

   a. Should be uppercase and lowercase, numbers, and special characters

   b. Should be complex and documented someplace

   c. Should be common words all strung together

   d. Should be documented so that you can reference them

   e. All of these answers are correct.

2. Which of the following are the main reasons why security attacks occur?

   a. Lack of effective network security policy

   b. Insecure physical premises

   c. Network configuration weaknesses

   d. Technology weaknesses

   e. Improperly documented changes

3. Which of the following are the main categories of threats?

   a. Categorized

   b. Structured

   c. Open

   d. Closed

   e. Unstructured

   f. Uncategorized

4. Which of the following are major network attack types?

   a. Reconnaissance

   b. Access

   c. Distributed

   d. Aggressive

   e. DoS

5. Which of the following are considered to be intruders on a computer system?

   a. Crackers

   b. Hackers

   c. Phreakers

   d. Script kiddies

   e. All of these answers are correct.

6. An intruder who enjoys the challenge of being able to bypass security measures is considered intruding for which of the following reasons?

   a. Curiosity

   b. Fun and pride

   c. Revenge

   d. Profit

   e. Political purpose

   f. None of these answers are correct.

7. Which of the following areas of the network are the most susceptible to configuration errors affecting security?

   a. Firewall settings

   b. DHCP settings

   c. SNMP settings

   d. IPS/IDS rules

   e. IP assignment settings

8. Which of the following are methods for performing a fabrication access attack? (Select all that apply)?

   a. Virus

   b. DoS

   c. Worm

   d. Spoofing

   e. Trojan horses

The answers to the "Do I Know This Already?" quiz are found in Appendix A. The suggested choices for your next step are as follows:

- **6 or less overall score:** Read the entire chapter. This includes the "Foundation Topics" and the "Exam Preparation" sections.

- **7 or 8 overall score:** If you want more review on these topics, skip to the "Exam Preparation" section. Otherwise, move on to Chapter 3, "Network Foundation Protection (NFP) Overview."

Foundation Topics

Computer systems are a fundamental component of nearly every organization today. Large and small corporations, government agencies, and other organizations devote significant resources to maintaining their networks, and even the smallest organization is likely to use a computer to maintain its records and financial information. Because these systems can perform functions rapidly and accurately and because they make it easy to facilitate communication between organizations, computer networks continue to grow and become more interconnected. Any organization that wants to provide some public access to its network usually maintains an Internet connection; this access comes with certain risks. This chapter defines some of the risks to networks and explains how an ineffective network security policy can further increase the chance of a network security breach. The key issues in securing and maintaining a computer network are confidentiality, integrity, and availability.

Vulnerabilities

To understand cyberattacks, you must remember that a computer, no matter how advanced, is a machine that operates based on predetermined instruction sets. The operating systems and other software packages are compiled instruction sets that the computer uses to transform input into output. A computer cannot determine the difference between authorized and unauthorized input unless specific filters and detection engines are in place to look for them. Any point in a software package that enables a user to alter the software or gain access to a system (that was not specifically designed into the software) is called a *vulnerability*. In many cases, crackers can exploit vulnerabilities and thus gain access to a network or computer. (See the section, "Threats.") It is possible to remotely connect to a TCP/IP computer on any of 65,535 available ports. As hardware and software technology continues to advance, this "dark side" continues to search for and discover new vulnerabilities. For this reason, most software manufacturers continue to produce patches for their products as vulnerabilities are discovered.

Self-Imposed Network Vulnerabilities

Most computer networks contain a combination of public and private data. A properly implemented security scheme protects all the data on the network while allowing some data to be accessed by outside entities, usually without the ability to change that data (for example, a corporate website). Other data, such as payroll information, should not be made available to the public and should be restricted only to specific users within the organization. Network security, when properly implemented, secures the corporate data, reduces the effectiveness of hacking attempts, and ensures that systems are used for their intended purposes. Networks designed to be freely available to the public need to be secured to ensure confidentiality and integrity of the information and availability to the public. Additionally, properly securing a network ensures that network resources are not used as an attack point against other networks.

Security attacks occur and damage networks because of the following main reasons:

- Lack of effective network security policy
- Network configuration weaknesses
- Technology weaknesses

Lack of Effective Network Security Policy

Because a network security policy directs administrators and engineers regarding how communications should be enabled and implemented, this policy serves as the basis for all security efforts. Security policies have weaknesses for numerous reasons, including the following:

- **Politics:** Politics within an organization can cause a lack of consistency within the security policies or, worse, a lack of uniform application of the security policies. Many security policies make so many exceptions for management and business owners that they become meaningless.

- **Lack of a written security policy:** The lack of a written security policy is essentially the same as not having a policy. Publishing and widely distributing the security policy, along with a thorough training program, prevents confusion about it within the organization.

- **Lack of continuity:** When personnel change too frequently, people often take less care regarding the enforcement of security policies. When a system administrator leaves a position, for example, all the passwords used by that administrator need to be changed. In an organization that changes administrators several times each year, there is a natural reluctance to change the passwords because users know they will be changed again soon because of administrator turnover.

- **Lack of disaster recovery planning:** A good disaster recovery plan must include contingencies for both physical and virtual security breaches. Confusion that results from a disaster can hamper the success of forensics efforts because administrators might not be careful in their recovery efforts.

- **Lack of patch management within the security policy:** A good security policy allows frequent hardware and software upgrades. A detailed procedure for implementing new hardware and software ensures that security does not become forgotten while implementing new equipment and software.

- **Lack of monitoring:** Failure to monitor logs from all available equipment exposes many organizations to attack without any knowledge that those attacks are occurring. Almost all equipment has the ability to log everything from simple events to security breaches; this information should be carefully monitored to ensure quick response.

- **Lack of proper access controls:** Unauthorized network access is made easier when poorly designed access controls are implemented on the network. Improper password length, infrequent password changes, passwords written on sticky notes adhered to monitors, and freely shared passwords are security risks that potentially can lead to security breaches. These can all be remedied when a thorough training program is used to educate users as to the risks of performing these actions.

The existence of all these different vulnerabilities is why Cisco developed the SAFE methodology and why it is best to follow the recommendations laid out in the methodology. There are so many pieces that exist within a network that in the past, much of the design was focused on the functionality of the network and had security added as an afterthought. With today's networks and threats to them, it is best that these networks be designed with integrated security technologies.

Network Configuration Weakness

As network devices become increasingly complex, the knowledge base required to configure systems correctly increases, too. This complexity represents more of an issue in smaller organizations in which a single administrator might be responsible for the LAN, WAN, servers, and workstations. In any organization, the most effective way to overcome network and system configuration issues is to establish and enforce a standardized baseline for all configurations. Configuration weaknesses normally fall into one of the following categories:

Key
Topic

- **Misconfigured equipment:** A simple misconfiguration can cause severe security issues. Whether the error is caused by a lack of knowledge of the system or a lack of attention to detail, the result might be an open vulnerability that leaves the system or network exposed to security threats and potential damage. Some areas of networking that are most susceptible to configuration errors are the firewall settings, access lists, intrusion prevention system/intrusion detection system (IPS/IDS) rules, Simple Network Management Protocol (SNMP) settings, and routing protocols.

- **Weak or exposed passwords:** Passwords that are too short, easily guessed, or consist of common words make it easy for an intruder to gain access to company resources, networks, and data. A "strong" password must consist of at least eight characters and include uppercase and lowercase letters, as well as numbers and special characters. Additionally, using the default password on administrator accounts is an especially poor practice. It is also important that users do not create a password that is too complex to remember. In such a scenario, users tend to write down their password on a sticky note, defeating the purpose of the password in the first place, and affix it to their monitor. One common method for creating and remembering passwords is the "vanity plate" method: Think of a word or phrase and convert it into the characters used on a vanity license plate, and then change the case of a letter or two and substitute one or more numbers for letters. Here is an example: In Virginia, for example, a Honda owner is apparently not fond of mayonnaise. The Honda owner's license plate reads IH8 Mayo. You can drop in an underscore and an exclamation point and you get IH8_Mayo!. Not too fancy and easy to remember. Another password technique that poses a risk is the use of "common accounts" shared by many users. Common accounts prevent accurate accounting of which actions were taken by specific users and make it impossible to determine (to a legal standard) whether a specific user is responsible for a specific action.

- **Misconfigured Internet services:** Hypertext Transfer Protocol (HTTP), File Transfer Protocol (FTP), Terminal Network (Telnet), and other service security settings can all be configured in ways that are considered unsafe. Knowing exactly which services are required and which services are running ensures that Internet services do not create potential network security breaches.

- **Using default settings:** The default settings of many products are designed to assist in device configuration and production environment placement. One of the most common default settings is the default password, or the lack of a password by default. Examples of default configuration settings include the following:

    - On initial configuration, there are no access lists limiting Telnet access on Cisco routers; if Telnet is enabled, you must ensure that the access is limited to authorized source addresses only (from your management network).

    - On the Cisco Linksys line of routers, the default password is "admin" and the default SSID on wireless devices is "linksys." Both of these make configuring and accessing them very easy but make their initial configuration very insecure.

These are just two examples of how default settings prove to be insufficient for production use.

Technology Weakness

All technologies have intrinsic weaknesses. These weaknesses can reside in the operating system, within the protocol, or within the networking equipment. Each of these weaknesses is discussed further in the following list:

- **Operating system weakness:** This weakness was discussed earlier in the "Vulnerabilities" section. Operating systems are complex, coded instructions written for the computer. If an intruder can inject additional instructions into the system by exploiting a vulnerability within the operating system, the intruder might be able to affect how that system functions. Entire organizations are dedicated to discovering and exploiting operating system vulnerabilities. Some operating systems tend to present a greater challenge and therefore receive significantly more attention from hackers, crackers, and script kiddies. This is most likely the reason why operating system developers dedicate tremendous resources to identifying and resolving possible vulnerabilities in a timely manner by releasing software patches. Many manufacturers have implemented an automated method to distribute patches and updates, such as Microsoft Windows Update, Linux up2date, Fedora YUM (Yellowdog Updater Modified), and Debian apt-get. It is now easier to immediately implement patches throughout the enterprise using automated techniques, thus ensuring the security posture of the network against the emerging threats that take advantage of new vulnerabilities. The flip side to this added security, however, is that some security patches have and will continue to be released without thorough testing. At times, this lack of up-front testing causes more problems than it fixes and should be considered as part of the security policy.

Key
Topic

- **Protocol weakness:** Some protocol suites, such as Transmission Control Protocol/Internet Protocol (TCP/IP), were designed without an emphasis on security aspects. Some of the security weaknesses of protocols are as follows:

    - As discussed in the previous section, some manufacturers receive significantly more attention from the hacker community. Microsoft has received more than its fair share of attention in this area. As a result, a significant number of vulnerabilities have been identified within the Microsoft Windows operating system, Microsoft Windows products, and Microsoft networking. It is common for perimeter firewalls to block nearly all the ports utilized for Microsoft networking to help protect against this common vulnerability.

■ The TCP/IP suite consists of Internet Control Message Protocol (ICMP), User Datagram Protocol (UDP), and Transmission Control Protocol (TCP) and has several inherent weaknesses. For example, the header and footer of an IP packet can be intercepted and modified without leaving evidence of the change. ICMP packets are routinely used in denial of service (DoS) attacks, as discussed in the "Types of Network Attacks" section.

■ As routing protocols were being developed, the emphasis was on functionality and communication and less on security. The lack of security in routing protocols resulted in a vulnerability that made it possible to inject incorrect information into the protocol and force a network disruption. There has been an increased emphasis on the security of routing protocols, along with the general elevation in the priority of network security.

■ **Application weaknesses:** Many applications continue to be written without regard to security. Sometimes, this is caused by a lack of programming experience and sometimes, the company's timelines restrict the time for coding securely. Because the primary objective of application development is functionality, security can easily become an item that is not heavily prioritized. Service packs, upgrades, and patches are normally released by the application developer as vulnerabilities are identified. As technology continues to develop, however, security is becoming a greater priority and is now being written into newly created applications during design. Another factor that affects the relative strength of an application is the application's production timeline. The tremendous competition to get products to market sometimes forces software manufactures to introduce products that have not been thoroughly tested. In this case, the actual product testing might occur in a production environment.

■ **Network equipment weakness:** Although all manufacturers strive to produce the best product possible, any system of sufficient complexity is prone to configuration errors or system design vulnerabilities. Additionally, all systems have their particular strengths and weaknesses. For example, one product might be efficient and secure when it processes a specific protocol or traffic for a specific application, but it might be weak or not support a different protocol or application. It is important to focus on exactly which type of network traffic you need to support and ensure that you implement the correct device in the correct location on the network. Additionally, always test your systems to ensure that they perform their functions as expected. Administrators who know the strengths and weaknesses of their equipment can overcome these shortcomings through the proper deployment and configuration of equipment.

Threats

Potential threats are divided into the following two categories, but their motivations tend to be more diverse and are detailed in the next section:

■ **Structured threats:** A structured threat is an organized effort to breach a specific target. This can be the most dangerous threat because of its organized nature. Structured threats are preplanned attacks by a person or group seeking a specific target.

■ **Unstructured threats:** Unstructured threats are by far the most common. They are usually a result of scanning the Internet by persons seeking targets of opportunity. Many different types of scanning files or "scripts" are available for download from the Internet and can be used to scan a host or network for vulnerabilities. Although the threat does not change, the attacker might change his methodology after vulnerabilities are identified.

Intruder Motivations

Several motivations might prompt someone to intrude on another's network. Although no text can list all the reasons why someone would decide to steal or corrupt data, some common themes become evident when looking at the motivations of previous intruders. To refine the discussion of intruder motivations, it is first necessary to define some terms. In the context of this chapter, an *intruder* refers to someone who attempts to gain access to a network or computer system without authorization. Intruders can be further classified as follows:

■ **Phreaker:** Phreakers are individuals who have extensive knowledge of telephone networks and switching equipment. Their goal is to gain free access to telephone networks so that they can make local and long-distance calls.

■ **Cracker:** Crackers use an advanced knowledge of networking and the Internet to compromise network security without proper authorization. Crackers are usually thought of as having a malicious intent.

■ **Hacker:** Hackers investigate the integrity or security of a network or operating system, usually relying on advanced programming techniques. *Ethical hacker* (white hats) is a term that refers to security consultants or those with good intentions; companies often hire ethical hackers to test current defenses (and thus perhaps expose weaknesses). Hackers with mixed priorities between good and bad objectives are called grey hats, and hackers with malicious intent are referred to as black hats.

■ **Script kiddie:** Script kiddies are novice hackers who rely heavily on publicly available scripts to test the security of a network and scan for vulnerabilities and weaknesses.

The dividing line between phreakers, crackers, hackers, and script kiddies is that phreakers, crackers, and hackers tend to be more skilled and normally develop their own tool sets; script kiddies, on the other hand, tend to be less skilled and use publicly available scripts. The motivation for someone to attempt to access, alter, or disrupt a network differs for each intruder. Some of the most common motivations are discussed in the sections that follow.

Lack of Understanding of Computers or Networks

Not all network or system intrusions are a directed effort. Sometimes, a user initiates a security breach through a lack of understanding. For example, an uneducated user with administrative rights on a Microsoft Windows Vista or Microsoft Windows 7 system can easily remove or change critical settings, resulting in an unusable system. Having too much trust combined with a lack of understanding can be equally dangerous. Often, network administrators open their entire network to someone else when access to a single machine is all that is required. A poorly trained or inexperienced firewall administrator can easily open connectivity to a point that the firewall becomes ineffective. Another possibility is that a temporary firewall opening becomes a permanent opening because of a lack of procedures to ensure that temporary openings are closed after the need has passed. Although some security breaches occur without malicious intent, a good security policy can help prevent them.

Intruding for Curiosity

Sometimes, people are just curious about data contained in a system or network. One incident typical of this type is a 14-year-old boy who accessed a credit-card company's computer systems. When asked why he broke into the system, he said that he wanted to see whether he could get in and he wanted to see what was there. Employees, for example, might attempt to access the payroll system to see whether their pay accords with coworkers. Alternatively, an employee might be curious about the financial status of the company or wonder whether employee personnel files contain anything interesting. Despite the focus of the curiosity, the common theme among those intruding because of curiosity is that the data usually suffers little or no damage.

Intruding for Fun and Pride

Some intruders enjoy the challenge of bypassing security measures. Many times, the more sophisticated the security measures, the greater the challenge. Whether these intruders are crackers, hackers, or script kiddies, their motivation is fun, pride, or a combination of the two. When George Leigh Mallory was asked why he wanted to climb Mount Everest, his reply was, "Because it is there." This seems to be the motivation for a number of potential intruders. On several bulletin boards and in several discussion groups, members list their latest conquests and the challenges posed to breaking into an organization's systems. The members of these groups applaud successful attempts and guide those who are unsuccessful. Additionally, many hacker websites publish tools, scripts, and code used to create viruses, worms, and Trojans. These websites are good places for a security administrator to monitor for information on the latest vulnerabilities and new techniques used for breaking into networks and systems.

Intruding for Revenge

Revenge can be powerful motivation. Disgruntled or former employees who have a good understanding of the network and know specific assets they want to target can cause substantial problems for an organization. Therefore, organizations should establish and enforce an "out-processing" procedure for employees to ensure that all the user accounts are removed or disabled and that any passwords for common accounts (which are not recommended in the first place) are changed. Whenever key personnel leave the organization, pay additional attention to network monitoring and intrusion detection to ensure that the former employee is not attempting to access the network using his knowledge of the network or perhaps any back-door access that might have been put in place during his employment.

Intruding for Profit

Profit is a powerful motivator for breaking into computer networks and systems. Credit-card information, unauthorized bank transfers, and manipulation of billing information can be extremely profitable if successful; however, not all intrusions for profit are based on money. A perfect example of this is the TJX companies' identity theft case, which has been in the news over the past few years. In this case, hackers compromised 45.7 million accounts over a two-year time period. The hackers involved in this case were caught, but the magnitude of such a breach is obviously large.

Intruding for Political Purposes

Because economies depend largely on electronic transactions, those economies are vulnerable to disruptions by an attacker. Cyberwarfare does exist and can pose a real threat to an economy. If disruption of an economy is desired, doing so through electronic means might become the ideal method for a number of reasons. These reasons include the ability to launch an attack from virtually any location, low equipment cost, low connectivity cost, and a lack of sufficient protection. A good example of this type of attack was the breach of the U.S. energy grid by foreign entities (China and Russia are accused). If these hackers were able to get in and deposit enough code to alter security and/or were able to map the infrastructure of the grid, much of the security that people take for granted could easily be circumvented. Another more common political motivation is known as *hactivism*, which is the act of targeting an organization and disrupting its communications or defacing its website for political purposes. A good example of this is the recent hacking of Sarah Palin's email accounts; these accounts were hacked by a person attempting to expose what he thought was her political hypocrisy.

Types of Network Attacks

Before learning about the characteristics of specific network attacks, you need to understand the different types of attacks. Attacks are defined by the goal of the attack rather than the motivation of the attacker. The three major types of network attacks, each with its own specific goal, are as follows:

- **Reconnaissance attacks:** A reconnaissance attack is designed not to inflict immediate damage to a system or network but only to map out the network and discover which address ranges are used, which systems are running, and which services are on those systems. One must "access" a system or network to some degree to perform reconnaissance, but normally the attacker does not cause any damage at that time.

- **Access attacks:** An access attack is designed to exploit vulnerability and gain access to a system on a network. When access is gained, the user can do the following:

- Retrieve, alter, or destroy data

- Add, remove, or change network resources, including user access

- Install other exploits that can be used later to gain access to the system or network

- **DoS attacks:** A DoS (and DDos) attack is designed solely to cause an interruption to a system or network.

Reconnaissance Attacks

The goal of a reconnaissance attack is to perform reconnaissance of a system or network, and the goal of the reconnaissance is to determine the makeup of the targeted system or network and to search for and map any vulnerabilities. A reconnaissance attack indicates potential for other, more invasive attacks. Many reconnaissance attacks have been written into scripts that enable novice hackers or script kiddies to launch attacks on networks with a few mouse clicks. The following list identifies the more common reconnaissance attacks:

- **DNS queries:** A Domain Name System (DNS) query can provide a tremendous amount of information about an organization because the DNSs are designed to resolve IP address space to DNS names. Most DNS information is publicly available and simple to query. The two most informative DNS queries are the "DNS lookup" and the "whois query." The DNS lookup provides you with the specific IP address information for servers using a specific domain name. A whois query provides the unauthorized user with the following information:

  - Organization name

  - Organization ID (assigned by the American Registry of Internet Numbers)

  - Street address

  - Assigned public IP address space

  - Public name server addresses

  - Technical contact name, telephone number, and email address

- **Ping sweep:** The output from a ping sweep can tell the unauthorized user the number of hosts active on a network.

- **Vertical scans:** Vertical scans scan the service ports of a single host and request different services at each port. This method enables the unauthorized user to determine which type of operating system is running and which services are running on the system.

- **Horizontal scans:** Horizontal scans scan an address range for a specific port or service. A common horizontal scan is the FTP sweep, which is the process of scanning a network segment, searching for replies to connection attempts on port 21.

■ **Block scans:** Block scans are a combination of the vertical and horizontal scans. In other words, they scan a network segment and attempt connections on multiple ports of each host on that segment.

Access Attacks

As the name implies, the goal of an access attack is to gain access to a system or a network. Having gained access, the user can perform many different functions. These functions fall into three distinct categories:

■ **Interception:** If the unauthorized user can capture traffic going from the source to the destination, that user can store the data for later use. The data might be anything crossing the network segment connected to the sniffer (including confidential data such as personnel records, payroll, or research and development projects). If network management data is crossing the network, it is possible to acquire passwords for specific components and take control of that equipment. For example, this is why it is so important to use Secure Shell (SSH) over Telnet for device management. The methods used for intercepting traffic vary but usually require physical connectivity with the network. The most effective way to protect your sensitive data is to save it in an encrypted format or to send it through an encrypted connection. The encryption prevents the intruder from being able to read the data. Figure 2-1 and Figure 2-2 show how interceptions can occur.

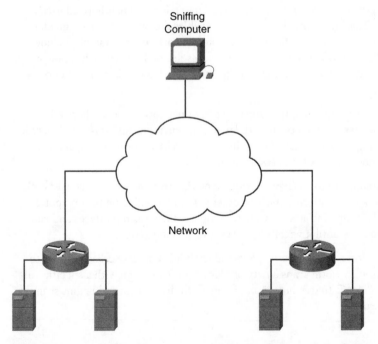

Figure 2-1   *A Computer Physically Connected Inline to "Sniff" Traffic*

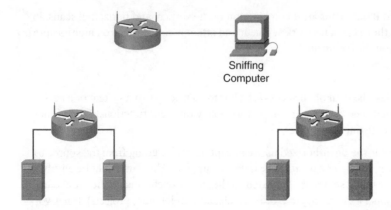

Figure 2-2   *A Computer Connected Wirelessly to "Sniff" Traffic*

- **Modification:** Having access, the unauthorized user can now alter the resource. This not only includes altering file content, but it also includes system configurations, unauthorized system access, and unauthorized privilege escalation. Unauthorized system access is completed by exploiting vulnerabilities in either the operating system or another application running on that system. Unauthorized privilege escalation refers to a user with a low level but authorized account attempting to gain higher-level or more privileged user account information to raise the unauthorized user's privilege level. This higher-privilege level then enables the intruder to have greater control of the target system or network. A more network central example includes router and switch spoofing along with Address Resolution Protocol (ARP) poisoning. These different attacks offer the attacker the ability to change a large number of network variables.

- **Fabrication:** Having access to the target system or network, the unauthorized user can create false objects and introduce them into the environment. This could include altering data or inserting packaged exploits such as a virus, worm, or Trojan horse that can continue to attack the network from within:

  - **Virus:** A computer virus can range from annoying to destructive. It consists of computer code that attaches itself to other software running on the computer. This way, each time the attached software opens, the virus reproduces and can continue to grow until it wreaks havoc on the infected system.

  - **Worm:** A worm is a virus that exploits vulnerabilities on networked systems to replicate itself. A worm scans a network looking for a system with a specific vulnerability. When it finds a host, it copies itself to that system and begins scanning from there, too.

- **Trojan horse:** A Trojan horse is a program that usually claims to perform one function (such as a game) but does something completely different in addition to the claimed function (such as corrupting the data on your hard disk). Many different types of Trojan horses get attached to systems, and the effects of these programs range from a minor irritation for the user to total destruction of the computer file system. Trojan horses are sometimes used to exploit systems by creating user accounts on systems that enable unauthorized users to gain access or upgrade their privilege level. Some Trojan horses capture data from the host system and send it back to a location where it can be accessed by the attacker. One of the most popular Trojan horses is used on computers to make them part of a botnet. After being compromised, these computers can be used along with others in any number of different attack types including identity theft.

DoS Attacks

A denial of service (DoS) attack is designed to deny user access to systems or networks. These attacks usually target specific services and attempt to overwhelm them by making numerous requests concurrently. If a system is not protected and cannot react to a DoS attack, it can be easy to overwhelm that system by running scripts that generate multiple requests. It is possible to greatly increase the magnitude of a DoS attack by launching the attack from multiple systems (botnets) against a single target. This practice is referred to as a *distributed DoS* (DDoS) attack.

Exam Preparation

As mentioned in the section, "How to Use This Book," in the Introduction, you have several choices for exam preparation: the exercises here, the memory tables in Appendix D, the final exam preparation chapter, and the exam simulation questions on the CD-ROM. The following questions present a bigger challenge than the exam itself because they use an open-ended question format. By using this more difficult format, you exercise your memory better and prove your conceptual and factual knowledge of this chapter. You can find the answers to these questions in Appendix A, "Answers to the DIKTA Quizzes and Fill in the Blanks Questions."

Review All Key Topics

Review the most important topics in this chapter, noted with the Key Topics icon in the margin. Table 2-2 lists a reference of these key topics and the page numbers on which each is found.

Table 2-2 *Key Topics*

Key Topic Element	Description	Page
List	Security policy weaknesses	25
List	Network configuration weaknesses	26
List	Technology weaknesses	27
List	Threat categories	29
List	Intruder types	29
List	Network attack types	31

Complete Tables and Lists from Memory

Print a copy of Appendix C, "Memory Tables" (found on the CD), or at least the section for this chapter, and complete the tables and lists from memory. Appendix D, "Memory Table Answers," also on the CD, includes completed tables and lists to check your work.

Define Key Terms

Define the following key terms from this chapter, and check your answers in the Glossary:

structured threats, unstructured threats, phreaker, cracker, hacker, script kiddie, reconnaissance attacks, access attacks, denial of service (DoS) attacks, virus, worm, Trojan horse

Fill in the Blanks

1. Politics within an organization can cause a lack of _____ within the security policies.
2. A good disaster recovery plan must include contingencies for both _____ and _____ security breaches.
3. Unauthorized network access is made easier when _____ are implemented on the network.
4. _____ are individuals who have extensive knowledge of telephone networks and switching equipment.
5. Hackers with malicious intent are referred to as _____ .
6. _____ scans scan the service ports of a single host and request different services at each port.
7. The most effective way to protect your sensitive data is to save it in an _____ format or to send it through an _____ connection.
8. The five core reasons for intruding on a system or network include _____ .

This chapter covers the following subjects:

- **Overview of device functionality planes:** This section describes the three functional planes of a router, each of which plays a vital role in the router's ability to provide a stable network infrastructure that in turn allows continuous service delivery.

- **Identifying network foundation protection deployment models:** This section describes the deployment of Network Foundation Protection in enterprise, SMB, and service provider–based networks, with a focus on the different security control considerations of each environment.

- **Identifying network foundation protection feature availability:** This section provides detailed information about the availability of Network Foundation Protection security controls on the wide array of Cisco devices.

CHAPTER 3

Network Foundation Protection (NFP) Overview

Cisco Network Foundation Protection is a strategy that provides security features in Cisco IOS Software that security professionals can employ to secure the network infrastructure. It provides a systematic approach to protect the router's functional planes that provide essential network services.

"Do I Know This Already?" Quiz

The "Do I Know This Already?" quiz helps you decide whether you really need to read the entire chapter. If you already intend to read the entire chapter, you do not necessarily need to answer these questions now.

The ten-question quiz, derived from the major sections in the "Foundation Topics" portion of this chapter, helps you determine how to spend your limited study time.

Table 3-1 outlines the major topics discussed in this chapter and the "Do I Know This Already?" quiz questions that correspond to those topics.

Table 3-1 *"Do I Know This Already?" Foundation Topics Section-to-Question Mapping*

Foundation Topics Section	Questions Covered in This Section
Overview of Device Functionality Planes	1–4
Identifying Network Foundation Protection Deployment Models	5, 6
Identifying Network Foundation Protection Feature Availability	7–10

Caution: The goal of self-assessment is to gauge your mastery of the topics in this chapter. If you do not know the answer to a question or are only partially sure of the answer, you should mark this question wrong for purposes of the self-assessment. Giving yourself credit for an answer that you correctly guess skews your self-assessment results and might provide you with a false sense of security.

1. Which of the following is the functional device plane that provides the ability to allow network administrators to connect to the device to execute configuration commands?

   a.   Data plane

   b.   Control plane

   c.   Management plane

   d.   Router plane

2. Which functional device plane is responsible for building the necessary information that is required to forward data properly?

   a.   Control plane

   b.   Management plane

   c.   Data plane

   d.   Back plane

3. Which of the following functional planes forwards data through the device and can apply services such as security or QoS to the data as well?

   a.   Management plane

   b.   Control plane

   c.   Data plane

   d.   Router plane

4. Which are the three functional planes on Cisco IOS devices?

   a.   Data plane

   b.   Control plane

   c.   Switch backplane

   d.   Management plane

5. Which of the following security controls are found in the core layer of the enterprise deployment model? (Select two.)

   a.   802.1x user authentication

   b.   VLAN segmentation

   c.   Device hardening

   d.   Routing protocol authentication

6. What three Network Foundation Protection deployment models are discussed in this chapter?

   a.   Enterprise model

   b.   SMB model

   c.   Branch model

   d.   Service provider model

   e.   Data center model

7. On the Cisco Catalyst switch, data plane functions are performed almost exclusively on hardware Application Specific Integrated Circuits.

   a. True

   b. False

8. What tool provides the ability to configure and monitor Cisco Integrated Services Routers through a simple GUI interface and includes many configuration wizards?

   a. Cisco Security Device Manager

   b. Cisco Secure Access Control Server

   c. Cisco IPS Manager Express

   d. Cisco Configuration Professional

9. What application allows the management of Cisco security devices in very large environments and includes policy-based management?

   a. Cisco MARS

   b. Cisco IOS Software Certificate Server

   c. Cisco Security Manager

   d. Cisco Secure Access Control Server

10. Which management application provides authentication, authorization, and accounting services and integrates with virtually every area of your environment?

   a. Cisco MARS

   b. Cisco IOS Software Certificate Server

   c. Cisco Security Manager

   d. Cisco Secure Access Control Server

The answers to the "Do I Know This Already?" quiz are found in Appendix A. The suggested choices for your next step are as follows:

■ **8 or less overall score:** Read the entire chapter. This includes the "Foundation Topics" and "Exam Preparation" sections.

■ **9 or 10 overall score:** If you want more review on these topics, skip to the "Exam Preparation" sections. Otherwise, move on to Chapter 4, "Configuring and Implementing Switched Data Plane Security Solutions."

Foundation Topics

It is almost impossible to find an organization that does not rely on connectivity to the Internet for the success of its business. Whether it uses the Internet as a means of connecting remote sites to its corporate headquarters through Virtual Private Networks (VPN) or it uses the Internet to maintain websites for e-commerce and/or marketing, the Internet has become interwoven into almost every facet of business today. This proliferation of connectivity also introduces risk to these organizations. Information security professionals are continually challenged today to protect the intellectual assets of their company. Securing the network infrastructure itself is paramount to being able to successfully maintain network service delivery.

The following sections provide basic descriptions of router/switch functional planes as described by Cisco Network Foundation Protection as well as high-level descriptions of deployment models and supported features on various Cisco devices.

Overview of Device Functionality Planes

The router is separated into three functional planes. Each plane plays a vital role in the router's ability to provide a stable network infrastructure, which in turn allows continuous service delivery. Delivering continuous service requires that the infrastructure device be able to route traffic, forward traffic, and provide management capabilities.

Table 3-2 lists the functional planes on a Cisco IOS Software router or switch along with the capabilities they provide.

Table 3-2 *Cisco IOS Software Network Device Functional Planes*

Functional Plane	Description
Control plane	Provides the capability to route traffic
Data plane	Provides the capability to forward traffic
Management plane	Provides the capability to manage devices

The *control plane* provides the functionality that builds the tables that are necessary to properly forward traffic. These tables, which include the routing table, forwarding table, MAC address table, and so on, provide the information required for the data plane to operate correctly and efficiently. The *data plane* forwards network traffic as well as applies various services to it such as security, QoS, accounting, and so on. The *management plane* provides the facilities through which the device is configured for initial deployment and then monitored and maintained thereafter.

Protecting each plane is crucial to the device's capability to provide a stable infrastructure. A successful compromise of any of the functional planes will result in degradation, or even worse, denial of service (DoS) of infrastructure availability.

Control Plane

The control plane must be looked at from a Layer 2 and Layer 3 perspective. Cisco IOS routers and certain switches operate at Layer 3 and certain IOS-based switches operate at Layer 2.

Table 3-3 lists some common control plane attacks on a Cisco IOS Software router or switch and the mitigation techniques used to prevent them.

Table 3-3 *Control Plane Attacks and Mitigation Techniques*

Key Topic

Type of Attack	Mitigation Technique
Router	
Routing protocol spoofing	Routing protocol authentication
	Routing protocol filtering
Control plane flooding	Control plane filtering and rate-limiting
Switch	
Spanning Tree Protocol (STP) poisoning	STP Protection
VLAN Trunking Protocol (VTP) spoofing	VTP Authentication
Control plane flooding	Control plane filtering and rate-limiting

Essentially, two types of attacks are most commonly launched against the control plane:

- The first type involves using commonly used legitimate protocols in a malicious manner. These common protocols, or signaling protocols, are what is used to build the information needed to properly forward traffic. These include Spanning Tree Protocol (STP), VLAN Trunking Protocol (VTP), and all routing protocols. As shown in Table 3-3, following best practices in most cases will help you protect yourself from these types of attacks. This means utilizing message digest algorithm 5 (MD5) authentication between routing peers and filtering any inbound route advertisements so that you only accept information that you know is legitimate. Protecting STP can be done with a proper STP deployment. This includes configuration items, such as specifying which device is the STP root bridge and using other tools, such as BPDU Guard, BPDU Filter, and BPDU Root Guard, as described in the Implementing Cisco IP Switched Networks course.

- The second type of attack is essentially a denial of service (DoS) attack against the control plane. Attacking the router with a large number of legitimate packets can possibly make the CPU on the device too busy to handle normal traffic. The use of access control lists (ACL), Control Plane Protection (CPPr), and Control Plane Policing (CoPP) can mitigate these types of attacks.

Chapter 9, "Implementing and Configuring Cisco IOS Control Plane Security," provides more detail about protecting the control plane.

Data Plane

The data plane performs the forwarding of traffic and can apply services to data, such as security, QoS, and so on. As with the control plane, attacks aimed at the data plane and the proper mitigation strategies are specific to whether the device is a router or a switch.

Table 3-4 lists some common data plane attacks on a Cisco IOS Software router or switch and the mitigation techniques used to prevent them.

Table 3-4   *Data Plane Attacks and Mitigation Techniques*

Type of Attack	Mitigation Technique
Router	
Device attacks	Device hardening
Link flooding	Access control lists (ACL)
	Flexible packet matching (FPM)
	QoS
	Unicast Reverse Path Forwarding (uRPF)
	Remotely Triggered Black Hole (RTBH)
	Intrusion Protection Systems (IPS)
Traffic interception	Cryptography
Switch	
MAC spoofing	Address Resolution Protocol (ARP) inspection
IP spoofing	Port security/802.1x
CAM table flooding	
DHCP spoofing	DHCP snooping
ARP spoofing	ARP inspection
Unauthorized network access	802.1x

Like the control plane, the attacks on the data plane can be placed into two categories. One is which the attack attempts to adversely affect the links connected to the device or the device itself, and the other category is for attacks that can be considered as some form of impersonation. From Table 3-4, you can see several different types of *spoofing*, which is an attempt to impersonate something that is considered legitimate, such as the MAC address, IP address, ARP table entry, and so forth. The table lists the various mitigation techniques as well.

Chapter 8, "Implementing and Configuring Cisco IOS Routed Data Plane Security," covers advanced topics in identifying and mitigating attacks that target the data plane.

Management Plane

The management plane is comprised of the processes that run at the process level on the CPU of a network device. These processes provide management functions for the network device and management access to the network device.

Cisco IOS Software running on routers and switches provides features to protect the device management plane from attacks.

Table 3-5 lists some common management plane attacks on a Cisco IOS Software router or switch and the mitigation techniques used to prevent them.

Table 3-5 *Management Plane Attacks and Mitigation Techniques*

Type of Attack	Mitigation Technique
Abuse of management features	Strong authentication, authorization, and accounting (AAA)
Management session spoofing	Protect management access

The attacks and controls revolving around the management plane are the same for routers and switches. One of the methods used to affect the management plane is for an authenticated user to execute commands on a device that is above his privilege level. A disgruntled user doing the same thing ends up with the same result. Without strong AAA, you do not have the proper mechanism to ensure that the administrators really are who they say they are, and you cannot limit their actions to those needed to successfully perform the duties of their role. Using Role-Based Access Control and ensuring that all administrator actions are logged for auditing and investigative purposes are two other things that should be done to protect the management plane functionality.

Protecting management access to the device means protecting the network path used, whether local or remote, by the administrator to reach the device. Protocols used to access Cisco IOS routers and switches include Secure Shell (SSH), Telnet, Simple Network Management Protocol (SNMP), HTTP, and HTTPS. If the path to the device is not trusted, that path should be protected using cryptography to ensure that management sessions are not compromised.

Chapter 10, "Implementing and Configuring Cisco IOS Management Plane Security," covers advanced topics regarding the security of the management plane.

Identifying Network Foundation Protection Deployment Models

Network Foundation Protection (NFP) is typically deployed the same way in all environments. Some factors that will influence the deployment are network size, network type (enterprise, service provider, small/medium business), and the type of equipment being deployed because this will determine the availability of NFP features.

For enterprise networks that are large enough to have all three layers of the Cisco Hierarchical Network design model, employing security measures at the appropriate layer is important. Most of the techniques are configured at the access layer because that is typically the point at which most attacks, whether intentional or not, will occur. The deployment of the security tools is similar to how you deploy network features in the hierarchical design model. The core layer is where you focus on moving traffic at the highest rates possible so that there are minimal services at this layer. The core will have only device hardening and routing protocol authentication. Device hardening and routing protocol authentication are also important at the distribution layer, but there are other controls, such as Netflow Telemetry Export, for traffic analysis at the distribution layer. The access layer is where you configure the bulk of the security controls. This is the point at which users first enter your network. Therefore, this is where you want to have the controls that will prevent malicious actions as well as innocent mistakes. Figure 3-1 shows the enterprise model with each layer's security controls.

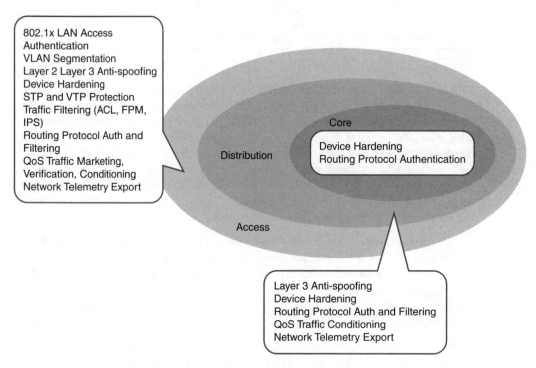

Figure 3-1   *Network Foundation Protection: Enterprise Model*

Small and medium businesses (SMB) will not typically have the network deployed using the Cisco Hierarchical Network design model. These smaller networks will not always have dedicated routers and switches at each layer. This means that the services of the three layers will be configured on the same devices, which in turn means that the security controls found at the access layer of the enterprise model will need to be configured on all devices in this scenario.

Figure 3-2 shows the SMB model and describes the controls that are deployed on all devices because of the collapsed nature of the model.

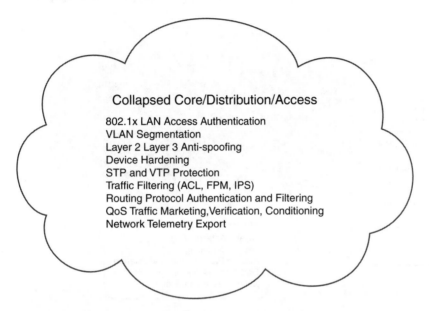

Collapsed Core/Distribution/Access

802.1x LAN Access Authentication
VLAN Segmentation
Layer 2 Layer 3 Anti-spoofing
Device Hardening
STP and VTP Protection
Traffic Filtering (ACL, FPM, IPS)
Routing Protocol Authentication and Filtering
QoS Traffic Marketing,Verification, Conditioning
Network Telemetry Export

Figure 3-2   *Network Foundation Protection: SMB Model*

The service provider network will generally be deployed using the Cisco Hierarchical Network design model. The deployment of the Network Foundation Protection strategy will follow the same principles as the enterprise model, with the following differences:

■ Service providers can use dedicated links, Point-to-Point Protocol (PPP), or PPP over Ethernet (PPPoE) to authenticate users prior to allowing access to services.

■ Service providers should provide separation between customers so that attacks cannot propagate from one customer to another.

■ Service providers will benefit from infrastructure ACLs that will prevent undesired traffic from being sent directly to service provider device's control planes.

Figure 3-3 shows the similarity of the service provider to the enterprise model, with some features that are specific to the service provider.

Reference material to assist network and security professionals with deploying the Cisco Network Foundation Protection are found in the following documents:

■ "SAFE - Network Foundation Protection" design guide

■ "SAFE - Enterprise Branch" design guide

■ Service Provider Infrastructure Security Techniques

■ Cisco IOS Network Foundation Protection white papers

Links to these resources can be found in the "References" section.

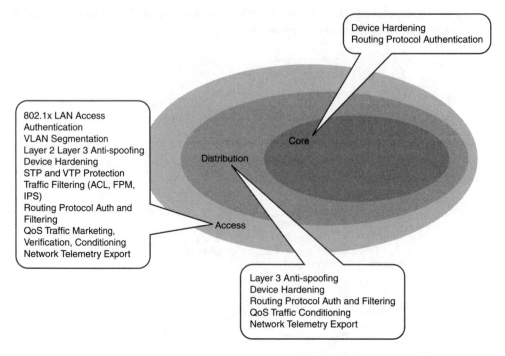

Figure 3-3   *Network Foundation Protection: Service Provider Model*

Identifying Network Foundation Protection Feature Availability

The following sections provide detailed information about the availability of Network Foundation Protection security controls on the wide array of Cisco devices.

Cisco Catalyst Switches

Generally, the security features found in the control and management planes are the same on almost all the platforms; however, data plane security features are highly platform independent.

Cisco Catalyst switches offer a comprehensive set of security features in the architecture of their control plane, data plane, and management plane.

Almost all the data plane functions are executed in hardware Application Specific Integrated Circuits (ASIC). Each platform will have hardware ASICs that are specific to that platform's functional design. In other words, the different switch platforms (access switch, data center switch, enterprise distribution/core switch) will have different ASICs, which in turn explains why the differences in data plane security control availability are highly platform specific.

Table 3-6 shows each functional plane on a Cisco Catalyst IOS switch and its corresponding available security control.

Table 3-6   *Cisco Catalyst IOS Switch Security Features*

Management Plane	Control Plane	Data Plane
Rich AAA functions	BPDU Guard	Port security
Role-Based Access Control (RBAC)	VTP authentication	Port ACLs
Secure management protocols (SSH, HTTPS, SNMPv3)	Routing protocol authentication	VLAN ACLs
	Routing protocol filtering	Private VLANs
		ARP inspection
		DHCP snooping
		802.1x
		Identity-based network security

Caution: Before investing in a Cisco Catalyst platform, make sure to research feature availability to ensure that the platform meets the needs of your environment.

Cisco Integrated Services Routers (ISR)

Unlike on the Cisco Catalyst switches, almost all the security features are available on the ISR because of the absence of the special ASICs that are found on the Cisco Catalyst switches. On ISRs, except for some special functions that can be processed on certain hardware processors, all the security functionality is handled by the main CPU on the router.

Because the ISR uses the main CPU to process its features, it provides a much broader set of security features. An organization can benefit by purchasing Cisco devices in the ISR family and be guaranteed to have all the Network Foundation Protection security features available for securing its infrastructure. There is another factor created by handling everything with the router's main CPU. As opposed to your available security feature set being limited by a specific type of ASIC, owners of the ISR models are only limited by the processor speed and memory in the device.

As mentioned earlier, there are some exceptions to the CPU handling all security features. Data plane functions for VPN traffic can be offloaded to a hardware module. Implementing cryptography on this specialized hardware module will move the processor-intensive load that is required to encrypt and decrypt ingress and egress traffic from the main CPU to the hardware module. Intrusion Prevention System (IPS) features can be processed either in software on the main processor or on a dedicated hardware module as with the VPN functionality. The IPS module makes available additional IPS features and improves performance because of the dedicated nature of the hardware module.

Table 3-7 shows the availability of security features and the functional plane to which they belong on a Cisco IOS Integrated Services Router (ISR).

Table 3-7 *Cisco Integrated Service Router Features*

Management Plane	Control Plane	Data Plane
Rich AAA functions	CoPP/CPPr	ACLs
Role-Based Access Control (RBAC)	Routing protocol authentication	Flexible Packet Matching (FPM)
Secure management protocols (SSH, HTTPS, SNMPv3)	Routing protocol filtering	uRPF
Management plane protection (MPP)		Infrastructure-based IPS
		VPN traffic protection
		Network export

Cisco Supporting Management Components

The following sections discuss the various Cisco Supporting Management components that complement the Cisco IOS Software Catalyst switches and the Cisco Integrated Services Routers (ISR).

Cisco Configuration Professional (CPP)

The Cisco Configuration Professional (CPP) is a GUI device management application for Cisco ISRs. It is provided by Cisco at no charge. It makes performing several complex configuration tasks very simple through the use of built-in wizards. Configuration tasks that can be completed using smart wizards include general router and firewall configurations, IPS, VPN, and Unified Communications features. Also included is a feature that hardens a router by automatically implementing a wide array of security features that essentially "lock down" the router without having to configure the features individually. Another feature included in CPP is an auditing feature in which the device's security configuration is checked and recommendations are made based on best practices provided by the Cisco Technical Assistance Center (TAC).

Cisco Security Manager (CSM)

Cisco Security Manager (CSM) is an application that can be used to deploy and manage security features on Cisco devices. CSM is designed to help large enterprise customers or service providers deploy their Cisco Network Foundation Protection strategy with more ease and consistency than they could if they performed the tasks manually. CSM gives organizations the capability to deploy and manage Cisco firewalls, VPNs, IPS sensors, and the Cisco IOS Software firewall and IPS features on the ISRs. CSM includes a workflow process with approval features as well as integrates with Cisco Secure Access Control Server (ACS) and Cisco Security Monitoring, Analysis, and Response System (CS-MARS) to provide RBAC and correlate events with firewall rules, respectively.

Cisco Secure Access Control Server (CS ACS)

The Cisco Secure Access Control Server (CS ACS) is an authentication server that supports TACACS and RADIUS protocols. Despite the growing complexities in today's networks,

Cisco Secure ACS provides authentication, authorization, and accounting (AAA) services for several connection types, devices, and user/groups:

■ CS ACS provides AAA services for device administration by authenticating users and authorizing commands while maintaining logs that provide audit trails.

■ CS ACS integrates with remote access devices to provide adherence to corporate security policies for remote access users and external connections to third-party vendors and partners.

■ CS ACS provides authentication and authorization for wireless users and devices to mitigate any possible attacks being launched through wireless connections.

■ CS ACS integrates with Network Admission Control access servers to validate and enforce posture requirements and access restrictions.

■ CS ACS provides a centralized platform from which security administrators can manage a wide range of security policies, protocols, and other requirements.

■ CS ACS provides support for other authentication platforms such as Microsoft Windows Active Directory, Lightweight Directory Access Protocol (LDAP) servers, and so on and allows organizations to capitalize on technologies that are already in place in an environment.

■ CS ACS can be deployed in an environment in a software (a Microsoft Windows Server application), hardware (an appliance), or a virtual appliance (VMware vSphere) format.

Cisco IOS Software Certificate Server

Cisco also provides a limited-functionality certificate server. The Cisco IOS Software Certificate Server is a certificate server that runs inside the Cisco IOS Software. The benefits are as follows:

■ Easier deployment of public-key infrastructure (PKI)–based services using the built-in support for device default behaviors.

■ This software is integrated with the Cisco IOS Software, which alleviates the need to purchase a separate server or appliance.

Cisco Security Monitoring, Analysis, and Response System (CS-MARS)

With the new heightened awareness of the need for security controls comes an ever-increasing amount of security log data. Log data received from devices such as firewalls, intrusion prevention systems, authentication servers, and so on is received at alarming rates. The task of monitoring these logs is daunting to say the least. In fact, in larger organizations, it is not even feasible to attempt to try to keep up with analysis of the log data manually.

The Cisco Security Monitoring, Analysis, and Response System (CS-MARS) is an application that performs the analysis of log data and transforms it into usable graphical information that can be used by security administrators to react efficiently to attacks and breaches:

■ CS-MARS can identify threats by using the information it receives to become aware of your environment.

■ Using the awareness and event correlation, CS-MARS makes recommendations for actions that can be taken to mitigate current threats.

■ Integration with Cisco Security Manager allows administrators to simply approve the mitigation technique recommended by CS-MARS, and the change is deployed to stop the threat.

Cisco IPS Manager Express

Cisco IPS Manager Express is a free event-monitoring solution for Cisco IPS events, including the IPS functionality provided by Cisco IOS Software running on a Cisco ISR. The application can assist in configuring, managing, and tuning Cisco IOS sensors, Cisco Advanced Inspection and Prevention Security Modules, Cisco Catalyst 6500 Series Intrusion Detection System Modules, Cisco IDS Network Modules, and Cisco IOS IPS software and modules. Besides reporting capabilities, the software also has a real-time event viewer for troubleshooting current events.

Exam Preparation

As mentioned in the section, "How to Use This Book," in the Introduction, you have several choices for exam preparation: the exercises here, the memory tables in Appendix C, the final exam preparation chapter, and the exam simulation questions on the CD-ROM. The following questions present a bigger challenge than the exam itself because they use an open-ended question format. By using this more difficult format, you exercise your memory better and prove your conceptual and factual knowledge of this chapter. You can find the answers to these questions in Appendix A, "Answers to the DIKTA Quizzes and Fill in the Blanks Questions."

Review All Key Topics

Review the most important topics in this chapter, noted with the Key Topics icon in the margin of the page. Table 3-8 lists a reference of these key topics and the page numbers on which each is found.

Table 3-8   *Key Topics*

Key Topic Element	Description	Page
Table 3-2	Cisco IOS software network device functional planes	42
Table 3-3	Control plane attacks and mitigation techniques	43
Table 3-4	Data plane attacks and mitigation techniques	44
Table 3-5	Management plane attacks and mitigation techniques	45

Complete Tables and Lists from Memory

Print a copy of Appendix C, "Memory Tables" (found on the CD), or at least the section for this chapter, and complete the tables and lists from memory. Appendix D, "Memory Table Answers," also on the CD, includes completed tables and lists to check your work.

Define Key Terms

Define the following key terms from this chapter, and check your answers in the Glossary:

control plane, data plane, management plane

Fill in the Blanks

1. Cisco Integrated Services Routers (ISR) differ from the Catalyst switches in that the security features are handled by the _____ in the router as opposed to specialized ASICs.

2. The Cisco Configuration Professional (CPP) is a GUI device-management application for _____.

3. _____ is an application from Cisco that can be used to deploy and manage security features on Cisco devices.

4. _____ is the process of determining that a user is who he says he is.

5. Ensuring that a user can only execute commands for which he has the proper privilege level is called _____.

6. _____ scans scan the service ports of a single host and request different services at each port.

7. _____ is a free event-monitoring solution for Cisco IPS events, including the IPS functionality provided by Cisco IOS Software running on a Cisco ISR.

8. Availability of security features on the Cisco IOS Software Catalyst switch is very _____ dependent.

References

For additional information, refer to these resources:

Cisco Systems, Inc. Cisco Network Foundation Protection, www.cisco.com/go/nfp.

SAFE - Network Foundation Protection, www.cisco.com/US/docs/solutions/Enterprise/Security/SAFE_RG/chap2.html.

SAFE - Enterprise Branch, www.cisco.com/US/docs/solutions/Enterprise/Security/SAFE_RG/chap8.html.

Service Provider Infrastructure Security Techniques, www.cisco.com/web/about/security/intelligence/sp_infrastruct_scty.html.

Cisco IOS Network Foundation Protection White Papers, www.cisco.com/en/US/products/ps6642/prod_white_papers_list.html.

This chapter covers the following subjects:

- **Switched data plane attack types:** This section reviews the different types of attacks that are focused on the data plane of switches.

- **Switched data plane security technologies:** This section goes over the specific technologies that can be used to mitigate the various attack types and describes how to configure them.

CHAPTER 4

Configuring and Implementing Switched Data Plane Security Solutions

An attacker can attempt to exploit a network in numerous ways. This chapter looks at the ways that target the technologies that are used on switches and are aimed at those used on the data plane. These technologies include Content Addressable Memory (CAM) tables, Address Resolution Protocol (ARP), Spanning Tree, virtual local-area networks (VLAN), and Dynamic Host Configuration Protocol (DHCP). This chapter also covers the configuration of these technologies so that they can be configured in a way that offers the smallest risk of attack.

"Do I Know This Already?" Quiz

The "Do I Know This Already?" quiz helps you decide whether you really need to read the entire chapter. If you already intend to read the entire chapter, you do not necessarily need to answer these questions now.

The ten-question quiz, derived from the major sections in the "Foundation Topics" section of this chapter, helps you determine how to spend your limited study time.

Table 4-1 outlines the major topics discussed in this chapter and the "Do I Know This Already?" quiz questions that correspond to those topics.

Table 4-1 *"Do I Know This Already?" Foundation Topics Section-to-Question Mapping*

Foundation Topics Section	Questions Covered in This Section
Switched Data Plane Attack Types	1, 2, 5, 6
Switched Data Plane Security Technologies	3, 4, 7–10

Caution: The goal of self-assessment is to gauge your mastery of the topics in this chapter. If you do not know the answer to a question or are only partially sure of the answer, you should mark this question wrong for purposes of the self-assessment. Giving yourself credit for an answer that you correctly guess skews your self-assessment results and might provide you with a false sense of security.

1. What is the default inactivity expire time period on a Cisco Catalyst switch CAM table?

   a. 1 minute

   b. 5 minutes

   c. 10 minutes

   d. 50 minutes

2. Which of the following attack types describes when an attacker tries to take over the root bridge functionality on a network?

   a. STP spoofing

   b. VLAN hopping

   c. CAM flooding

   d. ARP spoofing

3. Which command enables port security on an interface?

   a. **switchport mode port-security**

   b. **switchport mode interface-security**

   c. **switchport interface-security**

   d. **switchport port-security**

4. What is the default action mode for security violations?

   a. Protect

   b. Restrict

   c. Shutdown

5. The DTP state on a trunk port can be set to what?

   a. Auto, on, off, undesirable, or non-negotiate

   b. Auto, on, off, desirable, or non-negotiate

   c. Auto, on, off, desirable, or negotiate

   d. Auto, on, off, undesirable, or negotiate

6. What are the two different types of VLAN hopping attacks?

   a. Switch spoofing and double tagging

   b. Switch goofing and double teaming

   c. Switch impersonation and double grouping

   d. Switch imitation and double alliance

7. Which features of Cisco IOS Software enable you to mitigate STP manipulation? (Select two.)

    a. spanning-tree bpduguard

    b. spanning-tree guard root

    c. set spantree global-default loopguard enable

    d. set udld enable

8. What are the three types of private VLAN ports?

    a. Neighborhood, remote, and loose

    b. Community, isolated, and promiscuous

    c. Communal, remote, and licentious

    d. Area, secluded, and wanton

9. Which of the following databases is used by Dynamic ARP inspection?

    a. DAI group table

    b. IPSG snooping table

    c. DHCP snooping binding table

    d. CAM filtering table

10. Which of the following PVLAN edge ports is unable to communicate with other PVLAN edge ports?

    a. Isolated port

    b. Nonprotected port

    c. Secluded port

    d. Protected port

The answers to the "Do I Know This Already?" quiz are found in Appendix A. The suggested choices for your next step are as follows:

- **8 or less overall score:** Read the entire chapter. This includes the "Foundation Topics" and the "Exam Preparation" sections.

- **9 or 10 overall score:** If you want more review on these topics, skip to the "Exam Preparation" section. Otherwise, move on to Chapter 5, "802.1X and Cisco Identity-Based Networking Services (IBNS)."

Foundation Topics

Switched Data Plane Attack Types

It is first important to understand the different types of attacks that are being used before really learning about the security technologies that are available to mitigate them. The switched infrastructure is every bit as vulnerable to attack as the traditional routed infrastructure. With modern switches taking over many of the duties that have been traditionally reserved for the routers on the network, it is even more of a target than before because they are now serving multiple layers.

The most common types of switched data plane attacks are as follows:

- VLAN hopping

- CAM flooding

- MAC address spoofing

- STP spoofing

- DHCP "starvation"

- DHCP server spoofing

- ARP spoofing

- IP spoofing

VLAN Hopping Attacks

VLANs are a simple way to segment the network within an enterprise to improve performance and simplify maintenance. Each VLAN consists of a single broadcast domain. Ports are restricted to receiving only packets that are part of their assigned VLAN. The VLAN information can also be carried between switches in a LAN using trunk ports by tagging packets with an identification header. Trunk ports have access to all VLANs by default. They route traffic for multiple VLANs across the same physical link. Two types of trunking protocols include 802.1Q and Inter-Switch Link (ISL), with 802.1Q being primarily used.

The switchport trunking mode (trunk or access) can be sensed using Dynamic Trunking Protocol (DTP), which automatically senses whether the adjacent device to the port is capable of trunking. If so, it synchronizes the trunking mode on the two ends. The DTP state on a trunk port can be set to auto, on, off, desirable, or non-negotiate.

One of the areas of concern with Layer 2 security is the variety of mechanisms by which packets that are sent from one VLAN can be intercepted or redirected to another VLAN, which is called *VLAN hopping*. VLAN hopping attacks are designed to allow attackers to bypass a Layer 3 device when communicating from one VLAN to another. The attack works by taking advantage of an incorrectly configured trunk port.

It is important to note that this type of attack does not work on a single switch because the frame will never be forwarded to the destination; however, in a multiswitch environment, a trunk link could be exploited to transmit the packet. There are two different types of VLAN hopping attacks:

- **Switch spoofing:** The network attacker configures a device to spoof a switch by emulating either ISL or 802.1Q, and DTP signaling. This makes the attacker device appear to be a switch with a trunk port and therefore a member of all VLANs.

- **Double tagging:** Another variation of the VLAN hopping attack involves tagging the transmitted frames with two 802.1Q headers, with the outer 802.1Q header matching the configured trunk native VLAN. When the first switch sees that the first tag on the double-tagged frame is equal to that of the native VLAN, it strips this first tag off the frame and then forwards it with the inner 802.1Q tag intact across the trunk. The second switch then forwards the packet based on the VLAN ID in the second 802.1Q header, as illustrated in Figure 4-1.

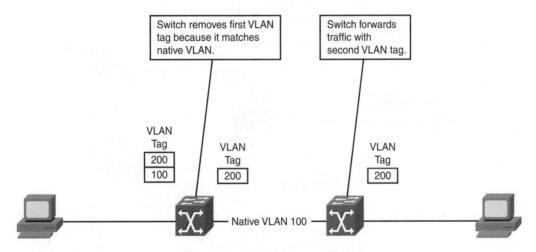

Figure 4-1   *Double-Tagging VLAN Hopping Attack*

CAM Flooding Attacks

The CAM table in a switch stores information, such as MAC addresses, switchport, and associated VLAN parameters. It is similar to a router's routing table. CAM tables have a fixed size and are populated when devices connect to the switch.

When a Layer 2 switch receives a frame, the switch looks in the CAM table for the matching destination MAC address. If an entry exists for that MAC address, the switch forwards the frame to the port identified in the CAM table for that MAC address. If the MAC address is not in the CAM table, the switch forwards the frame out all ports on the switch. If the switch sees a response as a result of the forwarded frame, it updates the CAM table with the port on which the communication was received.

Figure 4-2 shows the CAM table operation.

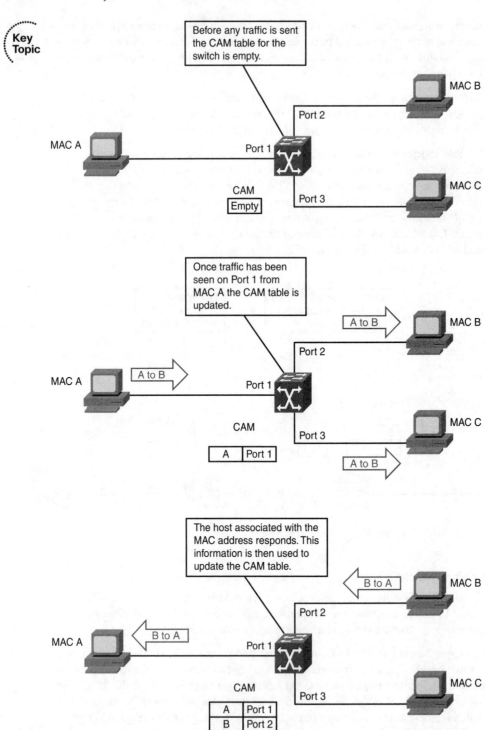

Figure 4-2   *CAM Table Operation*

The CAM table has a limited size, and these entries expire after a certain inactivity period (the default CAM aging timer on the Cisco Catalyst switch is 5 minutes). If enough MAC addresses are flooded to a switch before existing entries expire, the CAM table fills up and new entries are not accepted. Keep in mind, however, that on modern large switches, the size of the tables is typically over 100,000 addresses. When the CAM table is full, the switch starts flooding the packets out all ports. This scenario is called a *CAM table overflow* or *CAM flooding*.

In a CAM flooding attack, an attacker sends thousands of bogus MAC addresses from one port, which looks, to the switch, like valid hosts' communication. The goal is to flood the switch with traffic that fills the CAM table with false entries. When the CAM table is full, the switch broadcasts traffic without a CAM entry out all its ports; this broadcasting out all ports allows the attacker to see traffic not normally sent to their port. However, this flooding is limited to those ports that are configured into the same VLAN as the source attack port.

Figure 4-3 shows a CAM flooding attack.

MAC Address Spoofing

MAC address spoofing involves the use of a known MAC address of another host that is authorized to access the network. The attacker attempts to make the target switch forward frames destined for the actual host to be forwarded to the attacker device instead. This is done by sending a frame with the other host's source Ethernet address, with the objective to overwrite the CAM table entry. After the CAM is overwritten, all the packets destined for the actual host will be diverted to the attacker. If the original host sends out traffic, the CAM table will be rewritten again, moving the traffic back to the original host port.

Figure 4-4 shows how MAC spoofing works.

Spanning Tree Protocol (STP) Spoofing Attacks

STP prevents bridging loops in a redundant switched network environment. By avoiding loops, you can ensure that broadcast traffic does not become a traffic storm.

STP is a hierarchical tree-like topology with a "root" switch at the top. A switch is elected as root based on the lowest configured priority of any switch (0 through 65,535). When a switch boots up, it begins a process of identifying other switches and determining the root bridge. After a root bridge is elected, the topology is then established from its perspective of the connectivity. The switches determine the path to the root bridge, and all redundant paths are blocked. STP sends configuration and topology change notifications and acknowledgments (TCN/TCA) using bridge protocol data units (BPDU).

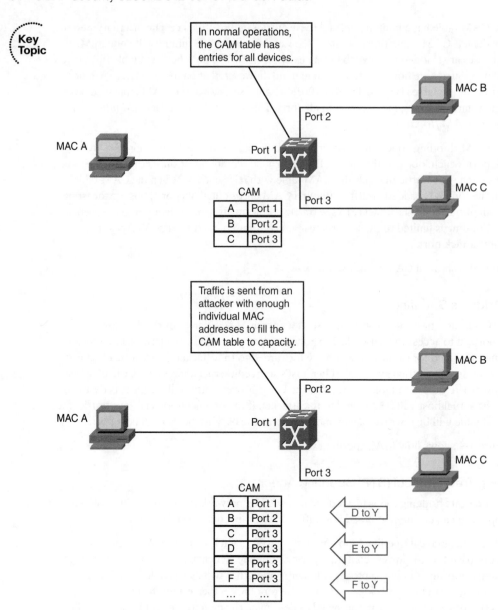

Figure 4-3 *CAM Flooding Attack*

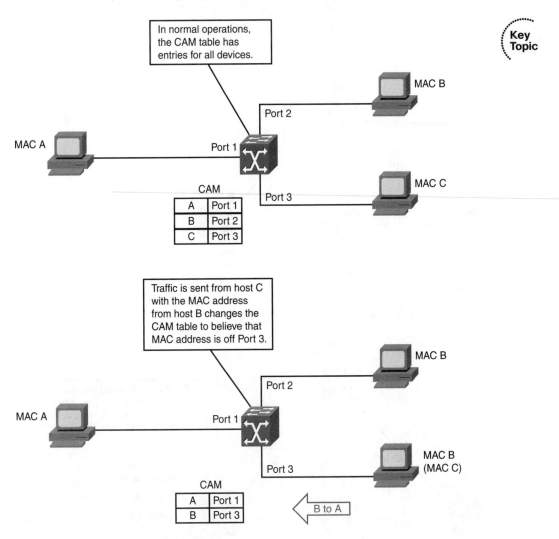

Figure 4-4 *MAC Address Spoofing Attack*

An STP attack involves an attacker spoofing the root bridge in the topology. The attacker broadcasts out an STP configuration/topology change BPDU in an attempt to force an STP recalculation. The BPDU sent out announces that the attacker's system has a lower bridge priority. This lower switch priority will prompt STP to perform a root election, resulting in the switch with the lower priority winning. The attacker (acting as the root switch) can then see a variety of frames forwarded from other switches to it. Besides the capability to take over the root switch, the capability to cause STP recalculation can also cause a denial of service (DoS) condition on the network by causing an interruption of 30 to 45 seconds each time the root bridge changes, depending on the version of STP implemented.

Figure 4-5 shows an attacker using STP network topology changes to force its host to be elected as the root bridge.

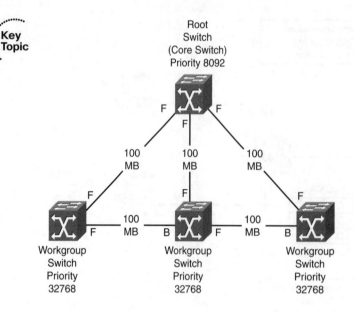

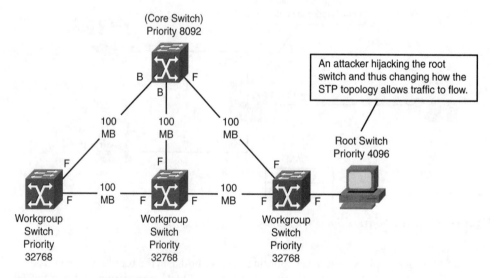

Figure 4-5   *STP Spoofing Attack*

DHCP Starvation Attacks

A DHCP server dynamically assigns IP addresses to hosts on a network. The administrator creates pools of addresses available for assignment, and then a lease time is associated with the addresses. A DHCP starvation attack works by broadcasting DHCP requests with spoofed MAC addresses; what this does, from the perspective of the DHCP server, is completely allocate the number of available IP addresses. If new clients are then unable to gain access to an IP address for the network, they will be unable to use network resources.

DHCP Server Spoofing

With DHCP server spoofing, the attacker can set up a rogue DHCP server and respond to DHCP requests from clients on the network. This type of attack can often be grouped with a DHCP starvation attack because the victim server will not have any new IP addresses to give out, which raises the chance of new clients using the rouge DHCP server. This information, which is given out by the rogue DHCP server, could send all the traffic through a rogue gateway, which can then capture the traffic for further analysis.

ARP Spoofing

Another method of spoofing MAC addresses is to use Address Resolution Protocol (ARP), which is used to map IP addresses to MAC addresses residing on one LAN segment. When a host sends out a broadcast ARP request to find a MAC address of a particular host, an ARP response comes from the host whose address matches the request. The ARP response is cached by the requesting host. An attacker can abuse this mechanism by responding as though they are the requested host. This method can be considered more threatening than MAC address spoofing because, while the CAM table stores these addresses for only 5 minutes (by default), most Cisco devices default to holding their ARP table associations for 4 hours.

ARP also has another method of identifying host IP-to-MAC associations, which is called Gratuitous ARP (GARP). With GARP, a broadcast packet is used by hosts to announce their IP address to the LAN to avoid duplicate IP addresses on the network. GARP can be exploited maliciously by an attacker to spoof the identity of the device by announcing a new IP-to-MAC association for the device on a LAN segment.

Figure 4-6 shows an attacker sending an altered GARP packet to have traffic to 192.168.1.3 rerouted to Host A.

IP Spoofing

With IP spoofing, an attacker attempts to send and receive traffic on the network using an IP address of another known host or known network. The attacker is then able to use network resources that are associated with that specific IP address. As with any of the other spoofing threats, an attacker can use this access for many purposes.

Switched Data Plane Security Technologies

The following sections review the different security technologies that can be used to mitigate the attacks discussed in the previous sections.

Port Configuration

With some basic configuration, a switchport can do a lot to improve the security of the network. Each switchport is configured to be in a specific mode; the default mode is dependent on the specific device.

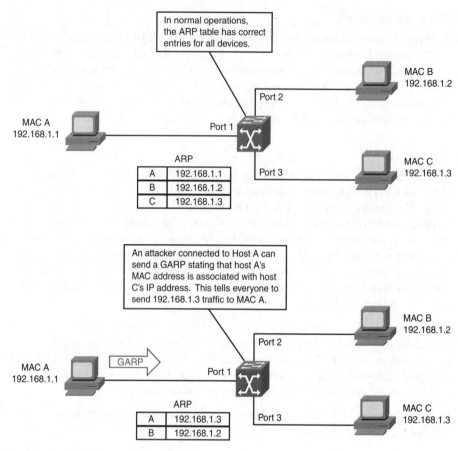

Figure 4-6   *ARP Spoofing Attack*

The switchport modes are as follows:

- **Access:** This mode is used when a single host is attached to the switchport; no trunking of any kind is permitted.

- **Trunk:** This mode statically configures the switchport as a trunk.

- **Dynamic auto:** This mode allows the port to become a trunk should the other side of the connection request it; if no request is made, it leaves the port in access mode.

- **Dynamic desirable:** This mode allows the port to become a trunk and actively attempts to make it a trunk; if unsuccessful, the port remains in access mode.

When the switchport is in either of the dynamic modes available, it relies on the Dynamic Trunking Protocol (DTP) to negotiate the port into a trunk mode. Another way of securing the switchport is to disable DTP; when this is done, the switchport must be manually configured as a trunk on both sides of the connection for the trunk to work.

Table 4-2 displays some of the basic commands that can be used to change switchport configuration and to display switchport information.

Table 4-2 *Configuring Ports*

Task	Command Syntax
Set the interface mode	Switch(config-if)#**switchport mode** {**access**	**trunk**	**dynamic auto**	**dynamic desirable**}
Disable DTP on the specified switchport	Switch(config-if)#**switchport nonegotiate**
Configure the VLAN for the specified access switchport	Switch(config-if)#**switchport access vlan** *vlan-id*
Configure the native VLAN for the specified trunk switchport	Switch(config-if)#**switchport trunk native vlan** *vlan-id*
Display the status of a switchport	**show interfaces** *interface* **switchport**
Display the status of a configured trunk	**show interfaces** *interface* **trunk**
Display information about a specific VLAN	**show vlan** *vlan-id*

Example 4-1 shows the configuration of a switchport into access mode; this would be the typical configuration of a port connecting to a single host device. Any potential attacker trying to gain access to information from multiple VLANs would be unable to get this information from this switchport.

Example 4-1 *Configuring Switchport Mode (Access)*

```
Switch# configure terminal
Switch(config)# interface fastethernet0/0
Switch(config-if)# switchport mode access
```

Example 4-2 shows the configuration of a switchport set to trunk mode. In this mode, the switchport is assumed to be connected to another trunk port of a neighboring switch. To quickly review, a trunk link is able to transport multiple VLANs from one switch to another so that VLANs can expand across multiple switches.

Example 4-2 *Configuring Switchport Mode (Trunk)*

```
Switch# configure terminal
Switch(config)# interface fastethernet0/0
Switch(config-if)# switchport mode trunk
```

Example 4-3 shows the configuration of two different switches, SwitchA and SwitchB. In this scenario, SwitchA would initiate a DTP negotiation with SwitchB to make the link between them a trunk. SwitchB would respond to this negotiation and form a trunk between them. In this case, SwitchA would always be the initiating switch.

Example 4-3   *Configuring Switchport Mode (Dynamic)*

```
SwitchA# configure terminal
SwitchA(config)# interface fastethernet0/0
SwitchA(config-if)# switchport mode dynamic desirable

SwitchB# configure terminal
SwitchB(config)# interface fastethernet0/0
SwitchB(config-if)# switchport mode dynamic auto
```

Example 4-4 shows the switchport being configured to not utilize DTP for trunk negotiation. An error will occur should this command be entered on a switchport that is configured in either of the dynamic modes. When using this command, the trunk must be statically configured.

Example 4-4   *Configuring Switchport Nonegotiate*

```
SwitchA# configure terminal
SwitchA(config)# interface fastethernet0/0
SwitchA(config-if)# switchport nonegotiate
```

The next part of the configuration involves the configuration of specific VLANs that are associated with specific ports. By default, all switchports are assigned into VLAN 1, and this includes the native VLAN on trunk links. A VLAN configured on an access port is assigned to all traffic coming from that specific switchport.

Example 4-5 shows an access switchport being configured into VLAN 100.

Example 4-5   *Configuring Access Switchport VLAN*

```
SwitchA# configure terminal
SwitchA(config)# interface fastethernet0/0
SwitchA(config-if)# switchport access vlan 100
```

A native VLAN on a trunk port is used to internally notate a VLAN for untagged traffic; the traffic on this native VLAN is transported across the link untagged. Traffic that comes into the switch to be transported across the trunk link with a VLAN tag number matching the native VLAN number has its tag stripped and goes across the trunk link untagged. This default behavior can be used by an attacker to perform a double-tagging VLAN hopping attack.

Three main methods can be used to eliminate this attack:

■   Never have a native trunk VLAN number that matches any access VLAN number.

■   Prune the native VLAN configured from being transported across the trunk (breaks native VLAN functionality).

■   Configure the switch to always tag native VLAN traffic (thus, all traffic is given a VLAN tag across the trunk).

Example 4-6 shows the native VLAN of a trunk being configured into VLAN 555 and the various mitigation techniques.

Example 4-6   *Configuring Native Trunk VLAN and Security Options*

```
Switch# configure terminal
Switch(config)# interface fastethernet0/0
Switch(config-if)# switchport trunk native vlan 555


Removes the native VLAN 555 from being transported over the trunk
Switch(config-if)# switchport trunk allow vlan remove 555


Configures the switch or switchport to autmatically tag all traffic on the
native VLAN
Switch(config)# vlan dot1q vlan native


Or


Switch(config-if)# switchport trunk vlan native tag
```

When you put all of this together, you get a solution for mitigating VLAN hopping attacks. The following list includes good guidelines to follow when setting up a switch securely and avoiding VLAN hopping attack risks:

■   Disable all unused ports and place them in an unused VLAN.

■   Set all user ports to nontrunking mode by disabling DTP. (It is not a bad idea to set all ports by default to access mode and then reconfigure the trunking ports as needed.)

■   For backbone switch-to-switch connections, explicitly configure trunking and disable DTP.

■   Do not use VLAN 1 as the switch management VLAN.

Port Security

You can mitigate CAM flooding, MAC address spoofing, and DHCP starvation attacks using different features available with port security. It is important to explain and understand these features and describe how they work to properly implement them. Port security classifies MAC addresses into three different groups:

■   **Static secure MAC addresses:** A switchport can be manually configured with the specific MAC address of the device that connects to it.

■   **Dynamic secure MAC addresses:** The maximum number of MAC addresses that will be learned on a single switchport is specified. These MAC addresses are dynamically learned, stored only in the address table, and removed when the switch restarts.

■   **Sticky secure MAC addresses:** The maximum number of MAC addresses on a given port can be dynamically learned or manually configured. Those addresses that are dynamically learned become sticky addresses that will be stored in the address table and added to the running configuration (as static entries). If the addresses are saved in the configuration file, the interface does not need to dynamically relearn them when the switch restarts.

A specific action is taken when a port security violation occurs. These actions include

- **Protect:** If the number of secure MAC addresses reaches the limit allowed on the port, frames with unknown source addresses are dropped until a number of MAC addresses are removed or the number of allowable addresses is increased; you receive no notification of the security violation.

- **Restrict:** If the number of secure MAC addresses reaches the limit allowed on the port, frames with unknown source addresses are dropped until some number of secure MAC addresses are removed or the maximum number of allowable addresses is increased. In this mode, a security notification is sent to the Simple Network Management Protocol (SNMP) server (if configured), a syslog message is logged, and the violation counter is incremented.

- **Shutdown:** If a port security violation occurs, the interface changes to error-disabled and the LED is turned off. It sends an SNMP trap, logs to a syslog message, and increments the violation counter. This is the default behavior.

Table 4-3 displays some of the basic commands that can be used to change port security configuration and to display port security information.

Key Topic

Table 4-3   *Configuring Port Security*

Task	Command Syntax
Enable port security on the interface.	Switch(config-if)# **switchport port-security**
Set the maximum number of secure MAC addresses for the interface. The active Switch Database Management (SDM) template determines the maximum number of available addresses. The default is 1.	Switch(config-if)# **switchport port-security** [*maximum value* [**vlan** {*vlan-list*	{**access**	**voice**}}]]
Set the action to be taken when a security violation is detected. The default mode for security violations is to shut down the interface.	Switch(config-if)# **switchport port-security violation** {**protect**	**restrict**	**shutdown**}

Table 4-3 *Configuring Port Security*

Task	Command Syntax
Set a secure MAC address for the interface. This command can be used to enter up to the allowed maximum number of secure MAC addresses. If fewer secure MAC addresses are configured than the maximum allowed, the remaining MAC addresses are dynamically learned.	Switch(config-if)# **switchport port-security** [mac-address *mac-address* [**vlan** {*vlan-id* | {access | voice}}]
Enable sticky learning on the interface.	Switch(config-if)# **switchport** *port-security mac-address* **sticky**
Display information about the current port-security settings.	**show port-security**

Note: When a secure port is in the error-disabled state, you can bring it out of this state automatically by using the **errdisable recovery** global configuration command, or you can manually reenable it by entering the **shutdown** and **no shutdown** interface configuration commands.

Both CAM flooding and DHCP starvation attacks can be mitigated by limiting the total number of allowed MAC addresses for an individual port. This eliminates the threat of CAM flooding because the maximum number of MAC addresses assigned would typically be much lower than what is available in the switch's CAM table. DHCP starvation attacks can be mitigated with this same feature because it limits the number of falsified clients on an individual port. The DHCP starvation attack could still happen but be limited in its scope.

MAC address spoofing attacks can be mitigated with port security by locking down which specific MAC addresses are allowed on an individual port. The attacker is then unable to plug into another port on the switch and utilize the spoofed MAC address.

The following example configures a switchport as an access port and sets dynamic port security with maximum number of addresses learned to 20. The violation mode is the default shutdown mode, sticky learning is enabled, and no static MAC addresses are configured. In the scenario where a twenty-first computer tries to connect, the port will be placed in error-disabled state and will send out an SNMP trap notification.

With the configuration shown in Example 4-7, both CAM flooding and DHCP starvation would be limited to 20 total CAM entries coming from interface fastethernet 0/0.

Example 4-7 *Configuring Dynamic Port Security (Maximum Addresses)*

```
Switch# configure terminal
Switch(config)# interface fastethernet0/0
Switch(config-if)# switchport mode access
Switch(config-if)# switchport port-security
Switch(config-if)# switchport port-security maximum 20
Switch(config-if)# switchport port-security mac-address sticky
```

With the configuration shown in Example 4-8, the port is configured with one specific MAC address. If any other device plugs into this interface not using that specific MAC address, the port will go into an err-disabled state that must be cleared by an administrator.

Example 4-8 *Configuring Static Port Security*

```
Switch# configure terminal
Switch(config)# interface fastethernet0/0
Switch(config-if)# switchport mode access
Switch(config-if)# switchport port-security
Switch(config-if)# switchport port-security mac-address 0123.4567.8910
```

Root Guard, BPDU Guard, and PortFast

To mitigate STP manipulation, two different features can be used. The Root Guard feature is configured on a switchport that should never become a root port, or in other words, the port that forwards traffic going toward the root bridge. A good example of this would be a connection between a distribution layer switch and an access layer switch. In this scenario, the port on the distribution switch going toward the access layer should never become a root port because the access layer switch should never become the root switch. If the switchport does receive a superior BPDU, the port will go into root-inconsistent state, indicating that another switch is attempting to become the root switch.

The other feature is BPDU Guard; this feature is typically implemented with PortFast. The PortFast feature is used on access ports to speed the transition of the port into STP forwarding state. PortFast and BPDU Guard are implemented on a switchport or interface. BPDU Guard should be implemented on a switchport or interface that should never receive a BPDU packet. Should the port be configured with BPDU Guard and receive a BPDU, the port will go into the error-disable state. All access ports should never receive a BPDU and can be configured with BPDU Guard to eliminate an attacker plugging into an access port and acting as a superior switch.

Table 4-4 displays some of the basic commands that can be used to configure the Root Guard, PortFast, and BPDU Guard features and to display feature information.

Table 4-4 *Configuring Root Guard and BPDU Guard*

Task	Command Syntax
Enables the Root Guard feature on a switchport	Switch(config-if)# **spanning-tree guard root**
Changes the default behavior to enable the PortFast feature on all switchports	Switch(config)#[no] **spanning-tree portfast default**
Changes the default behavior to enable the BPDU Guard feature on all PortFast switchports	Switch(config)# **spanning-tree portfast bpduguard default**
Enables the use of the PortFast feature on a switchport	Switch(config-if)# [no] **spanning-tree portfast**
Enables the use of the BPDU Guard feature on a switchport	Switch(config-if)# **spanning-tree bpduguard {enable	disable}**
Displays all switchports currently in root-inconsistent state; this condition can be caused by the Root Guard feature	**show spanning-tree inconsistent-ports**
Displays a summary of switchport states	**show spanning-tree summary**

Example 4-9 demonstrates enabling Root Guard and BPDU Guard. The switchport fastethernet0/0 is configured to not accept superior BPDUs and is configured to not use BPDU Guard, while all other ports are enabled by default.

Example 4-9 *Configuring Root Guard and BPDU Guard*

```
Switch# configure terminal
Switch(config)# spanning-tree portfast bpduguard default
Switch(config)# interface fastethernet 0/0
Switch(config-if)# spanning-tree guard root
Switch(config-if)# spanning-tree bpdu-guard disable
```

DHCP Snooping

One main feature can be used to mitigate DHCP server spoofing and offer additional protection from DHCP starvation attacks: DHCP snooping. DHCP snooping is a DHCP security feature that provides network security by filtering untrusted DHCP messages using a DHCP snooping binding database that it builds and maintains (referred to as the *DHCP snooping binding table*). This binding table includes the client MAC address, IP address, DHCP lease time, binding type, VLAN number, and interface information on each untrusted switchport or interface. An untrusted switchport or interface should be configured when it comes from an untrusted part of the network that should not contain a DHCP server; by default, all switchports are untrusted. A trusted switchport or interface should be configured to receive messages only from a trusted DHCP source or a network that contains a trusted DHCP source.

When a switch receives a packet on an untrusted switchport or interface and DHCP snooping is enabled on that interface or VLAN, the switch compares the source packet information with that held in the DHCP snooping binding table. In certain situations, the switch will permit or deny the packet based on this information. The following situations dictate when a packet is denied:

■   A packet from a DHCP server is received on an untrusted switchport or interface.

■   A packet is received on an untrusted switchport or interface that does not match the contents of the DHCP snooping binding table.

■   A packet is received from a DHCP relay-agent that does not match 0.0.0.0, or the DHCP relay agent forwards a packet that includes option-82 information on an untrusted switchport or interface.

DHCP snooping also has a rate-limiting function that limits the number of DHCP messages allowed on a switchport or interface per second. This capability can be used to further mitigate the risk of DHCP starvation attacks.

Table 4-5 displays some of the basic commands that can be used to configure DHCP snooping and display DHCP snooping information.

Table 4-5   *Configuring DHCP Snooping*

Task	Command Syntax
Enable the DHCP Snooping feature globally	Switch(config)# **ip dhcp snooping**
Enable the DHCP Snooping feature on a specific VLAN or VLAN range	Switch(config)# **ip dhcp snooping vlan** *vlan-id*
Enable the DHCP Snooping MAC verification feature globally; this is enabled by default	Switch(config)# **ip dhcp snooping verify mac-address**
Configure a static DHCP snooping binding entry	Switch(config)# **ip dhcp snooping binding** *mac-address* **vlan** *vlan-id ip-address* **interface** *interface* **expiry** *seconds*
Enable the DHCP snooping rate limit feature, which limits the number of DHCP packets received on an interface per second	Switch(config-if)# **ip dhcp snooping limit rate** *rate*
Configure the switchport or interface as trusted	Switch(config-if)# **ip dhcp snooping trust**
Display the current DHCP Snooping configuration	**show ip dhcp spoofing**
Display the current DHCP binding entries	**show ip dhcp snooping binding**
Display the status of the DHCP database agent	**show ip dhcp snooping database**

Example 4-10 shows the configuration for enabling DHCP snooping globally on the switch, enabling it on VLAN 34, and configuring a rate limit of 70 packets per second on the fastethernet0/0 interface.

Example 4-10 *Configuring DHCP Snooping*

```
Switch# configure terminal
Switch(config)# ip dhcp snooping
Switch(config)# ip dhcp snooping vlan 34
Switch(config)# interface fastethernet0/0
Switch(config-if)# ip dhcp snooping limit rate 70
```

Dynamic ARP Inspection (DAI)

The feature that can be used to mitigate ARP spoofing attacks is Dynamic ARP Inspection (DAI). DAI is a security feature that intercepts and verifies IP-to-MAC address bindings and discards invalid ARP packets. DAI uses the DHCP snooping database to validate bindings. It associates a trust state with each switchport or interface on the switch. Packets arriving on trusted interfaces bypass all DAI validation checks, and those arriving on untrusted interfaces undergo the DAI validation process. In a typical network, all ports on the switch connected to the host are configured as untrusted, and switchports or interfaces connected to other switches are considered trusted.

Table 4-6 displays some of the basic commands that can be used to configure DAI and to display DAI information.

Table 4-6 *Configuring Dynamic ARP Inspection*

Task	Command Syntax
Enable DAI on a specific VLAN	Switch(config)# **ip arp inspection vlan** *vlan-id*
Enable additional validation DAI checks	Switch(config)# **ip arp inspection validate {[src-mac]|[dst-mac]|[ip]}**
Configure a specific switchport or interface as trusted	Switch(config-if)# **[no] ip arp inspection trust**
Configure an ARP packet rate limit, in packets per second	Switch(config-if)# **ip arp inspection limit rate** *rate-pps*
Create a new ARP ACL and enters ARP access list configuration mode	Switch(config)# **arp access-list** *acl-name*
Apply an ARP ACL for a VLAN	Switch(config)# **ip arp inspection filter** *acl-name* **vlan** *vlan-id*
Configure a specific IP/MAC pair that is permitted	**permit ip host** *sender-ip* **mac host** *sender-mac*

Table 4-6   *Configuring Dynamic ARP Inspection*

Task	Command Syntax
Display the DAI status for a specific range of VLANs	**show ip arp inspection** [vlan-id]
Display the trust state and rate limit configured for a specific switchport or interface	**show ip arp inspection interfaces**
Display the configured ARP access lists	**show arp access-list** [acl-name]

Example 4-11 shows a basic DAI configuration that enables DAI on VLAN 34 and configures the fastethernet0/0 switchport/interface as trusted.

Example 4-11   *Configuring Dynamic ARP Inspection*

```
Switch# configure terminal
Switch(config)# ip arp inspection vlan 34
Switch(config)# interface fastethernet0/0
Switch(config-if)# ip arp inspection trust
```

DAI has the capability to perform additional checks on the ARP packets received. These additional validation checks enable further verification of the proper ARP use. The three additional checks that can be configured are as follows:

- **Source MAC address:** This validation check verifies that the source MAC address in the Ethernet header matches the sender MAC address in the ARP body.

- **Destination MAC address:** This validation check verifies that the destination MAC address in the Ethernet header matches the target MAC address in the ARP body.

- **IP address:** This validation check verifies that the address used is not invalid or unexpected.

Example 4-12 shows a DAI configuration that is enabled on VLAN 55 and performs additional validation of the source MAC address.

Example 4-12   *Configuring Dynamic ARP Inspection (Validation)*

```
Switch# configure terminal
Switch(config)# ip arp inspection vlan 55
Switch(config)# ip arp inspection validate src-mac
```

DAI can also perform rate limiting of ARP packets. This is useful if an attacker is trying to perform DoS attacks on a switchport or interface.

Example 4-13 shows a DAI configuration that limits the speed of ARP packets to 50 packets per second (pps).

Example 4-13 *Configuring Dynamic ARP Inspection (Rate Limit)*

```
Switch# configure terminal
Switch(config)# ip arp inspection rate 50
```

In situations where DHCP is not used or where some devices are statically configured, DAI must be configured using ARP access lists. These access lists define specific MAC/IP pairs that are allowed.

Example 4-14 shows a DAI configuration where the MAC/IP pair 192.168.1.50/ABCD.EF01.1234 is enabled on VLAN 100 as valid.

Example 4-14 *Configuring Dynamic ARP Inspection (Static ARP)*

```
Switch# configure terminal
Switch(config)# arp access-list DAI_example
Switch(config-arp-acl)# permit ip host 192.168.1.50 mac host abcd.ef01.1234
Switch(config-arp-acl)# exit
Switch(config)# ip arp inspection filter DAI_example vlan 100
```

IP Source Guard

The IP Source Guard (IPSG) feature mitigates the chances of IP spoofing. The IPSG feature works on Layer 2 ports by restricting IP traffic based on the entries that exist in the DHCP snooping binding table. When enabled, IPSG will not allow any IP traffic over the switchport except for that traffic coming from the entry listed in the DHCP snooping table. A port access list will then be dynamically created based on the DHCP binding. IPSG also offers the capability to configure a static IP source binding that can be used in situations without the use of the DHCP snooping binding table.

The behavior of IP Source Guard depends on how it is enabled; the two available options include

- **Source IP address filtering:** When using this type of filtering, IPSG allows packets with an IP source address that is in the DHCP snooping binding database.

- **Source IP and MAC address filtering:** When using this type of filtering, IPSG allows packets whose IP address and MAC address match the DHCP snooping binding table.

Table 4-7 displays some of the basic commands that can be used to configure IPSG and display IPSG information.

Table 4-7 *Configuring IPSG*

Key Topic

Task	Command Syntax
Enable the use of IPSG on a specific switchport. The **port-security** keyword is used to configure the use of MAC filtering and IP filtering.	Switch(config-if)# **ip verify source vlan dhcp-snooping [port-security]**

Table 4-7 *Configuring IPSG*

Task	Command Syntax
Configure a static IP source binding.	Switch(config)# **ip source binding** *mac-address* **vlan** *vlan-id ip-address* **interface** *interface*
Display the IPSG configuration for an interface or all interfaces.	**show ip verify source** [*interface*]
Display the IP source bindings.	**show ip source binding** [*ip-address*] [*mac-address*][**interface** *interface*][**vlan** *vlan-id*]

Example 4-15 shows IPSG configuration on interface fastethernet0/0 using source IP address filtering and a static source binding with a MAC address of 0123.4567.890a, an IP address of 192.168.1.200, and using VLAN 200 and interface fastethernet0/0. With this configuration, traffic will only be allowed from addresses with matching entries in the DHCP snooping binding table or matching the statically configured entry.

Example 4-15 *Configuring IPSG*

```
Switch# configure terminal
Switch(config)# interface fastethernet0/0
Switch(config-if)# ip verify source
Switch(config-if)# exit
Switch(config)# ip source binding 0123.4567.890a vlan 200 192.168.1.200 interface
fastethernet 0/0
```

Private VLANs (PVLAN)

The use of VLANs is common in many modern networks to isolate the various parts of the network. These parts are typically separated by administrative use or by the type of endpoint device. Each of these VLANs must be assigned a separate IP subnet, with a common Layer 3 device performing the routing between them and providing any security filtering. In situations where the number of different VLANs becomes excessive because of traffic isolation requirements, there is another alternative. The private VLAN feature offers the ability to isolate different devices within the same VLAN and IP subnet. This works by defining ports into three different classifications, which are as follows:

Key Topic

- **Promiscuous ports:** Communicate with all other port types. Configured in a primary VLAN.

- **Community ports:** Communicate with other devices inside the same community and with all promiscuous ports. Configured in a secondary VLAN that is tiered to a primary VLAN.

- **Isolated ports:** Communicate only with other promiscuous ports. Configured in a secondary VLAN that is tiered to a primary VLAN.

The private VLAN feature can also be used across switches as long as the trunks between the switches support the 802.1Q trunking standard; however, the private VLAN feature is not supported by Cisco VLAN Trunking Protocol (VTP). All devices using the private VLAN feature must be configured as VTP transparent.

Table 4-8 displays some of the basic commands that can be used to configure private VLANs and display private VLAN information.

Table 4-8   *Configuring Private VLANs*

Key Topic

Task	Command Syntax
Configure a VLAN as private primary, community, or isolated	Switch(config-vlan)# **private-vlan [community | isolated | primary]**
Associate a secondary VLAN with a primary VLAN	Switch(config-vlan)# **private-vlan association** *secondary-vlan-list* [**add** *secondary-vlan-list*] [**remove** *secondary-vlan-list*]
Configure the interface to use the associated private VLAN mapping or association	Switch(config-if)# **switchport mode private-vlan [host | promiscuous]**
Map the secondary VLANs to a Layer 2 primary interface	Switch(config-if)# **switchport private-vlan mapping primary-vlan** *secondary-vlan-list* [**add** *secondary-vlan-list*] [**remove** *secondary-vlan-list*]
Associate the primary VLAN to Layer 2 secondary switchport(s)	Switch(config-if)# **switchport private-vlan host-association primary-vlan secondary-vlan-list**
Map the secondary VLANs to a Layer 3 primary VLAN switched virtual interface (SVI)	Switch(config-if)# **private-vlan mapping** [*secondary-vlan-list* | **add** *secondary-vlan-list* | **remove** *secondary-vlan-list*]

The configuration process to implement the private VLAN feature involves the creation of the primary and secondary VLANs, associating these VLANs to each other, and then associating these VLANs to switchports or interfaces. Only one isolated secondary VLAN can be associated with a single primary VLAN, but multiple community VLANs can be assigned to a single primary VLAN.

Example 4-16 shows the configuration of private VLANs, with a primary VLAN 100 being configured on interface fastetherent0/0, a community secondary VLAN 200 being configured on interface fastethernet0/1, and an isolated secondary VLAN 300 being configured on interface fastethernet0/2.

Example 4-16   *Configuring Private VLANs*

```
Switch# configure terminal
Switch(config)# vtp mode transparent
Switch(config)# vlan 200
```

```
Switch(config-vlan)# private-vlan community
Switch(config-vlan)# vlan 300
Switch(config-vlan)# private-vlan isolated
Switch(config-vlan)# vlan 100
Switch(config-vlan)# private-vlan primary
Switch(config-vlan)# private-vlan association 200,300
Switch(config-vlan)# exit
Switch(config)# interface fastethernet0/0
Switch(config-if)# switchport mode private-vlan promiscuous 100 200,300
Switch(config-if)# interface fastetherent0/1
Switch(config-if)# switchport mode private-vlan host-association 100 200
Switch(config-if)# interface fastethernet0/2
Switch(config-if)# switchport mode private-vlan host-association 100 300
```

When trying to configure Layer 3 switching for private VLAN ingress traffic, the secondary VLANs must be mapped with the primary VLAN's switched virtual interface (SVI).

Example 4-17 shows the configuration that would be required to perform this mapping.

Example 4-17   *Configuring Private VLANs*

```
Switch# configure terminal
Switch(config)# interface vlan 200
Switch(config-if)# private-vlan mapping add 200,300
```

PVLAN Edge

Although private VLANs can be used in a variety of situations, they are not supported on all Catalyst switches. On the lower-end switches that do not support private VLANs, an alternative can be used called *PVLAN Edge*. This feature mimics the functionality of a private isolated VLAN. Each port that you want to be isolated is configured as a protected port. Protected ports are unable to exchange traffic directly between each other without a Layer 3 device. They can, however, exchange traffic normally with any unprotected ports.

Table 4-9 displays some of the basic commands that can be used to configure PVLAN Edge and to display PVLAN Edge information.

Key Topic

Table 4-9   *Configuring Private Edge Ports*

Task	Command Syntax
Configure a VLAN as private primary, community, or isolated	Switch(config-if)# **[no] switchport protected**
Display the current protected configuration of a switchport	**show interfaces interface switchport**

Example 4-18 shows the configuration of PVLAN Edge protected ports. In this example, switchports fastethernet0/0 and 0/1 would be unable to exchange traffic directly but could exchange traffic directly with all other switchports.

Example 4-18   *Configuring PVLAN Edge*

```
Switch# configure terminal
Switch(config)# interface fastetherent0/0
Switch(config-if)# switchport protected
Switch(config-if)# interface fastethernet0/1
Switch(config-if)# switchport protected
```

Exam Preparation

As mentioned in the section, "How to Use This Book," in the Introduction, you have several choices for exam preparation: the exercises here, the memory tables in Appendix D, the final exam preparation chapter, and the exam simulation questions on the CD-ROM. The following questions present a bigger challenge than the exam itself because they use an open-ended question format. By using this more difficult format, you exercise your memory better and prove your conceptual and factual knowledge of this chapter. You can find the answers to these questions in Appendix A, "Answers to the DIKTA Quizzes and Fill in the Blanks Questions."

Review All Key Topics

Review the most important topics in this chapter, noted with the Key Topics icon in the margin of the page. Table 4-10 lists a reference of these key topics and the page numbers on which each is found.

Table 4-10   *Key Topics*

Key Topic Element	Description	Page
List	Common switched data plan attacks	60
List	Types of VLAN hopping attacks	61
Figure 4-2	CAM table operation	62
Figure 4-3	CAM flooding attack	64
Figure 4-4	MAC address spoofing attack	65
Figure 4-5	STP spoofing attack	66
Figure 4-6	ARP spoofing attack	68
List	Switchport modes	68
Table 4-2	Configuring ports	69
Table 4-3	Configuring port security	72
Table 4-4	Configuring root guard and BPDU Guard	75
Table 4-5	Configuring DHCP snooping	76
Table 4-6	Configuring Dynamic ARP Inspection	77
Table 4-7	Configuring IP Source Guard	79
List	Private VLAN: Port classifications	80
Table 4-8	Configuring private VLANs	81
Table 4-9	Configuring private edge ports	82

Complete Tables and Lists from Memory

Print a copy of Appendix C, "Memory Tables" (found on the CD), or at least the section for this chapter, and complete the tables and lists from memory. Appendix D, "Memory Table Answers," also on the CD, includes completed tables and lists to check your work.

Define Key Terms

Define the following key terms from this chapter, and check your answers in the Glossary:

CAM table, ARP, VLAN, DHCP, STP, BPDU, DTP

Use Command Reference to Check Your Memory

Table 4-16 and Table 4-17 list the important commands from this chapter. To test your memory, cover the right side of the table with a piece of paper, read the description on the left side, and see how much of the command you can remember.

Table 4-16   *Command Reference*

Task	Command Syntax
Set the interface mode.	Switch(config-if)# **switchport mode {access | trunk | dynamic auto | dynamic desirable}**
Disable DTP on the specified switchport.	Switch(config-if)# **switchport nonegotiate**
Configure the VLAN for the specified access switchport.	Switch(config-if)# **switchport access vlan** *vlan-id*
Configure the native VLAN for the specified trunk switchport.	Switch(config-if)# **switchport trunk native vlan** *vlan-id*
Enable port security on the interface.	Switch(config-if)# **switchport port-security**
Set the maximum number of secure MAC addresses for the interface. The active Switch Database Management (SDM) template determines the maximum number of available addresses. The default is 1.	Switch(config-if)# **switchport port-security** [**maximum value** [**vlan** {*vlan-list* | {**access** | **voice**}}]]
Set the action to be taken when a security violation is detected. The default mode for security violations is to shut down the interface.	Switch(config-if)# **switchport port-security violation {protect | restrict | shutdown}**

Table 4-16 *Command Reference*

Task	Command Syntax
Set a secure MAC address for the interface. This command can be used to enter up to the allowed maximum number of secure MAC addresses. If fewer secure MAC addresses are configured than the maximum allowed, the remaining MAC addresses are dynamically learned.	Switch(config-if)# **switchport port-security** [**mac-address** *mac-address* [**vlan** {*vlan-id* | {**access** | **voice**}}]
Enable sticky learning on the interface.	Switch(config-if)# **switchport port-security mac-address sticky**
Enable the Root Guard feature on a switchport.	Switch(config-if)# **spanning-tree guard root**
Change the default behavior to enable the PortFast feature on all switchports.	Switch(config)# [**no**] **spanning-tree portfast default**
Change the default behavior to enable the BPDU Guard feature on all PortFast switchports.	Switch(config)# **spanning-tree portfast bpduguard default**
Enable the use of the PortFast feature on a switchport.	Switch(config-if)# [**no**] **spanning-tree portfast**
Enable the use of the BPDU Guard feature on a switchport.	Switch(config-if)# **spanning-tree bpduguard** {**enable** | **disable**}
Enable the DHCP Snooping feature globally.	Switch(config)# **ip dhcp snooping**
Enable the DHCP Snooping feature on a specific VLAN or VLAN range.	Switch(config)# **ip dhcp snooping vlan** *vlan-id*
Enable the DHCP Snooping MAC verification feature globally; this is enabled by default.	Switch(config)# **ip dhcp snooping verify mac-address**
Configure a static DHCP snooping binding entry.	Switch(config)# **ip dhcp snooping binding** *mac-address* **vlan** *vlan-id ip-address* **interface** *interface* **expiry** *seconds*
Enable the DHCP snooping rate limit feature, which limits the number of DHCP packets received on an interface per second.	Switch(config-if)#**ip dhcp snooping limit rate** *rate*
Configure the switchport or interface as trusted.	Switch(config-if)# **ip dhcp snooping trust**

Table 4-16 *Command Reference*

Task	Command Syntax
Enable DAI on a specific VLAN.	Switch(config)# **ip arp inspection vlan** *vlan-*
Enable additional validation DAI checks.	Switch(config)# **ip arp inspection validate** {[**src-mac**][**dst-mac**][**ip**]}
Configure a specific switchport or interface as trusted.	Switch(config-if)# [**no**] **ip arp inspection trust**
Configure an ARP packet rate limit, in packets per second.	Switch(config-if)# **ip arp inspection limit rate** *rate-pps*
Create a new ARP ACL and enter ARP access list configuration mode.	Switch(config)# **arp access-list** *acl-name*
Apply an ARP ACL for a VLAN.	Switch(config)# **ip arp inspection filter** *acl-name* **vlan** *vlan-id*
Configure a specific IP/MAC pair that is permitted.	**permit ip host** *sender-ip* **mac host** *sender-mac*
Enable the use of IP Source Guard on a specific switchport. The **port-security** keyword is used to configure the use of MAC filtering as well as IP filtering.	Switch(config-if)# **ip verify source vlan dhcp-snooping** [**port-security**]
Configure a static IP source binding.	Switch(config)# **ip source binding** *mac-address* **vlan** *vlan-id ip-address* **interface** *interface*
Configure a VLAN as private primary, community, or isolated.	Switch(config-vlan)# **private-vlan** [**community** | **isolated** | **primary**]
Associate a secondary VLAN with a primary VLAN.	Switch(config-vlan)# **private-vlan association** *secondary-vlan-list* [**add** *secondary-vlan-list*] [**remove** *secondary-vlan-list*]
Configure the interface to use the associated private VLAN mapping or association.	Switch(config-if)# **switchport mode private-vlan** [**host** | **promiscuous**]
Map the secondary VLANs to a Layer 2 primary interface.	Switch(config-if)# **switchport private-vlan mapping primary-vlan** *secondary-vlan-list* [**add** *secondary-vlan-list*] [**remove** *secondary-vlan-list*]
Associate the primary VLAN to Layer 2 secondary switchport(s).	Switch(config-if)# **switchport private-vlan host-association primary-vlan secondary-vlan-list**

Table 4-16   *Command Reference*

Task	Command Syntax
Map the secondary VLANs to a Layer 3 primary VLAN switched virtual interface (SVI).	Switch(config-if)# **private-vlan mapping** [*secondary-vlan-list*	**add** *secondary-vlan-list*	**remove** *secondary-vlan-list*]
Configure a VLAN as private primary, community. or isolated.	Switch(config-if)# [no] **switchport protected**

Table 4-17   show *Command Reference*

Task	Command Syntax
Display the status of a switchport.	**show interfaces** *interface* **switchport**
Display the status of a configured trunk.	**show interfaces** *interface* **trunk**
Display information about a specific VLAN.	**show vlan** *vlan-id*
Display information about the current port security settings.	**show port-security**
Display all switchports currently in root-inconsistent state; this condition can be caused by the Root Guard feature.	**show spanning-tree inconsistentports**
Display a summary of switchport states.	**show spanning-tree summary**
Display the current DHCP snooping configuration.	**show ip dhcp spoofing**
Display the current DHCP binding entries.	**show ip dhcp snooping binding**
Display the status of the DHCP database agent.	**show ip dhcp snooping database**
Display the DAI status for a specific range of VLANs.	**show ip arp inspection** [*vlan-id*]
Display the trust state and rate limit configured for a specific switchport or interface.	**show ip arp inspection interfaces**
Display the configured ARP access lists.	**show arp access-list** [*acl-name*]
Display the IPSG configuration for an interface or all interfaces.	**show ip verify source** [*interface*]
Display the IP source bindings.	**show ip source binding** [*ip-address*] [*mac-address*][**interface** *interface*][**vlan** *vlan-id*]
Display the current protected configuration of a switchport.	**show interfaces interface switchport**

Fill in the Blanks

1. The trunking mode on a switchport can be sensed using _____.

2. The _____ in a switch stores information, such as MAC addresses, switchport, and associated VLAN parameters.

3. The default CAM aging timer on the Cisco Catalyst switch is _____.

4. _____ prevents bridging loops in a redundant switched network environment.

5. A _____ server dynamically assigns IP addresses to hosts on a network.

6. ARP also has another method of identifying host IP-to-MAC associations, which is called _____.

7. The switchport mode that actively attempts to make a switchport a trunk is _____.

8. The _____ switchport security classification includes dynamically learned addresses that are automatically added to the running configuration.

9. The _____ includes the client MAC address, IP address, lease time, binding type, VLAN number, and interface information.

10. The three different private VLAN classifications are _____, _____, and _____.

This chapter covers the following subjects:

- **Identity-Based Networking Services (IBNS) and IEEE 802.1x overview:** Describes Cisco IBNS and IEEE 802.1x and discusses how IBNS extends on 802.1x.

- **802.1x internetworking:** Covers the detailed interworking of the 802.1x specification.

- **EAP type selection:** Covers the most commonly used EAP types that are deployed.

CHAPTER 5

802.1X and Cisco Identity-Based Networking Services (IBNS)

Cisco Identity-Based Networking Services (IBNS) is a technology framework for delivering logical and physical network access authentication. IBNS combines several Cisco products that offer authentication, user policies, and access control to provide a comprehensive solution for increasing network access security. An identity-based network (IBN) incorporates capabilities defined in the IEEE 802.1x standard. The 802.1x standard is a framework defined by the IEEE 802.1 working group to provide a standard link layer protocol for port-based access control and authentication.

This chapter discusses IBNS and 802.1x features and functionality.

"Do I Know This Already?" Quiz

The "Do I Know This Already?" quiz helps you decide whether you really need to read the entire chapter. If you already intend to read the entire chapter, you do not necessarily need to answer these questions now.

The ten-question quiz, derived from the major sections in "Foundation Topics" section of this chapter, helps you determine how to spend your limited study time.

Table 5-1 outlines the major topics discussed in this chapter and the "Do I Know This Already?" quiz questions that correspond to those topics.

Table 5-1 *"Do I Know This Already?" Foundation Topics Section-to-Question Mapping*

Foundation Topics Section	Questions Covered in This Section
Identity-Based Networking Services (IBNS) and IEEE 802.1x Overview	1–4
802.1x Internetworking	5–9
EAP Type Selection	10

Cauton: The goal of self-assessment is to gauge your mastery of the topics in this chapter. If you do not know the answer to a question or are only partially sure of the answer, you should mark this question wrong for purposes of the self-assessment. Giving yourself credit for an answer that you correctly guess skews your self-assessment results and might provide you with a false sense of security.

1. Which of the following is a framework defined by the IEEE 802.1 working group that provides a standard link layer protocol for port-based access control and authentication?

   a. 802.1q

   b. 802.11b

   c. 802.1x

   d. 802.1w

2. What are the three roles the IEEE 802.1x framework defines in the authentication process?

   a. Authentication server

   b. Administrator

   c. Authenticator

   d. Supplicant

   e. Client

   f. Object

3. Prior to the client authentication, which protocols are allowed to pass through a port? (Select three.)

   a. EAPOL

   b. RADIUS

   c. CDP

   d. TACACS+

   e. SNMP

   f. Spanning Tree Protocol (STP)

4. Which of the following are valid IBNS deployment modes?

   a. Monitor Mode

   b. High-Security Mode

   c. Low-Security Mode

   d. Unlocked Mode

   e. Low-Impact Mode

5. Which of the following are valid EAP packet types?

   a. EAPOL-Alert

   b. EAPOL-Start

   c. EAPOL-Logoff

   d. EAPOL-Private

   e. EAP-Packet

6. Which of the following are valid configurable 802.1x port states?

   a. Auto

   b. Unauthorized

    c. Forced-Authorized

    d. Authorized

    e. Forced-Unauthorized

7. Which of the following port authentication host modes allows a single data and single voice host to be authenticated?

    a. Single-Host

    b. Multi-Host

    c. Multi-Domain

    d. Multi-Auth

    e. Open

8. Which of the following is the correct Ethernet type value used with EAPOL?

    a. 88:8E

    b. 08:00

    c. 88:E5

    d. 86:DD

    e. 88:08

9. Which field in the EAP frame format is 1 octet and aids in matching responses with requests?

    a. Code

    b. Identifier

    c. Length

    d. Data

10. Which of the following EAP types utilizes tunnels to encapsulate EAP traffic?

    a. PEAP

    b. EAP-TLS

    c. EAP-TTLS

    d. EAP-FAST

The answers to the "Do I Know This Already?" quiz are found in Appendix A. The suggested choices for your next step are as follows:

■ **8 or less overall score:** Read the entire chapter. This includes the "Foundation Topics" and "Exam Preparation" sections.

■ **9 or 10 overall score:** If you want more review on these topics, skip to the "Exam Preparation" section. Otherwise, move on to Chapter 6, "Implementing and Configuring Basic 802.1X."

Foundation Topics

Identity-Based Networking Services (IBNS) and IEEE 802.1x Overview

IEEE 802.1x is a standard set by the IEEE 802.1 working group. It is a data link layer (Layer 2) protocol designed to provide port-based network access control using authentication unique to a device or user. This service is called port-level authentication.

In today's network environments, many enterprises have implemented virtual LANs (VLAN), wireless LANs (WLAN), Dynamic Host Configuration Protocol (DHCP), and other dynamic technologies to accommodate user mobility and flexibility. Although these technologies have increased the benefits for the users in terms of network availability, they also render the corporate networks vulnerable to unauthorized access. In an unsecured environment, it is much easier for hackers and unauthorized entities to launch denial of service (DoS), hijack, or other types of attacks.

Cisco IBNS is an IEEE 802.1x-based technology solution that increases network security by authenticating users based on personal identity in addition to device MAC and IP address verification. IBNS controls who and what is on the network, keeping outsiders out through authentication and authorization, keeping the insiders honest through accountability, and increasing the overall network visibility.

IBNS also defines a framework for deployment that allows a smooth transition to a fully enforced environment. This framework operates by defining three modes that are used at each transitional point in implementation and are detailed in Table 5-2.

Table 5-2 *IBNS Deployment Modes[1]*

Mode	Description
Monitor Mode	Provides visibility into access on your network. Includes a pre-access-control deployment assessment and a policy evaluation.
Low-Impact Mode	Reduces known issues with other protocol timeouts and networked services. Enables differentiated access through policy-driven downloadable access control lists (dACL) based on identity or group.
High-Security Mode	Provides the highest level of LAN-based access security for environments where access cannot be granted without authentication.

IBNS and 802.1x Enhancements and Features

Several enhancements to the IEEE 802.1x standard are offered by Cisco IBNS, including the following:

- **VLAN assignments:** In a standard 802.1x implementation, authenticated users are placed in a VLAN preconfigured for the connected port. With IBNS, VLAN assignments can be obtained through the user or device identity. This is accomplished using the username-to-VLAN and device-to-VLAN association maintained in the RADIUS server. When the user successfully authenticates, the RADIUS server sends the VLAN information to the switch, and the switch dynamically configures the attached port for the specific VLAN.

■ **802.1x guest VLAN:** This is an important feature in environments where there is a mix of 802.1x clients and clients that *do not* support 802.1x. Using this feature, the non-802.1x-compatible users or devices gain access to network resources through the guest VLAN. A guest VLAN normally provides restricted access for basic network resources that would allow limited functions such as browsing, email, or access to an 802.1x client.

■ **Restricted VLAN:** This feature allows 802.1x-compatible clients to still gain some restricted access, even if they fail authentication. If the client fails authentication three times, it will be automatically put into the restricted VLAN; without a success-ful authentication, the port will remain in the restricted VLAN indefinitely. After the client is put into the restricted VLAN, a fake Extensible Authentication Protocol (EAP) success message is sent to the client to stop constant reauthentication. The level of access given to this VLAN is configurable depending on the needs of the spe-cific organization. For example, it is possible to make a guest and a restricted user have the same access.

■ **Port security:** 802.1x provides the option to enable port security on a switch port. If this feature is enabled to allow only a single MAC address on the port, it will deny multiple MAC addresses to be used on that port. This eliminates the risk of users at-taching hubs to a switch port to add more devices to the same port.

■ **Voice VLAN ID:** This is a feature that incorporates the benefits of Voice over Internet Protocol (VoIP) and dynamic port security mechanisms such as 802.1x. It enables ad-ministrators to configure an auxiliary VLAN for voice VLAN ID.

■ **Access control list (ACL) assignment:** ACLs can be dynamically assigned using 802.1x authentication policy. This feature enables administrators to restrict the user to specific network segments or limit access to sensitive resources to specific users without compromising user mobility.

■ **Inaccessible Authentication Bypass:** This feature allows devices attached to criti-cal ports to still be authenticated and allowed to pass traffic even if the RADIUS server(s) is (are) inaccessible. When the RADIUS server(s) become accessible again, the ports are then automatically reauthenticated using the server.

■ **MAC Authentication Bypass (MAB):** When using this feature, it is possible for a device to be authenticated without 802.1x support. This is done by referencing a MAC database that is held on the RADIUS server. The MAB feature is only enabled after the client fails to respond to Extensible Authentication Protocol over LAN (EAPOL) requests and causes a timeout.

■ **Network Admission Control Layer 2 Validation:** When using this feature, it is possible to check the posture of the client before granting access to the client. This can be used to verify items such as firewall settings and the status of virus and spam software updates.

- **Web Authentication (WebAuth) with Automatic MAC Check:** This feature provides the capability to authenticate a port through a web browser. The automatic MAC check feature allows the automatic authentication of devices based on their MAC address; this is typical for devices like printers that do not support 802.1x.

- **Flexible Authentication Sequencing (FlexAuth):** FlexAuth provides the ability to change the default behavior in making authentication decisions. By default, the port attempts 802.1x authentication, then MAB, and then WebAuth.

- **Open Access:** When using this feature, the clients have the ability to authenticate using 802.1x or MAB; however, regardless of the outcome, the port will always allow normal access. This feature is typically used to perform a running audit of the clients on the network that support 802.1x. Typically, this is used during a transition to full 802.1x/IBNS enforcement.

- **Multi-Domain Authentication:** When using this port host mode, the port allows a device to be authenticated to both the data and the voice domains.

- **Multiple Authentications (MultiAuth):** When using this port mode, the port allows multiple devices to be separately authenticated while attaching through the same port. By default, the first device on a port authenticates the port for everyone else on the port. If that client goes offline, the access for the other clients is cut off until authentication from another client takes place.

- **Remote Site IEEE 802.1x Local Authentication Service:** This feature enables you to configure an access point or wireless-aware router to act as a local RADIUS server. This capability provides backup authentication in the event that the WAN link or the central RADIUS server fails.

802.1x Components

The IEEE 802.1x framework defines three roles in the authentication process. The terminology for these roles is as follows:

- **Supplicant:** The endpoint requesting access to the network. For example, this could be an end-user device, a printer, or an IP phone.

- **Authentication server:** The entity that validates the identity of the supplicant and notifies the authenticator to allow or deny the client request for access. For example, a RADIUS server, such as ACS, can provide authentication server services.

- **Authenticator:** The device between the supplicant and the authentication server that facilitates authentication. The client is normally directly connected to the authenticator. For example, a switch or a wireless access point would provide authenticator services to clients attempting to access LAN.

Figure 5-1 shows the specific roles of the devices in the network during 802.1x port-based authentication.

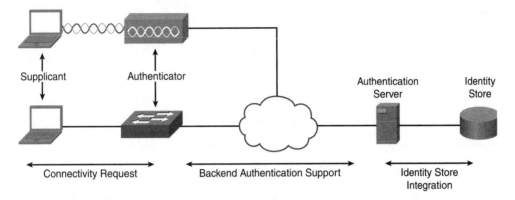

Figure 5-1 *802.1x Device Roles*

Prior to the client authentication, the port will only allow EAPOL, Cisco Discovery Protocol (CDP), and Spanning Tree Protocol (STP) traffic through the connected port. After the authentication is successful, normal traffic can pass through the port.

802.1x Interworking

The following sections go over the basic topics that are used when implementing 802.1x internetworking.

Extensible Authentication Protocol (EAP)

EAP is the transport mechanism used in 802.1x to authenticate supplicants against a backend data store, typically a RADIUS server. EAP was initially defined in RFC 2284 as a general authentication framework running over Layer 2 Point-to-Point Protocol (PPP). In RFC 3748, the EAP definition has been updated to include IEEE 802 as a link layer. The IEEE 802 encapsulation of EAP does not involve PPP, and IEEE 802.1X does not include support for link or network layer negotiations. As a result, within IEEE 802.1X, it is not possible to negotiate non-EAP authentication mechanisms, such as Password Authentication Protocol (PAP) or Challenge Handshake Authentication Protocol (CHAP), without specialized tunneling support. EAP does not select a specific authentication mechanism during the link layer phase but rather postpones it until the authentication phase. Figure 5-2 depicts the EAP packet format.

EAP Code (1 Byte)	EAP Identifier (1 Byte)	EAP Packet Length (2 Bytes)
EAP Data (0 + Bytes)		

Figure 5-2 *EAP Packet Format*

The field descriptions are as follows:

- **Code:** The Code field is 1 byte and identifies the type of EAP packet. Table 5-3 shows the assigned EAP codes.

Table 5-3 *EAP Codes*

Code	Description
1	Request
2	Response
3	Success
4	Failure

Any EAP packets with other codes are silently discarded.

■   **Identifier:** The Identifier field is 1 byte and aids in matching responses with requests.

■   **Length:** The Length field is 2 bytes and indicates the length, in bytes (octets), of the EAP packet, including the Code, Identifier, Length, and Data fields. Bytes outside the range of the Length field should be treated as data link layer padding and will be ignored upon reception. A message with the Length field set to a value larger than the number of received bytes will be silently discarded.

■   **Data:** The Data field is 0 or more bytes. The Code field determines the format of the Data field.

EAP over LAN (EAPOL)

On LAN media, the supplicant and the authenticator communicate using an encapsulation technique known as EAPOL. EAPOL supports various media types including Ethernet, Token Ring, Fiber Distributed Data Interface (FDDI), and WLANs. EAPOL provides the capability to encapsulate EAP messages that can be handled directly by a LAN MAC service.

The EAPOL frame is rather simple, as shown in Figure 5-3. The EAP packet is encapsulated within the frame and is located in the Packet Body field.

1	2	3	4	5	6	7	8	9	10	11	12	13	14	15	16	17	18	19	20	21	22	23	24	25	26	27	28	29	30	31	32
Destination MAC Address (6 Bytes)																															
																Source MAC Address (6 Bytes)															
PAE Ethernet Type (2 Bytes)																Protocol Version (1 Byte)								Packet Type (1 Byte)							
Packet Body Length (2 Bytes)																Packet Body (0 + Bytes)															

Figure 5-3 *EAPOL Frame Format*

The Destination and Source MAC Address fields are both 6 bytes and are used the same as with all normal Ethernet traffic; however, the Destination MAC Address field always holds the Port Access Entity (PAE) group address, which is defined as 01:80:C2:00:00:03.

The PAE Ethernet Type field is 2 bytes, taken to represent an unsigned binary number and always set to 88:8E.

The Packet Type field is 1 byte in length, taken to represent an unsigned binary number. Its value determines the type of packet being transmitted. Table 5-4 displays the types that are defined.

Table 5-4 *EAPOL Packet Types*

Type	Value
EAP-Packet	0000 0000 (0)
EAPOL-Start	0000 0001 (1)
EAPOL-Logoff	0000 0010 (2)
EAPOL-Key	0000 0011 (3)
EAPOL-Encapsulated-ASF-Alert	0000 0100 (4)

The Packet Body Length is 2 bytes, taken to represent an unsigned binary number and defines the length of the packet body. The field being set to 0 indicates that the Packet Body field is not present.

The Packet Body field is only present when the Packet Type field is set to EAP-Packet, EAPOL-Key, or EAPOL-Encapsulated-ASP-Alert.

EAP Message Exchange

EAP message exchange can be complex to understand. Figure 5-4 shows an example EAP exchange using the One-Time Password EAP method. It is important to understand that the EAP packets are only encapsulated by EAPOL from the supplicant to the authenticator; from the authenticator to the authentication server, the EAP packets are encapsulated within the RADIUS packets.

The following list describes what happens in each step of an EAP conversation:

Step 1.   The supplicant sends an EAPOL-Start frame to the authenticator to notify that it is ready to authenticate. If the authenticator initiates the connection, there will be no EAPOL-Start message sent.

Step 2.   The authenticator sends an EAP-Request/Identity packet to the supplicant as soon as it detects that the link is active (for example, the client has connected to a switch port).

Step 3.   The supplicant sends an EAP-Response/Identity packet to the authenticator, which is then passed on to the authentication (RADIUS) server. Communications between the supplicant and authentication server also leverage the RADIUS protocol carried over User Datagram Protocol (UDP).

Step 4.   The authentication server sends back a challenge to the authenticator, such as with a token password system. The authenticator unpacks this from IP and repackages it into EAPOL and sends it to the supplicant. Different authentication methods will vary this message and the total number of messages. EAP supports client-only authentication and strong mutual authentication. Only strong mutual authentication is considered appropriate in wireless environments.

Step 5. The supplicant responds to the challenge through the authenticator and passes the response on to the authentication server.

Step 6. If the supplicant provides proper identity, the authentication server responds with a success message, which is then passed on to the supplicant. The authenticator now allows access to the LAN, possibly restricted based on attributes that came back from the authentication server. For example, the authenticator might switch the supplicant to a particular VLAN or install a set of access control rules.

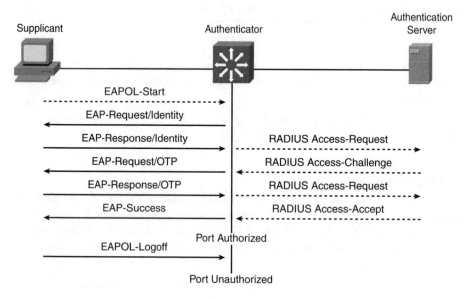

Figure 5-4 *Sample EAP Conversation*

Port States

When using 802.1x, there are three defined port states, as described in Table 5-5.

Table 5-5 *802.1x Port States*

State	Description
Auto	In this mode, the port begins in the unauthorized state and allows only EAPOL, CDP, and STP traffic. After the supplicant is authenticated, the port transitions to the authorized state and normal traffic is allowed.

Table 5-5 *802.1x Port States*

State	Description
Forced-Authorized	In this state, 802.1x is disabled on the port. All traffic is allowed as normal without restriction. This is the default port state when 802.1x is not globally enabled.
Forced-Unauthorized	In this state, the port ignores all traffic, including any attempts to authenticate.

If IEEE 802.1x is configured on a switch port, the port starts in the automatic port authentication state (Auto). When in the Auto state, the port will start in the *unauthorized* state and require the supplicant to successfully authenticate. After the supplicant authenticates, the port changes to the *authorized* state and allows through traffic from the client to network resources. If the client does not support IEEE 802.1x, the switch cannot authenticate the client unless MAB is configured to be used or a guest VLAN is preconfigured to provide some level of necessary network access.

Port Authentication Host Modes

Numerous host modes of operation are supported for 802.1x port authentication, as outlined in Table 5-6.

Table 5-6 *Port Authentication Host Modes*

Key
Topic

Mode	Description
Single-Host	Only allows a single host to be authenticated for a single port; if more than one attempts to authenticate, an error message is generated.
Multi-Host	After a single host is able to authenticate for a single port, multiple hosts are able to use the port while that host is authenticated. If that host closes its connection and becomes unauthorized, the port will transition back to an unauthorized state.
Multi-Domain	Allows a host to be authenticated for the data and voice domains. This is used when there is a computer and an IP phone attached through the same port.
Multi-Auth	Allows multiple hosts to be independently authenticated while using the same port. In situations where there are multiple hosts, the port can't be configured into more than one data VLAN at the same time. The VLAN configured with the first host will be used in these situations. In this situation, it is best for ACLs to be used to maintain security restrictions.
Open	In this mode, no access restrictions are assigned to the port.

EAP Type Selection

There are several types of EAP authentication available for wired and wireless networks. The most used types and methods for EAP authentication include the following:

- EAP-MD5

- PEAPv0-MSCHAPv2

- LEAP

- EAP-TLS

- EAP-TTLS

- EAP-FAST

The following sections describe the most common methods of 802.1x authentication.

EAP–Message Digest Algorithm 5

EAP-MD5 uses message digest algorithm 5 (MD5)–based challenge-response for authentication. Using this method, the client identity is transmitted over the network, but a hash is sent in lieu of a password. The server generates a random string and sends it to the user as a challenge. The client MD5 hashes the challenge using its password as the key and sends it back to the server. The server then authenticates the subscriber by verifying this hash.

This type of authentication is well supported and provides a simple mechanism for authentication using username and passwords. It also does not burden the server or the client because of its lightweight processing requirements.

The cons of using MD5 are the security weaknesses inherent in this authentication method. MD5 requires the storage of plain-text or reversible passwords on the authentication server.

Figure 5-5 displays a sample of the EAP data field.

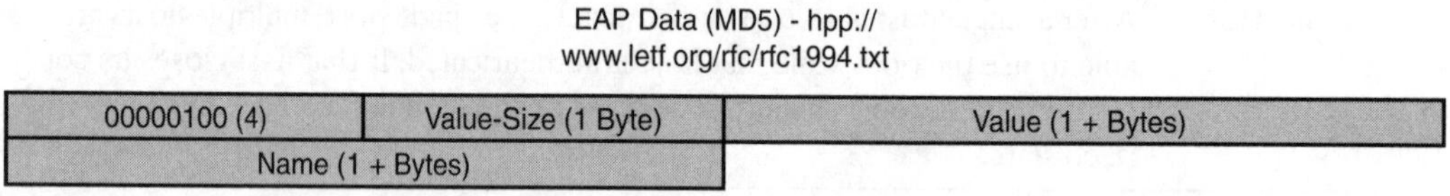

EAP Data (MD5) - hpp://
www.letf.org/rfc/rfc1994.txt

00000100 (4)	Value-Size (1 Byte)	Value (1 + Bytes)
Name (1 + Bytes)		

Figure 5-5 *EAP-MD5 Data Field Example*

Protected EAP w/MS-CHAPv2

Protected EAP (PEAP) is an IETF draft RFC submitted by Cisco Systems, Microsoft, and RSA Security. It supports various EAP-encapsulated methods within a protected Transport Layer Security (TLS) tunnel.

PEAP supports an extensible set of user authentication methods, such as one-time token authentication and password change or aging. It uses server-side digital certificate authentication based on the public-key infrastructure (PKI) standard. In environments where certificates are not issued to every client, PEAP can use a Microsoft Windows username and password instead by querying the Windows domain controller, Active Directory, or other existing user database.

PEAP uses two phases:

■ Phase 1 of the authentication sequence is the same as that for EAP-TLS (server-side TLS). A server-side TLS authentication is performed to create an encrypted tunnel and complete server-side authentication. At the end of Phase 1, an encrypted TLS tunnel is created between the user and the RADIUS server for transporting EAP authentication messages.

■ In Phase 2, the RADIUS server authenticates the client through the encrypted TLS tunnel through another EAP type, the most common being MS-CHAP version 2 (as defined by the PEAP draft). The RADIUS server will relay the MS-CHAP credentials to a server to validate the user login. When this is complete, an EAP-Success message is sent to the client.

Figure 5-6 displays a sample of the EAP data field.

EAP Data (PEAP/MS-CHAPv2)

00011001 (25)	Flags (5 Bits)	Version	TLS Message Length (4 Bytes)	
			EAP Code (1 byte)	EAP Identifier (1 Byte)
EAP Packet Length (2 Bytes)			00011101 (29)	MS-CHAP Type (1 Byte)
MS-CHAP Data (1 + Bytes)				

EAP Data (PEAP/MS-CHAPv2) – Windows XP Implementation

00011001 (25)	Flags (5 Bits)	Version	TLS Message Length (4 Bytes)	
			00011101 (29)	MS-CHAP Type (1 Byte)
MS-CHAP Data (1 + Bytes)				

Figure 5-6 *PEAP with MS-CHAPv2 Data Field Example*

Cisco Lightweight EAP

Cisco Lightweight Extensible Authentication Protocol (LEAP) uses the concept of mutual authentication to validate a user. Mutual authentication relies on a shared secret and the user's password, which is known by the client and the network. The authentication server sends a challenge to the client. The client uses a one-way hash of the user password to send a response to the challenge. The server creates its own response based on the user database information and compares it to the response received from the client. When the server authenticates the client, the same process is repeated in reverse so that the client can authenticate the server. When this process is completed, an EAP-Success message is sent to the client.

EAP–Transport Layer Security

EAP-TLS is a standard developed by Microsoft and accepted by the Internet Engineering Task Force (IETF) as RFC 2716. It is based on the Transport Layer Security (TLS) protocol as described in another standard (RFC 2246).

Similar to the Cisco LEAP method, EAP-TLS mutually authenticates the client and the server; however, in this case, passwords are not used. Instead, public key cryptography based on the Rivest, Shamir, and Adelman (RSA) handshake is used. EAP-TLS uses digital certificates or smart cards to validate both the user's and the server's identity.

The RADIUS server sends its certificate to the client in Phase 1 of the authentication sequence (server-side TLS). The client validates the RADIUS server certificate by verifying the issuer of the certificate, a certificate authority (CA) server entity, and the contents of the digital certificate. When this is complete, the client sends its certificate to the RADIUS server in Phase 2 of the authentication sequence (client-side TLS). The RADIUS server validates the client's certificate by verifying the issuer of the certificate (CA server entity) and the contents of the digital certificate. When this is complete, an EAP-Success message is sent to the client.

The advantage of EAP-TLS is that it can be configured for two-factor authentication systems; it is one of the strongest forms of authentication available today.

The cons of EAP-TLS are that it can be more complex to deploy because of the various components, such as a certificate authority (CA). It is also more computationally intensive on both the client and the server.

Figure 5-7 displays a sample of the EAP data field.

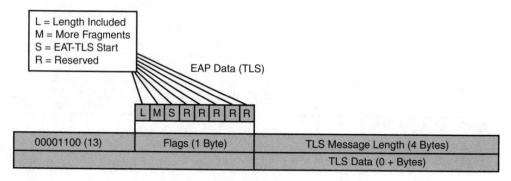

Figure 5-7   *EAP-TLS Data Field Example*

EAP–Tunneled Transport Layer Security

EAP-TTLS is defined in RFC 5281, extends on the concepts used for EAP-TLS, works similarly to PEAP, and uses two phases. Like EAP-TLS, EAP-TTLS utilizes TLS to form a tunnel between the authentication server and the supplicant and is created in Phase 1. Like PEAP, EAP-TTLS utilizes the TLS tunnel to encapsulate another form of EAP authentication but differs from PEAP in that it also can support non-EAP methods like PPP Authentication

Protocol (PAP) and PPP Challenge Handshake Authentication Protocol (CHAP). However, unlike EAP-TLS, EAP-TTLS does not require that both the server and client be authenticated, which makes configuration easier.

Figure 5-8 displays a sample of the EAP data field.

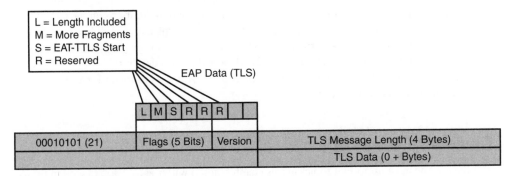

Figure 5-8   *EAP-TTLS Data Field Example*

EAP–Flexible Authentication via Secure Tunneling

EAP–Flexible Authentication via Secure Tunneling (EAP-FAST) was developed by Cisco and is documented in RFC 4851. Cisco developed EAP-FAST to support customers that require strong password policy enforcement but do not want to deploy digital certificates. EAP-FAST provides protection against a variety of network attacks, including man-in-the-middle, replay, and dictionary attacks.

Phase 1 establishes a mutually authenticated tunnel. The client and server use a Protected Access Credential (PAC) to authenticate each other and establish a secure tunnel.

Phase 2 performs client authentication in the established tunnel. The client sends a username and password to authenticate and establish client authorization policy.

EAP-FAST tunnel establishment relies on a PAC that can be provisioned and managed dynamically by EAP-FAST through the authentication server during Phase 2.

Figure 5-9 displays a sample of the EAP data field.

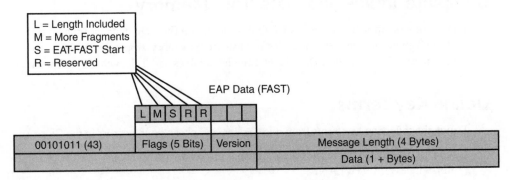

Figure 5-9   *EAP-FAST Data Field Example*

Exam Preparation

As mentioned in the section, "How to Use This Book," in the Introduction, you have several choices for exam preparation: the exercises here, the memory tables in Appendix D, the final exam preparation chapter, and the exam simulation questions on the CD-ROM. The questions that follow present a bigger challenge than the exam itself because they use an open-ended question format. By using this more difficult format, you exercise your memory better and prove your conceptual and factual knowledge of this chapter. You can find the answers to these questions in Appendix A, "Answers to the DIKTA Quizzes and Fill in the Blanks Questions."

Review All Key Topics

Review the most important topics in this chapter, noted with the Key Topics icon in the margin of the page. Table 5-7 lists a reference of these key topics and the page numbers on which each is found.

Table 5-7   *Key Topics*

Key Topic Element	Description	Page
Table 5-2	IBNS deployment modes	94
802.1x components	Lists and describes the three main 802.1x components	96
Figure 5-2	EAP packet format	97
Figure 5-3	EAPOL frame format	98
Table 5-5	802.1x port states	100
Table 5-6	Port authentication host modes	101

Complete Tables and Lists from Memory

Print a copy of Appendix C, "Memory Tables" (found on the CD), or at least the section for this chapter, and complete the tables and lists from memory. Appendix D, "Memory Table Answers," also on the CD, includes completed tables and lists to check your work.

Define Key Terms

Define the following key terms from this chapter, and check your answers in the Glossary:

Cisco Discovery Protocol (CDP), hash, Transport Layer Security (TLS), Voice over IP (VoIP), wireless LAN (WLAN)

Fill in the Blanks

1. The _____ deployment mode reduces known issues with other protocols' timeouts and networked services.

2. The _____ feature provides the ability for a host without 802.1x support to gain full network access.

3. The _____ feature provides the ability for a host to gain some network access even after failing authentication.

4. When implementing 802.1x, the _____ is the entity that validates the identity of the requesting host.

5. The _____ and _____ protocols are not supported by 802.1x natively without external tunneling support.

6. In a LAN environment, the _____ protocol is used to transport EAP traffic.

7. When the supplicant initiates the 802.1x connection, it sends an _____ frame to start the connection.

8. When using EAP-MD5, a _____ is sent in lieu of a password on the network.

9. The _____ is relied on by EAP-FAST to help establish tunneling.

10. When using EAPOL, the PAE group address is always set to _____ .

References

For additional information, refer to these resources:

[1] http://www.cisco.com/go/ibns

This chapter covers the following subjects:

■ **Plan basic 802.1X deployment on Cisco Catalyst IOS Software:** Covers the details of a basic 802.1X deployment.

■ **Configure and verify Cisco Catalyst IOS Software 802.1X authenticator:** Learn how to configure and verify the 802.1X authenticator on Cisco Catalyst IOS Software.

■ **Configure and verify EAP-FAST on Cisco Secure ACS:** The steps necessary to provide EAP-FAST support on Cisco Secure ACS are covered in this section.

■ **Configure and verify the Cisco Secure Services Client (CSSC) 802.1X supplicant:** The 802.1X supplicant is configured in this section.

■ **Troubleshoot 802.1X on Cisco Identity-Based Network Services (IBNS) components:** You learn a process for troubleshooting issues with 802.1X implementations.

CHAPTER 6

Implementing and Configuring Basic 802.1X

This chapter discusses the features of 802.1X authentication. The criticality of authenticating and authorizing access to information assets has never been more important than it is today. Organizations rely more heavily on digital information to increase their success. However, access to that same digital information by the wrong party can also bring about the demise of organizations. Cisco Identity-Based Network Services (IBNS) can use the features of 802.1X to ensure that users and machines that access a company's resources are properly authenticated and authorized before that access is granted.

"Do I Know This Already?" Quiz

The "Do I Know This Already?" quiz helps you decide whether you really need to read the entire chapter. If you already intend to read the entire chapter, you do not necessarily need to answer these questions now.

The ten-question quiz, derived from the major sections in the "Foundation Topics" portion of this chapter, helps you determine how to spend your limited study time.

Table 6-1 outlines the major topics discussed in this chapter and the "Do I Know This Already?" quiz questions that correspond to those topics.

Table 6-1 *"Do I Know This Already?" Foundation Topics Section-to-Question Mapping*

Foundation Topics Section	Questions Covered in This Section
Plan Basic 802.1X Deployment on Cisco Catalyst IOS Software	1–4
Configure and Verify Cisco Catalyst IOS Software 802.1X Authenticator	5, 6
Configure and Verify EAP-FAST on Cisco Secure ACS	7, 8
Configure and Verify the Cisco Secure Services Client (CSSC) 802.1X Supplicant	9, 10

Caution: The goal of self-assessment is to gauge your mastery of the topics in this chapter. If you do not know the answer to a question or are only partially sure of the answer, you should mark this question wrong for purposes of the self-assessment. Giving yourself credit for an answer that you correctly guess skews your self-assessment results and might provide you with a false sense of security.

1. Which of the following three components comprise Cisco 802.1X authentication?

   a.   Cisco IOS Software 802.1X authenticator

   b.   Cisco Secure ACS 4.2 Server

   c.   Cisco Secure Services Client wired 802.1X supplicant

   d.   Cisco MARS

   e.   Microsoft SQL Server

2. Which 802.1X component is also known as the client?

   a.   Cisco IOS Software 802.1X authenticator

   b.   Cisco Secure ACS 4.2 Server

   c.   Cisco Secure Services Client wired 802.1X supplicant

   d.   Cisco MARS

   e.   The user

3. Which 802.1X component is the switch or router between the client and the AAA server?

   a.   Cisco IOS Software 802.1X authenticator

   b.   Cisco Secure ACS 4.2 Server

   c.   Cisco Secure Services Client wired 802.1X supplicant

   d.   Cisco MARS

   e.   The user

4. Which 802.1X component is also known as the AAA server?

   a.   Cisco IOS Software 802.1X authenticator

   b.   Cisco Secure ACS 4.2 Server

   c.   Cisco Secure Services Client wired 802.1X supplicant

   d.   Cisco MARS

   e.   The user

5. Which command adds a RADIUS server to an IOS device's configuration?

   a.   router (config)# **RADIUS server add**

   b.   router (config)# **aaa authentication server RADIUS**

   c.   router (config-if)# **ip aaa RADIUS host**

   d.   router (config)# **radius-server host**

6. What UDP ports are used by Cisco as the default authentication and accounting ports?

    a. 67 and 68

    b. 1645 and 1646

    c. 1812 and 1813

    d. 20 and 21

    e. None of the answers are correct.

7. What must the Shared Secret field on the Network Configuration screen in Cisco Secure ACS match?

    a. The cryptographic key that was entered on the IOS-based switch when defining the RADIUS server

    b. The IP address of the switch

    c. The password that was entered for the user in the Protected Access Credential file

    d. The passphrase used to encrypt data between the AAA server and the authenticator

    e. The password entered on the supplicant

8. If the network between the supplicant and the AAA server is trusted, you can deploy user PAC files using which method?

    a. Manually by importing a PAC file into each client's supplicant.

    b. Configure the switch to copy the PAC from its flash to the client.

    c. Push the PAC to the user from the Windows Server Active Directory store.

    d. Automatic (anonymous).

9. What is the tool used to create the CSSC configuration profile?

    a. Cisco Secure ACS CSUtil command-line utility

    b. **dot1x test eapol-capable** command

    c. CSSC Management Utility

    d. Cisco Security Device Manager

10. From where are the CSSC supplicant and the CSSC Management Utility obtained?

    a. Included in the IOS image

    b. Included in Microsoft Windows Operating Systems

    c. Downloaded from Cisco.com

    d. Obtain from a TAC engineer

The answers to the "Do I Know This Already?" quiz are found in Appendix A. The suggested choices for your next step are as follows:

■ **8 or less overall score:** Read the entire chapter. This includes the "Foundation Topics" and the "Exam Preparation" section.

■ **9 or 10 overall score:** If you want more review on these topics, skip to the "Exam Preparation" section. Otherwise, move on to Chapter 7, "Implementing and Configuring Advanced 802.1X."

Foundation Topics

802.1X is an IEEE standard that provides a framework for authenticating and authorizing network devices connected to LAN ports and for preventing access in the event that the authentication and authorization fail. The authentication and authorization process requires a supplicant (client), an authenticator (router, switch, wireless AP, and so on), and an authentication server. This chapter covers basic 802.1X features. You will be able to plan basic 802.1X, perform basic configuration tasks, and troubleshoot basic functionality on Cisco IBNS components.

Figure 6-1 shows the components that come into play when considering 802.1X authentication.

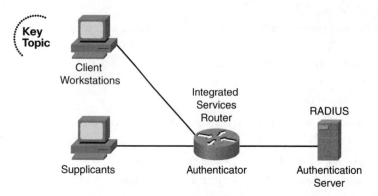

Figure 6-1   *Components Included in 802.1X Authentication Process*

This client-server-based access control and authentication protocol authenticates each client prior to making any services available to that port. Before a port enters an authorized state, 802.1X allows only Extensible Authentication Protocol over LAN (EAPOL), Cisco Discovery Protocol (CDP), and Spanning Tree Protocol (STP) packets to traverse the port.

Configuring 802.1X port authentication is supported on Layer 2 static access ports, voice VLAN–enabled ports, and Layer 3 routed ports. It is not supported on dynamic ports, trunk ports, or Switched Port Analyzer (SPAN) or Remote SPAN (RSPAN) ports.

Plan Basic 802.1X Deployment on Cisco Catalyst IOS Software

In this chapter, the basic 802.1X deployment includes configuring bidirectional, basic authentication on the network edge. The process authenticates the user to the network and the network to the user. The supplicant authenticates the user on the computer but not the computer itself. Machine authentication is discussed in Chapter 7. The credentials in this scenario will be shared secrets (passwords) and utilize EAP-FAST as the protocol between the supplicant and the authentication server. A basic 802.1X deployment involves gathering input parameters, making configuration choices, performing basic configuration tasks, and following some general deployment guidelines.

The Cisco IBNS components discussed are as follows:

- Cisco Catalyst IOS Software 802.1X authenticator

- Cisco Secure ACS 4.2 authentication, authorization, and accounting (AAA) server

- Cisco Secure Services Client (CSSC) 802.1X wired supplicant

Gathering Input Parameters

Because 802.1X authentication requires several technologies to work together, up-front planning helps ensure the success of the deployment. Part of this planning involves gathering important input information:

- Determine the list of LAN switches that currently allow unauthorized users full access to the network. Use this list to determine which of these devices should be configured with 802.1X and the feature availability on the switches.

- Determine what authentication database (such as Windows AD) is being used for user credentials. This allows you to determine whether you can leverage the same one and make the 802.1X deployment transparent to your users.

- Determine the types of clients being used on the network (platform and operating systems). This is required to choose a compatible supplicant and to configure it appropriately.

- Determine the software distribution mechanism in use by the organization. This will affect provisioning and supporting the supplicant on current and future client workstations.

- Determine whether the network path between the supplicant and the authentication server is trusted. A trusted network path allows an anonymous EAP-FAST implementation, whereas a nontrusted network path requires separate EAP-FAST credentials.

Deployment Tasks

Deploying basic 802.1X authentication involves the following deployment steps:

Step 1. Configure the 802.1X authenticator on a Cisco Catalyst IOS Software switch.

Step 2. On the switch, configure a guest VLAN or a restricted VLAN or tune 802.1X timers (optional).

Step 3. Configure the Cisco Secure ACS AAA server to support EAP-FAST and add a user account to its local database.

Step 4. Configure and deploy the 802.1X supplicant to the client machine. The following section discusses the Cisco Secure Services Client (CSS) on the Windows operating system.

Deployment Choices

Based on the systems and networks in your environment, you need to make some deployment choices when deploying basic 802.1X authentication:

- **Choice of EAP method:** There are several EAP methods from which to choose. If you use passwords or one-time passwords, use the following guidelines:
  - If you simply use passwords, you can use EAP-Flexible Authentication via Secure Tunneling (FAST) as the outer EAP method and EAP-Microsoft Challenge Handshake Authentication Protocol (MS-CHAPv2) as the inner method. EAP-FAST provides identity protection in that attackers cannot determine the client's identity. If this does not pose a risk for your environment, you can implement EAP-MSCHAPv2 without the EAP-FAST tunnel protection.

  - If you use one-time passwords, you can use EAP-Generic Token Card (GTC) inside EAP-FAST or inside Protected Extensible Authentication Protocol (PEAP). Never deploy standalone EAP-GTC.

- **Choice of supplicant:** You can choose to use the 802.1X supplicant that is provided by the operating system or a third-party supplicant, such as the Cisco Secure Services Client (CSSC). Consider the following:
  - Use the native 802.1X supplicant that is included in the operating system if it provides all the features and functionality that you require and makes provisioning in your environment easier.

  - Use the CSSC if you need support for many authentication protocols and a single supplicant that works for wired and wireless authentication.

General Deployment Guidelines

Use the following general guidelines when deploying basic 802.1X authentication:

- Use a single sign-on (SSO) solution for 802.1X that is scalable for your environment. Ensure that your authentication database enforces a policy that requires strong credential strength.

- Ensure proper analysis prior to deployment. Use a deployment plan that has tested successfully because incorrect parameters or configuration items can deny access to large numbers of users all at once.

- Run a pilot deployment and troubleshoot compatibility issues prior to deploying to the entire production environment.

- Ensure that the many different areas of the organization are represented in the pilot so that your testing mimics production as close as possible.

Configure and Verify Cisco Catalyst IOS Software 802.1X Authenticator

There are several tasks involved in configuring the Cisco Catalyst IOS Software 802.1X authenticator:

Key Topic

Task 1. Configure a RADIUS server on the network switch and the AAA server.

Task 2. Configure the switch to use AAA and the RADIUS protocol for authentication.

Task 3. Enable 802.1X globally on the switch.

Task 4. Enable 802.1X on access ports that require user authentication on the switch.

Task 5. (Optional) Configure periodic reauthentication.

Task 6. (Optional) Tune timers and thresholds.

Task 7. (Optional) Configure a guest policy on the switch if one is needed.

Configuration Choices

You have to make some configuration choices when configuring the authenticator:

- **You can optionally tune 802.1X EAPOL timers.** The default timers set in Cisco IOS Software are configured very conservatively. If you have clients that are not receiving their IP address from the DHCP server, it could be from a lengthy 802.1X authentication process.

- **You can optionally configure reauthentication.** Optional reauthentication is similar to using a heartbeat connection. In some cases, the switch port to which the host connects is not configured with 802.1X authentication and authentication takes place on an upstream switch. Configuring reauthentication will cause a period of verification to take place, thus ensuring that the client it still connected and that the port remains in the authenticated state.

- **You can optionally create a guest network.** This can be used for hosts that do not have an 802.1X supplicant or for hosts that fail authentication. The guest network can also be used for users who are not part of the authenticated network. These "guest" users might still need to connect and have limited access, such as connectivity to the Internet, but no connectivity to any internal resources.

Configuration Scenario

The configuration scenario, shown in Figure 6-2, will be to configure the Cisco Catalyst IOS Software 802.1X authenticator using the following information:

- The corporate user will be using an 802.1X supplicant, and there will be a guest without a supplicant that connect to a LAN switch that requires authentication on its user ports.

- The router/authenticator is running the Cisco IOS Software and is configured with 192.168.1.1 as its management IP address.

- VLAN 100 is used for the guest network and will only provide access to the public Internet.

■   The AAA server is Cisco Secure ACS 4.2, is running on Windows Server with an IP address of 10.1.1.1, and is configured with RADIUS for 802.1X communications.

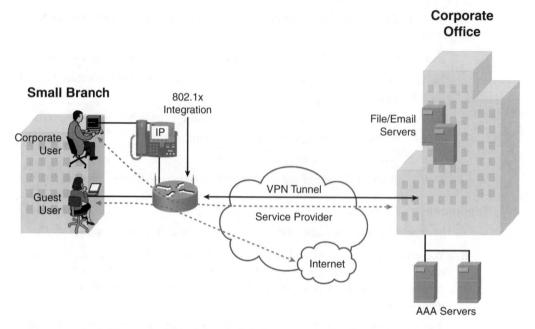

Figure 6-2 *Configuration Scenario*

Task 1: Configure RADIUS Server

The first task for enabling the Cisco IOS Software 802.1X authenticator is to configure a RADIUS server:

Step 1.   Enter the **radius-server host** command to specify the IP address of the RA-DIUS server with which the switch will communicate to authenticate 802.1X clients. This command also specifies the cryptographic authentication key that is used to protect the session.

> **Note:**   Configure two RADIUS servers to provide a redundant set of AAA servers. Also, use a strong value for the authentication key and consider using different authentication keys for each 802.1X switch, in case one of them gets compromised.

Step 2.   Optionally, you can change the authentication and accounting ports from the defaults, UDP 1645 and 1646, which are used by Cisco Secure ACS to the standard RADIUS ports, UDP 1812 and 1813.

Example 6-1 shows the configuration of a RADIUS server at 10.1.1.1, using the standard RADIUS ports, UDP 1812 and 1813, and specifying an authentication key of "rad123."

Example 6-1 *Configure a RADIUS Server on the Cisco Catalyst IOS Software Switch*

```
Router# configure terminal
Router(config)# radius-server host 10.1.1.1 auth-port 1812 acct-port 1813 key rad123
Router(config)# exit
Router# copy running-config startup-config
```

Task 2: Enable AAA and Use RADIUS for Authentication

In Task 2, you enable AAA and configure an AAA authentication method that uses RADIUS for interfaces that will be running 802.1X port security:

Step 1.   Enable AAA globally on the switch with the **aaa new-model** command.

Step 2.   Configure an AAA authentication method that specifies that 802.1X authentication requests should be sent to the configured RADIUS servers.

Example 6-2 shows the commands that will enable AAA globally on the switch and then create an AAA authentication method that will send 802.1X authentication requests to the configured RADIUS servers.

Example 6-2 *Enable AAA Globally and Use RADIUS for Authentication*

```
Router# configure terminal
Router(config)# aaa new model
Router(config)# exit
Router(config)# aaa authentication dot1x default group radius none
Router# copy running-config startup-config
```

Tasks 3 and 4: Enable 802.1X Globally and on Individual User Ports

Tasks 3 and 4 configure 802.1X globally and then enable 802.1X on user (access) ports on the switch:

Step 1.   Enable 802.1X globally on the switch with the **dot1x system-auth-control** global command.

Step 2.   On the ports that will require 802.1X authentication, ensure that the interface is configured as a Layer 2 access port with the **switchport mode access** interface command.

Step 3.   Make sure that the user interfaces are assigned to a proper access VLAN with the **switchport access vlan** *vlan-id* interface command.

Step 4.   Enable 802.1X port control on the user interfaces using the **authentication port-control** interface command.

Example 6-3 shows the commands that will enable AAA globally on the switch and then create a AAA authentication method that will send 802.1X authentication requests to the configured RADIUS servers.

Example 6-3 *Enable 802.1X Globally and Add New RADIUS Authentication Method*

```
Router# configure terminal
Router(config)# dot1x system-auth-control
Router(config)# interface FastEthernet 2/1
Router(config-if)# switchport mode access
Router(config-if)# switchport access vlan 90
Router(config-if)# authentication port-control auto
Router(config)# end
Router# copy running-config startup-config
```

Task 5: (Optional) Configure Periodic Reauthentication

Task 5 is an optional task that you can configure on an interface or range of interfaces. By default, 802.1X reauthentication is not enabled. This can cause problems in an environment in which not all switches perform authentication. For example, if your distribution switches perform 802.1X authentication, the switch will not detect that the client has disconnected and leave the port in an authenticated state. Periodic reauthentication can alleviate this by forcing the client to periodically reauthenticate to the AAA server.

Step 1. Enable periodic reauthentication on a user interface or range of interfaces with the **authentication periodic** interface command. The default is that periodic reauthentication is disabled.

Step 2. You can adjust the timer on the periodic reauthentication attempts with the **authentication timer reauthenticate** interface command. The default time between attempts is 3600 seconds. Reducing the time causes your user ports to be reauthenticated more often. This would be considered good from a security standpoint but will add extra load on your RADIUS servers. Proceed with caution, because a high load could cause legitimate clients to be denied access to your network if your AAA servers are too busy to process 802.1X authentication requests.

Example 6-4 shows the commands that enable periodic reauthentication and adjust the time between periodic reauthentication attempts.

Example 6-4 *Enable 802.1X Periodic Reauthentication and Adjust the Time Between Reauthentication Attempts*

```
Router# configure terminal
Router(config)# interface FastEthernet 2/1
Router(config-if)# authentication periodic
Router(config-if)# authentication timer reauthentication 600
Router(config)# end
Router# copy running-config startup-config
```

Task 6: (Optional) Tune Timers and Thresholds

Task 6 is an optional task in which you can adjust EAPOL timers to optimize the 802.1X authentication exchange between the supplicant and the authenticator.

Figure 6-3 shows the message exchange between the supplicant and the authenticator (ISR) and the authenticator (ISR) and the authentication server.

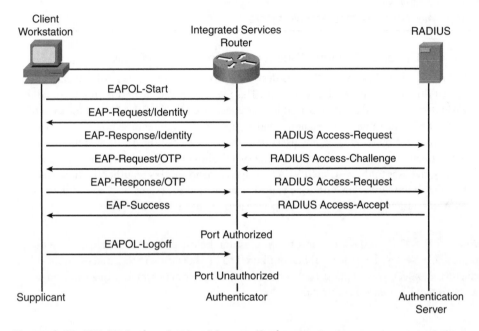

Figure 6-3   *802.1X Authentication Message Exchange*

Note: EAPOL is used between the supplicant and the authenticator, while RADIUS is used between the authenticator and the authentication server.

The authenticator expects to receive the EAP-Response/Identity frame as a response to its EAP-Request/Identity frame. If it has not received this frame within the default retransmission time, it will resend the Request frame. The default retransmission timer is 30 seconds. You can adjust this time to increase response times, which will allow a faster 802.1X authentication process. The retransmission timer is changed with the **dot1x timeout tx-period** interface command.

If the switch fails to authenticate a client, such as the user entering a bad password, the switch waits a period of time before trying again. The default value for this quiet timer is 60 seconds. You can lower this value, thus giving the client a faster response time with the **dot1x timeout quiet-period seconds** interface configuration command.

Example 6-5 shows the commands that change the retransmission and quiet 802.1X timers.

Example 6-5 *Change the Default Retransmission and Quiet Timers*

```
Router# configure terminal
Router(config)# interface FastEthernet 2/1
Router(config-if)# dot1x timeout tx-period 10
Router(config-if)# dot1x timeout quiet-period 10
Router(config)# end
Router# copy running-config startup-config
```

Task 7: (Optional) Configure Guest and Authentication Failed Policy

In Task 7, a special-purpose VLAN is designated for clients that either fail authentication or that do not have an 802.1X supplicant. This means that the client does not respond to EAPOL requests and must be placed into a "guest" VLAN. The VLAN used for each of these can be the same or different depending upon your architecture; however, it must exist on the switch before assigning users to it. In the case of authentication failure, you must specify the number of times that the switch should retry authentication before assigning the user to the restricted VLAN. The command for this is **authentication event fail retry** *number* **action authorize vlan**. The command to assign a user to the guest VLAN is **authentication event no-response action authorize VLAN.**

Note: The 802.1X authentication attempt must fail before the switch will assign the user to the guest VLAN. This time can be configured to be shorter on the interfaces upon which you expect to have guest connections by using the **dot1x timeout quiet-period** and **dot1x timeout tx-period** commands.

Example 6-6 shows the commands that assign an interface to a special VLAN for either guests or clients that fail authentication.

Example 6-6 *Commands to Configure Guest and Authentication Failed Policy*

```
Router# configure terminal
Router(config)# interface FastEthernet 2/1
Router(config-if)# authentication event fail retry 2 action authorize vlan 100
Router(config-if)# authentication event no-response action authorize vlan 100
Router(config)# end
Router# copy running-config startup-config
```

Implementation Guidelines for 802.1X Authentication Configuration

Misconfiguration of the 802.1X authenticator can render entire sections of the network unreachable to your users. Extreme caution and planning must be employed when configuring 802.1X authentication. Some guidelines to consider are as follows:

■   Adjusting EAPOL timers on interfaces configured with guest policies must be tested prior to implementing in production. Trying to speed up the process for guest users (because authentication must time out) by shortening the time that a switch waits could cause your legitimate users to be placed in the guest VLAN.

- Adjusting timers on the switch might require adjusting timers on the client supplicant as well.

- Ensure that you utilized several security layers in your design to adequately protect the rest of your network from the guest VLAN. You might even consider putting them in a separate Virtual Routing and Forwarding (VRF) instance. VRFs are configurations on Cisco IOS Software routers and switches that can be used to provide traffic separation, making them a good solution to keep guest traffic segregated from your corporate traffic.

Verify Basic 802.1X Functionality

To verify the operational status of the 802.1X configuration on your device, use the **show dot1x** command, which will show the current state of the authenticator as Enabled. Example 6-7 displays the output of the **show dot1x** command.

Example 6-7   show dot1x *Command Output*

```
Router# show dot1x


Sysauthcontrol              Enabled
Dot1x Protocol Version    2
```

The **show dot1x all summary** command, shown in Example 6-8, shows the authorization state of each of the interfaces on which you have 802.1X authentication configured.

Example 6-8   show dot1x all summary *Command Output*

```
Router# show dot1x all summary


Interface          PAE              Client            Status
--------------------------------------------------------------------------------
--------
Fa1                AUTH             000d.bcef.bfdc        AUTHORIZED
```

Configure and Verify Cisco ACS for EAP-FAST

Extensible Authentication Protocol - Flexible Authentication via Secured Tunnel (EAP-FAST) is a client-server security architecture that protects EAP transactions by use of a Transport Layer Security (TLS) tunnel. These tunnels are built using shared secrets that are called Protected Access Credentials (PAC).

There are several tasks involved in configuring Cisco Secure ACS for EAP-FAST:

Task 1.   Configure a RADIUS server on the network switch and the AAA server.

Task 2.   Configure EAP-FAST on the AAA server.

Task 3.   Populate the user authentication database on the AAA server.

Task 4.   (Optional) Generate user PAC files.

Task 5.   (Optional) Configure Network Access Restrictions (NAR) for 802.1X users.

Task 6.   Enable logging of passed authentications.

Configuration Choices

Prior to implementation, several configuration choices must be made:

- Deciding whether to use Network Access Restrictions (NAR). NAR can be used to impose additional restrictions on your users before permitting them to be successfully authenticated. For example, you can restrict them to access the network only from a certain network address space. There are many options available when configuring NAR.

- Deciding how to provision the Protected Access Credential (PAC) files is important. If the network between the AAA server and the switch is a fully trusted path, you can use automatic provisioning of the PAC files. If the path is not trusted, you should provision the PAC files manually.

- Deciding where you user credentials database will reside is also a very important design consideration. Use the Cisco Secure ACS internal database or use an external database that Cisco Secure ACS will contact for authentication validation. Using an external database, such as Windows Active Directory, will make administration much easier and enable single sign-on for the users.

Configuration Scenario

The configuration scenario will be to configure the Cisco Secure ACS EAP-FAST server using basic 802.1X. The client will either be using an 802.1X supplicant or will be a guest without a supplicant. Additionally, the client will connect to a LAN switch that requires authentication on its user ports and will use usernames and passwords to authenticate to the AAA server using EAP-MSCHAPv2 tunneled inside EAP-FAST. The router/authenticator is running the Cisco IOS Software and is configured with 192.168.1.1 as its management IP address. VLAN 100 is used for the guest network and will only provide access to the public Internet. The AAA server is Cisco Secure ACS 4.2 and is running on Windows Server with an IP address of 10.1.1.1 and is configured with RADIUS for 802.1X communications.

Task 1: Configure a RADIUS Server

For Cisco Secure ACS to authenticate 802.1X clients, the 802.1X-enabled switch/router/AP must be added as a AAA client on the Cisco Secure ACS server. For the first task of configuring the switch/router/AP as a RADIUS AAA client on Cisco Secure ACS, refer to Figure 6-4 and perform the following steps:

Step 1.   Click Network Configuration in the navigation bar. The Network Configuration window, shown in Figure 6-4, opens.

Step 2.   Click Add Entry below the AAA clients table.

Step 3.   Enter the name of the switch in the AAA Client Hostname field.

Step 4.   Enter the IP address of the switch in the AAA Client IP Address field.

Step 5.   Enter the session key in the Key field. This is the same key that you configured on the switch in the **aaa-server host** command used to add the RADIUS server to the switch.

Step 6.   Choose RADIUS (Cisco IOS/PIX) from the Authenticate Using drop-down box.

Step 7.   Click the Submit + Restart button.

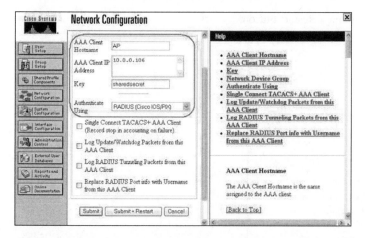

Figure 6-4   *Network Configuration on Cisco Secure ACS Server*

Figure 6-4 shows a AAA client named AP with an IP address of 10.0.0.106 being added to the Cisco Secure ACS server using a shared key of sharedsecret. The protocol used to communicate between the AAA server and the switch is RADIUS (Cisco/PIX).

Note: Failure to add the switch/router/AP to the Cisco Secure ACS server as a AAA client causes authentication attempt from your clients to fail. The AAA server treats the request as coming from an unknown source.

Task 2: Configure EAP-FAST on the AAA Server

In the second configuration task, refer to Figure 6-5 to enable EAP-FAST on Cisco Secure ACS and configure some of its basic properties.

Step 1.   Click System Configuration in the navigation bar. The System Configuration window opens (not shown).

Step 2.   Click Global Authentication Setup. The **System Configuration > Global Authentication Setup** window opens (not shown).

Step 3.   Enable EAP-FAST by selecting the check box next to the appropriate option.

Step 4.   In the Authority ID Info field, enter a unique name for this server, such as its host name. The example in Figure 6-5 has entered Cisco as the Authority ID.

Step 5.   Select the check box next to Allow Anonymous In-band PAC Provisioning if you are using a completely trusted link over which PAC files can be distributed anonymously (without authentication). If the link is not trusted, you should leave this deselected and use manual distribution of the PAC files. The PAC files must be manually imported into the 802.1X supplicant on the client.

Step 6. In the Protocols section of the Network Access Profile (NAP) configuration window (not shown), select the check box next to EAP-MSCHAPv2 under Allowed Inner Methods. This chooses EAP-MSCHAPv2 as the inner authentication method that will authenticate the user to the AAA server.

Step 7. Click the Submit + Restart button.

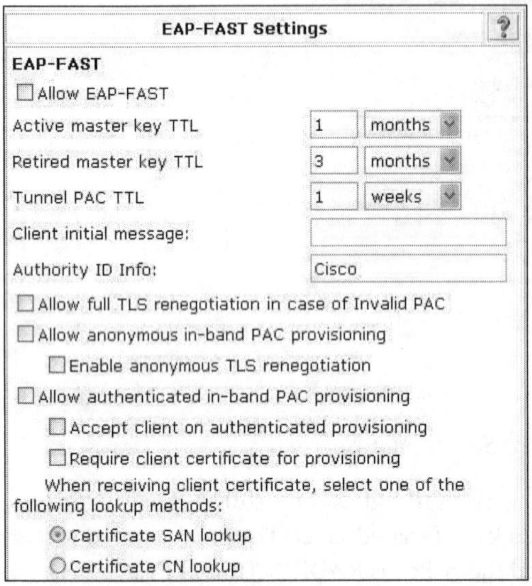

Figure 6-5 *System Configuration > Global Authentication Setup*

Task 3: Populate the User Authentication Database

Perform the following steps to create user accounts in the internal Cisco Secure ACS database. An external authentication database can be used instead. The third configuration task details how to create user accounts, as shown in Figure 6-6.

Step 1. Click User Setup in the navigation bar. The User Setup window opens, as shown in Figure 6-6.

Step 2. Enter a unique username in the User field and click Add/Edit. The Edit User window opens (not shown).

Step 3. In the Edit User screen, provide a password for the user and add the user to a group.

Step 4. Click Submit.

Task 4: (Optional) Generate User PAC Files

If the network path between the supplicant and the AAA server is not fully trusted, recommended practice dictates manually distributing user PAC files. To use the manual distribution process, PAC files must be generated. In Task 4, the Protected Access Credential (PAC) files for EAP-FAST must be generated and distributed to users to enable the EAP-FAST secure authentication process:

Step 1.   Open a command prompt window on the Cisco Secure ACS server as an administrator, as shown in Figure 6-7. Change the directory to a temporary folder.

Figure 6-6   *ACS User Setup Window*

Figure 6-7   *Command Prompt Window for CSUtil*

Step 2.   Run the **CSUtil** command with the **-t** and **-a** options to generate PAC files.

Step 3.   Import the PAC files located in the temporary folder from Step 2 into the supplicant on each user client.

Note: If you use automatic (anonymous) distribution of PAC files, they are transferred to the client during the first EAP-FAST authentication. Manual distribution requires that the files are imported into the 802.1X supplicant for each user.

Task 5: (Optional) Configure Network Access Restrictions

If the users must be restricted to authentication only from specific RADIUS clients, Network Access Restrictions (NAR) can provide this control. The optional Task 5 shows how to configure NAR to control the locations from which RADIUS users can authenticate:

Step 1.   Click Group Setup from the navigation bar. The Group Setup window opens.

Step 2.   Click the group that contains the 802.1X user accounts that you want to limit. Click Edit Settings, and the Group Settings page opens.

Step 3.   In the Group Settings windows, scroll down to Network Access Restrictions and select the check box to enable Define CLI/DNIS-based Access Restrictions. In the next box, click the device (or device group) from which you want to allow authentication and enter * in the Port, CLI, and DNIS fields. Click Enter to add entries to the list. Figure 6-8 shows this step.

Step 4.   Click Submit + Restart. Repeat this process for any additional groups to which a NAR must be applied.

Task 6: Enable Logging of Passed Authentications

Cisco Secure ACS can log successful as well as failed authentication attempts by users. Logging of successful authentication is disabled by default. To verify proper EAP-FAST authentication, follow the steps in Task 6, referring to Figure 6-9, to configure logging of passed authentications:

Step 1.   Click System Configuration on the navigation bar. The System Configuration window opens (not shown).

Step 2.   Click Logging to open the Logging Configuration window (not shown).

Step 3.   Click Configure in the CSV column in the ACS Reports section, and the CSV Passed Authentication File Configuration page opens (not shown).

Step 4.   Select the Log to CSV check box.

Step 5.   Click Submit.

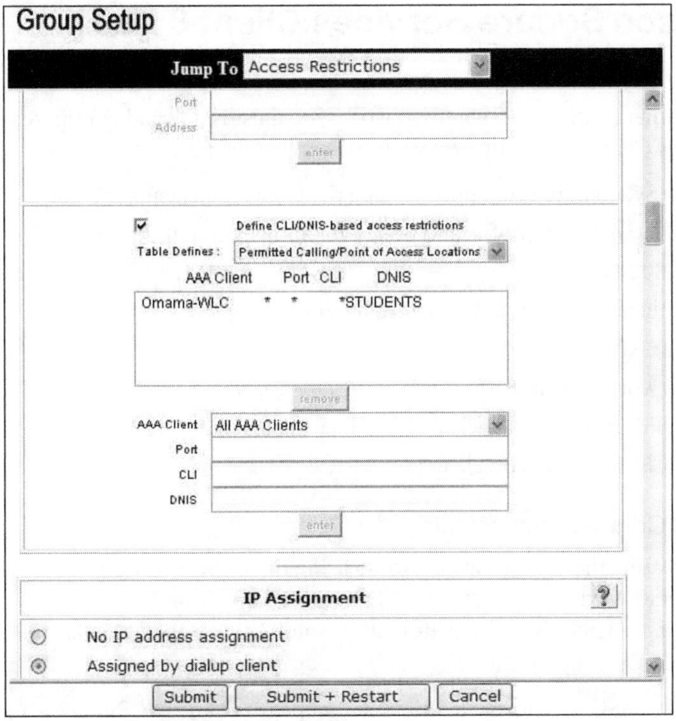

Group Setup

Jump To Access Restrictions

Port
Address

enter

☑   Define CLI/DNIS-based access restrictions

Table Defines :   Permitted Calling/Point of Access Locations

AAA Client   Port   CLI   DNIS

Omama-WLC   *   *   *STUDENTS

remove

AAA Client   All AAA Clients

Port

CLI

DNIS

enter

IP Assignment   ?

○   No IP address assignment

◉   Assigned by dialup client

Submit   Submit + Restart   Cancel

Figure 6-8 *ACS Group Setup Screen*

Figure 6-9 *ACS: Enable Logging of Passed Authentications*

Configure the Cisco Secure Services Client 802.1X Supplicant

To provide EAP-FAST authentication on a wired network, you must install and configure the Cisco Secure Services Client (CSSC) by performing the following tasks:

Task 1.   Create a CSSC configuration profile using the CSSC Management Utility.

Task 2.   Create a wired network profile and policy for authentication.

Task 3.   Configure 802.1X timers.

Task 4.   Choose authentication mode (user/machine/both).

Task 5.   Choose an EAP method.

Task 6.   Choose network authentication and login credentials.

Task 7.   Create a CSSC installation package including a configuration profile.

Task 8.   Install the CSSC package on clients.

Task 1: Create the CSSC Configuration Profile

The first task involves creating the configuration profile using the CSSC Management Utility. Download the CSSC Management Utility and the CSSC supplicant from Cisco.com. The output of the CSSC Management Utility is an XML file that contains the necessary settings for the client supplicant:

Step 1.   Download the CSSC Management Utility and unpack the archive. Run the ssc-ManagementUtility file to open the main screen.

Step 2.   Choose Create New Configuration Profile on the main screen.

Step 3.   Choose the version of CSSC being used. This chapter uses version 5.1.

Task 2: Create a Wired Network Profile

The second task creates a wired network profile inside the CSSC configuration profile. Using the CSSC Management Utility, as displayed in Figures 6-10 and 6-11, complete the following steps:

Step 1.   Choose a CSSC license option. Using the CSSC for wired only connectivity does not require a license, but if you plan to use the supplicant for both wired and wireless, a CSSC license must be provided on the Client Policy page.

Step 2.   Choose Attempt Connection After User Login in the Connection Setting section.

Step 3.   Choose to Allow Wired Media and click the Next button.

Step 4.   Choose EAP-FAST in the Allowed Authentication Modes on the Authentication Policy page, leaving all other options deselected. Click Next to continue.

Step 5.   Click Add Network on the Networks page to add a new network profile.

Step 6.   Leave the Wired Network Setting as the default on the Network Media page, and click the Next button.

Step 7.   Assign a name to the new network profile on the Wired Network Settings page. Specify the network as an authenticating network by clicking the appropriate radio button in the Security Level section, and then click the Next button.

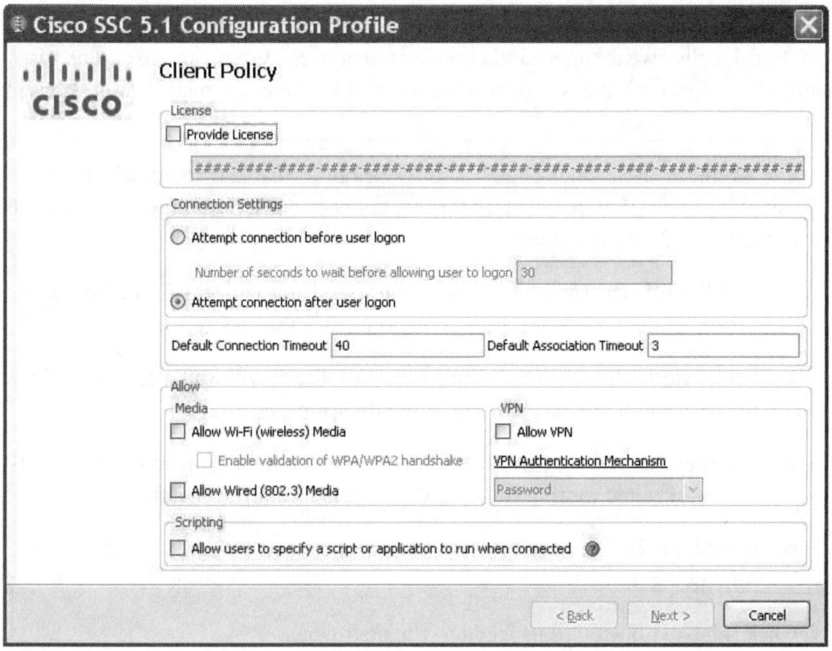

Figure 6-10 *CSSC Client Policy*

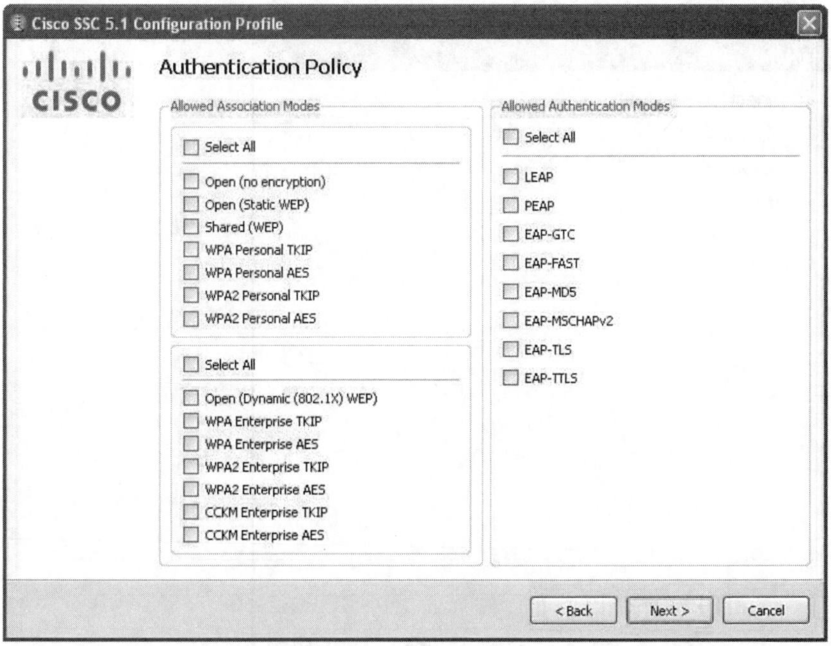

Figure 6-11 *CSSC Authentication Policy*

Tasks 3 and 4: (Optional) Tune 802.1X Timers and Authentication Mode

Tasks 3 and 4 optionally tweak timers and choose among user, system, and user plus system authentication. This example will be leaving the 802.1X timers at their default values but will set the authentication mode to user only:

Step 1.   The Connection Settings page has four options available through which to tune 802.1X EAPOL parameters for this connection. The parameters, as shown in Figure 6-12, are as follows:

- **authPeriod:** The time (in seconds) the supplicant will stay in the "authenticating" state while waiting for a response from the switch

- **heldPeriod:** The time (in seconds) the supplicant will wait after failing authentication before attempting authentication again

- **startPeriod:** The time (in seconds) the supplicant will stay in the "connecting" state while waiting for an EAP response from the switch

- **maxStart:** The number of times the supplicant will try to authenticate before giving up

Step 2.   Click the Next button to proceed to the next page.

Step 3.   Choose the User Connection type on the Network Connection Type page. This causes the connection to only attempt to authenticate the user, not the system.

Figure 6-12   *Connection Timers*

Task 5: Configure the Inner and Outer EAP Mode for the Connection

Task 5 configures the EAP mode that will be used for both the inner and outer authentication types for this connection. The example here chooses EAS-MSCHAPv2 tunneled inside EAP-FAST:

Step 1. Choose EAP-FAST as the outer EAP mode on the User Authentication page, as shown in Figure 6-13. Clicking the Configure button opens the EAP-FAST Settings window, shown in Figure 6-14, and permits you to configure EAP-FAST parameters.

Step 2. Select the Validate Server Identity check box in the EAP Settings window to make the supplicant authenticate the AAA server. In the Credentials Sections of the Inner Method section, choose Authenticate Using a Password and choose EAP-MSCHAPv2 as the inner EAP mode.

Step 3. This step is only required if you are manually distributing user PAC files. Select the Use PACs check box and import the specific PAC file for this user by clicking the Add PAC File button. This file was generated using the CSUtil CLI Utility.

Step 4. Leave all other settings at their default value and click OK.

Step 5. Click the Next button to go to the next page.

Figure 6-13 *User Authentication*

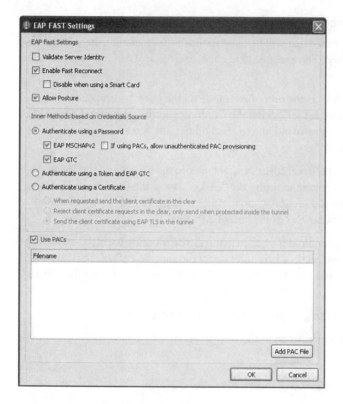

Figure 6-14 *EAP-FAST Settings*

Task 6: Choose the Login Credentials to Be Used for Authentication

Task 6 involves configuring the credentials that will be used to authenticate users to the network (AAA server). Perform the following steps to accomplish this:

Step 1. Click the Next button on the first User Server Validation page because password-based EAP-FAST mode does not require any configuration.

Step 2. On the second User Server Validation page, simply click the Next button again because password-based EAP-FAST authentication does not require trusted certificate authorities.

Step 3. The User Credentials page specifies how the CSSC will get the user's identity information (username) and authentication credentials (password). Enter a username in the Protected Identity Pattern field. You can optionally enter "[user]" to have a macro automatically select the user's current Microsoft Windows username as the username.

Step 4. On the same page, select the Prompt for Credentials option and pick the Remember While the User is Logged On option to cache the user's password. Optionally, you can pick the Use Single Sign On Credentials option to have the Microsoft Windows username and password be used for 802.1X authentication or statically enter the password in the Use Static Credentials option.

Step 5.   Click Finish to complete the CSSC Configuration Profile creation.

Task 7: Create the CSSC Installation Package

Task 7 executes the steps needed to create the CSSC Installation Package by bundling the CSSC Configuration Profile created in the previous steps with a CSSC installer to make a custom CSSC installation package for use on a client. Use Figure 6-15 for a visual aid and perform the following steps:

Step 1.   Run the sscManagementUtility executable to open the CSSC Management Utility again. The main window will open (not shown).

Step 2.   Choose Create Pre-Configured Client Component, and the Select Pre-Configured Client Components window opens (not shown).

Step 3.   Specify the path to the CSSC MSI software installer in the Select Pre-Configured Client Components window. This file would have been downloaded from Cisco.com. The path is specified in the Client Source Package File field.

Step 4.   Specify the path to the CSSC configuration profile that was created in the previous steps in the Processed and Signed Configuration File field.

Step 5.   Specify the location to which the custom CSSC Installation Package will be saved in the Client Destination Package File field.

Step 6.   Click Finish to create the custom package.

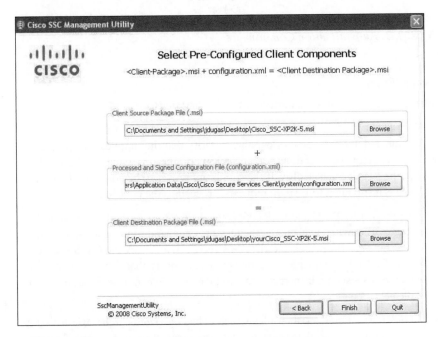

Figure 6-15   *Create a Preconfigured Client Package*

Network Login

If everything was configured correctly, the next time an attempt is made to connect to an 802.1X-authenticated network, the CSSC supplicant will start automatically and a pop-up window will appear asking for a password to be entered. Type in the password, and the client will be authenticated and granted access to the network.

Verify and Troubleshoot 802.1 X Operations

To successfully troubleshoot 802.1X authentication issues, you must consider all the components. These components include the supplicant, the authenticator, and the AAA server and the network connectivity between them. Figure 6-16 depicts the 802.1X authentication components.

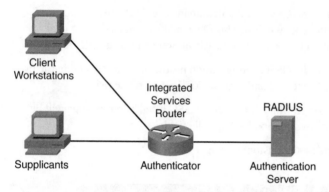

Figure 6-16 *802.1X Authentication Components*

Troubleshooting Flow

To troubleshoot 802.1X operation, perform the following steps:

Step 1. Verify the configuration of the client's supplicant. Use the Cisco IOS Software command **dot1x test eapol-capable** to verify that the supplicant responds to EAPOL requests. If it does not, check its configuration using the CSSC GUI or the Management Utility. If the supplicant proves to be configured correctly and is responding to EAPOL requests, proceed to the next step.

Step 2. Verify that RADIUS and EAP connections are set up correctly. Checking the logs on the switch while using the **test aaa** command can reveal RADIUS issues between the switch and the AAA server. Also, check the Cisco Secure ACS Failed Authentication Attempts report to verify that there are no errors on the AAA server. If there appears to be no problem in these areas, move to the next step.

Step 3. Look for user credential problems such as bad passwords in the ACS Failed Attempts log. Also, look for external database errors if using an external authentication database such as Microsoft Windows Active Directory.

Successful Authentication

By default, 802.1X authentication issues will be logged by Cisco IOS Software. Check logging messages by running the **show logging** command to verify successful authentication.

Verify Connection Status

The Cisco Secure Services Client (CSSC) installs a system tray icon that can be used to gather information regarding connection status. The tray icon's color and shape give indication to connection status. In addition, right-clicking the icon provides detailed connection status by choosing the Connection Status icon from the context menu.

Verify Authentication on AAA Server

The Cisco Secure ACS server provides detailed audit information in the Passed Authentication report. The report shows all successful authentications, whether they are against the internal database or against an external authentication database.

Verify Guest/Restricted VLAN Assignment

Verifying that interfaces utilized by guest users are assigned to the designated guest VLAN is a very important security requirement. You do not want a misconfiguration to allow a guest user to be connected to an internal production network. The **show interfaces status** command will show the connected status of your interfaces along with the VLAN to which the interfaces is assigned.

802.1X Readiness Check

The Cisco IOS Software command **dot1x test eapol-capable** can verify that the 802.1X authentication infrastructure is functioning properly before enforcing it. This test verifies the supplicant, the authenticator, and the AAA server. The output of the command will show which interfaces have an EAPOL-capable client attached. The switch will wait 10 seconds by default for a response from the supplicant on the client. The **dot1x test timeout** command can be used to change this timeout to a value range of 1 to 65,535 seconds.

Unresponsive Supplicant

The Cisco IOS Software logging mechanism will provide detailed information to use when troubleshooting a nonresponsive supplicant. Log messages can reveal messages that can indicate that no response was received from the supplicant, a response was received but authentication configurations between the supplicant and the AAA server are mismatched, successful authentications, and so on.

Failed Authentication: RADIUS Configuration Issues

When there is a configuration issue between the RADIUS configuration on the switch and the Cisco Secure ACS server, consult the switch logs as well as the Failed Authentication Attempts report. This report provides detailed messages that can be used to resolve issues.

Failed Authentication: Bad Credentials

When a user supplies invalid credentials, the Cisco IOS Software logs will display a failed authentication message. The authenticator (switch) will be notified of the invalid credentials in the form of a RADIUS message sent from the AAA server to the switch. The Cisco Secure ACS server Failed Authentication Attempts report will also indicate bad passwords.

Exam Preparation

As mentioned in the section, "How to Use This Book," in the Introduction, you have several choices for exam preparation: the exercises here, the memory tables in Appendix D, the final exam preparation chapter, and the exam simulation questions on the CD-ROM. The following questions present a bigger challenge than the exam itself because they use an open-ended question format. By using this more difficult format, you exercise your memory better and prove your conceptual and factual knowledge of this chapter. You can find the answers to these questions in Appendix A, "Answers to the DIKTA Quizzes and Fill in the Blanks Questions."

Review All Key Topics

Review the most important topics in this chapter, noted with the Key Topics icon in the margin of the page. Table 6-2 lists a reference of these key topics and the page numbers on which each is found.

Table 6-2   *Key Topics*

Key Topic Element	Description	Page
Figure 6-1	Components included in 802.1X authentication process	112
Task list	Configuration choices for configuring the 802.1X authenticator	115
Note	Describes protocols used between supplicant and authenticator and authenticator and authentication server	119

Complete Tables and Lists from Memory

Print a copy of Appendix C, "Memory Tables" (found on the CD), or at least the section for this chapter, and complete the tables and lists from memory. Appendix D, "Memory Table Answers," also on the CD, includes completed tables and lists to check your work. Although there were no memory tables in this chapter, you will find some for other chapters.

Define Key Terms

Define the following key terms from this chapter, and check your answers in the Glossary:

EAPOL, 802.1X readiness check

Fill in the Blanks

1. _____ is an IEEE standard that provides a framework for authenticating and authorizing network devices connected to LAN ports and for preventing access in the event that the authentication fails.

2. Configuring _____ causes a period verification to take place, thus ensuring that the client is still connected and the port should remain in the authenticated state.

3. Enable 802.1X globally on the switch with the _____ global command.

4. Verify the operational status of the 802.1X configuration on your device by using the _____ command.

5. _____ can be used to restrict 802.1X users to only access the network from a certain network address space.

6. The Cisco IOS Software _____ command can be used to verify that the 802.1X authentication is functioning properly.

References

NIST Special Publication 800-120 - Recommendation for EAP Methods Used in Wireless Network Access Authentication, http://csrc.nist.gov/publications/nistpubs/800-120/sp800-120.pdf.

802.1X IEEE Standard for Local and Metropolitan Area Networks – Port-based Network Access Control, http://standards.ieee.org/getieee802/download/802.1X-2004.pdf.

Configuring IEEE 802.1x Port-Based Authentication - Cisco IOS Configuration Guide 12.4, www.cisco.com/en/US/docs/ios/sec_user_services/configuration/guide/sec_cfg_ieee802_pba_ps6441_TSD_Products_Configuration_Guide_Chapter.html.

Catalyst 6500 Release 12.2SXH and Later Software Configuration Guide; Configuring IEEE 802.1X Port-Based Authentication, www.cisco.com/en/US/partner/docs/switches/lan/catalyst6500/ios/12.2SX/configuration/guide/dot1x.html.

Cisco Secure ACS: Network Access Restrictions with AAA Clients for Users and User Groups, www.cisco.com/en/US/partner/products/sw/secursw/ps2086/products_tech_note09186a0080858d3c.shtml.

This chapter covers the following subjects:

- **Plan the deployment of Cisco Advanced 802.1x authentication features:** Learn what is involved in planning the deployment of advanced 802.1x features.

- **Configure and verify EAP-TLS authentication on Cisco IOS components and Cisco Secure ACS:** Learn how to configure EAP-TLS authentication in this section.

- **Deploying user and machine authentication:** Covers the deployment of user and machine authentication. You also learn when to use each of them.

- **Deploying VLAN and ACL assignment:** For granular control of user access, you can use dynamically assigned VLANs and ACL assignment.

- **Configure and verify Cisco Secure ACS MAC address exception policies:** Covers configuring MAC Authentication Bypass for your non-802.1X clients.

- **Configure and verify web authentication on Cisco IOS Software LAN switches and Cisco Secure ACS:** Web authentication is another method for authentication of non-802.1x clients. This section covers configuring and verifying web authentication.

- **Choose a method to support multiple hosts on a single port:** Covers the information needed for you to provide authentication support for multiple hosts on the same port.

- **Configuring fail-open policies:** Learn how to configure fail-open policies for times when the default fail-close policy does not apply to your environment.

- **Resolve 802.1x compatibility issues:** Covers what you can do to overcome incompatibility issues when deploying 802.1x authentication in your network.

CHAPTER 7

Implementing and Configuring Advanced 802.1X

Chapter 6, "Implementing and Configuring Basic 802.1X," covered the basic configuration and troubleshooting of 802.1X authentication. Securing information assets is more important now than it has ever been in the past. Criminals have become more sophisticated in their types of attacks on organizations, and this requires the deployment of more advanced security features. This chapter discusses some advanced features of 802.1X authentication that will provide the capability to combat the newer, more prevalent attacks. The advanced 802.1X features will enhance basic authentication by adding things such as the use of certificates, machine authentication, automatic assignment of VLANs and ACLs, web authentication, and so on.

"Do I Know This Already?" Quiz

The "Do I Know This Already?" quiz helps you decide whether you really need to read the entire chapter. If you already intend to read the entire chapter, you do not necessarily need to answer these questions now.

The nine-question quiz, derived from the major sections in the "Foundation Topics" portion of this chapter, helps you determine how to spend your limited study time.

Table 7-1 outlines the major topics discussed in this chapter and the "Do I Know This Already?" quiz questions that correspond to those topics.

Table 7-1 *"Do I Know This Already?" Foundation Topics Section-to-Question Mapping*

Foundation Topics Section	Questions Covered in This Section
Plan the Deployment of Cisco Advanced 802.1X Authentication Features	1
Configure and Verify EAP-TLS Authentication on Cisco IOS Components and Cisco Secure ACS	2
Deploying User and Machine Authentication	3
Deploying VLAN and ACL Assignment	4

Table 7-1 *"Do I Know This Already?" Foundation Topics Section-to-Question Mapping*

Foundation Topics Section	Questions Covered in This Section
Configure and Verify Cisco Secure ACS MAC Address Exception Policies	5
Configure and Verify Web Authentication on Cisco IOS Software LAN Switches and Cisco Secure ACS	6
Choose a Method to Support Multiple Hosts on a Single Port	7
Configuring Fail-Open Policies	8
Resolve 802.1X Compatibility Issues	9

Caution: The goal of self-assessment is to gauge your mastery of the topics in this chapter. If you do not know the answer to a question or are only partially sure of the answer, you should mark this question wrong for purposes of the self-assessment. Giving yourself credit for an answer that you correctly guess skews your self-assessment results and might provide you with a false sense of security.

1. To provide per-user services, such as downloadable ACLs, which of the following must be deployed? (Select all that apply.)

    a. User authentication

    b. Machine authentication

    c. Combination of user and machine authentication

    d. One-time passwords

    e. All of these answers are correct.

2. In EAP-TLS implementations, which kind of certificate is used to verify identity certificates?

    a. The identity certificate belonging to each entity

    b. Supplicant certificate

    c. Certificate Authority (CA) certificate

    d. SSL certificate

3. What identifies the hardware (computer) as opposed to the user identity that is used to identify users that are logged in to the machine?

    a. SNMP

    b. Host name

    c. CA certificate

    d. User identity

    e. Machine identity

4. Cisco IBNS components can dynamically assign what two features to increase security in the environment?

    a. Physical tokens

    b. Access controls lists (ACL)

    c. Identity certificates

    d. VLAN assignment

    e. Kerberos ticket

5. If MAB is enabled, when will the switch try to authenticate the non-802.1X-capable client by using its MAC address?

    a. As soon as the switch receives the first EAPOL frame.

    b. After 802.1X authentication times out.

    c. It will not authenticate non-802.1X-capable clients.

    d. After the client sends an authentication request.

    e. None of these answers are correct.

6. How can web authentication be verified?

    a. Use **show ip admission cache** in the CLI.

    b. Call the user and ask him.

    c. In the Passed Authentication report in Cisco Secure ACS.

    d. Consult the logs on the web server.

    e. None of these answers are correct.

7. Which multihost authentication mode allows multiple hosts to forward traffic through a single port but does not require authentication after the first host authenticates?

    a. Multidomain mode

    b. Single-host mode

    c. Multihost mode

    d. Multi-auth mode

    e. None of these answers are correct.

8. The default, fail-closed mode of the Cisco Catalyst IOS Software 802.1X authenticator can be changed by enabling which optional fail-open features?

    a. Inaccessible Authentication Bypass feature

    b. MAC Authentication Bypass

    c. Open Authentication feature

    d. Multi-auth mode

9. Which of the following will not work with 802.1X authentication by default? (Select all that apply.)

    a. Wake-on-LAN (WOL)

    b. Non-802.1X IP phones

    c. Preboot Execution Environment (PXE)

    d. None of these answers are correct.

The answers to the "Do I Know This Already?" quiz are found in Appendix A. The suggested choices for your next step are as follows:

- **6 or less overall score:** Read the entire chapter. This includes the "Foundation Topics" and the "Exam Preparation" section.

- **7 through 9 overall score:** If you want more review on these topics, skip to the "Exam Preparation" section. Otherwise, move on to Chapter 8, "Implementing and Configuring Cisco IOS Routed Data Plane Security."

Foundation Topics

802.1X is an IEEE standard that provides a framework for authenticating and authorizing network devices connected to LAN ports and for preventing access in the event that the authentication and authorization fail. The authentication and authorization process requires a supplicant (client), an authenticator (router, switch, wireless AP, and so on), and an authentication server. In this chapter, advanced 802.1X features will be discussed. This chapter will discuss topics that enable additional security features on top of the basic 802.1X configurations that were covered in Chapter 6. The enhancements that will be covered include

- Configuring authentication of users and the network with certificate-based EAP-TLS

- Machine authentication

- Using VLANs or access control lists (ACL) to restrict authorization levels

- Providing support for multiple hosts on a single interface

- Providing support for non-802.1X devices

The Cisco Identity-Based Networking Services (IBNS) components on which these features will be configured will be the Cisco Catalyst IOS Software 802.1X authenticator, the Cisco Secure ACS 4.2 Server, and the Cisco Secure Services Client and Microsoft Windows wired 802.1X supplicants.

Plan the Deployment of Cisco Advanced 802.1X Authentication Features

The planning of Cisco 802.1X deployments is as important as the implementation. Information about your existing environment must be gathered, and some decisions must be made.

Gathering Input Parameters

Gathering important information about the environment into which 802.1X authentication will be deployed is needed to successfully deploy 802.1X on Cisco IBNS components. Information that you should gather includes the following:

- To use user or machine certificates, you should gather information about existing certificate architectures. Information about the existing Microsoft Active Directory or Public-Key Infrastructure (PKI) is important.

- Determine whether the deployment will employ user and/or machine authentication. This will help plan for certificate needs and Extensible Authentication Protocol (EAP) mode requirements.

- Determine any additional restrictions that will be deployed as part of the 802.1X authentication process, such as assigning VLANs or ACLs to users upon authentication.

- Gather a list of the types of clients that will be connecting to the network to determine if there are any non-802.1X-capable devices in the environment.

Deployment Tasks

Deploying advanced 802.1X authentication revolves around advanced EAP modes but includes several optional configuration items, including the following:

Step 1. Deploy advance EAP mode configurations.

Step 2. (Optional) Configure machine or machine and user authentication.

Step 3. (Optional) Configure authorization policies.

Step 4. (Optional) Configure features, if needed, to support non-802.1X host and special LAN features.

Deployment Choices

Choices must be made that depend upon an organization's environment and architecture, including the following:

- **Choice of EAP method:** As with the basic 802.1X configuration discussed earlier, the EAP method that satisfies authentication requirements must be chosen. Consider the following scenarios:
  - If the environment is one in which users and/or computers already have adequate certificates and a trusted certificate management process is in place, use Extensible Authentication Protocol–Transport Layer Security (EAP-TLS) (or, if you prefer inner and outer authentication layers, EAP-TLS tunneled inside Protected EAP [PEAP] or EAP–Flexible Authentication via Secure Tunneling [EAP-FAST]) as your authentication method.

  - Similarly, if you want to build a new certificate infrastructure to provide a stronger authentication mechanism, use EAP-TLS (or, if you prefer inner and outer authentication layers, EAP-TLS tunneled inside PEAP or EAP-FAST) as your authentication method.

  - Use EAP–Generic Token Card (EAP-GTC) tunneled inside PEAP if you prefer one-time passwords to authenticate users.

  - To use static passwords and avoid EAP-FAST because of the complexities of PAC deployment in your environment, use EAP–Microsoft Challenge Handshake Authentication Protocol version 2 (EAP-MSCHAPv2) inside PEAP because it only requires configuration of ACS or root CA certificates on the clients.

- **Type of authentication:** Choose whether to require user or machine authentication. It is also possible to choose to require both user and machine authentication. Consider the following:
  - Use machine authentication if you only need to tell the difference between a managed 802.1X machine and nonmanaged machines.

  - Decide whether automatic assignment of VLANs or ACLs to users is required. If so, plan to authenticate users with a combination of machine and user authentication.

Configure and Verify EAP-TLS Authentication on Cisco IOS Components and Cisco Secure ACS

Extensible Authentication Protocol–Transport Layer Security (EAP-TLS) is a good authentication choice when there is a requirement for mutual authentication using identity certificates.

EAP-TLS consists of two parties that each have a certificate with which to identify themselves and a Certificate Authority (CA) certificate with which it verifies the certificates of other parties.

In an EAP-TLS 802.1X authentication exchange, there are two authenticating parties:

- Supplicant (client)

- Server (the network), which is the Cisco Secure ACS server

This means that the client is requesting authentication to access network resources, but it also authenticates the network as well, thus the term *mutual* authentication. Each party sends its identity certificate to the other party. It can then use its CA certificate to verify the identity certificate.

Upon successful authentication, the ACS server notifies the authenticator (the switch), which then authorizes the port on which the supplicant is connected. Figure 7-1 shows the supplicant, authenticator, and authentication server.

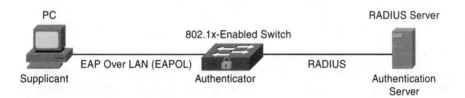

Figure 7-1 *802.1X Components*

EAP-TLS with 802.1X Configuration Tasks

To configure EAP-TLS with 802.1X on Cisco IBNS components, complete the following tasks:

Task 1.   Configure the Cisco IOS Software Catalyst switch authenticator and the RADIUS server (ACS).

Task 2.   Install identity certificate and CA certificate on all clients.

Task 3.   Install identity certificate and CA certificate on the Cisco Secure ACS server.

Task 4.   Configure the Cisco Secure ACS server for EAP-TLS support.

Task 5.   (Optional) Configure a network access profile to support EAP-TLS on the Microsoft Windows native 802.1X supplicant.

Task 6.   (Optional) Configure a network access profile to support EAP-TLS on the Cisco Secure Services Client supplicant.

Configuration Scenario

The configuration scenario shown in Figure 7-2 illustrates the tasks needed to configure EAP-TLS. The client will either be using the Microsoft Windows native 802.1X supplicant or the Cisco Secure Services Client (CSSC) supplicant. The authenticator is running Cisco IOS Software and is configured with 192.168.254.1 as its management IP address. The client will use an identity certificate to authenticate to the ACS server and a CA certificate to verify the ACS server's identity certificate. The ACS server will obtain its identity certificate from a Public Key Infrastructure (PKI) and use a CA certificate to verify the client's identity certificate. The ACS server is at IP address 10.1.1.1. It is assumed that the RADIUS configuration exists on both the switch and the ACS server and that basic 802.1X port authentication is already configured on the switch, as discussed in the previous chapter.

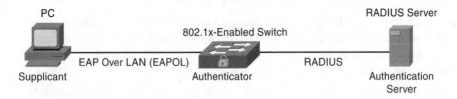

Figure 7-2   *Components in EAP-TLS with 802.1X Configuration*

Configuration Choices

You have to make the following configuration choices when configuring EAP-TLS:

■   The first decision is to determine what kind of identity certificate to use on the Cisco Secure ACS server. One option is to use a self-signed certificate, which is where the ACS server issues one to itself. The use of self-signed certificates should be limited to test scenarios because they must be manually imported to all clients and they are more difficult to revoke as compared to certificates obtained automatically from certificate servers. It is important to be able to revoke certificates in the event that the certificate becomes compromised by potential attackers. Obtaining identity certificates automatically by enrolling the ACS server with a certificate server provides automatic retrieval, renewal, and revocation of identity certificates.

■   The second decision is whether to use one-way or two-way authentication inside EAP-TLS. One-way and two-way are also known as unidirectional and bidirectional, respectively. Unidirectional authentication involves the client being authenticated by the authentication server (ACS), but the client does not authenticate the authentication server. This can be acceptable in a highly trusted network, where other security controls are used to mitigate the possibility of interception and spoofing attacks. Because the client does not authenticate the ACS server, there is no need for provisioning certificate authority certificates to clients. This can make deployment and maintenance of EAP-TLS much easier, but it should not be used in environments that are not fully trusted. Bidirectional authentication should be used in production and other environments where there are no mitigating security controls in place.

Task 1: Configure RADIUS Server

The first task is to configure a RADIUS server on the authenticator (switch) and configure the authenticator (switch) as an authentication, authorization, and accounting (AAA) client on the RADIUS server. This task is the same as the procedure in the previous chapter. See Chapter 6 for details.

Task 2: Install Identity and Certificate Authority Certificates on All Clients

The procedure for installing identity certificates and CA certificates on clients is specific to the certificate authority and the client operating system. Consult the vendor documentation for this procedure.

Task 3: Configure an Identity Certificate on the Cisco Secure ACS Server

Task 3 includes the necessary steps to successfully create an identity certificate and a CA certificate on the Cisco Secure ACS server. There are two subsets of configuration steps for this task. The CA certificate will be used by the ACS server to validate client identity certificates. Configure the following items:

Step 1. Log on to the Cisco Secure ACS server with administrative privileges and navigate to **System Configuration > ACS Certificate Setup > ACS Certificate Authority Setup.**

Step 2. The CA certificate must be imported to the Cisco Secure ACS server. Obtain the certificate from the CA administrator in the form of a file. This should be the file that the CA used to provision client certificates. This is the CA certificate that the ACS server will use to verify client certificates. After you have the file, enter the full pathname to the file in the CA Certificate File field and click Submit to continue.

Step 3. This step, as shown in Figure 7-3, configures a Certificate Signing Request (CSR) by enrolling with the organization's PKI:
  a. Enter a unique X.500 name in the Certificate Subject field.
  b. In the Private Key File field, specify the full pathname to the location where the ACS will store its private RSA key.

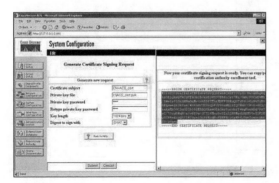

Figure 7-3 *Generate Certificate Signing Request*

    c. In the Private Key Password field, enter a strong password that will be used to encrypt the ACS server's private key.

    d. Re-enter the password in the Retype Private Key Password field.

    e. Enter the length of the RSA private and public keys in the Key Length field. A key length of 2048 bits is recommended.

    f. Specify the SHA-1 hashing algorithm in the Digest to Sign With field.

Step 4.   Click Submit to generate the Certificate Signing Request (CSR).

The CSR is a block of text that must be sent to the PKI to have a server identity certificate generated. The particular PKI in use will have procedures for importing a CSR and should then issue an identity certificate for the ACS server. The identity certificate should be in the form Base 64-encoded. After you have the identity certificate, refer to Figure 7-4 and follow these steps:

Step 1.   Navigate to **System Configuration > ACS Certificate Setup > Install ACS Certificate** and select the Install New Certificate option. The ACS server should already have a self-signed certificate, but this will be overridden with the newly obtained PKI-issued certificate. There can be only one identity certificate.

Step 2.   On the Install New Certificate page, choose the Read Certificate from File option and provide the full pathname to the location where the ACS identity certificate is stored. Also, in the bottom section, provide the path to the file containing the ACS server's private key and the password to decrypt the file. These were configured in previous steps. Click the Submit button to continue.

Step 3.   The ACS server will read the certificate and then install it. If the process is successful, the new certificate will be shown in the Installed Certificate Information section. Verify the Issued To and Issued By fields and make sure that Validity is set to OK.

Step 4.   Restart the Cisco Secure ACS after installing a new certificate.

Figure 7-4 *Install New Certificate in Cisco Secure ACS*

Note: To restart the system, navigate to **System Configuration > Service Control** and click Restart. This does not reboot the server. It restarts the Cisco Secure ACS services.

Task 4: Configure Support of EAP-TLS on the Cisco Secure ACS Server

Task 4 configures support of EAP-TLS on the Cisco Secure ACS server. Task 4 is comprised of two subsets of steps. The first set configures EAP-TLS and some of its basic properties. The second set configures user accounts for comparison to identity certificates received from supplicants.

To configure EAP-TLS and some of its basic properties, follow these steps:

Step 1.   Navigate to **System Configuration > Global Authentication Setup.**

Step 2.   From the resulting screen shown in Figure 7-5, select the Allow EAP-TLS option in the EAP-TLS section of the Global Authentication Setup page.

Figure 7-5   *EAP-TLS on Cisco Secure ACS*

Step 3.   Select the Certificate CN Comparison option in the EAP-TLS section to specify which field in the certificate will be compared against the ACS internal or external database. This step is to verify that the user specified in the client identity certificate does exist in an authentication database.

Step 4.   Click Submit + Restart.

Next, you need to create the user account in the ACS internal database, as shown in Figure 7-6. Alternatively, you can use an external database such as Active Directory. Either way, the user account that is read from the client's identity certificate must match an account that exists. Perform the following steps to create user accounts in the ACS internal database:

Step 1.   Click User Setup, and the User Setup screen opens.

Step 2.   In the User field, enter a unique name and click the Add/Edit button. The Edit User page opens. The username should match the format of the username in the identity certificate. For example, if the name in the certificate is in the *user@domain.com* format, the username created in ACS must also be created in that format.

Step 3.   Even though the user's password will never be used for EAP-TLS, because authentication is verified by certificates, enter a password in the user's password field. The password chosen should be a strong password with adequate length in case the user account is ever used for an authentication purpose that uses the password.

Step 4.   Click Submit.

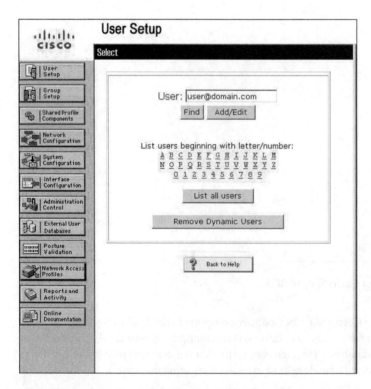

Figure 7-6   *User Setup in Cisco Secure ACS*

Task 5: (Optional) Configure EAP-TLS Support Using the Microsoft Windows Native Supplicant

Task 5 provides the steps necessary to configure support of EAP-TLS on the Microsoft Windows native 802.1X supplicant. You can configure the supplicant to support EAP-TLS in the LAN adapter properties window, as shown in Figure 7-7. Perform the following steps to complete this task:

Step 1. Open the properties dialog box of the LAN adapter that will be authenticating using 802.1X, and then click the Authentication tab.

Step 2. On the Authentication tab, select the Enable IEEE 802.1X Authentication check box, choose the Smart Card or Other Certificate EAP type, and make sure that both the Authenticate as Computer When Computer Information Is Available and the Authenticate as Guest When User or Computer Information Is Available options are not selected.

Step 3. Click the Properties button to open the EAP-TLS properties window.

Step 4. Select the Use a Certificate on This Computer option.

Step 5. To enable bidirectional authentication and ensure that the client authenticates the network (authentication server), choose the Validate Server Certificate option.

Step 6. Select the Connect to These Servers option and enter the name in the canonical name (CN) field on the ACS server's identity certificate.

Step 7. Find and select the installed CA certificate that issued the ACS certificate in the Trusted Root Certificate Authorities section.

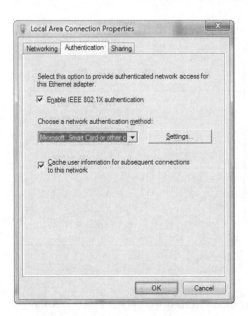

Figure 7-7   *Configure Windows Native 802.1X Client*

The supplicant should now be configured to support authentication with EAP-TLS and 802.1X.

Task 6: (Optional) Configure EAP-TLS Support Using the Cisco Secure Services Client (CSSC) Supplicant

Task 6 provides the steps necessary to configure support of EAP-TLS on the CSSC 802.1X supplicant. The following steps show how to configure support of the 802.1X supplicant. Chapter 6 provided full guidance of CSSC profile configuration:

Step 1.   In the Allowed Authentication Modes section, on the Authentication Policy page, select the EAP-TLS protocol as the outer EAP mode and leave all other choices deselected.

Step 2.   On the User Authentication page, select EAP-TLS as the outer EAP mode. Click the Configure button to configure EAP-TLS-specific parameters.

Step 3.   Select the Validate Server Certificate option in the EAP-TLS Settings window, as shown in Figure 7-8.

Step 4.   The Enable Fast Reconnect option can be selected to allow reauthentication between the supplicant and the ACS server. Essentially the TLS session keys are cached, thus allowing faster reauthentication by not having to perform a full TLS handshake. This is an optional setting that must be configured on the ACS server and the supplicant if used.

Step 5.   On the User Server Validating page, choose the Common Name value in the Certificate field, choose the Exactly Matches option in the Match field, and enter the name that exactly matches the canonical name (CN) as it was entered on the ACS identity certificate.

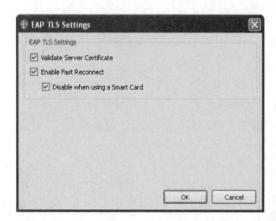

Figure 7-8   *EAP-TLS on Cisco Secure Services Client*

The supplicant should now be configured to support authentication with EAP-TLS and 802.1X.

Implementation Guidelines

Consider the following when deploying EAP-TLS:

- Using certificates to verify the authenticity of another party is much more demanding than other cryptographic methods that use passwords (EAP-MSCHAPv2 or EAP-FAST). The computational requirements placed on the ACS server will require that the platform be sized appropriately to handle the load.

- When using certificates, recommended practice dictates that both the ACS server and the clients be configured properly to use Certificate Revocation Lists (CRL). This will permit the device to automatically deny authentication requests that use expired or otherwise revoked certificates.

Feature Support

Minimum versions that support EAP-TLS features are v3.2 for Cisco Secure ACS and v4.0 for Cisco Secure Services Client (CSSC).

Verifying EAP-TLS Configuration

You can verify EAP-TLS authentication through the Passed Authentications report on Cisco Secure ACS. The report shows successful authentications of each 802.1X client and provides the username, MAC address, and 802.1X-enabled switch that is the authenticator. This report should be used to ensure that the client had the correct identity as well as the correct EAP mode.

Deploying User and Machine Authentication

Most of today's current operating systems have a machine identity and user identities. Note that the user identities are plural while the machine identity is not. The machine identity identifies the hardware (computer), while the user identity is used to identify users that are logged in to the machine. Having multiple user identities is possible because most modern operating systems support multiple users.

The 802.1X supplicant has the capability to distinguish between a machine authenticating to the network and a user authenticating to the network. The different approaches to authenticating entities from the viewpoint of the supplicant are as follows:

- **User authentication:** This approach involves the user logging in to the machine, which in turn provides authenticated access to the network. If a user is not logged in (successfully authenticated), the machine cannot access network resources.

- **Machine authentication:** The computer has its own credentials, such as a password or certificate, with which it can authenticate itself to the network. The machine has access to the network even when there is no user logged in.

- **User and machine authentication:** This approach is a combination of both methods. The computer will be authenticated to the network using its credentials while there is no user logged in. When a user logs in, the machine authentication is revoked and the computer has access to the network through the user's authentication.

When the user logs out, the computer can once again authenticate itself using its own credentials.

When would you use machine authentication by itself, and when would you use user and machine authentication? Table 7-2 provides some guidelines to help you make that decision.

Key Topic

Table 7-2   *Machine Authentication Versus User and Machine Authentication*

Machine Authentication	User and Machine Authentication
To authenticate single-user computers and not require users to log in	When the machine must be reachable at all times, but unique user policies, such as VLAN or ACL assignment, is required
To make a machine reachable on the network without requiring user authentication	When the machine must be reachable at all times but logging activities by the user are necessary for auditing purposes
To verify that the machine is managed through an Active Directory domain	

Configuring User and Machine Authentication Tasks

The tasks that must be configured on Cisco IBNS components to support user and machine authentication are as follows:

Task 1.   Install user and/or machine credentials (password or certificates) on client systems.

Task 2.   Configure EAP-TLS features on Cisco Secure ACS.

Task 3.   Configure support of machine authentication on the Cisco Secure ACS.

Task 4.   (Optional) Configure support for machine (computer) authentication on the Microsoft Windows native 802.1X supplicant if required.

Task 5.   (Optional) Configure support for machine (computer) authentication on the Cisco Secure Services Client (CSSC) 802.1X supplicant if required.

Task 6.   (Optional) Configure user authentication in addition to machine authentication if a combination of both authentication methods is required.

Configuration Scenario

Figure 7-9 shows the configuration that will be used to accompany the configuration tasks that will be performed in this section.

Assume the following:

■   Clients can automatically retrieve user and machine identity certificates from Active Directory certificate services.

■   The Cisco Secure ACS has its identity certificate from PKI.

■   EAP-TLS will be used for mutual authentication.

■ RADIUS is configured on the switch and ACS server.

■ EAP-TLS support is configured on the ACS server.

■ Switch ports are configured with 802.1X port control.

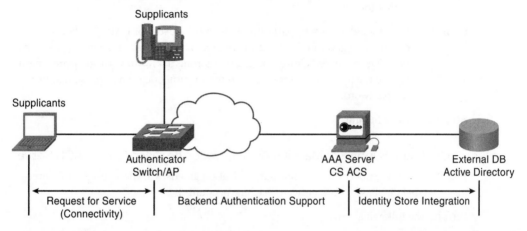

Figure 7-9 *Components and Sections of an EAP-TLS with 802.1X Authentication*

Task 1: Install Identity and Certificate Authority Certificates on All Clients

The procedure for installing identity certificates and CA certificates on clients is specific to the certificate authority and the client operating system. Consult the vendor documentation for this procedure.

Task 2: Configure Support of EAP-TLS on Cisco Secure ACS Server

Task 2 configures support of EAP-TLS on Cisco Secure ACS Server. Task 2 is comprised of two subsets of steps. The first set configures EAP-TLS and some of its basic properties. The second set configures user accounts for comparison to identity certificates received from supplicants:

Step 1.   Navigate to **System Configuration > Global Authentication Setup.**

Step 2.   Select the Allow EAP-TLS option in the EAP-TLS section of the Global Authentication Setup page.

Step 3.   Select the Certificate CN Comparison option in the EAP-TLS section to specify which field in the certificate will be compared against the ACS internal or external database. This step is to verify that the user specified in the client identity certificate does exist in an authentication database.

Step 4.   Click Submit + Restart.

The second subset of tasks creates the user account in the ACS internal database. Alternatively, an external database such as Active Directory can be used. Either way, the user account that is read from the client's identity certificate must match an account that exists. Use the following steps to create user accounts in the ACS internal database:

Step 1.   Click User Setup, and the User Setup screen opens.

Step 2.   In the User field, enter a unique name and click the Add/Edit button. The Edit User page opens. The username should match the format of the username in the identity certificate. For example, if the name in the certificate is in the *user@domain.com* format, the username created in ACS must also be created in that format.

Step 3.   Even though the user's password will never be used for EAP-TLS, because authentication is verified by certificates, enter a password in the user's password field. The password chosen should be a strong password with adequate length in case the user account is ever used for an authentication purpose that uses the password.

Step 4.   Click Submit.

Task 3: Configure Support of Machine Authentication on Cisco Secure ACS Server

Task 3 configures support of machine authentication and uses a Microsoft Active Directory external database to authenticate machine accounts.

Perform the following steps:

Step 1.   Navigate to **External User Databases > Unknown Uses Policy**.

Step 2.   Select the Check the Following External Databases option, and move the Windows database from the External databases pane to the Selected Databases pane.

Step 3.   Navigate to **External User Databases > Database Configuration > Windows Database > Configure** and choose the Enable EAP-TLS Machine Authentication option.

Task 4: Configure Support of Machine Authentication on Microsoft Windows Native 802.1X Supplicant

Task 4 provides the steps necessary to configure machine authentication on the Microsoft Windows native 802.1X supplicant. The supplicant is configured in the LAN adapter properties window.

Perform the following steps:

Step 1.   Open the properties dialog box of the LAN adapter that will be authenticating using 802.1X and click the Authentication tab.

Step 2.   On the Authentication tab, select the Enable IEEE 802.1X Authentication check box, choose Smart Card or Other Certificate EAP type, and make sure that the Authenticate as Computer When Computer Information Is Available option is selected and that the Authenticate as Guest When User or Computer Information Is Available option is not selected.

Step 3.   Click the Properties button to open the EAP-TLS properties window.

Step 4.   Select the Use a Certificate on This Computer option in the When Connecting screen.

Step 5.   To enable bidirectional authentication and ensure that the client authenticates the network (authentication server), select the Validate Server Certificate option, as shown in Figure 7-10.

Step 6.   Select the Connect to These Servers option, and enter the name in the canonical name (CN) field on the ACS server's identity certificate.

Step 7.   Find and select the installed CA certificate that issued the ACS certificate in the Trusted Root Certificate Authorities section.

The supplicant should now be configured to support machine authentication.

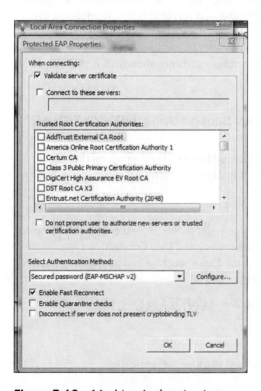

Figure 7-10   *Machine Authentication*

Task 5: (Optional) Configure Machine Authentication Support Using the Cisco Secure Services Client (CSSC) Supplicant

Task 5 provides the steps necessary to configure the support of machine authentication on the CSSC 802.1X supplicant.

Perform the following steps:

Step 1.   On the Network Connection Type page, select the option that makes this connection type a Machine Connection type, which will result in the supplicant performing only machine authentication without trying user authentication.

Step 2.   On the Machine Authentication (EAP) Method page, select EAP-TLS as the protocol. Click the Configure button to configure EAP-TLS specific settings.

Step 3.   Select the Validate Server Certificate option in the EAP-TLS Settings window. The Enable Fast Reconnect option can be selected to allow reauthentication between the supplicant and the ACS server. Essentially, the TLS session keys are cached, thus allowing faster reauthentication by not having to perform a full TLS handshake. This is an optional setting that must be configured on the ACS server and the supplicant if used.

Step 4.   On the Machine Credentials page, select the Use Machine Credentials option to use the machine certificate that the ACS server obtained from the Active Directory Certificate Service.

The supplicant should now be configured to support authentication with EAP-TLS and 802.1X.

Task 6: (Optional) Configure Additional User Support Using the Cisco Secure Services Client (CSSC) Supplicant

Task 6 provides the steps necessary to configure additional user support on the CSSC 802.1X supplicant. This would be necessary if machine and user authentication is required.

Perform the following steps:

Step 1.   From the Network Connection Type page, shown in Figure 7-11, select the option that makes this connection a Machine and User Connection type, which will result in the supplicant performing only machine and user authentication depending upon whether a user is logged in.

Step 2.   On the User Authentication page, select EAP-TLS as the protocol.

Implementation Guidelines

Consider the following when deploying user and machine authentication:

■   Using both authentication methods adds complexity to your authentication mechanism and to the resources needed to process authentication requests. Unless necessary, only use one or the other method, if possible.

■   All the authentication configuration and other details covered thus far have been done under the assumption of a wired connection. The same configuration tasks can be extended to 802.11 wireless networks using the same EAP modes and authentication credentials.

Feature Support

Minimum versions to support machine and user authentication features are v3.1 for Cisco Secure ACS and all versions of the Cisco Secure Services Client (CSSC).

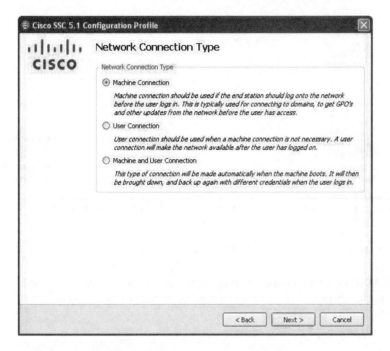

Figure 7-11 *Deploy Machine and User Authentication*

Deploying VLAN and ACL Assignment

Dynamic assignment of VLAN or ACL can be made possible through interaction between the Cisco Catalyst IOS Software–based switch and the Cisco Secure ACS server. The process of assigning a user to a specific VLAN or applying an ACL to that user's access is handled by the ACS server. After 802.1X authentication is successful, these dynamic features are assigned to users by the ACS server sending the information to the authenticator (switch) in the form of a RADIUS attribute, and the switch enforces the assignments.

Deploying VLAN and ACL Assignment Tasks

The tasks to configure dynamic VLAN and ACL assignments are as follows:

Task 1.   Configure Cisco IOS Software 802.1X authenticator authorization.

Task 2.   (Optional) Configure VLAN assignment on a Cisco Secure ACS server.

Task 3.   (Optional) Configure the Cisco IOS Software switch for ACL assignment.

Task 4.   (Optional) Configure ACL assignment on a Cisco Secure ACS server.

Configuration Scenario

Figure 7-12 shows the configuration that will be used to accompany the configuration tasks that will be performed in this section.

Cisco Secure ACS will dynamically assign the client supplicant switch port to VLAN 10 and dynamically assign an ACL that allows HTTP, DNS, and PING access to the network to users in Group 1 of the ACS database.

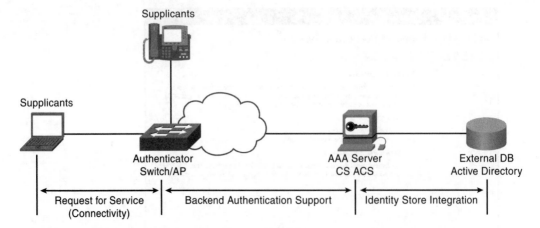

Figure 7-12 *Components and Sections of an EAP-TLS with 802.1X Authentication*

Assume that the RADIUS configuration exists on both the switch and the ACS server and that basic 802.1X port authentication is already configured on the switch, as discussed in the previous chapter.

Configuration Choices

You have to make some choices when configuring VLAN and ACS assignment, including the following:

■   Dynamic VLAN assignment should be used when there are other security controls in place in the environment to provide access control between the users and other resources.

■   If the other security controls do not exist, consider using dynamic ACL assignment instead of or in addition to the dynamic VLAN assignment.

Task 1: Configure Cisco IOS Software 802.1X Authenticator Authorization

Task 1 provides the steps necessary to configure the 802.1X switch with basic authorization features. Consult the vendor documentation for this procedure.

Perform the following steps:

Step 1.   Enable default network AAA authorization using the **aaa authorization network default** global configuration command. Example 7-1 shows how to configure the switch with global authorization to use the default RADIUS servers (**group radius**) to provide authorization to all 802.1X ports.

Example 7-1 *Commands to Enable Default Network Authorization Using RADIUS*

```
Router# configure terminal
Router(config)# aaa authorization network default group radius
Router(config)# exit
Router# copy running-config startup-config
```

Step 2.   As an option, configure an access VLAN that has very restricted access. This will be the default VLAN assigned to clients if 802.1X is not configured on the switch or automatic VLAN assignment is not configured on the ACS server. Example 7-2 shows the commands for configuring the port in a default VLAN with limited access.

Example 7-2 *Commands to Put Interface in Default Access VLAN*

```
Router# configure terminal
Router(config)# interface range GigabitEthernet0/1-24
Router(config-if-range)# switchport access vlan 99
Router# copy running-config startup-config
```

Task 2: (Optional) Configure VLAN Assignment on Cisco Secure ACS

Task 2 provides the steps necessary to configure the optional assignment of VLAN membership for an interface that is authenticated by a user or group of users in ACS.

Perform the following steps:

Step 1.   Enable VLAN assignment globally in the Cisco Secure ACS by including the option in the user interface. Log in to ACS with administrative access and choose Interface Configuration.

Step 2.   From the Interface Configuration window, choose RADIUS (IEFT).

Step 3.   Enable the following tunnel attributes for the group by selecting their check boxes in an ACS group profile:

- [064] Tunnel-type
- [065] Tunnel-Medium-type
- [081] Tunnel-Private-Group-ID

Step 4.   Select the Submit button and restart Cisco Secure ACS to enable the changes.

Step 5.   From the ACS home page, select Group Setup.

Step 6.   On the Group Setup page, choose Group 1 and click Edit.

Step 7.   On the Edit page, scroll down and find the IETF RADIUS Attributes section. Select the three tunnel attributes and complete their values as shown in IETF:

- Tunnel-Type (64), Tag 1 Value = VLAN
- Tunnel-Medium-Type (65), Tag 1 Value = 802
- Tunnel-Type (81), Tag 1 Value = 10

The value for the Tunnel-Type (81) is the name or number of the VLAN that is dynamically assigned to the interface upon successful authentication.

Task 3: (Optional) Configure and Prepare for ACL Assignment on Cisco IOS Software Switch

Task 3 provides the steps necessary to configure the optional assignment of an ACL to an authenticated entity. Several things must be accomplished on the switch, such as tuning RADIUS settings, enabling the IP device tracking feature, and assigning a default port to 802.1X-enabled user ports.

Perform the following steps:

Step 1.   Enable default network AAA authorization with the **aaa authorization network default** global command.

Step 2.   Configure the RADIUS client (switch) to send and also recognize vendor-specific attributes (VSA) that are needed for ACL assignment by using the **radius-server vsa send authentication** global configuration command.

Step 3.   Enable the IP tracking feature, which is needed to learn and verify the presence of MAC and IP addresses on ports. This is done with the **ip device tracking** global configuration command.

Step 4.   Configure and apply a default ACL using the **ip access-group** interface command. This default port ACL is required and will specify the traffic that is allowed by default on the port. At a minimum, it should allow Dynamic Host Configuration Protocol (DHCP) traffic.

Example 7-3 shows the commands discussed in this task being used to apply an ACL named "inbound-ACL" to interface FastEthernet 0/1 as well as the commands needed to enable ACL assignment.

Example 7-3   *Preparing 802.1X Authenticator for Automatic ACL Assignment*

```
Router# configure terminal
Router(config)# aaa authorization network default group radius
Router(config)# radius-server vsa send authentication
Router(config)# ip device tracking
Router(config)# interface FastEthernet0/1
Router(config-if)# ip access-group inbound-ACL in
Router(config)# end
Router(config)# copy running-config startup-config
```

Task 4: (Optional) Configure ACL Assignment on Cisco Secure ACS Server

Task 4 consists of two sets of steps. With the Cisco IOS Software authenticator prepared to receive downloadable ACLs, the Cisco Secure ACS server can now be configured. The first set of steps creates the downloadable ACL on Cisco Secure ACS, and the second set of steps configures assignment of the ACL for a group of users in Cisco Secure ACS. When configuring downloadable ACLs to be assigned to users upon authentication, always use **any** as the source IP address.

Perform the following steps:

Step 1. Create a downloadable ACL by logging in to Cisco Secure ACS as an administrator, navigating to **Shared Profile Components > Downloadable IP ACLs**, and then selecting Add to create a new ACL.

Step 2. On the Downloadable IP ACLs page, enter a name for the downloadable ACL (inbound-ACL is used in the example) and then click the Add button to add rules to the downloadable ACL.

Step 3. On the Downloadable IP ACLs page, as shown in Figure 7-13, enter a name for the first set of rules in the downloadable ACL and then enter the required access control elements (ACE) in the format of a Cisco IOS Software extended ACL in by clicking the Add button..

Step 4. Click the Submit button to save the downloadable ACL.

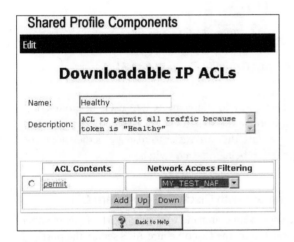

Figure 7-13 *Downloadable ACLs on Cisco Secure ACS*

The second set of rules will assign the downloadable ACL to a user or group of users in Cisco Secure ACS. The downloadable ACL has no size limitation except for that posed by the resource limitation of the authenticator to which it will be downloaded.

Perform the following steps:

Step 1. From the ACS home page, select Group Setup.

Step 2. On the Group Setup page, choose Group 1 and click Edit.

Step 3. On the Edit page, scroll down and find the Downloadable ACLs section, select the Assign IP ACL option, as shown in Figure 7-14, and select the downloadable ACL with the name that was used when creating the ACL.

Step 4. Click the Submit button to save the configuration.

This completes the configuration for ACL assignment. You can test the assignment of the ACL by reauthenticating the users to the authenticator (switch).

Figure 7-14   *Assign Downloadable ACL to a Group in Cisco Secure ACS*

Note: Downloadable ACLs are not the only way to assign an ACL to users or groups of users. Alternatively, an ACL that exists locally on the switch can be assigned. Downloadable ACLs are a better choice because they are easier to manage as they are centrally located on the ACS server as opposed to being on each switch.

Verification of VLAN and ACL Assignment with Cisco IOS Software CLI

To verify VLAN assignment, use the **show vlan** command to display port VLAN memberships. After the user has been authenticated by the Cisco Secure ACS server, the port should show membership in the correct dynamically assigned VLAN.

To verify ACL assignment, use the **show epm session ip** command with the argument of the user's IP address to display the dynamically generated per-user ACL that is applied to the user's session. The **show access-list** command can be used to display the contents of the assigned ACL. Example 7-4 shows the usage of both of these Cisco IOS Software commands.

Example 7-4   show vlan *and* show access-list *Commands to Verify VLAN and ACL Assignment*

```
Switch# show vlan


VLAN Name                             Status                          Ports
---- -------------------------------- ------------------------------- ----------------
1    default                          active
10   USERS                            active                          Gi0/1
```

```
Switch# show epm sessions ip 192.168.254.3
Admission feature         : DOT1X
AAA Policies              :
ACS ACL                   : xACSACLx-IP-inboundACL-4b834e1a


Switch# show access-list xACSACLx-IP-inboundACL-4b834e1a
Extended IP access list xACSACLx-IP-inboundACL-4b834e1a (per-user)
        10 permit tcp any any eq www
        20 permit udp any host 172.16.1.10 eq domain
        30 permit icmp any any echo
```

Verification of VLAN and ACL Assignment on Cisco Secure ACS

Select the Downloadable ACL field in the Passed Authentications report to verify correct assignment to authenticating users.

Configure and Verify Cisco Secure ACS MAC Address Exception Policies

There will be cases in which devices that do not support 802.1X authentication will need network connectivity. Examples of these devices include printers, PDAs, or some operating systems that do not support 802.1X or possibly the EAP method that is deployed in an environment. There are several ways in which exceptions can be made for these devices:

- Disable 802.1X on ports where these devices will connect and assign the same VLAN to the port as the 802.1X users receive upon authentication. There is risk associated with this approach. Unless these devices are static and the ports are physically secured, anyone can disconnect his network connection and connect an unauthorized machine and receive unauthenticated access to network resources.

- Disable 802.1X on ports where devices will connect and assign a VLAN that has access restrictions. This is similar to the previous option but mitigates some of the risks associated with unauthorized connections.

- The decision to authenticate a device can be made based upon the MAC address of the device. This option has the risk of being susceptible to MAC address spoofing but can be used in conjunction with dynamic VLAN or ACL assignment as well.

- Utilize web-based authentication to have users authenticate using a web interface, which provides the opportunity to authenticate to gain access to network resources.

Cisco Catalyst IOS Software MAC Authentication Bypass (MAB)

The MAC Authentication Bypass (MAB) configuration enables the switch to authorize clients based on their client MAC address. If MAB is enabled, the switch will try to authenticate the client by using MAB after the 802.1X authentication times out because of failure to receive the EAP response from the client.

Key Topic

With MAB enabled, the switch uses the client's MAC address as the client identity. The authentication server has a database of MAC addresses that are allowed to access the network against which the client's MAC address will be checked. When a device connects to a port on which 802.1X is configured, it will wait for an Ethernet packet from the client. The switch will send a RADIUS access/request frame with a username and password that are based on the MAC address to the authentication server. Successful authorization results in the switch granting access to the client, whereas a failed authorization results in the switch either assigning the port to a guest VLAN if one exists or the switch does not grant access to the client.

Reauthentication of clients is possible for clients that authenticate using MAB. The process is the same as it is for 802.1X clients. The Session-Timeout RADIUS attribute is used as the basis of reauthentication; the authorization period ends and connectivity will be lost to the client during reauthentication.

If an EAP over LAN (EAPOL) packet is received on a port that was authenticated using MAC Authentication Bypass, the switch determines that the connected client is an 802.1X supplicant and will use 802.1X to authorize the interface. If the interface is already authorized using MAB and detects an 802.1X supplicant, the client will not be deauthorized and disconnected. The switch will use 802.1X at the time of reauthentication instead of MAB.

MAB will interact with the following features:

- **802.1X authentication:** MAB can be enabled only if 802.1X authentication is enabled on the port.

- **Guest VLAN:** If a client has an invalid MAC address ID, the switch will assign the user to the guest VLAN if one exists.

- **Restricted VLAN:** Restricted VLANs are not supported for a client that authenticates through MAB on a port configured for 802.1X authentication.

- **Port security:** MAB can be used in conjunction with port security.

- **Voice VLAN:** MAB can be used along with voice VLANs.

- **VLAN Membership Policy Server (VMPS):** 802.1X and VMPS are mutually exclusive and, therefore, not used together.

- **Private VLANs (PVLAN):** It is possible to place a port in a PVLAN and then configure it for MAB.

Configuration Tasks

The tasks that are required to configure MAB exception policies are as follows:

Task 1.   Configure MAB on the authenticator (switch).

Task 2.   Configure MAB on Cisco Secure ACS.

Configuration Scenario

Figure 7-15 depicts the scenario used in the configuration tasks that follow. In this scenario, Cisco Secure ACS will permit a host with a MAC address of 000a.3453.cf2d to bypass the 802.1X authentication process. The switch and ACS are configured with their RADIUS association, EAP is enabled and configured, and the access ports on the switch are configured with 802.1X port control.

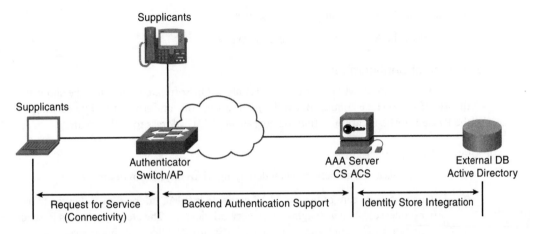

Figure 7-15 *Network Topology for Configuration Scenario*

Tasks 1 and 2: Configure MAC Authentication Bypass on the Switch and ACS

The steps that are required to configure MAB exception policies on the switch are as follows:

Step 1.   Enter either interface or interface range configuration mode on the switch.

Step 2.   Use the **authentication order** command to set the order of authentication processes on the interfaces. In the example, the switch will first perform a MAB check based on the client's MAC address and falls back to normal 802.1X EAP if needed.

Step 3.   Use the **mab** interface configuration command to enable the MAC Authentication Bypass feature.

Building a database of MAC addresses can be a challenging part of setting up MAB on the ACS server. If the number of hosts is relatively small, it might be feasible to simply add them individually to the Cisco Secure ACS internal database:

Step 1.   Click User Setup on the navigation pane from the ACS home page.

Step 2.   Enter the MAC address of the device without any symbols or special characters in the User field. Click the Add/Edit button.

Step 3.   Enter the MAC address of the device without any symbols or special characters in the Password and Confirm Password fields.

Step 4.   Click the Submit button when finished to create the MAC address-based user.

There are several ways that are beyond the scope of this material to populate the Cisco Secure ACS internal database with MAC address–based user accounts if the number of hosts is too large for manual entry, including

■ Creating the MAC database by using existing ACS tools

■ Creating the MAC database from log files

■ Creating the MAC database using third-party tools

Verification of Configuration

To verify operation of MAB on the Cisco Catalyst IOS Software switch, use the **show authentication interface** command. On the ACS server, you can verify MAB by checking the **Passed Authentication** to find the hosts using MAC address to authenticate.

Implementation Guidelines

Consider the following guidelines when deploying MAB in your environment:

■ Ensure that users cannot use the MAB credentials (MAC address) to authenticate to other processes, such as logging on to network devices. The Network Access Restriction feature can be configured on the Cisco Secure ACS to limit this access.

■ If MAB is placed before 802.1X authentication in the interface configuration, it will optimize the speed of MAB authentication at the expense of excess load on the ACS server because the ACS server must answer two queries from the user (a MAB query and an EAP query). Ensure that the ACS servers are sized appropriately.

■ Consider that you can use the guest VLAN and the restricted/authentication failed VLAN when both MAB and 802.1X fail for a user.

■ When adjusting 802.1X EAPOL timers to optimize authentication speed, be careful to not be too aggressive because this could allow 802.1X-capable machines to authenticate using MAB before 802.1X can respond to EAPOL identity requests.

In addition to the **authentication order** command, the **authentication priority** command can be used to choose a preferred authentication method over another. An example would be to use the **authentication order** command to first perform MAB and then 802.1X, but the **authentication priority** command would prefer the 802.1X authentication result over the MAB authentication result. These advanced configurations are beyond the scope of this study guide. See the "Flexible Authentication Order, Priority, and Failed Authentication" white paper for more information. The link is located in the "References."

Configure and Verify Web Authentication on Cisco IOS Software LAN Switches and Cisco Secure ACS

The web authentication feature puts in place a web-based access control on an 802.1X network. Web authentication can be used in conjunction with 802.1X authentication or as a replacement for 802.1X authentication for hosts that do not support it. One method is to configure the port to try 802.1X authentication first and then use web authentication if the client has no 802.1X supplicant.

The web authentication process is as follows:

■ The user is allowed basic DHCP connectivity on a port configured with a restrictive ACL.

■ The user's HTTP session is intercepted by the authenticator (the switch).

■ The user authenticates to the AAA server and is assigned a per-user ACL.

Note: The VLAN of the port cannot be changed with web authentication.

After an 802.1X EAP Request/Identity times out, the switch will put a preconfigured ACL on the port to control access to the network until the web authentication is successful. The switch intercepts the user's HTTP request and redirects the browser to a login page that is provided by the switch. Upon successful authentication, the switch downloads the per-user ACL from the Cisco Secure ACS server and adds it to the existing ACL. The browser then redirects the user to the original URL. Reauthentication takes place when the client does not respond to an Address Resolution Protocol (ARP) probe for Layer 2 interfaces and when the client does not send traffic within the idle timeout for Layer 3 interfaces.

If the web authentication fails, the user is presented with a Login-Fail web page that prompts the user to retry the login attempt.

Configuration Tasks

Deploying web authentication on Cisco IBNS components consists of the following tasks:

Task 1. Configure web authentication support on the authenticator (switch).

Task 2. Configure web authentication support on Cisco Secure ACS.

Configuration Scenario

Figure 7-16 shows the process involved in web authentication:

In this scenario, the switch will assign users that cannot authenticate using 802.1X to the guest VLAN of 700 (not shown). The port will be configured with an ACL that only permits DHCP requests. Cisco Secure ACS will use a unique group for web authentication users and assign an ACL to successfully authenticated users that allow HTTP access to 172.16.1.80 and DNS access to 172.16.1.53. User authentication will use a password as its authentication credential. Assumptions include that the switch and ACS are configured for RADIUS, that the EAP method is enabled, and that the basic 802.1X port control is already in place.

Task 1: Configure Web Authentication on the Switch

In Task 1, support of web authentication will be enabled on the 802.1X authenticator switch, and local AAA and RADIUS parameters will be configured. Also, the switch HTTP server, IP device tracking, and web authentication interception will be enabled. Perform the following steps:

Step 1. Log in to the switch and enter global configuration mode.

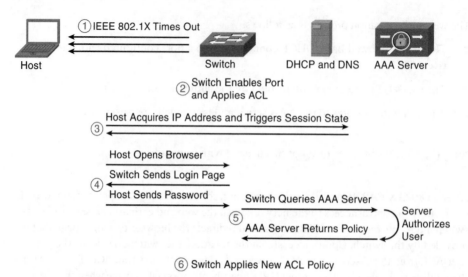

Figure 7-16 *Web Authentication Scenario*

Step 2.   Enable default AAA login authentication using the **aaa authentication login default** global configuration command and set it to use the local RADIUS client. In the example, the switch will use all the configured RADIUS servers in the default group (**group-radius**).

Note: It is recommended that any changes to the AAA configuration be made from a console connection until connectivity can be verified after making the changes. It is extremely easy to lock yourself out of a router/switch when modifying AAA configurations.

Step 3.   Enable default AAA authorization for the auth-proxy that is used by web authentication. It is enabled with the **aaa authorization auth-proxy default** global configuration command. In the example, the switch will use all the configured RADIUS servers in the default group (**group-radius**).

Step 4.   Configure the local RADIUS client to send and recognize vendor-specific attributes (VSA) required for dynamic ACL assignment using the **radius-server vsa send authentication** global configuration command.

Step 5.   Configure a new IP admission ruleset for proxy HTTP using the **ip admission name** command in global configuration command. The example uses the WEBAUTH name for this ruleset.

Step 6.   Enable the HTTP server on the switch using the **ip http server** command.

Step 7.   Enable IP tracking, which is required to learn and periodically verify the existence of hosts' MAC and IP addresses on interfaces. This is enabled with the **ip device tracking** global configuration command.

Step 8.   On all 802.1X ports, enable web authentication as the last method using the **webauth** and **authentication order** interface commands. Configure a default input ACL that permits minimal traffic (restrict to DHCP) using the **ip access-group** interface command and apply the IP admission ruleset using the **ip admission** interface command.

Example 7-5 shows the command usage from Steps 1–5.

Example 7-5   *Web Authentication on Cisco Catalyst IOS Software Switch*

```
Router# configure terminal
Router(config)# aaa authentication login default default group radius
Router(config)# aaa authorization auth-proxy default group radius
Router(config)# radius-server vsa send authentication
Router(config)# ip admission name WEBAUTH proxy http
Router(config)# ip http server
Router(config)# ip device tracking
Router(config)# interface range GigabitEthernet0/1 - 24
Router(config-if)# authentication order mab dot1x webauth
Router(config-if)# ip access-group DEFAULT-ACL in
Router(config-if)# ip admission WEBAUTH
```

Task 2: Configure Web Authentication on the Cisco Secure ACS Server

In Task 2, user accounts that are to be used by web authentication users will be configured on the Cisco Secure ACS server. The accounts are the same as other accounts except for the ACL that will be downloaded to the switch to provide additional access to web authentication users:

Step 1.   Log in to the Cisco Secure ACS with administrative privilege.

Step 2.   Navigate to the Edit Settings page in Group Setup for the group being configured.

Step 3.   Scroll down to the Cisco IOS/PIX 6.X RADIUS Attributes section and select the [009/001] cisco-av-pair option. In the Attributes Content field, enter the following to enforce the desired policy (web access to 172.16.1.80 and DNS access to 172.16.1.53):

- **Priv-lvl=15** to enable the execution of the following commands at the enable levels.

- Multiple **proxyacl** lines with a sequence number. Each proxyacl line represents a line (access control element [ACE]) in the dynamic ACL that is applied to the interface upon authentication. The syntax is **proxyacl#sequencenumber=ACE**.

Web Authentication Verification

In the CLI on a Cisco IOS Software device, the **show ip admission cache** command will show the client's IP address. In the Cisco Secure ACS, consult the Passed Authentication report to see authentication records (logs) of web authentication users.

User Experience

When the user sends an HTTP request to the web server, the switch intercepts the user's HTTP session request and presents the user with a pop-up dialog box that has a username and password field. After being authenticated successfully, the user is redirected to the original URL that was requested.

Choose a Method to Support Multiple Hosts on a Single Port

To support scenarios in which there might be more than one host per 802.1X port, Cisco Catalyst IOS Software provides several 802.1X authenticator modes:

- **Default single-host mode:** The authenticator authorizes the port and allows only the authenticated host's MAC address to forward traffic through the port.

- **Multihost mode:** The switch allows multiple hosts on a port where all MAC addresses are allowed to forward traffic after the first host authenticates.

- **Multi-auth mode:** The switch allows multiple hosts on a port, but each host must authenticate individually by using EAPOL to authenticate to the network.

- **Multidomain mode:** The switch allows multiple hosts on a port that are in multiple VLANs (a trunk port), such as a user computer and an IP phone.

Multiple Hosts Support Guidelines

Each of these modes supports various requirements. Some examples are provided to assist in determining which authentication mode is appropriate for a given set of requirements. The default single-host mode is for when there will only be a single host on each switch port. Multihost mode is used when there are several hosts per port and they are all considered authenticated by virtue of the initial authentication. This mode is appropriate for supporting virtual machines running in bridged mode.

The multi-auth mode is essentially for when there is another multiport device such as a hub connected to the port that is configured with 802.1X authentication port control. The "secondary" multiport device cannot be a switch unless it has the capability to forward EAPOL frames. Typically a switch will not forward EAPOL frames. Finally, multidomain authentication mode is to support IP phones that require the use of trunking to allow separate VLANs for the IP phone and the user's computer on the same switch port.

Configuring Support of Multiple Hosts on a Single Port

The default *single-host* mode requires no additional configuration.

Configuring *multihost* mode requires using the **dot1x host-mode multi-host** interface command. It is also recommended to use port security to limit the number of additional hosts that are allowed to forward traffic based off of the initial host's authentication. Example 7-6 shows its usage.

Example 7-6 *Configuring Multihost Authentication Mode*

```
Router# configure terminal
Router(config)# interface FastEthernet0/1-24
Router(config-if)# dot1x host-mode multi-host
Router(config-if)# switchport port-security
Router(config-if)# switchport port-security maximum 3
Router(config-if)# switchport port-security aging time 1
Router(config-if)# end
Router# copy running-config startup-config
```

Configuring *multi-auth* mode requires using the **dot1x host-mode multi-auth** interface command. Implementing port security with this mode in unnecessary because all hosts must authenticate to gain access to network resources. Example 7-7 shows its usage.

Example 7-7 *Configuring Multi-Auth Authentication Mode*

```
Router# configure terminal
Router(config)# interface FastEthernet0/1-24
Router(config-if)# dot1x host-mode multi-auth
Router(config-if)# end
Router# copy running-config startup-config
```

Configuring *multidomain* mode requires using the **dot1x host-mode multi-domain** interface command. Example 7-8 shows its use along with configuring VLAN 10 for the data VLAN and VLAN 20 for IP phone traffic.

Example 7-8 *Configure Multihost Authentication Mode*

```
Router# configure terminal
Router(config)# interface FastEthernet0/1-24
Router(config-if)# dot1x host-mode multi-domain
Router(config-if)# switchport access vlan 10
Router(config-if)# switchport voice vlan 20
Router(config-if)# end
Router(config)# copy running-config startup-config
```

Note: Prior to Release 12.2(33) SXI, the interface command to configure support for multiple hosts on a single port was the **dot1x host-mode** interface command. After Release 12.2(33) SXI, the **authentication host-mode** command replaced the **dot1x host-mode** command.

Configuring Fail-Open Policies

The Cisco Catalyst IOS Software 802.1X authenticator will, by default, not allow traffic to traverse a port that is not in the authorized state. RADIUS server failures, network outages, or any other reason that prevents a user from being authenticated will cause the port to remain in the unauthorized state.

This default, fail-closed mode can be changed to enable an optional fail-open behavior. This can be helpful in certain situations:

- **Critical ports:** For parts of the network that have unreliable connectivity to the RADIUS server and the risk of authentication failure exists, a permanent solution involves enabling the Inaccessible Authentication Bypass feature, which can authorize access to critical ports. This feature will place an interface in the authorized state if all configured RADIUS servers are unreachable.

- **Open Authentication:** Fail-open policies can alternatively be temporarily enabled, for example, during deployment, to work out any problems with the deployment. The Open Authentication feature implements this by allowing 802.1X verification without enforcing any access control on ports that fail to authorize.

Configuring Critical Ports

With the Inaccessible Authentication Bypass feature enabled, the switch checks the availability of the configured RADIUS servers. The switch will authenticate the user if a server is available. If none of the servers are available, the switch allows network access by placing the port in critical authentication state. The port must have transitioned to "critical" state to bypass authentication. The behavior of this bypass feature depends on the authorization state of the interface:

- If a host connected to a critical port tries to authenticate while the port is unauthorized and no RADIUS server is available, the switch puts the port in critical authentication state and places the port in the user-specified access VLAN.

- If the port is already authorized and a host attempts reauthentication, the switch places the port in the critical authentication state in the current VLAN, which could be the VLAN previously assigned by a RADIUS server.

- If the switch loses connectivity with the RADIUS server in the middle of an authentication attempt, the exchange will time out and the switch will put the interface in critical authentication state during the next authentication attempt.

When using the Inaccessible Authentication Bypass feature, consider using a special VLAN with access that is restricted to only critical assets.

Perform the following steps to configure ports as critical and enable Inaccessible Authentication Bypass:

Step 1. (Optional) Use the **authentication critical recovery delay** global configuration command to optionally set the time the switch will wait to reinitialize a port when a previously unavailable RADIUS server becomes available. The example sets this duration to 2 seconds.

Step 2. Label the port as critical and authorize the port to a specific VLAN using the **authentication event server dead action authorize vlan** interface configuration command.

Step 3. (Optional) Configure the port to reauthenticate immediately when a RADIUS server becomes available again using the **authentication event server alive reinitialize** interface configuration command.

Example 7-9 shows how to configure Inaccessible Authentication Bypass.

Example 7-9 *Configure Critical Ports*

```
Router# configure terminal
Router(config)# authentication critical recovery delay 2000
Router(config)# interface FastEthernet0/1-24
Router(config-if)# authentication event server dead action authorize vlan 10
Router(config-if)# authentication event server alive action reinitialize
Router(config-if)# end
Router(config)# copy running-config startup-config
```

The Inaccessible Authentication Bypass feature interacts with other features in the following ways:

- **Guest VLAN:** Inaccessible Authentication Bypass is compatible with guest VLANs. The interactions are

  - If at least one RADIUS server is reachable, the switch assigns a host to the guest VLAN if it does not receive a response to its EAP Request/Identity frame or when there are no EAPOL packets from the client.

  - If no RADIUS server is available and the client is connected to a critical port, the switch authenticates the client and puts the interface in the critical authenticated state and in the user-specified access VLAN.

  - If no RADIUS server is available and the client is not connected to a critical port, the switch assigns hosts to the guest VLAN if one is configured.

  - If no RADIUS server is available and the client is connected to a critical port and was previously assigned to the guest VLAN, the switch will keep the port assigned to the guest VLAN.

- **Restricted VLAN:** If no RADIUS server is available and the interface is already authorized in a restricted VLAN, the switch puts the interface in the critical authentication state and leaves it in the restricted VLAN.

- **802.1X accounting:** Accounting will not be affected by the RADIUS server being unreachable.

- **PVLAN:** Inaccessible Authentication Bypass can be configured on a PVLAN port as long as the VLAN is a secondary PVLAN.

- **Voice VLAN:** Inaccessible Authentication Bypass is compatible with voice VLANs, but the access VLAN and voice VLAN must be different.

- **RSPAN:** The Remote SPAN (RSPAN) VLAN should never be configured as the access VLAN on an interface configured with Inaccessible Authentication Bypass.

Configuring Open Authentication

Open authentication assists with deploying a Cisco IBNS 802.1X solution more smoothly. It is typically used temporarily and only during the initial implementation phase. However, it can be considered as an alternative to Inaccessible Authentication Bypass for locations with unstable connectivity to the RADIUS infrastructure. If this feature is deployed permanently, consider using per-user ACLs that provide additional access upon authentication.

To enable open authentication, use the **authentication open** interface configuration command.

Resolve 802.1X Compatibility Issues

There are several situations in which configuring 802.1X authentication on a switch port can create unanticipated problems. Cisco IOS Software provides solutions that can fix these issues.

Wake-on-LAN (WOL)

Wake-on-LAN is a networking standard that defines a specific type of packet, known as a "magic" packet, that allows a computer to be turned on or "woken" up upon receiving this magic packet. Switch ports that have 802.1X port control configured on them will not allow traffic to pass through an interface that is in the unauthorized state. The computer cannot wake up to authenticate, but yet it cannot receive that packet that is intended to wake it up. Cisco Catalyst IOS Software provides a solution to this by configuring an interface as unidirectionally controlled by using the **authentication control-direction in** interface command. In this configuration, the switch will still not allow ingress packets to traverse unauthenticated ports but will allow egress packets to flow through them. This allows the magic packet to be received and "wake up" the host. Example 7-10 shows the command in use.

Example 7-10 *Configure Interface as Unidirectionally Controlled*

```
Router# configure terminal
Router(config)# interface FastEthernet0/1-24
Router(config-if)# authentication control-direction in
Router(config-if)# end
Router(config)# copy running-config startup-config
```

Non-802.1X IP Phones

Most Cisco IP Phones support an 802.1X supplicant, enabling them to authenticate to the network using multidomain authentication on switch ports, as discussed earlier in this chapter. As depicted in Example 7-11, you can use multidomain authentication with MAB to authenticate these non-802.1X IP phones based on their MAC addresses.

Example 7-11 *Multidomain Authentication with MAB*

```
Router# configure terminal
Router(config)# interface FastEthernet0/1-24
Router(config-if)# dot1x host-mode multi-domain
Router(config-if)# switchport access vlan 10
Router(config-if)# switchport voice vlan 20
Router(config-if)# mab
Router(config-if)# end
Router(config)# copy running-config startup-config
```

Preboot Execution Environment (PXE)

Computers that are in a Preboot Execution Environment (PXE) need to use access to the network to boot themselves from a network resource. Switch ports configured with 802.1X port control will not let the necessary traffic pass because of the port being in an unauthorized state. Cisco Catalyst IOS Software provides two possible solutions to this:

■   Use open authentication with a default ACL, as shown in Example 7-12, that permits network boot traffic and then further restricts the traffic with a per-user downloadable ACL that will be applied after successful authentication.

■   Use MAB to initially authenticate the computer based on its MAC address, and use authentication order and authentication priority to prefer 802.1X authentication after the 802.1X supplicant is running.

Example 7-12 *Configure Interface as Unidirectionally Controlled*

```
Router# configure terminal
Router(config)# interface FastEthernet0/1-24
Router(config-if)# authentication open
Router(config-if)# ip access-group DHCP-PXE in
Router(config-if)# end
Router(config)# copy running-config startup-config
```

Exam Preparation

As mentioned in the section, "How to Use This Book," in the Introduction, you have several choices for exam preparation: the exercises here, the memory tables in Appendix D, the final exam preparation chapter, and the exam simulation questions on the CD-ROM. The following questions present a bigger challenge than the exam itself because they use an open-ended question format. By using this more difficult format, you exercise your memory better and prove your conceptual and factual knowledge of this chapter. You can find the answers to these questions in Appendix A, "Answers to the DIKTA Quizzes and Fill in the Blanks Questions."

Review All Key Topics

Review the most important topics in this chapter, noted with the Key Topics icon in the margin of the page. Table 7-3 lists a reference of these key topics and the page numbers on which each is found.

Table 7-3 *Key Topics*

Key Topic Element	Description	Page
List	List of input parameters that must be gathered prior to deploying advanced 802.1X	143
List	Deployment choice for EAP methods	145
List	List of tasks to configure EAP-TLS with 802.1X on Cisco Identity-Based Network components	146
Table 7-2	Differences between user and machine authentication	154
List	List of tasks to configure dynamic VLAN and ACL assignments	159
List	Implementation guidelines for deploying user and machine authentication	165
List	MAC Authentication Bypass interaction with other Cisco IOS features	166
List	Implementation guidelines for deploying MAC Authentication Bypass	168
List	Configuring critical ports	174
Paragraph	802.1X compatibility issues	176

Complete Tables and Lists from Memory

Print a copy of Appendix C, "Memory Tables" (found on the CD), or at least the section for this chapter, and complete the tables and lists from memory. Appendix D, "Memory Table Answers," also on the CD, includes completed tables and lists to check your work. Although there were no memory tables in this chapter, you will find some for other chapters.

Define Key Terms

Define the following key terms from this chapter, and check your answers in the Glossary:

mutual authentication, supplicant, Public-Key Infrastructure (PKI), public key cryptography, Certificate Signing Request (CSR), Certificate Authority (CA) certificate, user certificate, machine certificate

Fill in the Blanks

1. The _____ and _____ do not both authenticate to the network at the same time. _____ authentication is only needed when the user logs off.

2. With the _____ optional EAP-TLS parameter, the TLS session keys are essentially cached, thus allowing faster reauthentication by not having to perform a full TLS handshake.

3. The _____ command can be used to choose a preferred authentication method over another.

4. When the user sends an _____ request to the web server, the switch intercepts the user's HTTP session request and presents the user with a pop-up dialog box that has a username and password field.

5. Beginning with _____ of Cisco IOS Software, the **dot1x host-mode** command was replaced with the _____ command.

6. When configuring fail-open policies, label an interface as critical by using the _____ interface configuration command.

7. To handle Wake-on-LAN devices in an 802.1X environment, configure the interface as _____ by using the _____ interface command.

8. Use the _____ with _____ to authenticate non-802.1X IP phones based on their MAC addresses.

References

Cisco IOS Security Configuration Guide: Securing User Services, Release 12.4T, www.cisco.com/en/US/docs/ios/sec_user_services/configuration/guide/12_4T/sec_securing_user_services_12.4t_book.html.

Cisco IOS Security Command Reference - 12.4, www.cisco.com/en/US/docs/ios/security/command/reference/sec_book.html.

Cisco IOS Security Command Reference - 15.0M, www.cisco.com/en/US/partner/docs/ios/security/command/reference/sec_book.html.

Cisco IOS Security Configuration Guide: Securing User Services, Release 15.0, www.cisco.com/en/US/partner/docs/ios/sec_user_services/configuration/guide/15_0/sec_user_services_15_0_book.html.

Configuring IEEE 802.1X Port-Based Authentication - Cisco IOS Configuration Guide 12.4, www.cisco.com/en/US/docs/ios/sec_user_services/configuration/guide/sec_cfg_ieee802_pba_ps6441_TSD_Products_Configuration_Guide_Chapter.html.

Catalyst 6500 Release 12.2SXH and Later Software Configuration Guide: Configuring IEEE 802.1X Port-Based Authentication, www.cisco.com/en/US/partner/docs/switches/lan/catalyst6500/ios/12.2SX/configuration/guide/dot1x.html.

Flexible Authentication Order, Priority, and Failed Authentication, www.cisco.com/en/US/prod/collateral/iosswrel/ps6537/ps6586/ps6638/application_note_c27-573287_ps6638_Products_White_Paper.html.

This chapter covers the following subjects:

- **Routed data plane attack types:** Reviews the types of attack that are focused on the routed data plane.

- **Access control lists (ACL):** Covers the fundamentals of using ACLs and the configuration and verification commands to use.

- **Flexible Packet Matching (FPM):** Covers the steps involved in developing a traffic class and policy and assigning it to an interface. It also goes over the verification commands that can be used in configuration and troubleshooting.

- **Flexible NetFlow:** Reviews the fundamentals of Flexible NetFlow and describes the configuration and verification commands to use it.

- **Unicast Reverse Path Forwarding (Unicast RPF):** Covers the basics of how Unicast RPF functions and discusses the commands required to configure and verify it.

CHAPTER 8

Implementing and Configuring Cisco IOS Routed Data Plane Security

Several different parts of a network need to be secured from internal and external attack. The three planes as defined by Cisco include the data plane, management plane, and control plane, and these are split between those focused on the switched parts of the network and those focused on the routed parts of the network. This chapter addresses the routed data plane, including the Cisco IOS Software features that can be used to secure the network user data that traverses the network and discusses how to configure these features on the network devices within the network.

"Do I Know This Already?" Quiz

The "Do I Know This Already?" quiz helps you decide whether you really need to read the entire chapter. If you already intend to read the entire chapter, you do not necessarily need to answer these questions now.

The ten-question quiz, derived from the major sections in the "Foundation Topics" section of this chapter, helps you determine how to spend your limited study time.

Table 8-1 outlines the major topics discussed in this chapter and the "Do I Know This Already?" quiz questions that correspond to those topics.

Table 8-1 *"Do I Know This Already?" Foundation Topics Section-to-Question Mapping*

Foundation Topics Section	Questions Covered in This Section
Routed Data Plane Attack Types	1
Routed Data Plane Security Technologies	2–10

Caution: The goal of self-assessment is to gauge your mastery of the topics in this chapter. If you do not know the answer to a question or are only partially sure of the answer, you should mark this question wrong for purposes of the self-assessment. Giving yourself credit for an answer that you correctly guess skews your self-assessment results and might provide you with a false sense of security.

1. Which of the following are some of the most common types of routed data plane attacks?

   a. Routing protocol spoofing

   b. Slow-path denial of service

   c. STP spoofing

   d. Traffic flooding

2. Which of the following ACL ranges are used for standard access lists?

   a. 100–199

   b. 2000–2699

   c. 1–99

   d. 1300–1999

3. When using a reflexive access list, which of the following ACL types must be used?

   a. Standard IP ACL

   b. Extended IP ACL

   c. Extended IP named ACL

   d. Reflexive ACL

   e. Standard IP named ACL

4. Which of the following are valid steps required for the creation of an FPM filtering policy?

   a. Defining a service policy

   b. Loading of a PCFD

   c. Defining an access list

   d. Loading of a PHDF

5. Which command are used to load a traffic classification file (TCDF)?

   a. load protocol

   b. load classification

   c. load tcdf

   d. load class-file

6. Which commands are used to configure matching for a traffic class?

   a. match field

   b. match start

   c. match beginning

   d. match l2-layer

   e. match packet

7. Which of the following are restrictions when using FPM?

    a. Stateful inspection only

    b. IPv4/IPv6 unicast packets only

    c. IPv4 unicast packets only

    d. Cannot be used with IP options packets

8. Which of the following are benefits that are gained by using Flexible NetFlow?

    a. Flexible key and nonkey fields

    b. Version 5 export format

    c. Standardized key and nonkey fields

    d. Version 9 export format

9. Which of the following are Flexible NetFlow components?

    a. Flow sequencers

    b. Flow policers

    c. Flow monitors

    d. Flow samplers

10. Unicast RPF utilizes which of the following to compare source packet information?

    a. IP routing table

    b. CEF FIB

    c. Topology tables

    d. NetFlow records

The answers to the "Do I Know This Already?" quiz are found in Appendix A. The suggested choices for your next step are as follows:

■ **8 or less overall score:** Read the entire chapter. This includes the "Foundation Topics" section.

■ **9 or 10 overall score:** If you want more review on these topics, skip to the "Exam Preparation" section. Otherwise, move on to Chapter 9, "Implementing and Configuring Cisco IOS Control Plane Security."

Foundation Topics

Routed Data Plane Attack Types

As stated in previous chapters, understanding the attack makes the mitigation of the attack easier to accomplish. The routed infrastructure encompasses a large part of people's everyday lives, and because of this, it is a very large attack target. The following sections review the attacks that are targeted at the routed data plane.

The most common types of routed data plane attacks are

- IP spoofing
- Slow-path denial of service
- Traffic flooding

IP Spoofing

Although IP spoofing has been covered in earlier chapters, it is reviewed here. With IP spoofing, an attacker attempts to send and receive traffic on the network using an IP address of another known host or known network. The attacker is then able to use resources on the network that are associated with that specific IP address. IP spoofing is just as much of a threat on the routed network as it is with the switched network, but it is mitigated using different techniques and technologies. The three primary methods used to perform IP spoofing are as follows:

- Injecting packets with the IP address of an existing host
- Spoofing an existing host using source routing
- Injecting packets from nonexisting hosts to perform a denial of service attack.

Slow-Path Denial of Service

Generic denial of service attacks are well known because they are rather simple to understand. A host or group of hosts attempts to deny a specific service or services to their intended audience, typically through the flooding of traffic to the targeted sites. Slow-path denial of service looks to deny a service or services by sending a large number of packets through the routed pieces of equipment that are required to be process switched. Process switching compared with other alternatives is the "slow path" through the equipment. The CPU of each device is tasked to perform three functions:

- Process control plane traffic
- Process management plane traffic
- Process slow-path data plane traffic

This chapter focuses on the methods of mitigating slow-path data plane attacks.

Traffic Flooding

This attack type involves the flooding of packets at a specific target. Typically, these types of attack are focused on breaking down the functionality of the target host. The techniques described in this chapter can be used to mitigate traffic-flooding attacks on not only the data plane but also the control and management planes.

Routed Data Plane Security Technologies

A number of different security technologies can be used to mitigate the attacks covered in the previous sections. A description of these technologies and how to implement them will be covered in the following sections.

Access Control Lists (ACL)

ACLs are rules that deny or permit packets coming into or out of an interface. An ACL typically consists of multiple ACL entries (ACE), organized internally by the router. When a packet is subjected to access control, the router searches this linked list in order from top to bottom to find a matching element. The matching element is then examined to determine whether the packet is permitted or denied.

ACLs can be used to mitigate a number of attacks and can also be used in combination with other technologies to mitigate many more. ACLs can be used in small businesses or at the edge of larger businesses to mitigate both IP spoofing and slow-path denial of service attacks. These types of ACLs are called *infrastructure ACLs* because they look to protect not just the device but also the entire infrastructure. To mitigate IP spoofing attacks, an ACL is configured to automatically disallow inbound traffic that has a source IP address that is known to be inside the network. When being legitimately routed, these addresses, which are inside the network, will never be sourced outside the network. ACLs can also be used to screen traffic that has been sent in an effort to slow the device by forcing its traffic to be process switched. In small amounts, this is not an issue, but when a large number of packets need to be process switched, it has the chance of affecting the performance of the device.

Figure 8-1 shows the behavior of a router that has an ACL configured on its interfaces.

The function of ACLs includes their ability to

- Control the transmission of packets coming into or out of an interface

- Control virtual terminal line access

- Restrict contents of routing updates

- Define interesting traffic

There are two different methods to configure an ACL:

- **Numbered ACLs:** These are entered one line at a time, and the list is scanned for a match in that same order. If a change is required, the entire list must be reentered.

- **Named ACLs:** Theses provide a method of configuration that does not require the complete reentry of the ACL.

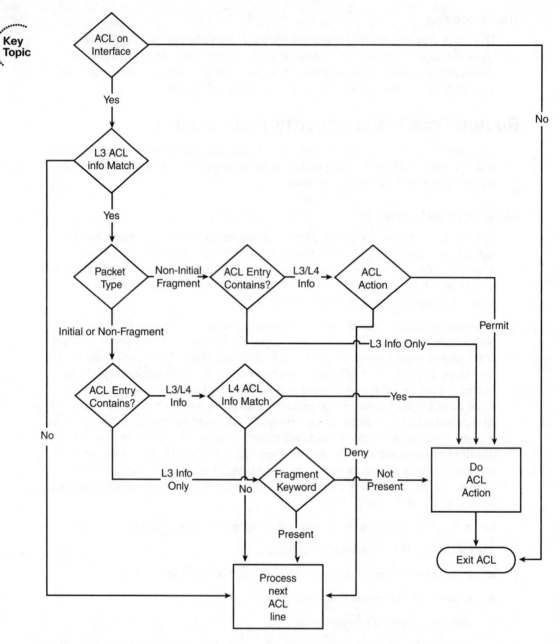

Figure 8-1   *High-Level Overview of How an ACL Is Processed by a Router*

The ACL criteria that can be used is quite large and includes information like the source and destination network layer information as well as a number of different fields provided by upper-layer protocols.

At the end of each ACL, there is an implied deny for traffic that has not been previously permitted. There must be at least one **permit** statement in an ACL; otherwise, all traffic will be blocked.

ACLs also have the capability to drop or ignore packets based on whether they contain any IP options. There are two ways in which this can be controlled: through the IP Options Selective Drop feature or through the use of the **option** keyword when creating an extended named access list. The IP Options Selective Drop feature is used by issuing the **ip options** {*drop* | *ignore*} **global configuration** command.

Determining Where and When to Configure Access Lists

To provide the security benefits of ACLs, at a minimum an ACL should be configured on the border routers, which are routers situated at the edges of the network. This setup provides a basic buffer from the outside network or from a less-controlled area of the network into a more sensitive area of the network.

An ACL can be configured so that inbound traffic or outbound traffic, or both, are filtered on an interface. ACLs should be defined on a per-protocol basis. In other words, an ACL should be defined for every protocol enabled on an interface if that protocols traffic is to be controlled.

Types of ACLs

Cisco IOS Software supports the following types of ACLs for IP:

- **Standard ACLs:** Use source addresses for matching operations.

- **Extended ACLs:** Use source and destination addresses for matching operations and optional protocol type information for finer granularity of control.

- **Reflexive ACLs:** Allow IP packets to be filtered based on session information. Reflexive ACLs contain temporary entries and are nested within extended-named IP ACLs.

- **Time-based ACLs:** As the name intuitively indicates, these ACLs are triggered by a time function.

Key Topic

The following sections discuss each type of ACL in detail.

Standard ACLs

Standard ACLs are the oldest type of ACLs, dating back as early as Cisco IOS Software Release 8.3. Standard ACLs control traffic by comparing the source address of the traffic to the addresses configured in the ACL.

The following is the command syntax format of a standard ACL:

```
router(config)# access-list access-list-number {permit | deny} {host | source
  source-wildcard | any} [log]
```

or

```
router(config)# ip access-list standard {access-list-number | access-list-name}
permit {host host | source source-wildcard | any} [log]
```

In all software releases, the access list number for standard IP access lists can be anything from 1 to 99. Table 8-2 shows the various protocol options and their corresponding number range for the ACL identification. In Cisco IOS Software Release 12.0.1, standard IP ACLs began using additional numbers (1300 to 1999). These additional numbers are referred to as *expanded IP ACLs*. In addition to using numbers to identify ACLs, Cisco IOS Software Release 11.2 and later added the ability to use the list *name* in standard IP ACLs.

Table 8-2 *Protocols and Their Corresponding Number Identification for an ACL*

Protocol	Range
Standard IP	1–99 and 1300–1999
Extended IP	100–199 and 2000–2699
Ethernet type code	200–299
Ethernet address	700–799
Transparent bridging (protocol type)	200–299
Transparent bridging (vendor code)	700–799
Extended transparent bridging	1100–1199
DECnet and extended DECnet	300–399
Xerox Network Systems (XNS)	400–499
Extended XNS	500–599
AppleTalk	600–699
Source-route bridging (protocol type)	200–299
Source-route bridging (vendor code)	700–799
Internetwork Packet Exchange (IPX)	800–899
Extended IPX	900–999
IPX Service Advertising Protocol (SAP)	1000–1099
Standard Virtual Integrated Network Service (VINES)	1–100
Extended VINES	101–200
Simple VINES	201–300

The **log** option enables the monitoring of how many packets are permitted or denied by a particular ACL, including the source address of each packet. The logging message includes the ACL number, whether the packet was permitted or denied, the source IP address of the packet, and the number of packets from that source permitted or denied in the prior 5-minute interval.

Wildcard masks are used in conjunction with IP addresses to identify the source address in an ACL. Wildcard masks are also known as *reverse netmasks* and are one of the topics that many people have considerable problem understanding. In an effort to make this a little clearer, an example will be shown. So, if the netmask normally is 255.255.255.0, it's this in binary:

11111111 11111111 11111111 00000000

Swapping the bits yields the reverse netmask, shown as follows:

00000000 00000000 00000000 11111111

or

0.0.0.255 (the wildcard mask)

Another way to calculate the wildcard mask is to take the network mask and subtract each octet from 255. If the network mask is 255.255.248.0, for example, the wildcard is calculated by subtracting it from 255 on each octet, yielding a 0.0.7.255 wildcard mask.

After defining an ACL, it must be applied to the interface (inbound or outbound):

```
router(config)# interface interface
router(config-if)# ip access-group number {in | out}
```

Example 8-1 shows the use of a standard IP ACL to block all traffic except that from source 192.168.100.x.

Example 8-1   *Sample ACL Configuration Permitting Network 192.168.100.0 into the FastEthernet 0/0 Interface and Implicitly Denying All Other IP Traffic*

```
router(config)# interface FastEthernet0/0
router(config-if)# ip address 192.168.100.1 255.255.255.0
router(config-if)# access-group 1 in
router(config)# access-list 1 permit 192.168.100.0 0.0.0.255
```

The terms *in*, *out*, *source*, and *destination* are used as referenced by the router. Traffic on the router could be compared to traffic on the highway. If a law enforcement officer in the United States wanted to stop a truck coming from Mexico and traveling to Canada, the truck's source would be Mexico and the truck's destination would be Canada. The roadblock could be applied at the U.S./Mexican border (in) or the U.S./Canadian border (out).

With regard to a router, these terms mean the following:

■ **In:** Traffic that is arriving on the interface and that will go through the router; the source is where it has been, and the destination is where it is going.

■   **Out:** Traffic that has already been through the router and is leaving the interface; the source is where it has been, and the destination is where it is going.

Extended IP ACLs

Extended IP ACLs were introduced in Cisco IOS Software Release 8.3. Extended IP ACLs can control traffic by not only comparing the source IP addresses but also comparing the destination IP address as well as other information, including the source and destination port numbers of the IP packets to those configured in the ACL.

The following is the command syntax format of extended IP ACLs:

```
router(config)# access-list access-list-number [dynamic dynamic-name [timeout
  minutes]]{deny | permit} protocol source source-wildcard destination
  destination-wildcard [precedence precedence] [tos tos] [log | log-input] [time-
  range time-range-name]
```

or

```
router(config)# ip access-list extended {access-list-number | access-list-name}
```

```
router(config-std-nacl)# [sequence-number] permit protocol source source-wildcard
destination destination-wildcard [option option-value] [precedence precedence]
[tos tos] [time-range time-range-name] [log]
```

or

```
router(config-ext-nacl)# [sequence-number] permit protocol source source-wildcard
destination destination-wildcard [option option-value] [precedence precedence]
[tos tos] [time-range time-range-name] [log]
```

In all software releases, the access list number for extended IP access lists can be 101 to 199. In Cisco IOS Software Release 12.0.1, extended IP ACLs began using additional numbers (2000 to 2699). These additional numbers are referred to as *expanded IP ACLs*. Cisco IOS Software Release 11.2 added the ability to use the list *name* in extended IP ACLs.

Example 8-2 shows an extended IP ACL used to permit traffic on the 192.168.100.x network (inside) and to receive ping responses from the outside while preventing unsolicited pings from people outside (permitting all other traffic).

Example 8-2   *Sample Configuration for an Extended IP ACL*

```
router(config)# access-list 101 deny icmp any 192.168.100.0 0.0.0.255 echo
router(config)# access-list 101 permit ip any 192.168.100.0 0.0.0.255
router(config)# interface FastEthernet0/0
router(config-if)# ip address 172.16.8.1 255.255.255.0
router(config-if)# ip access-group 101 in
```

Reflexive ACLs

Cisco IOS Software Release 11.3 introduced reflexive ACLs. Reflexive ACLs enable IP packets to be filtered based on upper-layer session information.

They are generally used in one of two ways:

- To allow outbound traffic out of an interface facing away from the internal network and filtering inbound traffic based on existing sessions originating inside the internal network

- To allow all inbound traffic to an interface facing toward the internal network and filtering outbound traffic based on the existing session originating inside the internal network

The former of these two is more typical with a network that does not utilize a demilitarized zone (DMZ). The latter is used to allow traffic into a DMZ but to not allow that traffic into the internal network without a previous connection initiated inside the internal network. Both of these are shown in Figures 8-2 and 8-3.

Reflexive ACLs can be defined only with extended named IP ACLs. They cannot be defined with numbered, standard named IP ACLs or with other protocol ACLs. Reflexive ACLs can be used in conjunction with other standard and static extended IP ACLs. The syntax for configuring a reflexive ACL is as follows:

```
router(config)# ip access-list extended {access-list-number | access-list-name}
  router(config-ext-nacl)# [sequence-number] permit protocol source source-wildcard
  destination destination-wildcard reflect name
```

and

```
router(config-ext-nacl)# evaluate
```

Example 8-3 demonstrates, by using Figure 8-2, the process of permitting all TCP traffic outbound and inbound TCP traffic that was initiated from inside the network.

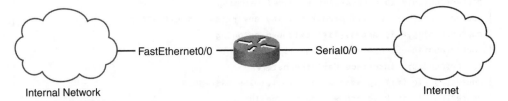

Figure 8-2   *Outbound Reflexive Diagram*

Example 8-3   *Sample Configuration for an Outbound Reflexive ACL*

```
router(config)# ip access-list extended outgoing
router(config-ext-nacl)# permit tcp any any reflect tcp-traffic
router(config)# ip access-list extended incoming
router(config-ext-nacl)# evaluate tcp-traffic
router(config)# interface Serial0/0
```

```
router(config-if)# ip address 192.168.100.1 255.255.255.0
router(config-if)# ip access-group incoming in
router(config-if)# ip accesss-group outgoing out
```

Example 8-4 demonstrates, by using Figure 8-3, the process of permitting all TCP traffic inbound and outbound TCP traffic that was initiated from inside the network.

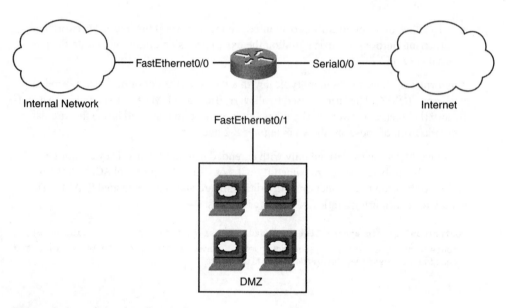

Figure 8-3 *Inbound Reflexive Diagram*

Example 8-4 *Sample Configuration for an Inbound Reflexive ACL*

```
router(config)# ip access-list extended incoming
router(config-ext-nacl)# permit tcp any any reflect tcp-traffic
router(config)# ip access-list extended outgoing
router(config-ext-nacl)# evaluate tcp-traffic
router(config)# interface FastEthernet0/0
router(config-if)# ip address 172.16.1.1 255.255.255.0
router(config-if)# ip access-group incoming in
router(config-if)# ip accesss-group outgoing out
```

Time-Based ACLs

Cisco IOS Software Release 12.0.1.T introduced time-based ACLs. Although similar to extended IP ACLs in function, they allow access control based on time. To implement time-based ACLs, a time range is created that defines specific times of the day and week. The time range is identified by a name and then referenced by a function. Therefore, the time restrictions are imposed on the function itself. The time range relies on the router's system clock. The router clock can be used solely, but the feature works best when Network Time Protocol (NTP) synchronization is used on the device.

Time-based ACL commands require the following syntax:

```
router(config)# time-range time-range-name
router(config-time-range)# periodic days-of-the-week hh:mm to [days-of-the-
  week] hh:mm
router(config-time-range)# absolute [start time date] [end time date]
```

and

```
router(config)# access-list access-list-number protocol source source-wildcard
  destination destination-wildcard [time-range time-range-name]
```

or

```
router(config)# ip access-list extended {access-list-number ¦ access-list-name}
router(config-ext-nacl)# [sequence-number] permit protocol source source-wildcard
  destination destination-wildcard [time-range time-range-name]
```

or

```
router(config)# ip access-list extended {access-list-number ¦ access-list-name}
router(config-ext-nacl)# [sequence-number] permit protocol source source-wildcard
  destination destination-wildcard [precedence precedence] [tos tos] [time-range
  time-range-name] [log]
```

Example 8-5 shows a Telnet connection permitted from the outside the network (172.16.1.0) to the inside of the network (192.168.1.0) on Monday, Tuesday, and Thursday during the hours of 7 a.m. through 6 p.m.

Example 8-5 *Sample Configuration for Time-Range ACL*

```
router(config)# interface FastEthernet0/0
router(config-if)# ip address 192.168.1.1 255.255.255.0
router(config)# interface FastEthernet0/1
router(config-if)# ip address 172.16.1.1 255.255.255.0
router(config-if)# ip access-group 101 in
router(config)# access-list 101 permit tcp 172.16.1.0 0.0.0.255 192.168.1.0
0.0.0.255 eq telnet time-range TelnetAccess
router(config)# time-range TelnetAccess
router(config-time-range)# periodic Monday Tuesday Thursday 7:00 to 18:00
```

Time ranges offer many possible benefits, including the following:

■ The network administrator has more control over permitting or denying a user access to resources. These resources include an application (identified by an IP address/mask pair and a port number), policy routing, or an on-demand link (identified as interesting traffic to the dialer).

- When provider access rates vary by time of day, it is possible to automatically reroute traffic cost-effectively.

- Service providers can dynamically change a committed access rate (CAR) configuration to support the quality of service (QoS) service-level agreements (SLA) that are negotiated for certain times of day.

- Network administrators can control logging messages. ACL entries can log traffic at certain times of the day but not constantly. Therefore, administrators can just deny access without analyzing the many logs generated during peak hours.

- Policy-based routing and queuing functions are enhanced.

ACL Verification

There are a number of different **show** commands that can be used to verify ACL configuration.

To display the contents of all current access lists, enter the following command:

```
show access-list [access-list-number | access-list-name}
```

To display the contents of all current IP access lists, enter the following command:

```
show ip access-list [access-list-number | access-list-name}
```

Flexible Packet Matching

Flexible Packet Matching (FPM) was created to be a more thorough and customized packet filter option. FPM enables the user to configure match parameters based on arbitrary bits of a packet and arbitrary depths within the packet header and payload. This technique can be used to mitigate several different types of attack, including slow-path denial of service and zero-day virus and malware.

FPM is implemented using a filtering policy that is divided into four tasks:

- Loading of a Protocol Header Description File (PHDF)

- Defining a class map and a specific protocol stack chain (traffic class)

- Defining a service policy (traffic policy)

- Application of a service policy on a specific interface

Key Topic

FPM Restrictions

As with all technologies, a number of different restrictions must be known before attempting to configure FPM. The main restrictions for FPM include

- FPM is stateless; it cannot keep track of traffic flows through the configured interface (for example, port numbers).

- FPM inspects only IPv4 unicast packets.

- FPM cannot classify packets with IP options.

- FPM is not supported on tunnel or Multiprotocol Label Switching (MPLS) interfaces.

- FPM cannot be configured on FlexWAN cards.

- Noninitial fragments will not be matched by FPM.

Protocol Header Description File

With FPM, two different methods can be used to match specific traffic: the use of a Protocol Header Description File (PHDF) and/or the direct matching of traffic based on length and offset, or a mix of the two. A PHDF is used to define the various field names within a specific protocol. For example, the IP.phdf file has a field defined for each field in an IP header (that is, Version, Header Length, ToS, and so on), and TCP.phdf has a field defined for each field in the TCP header (that is, Source and Destination Port, Sequence Number, Acknowledgment Number, and so on). To take advantage of these field names, this file must first be loaded with the **load protocol** global configuration command. Loading a PHDF file also provides the ability to use the **match field** class map configuration command, which provides the ability to match based on this PHDF field information. Without loading the PHDF file, only the **match start** class map configuration command is supported, which provides the capability to match based on specific length and offset information. Both of these commands provide different methods for matching specific information within the packet and will be covered in more depth in the following sections. It is also possible for PHDFs to be custom written for other protocols; PHDFs are XML files and can be easily adapted for these purposes. The specific command syntax required to load the PHDF files is as follows:

```
router(config)# load protocol location:filename
```

Example 8-6 demonstrates the loading of both the IP and TCP PHDF files for use with the **match field** command.

Example 8-6 *Sample Configuration for the* **load protocol** *Command*

```
router(config)# load protocol system:fpm/phdf/ip.phdf
router(config)# load protocol system:fpm/phdf/tcp.phdf
```

Defining a Traffic Class

When creating a traffic class, its purpose is to define a number of criteria that are used to match specific traffic based on stateless packet classification. A simple example of this would be to match based on TCP traffic with a port number equal to 80 (web traffic). Of course, this type of example is simple and can be accomplished with common access list commands that are used more often for these types of matches. However, FPM provides the capability to not only match based on a specific criteria like a TCP port number but also based on a specific set of criteria, such as TCP port 80, with an IP packet length of less than 400 bytes, with a specific pattern 4 bytes long at offset 400. Now at first glance, why would someone need this capability? Well in the modern world, a number of threats exist, many of which are being created every day. Many of these are caught and prevented using tools such as intrusion protection systems (IPS); however, some attacks are so new that a signature is not yet available for the IPS. This is where the flexibility of FPM comes in handy. If an attack is occurring and a pattern is able to be distinguished, FPM can be used to surgically drop these attack packets inline without interruption of other uninfected traffic.

With FPM, two different methods can be used to configure traffic classes:

- Traffic can be classified using a Traffic Classification Definition File (TCDF).

- Traffic can be classified through the CLI using class maps.

When using a TCDF, a file must be created and then loaded. The TCDF file uses XML and is rather simple to create. TCDFs offer a method of implementing the same matching criteria as the CLI commands, but allow them to be repetitively used over a number of different devices without the hassle of manually adding commands on each device. The steps used to create the match criteria are the same as when using the CLI. These specific steps will be covered in the text that follows in CLI terms, and specific examples will be included showing the correct TCDF format. Use of a TCDF requires the **load classification** command to load the TCDF file on the device. The command syntax required for this command is as follows:

```
router(config)# load classification location:filename
```

Because CLI configuration is the most commonly understood method of configuration, this type of configuration will be covered in depth. The first thing that must be configured with the CLI is a class map; this is done using the **class-map** command. This command is well known because it is used for many other tasks within IOS and is configured similarly. Two class map types are used with FPM:

Key Topic

- **Stack:** Specifies the specific protocol stacks that will be used to match (for example, IP, TCP, UDP) and can be only used with the **match-all** keyword.

- **Access control:** Matches specific patterns within the traffic of interest.

The command syntax required to create these class maps is as follows:

CLI:

```
router(config)# class-map type [stack | access-control] [match-all | match-any]
  class-map-name
```

TCDF:

```
<?xml version"1.0" encoding="UTF-8"?>
<tcdf>
    <class name="class-name" type="stack | access-control" match="any |
    all"></class>
    ...
</tcdf>
```

The second part of this process is configuring specific match criteria; to do this, the **match start** and the **match field** commands are used. As stated earlier, the **match field** command only works after a PHDF has been loaded. The **match field** command is used to match based on the PHDF fields loaded. The **match start** command is used to match a specific pattern based on a specific offset and length and whether to begin inspection at the beginning of the Layer 3 packet header or at the beginning of the Layer 2 frame header. The command syntax for these commands is as follows:

CLI:

```
router(config-cmap)# match field protocol protocol-field [eq | neq | gt | lt | range
  range] value next next-protocol

router(config-cmap)# match start [12-start | 13-start] offset offset size size
 [eq | neq | gt | lt | range range] value
```

TCDF:

```
<?xml version"1.0" encoding="UTF-8"?>
<tcdf>
    ...
      <match>
          <[eq | neq | gt | lt] field="field-name" value="value"></[eq | neq | gt
           | lt]>
          <range field="field-name" from="beginning-value" to="ending-
            value"></range>
      </match>
    ...
</tcdf>
```

To wrap up all the different commands required for a traffic class, Example 8-7 shows a sample configuration. In this example, two different separate class maps are being created:

- **tcp-class:** This class map is configured to match the IP protocol header field when it is equal to 0x6 (TCP) and tells FPM that the next protocol to be analyzed will be TCP.

- **sample-match:** This class map is configured to match traffic that has a TCP destination port that is equal to 0x50 (80) *and* has the contents "0x1234" at offset 200 in the IP packet.

Example 8-7 *Sample Traffic Class Configuration*

```
CLI:


router(config)# class-map type stack match-all tcp-class
router(config-cmap)# match field ip protocol eq 0x6 next tcp

router(config)# class-map type access-control match-all sample-match
router(config-cmap)# match field tcp dest-port eq 0x50
router(config-cmap)# match start 13-start offset 200 size 2 eq 0x1234


TCDF:


<?xml version"1.0" encoding="UTF-8"?>
<tcdf>
    <class name="tcp-class" type="stack" match="all">
```

```
            <match>
                <eq field="ip.protocol" value="0x6" next="tcp"></eq>
            </match>
        </class>
        <class name="sample-match" type="access-control" match="all">
            <match>
                <eq field="tcp.dest-port" value="0x50"></eq>
                <eq start="l3-start" offset="200" size="2" value="0x1234"></eq>
            </match>
        </class>
</tcdf>
```

Defining a Traffic Policy

The next step is to configure what to do with the traffic that was matched with the class map; this is done through the creation of a traffic policy. The policy must use one (or more) of the configured traffic classes to match specific traffic and then configure what to do with this traffic after it is found.

The first part required for the configuration of a traffic policy is the creation of a policy map using the **policy-map** command; the command syntax for this command is as follows:

CLI:

```
router(config)# policy-map type access-control policy-map-name
```

TCDF:

```
<?xml version"1.0" encoding="UTF-8"?>
<tcdf>
    ...
    <policy name="policy-name"></policy>
    ...
</tcdf>
```

The second part of the process is specifying a traffic class that is configured using the **class** command; the command syntax for this command is as follows:

CLI:

```
router(config-pmap)# class class-name
```

TCDF:

```
<?xml version"1.0" encoding="UTF-8"?>
<tcdf>
    ...
    <class name="policy-name"></class>
    ...
</tcdf>
```

The final part of the process is configuring what action will be taken should a match occur; the command syntax for this command is as follows:

CLI:

```
router(config-pmap-c)# drop
```

TCDF:

```
<?xml version"1.0" encoding="UTF-8"?>
<tcdf>
    ...
    <action>Drop</action>
    ...
</tcdf>
```

An additional part can be added to a traffic policy by nesting policies. To take advantage of this functionality, the **service-policy** command is used, and the syntax is as follows:

CLI:

```
router(config-pmap-c)# service-policy policy-map-name
```

TCDF:

```
<?xml version"1.0" encoding="UTF-8"?>
<tcdf>
    ...
    <action>service-policy policy-map-name</action>
    ...
</tcdf>
```

There also seems to be a caveat when utilizing nesting policies with a TCDF file: The action tag will only allow a policy map name of up to 16 characters, which is not true when configuring nesting using only the CLI.

To wrap up the different commands required for a traffic policy, Example 8-8 shows a sample configuration. In this example, two different policy maps are created. One of these policy maps is then configured to nest inside the other. This traffic policy would be processed like this:

Step 1. Within the tcp-policy policy map, all traffic that is matched with the class map tcp-class will be sent to the tcp-policy-nest policy. (This would include all TCP traffic.)

Step 2. Within the tcp-policy-nest policy map, all traffic matching the class map sample-match would be dropped. (This would include traffic with a TCP destination port 0x50 (80) *and* has the contents "0x1234" at offset 200 in the IP packet.)

Example 8-8 *Sample Traffic Policy Configuration*

```
CLI:


router(config)# policy-map type access-control tcp-policy-nest
router(config-pmap)# class sample-match
router(config-pmap-c)# drop


router(config)# policy-map type access-control tcp-policy
router(config-pmap)# class tcp-class
router(config-pmap-c)# service-policy tcp-policy-nest

TCDF:

<?xml version"1.0" encoding="UTF-8"?>
<tcdf>

    ...
    <policy type="access-control" name="tcp-policy-nest">
        <class name="sample-match"></class>
            <action>Drop</action>
    </policy>

    <policy type="access-control" name="tcp-policy">
        <class name="tcp-class"></class>
            <action>service-policy tcp-policy-nest</action>
    </policy>
    ...
</tcdf>
```

Application of a Traffic Policy

The final step in this process is the application of the traffic policy on a specific interface. This application can be configured in either an incoming (input) or an outgoing (output) direction. The **service-policy type access-control** command is used to apply a specific traffic policy to an interface; the syntax for this command is as follows:

```
router(config-if)# service-policy type access-control [input | output] policy-
    map-name
```

Example 8-9 shows the application of the tcp policy policy map onto the FastEthernet0/0 interface.

Example 8-9 *Sample Traffic Policy Application Configuration*

```
CLI:


router(config)# interface FastEthernet0/0
router(config-if)# service-policy type access-control input tcp-policy
```

FPM Verification

Many different **show** commands can be used to verify FPM configuration.

To show which specific PHDFs are loaded and which fields are supported, enter the following command:

```
show protocols phdf phdf-name
```

To display the current traffic classes configured and matching criteria, enter the following command:

```
show class-map type [stack | access-control]
```

To display the current traffic policies, enter the following command:

```
show policy-map type access-control {interface interface}
```

Flexible NetFlow

As the name suggests, Flexible NetFlow is a more flexible version of NetFlow that allows additional options that make it superior to the original in many ways. These additional benefits include

- Scalable, aggregatable high-capacity flow information

- Enhanced flow structure focused on additional security-monitoring capabilities

- Flexible key and nonkey field configuration

- NetFlow Version 9 export format (flexible structure)

- Comprehensive IP and BGP accounting

Both NetFlow and Flexible NetFlow work by identifying and recording flow information. A *flow* is a group of packets that have the same key fields. With the original version of NetFlow, these key fields were static and included: source and destination IP addresses, source and destination ports, protocol, interface, and class of service (CoS). Along with this key field information, nonkey fields, including the number of packets and number of total bytes, were also recorded. Flexible NetFlow allows these key and nonkey fields to be customizable and thus can be used in a large number of ways, depending on the specific information that is being sought.

So, the next question is "What can Flexible NetFlow be used for?" There are a number of things, from traffic accounting to capacity planning to security monitoring. This includes the ability to track slow-path and normal denial of service attacks and attack attempts. The following is a list (per Cisco) of typical Flexible NetFlow uses:

- Network monitoring

- Application monitoring and profiling

- User monitoring and profiling

- Network planning and analysis

- Security analysis

- Billing and accounting

- Data warehousing and data mining

Components

A couple of main components must be understood to configure Flexible NetFlow, as outlined in Table 8-3.

Table 8-3 *Flexible NetFlow Components*

Component	Description
NetFlow records	As information is collected by NetFlow, flows are defined by the configured key and nonkey fields. When there is a unique match of key fields, the matching traffic information will be recorded in a cache as a NetFlow record. As additional matching traffic occurs, the record is updated with this additional information (for example, byte counts increase if the field is configured). With Flexible NetFlow, there are predefined and user-defined record layout possibilities.
Flow monitors	Flow monitors are attached to interfaces and perform the network-monitoring tasks. The flow monitor is configured with a specific record format, an optional flow exporter, and a cache.
Flow exporters	A flow exporter's job is rather self explanatory: It exports data from the NetFlow cache to a remote system. With Flexible NetFlow, this is typically done using the NetFlow Data Export Format, V9.
Flow samplers	A flow sampler reduces the load on the network device. By default, NetFlow records flows based on all the traffic in a specific direction (or both if configured). Because this can constitute a large amount of traffic on busy devices, the concept of a flow sampler was created. A flow sampler is configured to change the number of packet captures from all packets to a sampled number of packets based on configuration (for example, every other packet—50%).

NetFlow Records

The first thing that must be covered with NetFlow records is key and nonkey fields and the difference between them. The difference is rather simple: A key field is used to identify a specific flow, whereas a nonkey field is simply recorded as part of an already identified flow. This difference is important when utilizing the user-defined options available with Flexible NetFlow.

Now with the original NetFlow, the key and nonkey fields were static and provided no flexibility. Flexible NetFlow resolved this by allowing user-defined record structures. However, because original NetFlow has an established configuration base, it was important to include backward compatibility. Table 8-4 displays the NetFlow Original/NetFlow IPv4 Original Input record format, and Table 8-5 displays the NetFlow IPv4 Original Output record format; both of the tables include key/nonkey field information.

Table 8-4 *NetFlow Original/NetFlow IPv4 Original Input Format*

Field	Key or Nonkey	Description
IP ToS	Key	Value of the IP ToS field
IP Protocol	Key	Value of the IP Protocol field
IP Source Address	Key	—
IP Destination Address	Key	—
Transport Source Port	Key	Transport layer source port
Transport Destination Port	Key	Transport layer destination port
Interface Input	Key	Receiving interface
Flow Sampler ID	Key	ID of the flow sampler (if used)
IP Source AS	Nonkey	Source Autonomous System Number
IP Destination AS	Nonkey	Destination Autonomous System Number
IP Next Hop Address	Nonkey	Next-hop IP address
IP Source Mask	Nonkey	—
IP Destination Mask	Nonkey	—
TCP Flags	Nonkey	Value of the TCP Flag field
Interface Output	Nonkey	Transmitting Interface
Counter Bytes	Nonkey	—
Counter Packets	Nonkey	—
Time Stamp System Uptime First	Nonkey	System uptime, when the first packet was switched
Time Stamp System Uptime Last	Nonkey	System uptime, when the last packet was switched

Table 8-5 *NetFlow IPv4 Original Output Format*

Field	Key or Nonkey	Description
IP ToS	Key	Value of the IP ToS field
IP Protocol	Key	Value of the IP Protocol field

Table 8-5   *NetFlow IPv4 Original Output Format*

Field	Key or Nonkey	Description
IP Source Address	Key	—
IP Destination Address	Key	—
Transport Source Port	Key	Transport layer source port
Transport Destination Port	Key	Transport layer destination port
Interface Output	Key	Transmitting interface
Flow Sampler ID	Key	ID of the flow sampler (if used)
IP Source AS	Nonkey	Source Autonomous System Number
IP Destination AS	Nonkey	Destination Autonomous System Number
IP Next Hop Address	Nonkey	Next-hop IP address
IP Source Mask	Nonkey	—
IP Destination Mask	Nonkey	—
TCP Flags	Nonkey	Value of the TCP Flag field
Interface Input	Nonkey	Receiving interface
Counter Bytes	Nonkey	—
Counter Packets	Nonkey	—
Time Stamp System Uptime First	Nonkey	System uptime, when the first packet was switched
Time Stamp System Uptime Last	Nonkey	System uptime, when the last packet was switched

As can be seen, a large amount of information was recorded in this original format. Flexible NetFlow provides the capability to pare down these fields to only those needed. To use only specific fields, a user-defined record format would be defined. The command syntax required to create this record format is as follows:

```
router(config)# flow record flow-record-name
```

To specify key fields:

```
router(config-flow-record)# match [ipv4 | ipv6 | datalink | routing | flow |
  interface} options
```

To specify nonkey fields:

```
router(config-flow-record)# collect [counter | ipv4 | ipv6 | datalink | routing |
  flow | interface | timestamp] options
```

Example 8-10 shows the commands that would be required to identify flows by the source and destination IP addresses and TCP source and destination port information and to record the packet and byte counts for each flow.

Example 8-10 *Sample Flow Record Configuration*

```
router(config)# flow record test-record-name
router(config-flow-record)# match ipv4 source address
router(config-flow-record)# match ipv4 destination address
router(config-flow-record)# match transport tcp source-port
router(config-flow-record)# match transport tcp destination-port
router(config-flow-record)# collect counter packets
router(config-flow-record)# collect counter bytes
```

Flow Monitors

The flow monitors attach to an interface where the traffic information is captured, either in an incoming (input) or outgoing (output) direction. However, before the flow monitor is assigned to an interface, it must be configured. The flow monitor requires that at least a NetFlow record format is configured to operate. At this point, a flow exporter can also be configured; this is covered in the next section. Also note that the support for IPv6 records was added in Release 12.3(20)T. The command syntax required for flow monitor configuration is as follows:

```
router(config)# flow monitor flow-monitor-name

router(config-flow-monitor)# record [flow-record-name | netflow | netflow-
  original] {ipv4 | ipv6} {original-input | original-output}
```

Example 8-11 shows the configuration of the test monitor name flow monitor with a custom flow record named test-record-name.

Example 8-11 *Sample Flow Monitor Configuration*

```
router(config)# flow monitor test-monitor-name
router(config-flow-monitor)# record test-record-name
```

Flow Exporter

A flow exporter is used to take the inactive (default = 15 seconds) or long-active (default = 30 minutes) records and export them to a remote system for analysis and/or storage. The command syntax required for flow exporter configuration is as follows:

```
router(config)# flow exporter flow-exporter-name

    router(config-flow-exporter)# destination [hostname | ip-address]
    router(config-flow-exporter)# transport udp port
```

```
router(config-flow-monitor)# exporter flow-exporter-name
```

Example 8-12 shows the configuration of a flow exporter named test-exporter-name with a destination address of 192.168.1.1 using UDP port 1234. This example then shows the flow exporter being applied to a flow monitor.

Example 8-12   *Sample Flow Exporter Configuration*

```
router(config)# flow exporter test-exporter-name
router(config-flow-exporter)# destination 192.168.1.1
router(config-flow-exporter)# transport udp 1234

router(config-flow-monitor)# exporter test-exporter-name
```

Flow Sampler

A flow sampler, as stated previously, is used when the amount of processing is either too much for the device to handle or is simply higher than acceptable. Two modes of sampling can be utilized:

Key Topic

- **Deterministic:** When using the deterministic mode, traffic is sampled at a configured interval; this mode requires less overhead than random mode. Deterministic mode is recommended when traffic patterns are random in nature.

- **Random:** When using random mode, traffic is sampled randomly; this mode should be used to eliminate any potential monitoring bias and to counter any user attempting to avoid monitoring.

The command syntax required for flow sampler configuration is shown as follows:

```
router(config)# sampler sampler-name
router(config-sampler)# mode {deterministic | random} 1 out-of window-size
```

Example 8-13 shows the configuration of a flow sampler named test-sampler with deterministic sampling with a window size of 2.

Example 8-13   *Sample Flow Sampler Configuration*

```
router(config)# sampler test-sampler
router(config-sampler)# mode deterministic 1 out-of 2
```

Application of a Flow Monitor

The final step in this process is the application of the flow monitor on a specific interface. This application can be configured in either an incoming (input) or an outgoing (output) direction. The **ip flow-monitor** command is used to apply a specific flow monitor to an interface; the syntax for this command is as follows:

```
router(config-if)# ip flow monitor flow-monitor-name {sampler sampler-name}
   [multicast | unicast] [input | output]
```

Example 8-14 shows the application of a flow monitor named test-monitor-name onto the FastEthernet0/0 interface using the flow sampler named test-sampler on input traffic.

Example 8-14 *Sample Flow Monitor Application Configuration*

```
router(config)# interface FastEthernet0/0
router(config-if)# ip flow monitor test-monitor-name sampler test-sampler input
```

Flexible NetFlow Verification

Many different **show** commands can be used to verify Flexible NetFlow configuration.

To verify flow monitor configuration, enter the following command:

```
show flow monitor
```

To verify that a flow monitor is enabled on an interface, enter the following command:

```
show flow interface interface
```

To verify flow exporter configuration, enter the following commands:

```
show flow exporter
show running-config flow exporter flow-exporter-name
```

To view the NetFlow cache, enter the following command:

```
show flow monitor name flow-monitor-name cache format [csv | record | table]
```

To view flow sampler configuration, enter the following command:

```
show sampler
```

Additional Flexible NetFlow Information

A lot more information is available at Cisco.com that was not possible to fit into this book. To gain access to this information, go to www.cisco.com/en/US/docs/ios/fnetflow/configuration/guide/12_4t/fnf_12_4t_book.pdf.

Unicast Reverse Path Forwarding (Unicast RPF)

On modern networks, one of the most common attack types involves the forging or spoofing of IP source addresses. The configuration of ACLs for this purpose on large networks can be very cumbersome and hard to maintain. In an attempt to develop a technology to deal with these issues, Unicast Reverse Path Forwarding (URPF) was developed. Unicast RPF provides a source validation step to packet handling; it does this by verifying the source information of a packet to information contained within the Cisco Express Forwarding (CEF) Forwarding Information Base (FIB). The CEF FIB is a table that contains packet-switching information that mirrors that of the routing table; this is used by the device to increase the speed of packets being forwarding through the device. Because Unicast RPF relies on CEF's FIB, CEF must be configured on the device before Unicast RPF is configured.

Unicast RPF operates in one of two modes:

Key Topic

- **Strict (normal):** When in strict mode, Unicast RPF verifies that the source address is in the FIB *and* that the source address was received on the best return route interface as determined by CEF. This operation, while thorough, can also be troublesome if routing is multihomed. This is because the best return path might not be the same as the receiving interface; because of this, strict Unicast RPF is limited to single-homed connections. Unicast RPF will also work in situations where there are multiple equal-metric best paths available; this includes Enhanced IGRP (EIGRP) configurations where metric variance is configured. The recommended applications for strict Unicast RPF include (a) where only single connections are available to enter/exit the network, including the edge of a network, or (b) where single-homed customer connections connect into the core network because this would meet the single-homed requirement.

- **Loose:** Loose mode verifies only that the source address exists within the FIB and *not* the interface. Loose mode allows additional flexibility to implement Unicast RPF in locations where multihoming is common, including within a network.

Another important thing to understand about Unicast RPF is that it only works on incoming (input) interfaces. So, if a single-homed connection existed between the network and an ISP, RPF would be configured to monitor traffic coming from the ISP only. The use of Unicast RPF also increases the performance of the device over using traditional ACL methods of spoofing protection; this is because, unlike ACLs, Unicast RPF operates at CEF forwarding rates. When configuring Unicast RPF on interfaces over 1 Mbps, this processing difference is important.

Unicast RPF Configuration

The first thing that must be configured before starting Unicast RPF configuration is to enable the use of CEF. The **ip cef** *distributed* command enables the use of CEF; the syntax for this command is as follows:

```
ip cef {distributed}
```

The next part requires enabling Unicast RPF on the incoming interface. The **ip verify uni-cast source reachable-via** command is used to enable the use of Unicast RPF on an interface; the syntax for this command is as follows:

```
ip verify unicast source reachable-via [rx | any] {access-list}
```

The use of the **rx** or **any** keyword determines which mode that Unicast RPF will operate in; **rx** is used for strict mode and **any** is used for loose mode. An access list can also be specified with this command; its purpose is to determine whether the traffic will be dropped (default behavior - deny) or forwarded (permit). It is important to understand that this access list is not considered unless the packet fails the Unicast RPF check.

Unicast RPF Verification

A few commands can be used to verify the operation of Unicast RPF.

To verify that Unicast RPF is operational, enter the following command:

```
show cef interface interface
```

To verify global Unicast RPF packet count, enter the following command:

```
show ip traffic
```

To verify the number of interface Unicast RPF packet drops (verification drops)/forwards (suppressed verification drops), enter the following command:

```
show ip interface interface
```

Exam Preparation

As mentioned in the section, "How to Use This Book," in the Introduction, you have several choices for exam preparation: the exercises here, the memory tables in Appendix D, the final exam preparation chapter, and the exam simulation questions on the CD-ROM. The following questions present a bigger challenge than the exam itself because they use an open-ended question format. By using this more difficult format, you exercise your memory better and prove your conceptual and factual knowledge of this chapter. You can find the answers to these questions in Appendix A, "Answers to the DIKTA Quizzes and Fill in the Blanks Questions."

Review All Key Topics

Review the most important topics in this chapter, noted with the Key Topics icon in the margin of the page. Table 8-6 lists a reference of these key topics and the page numbers on which each is found.

Table 8-6 *Key Topics*

Key Topic Element	Description	Page
Figure 8-1	High-level overview of how an ACL is processed by a router	188
List	ACL types	189
Table 8-2	Protocols and their corresponding number identification for an ACL	190
List	FPM restrictions	196
List	FPM class-map types	198
Table 8-3	Flexible NetFlow components	204
Table 8-4	NetFlow original/NetFlow IPv4 original input format	205
Table 8-5	NetFlow IPv4 original output format	205
List	Flow sampling modes	208
List	Unicast RPF modes	210

Complete Tables and Lists from Memory

Print a copy of Appendix C, "Memory Tables" (found on the CD), or at least the section for this chapter, and complete the tables and lists from memory. Appendix D, "Memory Table Answers," also on the CD, includes completed tables and lists to check your work.

Define Key Terms

Define the following key terms from this chapter, and check your answers in the Glossary:

access control list (ACL), stateless

Use Command Reference to Check Your Memory

Table 8-7 lists the important commands from this chapter. To test your memory, cover the right side of the table with a piece of paper, read the description on the left side, and then see how much of the command you can remember.

Table 8-7 *Command Reference*

Task	Command Syntax
Create a standard access list	**access-list** *access-list-number* {**permit** | **deny**} {*host* | *source source-wildcard* | **any**} **[log]**
	or
	ip access-list standard {*access-list-number* | *access-list-name*}
	permit {**host** *host* | *source source-wildcard* | **any**} **[log]**
Create an extended access list	**access-list** *access-list-number* [**dynamic** *dynamic-name* [**timeout** *minutes*]]{**deny** | **permit**} *protocol source source-wildcard destination destination-wildcard* [**precedence** *precedence*] [**tos** *tos*] [**log** | log-input] [**time-range** *time-range-name*]
	or
	ip access-list extended {*access-list-number* | *access-list-name*}
	[*sequence-number*] {**deny** | **permit**} *protocol source source-wildcard destination destination-wildcard* [**option** *option-value*] [**precedence** *precedence*] [**tos** *tos*] [**time-range** *time-range-name*] [**log**]
Assign an access list to an interface	**ip access-group** *number* {**in** | **out**}
Create a reflexive access list	**ip access-list extended** {*access-list-number* | *access-list-name*}
	[*sequence-number*] {**deny** | **permit**} *protocol source source-wildcard destination destination-wildcard* reflect *name*
	and
	evaluate

Table 8-7 *Command Reference*

Task	Command Syntax
Create a time-based access list	**time-range** *time-range-name*
	periodic *days-of-the-week hh:mm* **to** [days-of-the-week] *hh:mm*
	absolute [**start** *time date*] [**end** *time date*]
	access-list *access-list-number protocol source source-wildcard destination destination-wildcard* [**time-range** *time-range-name*]
	or
	ip access-list extended {*access-list-number* | *access-list-name*}
	[*sequence-number*] {**deny** | **permit**} *protocol source source-wildcard destination destination-wildcard* [**time-range** *time-range-name*]
Load a specific PHDF file	**load protocol** *location:filename*
Load a specific TCDF file	**load classification** *location:filename*
Create an FPM class map	**class-map type** [**stack** | **access-control**] [**match-all** | **match-any**] *class-map-name*
Match specific traffic to classify within a class map	**match field** *protocol protocol-field* [**eq** | **neq** | **gt** | **lt** | **range** range] *value* **next** *next-protocol*
	match start [**l2-start** | **l3-start**] **offset** *offset* **size** *size* [**eq** | **neq** | **gt** | **lt** | **range** range] *value*
Create an FPM policy map	**policy-map type access-control** *policy-map-name*
Associate a class map with a policy map	**class** *class-name*
Specify a policy map action	**drop**
	or
	service-policy *policy-map-name*
Assign a policy map to an interface	**service-policy type access-control** [**input** | **output**] *policy-map-name*
Create a user-defined NetFlow flow record format	**flow record** *flow-record-name*
Specify NetFlow key fields	**match** [**ipv4** | **ipv6** | **datalink** | **routing** | **flow** | **interface**} *options*

Table 8-7   *Command Reference*

Task	Command Syntax
Specify NetFlow nonkey fields	**collect** [**counter** | **ipv4** | **ipv6** | **datalink** | **routing** |**flow** | **interface** | **timestamp**] *options*
Configure a NetFlow flow monitor	**flow monitor** *flow-monitor-name*
Specify a NetFlow record format	**record** [*flow-record-name* | **netflow** | **netflow-original**] {**ipv4** | **ipv6**} {**original-input** | **original-output**}
Configure a NetFlow flow exporter	**flow exporter** *flow-exporter-name*
Specify a NetFlow flow exporter server	**destination** [*hostname* | *ip-address*]
Specify a NetFlow flow exporter server port	**transport udp** *port*
Configure a NetFlow flow exporter with a flow monitor	**exporter** *flow-exporter-name*
Configure a NetFlow flow sampler	**sampler** *sampler-name*
Specify a NetFlow flow sampler mode	**mode** {**deterministic** | **random**} **1 out-of** *window-size*
Associate a NetFlow flow monitor with an interface	**ip flow monitor** *flow-monitor-name* {**sampler** *sampler-name*} [**input** | **output**]
Enable CEF	**ip cef** {**distributed**}
Configure Unicast RPF on a specific interface	**ip verify unicast source reachable-via** [**rx** | **any**] {*access-list*}
Display the contents of all current access lists	**show access-list** [*access-list-number* | *access-list-name*]
Display the contents of all current IP access lists	**show ip access-list** [*access-list-number* | *access-list-name*]
Display which specific PHDFs are loaded and which fields are supported	**show protocols phdf** *phdf-name*
Display the current traffic classes configured and their matching criteria	**show class-map type** [**stack** | **access-control**]
Display the current traffic policies	**show policy-map type access-control** {**interface** *interface*}
Display NetFlow flow monitor configuration	**show flow monitor**
Display NetFlow flow monitor interface configuration	**show flow interface** *interface*

Table 8-7   *Command Reference*

Task	Command Syntax
Display NetFlow flow exporter configuration	**show flow exporter**
Display NetFlow cache	**show flow monitor name** flow-monitor-name **cache format [csv	record	table]**
Display NetFlow sampler configuration	**show sampler**
Display Unicast RPF status	**show cef interface** *interface*
Display global Unicast RPF packet count	**show ip traffic**
Display the number of interface Unicast RPF packet drops	**show ip interface** *interface*

Fill in the Blanks

1. There is a(n) _____ at the end of each access list.

2. An extended access list can use the number ranges of _____ and _____ .

3. The wildcard mask that would be used with a subnet mask of 255.255.255.192 would be _____ .

4. When assigning reflexive access lists to an interface, they are typically placed _____ on an interface facing away from the internal network or _____ on an interface facing toward the internal network.

5. Both PHDF and TCDF are formatted using _____ .

6. When using FPM, traffic can be classified using _____ files or using the _____ .

7. FPM is only able to inspect _____ unicast packets.

8. _____ fields are used by NetFlow to identify specific flows.

9. Unicast RPF can operate in _____ or _____ mode.

10. When configuring Unicast RPF, the first thing that must be configured is _____ .

This chapter covers the following subjects:

- **Control plane attack types:** Reviews the different types of attacks that are focused on the control plane.

- **Control plane security technologies:** Goes over the specific technologies that can mitigate the various attack types and describes how to configure them.

CHAPTER 9

Implementing and Configuring Cisco IOS Control Plane Security

The control plane of a device is the heart of each device and must be kept protected to keep everything else that relies on it protected. This chapter looks at the specific threats that are focused on the control plane and the technologies that can be used to mitigate these types of attacks.

"Do I Know This Already?" Quiz

The "Do I Know This Already?" quiz helps you decide whether you really need to read the entire chapter. If you already intend to read the entire chapter, you do not necessarily need to answer these questions now.

The ten-question quiz, derived from the major sections in "Foundation Topics" section of this chapter, helps you determine how to spend your limited study time.

Table 9-1 outlines the major topics discussed in this chapter and the "Do I Know This Already?" quiz questions that correspond to those topics.

Table 9-1 *"Do I Know This Already?" Foundation Topics Section-to-Question Mapping*

Foundation Topics Section	Questions Covered in This Section
Control Plane Attack Types	1, 3
Control Plane Security Technologies	2, 4–10

Caution: The goal of self-assessment is to gauge your mastery of the topics in this chapter. If you do not know the answer to a question or are only partially sure of the answer, you should mark this question wrong for purposes of the self-assessment. Giving yourself credit for an answer that you correctly guess skews your self-assessment results and might provide you with a false sense of security.

1. The central processing unit of each device is tasked to not do which of these?

    a. Process fast-path data plane traffic

    b. Process control plane traffic

    c. Process management plane traffic

    d. Process slow-path data plane traffic

2. The route processor is divided into which of the following parts?

    a. Distributed switch engine

    b. Management plane

    c. Central switch engine

    d. Control plane

3. The purpose of a slow-path denial of service attack is to force packets to be what?

    a. Distributed switched

    b. Process switched

    c. Routed

    d. Switched

4. When using Control Plane Policing, the two types of policing types include which of the following?

    a. Distributed control plane services

    b. Summarized control plane services

    c. Processed control plane services

    d. Aggregate control plane services

5. Which of the following traffic is classified as always destined for the control plane?

    a. Data traffic packets

    b. Routing protocol control packets

    c. Management protocol packets

    d. Marked QoS packets

6. When using Control Plane Protection, which of the following subinterfaces are not used to further refine control plane security?

    a. Control plane host subinterface

    b. Control plane transmit subinterface

    c. Control plane CEF-exception subinterface

    d. Control plane transit subinterface

7. Which of the following features were added with Control Plane Protection?

    a. Port filtering

    b. Queue thresholding

    c. Protocol filtering

    d. Port thresholding

8. Which of the CPPr features provide the ability to early-drop specific packets before they get to the process level?

    a. Queue thresholding

    b. Packet filtering

    c. Protocol filtering

    d. Port filtering

9. What security mechanism works by creating a hash that is then transmitted to verify authenticity?

    a. MD4

    b. CPPr

    c. MD5

    d. AES

10. Which of the following steps is not used by the MQC to create and deploy a traffic policy?

    a. Creation of a class map

    b. Application of a class map

    c. Creation of a policy map

    d. Application of a policy map

The answers to the "Do I Know This Already?" quiz are found in Appendix A. The suggested choices for your next step are as follows:

■ **8 or less overall score:** Read the entire chapter. This includes the "Foundation Topics" and the "Exam Preparation" sections.

■ **9 or 10 overall score:** If you want more review on these topics, skip to the "Exam Preparation" section.

Foundation Topics

Control Plane Attack Types

Although the data plane of a device is very important to protect, it is also vital to protect the control plane of the device. If the control plane of any device is exploited, the security of the device itself and all other actions to mitigate other threats become vulnerable to easy circumvention. The following sections review the major types of attack that are focused at the control plane.

Slow-Path Denial of Service

As stated in the previous chapter, slow-path denial of service attacks, when focused at the data plane, attempt to deny a service or services. This is done by sending a large number of packets through the device with the intention of having them be process switched. When the target is the control plane instead of the data plane, the concept is the same; in this case, the control plane is targeted with a large number of packets. As stated in the previous chapter, the CPU of each device is tasked to perform three functions:

- Process control plane traffic

- Process management plane traffic

- Process slow-path data plane traffic

A successful attack on any one of these three has the capability to affect the other two. The access control list (ACL) techniques shown in Chapter 8, "Implementing and Configuring Cisco IOS Routed Data Plane Security," can be used to secure the control plane as they do the data plane. This chapter focuses on the methods to mitigate attacks targeted specifically at the control plane.

Routing Protocol Spoofing

Because a routing protocol is responsible for making the decisions as to how data is routed across a given network, the security of the routing protocol is paramount. A spoofing attack on a routing protocol involves an attacker attempting to inject false routing information into the protocol with the intention of rerouting the traffic. The route that this traffic takes, after it is exploited, could be focused on denying the specific traffic a path, or it could involve routing the data so that it can be captured and reviewed.

Control Plane Security Technologies

The following sections describe the technologies available to mitigate the attacks covered in the previous sections and discusses how to configure them.

Control Plane Policing (CoPP)

One of the methods that can be used to mitigate attacks that are focused on the control plane is *Control Plane Policing (CoPP)*. CoPP works the same as normal traffic policing; this includes the capability to control which and how much traffic is able to gain access to the control plane. The first thing that you need to understand is what the control plane is and how the architecture of these devices is laid out with respect to the control plane.

The route processor (RP) of a device is divided into two main parts:

■ **Control plane:** Includes the group of processes that are run at the process level and that control most high-level control IOS functions.

■ **Central switch engine:** Responsible for the high-speed routing of packets that typically come from nondistributed line card interfaces. The high-speed routing of packets on distributed interfaces is typically handled at the processor on the line card.

CoPP takes advantage of this processing capability by offering a separate level of policing at the line card as well as on a level that is performed by the central switch engine. The two available control plane policing types include

■ Distributed control plane services

■ Aggregate control plane services

It is important to be aware that aggregate control plane services are configured to be used on all control plane traffic, including that coming from line cards that support distributed processing. Distributed control plane services are considered first, and then the conditioned traffic is passed through to aggregate control plane services.

It is also important to know that traffic is not subject to either of the control plane services until the packet has been determined to have the control plane as its destination. Input control plane services are executed only after a routing decision has been made. Output control plane services are applied after the packet exits the control plane and are available only with aggregate control plane services.

Traffic that is classified as destined for the control plane includes

■ Routing protocol control packets

■ Packets destined for a local IP address of the device

■ Packets from management protocols

The second thing that needs to be explained is how CoPP works. When using CoPP, the control plane is configured to act as a separate entity with its own input and output interface. The modular quality of service command-line interface (MQC) is then used to classify traffic into classes and to create policies that dictate the traffic action. The MQC is easy to learn and will be reviewed next.

Defining a Traffic Class

The first thing that is configured through MQC is the creation of a traffic class.

The configuration of the traffic class involves the creation of the class. The class is then configured to match specific traffic based on a number of available commands. Numerous commands are available to use within the MQC for classifying traffic. Some of the most commonly used commands with CoPP are covered in Table 9-2.

Table 9-2 *Configuring an MQC Traffic Class*

Task	Command Syntax
Create a class map (traffic class)	Router(config)# **class-map [match-all	match-any]** *class-map-name*
Match traffic based on a configured access list	Router(config-cmap)# **match access-group** *access-group*
Match traffic based on a DSCP classification	Router(config-cmap)# **match dscp** *dscp-value*
Match traffic based on an IP precedence classification	Router(config-cmap)# **match precedence** *precedence*
Match traffic based on a specific protocol	Router(config-cmap)# **match protocol** *protocol-name*
Display information about the configured traffic classes	**show class-map**

Example 9-1 shows the configuration of a traffic class based on an access list. The access list is configured to allow Secure Shell (SSH) traffic from the 10.10.10.0/24 network to enter the control plane without restriction and polices all other SSH traffic from other sources. At first glance, this looks reversed; however, the **deny** statement in this example exempts the 10.10.10.0/24 traffic from CoPP because this traffic is not matched.

Example 9-1 *Configuring a Traffic Class*

```
Router# configure terminal
Router(config)# access-list 110 deny tcp 10.10.10.0 0.0.0.255 any eq 22
Router(config)# access-list 110 permit tcp any any eq 22
Router(config)# class-map ssh-class
Router(config-cmap)# match access-group 110
```

Defining a Traffic Policy

The second thing that must be configured through MQC is the creation of a traffic policy.

The configuration of the traffic policy involves the creation of the policy. The policy is then configured to use a specific traffic class to identify packets that will then be subject to the traffic policy. The next part involves what to do with the traffic if it is matched with the traffic class. With CoPP, the available options include drop and police. Table 9-3 outlines the commands to configure an MQC traffic policy.

Table 9-3 *Configuring an MQC Traffic Policy*

Task	Command Syntax
Create a policy map (traffic policy)	Router(config)# **policy-map** *policy-map-name*

Table 9-3 *Configuring an MQC Traffic Policy*

Task	Command Syntax
Configure the use of a specific traffic class that is used to match traffic that is applied to this policy	Router(config-pmap)# **class** *class-map-name*
Configure the policy to police the matched traffic	Router(config-pmap-c)# **police bps** [**burst-normal**] [**burst-max**] **conform-action** *action* **exceed-action** *action* [**violate-action** *action*]
Configure the policy to drop the matched traffic	Router(config-pmap-c)# **drop**
Display information about the configured traffic policies	**show policy-map** [*policy-map-name*]

Example 9-2 shows the configuration of a traffic policy that uses the traffic class ssh-class defined in Example 9-1 to identify packets for the policy. The traffic policy then polices all other traffic by limiting the traffic rate to 100 kbps; if this rate is exceeded, those excessive packets are dropped.

Example 9-2 *Configuring a Traffic Policy*

```
Router# configure terminal
Router(config)# policy-map ssh-policy
Router(config-pmap)# class ssh-class
Router(config-pmap-c)# police 100000 conform-action transmit exceed drop
```

Applying a Traffic Policy

The application of the traffic policy on a specific interface is the final thing that must be configured through MQC. In this part of the process, the commands specific to CoPP are used. As stated previously, CoPP allows the control plane to be considered like a separate entity with its own input and output interface. When using the MQC to apply policies to a normal interface, the commands would be entered in interface configuration mode. When using CoPP, the commands are entered in control-plane configuration mode. Table 9-4 displays a list of the commands used to apply a traffic policy.

Table 9-4 *Applying an MQC Traffic Policy*

Task	Command Syntax
Enter control-plane configuration mode	Router(config)# **control-plane** [slot *slot-number*]
Configure a traffic policy onto the control plane	Router(config-cp)# **service-policy** [**input** | **output**] *policy-map-name*

Table 9-4   *Applying an MQC Traffic Policy*

Task	Command Syntax
Display information about the config-ured control plane traffic classes	**show policy-map control-plane** [**all** | **slot** *slot-number*] [**input** [**class** *class-name*] | **output** [**class** *class-name*]]

Note: When an output-aggregated control plane policy is used, those packets dropped by the policy do not create a system message; this is called *silent mode operation.*

Example 9-3 shows the application of the traffic policy ssh-policy on traffic entering the control plane; this is an example of aggregated control plane services.

Example 9-3   *Applying a Traffic Policy to the Control Plane*

```
Router# configure terminal
Router(config)# control-plane
Router(config-cp)# service-policy input ssh-policy
```

If there is a line card available that supports distributed control plane services, the syntax in Example 9-3 is slightly modified. Example 9-4 shows the application of the traffic pol-icy ssh-policy entering the control plane on the line card in slot 1; this is an example of distributed control plane services.

Example 9-4   *Applying a Traffic Policy to the Control Plane (Distributed)*

```
Router# configure terminal
Router(config)# control-plane slot 1
Router(config-cp)# service-policy input ssh-policy
```

Note: Although aggregated CoPP supports both input and output policies, distributed CoPP only supports input policies.

Control Plane Protection (CPPr)

The second method available to mitigate attacks that are focused on the control plane is Control Plane Protection (CPPr). The first piece of CPPr is essentially an extension of CoPP. With CPPr, the control plane interface is split into four pieces, an aggregate inter-face and three subinterfaces. The aggregate interface receives all traffic, which is then out-put into one of three different subinterfaces; this allows a finer level of control on traffic. At press time, the use of CPPr with distributed processing is not supported. The three subinterfaces are as follows:

- **Control plane host subinterface:** The host subinterface receives all control plane IP traffic that is directed at one of the device's interfaces. All the traffic that is processed on the host subinterface is terminated on and processed by the device.

- **Control plane transit subinterface:** The transit subinterface receives all control plane IP traffic that is software switched on the route processor. All of this traffic is not destined for the device directly but is transiting through the device.

- **Control plane CEF-exception subinterface:** The CEF-exception subinterface receives all traffic that is either redirected as a result of a configured input feature in the Cisco Express Forwarding (CEF) packet forwarding path for process switching or entered directly in the input queue by the interface driver (ATP, L2 keepalives, and all non-IP host traffic).

The second piece of CPPr includes the addition of two different features that extend the capability to block specific traffic and to limit traffic based on a specific protocol. These two CPPr features are as follows:

- **Port filtering:** Enhances control plane protection by providing the ability to drop packets early that are directed at closed or nonlistened-to ports.

- **Queue thresholding:** Enhances CPPr by providing a mechanism for limiting the number of unprocessed packets that a specific protocol can have at the process level. If configured, it is processed before port filtering.

Both the port-filtering and queue-thresholding features are supported only on the control plane host subinterface.

The configuration of CPPr using the aggregate interface is the same as with CoPP. The standard configuration of CPPr using the three additional subinterfaces is similar to that of CoPP; the main difference is in the application of the policy. The configuration of port filtering and queue thresholding still utilizes the MQC concepts but requires a modification of the commands that are specific to each; these will be discussed in their own sections. Table 9-5 displays the commands that are required to apply a traffic policy.

Table 9-5 *Applying an MQC CPPr Traffic Policy*

Task	Command Syntax
Enter control-plane configuration mode	Router(config)# **control-plane** [**host** | **transit** | **cef-exception**]
Configure a traffic policy onto the control plane	Router(config-cp)# **service-policy** [**input** | **output**] *policy-map-name*
Display information about the configuration and statistics of control plane traffic policies	**show policy-map control-plane** [**all** | **slot** *slot-number*] [**input** [**class** *class-name*] | **output** [**class** *class-name*]]

Example 9-5 displays the application of the ssh policy created in the previous section using the control plane host subinterface.

Example 9-5 *Applying a Traffic Policy to the Control Plane Host Subinterface*

```
Router# configure terminal
Router(config)# control-plane host
Router(config-cp)# service-policy input ssh-policy
```

Port Filtering

The port-filtering feature provides the capability to configure CPPr to drop specific packets before they even get to the process level (control plane IP input queue). Typically, these filters are configured to automatically drop all traffic that is destined for closed or nonlistened-to ports. However, port filtering can be configured to drop packets from any specific TCP or UDP port that is configured.

The configuration of the port-filtering feature is similar to that used by CoPP and still uses the same MQC class map, policy map, and service policy structure. The creation of a traffic class utilizes the same overall syntax but with the addition of the type **port-filter** parameter. Table 9-6 displays the commands required to configure a traffic class.

Table 9-6 *Configuring a Port Filter Traffic Class*

Task	Command Syntax
Create a class map (traffic class)	Router(config)# **class-map type port-filter** [**match-all** | **match-any**] *class-map-name*
Match automatically all closed ports on the device	Router(config-cmap)# **match closed-ports**
Match manually the TCP/UDP ports that you specify	Router(config-cmap)# **match port** *port-num*
Match manually the TCP port that you specify	Router(config-cmap)# **match tcp** *port-num*
Match manually the UDP port that you specify	Router(config-cmap)# **match udp** *port-num*
Display information about the configured control plane traffic classes	**show class-map type port-filter** [*class-map-name*]

Example 9-6 shows the configuration of a port filter class map that matches all closed ports on the router.

Example 9-6 *Configuring a Port Filter Traffic Class*

```
Router# configure terminal
Router(config)# class-map type port-filter portf-class
Router(config-cmap)# match closed-ports
```

The creation of a traffic policy utilizes the same overall syntax but with the addition of the type **port-filter** parameter. Table 9-7 displays the commands required to configure a traffic policy.

Table 9-7   *Configuring a Port Filter Traffic Policy*

Task	Command Syntax
Create a policy map (traffic policy)	Router(config)# **policy-map type port-filter** *policy-map-name*
Configure the use of a specific traffic class that is used to match traffic that is applied to this policy	Router(config-pmap)# **class** *class-map-name*
Configure the policy to drop the matched traffic	Router(config-pmap-c)# **drop**
Display information about the configured control plane traffic policies	**show policy-map type port-filter** [*policy-map-name* [**class** *class-map-name*]
Display configuration and statistics for a traffic class or classes in a traffic policy	**show policy-map control-plane type port-filter** [**host** | **transit** | **cef-exception**] [**input** [**class** *class-name*] | **output** [**class** *class-name*]]

Example 9-7 shows the configuration of a port filter policy map utilizing the portf-class class map defined in Example 9-6 for classification. It is important to note that when configuring a port filter policy map, the only available action is drop.

Example 9-7   *Configuring a Port Filter Traffic Policy*

```
Router# configure terminal
Router(config)# policy-map type port-filter portf-policy
Router(config-pmap)# class portf-class
Router(config-pmap-c)# drop
```

Like the traffic class and policy, the application of a port filter requires the addition of the **port-filter** parameter. The port filter feature is only able to be used on the control plane host subinterface. Table 9-8 displays the commands required to apply a traffic policy.

Table 9-8   *Applying a Port Filter Traffic Policy*

Task	Command Syntax
Enter control-plane configuration mode	Router(config)# **control-plane host**
Configure a port filter traffic policy onto the control plane	Router(config-cp)# **service-policy type port-filter input** *policy-map-name*
Display information about the configuration and statistics of control plane traffic policies	**show policy-map control-plane** [**input** [**class** *class-name*] | **output** [**class** *class-name*]]

Example 9-8 displays the application of the portf policy created previously using the control plane host subinterface.

Example 9-8 *Applying a Port Filter Traffic Policy*

```
Router# configure terminal
Router(config)# control-plane host
Router(config-cp)# service-policy type port-filter input portf-policy
```

Queue Thresholding

The queue-thresholding feature is used to limit the amount of traffic that can come from a given protocol into the control plane. The purpose of this is to limit the ability of a single protocol from overwhelming the process level (control-plane IP input queue) should it malfunction.

The queue-thresholding feature, like the port-filtering feature, continues to use the MQC structure, except with minor modification. The creation of a traffic class utilizes the same overall syntax but with the addition of the type **queue-threshold** parameter. Table 9-9 displays the commands required to configure a traffic class.

Table 9-9 *Configuring a Queue Threshold Traffic Class*

Task	Command Syntax
Create a class map (traffic class)	Router(config)# **class-map type queue-threshold [match-all	match-any]** *class-map-name*
Match an upper-layer protocol	Router(config-cmap)# **match protocol [bgp	dns	ftp	http	igmp	snmp	ssh	syslog	telnet	tftp |** *host-protocols*]
Display information about the configured control plane traffic classes	**show class-map**

Example 9-8 shows the configuration of a queue threshold class map that matches all HTTP traffic.

Example 9-8 *Configuring a Queue Threshold Traffic Class*

```
Router# configure terminal
Router(config)# class-map type queue-threshold queue-class
Router(config-cmap)# match protocol http
```

The creation of a traffic policy utilizes the same overall syntax as the port-filtering feature, as shown previously with the class map, but with the addition of the type **queue-threshold** parameter. Table 9-10 displays the commands required to configure a traffic policy.

Table 9-10 *Configuring a Queue Threshold Traffic Policy*

Task	Command Syntax
Create a policy map (traffic policy)	Router(config)# **policy-map type queue-threshold** *policy-map-name*
Configure the use of a specific traffic class that is used to match traffic that is applied to this policy	Router(config-pmap)# **class** *class-map-name*
Configure the policy to apply a queue threshold to the matched protocol packets	Router(config-pmap-c)# **queue-limit** *number*
Display configuration and statistics for a traffic class or classes in a traffic policy	**show policy-map control-plane type queue-threshold [host	transit	cef-exception] [input [class** *class-name***]	output [class** *class-name***]]**

Example 9-9 shows the configuration of a queue threshold policy map utilizing the queue-class class map defined in Example 9-8 for classification and limiting the number of packets to 50. It is important to note that when configuring a queue policy map, the only available action is queue limit. The queue limit can be set from 0 through 255 packets, which is the number of matched protocol packets allowed at the process level (control-plane IP input queue).

Example 9-9 *Configuring a Queue Threshold Traffic Policy*

```
Router# configure terminal
Router(config)# policy-map type port-filter queue-policy
Router(config-pmap)# class queue-class
Router(config-pmap-c)# queue-limit 50
```

Like the traffic class and policy, the application of a queue threshold requires the addition of the **queue-threshold** parameter. As stated previously, the queue threshold feature is able to be used only on the control plane host subinterface. Table 9-11 displays the commands required to apply a traffic policy.

Table 9-11 *Applying a Queue Threshold Traffic Policy*

Task	Command Syntax
Enter control-plane configuration mode	Router(config)# **control-plane host**
Configure a queue threshold traffic policy onto the control plane	Router(config-cp)# **service-policy type queue-threshold input** *policy-map-name*
Display information about the configuration and statistics of control plane traffic policies	**show policy-map control-plane [input [class** *class-name***]	output [class** *class-name***]]**

Example 9-10 displays the application of the queue policy created previously using the control plane host subinterface.

Example 9-10 *Applying a Queue Threshold Traffic Policy*

```
Router# configure terminal
Router(config)# control-plane host
Router(config-cp)# service-policy type queue-threshold input queue-policy
```

Routing Protocol Authentication

The security of the routing infrastructure is very important because it is responsible for determining the paths for all traffic using it. If an attacker was able to exploit this, the security of not only the routing infrastructure but also all devices relying on this infrastructure would be affected. One of the easiest ways to ensure the security of these routing protocols is through the use of routing protocol authentication. Typically this involves a configuration change on every routing device to exchange some type of shared secret (typically using message digest algorithm 5 [MD5]) to ensure neighbor authenticity.

MD5 works by creating a one-way hash out of a shared secret and sending this hash between the source and destination. The destination then calculates the hash from its configured shared secret and verifies the source authenticity. Because this is a one-way process, the process cannot be reversed to determine the originating shared secret.

The way that each routing protocol performs this authentication is slightly different. Each of the specific routing protocol configuration requirements will be covered in separate sections.

Key Chains

Because both Enhanced Interior Gateway Routing Protocol (EIGRP) and Routing Information Protocol version 2 (RIPv2) take advantage of the key chain functionality within IOS, it makes sense to review the use and configuration of a key chain. A key chain is essentially an electronic repository of keys and their respective shared secret and validity schedules. The key chain function supports over 2 billion configured keys, so the likelihood of running into a key storage issue is rather slim. Multiple keys can then be set up and configured to be used based on a specific time schedule. This makes it easy for keys to be routinely changed automatically within the configuration. Table 9-12 displays the commands required to configure a key chain.

Table 9-12 *Key Chain Configuration*

Task	Command Syntax
Create a key chain and enter key chain configuration mode	Router(config)# **key chain** *name-of-chain*
Create a key and enter key configuration mode	Router(config-keychain)# **key** *key-id*
Configure a shared secret key string	Router(config-keychain-key)# **key-string** *secret*

Table 9-12 *Key Chain Configuration*

Task	Command Syntax
Configure an acceptance lifetime for incoming key string authentication requests	Router(config-keychain-key)# **accept-lifetime** *start-time* {**infinite**	*end-time*	**duration** *seconds*}
Configure a send lifetime for outgoing key string authentication requests	Router(config-keychain-key)# **send-lifetime** *start-time* {**infinite**	*end-time*	**duration** *seconds*}
Display authentication key information	**show key chain**

Example 9-11 displays the creation of a key chain with a key number of 1 and a shared secret of "sharedsecret" that can be received and sent from October 29, 2008 at noon through January 27, 2009 at noon.

Example 9-11 *Key Chain Creation*

```
Router# configure terminal
Router(config)# key chain auth-chain
Router(config-keychain)# key 1
Router(config-keychain-key)# key-string sharedsecret
Router(config-keychain-key)# accept-lifetime 12:00:00 Oct 29 2008 12:00:00 Jan 27
2009
Router(config-keychain-key)# send-lifetime 12:00:00 Oct 29 2008 12:00:00 Jan 27 2009
```

EIGRP

As previously stated, EIGRP uses the key chain functionality that is built into IOS. After the key chains have been configured, EIGRP must be configured to use this information for authentication. Table 9-13 displays the commands required to configure EIGRP authentication.

Table 9-13 *EIGRP Authentication Configuration*

Task	Command Syntax
Configure the use of a key on a specific EIGRP autonomous system	Router(config-if)# **ip authentication key-chain eigrp** *as-number name-of-chain*
Configure the use of MD5 on a specific EIGRP autonomous system	Router(config-if)# **ip authentication mode eigrp** *as-number* **md5**
Display the EIGRP interface authentication information	**show ip eigrp interfaces detail**

Example 9-12 displays the configuration of EIGRP authentication on autonomous system 100 using interface fastethernet0/0 and key chain auth-chain. In this cast, this device and the remote neighbor device on the same network would require the same shared secret to communicate.

Example 9-12 *EIGRP Authentication Configuration*

```
Router# configure terminal
Router(config)# interface fastethernet0/0
Router(config-if)# ip authentication key-chain eigrp 100 auth-chain
Router(config-if)# ip authentication mode eigrp 100 md5
```

RIPv2

Like EIGRP, RIPv2 supports authentication using the key chain functionality and is configured very similarly to EIGRP authentication. RIPv2 also supports the use of clear-text authentication using the key chain functionality, although it is not recommended that this be used because it is so easily exploited. Table 9-14 displays the commands required to configure RIP authentication.

Table 9-14 *RIP Authentication Configuration*

Task	Command Syntax
Configure the use of a key on a specific EIGRP autonomous system	Router(config-if)# **ip rip authentication key-chain** *name-of-chain*
Configure the use of MD5 on a specific EIGRP autonomous system	Router(config-if)# **ip rip authentication mode {text | md5}**
Display the status RIP including the currently assigned key chain	**show ip protocols**

Example 9-13 displays the configuration of RIPv2 authentication using interface fastethernet0/0 and key chain auth-chain. As with EIGRP, the neighbors off of this interface will require a matching shared secret to communicate with this device.

Example 9-13 *RIP Authentication Configuration*

```
Router# configure terminal
Router(config)# interface fastethernet0/0
Router(config-if)# ip rip authentication key-chain auth-chain
Router(config-if)# ip rip authentication mode md5
```

OSPF

Open Shortest Path First (OSPF) authentication configuration does not use the key chain functionality and requires commands specifically used for OSPF. OSPF provides three different authentication options: null (no authentication), simple (clear text), and MD5. OSPF authentication also offers two different methods of configuration. One method is configured for all devices off of a specific segment (interface), and the other method is configured for an entire OSPF area. If both area- and segment-level OSPF authentication commands are used, the segment-level commands override the area-level commands. The choice of which one to choose depends on the specific network configuration.

When configuring OSPF area authentication, the method selected must be the same across the entire area, whether it be null, simple, or MD5. Table 9-15 displays the commands required to configure OSPF area authentication.

Table 9-15 *OSPF Area Authentication Configuration*

Task	Command Syntax
Configure a simple authentication key for OSPF authentication	Router(config-if)# **ip ospf authentication-key** *key*
Configure an MD5 authentication key for OSPF authentication	Router(config-if)# **ip ospf message-digest-key** *key-id* **md5** *key*
Configure the use of simple authentication on an OSPF area	Router(config-router)# **area** *area-id* **authentication**
Configure the use of MD5 authentication on an MD5 area	Router(config-router)# **area** *area-id* **authentication message-digest**
Display the status and configuration of OSPF including area authentication	**show ip ospf** [*process-id*]
Display the status and configuration of OSPF on an interface	**show ip ospf interface** *interface*

Example 9-14 displays the configuration of OSPF area 0 authentication with a shared secret of "sharedsecret" and using the MD5 hash method.

Example 9-14 *OSPF Area Authentication Configuration*

```
Router# configure terminal
Router(config)# interface fastethernet0/0
Router(config-if)# ip ospf message-digest-key 1 md5 sharedsecret

Router(config)# router ospf 10
Router(config-router)# area 0 authentication message-digest
```

OSPF also supports authentication on a specific network segment. This way, only those neighbors that share interfaces in the same segment must be configured for authentication. As with area authentication, segment authentication supports both simple and MD5 authentication methods. As stated previously, if configured with area authentication, segment authentication will override area authentication settings. Table 9-16 displays the commands required to configure OSPF segment authentication.

Table 9-16 *OSPF Segment (Network) Authentication Configuration*

Task	Command Syntax
Configure an interface to support either simple or MD5 segment authentication	Router(config-if)# **ip ospf authentication** [message-digest]
Configure a simple authentication key for OSPF authentication.	Router(config-if)# **ip ospf authentication-key** *key*
Configure an MD5 authentication key for OSPF authentication	Router(config-if)# **ip ospf message-digest-key** *key-id* **md5 key**
Display the status and configuration of OSPF on an interface	**show ip ospf interface** *interface*

Example 9-15 displays the configuration of OSPF segment authentication with a shared secret of "sharedsecret" and using the MD5 hash method.

Example 9-15 *OSPF Segment (Network) Authentication Configuration*

```
Router# configure terminal
Router(config)# interface fastethernet0/0
Router(config-if)# ip ospf message-digest-key 1 md5 sharedsecret
Router(config-if)# ip ospf authentication message-digest
```

BGP

In Border Gateway Protocol (BGP), the configuration of authentication (MD5) is done by configuring a shared secret between each BGP neighbor or peer. This can also be configured to work for an entire BGP peer group, which can simplify the configuration of multiple neighbors (peers). As with all other MD5 implementations, the devices exchanging the MD5 must have identical shared secrets to communicate. Table 9-17 displays the commands required to configure BGP authentication.

Table 9-17 *BGP Authentication Configuration*

Task	Command Syntax
Configure authentication between BGP neighbors/peers, or between members of a peer group	Router(config-router)# **neighbor** {*ip-address*	*peer-group-name*} **password** *key*
Display the status of a BGP neighbor (peer), look at the Option flags to verify MD5 configuration	**show ip bgp neighbors** *neighbor*

Example 9-16 displays the configuration of BGP neighbor (peer) authentication to neighbor 172.16.1.1 on BGP autonomous system 10000 with a shared secret of "sharedsecret."

Example 9-16 *BGP Authentication Configuration*

```
Router# configure terminal
Router(config)# router bgp 10000
Router(config-router)# neighbor 172.16.1.1 password sharedsecret
```

Exam Preparation

As mentioned in the section, "How to Use This Book," in the Introduction, you have several choices for exam preparation: the exercises here, the memory tables in Appendix D, the final exam preparation chapter, and the exam simulation questions on the CD-ROM. The following questions present a bigger challenge than the exam itself because they use an open-ended question format. By using this more difficult format, you exercise your memory better and prove your conceptual and factual knowledge of this chapter. You can find the answers to these questions in Appendix A, "Answers to the DIKTA Quizzes and Fill in the Blanks Questions."

Review All Key Topics

Review the most important topics in the chapter, noted with the Key Topics icon in the margin of the page. Table 9-18 lists a reference of these key topics and the page numbers on which each is found.

Table 9-18 *Key Topics*

Key Topic Element	Description	Page
List	Central processing unit functions	222
List	Route process parts	223
List	Control Plane Policing types	223
List	Classified control plane traffic	223
List	CPPr subinterfaces	226
List	CPPr features	227

Complete Tables and Lists from Memory

Print a copy of Appendix C, "Memory Tables" (found on the CD), or at least the section for this chapter, and complete the tables and lists from memory. Appendix D, "Memory Table Answers," also on the CD, includes completed tables and lists to check your work.

Define Key Terms

Define the following key terms from this chapter, and check your answers in the Glossary:

control plane, central switching engine, MQC, MD5

Use Command Reference to Check Your Memory

Table 9-19 lists the important commands from this chapter. To test your memory, cover the right side of the table with a piece of paper, read the description on the left side, and then see how much of the command you can remember.

Table 9-19 *Command Reference*

Task	Command Syntax
Create a class map (traffic class)	Router(config)# **class-map [match-all	match-any]** *class-map-name*
Match traffic based on a configured access list	Router(config-cmap)# **match access-group**
Match traffic based on a DSCP classification	Router(config-cmap)# **match ip dscp**
Match traffic based on an IP precedence classification	Router(config-cmap)# **match ip precedence**
Match traffic based on a specific protocol	Router(config-cmap)# **match protocol**
Create a policy map (traffic policy)	Router(config)# **policy-map** *policy-map-name*
Configure the use of a specific traffic class that is used to match traffic that is applied to this policy	Router(config-pmap)# **class** *class-map-name*
Configure the policy to police the matched traffic	Router(config-pmap-c)# **police bps [burst-normal] [burst-max] conform-action** *action* **exceed-action** *action* **[violate-action** *action]*
Configured the policy to drop the matched traffic	Router(config-pmap-c)# **drop**
Enter control-plane configuration mode	Router(config)# **control-plane [slot** *slot-number]*
Configure a traffic policy onto the control plane	Router(config-cp)# **service-policy [input	output]** *policy-map-name*
Enter control-plane configuration mode	Router(config)# **control-plane [host	transit	cef-exception]**
Configure a traffic policy onto the control plane	Router(config-cp)# **service-policy [input	output]** *policy-map-name*
Create a class map (traffic class)	Router(config)# **class-map type port-filter [match-all	match-any]** *class-map-name*
Match automatically all closed ports on the device	Router(config-cmap)# **match closed-ports**

Table 9-19 *Command Reference*

Task	Command Syntax
Match manually the TCP/UDP ports that you specify	Router(config-cmap)# **match port** *port-num*
Match manually the TCP port that you specify	Router(config-cmap)# **match tcp** *port-num*
Match manually the UDP port that you specify	Router(config-cmap)# **match udp** *port-num*
Create a policy map (traffic policy)	Router(config)# **policy-map type port-filter** *policy-map-name*
Configure the use of a specific traffic class that is used to match traffic that is applied to this policy	Router(config-pmap)# **class** *class-map-name*
Configure the policy to drop the matched traffic	Router(config-pmap-c)# **drop**
Enter control-plane configuration mode	Router(config)# **control-plane host**
Configure a port filter traffic policy onto the control plane	Router(config-cp)# **service-policy type port-filter input** *policy-map-name*
Create a class map (traffic class)	Router(config)# **class-map type queue-threshold [match-all | match-any]** *class-map-name*
Match an upper-layer protocol	Router(config-cmap)# **match protocol [bgp | dns | ftp | http | igmp | snmp | ssh | syslog | telnet | tftp | host-protocols]**
Create a policy map (traffic policy)	Router(config)# **policy-map type queue-threshold** *policy-map-name*
Configure the use of a specific traffic class that is used to match traffic that is applied to this policy	Router(config-pmap)# **class** *class-map-name*
Configure the policy to apply a queue threshold to the matched protocol packets	Router(config-pmap-c)# **queue-limit** *number*
Enter control-plane configuration mode	Router(config)# **control-plane host**
Configure a queue threshold traffic policy onto the control plane	Router(config-cp)# **service-policy type queue-threshold input** *policy-map-name*
Create a key chain and enter key chain configuration mode	Router(config)# **key chain** *name-of-chain*
Create a key and enter key configuration mode	Router(config-keychain)# **key** *key-id*

Table 9-19 *Command Reference*

Task	Command Syntax
Configure a shared secret key string	Router(config-keychain-key)# **key-string** *secret*
Configure an acceptance lifetime for incoming key string authentication requests	Router(config-keychain-key)# **accept-lifetime** *start-time* {**infinite** | *end-time* | **duration** *seconds*}
Configure a send lifetime for outgoing key string authentication requests	Router(config-keychain-key)# **send-lifetime** *start-time* {**infinite** | *end-time* | **duration** *seconds*}
Configure the use of key on a specific EIGRP autonomous system	Router(config-if)# **ip authentication key-chain eigrp** *as-number name-of-chain*
Configure the use of MD5 on a specific EIGRP autonomous system	Router(config-if)# **ip authentication mode eigrp** *as-number* **md5**
Configure the use of a key on a specific EIGRP autonomous system	Router(config-if)# **ip rip authentication key-chain** *name-of-chain*
Configure the use of MD5 on a specific EIGRP autonomous system	Router(config-if)# **ip rip authentication mode** {**text** | **md5**}
Configure a simple authentication key for OSPF authentication	Router(config-if)# **ip ospf authentication-key** *key*
Configure an MD5 authentication key for OSPF authentication	Router(config-if)# **ip ospf message-digest-key** *key-id* **md5** *key*
Configure the use of simple authentication on an OSPF area	Router(config-router)# **area** *area-id* **authentication**
Configure the use of MD5 authentication on an MD5 area	Router(config-router)# **area** *area-id* **authentication message-digest**
Configure an interface to support either simple or MD5 segment authentication	Router(config-if)# **ip ospf authentication** [**message-digest**]
Configure a simple authentication key for OSPF authentication	Router(config-if)# **ip ospf authentication-key** *key*
Configure an MD5 authentication key for OSPF authentication	Router(config-if)# **ip ospf message-digest-key** *key-id* **md5** *key*
Configure authentication between BGP neighbors/peers, or between members of a peer group	Router(config-router)# **neighbor** {*ip-address* | *peer-group-name*} **password** *key*
Display information about the configured traffic classes	**show class-map**

Table 9-19   *Command Reference*

Task	Command Syntax
Display information about the configured traffic policies	**show policy-map** [*policy-map-name*]
Display information about the configuration and statistics of control plane traffic policies	**show policy-map control-plane** [**all** | **slot** slot-number] [**input** [**class** *class-name*] | **output** [**class** *class-name*]]
Display information about the configured control plane traffic classes	**show class-map type port-filter** [*class-map-name*]
Display information about the configured control plane traffic policies	**show policy-map type port-filter** [*policy-map-name* [**class** *class-map-name*]
Display configuration and statistics for a traffic class or classes in a traffic policy	**show policy-map control-plane type port-filter** [**host** | **transit** | **cef-exception**] [**input** [**class** *class-name*] | **output** [**class** *class-name*]]
Display information about the configuration and statistics of control plane traffic policies	**show policy-map control-plane** [**input** [**class** *class-name*] | **output** [**class** *class-name*]]
Display information about the configured control plane traffic classes	**show class-map**
Display configuration and statistics for a traffic class or classes in a traffic policy	**show policy-map control-plane type queue-threshold** [**host** | **transit** | **cef-exception**] [**input** [**class** *class-name*] | **output** [**class** *class-name*]]
Display information about the configuration and statistics of control plane traffic policies	**show policy-map control-plane** [**input** [**class** *class-name*] | **output** [**class** *class-name*]]
Display authentication key information	**show key chain**
Display the EIGRP interface authentication information	**show ip eigrp interfaces detail**
Display the status RIP, including the currently assigned key chain	**show ip protocols**
Display the status and configuration of OSPF, including area authentication	**show ip ospf** [*process-id*]
Display the status and configuration of OSPF on an interface	**show ip ospf interface** *interface*
Display the status of a BGP neighbor (peer), look at the Option flags to verify MD5 configuration	**show ip bgp neighbors** *neighbor*

Fill in the Blanks

1. The control plane includes the group of processes that are run at the _____ level and control most high-level control IOS functions.

2. The _____ is responsible for the high-speed routing of packets that typically come from nondistributed interfaces.

3. _____ control plane services are considered first, and then the conditioned traffic is passed through to _____ control plane services.

4. Output control plane services are applied after the packet exits the control plane and are only available with _____ control plane services.

5. _____ allows the control plane to be considered like a separate entity with its own input and output interface.

6. With Control Plane Protection, the control plane interface is split into four pieces, an _____ and _____.

7. The _____ receives all control plane IP traffic that is directed at one of the device's interfaces.

8. The _____ feature enhances Control Plane Protection by providing a mechanism for limiting the number of matched protocol packets allowed at the process level.

9. _____ works by creating a one-way hash out of a shared secret and sending this hash between source and destination.

10. A _____ is essentially an electronic repository of keys and their respective shared secret and validity schedules.

This chapter covers the following subjects:

- **Management plane attack types:** Reviews the different types of attacks that are focused on the management plane.

- **Management plane security technologies:** Goes over the specific technologies that can be used to mitigate the various management place attack types and describes how to configure them.

CHAPTER 10

Implementing and Configuring Cisco IOS Management Plane Security

The management plane is a hard thing to protect in the production environments because it must remain open enough for legitimate management but stay closed enough to not be exploited. This chapter reviews the threats to the management plane and describes the available security technology options that are available to help in securing it.

"Do I Know This Already?" Quiz

The "Do I Know This Already?" quiz helps you decide whether you really need to read the entire chapter. If you already intend to read the entire chapter, you do not necessarily need to answer these questions now.

The ten-question quiz, derived from the major sections in the "Foundation Topics" section of this chapter, helps you determine how to spend your limited study time.

Table 10-1 outlines the major topics discussed in this chapter and the "Do I Know This Already?" quiz questions that correspond to those topics.

Table 10-1 *"Do I Know This Already?" Foundation Topics Section-to-Question Mapping*

Foundation Topics Section	Questions Covered in This Section
Management Plane Attack Types	1
Management Plane Security Technologies	2–10

Caution: The goal of self-assessment is to gauge your mastery of the topics in this chapter. If you do not know the answer to a question or are only partially sure of the answer, you should mark this question wrong for purposes of the self-assessment. Giving yourself credit for an answer that you correctly guess skews your self-assessment results and might provide you with a false sense of security.

1. Which type of management plane attack type works by creating or taking over a management session?

   a. Slow-path denial of service

   b. Management session spoofing

   c. Man-in-the-middle attacks

   d. DoS session spoofing

2. Which of the following type of password is used to secure SSH connections?

   a. Terminal line

   b. Console

   c. Async

   d. Enable

3. Which of the following is the highest level of privilege supported?

   a. 1

   b. 16

   c. 15

   d. 0

4. What is the minimum modulus (key size) that must be used to enable SSH version 2?

   a. 2048

   b. 512

   c. 1024

   d. 768

5. Which of the following SNMP components is run directly on the device?

   a. Manager

   b. Agent

   c. MIB

   d. Supervisor

6. Which of the following SNMP operations notify the manager of an event without requiring an acknowledgment?

   a. Get

   b. Trap

   c. Put

   d. Inform

7. Which of the following authentication mechanisms can be used with SNMP version 3?

    a. MD5

    b. 3DES

    c. AES

    d. SHA

8. Which of the following protocols are supported by MPP?

    a. CDP

    b. Rsync

    c. SSH

    d. FTP

9. Which of the following global services are disabled by the AutoSecure feature?

    a. HTTP server

    b. SSH

    c. NTP

    d. AAA

10. Which of the following are valid types of keys when using digitally signed Cisco software?

    a. Rollover

    b. Development

    c. Global

    d. Special

The answers to the "Do I Know This Already?" quiz are found in Appendix A. The suggested choices for your next step are as follows:

■ **8 or less overall score:** Read the entire chapter. This includes the "Foundation Topics" and the "Exam Preparation" sections.

■ **9 or 10 overall score:** If you want more review on these topics, skip to the "Exam Preparation" section.

Foundation Topics

Management Plane Attack Types

As with the other planes that were discussed in the previous chapters, it is important to understand the common types of attacks that are attempted toward the management plane. The following sections review these common attack types.

When setting up the management of network devices, it is important that those who are able to gain access to them have been authenticated and given the appropriate privileges to do their jobs. Depending on the size of the company and the network, these privileges can be set up to only permit those commands required to be used at each stage of the support structure. It is also important that whatever authentication is used is capable of securing the device not only from unauthorized internal users but also from outside attacks. A strong management structure is vital in maintaining these requirements. This chapter covers a number of different features that can be used to create a system that meets these requirements.

As much as a strong management system is important in maintaining the security of a device, it is also important to secure the device from potential spoofing attacks. These attacks are made possible by using management protocols that are inherently insecure and should not be used. These attacks work by creating or taking over a management session. The attacker can then perform the commands that were able to be performed by the exploited user.

Management Plane Security Technologies

You can use a number of different security technologies to mitigate the attacks alluded to in the previous section. A description of these technologies and how to implement them will be covered in the following sections.

Basic Management Security and Privileges

Some of the best ways to secure a networking device are the simplest things to configure. These include basic password management, the configuration of privileges, and the creation of access control lists (ACL) that are used to limit management access. This section reviews the available options and displays how to configure each of them.

Each device has a number of IOS modes that are used to display and configure it for a variety of operations; the main two are

- **User EXEC mode:** While in user EXEC mode, the user is limited to doing a number of limited display commands that can only be used to parse the simplest of device information.

- **Privileged EXEC mode:** By default, while in privileged EXEC mode, the user is allowed to do any of the commands available on the device, including all that display and configure the device.

On top of privileged EXEC mode are a number of configuration modes that can be used to configure the various features available on the device. The highest available configuration mode is global configuration mode, which is used to configure feature options for the entire device. From within global configuration mode, there are a number of different others modes that can be accessed to configure all the other available features on the device.

Password Management

On each device, there are a number of passwords that can be set to control access to the various parts of the device, which include the following:

- **Enable:** The enable password is used to control access to the privileged EXEC mode.

- **Console:** The console password is used to control access to user EXEC mode when connecting through the console port of the device.

- **Terminal line:** The terminal lines (also called virtual teletypewriter lines [VTY]) are mainly used to control access to the user EXEC mode when connecting through Telnet or Secure Shell (SSH).

On a Cisco device, there are two different methods that can be used to set the enable password; these include the **enable password** and **enable secret** commands. The difference between these two commands is the method that is used to store the password information when contained in the device configuration. By default, many of the passwords entered on these devices are entered into the configuration as plain text. This includes the enable password when configured with the **enable password** command. If a level of encryption on these passwords is required, two options exist:

- Configure the service password-encryption command. When this command is issued, all clear-text passwords will be stored in the configuration encrypted with a low-level reversible encryption. Because this encryption is easy to reverse, it is recommended only as a first level of password security.

- Configure the enable secret command. When using this command, the enable password is stored in the configuration using the message digest algorithm 5 (MD5) algorithm, which is not reversible and considerably harder to exploit.

Both the console and terminal line passwords are clear text by default and are affected by the **service password-encryption** command. However, neither of these passwords has an MD5 option like the enable password. With these passwords, the low-level encryption provided by the **service password-encryption** command is all that is available.

Table 10-2 describes the commands that are used to change each of these passwords.

Table 10-2 *Configuring Device Passwords*

Task	Command Syntax
Configure the enable password for a device using a clear-text or reversibly encrypted password	Router(config)# **enable password** *password*
Configure the enable password for a device using MD5	Router(config)# **enable secret** *password*

Table 10-2 *Configuring Device Passwords*

Task	Command Syntax
Enter console line configuration mode	Router(config)# **line console 0**
Enter terminal line configuration mode	Router(config)# **line vty 0 4**
Configure a password for console or terminal (VTY) lines	Router(config-line)# **password** *password*
Configure the use of reversible password encryption	Router(config)# **service password-encryption**

Example 10-1 shows the configuration of the enable password using MD5, enables password encryption, and configures the console and terminal line passwords.

Example 10-1 *Configuring Device Passwords*

```
Router# configure terminal
Router(config)# enable secret ciscopress
Router(config)# service password-encryption
Router(config)# line console 0
Router(config-line)# password ciscopress
Router(config-line)# line vty 0 4
Router(config-line)# password ciscopress
```

Privileges

Additional levels of protection are available through the use of privilege levels. By default, user EXEC mode is privilege level 1 and privileged EXEC mode is privilege mode 15. These levels, from 1 through 15, are available to be modified to suit the specific needs of an organization. There are three main ways in which privileges can be implemented: using different enable passwords that are each given a different level of authorization, through the use of usernames configured on the device, and using a server-based username solution. Obviously, the use of different enable passwords is easy, but quite configuration intensive should there be a number of different devices. The same is true of using usernames configured at each device. The best solution to use in large organizations is the use of server-based username authorization; however, this is outside the scope of this book. Table 10-3 outlines the configuration of privilege levels without the use of a server.

Table 10-3 *Configuring Privilege Levels*

Task	Command Syntax
Configure different privilege levels for specific commands	Router(config)# **privilege** *mode* [**all**] {**level** *level* | **reset**} *command-string*
Configure an enable password at a specific privilege level	Router(config)# **enable secret level** *level* *password*

Table 10-3   *Configuring Privilege Levels*

Task	Command Syntax
Create a user with a specific privilege level	Router(config)# **username** *username* **privilege** *level* **secret** *password*
Configure the use of the local authentication database (used with **username** command)	Router(config-line)# **login local**
Display the current privilege level	Router# **show privilege**

Note: Use the privilege **reset** option when trying to make command changes; there is no **no** form of the privilege command.

Example 10-2 shows the configuration of privilege level 7, which is configured to allow the **clear counters** command to be issued. An enable password and user "cisco" are configured to use privilege level 7 using "ciscopress" as a password.

Example 10-2   *Configuring Privilege Levels*

```
Router# configure terminal
Router(config)# privilege exec level 7 clear counters
Router(config)# enable secret level 7 ciscopress
Router(config)# username cisco privilege 7 secret ciscopress
```

Note: When changing passwords on Cisco devices, they are not verified, which can lead to lockouts. Ensure that the passwords that you enter are correct. A good safeguard is to have two sessions open to the device when changing passwords; use one of them to change the password and to test that it works correctly. If there is an entry problem, the second session will still be able to change the password.

RBAC

Role-Based Access Control (RBAC) is implemented on devices through the use of role-based CLI access. Role-based CLI access provides the ability to set up to 15 (not including the root view) CLI views that are configured to run commands that are configured for different job functions. The configuration is similar to setting up privileges but allows additional control that is not provided using privileges alone.

When using CLI views, all configurations are done using the root view. The root view has the privileges equivalent to level 15 but with the additional ability to configure CLI views. Role-based CLI access also allows the configuration of a superview that can be configured with the privileges from several existing CLI views; this can then be used by higher-level network operations personnel.

The configuration of a CLI view involves the creation of the CLI view, the setting of a password, and several commands that are used to specify the commands that will be allowed. Table 10-4 describes the different commands that are required to create and configure a CLI view.

Table 10-4   *Configuring a CLI View*

Task	Command Syntax
Enable the use of AAA on the device	Router(config)# **aaa new-model**
Enter a root or specific view name	Router# **enable** [**view** [*view-name*]]
Create a view and enter view configuration mode	Router(config)# **parser view** *view-name*
Configure a view password using MD5	Router(config-view)# **secret** *password*
Configure commands or interfaces that are accessible from within the configured view	Router(config-view)# **commands** *mode* {**include** | **include-exclusive** | **exclude**} [**all**] [*command*]
Display the current CLI view	Router# **show parser view**

Note: Unlike with user EXEC mode, which includes many basic CLI commands by default, a view, by default, is only allowed to perform the exact commands as specified by the configuration.

Example 10-3 shows the configuration of a new CLI view called ciscoview, shows a password of ciscopress, and allows the use of the **show version** command.

Example 10-3   *Configuring a CLI View*

```
Router# configure terminal
Router(config)# aaa new-model
Router(config)# end
Router# enable view
Router# configure terminal
Router(config)# parser view ciscoview
Router(config-view)# secret ciscopress
Router(config-view)# commands exec include show version
```

After the CLI views have been configured, the ability to create a superview is available. As stated previously, a superview is a view that is given the privileges of several existing CLI views. Table 10-5 describes the different commands that are required to create and configure a CLI superview.

Table 10-5 *Configuring a CLI Superview*

Task	Command Syntax
Enter a root or specific view name	Router# enable [**view** [*view-name*]]
Create a superview and enter view configuration mode	Router(config)# **parser view** *view-name* **superview**
Configure a view password using MD5	Router(config-view)# **secret** *password*
Associate a CLI view to the superview	Router(config-view)# **view** *view-name*
Display the current CLI view	Router# **show parser view**

Example 10-4 shows the configuration of a new CLI superview called ciscosuper, shows a password of ciscopress, and associates CLI views ciscoview and ciscoview_2. When logged in using this superview, the user will have access to the commands from both of these views.

Example 10-4 *Configuring a CLI Superview*

```
Router# enable view
Router# configure terminal
Router(config)# parser view ciscosuper superview
Router(config-view)# view ciscoview
Router(config-view)# view ciscoview_2
```

Management ACLs

Another method of securing the terminal lines into a device is through the use of an ACL that is configured on each terminal line into the device. These ACLs can be configured to only allow management traffic into these terminal lines from a specific host or network. Because ACLs were covered in Chapter 8, "Implementing and Configuring Cisco IOS Routed Data Plane Security," this section only reviews the application of an ACL on specific terminal lines. Table 10-6 describes the different commands that are required to create and configure a management ACL.

Table 10-6 *Configuring Management ACLs*

Task	Command Syntax
Configure an ACL on a specific terminal line	Router(config-line)# **access-class** *access-list-number* {**in**	**out**}
Display the configuration information about the device lines	Router# **show line**

Example 10-5 shows the configuration of access list 1 inbound on all terminal lines.

Example 10-5 *Configuring a Management ACL*

```
Router# configure terminal
Router(config)# access-list 1 permit 192.168.1.100
Router(config)# line vty 0 4
Router(config-line)# access-class 1 in
```

SSH

For a long time, the preferred method of managing devices was through the use of Telnet. The problem with Telnet is that it is not a secure protocol and can be easily intercepted, which can lead to significant security problems. The solution for this is the use of the Secure Shell (SSH) protocol, which provides an encrypted session between the device and the managing user.

Two different versions of SSH are supported on these devices: version 1 and version 2. Version 2 provides some additional capabilities, including support for larger bit modulus (key size) and RSA key enhancements.

There are two methods of SSH configuration. The first requires that both the device host name and the device domain name be configured before initial SSH configuration. This type of configuration is shown next. Table 10-7 describes the different commands that are required to create and configure SSH with a host name and domain name.

Table 10-7 *Configuring SSH with Host Name and Domain Name*

Task	Command Syntax
Configure a device host name	Router(config)# **hostname** *hostname*
Configure a device domain name	Router(config)# **ip domain-name** *domain-name*
Create an RSA key pair and enable the use of SSH version 1	Router(config)# **crypto key generate rsa modulus** *modulus*
Delete the current RSA key pair and disable the SSH server	Router(config)# **crypto key zeroize rsa**
Display information about the currently active SSH sessions	Router# **show ssh**
Display information about the current SSH configuration	Router# **show ip ssh**

Example 10-6 shows the configuration of SSH using a host name of device, a domain name of ciscopress.com, and a modulus of 512.

Example 10-6 *Configuring SSH with Host Name and Domain Name*

```
Router# configure terminal
Router(config)# hostname device
device(config)# ip domain-name ciscopress.com
device(config)# crypto key generate rsa modulus 512
```

By default, if a key pair is generated that has a modulus that is greater than or equal to 768, both version 1 and version 2 of SSH are enabled and both types of connection are honored. If only a specific version of SSH is intended, either a modulus less than 768 must be used (to enable SSH version 1) or it can be individually configured.

The second method of SSH configuration uses key pair labels (names); this method does not require the prior configuration of a host name or domain name. Table 10-8 describes the different commands that are required to create and configure SSH without a host name or domain name.

Table 10-8 *Configuring SSH Without a Host Name and Domain Name*

Task	Command Syntax
Configure the use of a specific key pair to be used with SSH (does not enable SSH until a key has been generated)	Router(config)# **ip ssh rsa keypair-name** *keypair-name*
Create an RSA key pair with a keypair name and enable the use of SSH version 2	Router(config)# **crypto key generate rsa usage-keys label** *keypair-name* **modulus** *modulus*
Configure the use of a specific SSH version	Router(config)# **ip ssh version {1	2}**
Delete the current or named RSA key pair and disable the SSH server	Router(config)# **crypto key zeroize rsa** [*keypair-name*]
Display information about the currently active SSH sessions	Router# **show ssh**
Display information about the current SSH configuration	Router# **show ip ssh**

Example 10-7 shows the configuration of SSH without a configured host name and domain name. This configuration includes a key pair name of ciscopair, with a modulus of 1024, and configures the use of only SSH version 2.

Example 10-7 *Configuring SSH Without a Host Name and Domain Name*

```
Router# configure terminal
Router(config)# ip ssh rsa keypair-name ciscopair
Router(config)# generate rsa usage-keys label ciscopair modulus 1024
Router(config)# ip ssh version 2
```

SNMP

The Simple Network Management Protocol (SNMP) is used by many organizations to keep a good management and monitoring capability for all their devices. SNMP can be used for a number of different things, from the monitoring and triggering of alerts to device configuration.

SNMP is broken down into three components:

- **SNMP manager:** The SNMP manager controls and monitors the devices within the network using SNMP.

- **SNMP agent:** The SNMP agent is the component that is run directly on the device and maintains data and reports this data (if needed) to the SNMP manager.

- **MIB:** The Management Information Base (MIB) is a virtual information storage location that contains collections of managed objects. Within the MIB, there are objects that relate to different defined MIB modules (for example, the interface module).

The use of these three components can make a network easy to monitor and maintain. To obtain information from the MIB on the SNMP agent, several different operations can be used:

- **Get:** Used to get information from the MIB from an SNMP agent

- **Set:** Used to get information to the MIB from an SNMP manager

- **Walk:** Used to list information from successive MIB objects within a specified MIB

- **Trap:** Used by the SNMP agent to send a triggered piece of information to the SNMP manager

- **Inform:** The same as a trap, but adds an acknowledgment that is not provided with a trap.

There are also three main versions of SNMP that have been defined:

- **Version 1:** This version was defined in RFC 1157 and utilizes community-based security.

- **Version 2c:** This version was defined in RFCs 1901, 1905, and 1906 and utilizes community-based security. Version 2c added some additional protocol operations and data types to version 1; these include a bulk retrieval mechanism.

- **Version 3:** This version was defined in RFCs 3413 through 3415 and defines a new security model that includes features that support message integrity, authentication and, encryption.

The community-based security method is known to be a large security vulnerability to versions 1 and 2 because of its lack of encryption and authentication (other than a simple community name). While the configuration of SNMP version 3 is more intensive, it should be preferred when traffic is routed over untrusted networks. Table 10-9 shows the various SNMP security models and levels.

Table 10-9 *SNMP Security Models and Levels*

Model	Level	Authentication	Encryption?
v1	noAuthnoPriv	Community String	No
v2c	noAuthNoPriv	Community String	No
v3	noAuthNoPriv	Username	No
v3	authNoPriv	MD5 or SHA	No
v3	authPriv	MD5 or SHA	Yes (DES, 3DES, or AES)

Basic SNMP Parameter Configuration

Typically, the first things that are configured on a device include the system contact, device location, and device serial number. The first SNMP command, which is used automatically, enables the SNMP agent on the device. Table 10-10 outlines the commands to configure the system contact, device location, and device serial number.

Table 10-10 *Configuring Basic SNMP*

Task	Command Syntax
Configure the SNMP contact information	Router(config)# **snmp-server contact** *text*
Configure the SNMP device location	Router(config)# **snmp-server location** *text*
Configure the SNMP device serial number	Router(config)# **snmp-server chassis-id** *number*
Display the current SNMP contact information	Router# **show snmp contact**
Display the current SNMP device location	Router# **show snmp location**
Display the current SNMP device serial number	Router# **show snmp chassis**

Example 10-8 shows the configuration of basic SNMP parameters, including a contact, device location, and device serial number.

Example 10-8 *Configuring Basic SNMP*

```
Router# configure terminal
Router(config)# snmp-server contact John Smith at (919) 555-1212
Router(config)# snmp-server location Raleigh, NC
Router(config)# snmp-server chassis-id 123456
```

SNMP View Configuration

To limit the amount of information that is available for those accessing the MIB objects on a device, a view can be configured. A view is configured with the MIB objects that are allowed (or disallowed) to be accessed by a specific community or group. It is through the configuration of multiple view entries that the access control of the MIB objects is controlled. Table 10-11 outlines the commands to configure an SNMP view.

Table 10-11 *Configuring SNMP Views*

Task	Command Syntax
Create and configure an SNMP view	Router(config)# **snmp-server view** *view-name* *oid-tree* [**included** | **excluded**]
Display information about the currently configured SNMP views	Router# **show snmp view**

Example 10-9 shows the configuration of the ciscoview SNMP view, which is configured to allow access to the entire MIB-II subtree.

Example 10-9 *Configuring SNMP Views*

```
Router# configure terminal
Router(config)# snmp-server view ciscoview mib-2 included
```

SNMP Community Configuration (Versions 1 and 2c)

With SNMP versions 1 and 2c, a community string is used as the only form of authentication. When configuring a community string, specific privileges can be given to those authenticating with the correct string. Access can be given broadly with global read-only and global read-write access as well as more specifically with an existing SNMP view. Access to the SNMP agent can also be restricted through the use of a standard IP access list. Table 10-12 describes the different commands that are required to create and configure SNMP communities.

Table 10-12 *Configuring SNMP Communities*

Task	Command Syntax
Create and configure an SNMP community	Router(config)# **snmp-server community** *string* [**view** *view-name*] [**ro** | **rw**] [*access-list-number*]
Display information about the currently configured SNMP communities	Router# **show snmp community**

Example 10-10 shows the configuration of two communities, the first with read-only access to the entire MIB and the second with access to only the MIB-II subtree as provided by the ciscoview view created in Example 10-9.

Example 10-10   *Configuring SNMP Communities*

```
Router# configure terminal
Router(config)# snmp-server community first ro
Router(config)# snmp-server community second view ciscoview
```

SNMP Version 3 Configuration

The configuration of SNMP version 3 is different from that of the other versions because the security mechanism is much more complex and offers a much higher level of security. Security is configured through the creation of users and groups; the groups are given access to specific SNMP MIB objects through views, and the users are assigned to specific groups. Version 3 also supports the use of both authentication (MD5 or Secure Hash Algorithm [SHA]) and encryption (Data Encryption Standard [DES], Triple DES [3DES], or Advanced Encryption Standard [AES]) of SNMP traffic. Users can be set up on the local device and/or on the remote management server. The security digests required for authenticating and encrypting packets utilize an EngineID that is automatically generated on the local device (local EngineID) but is required to be configured for each remote device/remote management server when exchanging packets (remote EngineID). Remote users can also be configured, but the remote EngineID is required before these users can be created to ensure proper security exchange information. Table 10-13 describes the different commands that are required to create and configure SNMPv3 users and groups.

Table 10-13   *Configuring SNMP v3 User and Groups*

Task	Command Syntax
Create and configure an SNMP v3 group	Router(config)# **snmp-server group** *group-name* {**v3** {**auth** | **noauth** | **priv**}} [**read** *read-view*] [**write** *write-view*] [**notify** *notify-view*] [**access** [*acl-number* | *acl-name*]]
Create and configure an SNMP v3 user	Router(config)# **snmp-server user** *username group-name* [**remote host** [**udp-port** *port*]] {**v3** [**encrypted**] [**auth** {**md5** | **sha**} *auth-password*]} [**priv** {**des** | **3des** | **aes** {**128** | **192** |**256**}} *privpassword*]
Configure the local EngineID	Router(config)# **snmp-server engineID local** *engineid-string*
Configure a remote EngineID	Router(config)# **snmp-server engineID remote** {*ipv4-ip-address* | *ipv6-address*}[**udp**-port *udp-port-number*] *engineid-string*
Display the currently configured SNMP groups	Router# **show snmp group**
Display the currently configured SNMP users	Router# **show snmp user**
Display the currently configured EngineIDs	Router# **show snmp engineID**

Example 10-11 shows the configuration of a new SNMP group called v3group that is used for authorization and provides a read view of ciscoview. This configuration also shows a new SNMP user called v3user configured to use MD5 for authorization with a password of ciscopass.

Example 10-11 *Configuring SNMP v3 User and Groups*

```
Router# configure terminal
Router(config)# snmp-server group v3group v3 auth read ciscoview
Router(config)# snmp-server user v3user v3group v3 auth md5 ciscopass
```

Basic Notification Configuration

One of the main capabilities with SNMP is the ability to have the devices send messages to a central server for recording purposes or to alert a device of a problem. These messages can be in the form of a trap or inform; the difference between the two is that an inform requires an acknowledgment from the server while a trap does not. An SNMP version 3 inform also requires that a remote EngineID is configured to ensure that the acknowledgment security information is able to be correctly calculated. Table 10-14 describes the different commands that are required to configure SNMP notifications.

Table 10-14 *Configuring SNMP Notifications*

Task	Command Syntax
Configure a remote SNMP v3 user	Router(config)# **snmp-server user** *username group-name* **remote** *host* [**udp-port** *port*]{**v3** [**encrypted**] [**auth** {**md5** | **sha**} *auth-password*]} [**priv** {**des** | **3des** | **aes** {**128** | **192** |**256**}} *privpassword*]
Configure an SNMP notification host (trap or inform)	Router(config)# **snmp-server host** {*hostname* | *ip-address*} [**traps** | **informs**] [**version** {**1** | **2c** | **3** [**auth** | **noauth** | **priv**]}] {*community-string* | *username*}[**udp-port** *port*] [*notification-type*]
Configure the notification types to be sent in a trap or inform (this command works with both traps and informs; the configuration of the **snmp-server** host command dictates which type is sent)	Router(config)# **snmp-server enable traps** [*notification-type*]
Display the currently configured notification hosts	Router# **show snmp host**

Example 10-12 shows the configuration of the EngineID for the remote network server at IP address 10.10.1.100 and with an EngineID string of 800000090300CA00144C0008, and configures a notification host at IP address 10.10.1.100. Then, it configures SNMP informs to be sent for alert events.

Example 10-12   *Configuring SNMP v3 Notifications*

```
Router# configure terminal
Router(config)# snmp-server engineID remote 10.10.1.100 800000090300CA00144C0008
Router(config)# snmp-server user v3remoteuser v3group remote 10.10.1.100 v3 auth
 md5 ciscopass
Router(config)# snmp=server host 10.10.1.100 informs version 3 auth v3remoteuser
Router(config)# snmp-server enable traps alert
```

CPU and Memory Thresholding

One of the ways to monitor whether an attack is occurring on a device is through the simple monitoring of device resources, including CPU and memory utilization. This is done by configuring the use of CPU or memory threshold monitoring. Both of these features can be combined with a remote management server to notify an organization when the CPU and memory conditions on a device become critical.

CPU Thresholding Configuration

The configuration of CPU thresholding utilizes two different types of threshold: rising and falling. The rising threshold is triggered when the CPU utilization exceeds a configured threshold. A falling threshold is triggered when the CPU utilization falls back below a configured threshold. Table 10-15 describes the different commands that are required to configure CPU thresholding.

Table 10-15   *Configuring CPU Thresholding*

Task	Command Syntax
Configure the use of a rising (and falling, if needed) CPU threshold	Router(config)# **process cpu threshold type** {**total** | **process** | **interrupt**} y *percentage* **interval** *seconds* [**falling** *fall-percentage* **interval** *seconds*]
Configure the use of an SNMP trap (or inform) should a CPU threshold message be triggered	Router(config)# **snmp-server enable traps cpu threshold**

Example 10-13 shows the configuration of a CPU threshold that triggers when the total CPU utilization goes above 70 percent and when it falls back below 40 percent and is checked in 5-second intervals.

Example 10-13   *Configuring CPU Thresholding*

```
Router# configure terminal
Router(config)# snmp=server host 10.10.1.100 traps first
Router(config)# snmp-server enable traps cpu threshold
Router(config)# process cpu threshold type total rising 70 interval 5 falling 40
 interval 5
```

Memory Threshold Configuration

The memory threshold feature also has two different options that can be configured. These include an ability to trigger a message when the device memory goes below a configured level and/or the ability to reserve an amount of memory to be used for critical notifications. Table 10-16 describes the different commands that are required to configure memory thresholding.

Table 10-16   *Configuring Memory Thresholding*

Task	Command Syntax
Configure the use of a memory threshold message should the device memory go below the configured level	Router(config)# **memory free low-water-mark** {**processor** *threshold*	**io** *threshold*}
Configure a memory reserve that is used to ensure that critical notifications can be sent	Router(config)# **memory reserve critical** *kilobytes*

Example 10-14 shows the configuration of memory threshold of 10 MB (less than 10 MB is available) and a reservation of 2 MB for critical notifications.

Example 10-14   *Configuring Memory Thresholding*

```
Router# configure terminal
Router(config)# memory free low-watermark processor 10000
Router(config)# memory reserve critical 2000
```

Management Plane Protection

In many situations, it is possible to know which device interface or interfaces will always be used for management traffic. It is in these situations when the Management Plane Protection (MPP) feature can be used. MPP enables you to limit the source of management traffic to a specific interface (or interfaces) on a device. This is important because many of these protocols are inherently insecure. This ability provides additional protection from management plane attacks that are sourced off of interfaces that should never contain management traffic.

To use the MPP feature, IP Cisco Express Forwarding (CEF) must be enabled on the device. Also note that if the management of a device is handled through the use of a loopback interface, the management interface to be used in MPP configuration is the physical interface where management traffic will be processed.

The MPP feature supports only the following specific management protocols:

- File Transfer Protocol (FTP)

- Hypertext Transfer Protocol (HTTP)

- Hypertext Transfer Protocol - Secure (HTTPS)

- Secure Shell (SSH), versions 1 and 2

- Simple Network Management Protocol (SNMP), all versions

- Telnet

- Trivial File Transfer Protocol (TFTP)

- Blocks Extensible Exchange Protocol (BEEP)

Table 10-17 describes the different commands that are required to configure management plane protection.

Table 10-17 *Configuring MPP*

Task	Command Syntax
Configure a specific interface to be specified for management traffic using Management Plane Protection (MPP)	Router(config-cp-host)# **management-interface** *interface* **allow** *protocols*
Display the current configured management interface and protocols allowed	Router# **show management-interface** [*interface* | **protocol** *protocol-name*]

Example 10-15 shows the configuration of MPP using interface fastethernet0/0 and allowing only the SSH protocol.

Example 10-15 *Configuring MPP*

```
Router# configure terminal
Router(config)# ip cef
Router(config)# control-plane host
Router(config-cp-host)# management-interface fastethernet0/0 allow ssh
```

AutoSecure

The AutoSecure feature can be used to disable many of the commonly exploited IP services on a device. The caveat is that many of these IP services are used for valid purposes and need to be left running. It is because of this that Cisco recommends that this feature not be used in a production environment but rather in a test environment as a reference to which services can be disabled and how to disable them.

Global Services

The following global services are disabled on a device without prompting when AutoSecure is enabled:

- Finger

- PAD

- Small Servers

- BOOTP Server

- HTTP Server

- Identification Service

- Cisco Discovery Protocol (CDP)

- Network Time Protocol (NTP)

- Source Routing

The following global services are enabled on a device without prompting when AutoSecure is enabled:

- **service password-encryption** is enabled.

- **service tcp-keepalives-in** and **service tcp-keepalives-out** are enabled.

Interface Services

The following interface services are disabled on a device without prompting when AutoSecure is enabled:

- Internet Control Message Protocol (ICMP) redirects

- ICMP unreachables

- ICMP mask reply messages

- Proxy ARP

- Directed Broadcast

- Maintenance Operations Protocol (MOP)

Secure Access

The following options are available on the device when AutoSecure is enabled:

- If a device banner does not exist, a prompt will ask for one.

- A login and password are configured for the console, AUX, VTY, and TTY lines (if available), and the EXEC timeout is set to 10 minutes.

- If the device has a crypto image, SSH and secure copy (SCP) are enabled, and the timeout and authentication retries are set to minimums.

- If run in noninteract mode, SNMP is disabled if the community strings are set to **public** or **private**; if run in interactive mode, it is prompted whether to disable SNMP regardless of the configured community strings.

- If authentication, authorization, and accounting (AAA) is not configured, it will be prompted to configure a local username and password.

Security Logging

The following logging options are available on the device when AutoSecure is enabled:

- Sequence numbers and time stamps are enabled on all debug and log messages.

- Logging messages will be generated for login-related events.

- The **logging console critical**, **logging buffered**, and **logging trap debugging** commands are issued.

Table 10-18 describes the different commands that are required to configure AutoSecure.

Table 10-18 *Configuring AutoSecure*

Task	Command Syntax
Secure the device according to the previous guidelines	Router# **auto secure [management	forwarding] [no-interact	full] [ntp	login	ssh	firewall	tcp-intercept]**
Display the AutoSecure configurations	Router# **show auto secure config**

Example 10-16 shows the configuration of the AutoSecure feature on all available options on a device without prompting.

Example 10-16 *Configuring AutoSecure*

```
Router# auto secure no-interact
```

Digitally Signed Cisco Software

A new feature that is only available in the new Cisco IOS Release 15.0.1M and later is digitally signed software. At the time of this writing, it is only supported by the 1900, 2900, and 3900 series routers.

Digitally signed software will come with an extension of .SPA or .SSA, depending on the type of image. The type of image can be calculated using the following key:

- **First character:** States that the image is digitally signed (S)

- **Second character:** Specifies which type of image (P = Production, S = Special)

- **Third character:** Indicates the key version

There are three different types of key:

- Production

- Special

- Rollover

The use and configuration of signed images are outside the scope of this book, but the information is provided because it will become more commonplace with newer versions of Cisco software.

Note: You can find additional information about the digitally signed software feature and configuration at www.cisco.com/en/US/docs/ios/fundamentals/configuration/guide/ cf_dgtly_sgnd_sw_ps10591_TSD_Products_Configuration_Guide_Chapter.html.

Exam Preparation

As mentioned in the section, "How to Use This Book," in the Introduction, you have several choices for exam preparation: the exercises here, the memory tables in Appendix C, the final exam preparation chapter, and the exam simulation questions on the CD-ROM. The following questions present a bigger challenge than the exam itself because they use an open-ended question format. By using this more difficult format, you exercise your memory better and prove your conceptual and factual knowledge of this chapter. You can find the answers to these questions in Appendix A, "Answers to the DIKTA Quizzes and Fill in the Blanks Questions."

Review All Key Topics

Review the most important topics in the chapter, noted with the Key Topics icon in the margin of the page. Table 10-19 lists a reference of these key topics and the page numbers on which each is found.

Table 10-19   *Key Topics*

Key Topic Element	Description	Page
List	IOS modes	248
List	Password configuration modes	249
Note	reset command	251
List	SNMP components	256
List	SNMP operations	256
List	SNMP versions	256
Table 10-9	SNMP security models and levels	257
List	MPP-supported protocols	263
List	AutoSecure disabled services	264

Complete Tables and Lists from Memory

Print a copy of Appendix C, "Memory Tables" (found on the CD), or at least the section for this chapter, and complete the tables and lists from memory. Appendix D, "Memory Table Answers," also on the CD, includes completed tables and lists to check your work.

Define Key Terms

Define the following key terms from this chapter, and check your answers in the Glossary:

management plane, key pair, SNMP manager, SNMP agent, MIB

Use Command Reference to Check Your Memory

Table 10-20 lists the important commands from this chapter. To test your memory, cover the right side of the table with a piece of paper, read the description on the left side, and then see how much of the command you can remember.

Table 10-20   *Command Reference*

Task	Command Syntax
Configure the enable password for a device using a clear-text or reversibly encrypted password	Router(config)# **enable password** *password*
Configure the enable password for a device using MD5	Router(config)# **enable secret** *password*
Enter console line configuration mode	Router(config)# **line console 0**
Enter terminal line configuration mode	Router(config)# **line vty 0 4**
Configure a password for a console or terminal (VTY) lines	Router(config-line)# **password** *password*
Configure the use of reversible password encryption	Router(config)# **service password-encryption**
Configure different privilege levels for specific commands	Router(config)# **privilege** *mode* **[all]** {**level** *level* | **reset**} *command-string*
Configure an enable password at a specific privilege level	Router(config)# **enable secret level** *level* *password*
Create a user with a specific privilege level	Router(config)# **username** *username* **privilege** *level* **secret** *password*
Configure the use of the local authentication database (used with **username** command)	Router(config-line)# **login local**
Enable the use of AAA on the device	Router(config)# **aaa new-model**
Enter a root or specific view name	Router# **enable [view [** *view-name* **]]**
Create a view and enter view configuration mode	Router(config)# **parser view** *view-name*
Configure a view password using MD5	Router(config-view)# **secret** *password*
Configure commands or interfaces that are accessible from within the configured view	Router(config-view)# **commands** *mode* {**include** | **include-exclusive** | **exclude**} **[all]** [*command*]
Enter a root or specific view name	Router# **enable [view [** *view-name* **]]**

Table 10-20 *Command Reference*

Task	Command Syntax
Create a superview and enter view configuration mode	Router(config)# **parser view** *view-name* **superview**
Configure a view password using MD5	Router(config-view)# **secret** *password*
Associate a CLI view to the superview	Router(config-view)# **view** *view-name*
Configure an ACL on a specific terminal line	Router(config-line)# **access-class** *access-list-number* {**in** | **out**}
Configure a device host name	Router(config)# **hostname** *hostname*
Configure a device domain name	Router(config)# **ip domain-name** *domain-name*
Create an RSA key pair and enable the use of SSH version 1	Router(config)# **crypto key generate rsa modulus** *modulus*
Delete the current RSA key pair and disable the SSH server	Router(config)# **crypto key zeroize rsa**
Configure the use of a specific key pair to be used with SSH (does not enable SSH until a key has been generated)	Router(config)# **ip ssh rsa keypair-name** *keypair-name*
Create an RSA key pair with a key pair name and enable the use of SSH version 2	Router(config)# **crypto key generate rsa usage-keys label** *keypair-name* **modulus** *modulus*
Configure the use of a specific SSH version	Router(config)# **ip ssh version** {**1** | **2**}
Delete the current or named RSA key pair and disable the SSH server	Router(config)# **crypto key zeroize rsa** [*keypair-name*]
Configure the SNMP contact information	Router(config)# **snmp-server contact** *text*
Configure the SNMP device location	Router(config)# **snmp-server location** *text*
Configure the SNMP device serial number	Router(config)# **snmp-server chassis-id** *number*
Create and configure an SNMP view	Router(config)# **snmp-server view** *view-name oid-tree* [**included** | **excluded**]
Create and configure an SNMP community	Router(config)# **snmp-server community** *string* [**view** *view-name*] [**ro** | **rw**] [*access-list-number*]

Table 10-20 *Command Reference*

Task	Command Syntax
Create and configure an SNMP v3 group	Router(config)# **snmp-server group** *group-name* {**v3** {**auth** | **noauth** | **priv**}} [**read** *read-view*] [**write** *write-view*] [**notify** *notify-view*] [**access** [*acl-number* | *acl-name*]]
Create and configure an SNMP v3 user	Router(config)# **snmp-server user** *username group-name* [**remote host** [**udp-port** *port*]] {**v3** [**encrypted**] [**auth** {**md5** | **sha**} *auth-password*]} [**priv** {**des** | **3des** | **aes** {**128** | **192** |**256**}} *privpassword*]
Configure the local EngineID	Router(config)# **snmp-server engineID local** *engineid-string*
Configure a remote EngineID	Router(config)# **snmp-server engineID remote** {*ipv4-ip-address* | *ipv6-address*}[**udp-port** *udp-port-number*] *engineid-string*
Configure a remote SNMP v3 user	Router(config)# **snmp-server user** *username group-name* **remote** *host* [**udp-port** *port*]{**v3** [**encrypted**] [**auth** {**md5** | **sha**} *auth-password*]} [**priv** {**des** | **3des** | **aes** {**128** | **192** |**256**}} *privpassword*]
Configure an SNMP notification host (trap or inform)	Router(config)# **snmp-server host** {*hostname* | *ip-address*} [**traps** | **informs**] [**version** {**1** | **2c** | **3** [**auth** | **noauth** | **priv**]}] {*community-string* | *username*}[**udp-port** *port*] [*notification-type*]
Configure the notification types to be sent in a trap or inform (this command works with both traps and informs; the configuration of the **snmp-server** host command dictates which type is sent)	Router(config)# **snmp-server enable traps** [*notification-type*]
Configure the use of a rising (and falling, if needed) CPU threshold	Router(config)# **process cpu threshold type** {**total** | **process** | **interrupt**} **rising** *percentage* **interval** *seconds* [**falling** *fall-percentage* **interval** *seconds*]
Configure the use of an SNMP trap (or inform) should a CPU threshold message be triggered	Router(config)# **snmp-server enable traps cpu threshold**
Configure the use of a memory threshold message should the device memory go below the configured level	Router(config)# **memory free low-water-mark** {**processor** *threshold* | **io** *threshold*}

Table 10-20 *Command Reference*

Task	Command Syntax
Configure a memory reserve that is used to ensure that critical notifications can be sent	Router(config)# **memory reserve critical** *kilobytes*
Configure a specific interface to be specified for management traffic using Management Plane Protection (MPP)	Router(config-cp-host)# **management-interface** *interface* **allow** *protocols*
Secure the device according to the previous guidelines	Router# **auto secure [management | forwarding] [no-interact | full] [ntp | login | ssh | firewall | tcp-intercept]**
Display the current privilege level	Router# **show privilege**
Display the current CLI view	Router# **show parser view**
Display the configuration information about the device lines	Router# **show line**
Display information about the currently active SSH sessions	Router# **show ssh**
Display information about the current SSH configuration	Router# **show ip ssh**
Display the current SNMP contact information	Router# **show snmp contact**
Display the current SNMP device location	Router# **show snmp location**
Display the current SNMP device serial number	Router# **show snmp chassis**
Display information about the currently configured SNMP views	Router# **show snmp view**
Display information about the currently configured SNMP communities	Router# **show snmp community**
Display the currently configured SNMP groups	Router# **show snmp group**
Display the currently configured SNMP users	Router# **show snmp user**
Display the currently configured engineIDs	Router# **show snmp engineID**
Display the currently configured notification hosts	Router# **show snmp host**
Display the currently configured management interface and protocols allowed	Router# **show management-interface** [*interface* | **protocol** *protocol-name*]
Display the AutoSecure configurations	Router# **show auto secure config**

Fill in the Blanks

1. The highest available configuration mode is _____, which is used to configure feature options for the entire device.

2. When using the **enable secret** command, the password is secured using the _____ algorithm.

3. Role-based CLI access provides the ability to set up as many as _____ CLI views, which are configured to run commands that are configured for different job functions.

4. The configuration of SSH without the use of labels requires that the _____ and _____ be configured first.

5. The _____ is a virtual information storage location that contains collections of managed objects.

6. The _____ and _____ versions of SNMP utilize community name-based security.

7. The _____ SNMP security model supports both authentication and encryption.

8. _____ gives you the ability to limit the source of management traffic to a specific interface on a device.

9. Cisco recommends that the _____ feature not be used in production environments.

10. A _____ threshold is triggered when the CPU utilization exceeds a configured threshold.

This chapter covers the following subject:

■ **Network Address Translation (NAT):** Describes the different types of NAT available and discusses how to configure them to meet the requirements of modern networks.

CHAPTER 11

Implementing and Configuring Network Address Translation (NAT)

The use of Network Address Translation (NAT) is widespread; it is used by millions of people every day, most without knowing it. The understanding of how NAT works is a vital part of securing a network because so many networks use its abilities. This chapter reviews the different types of NAT that are available and displays examples of how each of them would be configured in operation.

"Do I Know This Already?" Quiz

The "Do I Know This Already?" quiz helps you decide whether you really need to read the entire chapter. If you already intend to read the entire chapter, you do not necessarily need to answer these questions now.

The nine-question quiz, derived from the major sections in the "Foundation Topics" section of this chapter, helps you determine how to spend your limited study time.

Table 11-1 outlines the major topics discussed in this chapter and the "Do I Know This Already?" quiz questions that correspond to those topics.

Table 11-1 *"Do I Know This Already?" Foundation Topics Section-to-Question Mapping*

Foundation Topics Section	Questions Covered in This Section
Network Address Translation (NAT)	1–9

Caution: The goal of self-assessment is to gauge your mastery of the topics in this chapter. If you do not know the answer to a question or are only partially sure of the answer, you should mark this question wrong for purposes of the self-assessment. Giving yourself credit for an answer that you correctly guess skews your self-assessment results and might provide you with a false sense of security.

1. Which of the following are potential limitations of using NAT?

    a. Embedding address complications

    b. Private address support complications

    c. Logging complications

    d. Overlapping address complications

2. Which of the following are valid NAT interface types?

    a. Inside

    b. Internet

    c. Outside

    d. Broadcast

3. Which of the following NAT address types displays the address of the internal host as seen by external hosts?

    a. Outside global address

    b. Inside local address

    c. Outside local address

    d. Inside global address

4. Which of the following NAT types has a one-to-one relationship without a specific external address?

    a. Static

    b. Dynamic

    c. Overloaded

    d. Overlapping

5. Which command is used to configure static NAT?

    a. **ip nat inside source static** *local-ip remote-ip*

    b. **ip nat inside source static** *remote-ip local-ip*

    c. **ip nat inside static source** *local-ip remote-ip*

    d. **ip nat inside static source** *remote-ip local-ip*

6. Which command is used to configure a NAT pool?

    a. **ip nat pool** *pool-name ip-address* [**netmask** *mask* | **prefix-length** *prefix-length*]

    b. **nat pool** *pool-name start-ip end-ip* [**netmask** *mask* | **prefix-length** *prefix-length*]

    c. **nat pool** *pool-name ip-address* [**netmask** *mask* | **prefix-length** *prefix-length*]

    d. **ip nat pool** *pool-name start-ip end-ip* [**netmask** *mask* | **prefix-length** *prefix-length*]

7. Which of the following can be used as an alternative name for Port Address Translation?

   a. Dynamic NAT

   b. Static NAT

   c. Overloaded NAT

   d. Overlapping NAT

8. What is the default translation timeout when using dynamic NAT?

   a. 60 minutes

   b. 24 hours

   c. 5 minutes

   d. 10 minutes

9. Which command is used to configure an overlapping NAT configuration?

   a. **ip nat outside source static** *local-ip remote-ip*

   b. **ip nat inside source static** *local-ip remote-ip*

   c. **ip nat outside source static** *remote-ip local-ip*

   d. **ip nat inside source static** *remote-ip local-ip*

The answers to the "Do I Know This Already?" quiz are found in Appendix A. The suggested choices for your next step are as follows:

- **7 or less overall score:** Read the entire chapter. This includes the "Foundation Topics" and the "Exam Preparation" sections.

- **8 or 9 overall score:** If you want more review on these topics, skip to the "Exam Preparation" section.

Foundation Topics

Network Address Translation

Network Address Translation (NAT) provides the capability to translate one set of addresses to another; typically, this is done with internal private addresses and external public addresses. This can be used for a number of different reasons, including the ability to separate an internal network from an external one and the ability to translate an entire internal network to a few external addresses. In an environment where the number of Internet users continues to rise at a high rate, the number of IPv4 addresses available to be used has dwindled; it is only through the wide-scale implementation of NAT that has, up to this point, made the continued use of IPv4 addresses still a viable solution.

NAT can be used for many purposes, including the following:

- **Address migration:** If an organization is changing the way that its addresses are organized, an easy way to maintain connectivity is through the use of NAT during the migration.

- **Private address use:** In many organizational networks, it is an advantage to use private address space to have the most addressing flexibility. In these situations, it is required to translate these addresses to global public addresses for public (Internet) traffic.

- **Address overlap:** In some situations, an organization could be using other companies' legitimate public addresses for internal addressing. When these organizations connect to a public network, an address conflict can occur.

- **Load sharing:** It is possible to configure NAT to map a single external address to multiple internal devices; this is used to spread the load of network traffic and processing capability.

As with any technology, the use of NAT can introduce problems because some technologies do not support the use of NAT. These limitations include

- **Embedding address complications:** For the correct operation of NAT, it must understand the source and destination address information for each conversation. Some protocols obscure this information, which can be troublesome.

- **Encryption and authorization protocol support:** Because the point in many of these protocols is to ensure that a packet has not been interfered with in transit, the use of NAT in itself already breaks this requirement because it alters the original packet. Some protocols are likely to fail in situations where traffic traverses a NAT device.

- **Logging complications:** The use of NAT can complicate the way to view and interpret logs. As the address that is used for a specific packet changes from an inside to outside interface, this must be considered when using logging.

With typical NAT implementations, an inside and outside interface is defined. Each interface is described in Table 11-2 and illustrated in Figure 11-1.

Table 11-2 *NAT Interface Types*

Key Topic

Interface Type	Description
Inside Interface (Local)	Connects to the internal network, which is typically a stub network (not connected to the external network in another location).
Outside Interface (Global)	Connects to an external network; in many applications, this external network is also a public (Internet) network.

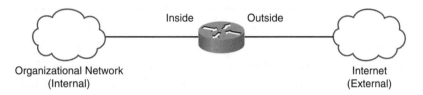

Figure 11-1 *NAT Interfaces*

Along with the NAT interfaces, there are definitions for the different addresses that are used. The typical NAT implementation includes a single internal (local) stub host (or network) that requires translation to an external (global) network. In this situation, the internal network address is referred to as the *inside local address*, and the address used by this host as it appears on the external network is called the *inside global address*. There is also an outside local address and outside global address. The *outside local address* is the address of the destination host address as seen by the local host, and the *outside global address* is the address as it was originally assigned. Table 11-3 describes these addresses.

Table 11-3 *NAT Address Types*

Key Topic

Address Type	Description
Inside local address	This is the address as it was assigned to the inside host.
Inside global address	This is the address of the inside host as seen by all outside hosts.
Outside local address	This is the address of the outside host as seen by all inside hosts.
Outside global address	This is the address as it was assigned to the outside host.

There are also three different types of NAT that can be configured. These include static, dynamic, and overloaded (Port Address Translation [PAT]) NAT, as described in Table 11-4. Static NAT is used when a single one-to-one mapping is required between inside and outside networks.

Table 11-4   *NAT Types*

NAT Type	Description
Static NAT	Used when a one-to-one static relationship is required between an inside and outside address.
Dynamic NAT	Used when a one-to-one relationship is required but without a static outside address requirement.
Overloaded (PAT)	Used when many internal addresses need to access an external network and few external addresses are available.

Static NAT Example

Figure 11-2 shows an example of static NAT with a connection that is established between the internal host 192.168.1.1 and the external host 64.28.85.16. The external host sees traffic come from the internal host with an address of 209.202.161.1, and the internal host sees the external host traffic as coming from 64.28.85.16 (or the original address without translation).

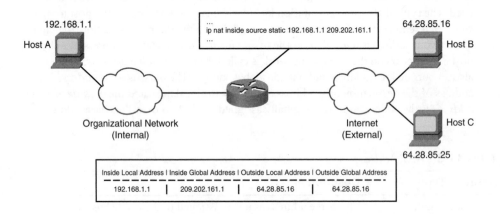

Figure 11-2   *NAT Addresses (Static NAT)*

Dynamic NAT Example

Dynamic NAT is used to map an internal local address to outside addresses by utilizing an outside address pool; in this configuration, there is still a one-to-one address relationship.

Figure 11-3 shows an example of dynamic NAT, with two different connections that include traffic from hosts 192.168.1.1 and 192.168.1.2 going to two different remote hosts 64.28.85.16 and 64.28.85.25. The NAT pool is configured to give out addresses 209.202.161.1 through 209.202.161.10. These addresses from the pool are assigned on a first-come, first-served basis. The host 192.168.1.1 initiates a connection to remote host 64.28.85.16; being the first to request NAT services, the first address from this pool is assigned for use with 192.168.1.1. After this, a connection is initiated from host 192.168.1.2 to the remote host 64.28.85.25; being the second to request NAT services, the second address from the pool is assigned for use with 192.168.1.2. From the perspective of the remote hosts, traffic comes from the addresses 209.202.161.1 (192.168.1.1) and 209.202.161.2 (192.168.1.2). From the perspective of the local hosts, the traffic comes from its original host addresses 64.28.85.16 and 64.28.85.25.

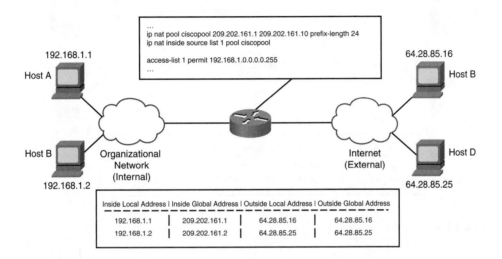

Figure 11-3   *Dynamic NAT*

PAT Example

Overloading, or PAT, is a form of dynamic NAT where multiple internal addresses are mapped to outside addresses by mapping not only the address but also mapping a specific port. In this configuration, the relationship is many-to-one, and each traffic conversation is assigned a specific port on the outside address used. All traffic conversations are kept separate by NAT and redirected to the original source port by NAT.

Figure 11-4 shows an example of overloading NAT (PAT) with two different connections that include traffic from hosts 192.168.1.1 and 192.168.1.2 going to a single remote host at address 64.28.85.16. The NAT pool is configured to give out address 209.202.161.1. This address and port assignments come from the pool on a first-come, first-served basis. The host 192.168.1.1 initiates an HTTP connection to remote host 64.28.85.16; being the first to request NAT services, the first available address/port combination is assigned (209.202.161.1, port 1). After this, the host 192.168.1.2 initiates an HTTP connection to the remote host 64.28.85.16; being the second to request NAT services, the second available address/port combination is assigned (209.202.161.1, port 2). From the perspective of the remote host, both connections come from the same addresses 209.202.161.1 but from different source ports. When the remote host sends back traffic, it will be sent to these separate remote ports; this is how the NAT device differentiates connections. From the perspective of the local hosts, the traffic comes from its original host address 64.28.85.16 and original port.

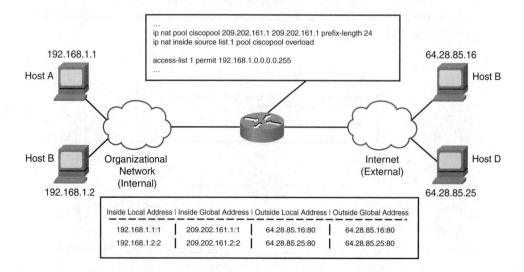

Figure 11-4 *Overloaded NAT (PAT)*

NAT Configuration

The configuration of NAT requires that a few pieces of information be available, including the following:

■ The type of NAT to be used

■ The list of systems requiring NAT services

■ The available addresses that can be used

■ A list of potential problem network applications

■ The location of each host in relation to the NAT device

Each NAT type requires a slightly different configuration that provides the correct NAT capabilities.

Figure 11-5 shows an example of a common configuration topology.

Static NAT Configuration

The configuration of static NAT requires a local address (inside local address) that will be translated and an external address (inside global address) that will be used in place of this local address on the outside network. Table 11-5 describes the different commands that are required to configure static NAT.

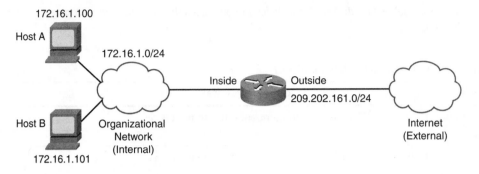

Figure 11-5 *Common Configuration Topology*

Table 11-5 *Configuring Static NAT*

Task	Command Syntax
Configure the inside NAT interface	Router(config-if)# **ip nat inside**
Configure the outside NAT interface	Router(config-if)# **ip nat outside**
Configure static NAT	Router(config)# **ip nat inside source static** *local-ip remote-ip*
Display the currently configured NAT translations	Router# **show ip nat translations**
Display the NAT translation actions as they occur	Router# **debug ip nat**

Example 11-1 shows the configuration of static NAT. The fastethernet0/0 interface is the inside interface, and the fastethernet0/1 interface is the outside interface. The local IP address 172.16.1.100 (inside local address) will be translated on the outside network to address 209.202.161.100 (inside global address).

Example 11-1 *Configuring Static NAT*

```
Router# configure terminal
Router(config)# ip nat inside source static 172.16.1.100 209.202.161.100
Router(config)# interface fastethernet0/0
Router(config-if)# ip nat inside
Router(config-if)# interface fastethernet0/1
Router(config-if)# ip nat outside
```

Dynamic NAT Configuration

The configuration of dynamic NAT is different because it requires the local addresses (inside local addresses) that will be translated and the external addresses (inside global addresses) that will be used in place of these local addresses on the outside network. With dynamic NAT, the source addresses are identified through the use of a standard IP access control list (ACL). The addresses to be used as the external addresses will be defined in a

NAT pool. Table 11-6 describes the different commands that are required to configure dynamic NAT.

Table 11-6 *Configuring Dynamic NAT*

Task	Command Syntax
Configure the inside NAT interface	Router(config-if)# **ip nat inside**
Configure the outside NAT interface	Router(config-if)# **ip nat outside**
Create a NAT pool	Router(config)# **ip nat pool** *pool-name start-ip end-ip* [**netmask** *netmask* | **prefix-length** *prefix-length*]
Create a standard IP access list	Router(config)# **access-list** *access-list-number* **permit** *source* [*source-wildcard-mask*]
Configure dynamic NAT	Router(config)# **ip nat inside source list** *access-list-number* **pool** *pool-name*
Display the currently configured NAT translations	Router# **show ip nat translations**
Display the NAT translation actions as they occur	Router# **debug ip nat**

Example 11-2 shows the configuration of dynamic NAT. The fastethernet0/0 interface is the inside interface, and the fastethernet0/1 interface is the outside interface. All addresses with a source address in the 172.16.1.0/24 network (inside local addresses) will be translated using NAT. The address range from 209.202.161.100 through 209.202.161.110 will be used for external addresses (inside global addresses); these are allocated in a first-come, first-served fashion. In this case, the first ten hosts that require a NAT translation will be successful, but the 11th host would be unsuccessful because no address would be available.

Example 11-2 *Configuring Dynamic NAT*

```
Router# configure terminal
Router(config)# access-list 1 permit 172.16.1.0 0.0.0.255
Router(config)# ip nat pool addresspool 209.202.161.100 209.202.161.110 prefix-
   length 24
Router(config)# ip nat inside source list 1 pool addresspool
Router(config)# interface fastethernet0/0
Router(config-if)# ip nat inside
Router(config-if)# interface fastethernet0/1
Router(config-if)# ip nat outside
```

Overloading NAT (PAT) Configuration

The configuration of overloading NAT is similar to that of dynamic NAT but works quite differently. When using overloading NAT, instead of having a one-to-one addressing relationship, multiple internal hosts share the same external address or addresses and are differentiated by the source port number allocated by the NAT device. As with dynamic NAT configuration, a standard IP access list is used to identify the source addresses to be translated. A pool is also configured with the available external addresses; however, unlike with dynamic NAT, a single address can be configured in the pool that can be used for multiple internal hosts. Table 11-7 describes the different commands that are required to configure PAT.

Table 11-7 *Configuring PAT*

Task	Command Syntax
Configure the inside NAT interface	Router(config-if)# **ip nat inside**
Configure the outside NAT interface	Router(config-if)# **ip nat outside**
Create a NAT pool	Router(config)# **ip nat pool** *pool-name start-ip end-ip* [**netmask** *netmask* | **prefix-length** *prefix-length*]
Create a standard IP access list	Router(config)# **access-list** *access-list-number* **permit** *source* [*source-wildcard-mask*]
Configure overloading NAT	Router(config)# **ip nat inside source list** *access-list-number* **pool** *pool-name* **overload**
Display the currently configured NAT translations	Router# **show ip nat translations**
Display the NAT translation actions as they occur	Router# **debug ip nat**

Example 11-3 shows the configuration of overloading NAT. The fastethernet0/0 interface is the inside interface, and the fastethernet0/1 interface is the outside interface. All addresses with a source address in the 17216.1.0/24 network (inside local addresses) will be translated using NAT. The address 209.202.161.100 will be used for the external address (inside global address). With each connection translated, a different source port number is assigned using the address in the pool; this enables the NAT device to distinguish the connections from each other.

Example 11-3 *Configuring Overloading NAT*

```
Router# configure terminal
Router(config)# access-list 1 permit 172.16.1.0 0.0.0.255
Router(config)# ip nat pool addresspool 209.202.161.100 209.202.161.100 prefix-
  length 24
```

```
Router(config)# ip nat inside source list 1 pool addresspool overload
Router(config)# interface fastethernet0/0
Router(config-if)# ip nat inside
Router(config-if)# interface fastethernet0/1
Router(config-if)# ip nat outside
```

NAT Timer Configuration

The amount of time that a specific NAT translation entry is assigned depends on the type of NAT that has been configured. By default, translation entry timeout is 24 hours with dynamic NAT. With overloading NAT, the translation entry timeout period depends on the specific protocol being translated. By default, the timeouts described in Table 11-8 are used.

Key Topic

Table 11-8 *Overloading NAT Timeouts*

Protocol	Timeout
UDP	5 minutes
TCP (Established Port)	24 hours
SYN	1 minute
FIN/RST	1 minute
DNS	1 minute
ICMP	1 minute

To change the timeouts from their defaults, use the commands outlined in Table 11-9.

Table 11-9 *Configuring NAT Timeouts*

Task	Command Syntax
Change the default dynamic translation timeout	Router(config)# **ip nat translation timeout** *seconds*
Change the default overloading User Datagram Protocol (UDP) timeout	Router(config)# **ip nat translation udp-timeout** *seconds*
Change the default overloading TCP port timeout	Router(config)# **ip nat translation tcp-timeout** *seconds*
Change the default overloading SYN timeout	Router(config)# **ip nat translation syn-timeout** *seconds*
Change the default overloading FIN/RST timeout	Router(config)# **ip nat translation finrst-timeout** *seconds*
Change the default overloading Domain Name System (DNS) timeout	Router(config)# **ip nat translation dns-timeout** *seconds*

Table 11-9 *Configuring NAT Timeouts*

Task	Command Syntax
Change the default overloading Internet Control Message Protocol (ICMP) timeout	Router(config)# **ip nat translation icmp-timeout** *seconds*

Overlapping NAT

With overlapping NAT, the internal addresses used could potentially overlap with external addresses (this is typical if internal addressing was assigned before an Internet connection was considered); this requires that the NAT configuration be altered. This is because with a typical NAT configuration, the internal network hosts see the unaltered external addresses. If there is an overlap and a connection is attempted to a remote device with one of the overlapping addresses, there will be a connection problem. The typical connection setup for a host would be to perform a DNS lookup of the specific external host. If no extra configuration is given, the address returned will be an address that the internal host sees as being on the internal network; a connection will then be attempted but to the internal host with the same overlapping address. Overlapping NAT configuration offers a solution to this problem. When configured, the NAT device will monitor the DNS traffic to and from the configured overlapping address or addresses. When a conflict occurs, the NAT device will alter the DNS response so that the internal client will not see it as a conflict. Traffic going to the altered DNS response IP will then be translated back as the connection is established.

Figure 11-6 shows a configuration where the internal host A has an address of 192.168.1.1 that conflicts with an external host C address, which is also assigned 192.168.1.1. When host A performs a DNS lookup for host C, the DNS response will be altered so that the internal host sees the address for host C as being 172.16.1.1. Traffic from host A will then be directed at 172.16.1.1 for host C, which is translated again on the NAT device to 192.168.1.1.

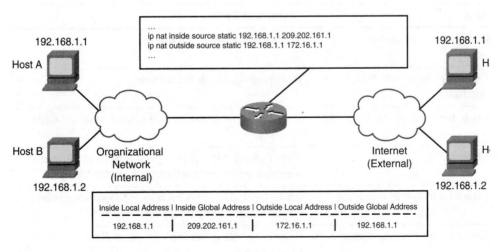

Figure 11-6 *Overlapping NAT*

The end result of this example would be that the traffic from host A to the NAT device would be using addresses 192.168.1.1 (host A) and 172.16.1.1; the traffic from the NAT device to host C would be using addresses 209.202.161.1 and 192.168.1.1 (host C). The translation happens in two different directions: outbound (toward host C) through the first command and inbound (toward host A) by the second command.

Tip: Trying to get your head around overlapping address examples can be difficult. The best way to get it straight is to perform a test in a lab environment.

Overlapping NAT Configuration

The configuration of overlapping NAT can be confusing because the configuration uses aspects of a typical NAT configuration as well as the configuration dealing with the overlapping address problems.

The configurations specific to the overlapping address problem are covered here because the other aspect of the configuration is covered in detail in previous sections. The configuration of an outside NAT command is similar to that of the inside NAT command, except instead of altering the inside source addresses to appear differently to the outside, the outside addresses are altered to appear differently to the inside. The other difference is in how the NAT device automatically alters DNS responses; this is not part of the inside NAT commands.

The overlapping NAT configuration can be configured statically or dynamically, as with typical NAT configurations.

Table 11-10 describes the different commands that are required to configure overlapping NAT.

Table 11-10   *Configuring Overlapping NAT*

Task	Command Syntax
Configure the inside NAT interface	Router(config-if)# **ip nat inside**
Configure the outside NAT interface	Router(config-if)# **ip nat outside**
Configure overlapping static NAT	Router(config)# **ip nat outside source static** *local-ip remote-ip*
Create a NAT pool	Router(config)# **ip nat pool** *pool-name start-ip end-ip* [**netmask** *netmask* | **prefix-length** *prefix-length*]
Create a standard IP access list	Router(config)# **access-list** *access-list-number* **permit** *source* [*source-wildcard-mask*]
Configure overlapping dynamic NAT	Router(config)# **ip nat outside source list** *access-list-number* **pool** *pool-name*

Table 11-10 *Configuring Overlapping NAT*

Task	Command Syntax
Display the currently configured NAT translations	Router# **show ip nat translations**
Display the NAT translation actions as they occur	Router# **debug ip nat**

Example 11-4 shows the configuration of overlapping dynamic NAT. In this example, all traffic from the outside interface (outside global addresses) will be translated to all inside hosts as from the 172.16.1.1–172.16.1.10 range (outside local addresses).

Example 11-4 *Configuring Overlapping Dynamic NAT*

```
Router# configure terminal
Router(config)# access-list 1 permit 192.168.1.0 0.0.0.255
Router(config)# ip nat pool addresspool 172.16.1.1 172.16.1.10 prefix-length 24
Router(config)# ip nat outside source list 1 pool addresspool
Router(config)# interface fastethernet0/0
Router(config-if)# ip nat inside
Router(config-if)# interface fastethernet0/1
Router(config-if)# ip nat outside
```

Exam Preparation

As mentioned in the section, "How to Use This Book," in the Introduction, you have several choices for exam preparation: the exercises here, the memory tables in Appendix C, the final exam preparation chapter, and the exam simulation questions on the CD-ROM. The following questions present a bigger challenge than the exam itself because they use an open-ended question format. By using this more difficult format, you exercise your memory better and prove your conceptual and factual knowledge of this chapter. You can find the answers to these questions in Appendix A, "Answers to the DIKTA Quizzes and Fill in the Blanks Questions."

Review All Key Topics

Review the most important topics in the chapter, noted with the Key Topics icon in the margin of the page. Table 11-11 lists a reference of these key topics and the page numbers on which each is found.

Table 11-11 *Key Topics*

Key Topic Element	Description	Page
Table 11-2	NAT interface types	279
Table 11-3	NAT address types	279
Table 11-4	NAT types	280
List	NAT information requirements	282
Table 11-8	Overloading NAT timeouts	286

Complete Tables and Lists from Memory

Print a copy of Appendix C, "Memory Tables" (found on the CD), or at least the section for this chapter, and complete the tables and lists from memory. Appendix D, "Memory Table Answers," also on the CD, includes completed tables and lists to check your work.

Define Key Terms

Define the following key terms from this chapter, and check your answers in the Glossary:

inside local address, inside global address, outside local address, outside global address, static NAT, dynamic NAT, PAT

Use Command Reference to Check Your Memory

Table 11-12 lists the important commands from this chapter. To test your memory, cover the right side of the table with a piece of paper, read the description on the left side, and then see how much of the command you can remember.

Table 11-12 *Command Reference*

Task	Command Syntax
Configure the inside NAT interface	Router(config-if)# **ip nat inside**
Configure the outside NAT interface	Router(config-if)# **ip nat outside**
Configure static NAT	Router(config)# **ip nat inside source static** *local-ip remote-ip*
Create a NAT pool	Router(config)# **ip nat pool** *pool-name start-ip end-ip* [**netmask** *netmask* | **prefix-length** *prefix-length*]
Create a standard IP access list	Router(config)# **access-list** *access-list-number* **permit** *source* [*source-wildcard-mask*]
Configure dynamic NAT	Router(config)# **ip nat inside source list** *access-list-number* **pool** *pool-name*
Configure overloading NAT	Router(config)# **ip nat inside source list** *access-list-number* **pool** *pool-name* **overload**
Change the default dynamic translation timeout	Router(config)# **ip nat translation timeout** *seconds*
Change the default overloading UDP timeout	Router(config)# **ip nat translation udp-timeout** *seconds*
Change the default overloading TCP port timeout	Router(config)# **ip nat translation tcp-timeout** *seconds*
Change the default overloading SYN timeout	Router(config)# **ip nat translation syn-timeout** *seconds*
Change the default overloading FIN/RST timeout	Router(config)# **ip nat translation finrst-timeout** *seconds*
Change the default overloading DNS timeout	Router(config)# **ip nat translation dns-timeout** *seconds*
Change the default overloading ICMP timeout	Router(config)# **ip nat translation icmp-timeout** *seconds*
Configure overlapping static NAT	Router(config)# **ip nat outside source static** *local-ip remote-ip*
Display the currently configured NAT translations	Router# **show ip nat translations**
Display the NAT translation actions as they occur	Router# **debug ip nat**

Fill in the Blanks

1. A typical NAT implementation includes a single _____ stub host that requires translation to an _____ network.

2. Three different types of NAT can be configured: _____, _____, and _____.

3. _____ has a many-to-one relationship with traffic conversations being differentiated by port number.

4. The configuration of _____ requires a local address that will be translated and an external address that will be used in place of this local address on the external network.

5. With dynamic NAT, the source address(es) is/are identified through the use of a _____.

6. By default, the translation entry timeout is _____ with dynamic NAT.

7. In a typical NAT configuration, the internal network hosts see the external host address _____.

This chapter covers the following subjects:

- **Zone-based policy firewall overview:** Describes the different types of NAT that are available and discusses how to configure them to meet the requirements of modern networks.

- **Zone-based Layer 3/4 policy firewall configuration:** Describes the concepts and configuration required for a Layer 3/4 firewall.

- **Zone-based Layer 7 policy firewall configuration:** Describes the concepts and configuration required for a Layer 7 firewall.

Implementing and Configuring Zone-Based Policy Firewalls

One of the most important pieces in securing a network is the implementation of a firewall. This system provides a wall of protection between the sensitive data held inside the organizational network and the potential outside attackers. Although it is only one of the pieces, it is important that the firewall be designed and implemented to mitigate a number of different potential threats. This chapter reviews the options that are available when designing and implementing a Cisco Zone-Based Policy Firewall.

"Do I Know This Already?" Quiz

The "Do I Know This Already?" quiz helps you decide whether you really need to read the entire chapter. If you already intend to read the entire chapter, you do not necessarily need to answer these questions now.

The ten-question quiz, derived from the major sections in the "Foundation Topics" section of this chapter, helps you determine how to spend your limited study time.

Table 12-1 outlines the major topics discussed in this chapter and the "Do I Know This Already?" quiz questions that correspond to those topics.

Table 12-1 *"Do I Know This Already?" Foundation Topics Section-to-Question Mapping*

Foundation Topics Section	Questions Covered in This Section
Zone-Based Policy Firewall Overview	1–4
Zone-Based Layer 3/4 Policy Firewall Configuration	5–8
Zone-Based Layer 7 Policy Firewall Configuration	9–10

Caution: The goal of self-assessment is to gauge your mastery of the topics in this chapter. If you do not know the answer to a question or are only partially sure of the answer, you should mark this question wrong for purposes of the self-assessment. Giving yourself credit for an answer that you correctly guess skews your self-assessment results and might provide you with a false sense of security.

1. The Context-Based Access Control (CBAC) applies policies using which of the following?

    a. **inspect** statements

    b. **cbac-policy** statements

    c. ACLs on interfaces

    d. ACLs on zones

2. ZBPFW applies using which of the following?

    a. MQC

    b. AIC

    c. ACLs

    d. C3PL

3. Traffic between zones is only permitted when?

    a. A zone pair is configured.

    b. The zone is configured.

    c. The zone is assigned to an interface.

    d. The ZBPFW feature is enabled.

4. Traffic that is sourced and destined within the same zone can be configured when using at least which IOS version?

    a. 12.4.24T

    b. 15.1.0M

    c. 15.0.1M

    d. 12.3.10

5. A parameter map is applied inside which of the following?

    a. Class map

    b. Service map

    c. Interface

    d. Policy map

6. Which of the following are valid methods for matching traffic with a class map?

    a. **match-all**

    b. **match-same**

    c. **match-any**

    d. **match-none**

7. Which of the following are valid inspect policy map actions?

  a. police

  b. ignore

  c. inspect

  d. deny

8. To configure the ZBPFW for management and control plane traffic, which of the following zones is used?

  a. Manage

  b. Self

  c. Router

  d. Entity

9. Which of the following are supported AIC protocols?

  a. AOL Instant Messenger

  b. TFTP

  c. MGCP

  d. H.323

10. Which of the following parameter map types is used along with HTTP inspection?

  a. GLOB

  b. Shell

  c. regex

  d. inspect

The answers to the "Do I Know This Already?" quiz are found in Appendix A. The suggested choices for your next step are as follows:

■ **8 or less overall score:** Read the entire chapter. This includes the "Foundation Topics" and the "Exam Preparation" sections.

■ **9 or 10 overall score:** If you want more review on these topics, skip to the "Exam Preparation" section.

Foundation Topics

Zone-Based Policy Firewall Overview

The Zone-Based Policy Firewall (ZBPFW) is the next Cisco implementation of a router-based firewall that runs in Cisco IOS Software. It was introduced in IOS Release 12.4(6)T and takes advantage of many new features that make the configuration and implementation of a firewall easier than was available previously.

The first obvious questions are "What is a firewall used for?" and "How does it perform its function?" A firewall is used to enforce an access policy between security domains. With the ZBPFW feature, these domains are represented by security zones. The previous Cisco IOS firewall feature was called Context-Based Access Control (CBAC), which applied policies through inspect statements and configured access control lists (ACL) between interfaces. ZBPFW applies policies using the Cisco Common Classification Policy Language (C3PL), which closely resembles the Modular QoS Command-Line Interface (MQC) structure. Security classification with C3PL is done through the use of class maps, which are then combined into a security policy that uses policy maps. These policy maps are then applied to a specific security zone pair.

As was supported by CBAC, the ZBPFW supports stateful inspection as well as Application Inspection and Control (AIC), which is also referred to as *Deep Packet Inspection (DPI)*. This includes inspection support for Layers 3 through 7.

Stateful inspection offers the capability to track the connection status of active connections going between the configured zone pair. The connections through the firewall can be tracked by inspecting the setup communications between the source and destination as well as using many other traffic attributes. The tracking database can also be used to allow valid return inbound connections back through the firewall.

AIC provides the ability to perform in-memory reassembly of Layer 4 sessions to obtain stream information between the two connected hosts. It also provides the ability to monitor application layer protocol information and verify that this information is conforming to established standards.

Note: When using both ACLs and zone policies, the ACLs will be considered before any zone polices will be enforced.

Zones/Security Zones

As mentioned previously, one of the main differences between a firewall using CBAC and ZBPFW is the use of *security zones*. These zones separate the specific security areas within a network. Each organization has its own specific security divisions that must be defined before the implementation of a ZBPFW is successful. A typical example would be a firewall that touches three main security zones:

- **Internal:** Internal organizational network

- **DMZ:** Where publicly available servers are located

- **External:** Includes all outside destinations

Figure 12-1 illustrates these three main security zones.

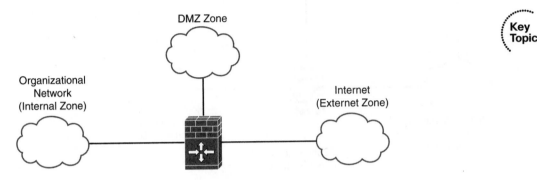

Key
Topic

Figure 12-1   *Basic Zones*

After the zones are created, the interfaces are then assigned to their specific zones, and traffic in and out of each zone interface is controlled by zone policy. A number of rules are used by default when configuring a ZBPFW, including the following:

- Intrazone traffic is freely permitted by default; only IOS Release 15.0.1M and higher will support intrazone policies.

Key
Topic

- Interzone traffic is not permitted by default; traffic is allowed only when configured within a zone policy.

- Interfaces are not required to be a member of a zone; however, traffic will not be permitted between an interface in a zone and an interface not in a zone regardless of policy.

ZBPFW is also Virtual Routing and Forwarding (VRF) aware and can be used between different VRFs. Interfaces that are configured in different VRFs should not be configured in the same zone, and thus all interfaces that are in a zone must be configured within the same VRF. If there is a common interface or interfaces that are used by multiple VRFs, a common zone should be created and individually paired with each zone (and thus with each VRF).

Zone Pairs

Traffic policy is applied unidirectionally between zones using zone pairs. When traffic needs to flow between zones, a zone pair is set up in the direction of the traffic flow. If a bidirectional traffic flow is required, two zone pairs are required, one in each direction. This second zone pair is not required if using stateful inspection and the only expected traffic is return traffic. The second zone pair is not required because this traffic is permitted by default. Figure 12-2 displays a possible configuration when using the three zones described in the previous section.

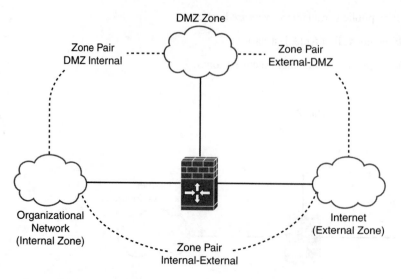

Figure 12-2 *Zone Pairs*

Zone pairs can also be set up to protect the control and management planes. This is done through the use of the system-defined self zone. The self zone includes all traffic that is directed at the device directly or traffic that is generated by the device, as illustrated in Figure 12-3. As with other zones, the self zone can be used as both the source or destination zone and is also configured unidirectionally.

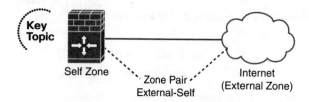

Figure 12-3 *Self Zone Zone Pair*

Prior to IOS Release 15.0.1M, all traffic that was sourced and destined for devices inside the same zone was freely permitted. With this IOS release, the ability to configure a zone pair with the same zone as both source and destination is possible; this enables you to apply policies for traffic traveling within the same zone across the device, as illustrated in Figure 12-4.

Transparent Firewalls

The ZBPFW also supports transparent firewalls, which utilize the bridging interface mode capability. After the bridge mode is configured, these bridged interfaces are then configured in the same way as with routed interfaces by placing the bridged interface into a zone. One big restriction with a transparent firewall is that Network-Based Application Recognition (NBAR) cannot be used.

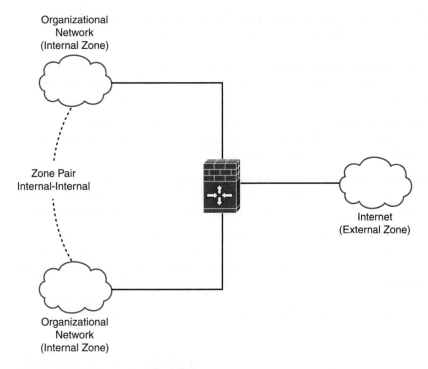

Figure 12-4   *Intrazone Zone Pair*

Zone-Based Layer 3/4 Policy Firewall Configuration

As stated previously, the configuration of ZBPFW uses the Cisco Common Classification Policy Language (C3PL). This structure should be familiar to many people because it closely resembles Modular Quality of Service Command-Line Interface (MQC). For ZBPFW, a class map is created to match the specific traffic that will be subject to the firewall policy. For Layer 3 and 4 traffic, this is done through the matching of a protocol or access group (ACL) or through a second nested class map. A policy is then created and an action assigned to the traffic matched with the class map.

A default class map is also supported that enables the creation of a *catchall* rule that is applied should the traffic not match any configured class map. This is useful when specific traffic is required to be dropped while all other permitted traffic needs to be inspected.

The default parameters of inspect type class and policy maps are often used because the parameters are correctly set for many situations. When these parameters need to be changed, a parameter map can be created and applied to the inspect action inside a policy map.

The ZBPFW feature also supports the use of Port to Application Matching (PAM). This feature can be used when nonstandard ports are used for common services. For example, if HTTP is configured to be used on port 8000 instead of 80, with PAM, port 8000 can be mapped as an HTTP port and be analyzed as a normal HTTP connection.

As with all configurations, a number of pieces of information are required before configuration should begin. For ZBPFW, these include

- **Security zone separation policy:** The specific zones that will be used within the organizational network must be researched and mapped out before configuration should continue.

- **Access rule definition:** After the specific zones have been defined, the rules that will be configured should be mapped out to ensure both the highest level of security and full operation of existing applications.

- **Dynamic application requirements definition:** Many protocols are dynamic in how they operate and are inspected in different ways. The requirements for these applications should be mapped out before the firewall is configured to ensure operability.

- **Management access requirements:** It is vital that the device itself has the highest level of security because it controls the access to the entire network. The specific management requirements for the device should be defined to ensure the security and access to the device.

Figure 12-5 will be used for the configurations displayed in the following sections.

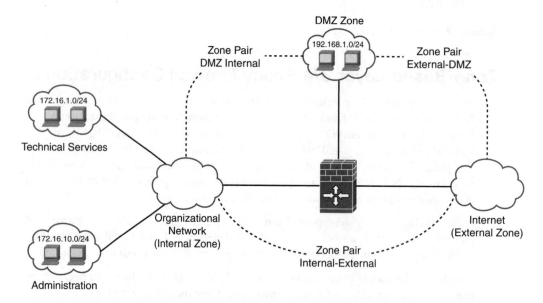

Figure 12-5 *Common Configuration Design*

Class Map Configuration

The traffic matched using a class map can be based on the protocol or access group (ACL) or through a second nested class map. With Layer 3 and 4 traffic, the class map type is always the inspect type. When configuring the **class-map** command, there are two different methods of matching traffic, which include the following parameters:

- **match-any:** When using the **match-any** parameter, traffic that meets any of the configured match criteria will be matched and be subject to the associated policy.

- **match-all:** When using the **match-all** parameter, for the traffic to be matched and be subject to the associated policy, it must match every **match** command.

Another important thing to keep in mind when using the **match-any** parameter is to make sure that the more specific **match** commands are entered before any less specific ones in order. This is to ensure that the traffic is handled and inspected in the most detailed way possible.

Table 12-1 displays the commands that can be used to configure a ZBPFW class map. The **class-map** command and at least one of the **match** commands are required.

Table 12-1   *Configuring a Layer 3/4 Class Map*

Task	Command Syntax
Create and configure a ZBPFW class map	Router(config)# **class-map type inspect** [**match-any** | **match-all**] *class-map-name*
Use an existing access list as matching criteria	Router(config-cmap)# **match access-group** [*access-group* | **name** *access-group-name*]
Match based on the specified protocol	Router(config-cmap)# **match protocol** *protocol-name*
Match based on the criteria defined in another existing class map	Router(config-cmap)# **match class-map** *class-map-name*
Display the currently configured inspect type class maps	Router# **show class-map type inspect**

Example 12-1 shows the configuration of a class map named DMZ-Internal-class. This matches traffic based on access list 150 *and* FTP as well as a class map named Internal-DMZ-class, which matches traffic based on access list 151 *and* FTP. This specifies the traffic that will be allowed between the DMZ and the internal zone.

Example 12-1   *Configuring a Layer 3/4 Class Map (DMZ-Internal)*

```
Router# configure terminal
Router(config)# access-list 150 permit any 192.168.1.0 255.255.255.0
Router(config)# access-list 151 permit 192.168.1.0 255.255.255.0 any
Router(config)# class-map type inspect DMZ-Internal-class
Router(config-cmap)# match access-group 150
Router(config-cmap)# match protocol ftp
```

```
Router(config)# class-map type inspect Internal-DMZ-class
Router(config-cmap)# match access-group 151
Router(config-cmap)# match protocol ftp
```

Example 12-2 shows the configuration of a class map named External-DMZ-class that matches traffic based on HTTP. This specifies the traffic that will be allowed between the external zone and the DMZ.

Example 12-2 *Configuring a Layer 3/4 Class Map (External-DMZ)*

```
Router# configure terminal
Router(config)# class-map type inspect External-DMZ-class
Router(config-cmap)# match protocol http
```

Example 12-3 shows the configuration of a class map named Internal-External-class that matches traffic based on protocols AOL and ICQ (instant messengers) and IRC (relay chat). This specifies the traffic that will be allowed between the internal zone and the external zone.

Example 12-3 *Configuring a Layer 3/4 Class Map (Internal-External)*

```
Router# configure terminal
Router(config)# class-map type inspect Internal-External-class
Router(config-cmap)# match protocol aol
Router(config-cmap)# match protocol icq
Router(config-cmap)# match protocol irc
```

Parameter Map Configurations

When using the inspect type policy map, the creation of a parameter map is optional and can be included within the policy map configuration. A number of different parameters can be altered within a parameter map that change the behavior of the stateful inspection engine. Table 12-2 displays the most commonly used parameter options and their default settings.

Table 12-2 *Parameter Map Options*

Task	Default	Command Syntax
Create and configure a parameter map (the default and global parameters were introduced in Release 15.1(1)T)	Not applicable	Router(config)# **parameter-map type inspect** [*parameter-map-name* | **default** | **global**]
Configure logging of the firewall packets (introduced in Release 15.1(1)T)	No logging	Router(config-profile)# **log** {**dropped-packets** {**disable** | **enable**} | **summary** [**flows** *number*] [**time-interval** *seconds*]}

Table 12-2 *Parameter Map Options*

Task	Default	Command Syntax
Enable IOS stateful packet inspection alert messages	Enabled	Router(config-profile)# **alert {on | off}**
Enable audit trail messages	No audit trail	Router(config-profile)# **audit trail {on | off}**
Configure the DNS idle timeout	5	Router(config-profile)# **dns-time-out** *seconds*
Configure the ICMP idle timeout	10	Router(config-profile)# **icmp idle-timeout** *seconds*
Configure the number of existing half-open sessions that are allowed	Unlimited	Router(config-profile)# **max-incomplete {low** *number-of-connections* **| high** *number-of-connections***}**
Configure the number of new un-established half-open sessions that are allowed	None	Router(config-profile)# **one-minute {low** *number-of-connections* **| high** *number-of-connections***}**
Configure the maximum number of sessions that are allowed to exit on a zone pair	Unlimited	Router(config-profile)# **sessions maximum** *sessions*
Configure the TCP-FIN timeout	5	Router(config-profile)# **tcp fin-wait-time** *seconds*
Configure the TCP idle timeout	3600	Router(config-profile)# **tcp idle-time** *seconds*
Configure the threshold and blocking time values for TCP denial of service (DoS) detection	Threshold= unlimited Block-time=0	Router(config-profile)# **tcp max-incomplete host** *threshold* **[block-time** *minutes***]**
Configure the amount of time that is given for a TCP session to be established	30	Router(config-profile)# **tcp syn-wait-time** *seconds*
Disable the TCP invalid window scale option check	Strict mode is enabled, the check is enabled	Router(config-profile)# **tcp window-scale-enforcement loose**
Configure the UDP timeout	30	Router(config-profile)# **udp idle-time** *seconds*
Display the currently configured inspect type parameter maps	—	Router# **show parameter-map type inspect**

Example 12-4 shows the configuration of a parameter map named example-parms that enables IOS stateful packet inspection alert messages.

Example 12-4 *Configuring a Parameter Map*

```
Router# configure terminal
Router(config)# parameter-map type inspect example-parms
Router(config-profile)# alert on
```

Policy Map Configuration

A policy map is used to configure the action that will be taken with the traffic that was matched within the class map configuration. Table 12-3 highlights a limited number of actions that are available when using ZBPFW.

Table 12-3 *Policy Map Actions*

Task	Command Syntax
Enable the use of IOS stateful packet inspection on the matched class map traffic	**inspect**
Pass all matched class map traffic	**pass**
Drop all matched class map traffic	**drop**
Police the amount of bandwidth available to the matched class map traffic	**police**
Nest a Layer 7 policy map inside a Layer 3/4 policy map	**service-policy**

Note: Policing is not permitted on zone pairs that have the self zone as source or destination.

Table 12-4 displays the commands that can be used to configure a ZBPFW policy map. The **policy-map** command and at least one of the **inspect,** pass, drop, or **police** commands is required. To nest a Layer 7 policy map using the **service-policy** command, the inspect action must be configured first.

Table 12-4 *Configuring a Layer 3/4 Policy Map*

Task	Command Syntax
Create and configure a ZBPFW policy map	Router(config)# **policy-map type inspect** *policy-map-name*
Configure a specific class map to be used in the policy	Router(config-pmap)# **class type inspect** *class-name*
Configure stateful packet inspection to be used on the matched traffic	Router(config-pmap-c)# **inspect**

Table 12-4   *Configuring a Layer 3/4 Policy Map*

Task	Command Syntax
Configure the passing of all matched traffic	Router(config-pmap-c)# **pass**
Configure the dropping of all matched traffic and optionally configure the logging of this traffic	Router(config-pmap-c)# **drop [log]**
Configure the policing of the matched traffic	Router(config-pmap-c)# **police rate** *bps* **burst** *size*
Configure a nested Layer 7 policy map (see the "Application of URL Filter" and "Application of HTTP Inspection" sections, later in this chapter, for further configuration)	Router(config-pmap-c)# **service-policy [urlfilter	http	im	imap	pop3	smtp]** *dpi-policy-map-name*
Display the currently configured inspect type policy maps	Router# **show policy-map type inspect**

Example 12-5 shows the configuration of two policies:

■ **DMZ-Internal-policy:** Automatically passes all traffic matched with the DMZ-Internal-class

■ **Internal-DMZ-policy:** Automatically passes all traffic matched with the Internal-DMZ-class

Example 12-5   *Configuring a Layer 3/4 Policy Map (DMZ-Internal)*

```
Router# configure terminal
Router(config)# policy-map type inspect DMZ-Internal-policy
Router(config-pmap)# class type inspect DMZ-Internal-class
Router(config-pmap-c)# pass
Router(config-pmap-c)# policy-map type inspect Internal-DMZ-policy
Router(config-pmap)# class type inspect Internal-DMZ-class
Router(config-pmap-c)# pass
```

Example 12-6 shows the configuration of a policy map named External-DMZ-policy that automatically passes all traffic matched with the External-DMZ-class.

Example 12-6   *Configuring a Layer 3/4 Policy Map (External-DMZ)*

```
Router# configure terminal
Router(config)# policy-map type inspect External-DMZ-policy
Router(config-pmap)# class type inspect External-DMZ-class
Router(config-pmap-c)# pass
```

Example 12-7 shows the configuration of a policy map named Internal-External-policy that automatically drops all traffic matched with the Internal-External-class and inspects all unmatched traffic using the example-parms parameter map.

Example 12-7 *Configuring a Layer 3/4 Policy Map (Internal-External)*

```
Router# configure terminal
Router(config)# policy-map type inspect Internal-External-policy
Router(config-pmap)# class type inspect Internal-External-class
Router(config-pmap-c)# drop
Router(config-pmap)# class class-default
Router(config-pmap-c)# inspect example-parms
```

Zone Configuration

The configuration of the zones is simple because it only requires the creation of the zone itself and the assignment of specific interfaces into the zone.

Table 12-5 displays the commands that can be used to create zones and assign interfaces into their assigned zone.

Table 12-5 *Configuring and Assigning Zones*

Task	Command Syntax
Create and configure a zone	Router(config)# **zone security** *zone-name*
Assign an interface into a specific zone	Router(config-if)# **zone-member security** *zone-name*
Display the currently configured security zones	Router# **show zone security**

Example 12-8 shows the creation of the DMZ, internal, and external zones.

Example 12-8 *Configuring Zones*

```
Router# configure terminal
Router(config)# zone security DMZ
Router(config-sec-zone)# zone security internal
Router(config-sec-zone)# zone security external
```

Example 12-9 shows the assignment of interfaces fastethernet0/0, 0/1, and 0/2 into their respective zones.

Example 12-9 *Assigning Interfaces into Zones*

```
Router# configure terminal
Router(config)# interface fastethernet0/0
Router(config-if)# zone-member security internal
Router(config-if)# interface fastethernet0/1
```

```
Router(config-if)# zone-member security DMZ
Router(config-if)# interface fastethernet0/2
Router(config-if)# zone-member security external
```

Zone Pair Configuration

The configuration of the zone pair is important because its configuration dictates the direction in which traffic is allowed to flow. As stated previously, a zone pair is unidirectional and is the part of the configuration that controls traffic between zones; this is referred to as *interzone*. If no zone pair is defined, traffic will not flow between zones. The only exception to the unidirectional behavior of zone pairs is with return traffic; this traffic is inspected and permitted based on the configured policy. The zone pair can also be configured to control the traffic permitted directly into the device; this includes control and management plane traffic. This is configured by creating a zone pair using the self zone as the source or destination zone. With the release of IOS 15.0.1M, it is also possible to control the traffic within the same zone; this is referred to as *intrazone*. This is configured by creating a zone pair with the same two zone names as both source and destination.

The zone pair configuration is also where the firewall policy is applied. Make sure to associate the correct firewall policy with the correct zone pair.

Table 12-6 displays the commands that can be used to create zone pairs and are used to apply a firewall policy to each specific zone pair.

Table 12-6   *Configuring Zone Pairs and Assigning Firewall Policy*

Task	Command Syntax
Create and configure a zone pair	Router(config)# **zone-pair security** *zone-pair-name* [source *source-zone-name* | **self**] **destination** [*destination-zone-name* | **self**]
Assign a firewall policy to a zone pair	Router(config-sec-zone-pair)# **service-policy type inspect** *policy-map-name*
Display the currently configured security zone pair and assigned firewall policy	Router# **show zone-pair security**

Example 12-10 shows the creation of two zone pairs, one going from the DMZ to the internal zone and the other from the internal zone to the DMZ. Both allow FTP traffic between the DMZ and internal zones in each direction.

Example 12-10   *Configuring Zone Pairs and Assigning Firewall Policy (DMZ-Internal)*

```
Router# configure terminal
Router(config)# zone-pair DMZ-Internal-pair source DMZ destination internal
Router(config-sec-zone-pair)# service-policy type inspect DMZ-Internal-policy
```

```
Router(config-sec-zone-pair)# zone-pair Internal-DMZ-pair source internal
  destination DMZ
Router(config-sec-zone-pair)# service-policy type inspect Internal-DMZ-policy
```

Example 12-11 shows the creation of two zone pairs, one going from the external zone to the DMZ and the other from the DMZ to the external zone. Both allow unrestricted HTTP traffic between the DMZ and internal zone in each direction. It was also possible to configure this differently by inspecting the traffic from the external zone into the DMZ. In this scenario, only one zone pair would be required because the traffic coming into the HTTP server would be monitored and only permitted return traffic would be allowed.

Example 12-11   *Configuring Zone Pairs and Assigning Firewall Policy (External-DMZ)*

```
Router# configure terminal
Router(config)# zone-pair External-DMZ-pair source external destination DMZ
Router(config-sec-zone-pair)# service-policy type inspect External-DMZ-policy
Router(config-sec-zone-pair)# zone-pair DMZ-Internal-pair source DMZ destination
external
Router(config-sec-zone-pair)# service-policy type inspect External-DMZ-policy
```

Example 12-12 shows the creation of a zone pair between the internal zone and external zone and is applied in the direction from the internal zone to the external zone. The Internal-External-policy firewall policy is then applied to the zone pair. In this case, the traffic is inspected, so the second zone pair is not needed for return traffic.

Example 12-12   *Configuring Zone Pair and Assigning Firewall Policy (Internal-External)*

```
Router# configure terminal
Router(config)# zone-pair Internal-External-pair internal DMZ destination external
Router(config-sec-zone-pair)# service-policy type inspect Internal-External-policy
```

Port to Application Mapping (PAM) Configuration

As discussed previously, Port to Application Mapping (PAM) enables you to use nonstandard ports for standard services. For example, if HTTP traffic was going to use port 8080 instead of 80, PAM could be used to associate port 8080 with HTTP. After this configuration is complete, commands such as **match protocol http** could be used to detect traffic on these ports as well as the standard ports.

System-defined port mapping cannot be changed or deleted. This means that, although it is possible to associate HTTP traffic with port 8080, it is not possible to associate it with another well-known port, such as 21 (FTP).

Table 12-7 shows a list of system-defined port mappings.

PAM can be configured in one of two ways:

■   On the service as a whole (all hosts)

■   Host-specific

The host-specific option enables you to associate different ports not only based on their port number but also based on the device. In this situation, port associations could be different from one host to another.

Table 12-7   *System-Defined Port Mappings*

Application	Port
File Transfer Protocol (FTP)	21
Telnet	23
Simple Mail Transfer Protocol (SMTP)	25
Trivial File Transfer Protocol (TFTP)	69
Hypertext Transfer Protocol (HTTP)	80
SUN Remote Procedure Call (sunrpc)	111
Microsoft Remote Procedure Call (msrpc)	135
Remote Process Execution (exec)	512
Remote Login (login)	513
Remote Command (shell)	514
SQL-NET	1521
Streamworks Protocol	1558
H.323	1720
Microsoft Netshow	1755
Media Gateway Control Protocol (MGCP)	2427
Session Initiation Protocol (SIP)	5060
VDOLive Protocol	7000
Realaudio and Realvideo	7070
CU-SeeMe Protocol	7648
Real-Time Streaming Protocol	8559

Table 12-8 displays the commands that can be used to configure PAMs.

Table 12-8   *Configuring PAMs*

Task	Command Syntax
Create a port-mapping entry; utilize an existing ACL to configure host-specific mapping	Router(config)# **ip port-map** *appl_name* **port [tcp	udp]** *port_num* [**list** *acl_num*]
Display information about the currently configured port maps (includes system-defined mappings)	Router# **show ip port-map**

Example 12-13 shows the mapping of the HTTP application to port 8080.

Example 12-13   *Configuring HTTP PAMs*

```
Router# configure terminal
Router(config)# ip port-map http port 8080
```

Zone-Based Layer 7 Policy Firewall Configuration

The use of the Layer 7 policies with a zone-based firewall is also supported. This capability allows the device to control the traffic through attributes that are provided at Layers 5–7. A requirement of these policies is that they must be nested under an existing Layer 3/4 policy map to be applied (using the **service-policy** command) and there must be an **inspect** action configured first.

A number of different protocols are supported using Application Inspection and Control (AIC):

- America Online (AOL) Instant Messenger
- eDonkey P2P protocol
- FastTrack traffic P2P protocol
- Gnutella Version 2 traffic P2P protocol
- H.323 VoIP Protocol version 4
- Hypertext Transfer Protocol (HTTP) (URL filtering and HTTP inspection)
- Internet Message Access Protocol (IMAP)
- I Seek You (ICQ) IM protocol
- Kazaa Version 2 P2P protocol
- MSN Messenger IM protocol
- Post Office Protocol version 3 (POP3)
- Session Initiation Protocol (SIP)
- Simple Mail Transfer Protocol (SMTP)

- Sun RPC (SUNRPC)

- Windows Messenger IM protocol

- Yahoo IM protocol

The URL filter and HTTP inspection features are covered in the following sections.

URL Filter

The URL Filter feature provides the ability to pass, drop, or log the traffic whose URL matches specific configured characteristics. These characteristics can be quite robust, including the capability to match traffic based on something as simple as a domain or something as complex as is provided by category matching (porn, gaming, weapons, and so on). The more complex configurations use an external URL filtering server, including support for Websense and N2H2. Unlike with the simpler Layer 3/4 configurations demonstrated in the previous section, the URL Filtering feature requires the configuration of a parameter map. The parameter map is used to define the specific parameters that will be referenced in the class map or policy map.

Parameter Map Configuration

Two different types of parameter maps can be configured for the URL Filter feature:

- **URL filter policy parameter map:** Sets up the different parameters to be used with the URL filter policy.

- **URL filter - GLOB parameter map:** Specifies a list of domains, URL keywords, or URL metacharacters when setting up a local whitelist or blacklist.

The options that are available using the URL filter policy parameter map depend on the type of URL filtering that is going to be used: local, N2H2, or Websense. N2H2 and Websense provide competing databases that can be referenced when performing URL filtering. Table 12-9 lists the available options.

Table 12-9 *Configuring URL Filter Policy Parameter Map*

Task	Command Syntax
Create and configure a URL filter policy parameter map.	Router(config)# **parameter-map type urlfpolicy** {**local**	**n2h2**	**websense**} *parameter-map-*
Turn off or on URL filtering alert messages at the console. Default is off.	**alert** {**on**	**off**}
Specify the behavior of the URL filter should the database become unreachable. When on, all unmatched URL requests are allowed. Off is default.	**allow-mode** {**on**	**off**}
Specify the blocked URL request response.	**block-page** {**message** *string*	**redirect-url** *url*}
Specify the entry cache table lifetime. Default is 24.	**cache-entry-lifetime** *hours*

Table 12-9   *Configuring URL Filter Policy Parameter Map*

Task	Command Syntax
Specify the maximum number of entries in the categorization cache. Default is 5000.	**cache-size maximum-entries** *number-of-entries*
Specify the maximum number of pending requests. Default is 1000.	**max-request** *number-of-requests*
Specify the number of HTTP responses that can be buffered. Default is 200.	**max-resp-pak** *number-of-responses*
Specify the URL-filtering server configuration.	**server** {*server-name* | *ip-address*} [**outside**] [**port** *port-number*] [**retrans** *retransmission-count*] [**timeout** *seconds*]
Specify the interface to be used for URL-filtering server traffic.	**source-interface** *interface*
Specify whether URLs will be truncated.	**truncate** {hostname | script-options}
Specify the use of the URL-filtering servers' logging.	**urlf-server-log** {on | off}

Example 12-14 shows the configuration of a URL filter policy parameter map using a local filtering database that enables URL filtering alert messages and changes the blocked page message to "Access Denied."

Example 12-14   *Configuring URL Filter Policy Parameter Map*

```
Router# configure terminal
Router(config)# parameter-map type urlfpolicy local local-urlf-parameter-map
Router(config-profile)# alert on
Router(config-profile)# block-page message "Access Denied"
```

The URL filter - GLOB parameter map is used to configure the specific traffic patterns that will be matched to server domains or URL keywords used inside the URL filter class map. The pattern matching is rather flexible. For matching server domains, a simple expression like "microsoft.com" will work to match URLs with "microsoft.com" in them. A URL keyword is matched against any part of the URL after the initial / character and between any later / characters. The pattern matching is only limited by matching the /, {, and } characters, which are not permitted. Table 12-10 shows the different expressions that are supported.

Table 12-10   *URL Filtering GLOB Expressions*

Character	Description
*	Matches any sequence of 0 or more characters.
[abc]	Matches any character in the brackets and is case sensitive. This example would match a, b, or c.
[a-c]	Matches any character inside the range in the brackets. This example would match a, b, or c. Support for noncontiguous letters is also supported. For example, [a-cx-z] would match a, b, c, x, y, or z.
[0-9]	Matches any number inside the brackets. This example would match 0, 1, 2, 3, 4, 5, 6, 7, 8, or 9.

Table 12-11 displays the commands that can be used to configure URL filtering.

Table 12-11   *Commands to Configure the URL Filter - GLOB Parameter Map*

Task	Command Syntax
Create and configure a URL Filter GLOB parameter map	Router(config)#**parameter-map type urlf-glob** *parameter-map-name*
Configure a pattern to be matched	Router(config-profile)# **pattern** *expression*

Example 12-15 shows the configuration of two expressions:

- **One matching the server domain:** The server domains to be matched would be the ones containing testing-1.com, testing-2.com, or testing-3.com.

- **One matching URL keywords:** The URL keyword to be matched would include a URL with the words *test* or *example* (For example, http://www.testing-1.com/test/index.html).

Example 12-15   *Configuring URL Filter - GLOB Parameter Map*

```
Router# configure terminal
Router(config)# parameter-map type urlf-glob glob_server_parameter_map
Router(config-profile)# pattern testing-[1-3].com
Router(config)# parameter-map type urlf-glob glob_keyword_parameter_map
Router(config-profile)# pattern test
Router(config-profile)# pattern example
```

Class Map Configuration

The class map is used to match the specific traffic, as described in the earlier sections. The options that are available using the class map depend on the type of URL filtering that is going to be used: local, N2H2, or Websense.

When setting up a local matching database, there are two available options: to match based on the server domain or to match based on a URL keyword. When setting up a remote URL-filtering solution, like N2H2 or Websense, only matching based on server response is supported.

Table 12-12 displays the commands that can be used to configure a URL filter class map.

Table 12-12 *Configuring URL Filter Class Map*

Task	Command Syntax
Create and configure a URL filter class map	Router(config)# **class-map type urlfilter [n2h2 | websense] [match-any]** *class-map-name*
Configure the match criteria for N2H2 and Websense	Router(config-cmap)# **match server-response any**
Configure the parameter map to be used for server domain matching	Router(config-cmap)# **match server-domain urlf-glob** *parameter-map-name*
Configure the parameter map to be used for URL keyword matching	Router(config-cmap)# **match url-keyword urlf-glob** *parameter-map-name*
Display the currently configured URL filter class maps	Router# **show class-map type urlfilter**

Example 12-16 shows the configuration of a URL filter class map that matches traffic based on the glob_server_parameter_map and glob_keyword_parameter_map parameter maps configured in Example 12-15.

Example 12-16 *Configuring URL Filter Class Map*

```
Router# configure terminal
Router(config)# class-map type urlfilter url_class_map
Router(config-cmap)# match server-domain urlf-glob glob_server_parameter_map
Router(config-cmap)# match url-keyword urlf-glob glob_keyword_parameter_map
```

Policy Map Configuration

The policy map is used to create the policy that will use all the different variables configured with the parameter maps and class map and dictates the behavior of the matched traffic. Table 12-13 lists the available policy actions.

Table 12-13 *URL Filter Policy Map Actions*

Task	Command Syntax
Permit the matched traffic	allow
Log the matched traffic	log
Reset the connection of the matched traffic	reset

Table 12-14 displays the commands that can be used to configure a URL filter policy map.

Table 12-14 *Commands to Configure a URL Filter Policy Map*

Task	Command Syntax
Create and configure a URL filter policy map	Router(config)# **policy-map type inspect urlfilter** *policy-map-name*
Configure the use of a URL filter policy parameter map	Router(config-pmap)# **parameter type urlfpolicy** {**local** | **n2h2** | **websense**} *parameter-map-name*
Configure the use of a class map for traffic matching	Router(config-pmap)# **class type urlfilter** *class-map-name*
Permit the matched traffic	Router(config-pmap-c)# **allow**
Log the matched traffic	Router(config-pmap-c)# **log**
Reset the connection of the matched traffic	Router(config-pmap-c)# **reset**
Display the currently exising URL filter policy maps	Router# **show policy-map type inspect urlfilter**

Example 12-17 shows the configuration of a URL filter policy map that uses the parameters in the local-urlf-parameter-map created in one of the previous sections, matches traffic based on the url_class_map defined in the previous section, and logs all matched traffic.

Example 12-17 *Configuring URL Filter Policy Map*

```
Router# configure terminal
Router(config)# policy-map type inspect urlfilter url_policy_map
Router(config-pmap)# parameter type urlfilter local local-urlf-parametermap
Router(config-pmap)# class type urlfilter url_class_map
Router(config-pmap-c)# log
```

Application of URL Filter

The application of a URL filter policy map can be confusing because it is not possible to directly associate it with a specific zone pair as is possible with a Layer 3/4 policy map. With a Layer 7 policy map, the URL filter policy map must be nested under an existing Layer 3/4 policy using the **service-policy** command.

To apply a URL filter policy to a Layer 3/4 policy map, enter the following command:

Router(config-pmap-c)# **service-policy urlfilter** *DPI_policy_map_name*

Example 12-18 shows the association of the url_policy_map created in the previous section with a Layer 3/4 policy.

Example 12-18   *Applying a URL Filter Policy*

```
Router# configure terminal
Router(config)# class-map type inspect http_class_map
Router(config-cmap)# match protocol http
Router(config-cmap)# exit
Router(config)# policy-map type inspect http_policy_map
Router(config-pmap)# class http_class_map
Router(config-pmap-c)# inspect
Router(config-pmap-c)# service-policy urlfilter url_policy_map
```

HTTP Inspection

The ability to inspect HTTP traffic directly is also possible with ZBPFW using AIC. As with the previous features, HTTP inspection is configured using the C3PL. The abilities of the HTTP inspection engine are quite vast and will be covered briefly in the following sections. For information on all the available features, check out Cisco.com.

Parameter Map Configuration

With HTTP inspection, only one parameter map needs to be configured if the class map requires pattern matching. The regex parameter map offers the ability to do very detailed pattern matching using a number of different variables. The pattern-matching abilities are not the same as URL filtering, as described in Table 12-15. Table 12-16 shows how a HTTP Inspection parameter map is created and configured.

Table 12-15   *HTTP Inspection Regex Expressions*

Character	Description
.	Matches a single character.
(xxx)	Provides the ability to segregate characters from their surrounding characters. For example, t(ilo)m will match tim or tom, while tilom will match ti or om.
|	Matches either expression that it separates.
?	A qualifier that indicates that there are 0 or 1 of the previous expression. For example, lo?ose will match lose or loose.

Table 12-15 *HTTP Inspection Regex Expressions*

Character	Description
*	A qualifier that indicates that there are 0, 1, or multiples of the previous expression. For example, lo*ose will match lose, loose, looose, and so on.
+	A qualifier that indicates that there are 1 or multiples of the previous expression. For example, lo+ose will match loose, looose, and so on.
{x}	Repeat exactly x times. For example, 12(3){3}4 will match '123334'.
{x,}	Repeat at least x times. For example, 12(3){3,}4 will match 123334, 1233334, and so on.
[abc]	Matches any character in the brackets. For example, [abc] will match a, b, or c.
[^abc]	Matches any character *not* in the brackets. For example, [^abc] would match any character that is not a, b, or c.
[a-c]	Matches any character in the range. For example, [a-d] would match a, b, c, or d.
" "	Preserves leading or trailing spaces in a string.
^	Specifies the beginning of a line.
\a	When preceding a literal character, matches the literal character. For example, \[matches [.
char	Matches a character that is not a literal character.
\r	Matches a carriage return 0x0d.
\n	Matches a new line 0x0a.
\t	Matches a tab 0x09.
\f	Matches a form feed 0x0c.
\xnn	Matches an ASCII character using HEX (two characters).
\nnn	Matches an ASCII character using octal (two characters).

Table 12-16 *Configuring HTTP Inspection Parameter Map*

Task	Command Syntax
Create and configure a regex parameter map	Router(config)# **parameter-map type regex** *parameter-map-name*
Configure a pattern to be matched	Router(config-profile)# **pattern** *expression*

Example 12-19 shows the configuration of a regex parameter map that matches either tim or tom.

Example 12-19   *Configuring HTTP Inspection Parameter Map*

```
Router# configure terminal
Router(config)# parameter-map type regex http_DPI_parameter_map
Router(config-profile)# pattern t(i¦o)m
```

Class Map Configuration

The HTTP inspection-matching abilities are quite extensive and include several options for the HTTP request, HTTP response, or both. There are also a couple of different options that can be used to detect other criteria, including non-HTTP traffic using HTTP ports and whether the traffic contains Java applet(s). Table 12-17 shows a number of the available options.

Table 12-17   *Configuring HTTP Inspection Class Map*

Task	Command Syntax
Create and configure an HTTP inspection class map	Router(config)# **class-map type inspect http** [**match-any** | **match-all**] *class-map-name*
Match HTTP traffic that is noncompliant	Router(config-cmap)# **match req-resp protocol violation**
Match based on the HTTP body length	Router(config-cmap)# **match req-resp body length** {**lt** | **gt**} {*bytes*}
Match based on the HTTP content type	Router(config-cmap)# **match req-resp header content-type** {**violation** | **mismatch** | **unknown**}
Match based on the HTTP encoding method	Router(config-cmap)# **match req-resp header transfer-encoding** {**chunked** | **compress** | **deflate** | **gzip** | **identity** | **all**}
Match based on the URI or argument length	Router(config-cmap)# **match request** {**uri** | **arg**} **length gt** *bytes*
Match based on the HTTP request method	Router(config-cmap)# **match request method** {**connect** | **copy** | **delete** | **edit** | **get** | **getattribute** | **getattributenames** | **getproperties** | **head** | **index** | **lock** | **mkdir** | **move** | **options** | **post** | **put** | **revadd** | **revlabel** | **revlog** | **revnum** | **save** | **setattribute** | **startrev** | **stoprev** | **trace** | **unedit** | **unlock**}
Match applications misusing the HTTP port	Router(config-cmap)# **match request port-misuse** {**im** | **p2p** | **tunneling** | **any**}
Match based on the URI or argument matching the regex expression	Router(config-cmap)# **match request** {**not**}{**uri**|**arg**} **regex** *parameter-map-name*

Table 12-17 *Configuring HTTP Inspection Class Map*

Task	Command Syntax
Match Java applets being used by the HTTP connection	Router(config-cmap)# **match response body java-applet**
Match based on the status line of the response message matching the regex expression	Router(config-cmap)# **match response status-line regex** *parameter-map-name*
Match based on the request, response, or both messages whose header count does not exceed a maximum number of fields	Router(config-cmap)# **match [request | response | req-resp] header [***header-name***] count gt** *number*
Match based on the request, response, or both message header length	Router(config-cmap)# **match [request | response | req-resp] header [***header-name***] length gt** *bytes*
Match based on the request, response, or both message header matching a regex expression	Router(config-cmap)# **match [request | response | req-resp] header [***header-name***] regex** *parameter-map-name*
Match based on the request, response, or both message body matching a regex expression	Router(config-cmap)# **match [request | response | req-resp] body regex** *parameter-map-name*
Display the existing HTTP inspection class maps	Router# **show class-map type inspect http**

Example 12-20 shows the configuration of an HTTP inspection class map that matches traffic that is misusing the HTTP port or traffic that contains tim or tom as configured in the regex_parameter_map.

Example 12-20 *Configuring HTTP Inspection Class Map*

```
Router# configure terminal
Router(config)# class-map type inspect http match-any http_DPI_class_map
Router(config-cmap)# match request port-misuse any
Router(config-cmap)# match req-resp body regex http_DPI_parameter_map
```

Policy Map Configuration

The policy map is used to create the policy that will then be enforced against the traffic matched in the class map. Table 12-18 lists the available policy actions.

Table 12-18 *HTTP Inspection Policy Map Actions*

Key Topic

Task	Command Syntax
Permit the matched traffic	allow
Log the matched traffic	log
Reset the connection of the matched traffic	reset

Table 12-19 displays the commands that can be used to configure an HTTP inspection policy map.

Table 12-19   *Commands to Configure HTTP Inspection Policy Map*

Task	Command Syntax
Create and configure an HTTP inspection policy map	Router(config)# **policy-map type inspect http** *policy-map-name*
Configure the use of a class map for traffic matching	Router(config-pmap)# **class type inspect http** *class-map-name*
Permit the matched traffic	Router(config-pmap-c)# **allow**
Log the matched traffic	Router(config-pmap-c)# **log**
Reset the connection of the matched traffic	Router(config-pmap-c)# **reset**
Display the existing HTTP inspection policy maps	Router# **show policy-map type inspect http**

Example 12-21 shows the configuration of an HTTP inspection policy map that matches traffic based on the http_DPI_class_map and resets the connection of this traffic.

Example 12-21   *Configuring HTTP Inspection Policy Map*

```
Router# configure terminal
Router(config)# policy-map type inspect http http_DPI_policy_map
Router(config-pmap)# class-map type inspect http http_DPI_class_map
Router(config-pmap-c)# reset
```

Application of HTTP Inspection

The application of an HTTP inspection policy map is completed in the same way as a URL-filtering policy:

```
Router(config-pmap-c)# service-policy http DPI_policy_map_name
```

Example 12-22 shows the association of the http_DPI_policy_map created in the previous section with a Layer 3/4 policy.

Example 12-22   *Applying an HTTP Inspection Policy*

```
Router# configure terminal
Router(config)# class-map type inspect http_class_map
Router(config-cmap)# match protocol http
Router(config-cmap)# exit
Router(config)# policy-map type inspect http_policy_map
Router(config-pmap)# class http_class_map
Router(config-pmap-c)# inspect
Router(config-pmap-c)# service-policy http http_DPI_policy_map
```

Exam Preparation

As mentioned in the section, "How to Use This Book," in the Introduction, you have several choices for exam preparation: the exercises here, the memory tables in Appendix C, the final exam preparation chapter, and the exam simulation questions on the CD-ROM. The following questions present a bigger challenge than the exam itself because they use an open-ended question format. By using this more difficult format, you exercise your memory better and prove your conceptual and factual knowledge of this chapter. You can find the answers to these questions in Appendix A, "Answers to the DIKTA' Quizzes and Fill in the Blanks Questions."

Review All Key Topics

Review the most important topics in the chapter, noted with the Key Topics icon in the margin of the page. Table 12-20 lists a reference of these key topics and the page numbers on which each is found.

Table 12-20 *Key Topics*

Key Topic Element	Description	Page
Figure 12-1	Basic zones	299
List	ZBPFW default rules	299
Figure 12-2	Zone pairs	300
Figure 12-3	Self zone zone pair	300
Figure 12-4	Intrazone zone pair	301
List	ZBPFW configuration information	302
Figure 12-5	Common configuration design	302
Table 12-3	Policy map actions	306
List	Supported AIC protocols	312
Table 12-13	URL filter policy map actions	317
Table 12-18	HTTP inspection policy map actions	321

Complete Tables and Lists from Memory

Print a copy of Appendix C, "Memory Tables" (found on the CD), or at least the section for this chapter, and complete the tables and lists from memory. Appendix D, "Memory Table Answers," also on the CD, includes completed tables and lists to check your work.

Define Key Terms

Define the following key terms from this chapter, and check your answers in the Glossary:

class map, interzone zone pair, intrazone zone pair, parameter map, policy map, security zone, stateful inspection, transparent firewall, zone pair

Use Command Reference to Check Your Memory

Table 12-21 lists the important commands from this chapter. To test your memory, cover the right side of the table with a piece of paper, read the description on the left side, and then see how much of the command you can remember.

Table 12-21   *Command Reference*

Task	Command Syntax
Create and configure a ZBPFW class map	Router(config)# **class-map type inspect [match-any	match-all]** *class-map-name*
Utilize an existing access list as matching criteria	Router(config-cmap)# **match access-group** [*access-group*	**name** *access-group-name*]
Match based on the specified protocol	Router(config-cmap)# **match protocol** *protocol-name*
Match based on the criteria defined in another existing class map	Router(config-cmap)# **match class-map** *class-map-name*
Create and configure a parameter map (the default and global parameters were introduced in Release 15.1(1)T)	Router(config)# **parameter-map type inspect** [*parameter-map-name*	**default**	**global**]
Configure logging of the firewall packets (introduced in Release 15.1(1)T)	Router(config-profile)# **log {dropped-packets {disable	enable}	summary [flows** *number*] **[time-interval** *seconds*]}**
Enable IOS stateful packet inspection alert messages	Router(config-profile)# **alert {on	off}**

Table 12-21 *Command Reference*

Task	Command Syntax
Enable audit trail messages	Router(config-profile)# **audit trail** {**on**	**off**}
Configure the DNS idle timeout	Router(config-profile)# **dns-timeout** *seconds*
Configure the ICMP idle timeout	Router(config-profile)# **icmp idle-timeout** *seconds*
Configure the number of existing half-open sessions that are allowed	Router(config-profile)# **max-incomplete** {**low** *number-of-connections*	**high** *number-of-connections*}
Configure the number of new unestablished half-open sessions that are allowed	Router(config-profile)# **one-minute** {**low** *number-of-connections*	**high** *number-of-connections*}
Configure the maximum number of sessions that are allowed to exit on a zone pair	Router(config-profile)# **sessions maximum** *sessions*
Configure the TCP-FIN timeout	Router(config-profile)# **tcp finwait-time** *seconds*
Configure the TCP idle timeout	Router(config-profile)# **tcp idle-time** *seconds*
Configure the threshold and blocking time values for TCP denial of service (DoS) detection	Router(config-profile)# **tcp max-incomplete host** *threshold* [**block-time** *minutes*]
Configure the amount of time that is given for a TCP session to be established	Router(config-profile)# **tcp synwait-time** *seconds*
Disable the TCP invalid window scale option check	Router(config-profile)# **tcp window-scale-enforcement loose**
Configure the UDP timeout	Router(config-profile)# **udp idle-time** *seconds*
Create and configure a ZBPFW policy map	Router(config)# **policy-map type inspect** *policy-map-name*
Configure a specific class map to be used in the policy	Router(config-pmap)# **class type inspect** *class-name*
Configure stateful packet inspection to be used on the matched traffic	Router(config-pmap-c)# **inspect**
Configure the passing of all matched traffic	Router(config-pmap-c)# **pass**
Configure the dropping of all matched traffic and optionally configure the logging of this traffic	Router(config-pmap-c)# **drop** [**log**]

Table 12-21 *Command Reference*

Task	Command Syntax
Configure the policing of the matched traffic	Router(config-pmap-c)# **police rate** *bps* **burst** *size*
Configure a nested Layer 7 policy map (see the Layer 7 configuration section for further configuration)	Router(config-pmap-c)# **service-policy** [**urlfilter** | **http** | **im** | **imap** | **pop3** | **smtp**] *dpi-policy-map-name*
Create and configure a zone	Router(config)# **zone security** *zone-name*
Assign an interface into a specific zone	Router(config-if)# **zone-member security** *zone-name*
Create and configure a zone pair	Router(config)# **zone-pair security** *zone-pair-name* [**source** *source-zone-name* | **self**] **destination** [*destination-zone-name* | **self**]
Assign a firewall policy to a zone pair	Router(config-sec-zone-pair)# **service-policy type inspect** *policy-map-name*
Create a port-mapping entry, utilize an existing ACL to configure host-specific mapping	Router(config)# **ip port-map** *appl_name* **port** [**tcp** | **udp**] *port_num* [**list** *acl_num*]
Create and configure a URL filter policy parameter map	Router(config)# **parameter-map type urlf-policy** {**local** | **n2h2** | **websense**} *parameter-map-name*
Turn off or on URL-filtering alert messages on the console. Default is off.	**alert** {**on** | **off**}
Specify the behavior of the URL filter should the database become unreachable. When on, all unmatched URL requests are allowed. Off is the default.	**allow-mode** {**on** | **off**}
Specify the blocked URL request response	**block-page** {**message** *string* | **redirect-url** *url*}
Specify the entry cache table lifetime. Default is 24.	**cache-entry-lifetime** *hours*
Specify the maximum number of entries in the categorization cache. Default is 5000.	**cache-size maximum-entries** *number-of-entries*
Specify the maximum number of pending requests. Default is 1000.	**max-request** *number-of-requests*
Specify the number of HTTP responses that can be buffered. Default is 200.	**max-resp-pak** *number-of-responses*
Specify the URL-filtering server configuration	**server** {*server-name* | *ip-address*} [**outside**] [**port** *port-number*] [**retrans** *retransmission-count*] [**timeout** *seconds*]

Table 12-21 *Command Reference*

Task	Command Syntax
Specify the interface to be used for URL-filtering server traffic	source-interface *interface*
Specify whether URLs will be truncated	truncate {hostname	script-options}
Specify the use of the URL-filtering servers' logging	urlf-server-log {on	off}
Create and configure a URL filter GLOB parameter map	Router(config)# parameter-map type urlf-glob *parameter-map-name*
Configure a pattern to be matched	Router(config-profile)# pattern *expression*
Create and configure a URL filter class map	Router(config)# class-map type urlfilter [n2h2	websense] [match-any] *class-map-name*
Configure the match criteria for N2H2 and Websense	Router(config-cmap)# match server-response any
Configure the parameter map to be used for server domain matching	Router(config-cmap)# match server-domain urlf-glob *parameter-map-name*
Configure the parameter map to be used for URL keyword matching	Router(config-cmap)# match url-keyword urlf-glob *parameter-map-name*
Create and configure a URL filter policy map	Router(config)# policy-map type inspect urlfilter *policy-map-name*
Configure the use of a URL filter policy parameter map	Router(config-pmap)# parameter type urlf-policy {local	n2h2	websense} *parameter-map-name*
Configure the use of a class map for traffic matching	Router(config-pmap)# class type urlfilter *class-map-name*
Permit the matched traffic	Router(config-pmap-c)# allow
Log the matched traffic	Router(config-pmap-c)# log
Reset the connection of the matched traffic	Router(config-pmap-c)# reset
Apply a URL filter policy to a Layer 3/4 policy map	Router(config-pmap-c)# service-policy urlfilter *DPI_policy_map_name*
Create and configure a regex parameter map	Router(config)# parameter-map type regex *parameter-map-name*
Configure a pattern to be matched	Router(config-profile)# pattern *expression*
Create and configure an HTTP inspection class map	Router(config)# class-map type inspect http [match-any	match-all] *class-map-name*

Table 12-21   *Command Reference*

Task	Command Syntax
Match HTTP traffic that is noncompliant	Router(config-cmap)# **match req-resp protocol violation**
Match based on the HTTP body length	Router(config-cmap)# **match req-resp body length** {**lt** | **gt**} {*bytes*}
Match based on the HTTP content type	Router(config-cmap)# **match req-resp header content-type** {**violation** | **mismatch** | **unknown**}
Match based on the HTTP encoding method	Router(config-cmap)# **match req-resp header transfer-encoding** {**chunked** | **compress** | **deflate** | **gzip** | **identity** | **all**}
Match based on the URI or argument length	Router(config-cmap)# **match request** {**uri** | **arg**} **length gt** *bytes*
Match based on the HTTP request method	Router(config-cmap)# **match request method** {**connect** | **copy** | **delete** | **edit** | **get** | **getattribute** | **getattributenames** | **getproperties** | **head** | **index** | **lock** | **mkdir** | **move** | **options** | **post** | **put** | **revadd** | **revlabel** | **revlog** | **revnum** | **save** | **setattribute** | **startrev** | **stoprev** | **trace** | **unedit** | **unlock**}
Match applications misusing the HTTP port	Router(config-cmap)# **match request port-misuse** {**im** | **p2p** | **tunneling** | **any**}
Match based on the URI or argument matching the regex expression	Router(config-cmap)# **match request** {**not**}{**uri**|**arg**} **regex** *parameter-map-name*
Match Java applets being used by the HTTP connection	Router(config-cmap)# **match response body java-applet**
Match based on the status line of the response message matching the regex expression	Router(config-cmap)# **match response status-line regex** *parameter-map-name*
Match based on the request, response, or both messages whose header count does not exceed a maximum number of fields	Router(config-cmap)# **match** [**request** | **response** | **req-resp**] **header** [*header-name*] **count gt** *number*
Match based on the request, response, or both message header length	Router(config-cmap)# **match** [**request** | **response** | **req-resp**] **header** [*header-name*] **length gt** *bytes*
Match based on the request, response, or both message header matching a regex expression	Router(config-cmap)# **match** [**request** | **response** | **req-resp**] **header** [*header-name*] **regex** *parameter-map-name*

Table 12-21   *Command Reference*

Task	Command Syntax
Match based on the request, response, or both message body matching a regex expression	Router(config-cmap)# **match [request | response | req-resp] body regex** *parameter-map-name*
Create and configure an HTTP inspection policy map	Router(config)# **policy-map type inspect http** *policy-map-name*
Configure the use of a class map for traffic matching	Router(config-pmap)# **class type inspect http** class-map-name
Permit the matched traffic	Router(config-pmap-c)# **allow**
Log the matched traffic	Router(config-pmap-c)# **log**
Reset the connection of the matched traffic	Router(config-pmap-c)# **reset**
Apply a URL filter policy to a Layer 3/4 policy map	Router(config-pmap-c)# **service-policy http** *DPI_policy_map_name*
Display the currently configured inspect type class maps	Router# **show class-map type inspect**
Display the currently configured inspect type parameter maps	Router# **show parameter-map type inspect**
Display the currently configured inspect type policy maps	Router# **show policy-map type inspect**
Display the currently configured security zones	Router# **show zone security**
Display the currently configured security zone pair and assigned firewall policy	Router# **show zone-pair security**
Display information about the currently configured port maps (includes system-defined mappings)	Router# **show ip port-map**
Display the currently configured URL filter class maps	Router# **show class-map type urlfilter**
Display the currently exising URL filter policy maps	Router# **show policy-map type inspect urlfilter**
Display the existing HTTP inspection class maps	Router# **show class-map type inspect http**
Display the existing HTTP inspection policy maps	Router# **show policy-map type inspect http**

Fill in the Blanks

1. A firewall is used to enforce an access policy between _____.

2. In IOS versions before 15.0.1M, intrazone traffic was _____ by default.

3. Traffic policy is applied _____ between zones using zone pairs.

4. Zone pairs can be set up to protect the control and management planes by using the _____.

5. The PAM feature is used to map _____ onto _____.

6. With Layer 3/4 traffic, the class map type is always the _____.

7. When using the inspect type policy map, the creation of a parameter map is _____.

8. If no zone pair is defined, traffic will _____ between zones.

9. The URL filter feature provides the ability to _____, _____, or ___ the traffic whose URL matches the configured characteristics.

This chapter covers the following subjects:

- **Configuration choices, basic procedures, and required input parameters:** Describes the difference between intrusion detection and intrusion prevention. It also covers the concept of signatures.

- **Choosing an IPS sensor platform:** Cisco provides many platforms through which you can deploy Cisco IOS intrusion prevention. The company's hardware and software implementations are covered in this section.

- **Deploying Cisco IOS Software IPS signature policies:** Covers creating and deploying signature policies.

- **Tuning Cisco IOS Software IPS signatures:** Covers tuning IPS signatures to fit your network.

- **Deploying Cisco IOS Software IPS signature updates:** Learn how to update the signatures for your intrusion prevention system in this section.

- **Monitoring Cisco IOS Software IPS events:** Covers the different methods to monitor events from the intrusion prevention system.

- **Troubleshooting Cisco IOS Software IPS sensor:** In the event that you have problems with your intrusion prevention deployment, troubleshooting guidelines and procedures are provided in this section.

CHAPTER 13

Implementing and Configuring IOS Intrusion Prevention System (IPS)

As the reliance on the Internet becomes more and more crucial to the success of businesses, the ability to secure and protect information assets becomes increasingly critical. Today's environments must stave off several different types of compromises such as disclosing privacy information, corporate espionage, or denial of service attacks to name a few. Deploying a layered approach to security implementations is the best way to protect a network from attack. Having the ability to proactively monitor traffic as it traverses networks adds an important layer of security. Actively inspecting data that passes through stateful firewalls can detect malicious packets and reduce the risk of exposure for corporations. Intrusion detection and prevention systems are security tools that provide the ability to inspect data as traffic flows through firewalls on permitted ports. Intrusion prevention and detection both analyze traffic based on signature matching. The main difference is that intrusion prevention can proactively take action to prevent malicious traffic from entering your network. Intrusion detection requires manual intervention by network administrators to stop traffic after the intrusion detection system triggers an event.

This chapter covers the Cisco IOS intrusion prevention system (IPS). Upon completing this chapter, you will have an understanding of how to configure intrusion prevention on a Cisco IOS router, which includes enabling Cisco IPS, understanding and updating signatures, and monitoring events with either syslog or Security Device Event Exchange (SDEE).

"Do I Know This Already?" Quiz

The "Do I Know This Already?" quiz helps you decide whether you really need to read the entire chapter. If you already intend to read the entire chapter, you do not necessarily need to answer these questions now.

The eight-question quiz, derived from the major sections in the "Foundation Topics" portion of this chapter, helps you determine how to spend your limited study time.

Table 13-1 outlines the major topics discussed in this chapter and the "Do I Know This Already?" quiz questions that correspond to those topics.

Table 13-1 *"Do I Know This Already?" Foundation Topics Section-to-Question Mapping*

Foundation Topics Section	Questions Covered in This Section
Configuration Choices, Basic Procedures, and Required Input Parameters	1, 2
Choosing an IPS Sensor Platform	3
Deploying Cisco IOS Software IPS Signature Policies	4
Tuning Cisco IOS Software IPS Signatures	5
Deploying Cisco IOS Software IPS Signature Updates	6
Monitoring Cisco IOS Software IPS Events	7
Troubleshooting Cisco IOS Software IPS Sensors	8

Caution: The goal of self-assessment is to gauge your mastery of the topics in this chapter. If you do not know the answer to a question or are only partially sure of the answer, you should mark this question wrong for purposes of the self-assessment. Giving yourself credit for an answer that you correctly guess skews your self-assessment results and might provide you with a false sense of security.

1. What types of security controls are capable of monitoring traffic to detect problems in the network?

     a. Intrusion prevention systems (IPS)

     b. Protocol analyzers

     c. Intrusion detection systems (IDS)

     d. Security policy

2. What security controls are capable of monitoring traffic to detect and prevent problems in the network?

     a. Intrusion detection systems (IDS)

     b. Wireless sniffers

     c. Intrusion prevention systems (IPS)

     d. None of these answers are correct.

3. The software-based IPS can support which of the same analysis features as the hardware IPS appliances?

     a. Some

     b. All

     c. None

     d. Most

4. It is highly recommended to deploy all selected signatures initially without putting which type of action in place to permit tuning the sensor for a particular environment to minimize false positive and false negative events?

   a. Remote

   b. Passive

   c. Preventative

   d. All of these answers are correct.

5. What is an indication of confidence in a signature's performance given the environment in which it is deployed?

   a. Attack Severity Rating (ASR)

   b. Signature Fidelity Rating (SFR)

   c. Target Value Rating (TVR)

   d. Event Risk Rating (ERR)

6. If a license on a router expires, it will no longer be able to do what after the license expiration date?

   a. Apply any signatures created

   b. Analyze traffic

   c. Take preventative action when a signature is matched

   d. None of these answers are correct.

7. SDEE uses what kind of communication model for event messages?

   a. Pull

   b. Push

   c. Manual

   d. None of these answers are correct.

8. What is one of the common issues found when deploying Cisco IOS Software IPS sensors to accommodate the signature database?

   a. Lack of router memory

   b. Insufficient router processor speed

   c. Insufficient interface throughput

   d. None of these answers are correct.

The answers to the "Do I Know This Already?" quiz are found in Appendix A. The suggested choices for your next step are as follows:

- **6 or less overall score:** Read the entire chapter. This includes the "Foundation Topics" and "Exam Preparation" sections.

- **7 or 8 overall score:** If you want more review on these topics, skip to the "Exam Preparation" section. Otherwise, move on to Chapter 14, "Introduction to Cisco IOS Site-to-Site Security Solutions."

Foundation Topics

This chapter discusses the Cisco IOS IPS. Unlike the Cisco IOS IDS, which was tightly integrated with the Cisco IOS Firewall feature set, IPS is an independent component of Cisco IOS Software Release 12.3T and later.

This chapter covers seven main topics that pertain to the Cisco IOS IPS, as covered in the following sections.

Configuration Choices, Basic Procedures, and Required Input Parameters

This section describes the Cisco IOS features and new enhancements.

Intrusion detection systems (IDS) are types of security controls that are capable of monitoring traffic to *detect* problems in the network. They are typically network devices called *sensors* that monitor traffic to or from (or both) a particular network segment and perform analysis to detect misuse of network resources. The analysis can be based on a set of signatures, anomalous traffic as compared to normal traffic, or a user-specified policy.

The following list describes some examples of common attacks, although this is by no means an exhaustive list:

■ Network sweeps and scans indicate a possible network reconnaissance attack that can be detected by network IDS components.

■ Certain anomalies in traffic patterns can be detected by network IDS. These are often referred to as malformed packets:

   ■ Invalid IP datagrams (for example, a "Christmas Tree" packet). This is a packet for which every single option is set regardless of the protocol.

   ■ Invalid TCP packets (for example, a source or destination port is set to 0).

   ■ Invalid application layer information such as instructions in an HTTP request that do not meet RFC specifications.

■ Denial of service (DoS) attacks, such as floods of Internet Control Message Protocol (ICMP) packets or TCP packets can cause performance degradation by rendering normal services unavailable.

■ Application layer attacks, such as buffer overflows and command injections.

Upon detection of these and other types of attacks, intrusion detection systems generate alerts. These alerts are either stored locally on the IDS but also can be retrieved by a management system. With IDS, security administrators must monitor alerts and make configuration changes manually to stop and prevent further attack traffic.

Intrusion prevention systems (IPS) are security controls that are capable of monitoring traffic to *detect and prevent* problems in the network. Cisco IPS is a solution designed to detect, classify, and stop malicious attacks. Action by administrators is typically not required because IPS sensors take immediate, real-time action to protect the network. It is recommended that administrative staff continue to monitor alerts generated by intrusion prevention systems for analysis.

Key Point:

IDS:

- Analyzes copies of the traffic stream
- Does not slow traffic throughput rate
- Does not prevent malicious traffic from entering the network

IPS:

- Works inline in real-time to analyze Layer 2 through Layer 7 traffic
- Must have throughput capacity to handle traffic rate so that IPS does not introduce unacceptable latency
- Prevents malicious traffic from entering the network

Intrusion Detection and Prevention with Signatures

Signatures are rules that are configured in a network IPS device that describe network traffic patterns that match a known type of malicious activity. Extensive research is conducted upon attacks and vulnerabilities to develop signatures to match certain attacks.

A signature-based network IPS uses a local database of known attack signatures against which it analyzes traffic flows. The signature-based network IPS looks inside packet headers and payloads in an attempt to match a possible string of bytes to a known signature. Consider the following examples:

- There are specific types of URLs that can be used to attack a web server. The signature-based network IPS will look inside HTTP packets to try to find these malicious data patterns.
- Buffer overflows inside the Multi-Purpose Internet Mail Extension (MIME) headers of an email message can be used in an attempt to attack an email client. The IPS will look for a particular series of bytes in the MIME part of a message to try to detect these types of attacks.

By definition, a signature-based network IPS can only detect attacks that are included in the signature database by the vendor or that are created by a network security administrator. Attack signatures that are not in the database typically go undetected by signature-based IPS devices. For this reason, signature-based IPS devices must have their signature databases updated frequently to stay current. IPS vendors will usually publish database updates that can be automatically downloaded and applied by the IPS device. However, network security administrators should always stay abreast of new attacks and ensure that their database signatures will match them. In some cases, administrators will need to create custom signatures to match them. Table 13-2 describes some of the advantages and disadvantages of IPS.

Table 13-2   *Advantages and Limitations: Signature-Based Intrusion Prevention Systems*

Advantage	Limitation
Low false positive rate after signatures have been properly tuned.	The signature-based network IPS will seldom detect an attack for which it has no signature. In some cases, very generic signatures could possibly detect an attack by matching a common string of malicious identifiable characters.
Updating the signature database is usually a fairly simple process. It is usually an automated process.	Signature-based IPS requires constant updating of its signature database to remain effective against most attack types.
The database of signatures also provides the ability to provide administrators with the names of attacks, proper mitigation techniques, and recommendations on how to patch vulnerable systems that can be susceptible to this attack.	In some environments, signatures must be tuned to avoid an overwhelming number of false positives because of different types of users and applications in a frequently changing environment.

A signature engine is a component of the sensors' analysis engine. The signature engine will inspect a specific type of traffic and support a specific category of signatures. Each signature within a Cisco IPS component is created and controlled by a signature engine that is designed for a particular type of traffic. An example would be the STRING.TCP engine, which is designed to analyze TCP connections and look for particular string patterns. An example of a signature supported by the STRING.TCP engine is provided next.

- Signature 3118, rwhoisd format-string, triggers when the engine detects an soa command being sent to an rwhois server with an abnormally large argument.

- Signature 3138 fires when a match to the C variant of the Bagle C virus email attachment is detected in an email attachment.

Each engine is made up of a parser and an inspector. There are a legal set of parameters with prescribed ranges or sets of values. These configurable engine parameters provide the ability to tune the signatures to match the current environment.

In Cisco IOS Software Release 12.4(11)T and later T-Train releases, IOS IPS signature provisioning is accomplished by selecting one of two signature categories: Basic or Advanced. Starting with IOS Release 15.0(1)M, a new category called "IOS IPS Default" will be also supported and released within IPS signature packages. At that time, the IOS Advanced category will be changed to contain exactly the same signatures as in the IOS Default category, allowing both category names to be used interchangeably for backward compatibility. Users can also add or remove individual signatures and/or can tune signature parameters through Cisco Configuration Professional (CCP) or Cisco Security Manager (CSM) management or through the command-line interface (CLI), which allows easy scripting to manage signature configuration for a large number of routers.

IOS Basic and Advanced/Default signature categories are preselected signature sets intended to serve as a good starting set for most users of IOS IPS. They contain the latest high-fidelity (low-false-positive) worm, virus, IM, or peer-to-peer blocking signatures for detecting security threats, allowing easier deployment and signature management. Cisco IOS IPS also allows the selection and tuning of signatures outside those two categories. Table 13-3 lists signature engines and their descriptions.

Table 13-3   *Signature Engines*

Signature Engine	Description
ATOMIC.IP	Used to examine IP, TCP, UDP, and ICMP headers and payloads
SERVICE.DNS	Examines Domain Name System (DNS) application layer sessions
SERVICE.RPC	Examines UNIX remote procedure call (RPC) application layer sessions
SERVICE.MSRPC	Examines Microsoft RPC application layer sessions
SERVICE.HTTP	Examines HTTP application layer sessions
SERVICE.FTP	Examines FTP application layer sessions
SERVICE.SMTP	Examines Simple Mail Transfer Protocol (SMTP) application layer sessions
STRING.TCP	Examines reassembled TCP sessions for data patterns
STRING.UDP	Examines UDP sessions for data patterns
STRING.ICMP	Examines ICMP sessions for data patterns
MULTI-STRING	Performs pattern matching in multiple sessions
NORMALIZER	Normalizes traffic, such as IP fragments and TCP segments, before processing by another engine
OTHER	Provides an internal engine to process miscellaneous signatures

Sensor Accuracy

Because of the complexity of today's network environments, security controls, such as IDS or IPS, can sometimes produce incorrect results that are due to either misconfigurations or something in the environment. All events should be vigorously investigated before assuming that an alert is incorrect.

There are four classifications into which the decisions made by IPS and IDS can fall:

- **True positives:** The IPS or IDS sensor triggered because of legitimate malicious activity. This is normal, desired operation.

- **False positives:** The IPS or IDS sensor triggered because of nonmalicious activity. This is usually because of errors caused by signatures that are configured to be too relaxed or broad in scope. In other words, the sensor mistook normal traffic patterns to be malicious.

- **True negatives:** The IPS or IDS sensor failed to trigger when there was no malicious activity. This is normal, desired operation.

- **False negatives:** The IPS or IDS sensor failed to trigger when there was malicious activity. This is usually because of errors caused by signatures that are configured to be too specific.

Care must be taken when tuning signatures. Adjusting signatures to be less restrictive to reduce the number of false positives can move your sensor closer to the possibility of missing legitimate attacks (false negatives).

Proper knowledge, research, and expertise in a specific environment are required to adjust signatures to a state where they successfully trigger on legitimate malicious activity, yet do not trigger on legitimate nonmalicious activity and block legitimate traffic.

Choosing a Cisco IOS IPS Sensor Platform

Key
Topic

The Cisco IOS Sensor functionality can be deployed in two different platforms. One platform is software based and uses the router's main CPU for processing, and the other is hardware based and takes advantage of special-purpose hardware processors.

Software-Based Sensor

Cisco Integrated Services Routers (ISR) can implement the Cisco IPS sensor functionality by using the router's main CPU to analyze packets. Software-based IPS only works in inline mode, meaning that packets are examined as they are forwarded by the router. The software-based IPS can support most of the same analysis features as the hardware IPS appliances. One of the benefits of it being inline is that it can drop traffic, block attacks, send alarms, and reset connections. This allows the router to respond immediately to detected security attacks.

The IOS Software–based IPS is limited by the router's CPU and memory performance, which are shared with other processes running on the router. Additionally, the Cisco IOS Software IPS requires a license to enable signatures after a certain date. The IPS signature update license is part of the IOS license configuration and is configured as any other Cisco IOS Software licensed feature.

This study guide covers the Cisco IOS Software IPS sensor that is available in all Cisco ISR routers.

Hardware-Based Sensor

There are two other options for deploying the intrusion prevention system on the Cisco ISR that offer a more granular, high-performance IPS solution. The Cisco IPS Advanced Integration Module and the Cisco IPS Network Module Enhanced are two other methods for implementing the intrusion prevention system on the Cisco ISR.

The Cisco IPS Advanced Integration Module and the Cisco IPS Network Module Enhanced are dedicated hardware IPS coprocessors for the Cisco ISR. The Advanced Integration

Module (AIM) is typically geared toward the small- to medium-sized businesses as well as for branch office implementations. The Network Module Enhanced (NME) is typically appropriate for small enterprises to large branch office deployments. Both modules run the same software as the IPS appliance and provide the full intrusion prevention feature set.

AIM-IPS and NME-IPS can both be implemented in both inline and promiscuous inspection modes. The modules are able to monitor and analyze traffic from any router interface as well as generic routing encapsulation (GRE) and IPsec traffic that is decrypted by the router; however, neither module supports policy virtualization.

Table 13-4 summarizes the characteristics of and supported models for the hardware-based sensors.

Table 13-4 *Cisco IPS Hardware Modules*

Module	Characteristics	Supported Models
Cisco AIM-IPS	Can be run in the Cisco ISR routers and provides up to 45 Mbps of intrusion services to the router	Cisco 1841, Cisco 2801, Cisco 2811, Cisco 2821, Cisco 2851, Cisco 3825, Cisco 3845
Cisco NME-IPS	Yields up to 75 Mbps of intrusion services in the router	Cisco 2811, Cisco 2821, Cisco 2851, Cisco 3825, Cisco 3845
		Cisco 2911˙, Cisco 2921˙, Cisco 2951˙, Cisco 3925˙, Cisco 3945˙

* The Cisco NME-IPS module requires an adapter card.

The Cisco NME-IPS module has one external Gigabit Ethernet port that is used as a command and control interface for out-of-band management. The AIM-IPS module does not have any external interfaces. These modules run the full Cisco IPS software and therefore are outside the scope of this chapter.

Deployment Tasks

There are several deployment tasks you must do to deploy the IPS on Cisco IOS Software devices. The following list summarizes what you must do for a successful implementation:

Step 1.   Configure a Cisco IOS Software IPS Signature policy, which means enabling a particular set of signatures on a specific router interface or interfaces.

Step 2.   Tune Cisco IOS Software IPS Signature policies to balance between and manage false positives and false negatives.

Step 3.   Deploy the Cisco IOS Software IPS Signature update feature, which configures the router to independently load new signatures as they become available.

Step 4.   Select a monitoring tool and use it to monitor intrusion events generated by the Cisco IOS Software IPS sensor.

Deployment Guidelines

The following guidelines should be considered when deploying Cisco IOS Software IPS:

- Consider using the Cisco IOS Software Release 15.0(1)M or later, because it supports lightweight signature engines, which allows the use of more active signatures with the same CPU and memory configuration as compared to older Cisco IOS Software releases.

- Deploy Cisco IOS Software IPS at the edge of the network to have the security control running where malicious software is most likely to enter the environment.

- If there will be a large number of Cisco IOS Software IPS sensors deployed in the environment, consider using a centralized Security Information Manager (SIM) application to effectively manage the event information.

- If there will be a large number of Cisco IOS Software IPS sensors deployed in the environment, consider using a tool that will centralize deployment and configuration of the sensors. The Cisco Security Manager supports provisioning Cisco IOS Software IPS sensor configurations in large, complex environments.

Deploying Cisco IOS Software IPS Signature Policies

The first deployment task you must complete is to deploy IPS signature policies. The configuration tasks that you must complete are listed next.

Configuration Tasks

The first deployment task for the Cisco IOS Software IPS sensor is to enable the IPS functionality globally on the router, designate the interfaces on which the router will inspect traffic, and select a signature set that will be tuned in a later task. The following configuration tasks cover this first deployment task:

Task 1: Import the RSA public key that the router will use to verify authenticity and integrity of all signature packages and updates to the router.

Task 2: Create the IPS ruleset that will be applied to interfaces.

Task 3: Apply the configured IPS ruleset to the router interfaces.

Task 4: From Cisco.com, download the basic signature package onto the router.

Task 5: Choose the initial signature set by specifying the signature categories that will be enabled by default and the category-based actions that will be assigned to these signatures.

Configuration Scenario

Prior to installing and configuring Cisco IOS IPS, you need to consider a few factors, as discussed in the following sections. Figure 13-1 shows the scenario used for the configuration tasks in this chapter.

The configuration tasks will enable the IPS function on the router to inspect traffic on the interface nearest the attacker. An initial signature set that will drop all packets containing malicious traffic will also be configured on the router.

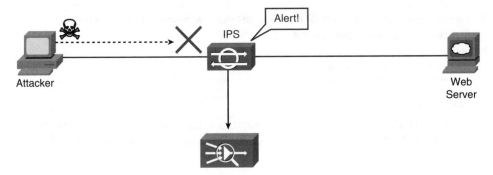

Figure 13-1 *Configuration Scenario*

The configuration steps in the chapter will assume that the Cisco ISR is already configured with a complete configuration to provide full connectivity between all involved networks.

Task 1

The first configuration task in this sequence is to import a known RSA public key whose private key is used by Cisco IPS engineering to digitally sign all signature packages and updates for Cisco IPS sensors. This public key will be used by the Cisco ISR to validate the digital signature of signature packages and updates as authentic. This is important because it is designed to prevent rogue updates from being deployed onto Cisco IPS sensors. This is not associated with the Cisco IPS licensing framework.

To install the known RSA public key, create an RSA public key chain on the router, using the **crypto key pubkey-chain rsa** command, and inside it, create a new named signature key with the name realm-cisco.pub using the **named-key** command. Then, enter the **key-string** command and paste the text from the realm-cisco.pub.key.txt file, which is found at Cisco.com. The commands are shown in Example 13-1.

Example 13-1 *Import RSA Key to Cisco ISR*

```
Router# configure terminal
Router(config)# crypto key pubkey-chain rsa
Router(config-pubkey-chain)# named-key realm-cisco.pub signature
Translating "realm-cisco.pub"
Router(config-pubkey-key)# key-string
Enter a public key as a hexadecimal number ....
! Note:   The $ to the left of the hex characters represent there are more
numbers present than would fit on one line.
Router(config-pubkey)# $2A864886 F70D0101 01050003 82010F00 3082010A 02820101
Router(config-pubkey)# $D6CC7A24 5097A975 206BE3A2 06FBA13F 6F12CB5B 4E441F16
Router(config-pubkey)# $912BE27F 37FDD9C8 11FC7AF7 DCDD81D9 43CDABC3 6007D128
Router(config-pubkey)# $085FADC1 359C189E F30AF10A C0EFB624 7E0764BF 3E53053E
Router(config-pubkey)# $0298AF03 DED7A5B8 9479039D 20F30663 9AC64B93 C0112A35
Router(config-pubkey)# $994AE74C FA9E481D F65875D6 85EAF974 6D9CC8E3 F0B08B85
Router(config-pubkey)# $5E4189FF CC189CB9 69C46F9C A84DFBA5 7A0AF99E AD768C36
Router(config-pubkey)# $A3B3FB1F 9FB7B3CB 5539E1D1 9693CCBB 551F78D2 892356AE
```

```
Router(config-pubkey)# $80CA4F4D 87BFCA3B BFF668E9 689782A5 CF31CB6E B4B094D3
Router(config-pubkey)# F3020301 0001
Router(config-pubkey)# quit
Router(config-pubkey-key)# end
```

Tasks 2 and 3

The second and third tasks involve creating and applying a named IPS ruleset. A default location for the IPS sensor configuration files in the router's local file system must be specified.

The majority of the Cisco IOS Software IPS sensor's configuration is not stored in the router's running configuration. It stores the signature definitions and other auxiliary files as XML files in the designated location in the file system. When a signature is updated or the signature policy is changed, these XML files are changed by the CLI or Cisco Configuration Professional configuration tasks that are executed.

Create the new directory on the router's local file system with the **mkdir** command. Then, enter configuration mode and specify the location of the new folder with the **ip ips config location** command.

Next, create a basic named IPS ruleset using the **ip ips name** command. Note that the only parameters to configure inside the named ruleset would be to specify an optional access list if there is a requirement to inspect only a portion of the traffic seen by the IPS function. To inspect all traffic, simply create the ruleset and apply it to all the interfaces that require inspection by IPS. The CLI commands are shown in Example 13-2.

Example 13-2   *Import RSA Key to Cisco ISR*

```
Router# configure terminal
Router(config)# ip ips config location flash:/ipsroot
Router(config)# ip ips name MY-IPS
Router(config)# interface GigabitEthernet0/0
Router(config-if)# ip ips MY-IPS in
Router(config-if)# ip ips MY-IPS out
Router(config-pubkey)# end
Router# copy running-config startup-config
```

Task 4

Task 4 loads a basic IPS signature package onto the router, which then compiles and creates the local signature database.

First, the signature package must be downloaded from Cisco.com. Go to the download section of Cisco.com and navigate to **Products > Security > Integrated Router/Switch Security > Integrated Threat Control > Cisco IOS Intrusion Prevention System Feature Software > IOS IPS Signature Data File**. Download the latest package, which should have a filename in the format IOS-S*xxx*-CLI.pkg. Put the file on the server from which you will transfer it to the router. Use the **copy** command to transfer the file to the router's **idconf** alias. This causes the router to download and unpack the contents of the file (XML files) into the folder that was specified in Task 2 of this section. The router compiles the files into the required internal format and displays any errors that occur.

Task 5

The last task of this sequence involves choosing signatures that will be included in the initial signature set. The most efficient way to choose signatures would be to choose them by category. Cisco IOS Software IPS provides categories for the IPS signatures based on attack type, operating system relevance, network protocol, and so on. Also, select the default action to be taken by the sensor for any entire category of signatures.

When a signature is matched by a packet in a session, the Cisco IOS IPS sensor will take any of the following configurable actions:

- Send an alarm

- Drop the offending packet

- Reset the connection

- Deny traffic for a particular source address

- Deny traffic for a particular connection (session)

For each category and for each individual signature in the signature database, two different states can be specified:

- Some signatures can be *disabled*. This signature is present in the router's memory but is not being used for traffic inspection. It can be enabled without the router needing to recompile the signature database.

- Some signatures can be *retired*. This signature is not present in the router's memory. Unretiring a retired signature requires that the router recompile the signature database. This can temporarily affect performance and take a long time with a large signature database.

This configuration task is completed by entering the signature category configuration mode using the **ip ips signature-category** command. See Example 13-3 for the relevant configuration. First, retire and disable all signatures because only the desired signatures will be enabled. This is achieved using the **category all** command. Then, use the **retired true** and **enabled false** commands to disable and retire all signatures by default. Next, enable all signatures that are designed to prevent attacks against Cisco IOS Software devices and assign a preventative action to them. Enter the category that comprises these signatures using the **category os ios** command and enable them by using the **retired false** and **enabled true** commands. Use the **event-action produce-alert deny-packet-inline** command to enable these signatures to generate an alert and drop the offending packets when they trigger.

Example 13-3 *Configure a Signature Set and Default Category Actions on the Cisco ISR*

```
Router# configure terminal
Router(config)# ip ips signature-category
Router(config-ips-category)# category all
```

```
Router(config-ips-category-action)# enabled false
Router(config-ips-category-action)# retired true
Router(config-ips-category-action)# exit
Router(config-ips-category)# category os ios
Router(config-ips-category-action)# retired false
Router(config-ipss-category-action)# exit
Router(config)# exit
Do you want to accept these changes?[confirm] yes
```

Verification

Verifying the signature policy configuration can be accomplished through the use of the **show ip ips configuration** command, as demonstrated in Example 13-4. This will show the database location, the signature database load times, and the signature categories that have been configured to create the initial signature set. Use the **show ip ips interfaces** command to view the interfaces on which the IPS functionality has been applied. You can use the **show ip ips statistics** command to view information such the number of packets audited and the number of interfaces configured for auditing.

Example 13-4   *Verifying a Signature Set and Default Category Actions on the Cisco ISR*

```
Router# show ip ips configuration
Event notification through syslog is enabled
Event notification through Net Director is enabled
Default action(s) for info signatures is alarm
Default action(s) for attack signatures is alarm
Default threshold of recipients for spam signature is 25
PostOffice:HostID:5 OrgID:100 Addr:10.2.7.3 Msg dropped:0
HID:1000 OID:100 S:218 A:3 H:14092 HA:7118 DA:0 R:0
     CID:1 IP:172.21.160.20 P:45000 S:ESTAB (Curr Conn)
Audit Rule Configuration
 Audit name AUDIT.1
     info actions alarm

show ip ips interface Command
Interface Configuration
 Interface Ethernet0
  Inbound IPS audit rule is AUDIT.1
    info actions alarm
  Outgoing IPS audit rule is not set
 Interface Ethernet1
  Inbound IPS audit rule is AUDIT.1
    info actions alarm
  Outgoing IPS audit rule is AUDIT.1
    info actions alarm
```

```
show ip ips statistics
Signature audit statistics [process switch:fast switch]
  signature 2000 packets audited: [0:2]
  signature 2001 packets audited: [9:9]
  signature 2004 packets audited: [0:2]
  signature 3151 packets audited: [0:12]
Interfaces configured for audit 2
Session creations since subsystem startup or last reset 11
Current session counts (estab/half-open/terminating) [0:0:0]
Maxever session counts (estab/half-open/terminating) [2:1:0]
Last session created 19:18:27
Last statistic reset never
HID:1000 OID:100 S:218 A:3 H:14085 HA:7114 DA:0 R:0
```

Guidelines

Consider the following guidelines when deploying the initial Cisco IOS Software IPS sensor policies:

- Rather than deploying a large number of signatures initially, it is recommended to configure a selection of critical signatures first and then add more signatures later if it is determined that the router's resources can handle them.

- It is highly recommended to deploy all selected signatures initially without a preventative action (drop packet, reset connection, deny connection) to permit tuning the sensor for a particular environment to minimize false positive and false negative events.

Tuning Cisco IOS Software IPS Signatures

In most cases, to manage the number of false positives and false negatives being received from the Cisco IOS Software IPS sensor, administrators need to tune the active signatures after they have been exposed to live network traffic. Individual signatures can be tuned using the CLI or the Cisco Configuration Professional. Signature parameters that can be tuned include

- Tuning trigger conditions
- Tuning response actions

Advanced tuning requires the Cisco IOS Software Signature Event Action Processor (SEAP) function. Advanced tuning is only possible using SEAP.

Manage false positives by creating address-based filters that selectively disable signatures for specific hosts whose legitimate traffic triggers signatures. This is similar to creating an exception based upon a host's address.

Create global actions for all signatures based on the risk level (covered later in this topic).

Event Risk Rating System Overview

The Cisco IOS Software IPS sensor uses a concept called *event risk rating (ERR)* to calculate and provide to administrators the severity of an event in a given network environment. The event risk rating is an integer with a value between 0 and 100. Values over 100 are capped at 100. The value is dynamically configured after the firing of a signature. The higher the value, the greater the security risk of the event.

Event Risk Rating Calculation

The ERR calculation, as shown in the formula in Figure 13-2, uses several components from an intrusion event. Some of these components must be manually configured, some of them are preconfigured and can be tuned, and some are collected automatically from the environment.

$$ERR = \frac{ASR * TVR * SFR}{10,000}$$

Figure 13-2 *Formula for Event Risk Rating Calculation*

Potential Damage

The Attack Severity Rating (ASR) is assigned to each signature by the Cisco IPS sensor. The ASR is determined by the severity configured for each signature. The severity level can be informational, low, medium, or high. Each of these severity levels has a numeric value that is associated with it that is used in the ERR calculation:

- Informational (25)

- Low (50)

- Medium (75)

- High (100)

Target Value Rating

The Target Value Rating (TVR) is assigned to each asset and is used to assign value to a particular asset. To the Cisco IPS sensor, each unique asset is identified by its IP address. Assets in the environment that are more important or mission critical would receive a higher value than those assets that are not as important. The target value rating level can be set to zero, low, medium, high, or mission critical. Each target level has a numeric value that is associated with it that is used in the ERR calculation:

- Zero (50)

- Low (75)

- Medium (100)

- High (150)

■   Mission Critical (200)

By default, the Cisco IPS sensors consider all assets as having a Medium TVR.

Signature Accuracy

The Signature Fidelity Rating (SFR) is assigned to each asset and is used to assign value. The SFR is an indication of confidence in a signature's performance given the environment in which it is deployed. The SFR has a value between 0 and 100.

Event Risk Rating Example

Figure 13-3 shows the calculation of event risk rating for a signature with the following properties:

■   Attack Severity Rating = 50 (Low)

■   Signature Fidelity Rating = 90

■   The target has a default TVR of 100.

Based on the data and the rating formula, the event risk for this particular occurrence is 45.

$$ERR = \frac{50 * 100 * 90}{10,000} = 45$$

Figure 13-3 *Event Risk Rating Calculation*

Signature Event Action Overrides (SEAO)

The SEAP signature event action overrides (SEAO) are a Cisco IOS Software IPS configuration tool that allows one or more actions to be added to all active signatures based on the calculated risk rating of each event.

Event action overrides provide a way to add actions globally without having to configure each signature or signature category. Each event action override is associated with an event risk rating range. If a signature event occurs and the event risk rating for the event falls within the configured range for the event action override, the action will be added to the event. For example, if you set the risk rating range for the "deny packet inline" action to 85–100, for every signature event that has an event risk rating calculation that falls within this range, the "drop packet inline" action will be added to the event.

Signature Event Action Filters (SEAF)

The SEAP signature event action filters are a Cisco IOS Software IPS configuration tool that allows one or more actions to be removed from all active signatures based on the attacker and/or target (source and destination) address and event risk rating criteria.

Signature event action filters are typically used to remove one, several, or all actions from a particular signature when certain circumstances are met, such as when triggered by a specific source IP address.

Configuration Tasks

The second deployment task for the Cisco IOS Software IPS sensor is to tune the IPS sensor's signature policies to adapt them to the installed environment. This involves the four following configuration tasks:

Task 1: Optionally, tune individual signatures.

Task 2: Configure Target Value Ratings for your environment.

Task 3: Configure SEAP signature event action overrides to globally add actions to signatures.

Task 4: Configure SEAP signature event action filters to remove actions from events to address false positive events.

Configuration Scenario

The scenario in which the configuration tasks will be implemented will include the following information:

- Tune the "IOS FTPd Successful Login" signature (signature ID 5860, subsignature ID 1) to only produce alerts. Additionally, set its Signature Fidelity Rating to 40 and its severity to Low.

- Using SEAP, filter the "Malformed MGCP Packet" signature (signature ID 6179, subsignature ID 0) to not trigger if traffic is sourced from 10.1.1.10.

- Assign a Mission Critical Target Value Rating (TVR) for hosts in the 10.10.10.0/25 subnet.

- For configured signatures of any category, add the "Deny attacker inline" action if the event risk rating exceeds 90. This causes the attacker to be temporarily blocked by the IPS-enabled router.

The configuration steps in the chapter will assume that the Cisco ISR is already configured with a complete configuration to provide full connectivity among all involved networks.

Task 1: Tune Individual Signatures Using the Cisco IOS Software CLI

The first task involves tuning an individual signature to change its event actions and signature parameter. First, enter signature configuration mode using the **ip ips signature-definition** command. Specify the signature that needs to be configured using the **signature** command by specifying its signature and subsignature ID ("IOS FTPd Successful Login," signature 5860, subsignature ID 0).

Example 13-5 shows the commands used to produce an alert as the event action and set the fidelity rating to 40.

Example 13-5 *Tune Individual Signatures Using the CLI*

```
Router# configure terminal
Router(config)# ip ips signature-definition
Router(config-sigdef-sig)# signature 5860 1
```

```
Router(config-sigdef-action)# engine
Router(config-sigdef-action-engine)# event-action produce-alert
Router(config-sigdef-action)# alert-severity low
Router(config-sigdef-action)# fidelity-rating 40
Router(config-if)# ^Z
Do you want to accept these chagnes:[confirm] y
```

Inside the signature configuration mode, enter the signature engine configuration mode by entering the **engine** command and only specify the **produce-alert** action for this signature. Exit from the signature engine configuration mode by using the **exit** command. Back in signature configuration mode, alter the default ASR and SFR values for this signature by using the **alert-severity** and **fidelity-rating** commands. Refer to the "References" section, later in this chapter, for links to Cisco IOS command references.

Task 1 (Continued): Tune Individual Signatures Using the Cisco Configuration Professional

Cisco Configuration Professional (CCP) can also be used to edit the parameters of individual signatures. Refer to Figure 13-4 and complete the following steps in CCP:

Step 1.   Navigate to **Configure > Security > Advanced Security > Intrusion Prevention > Edit IPS > Signatures**.

Step 2.   Under Signatures, select the **All Categories > OS > Windows > IOS** category to display all enabled signatures for this category.

Step 3.   Find the signature to be configured ("IOS FTPd Successful Login," signature ID 5860, subsignature ID 1), select it, and click the Edit button.

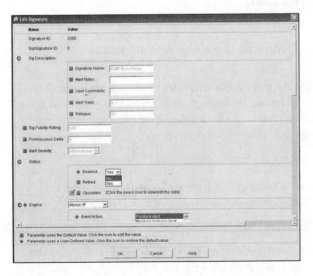

Figure 13-4   *Tune Signature in Cisco Configuration Professional*

Step 4. In the Edit Signature window, change the Alert Severity, Sig Fidelity Rating, and Event Action values in their corresponding fields.

Step 5. Click OK and then click Apply Changes to confirm the changes to the signature.

Task 2: Configure Target Value Ratings

Task 2 allows the optional configuration of the Target Value Ratings for the hosts (assets) in the network. Note, by default, that all hosts are assigned a Target Value Rating of 100.

You can adjust the Target Value Rating for a host or an address range by entering the SEAP configuration mode using the **ip ips event-action-rules** command. Inside the SEAP configuration mode, use the **target-value** command to set the TVR for a host or a network. Example 13-6 shows the configuration using Cisco IOS CLI commands, and the following steps detail the process in Cisco Configuration Professional:

Step 1. Navigate to **Configure > Security > Advanced Security > Intrusion Prevention > Edit IPS > SEAP Configuration > Target Value Rating**.

Step 2. Click Add to add a new TVR rule.

Step 3. In the Add Target Value Rating window, select the Target Value Rating and specify the address or address range for this Target Value Rating.

Step 4. Click OK and then click Apply Changes to confirm the Target Value Rating rule.

Example 13-6 *Tune Individual Signatures Using the CLI*

```
Router# configure terminal
Router(config)# ip ips event-action-rules
Router(config)# target-value mission-critical target-address 10.10.10.0/24
Router(config-pubkey)# end
Router# copy running-config startup-config
```

Task 3: Create Event Action Overrides Using Cisco Configuration Professional

Task 3 illustrates how to create SEAP event action overrides to add actions to signatures that trigger based on the event risk rating. The example includes adding a "Deny attacker inline" action if the ERR exceeds 90. Interactively creating SEAP event action overrides can only be accomplished using Cisco Configuration Professional.

The following steps detail the process in Cisco Configuration Professional:

Step 1. Navigate to **Configure > Security > Advanced Security > Intrusion Prevention > Edit IPS > SEAP Configuration > Event Action Overrides**.

Step 2. Select the Use Event Action Override check box.

Step 3. Click Add to create a new event action override. The Add Event Action Override window opens, as shown in Figure 13-5. It is possible to create multiple event action overrides to add multiple actions.

Step 4.   Select the event action to be added to a signature event from the Event Action list.

Step 5.   To enable the event action, select the Yes radio button in the Enabled field.

Step 6.   In the Risk Rating field, assign a risk rating range to the action override.

Step 7.   Click the OK button. The new event action override now appears in the list on the Event Action Overrides tab (not shown).

Step 8.   Click OK and then click Apply Changes to confirm the event action override rule.

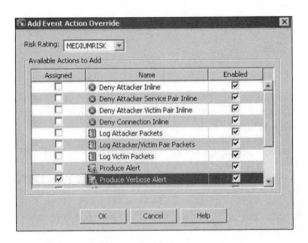

Figure 13-5   *Configure Event Action Override*

Task 4: Create Event Action Filters Using Cisco Configuration Professional

Task 4 illustrates how to create SEAP event action filters to remove actions from signatures that trigger based on the source and/or destination IP address and the event risk rating. Interactively creating SEAP event action filters can only be accomplished using Cisco Configuration Professional.

The following steps detail the process in Cisco Configuration Professional:

Note: Event action filters are processed as an ordered list, and filters can be moved up and down the list. A filter that removes all actions from an event effectively disables the signature in the defined context.

Step 1.   Navigate to **Configure > Security > Advanced Security > Intrusion Prevention > Edit IPS > SEAP Configuration > Event Action Filters**.

Step 2.   Select the Use Event Action Filters check box.

Step 3.   Click Add, and the Add Event Action Filter window opens, as shown in Figure 13-6.

Figure 13-6 *Configure Event Action Filter*

Step 4. In the Name field, enter a name for the event action filter. A default name is always supplied, but it can be changed to have a more meaningful name.

Step 5. To enable the event action filter, select the Yes radio button in the Enabled field.

Step 6. In the Signature ID field, enter the signature IDs of all signatures to which this filter should be applied.

Step 7. In the Subsignature field, enter the subsignature IDs of the subsignatures to which this filter should be applied.

Step 8. In the Attacker Address field, enter the IP address of the source host. This can be entered as a specific host IP address or as a range of IP addresses, such as 0.0.0.0-255.255.255.255.

Step 9. In the Attacker Port field, enter the port number used by the attacker to send the offending packet. The default value is all ports.

Step 10. In the Victim Address field, enter the IP address of the destination host. This can be a specific host or a range of IP addresses such as 0.0.0.0-255.255.255.255.

Step 11. In the Victim Port field, enter the port number used by the victim host to receive the offending packet. The default value is all ports.

Step 12. In the Risk Rating field, specify a risk rating range for this filter.

Step 13. In the Actions to Subtract field, select the actions to remove from the signature event.

Step 14. In the Stop on Match field, select one of the following radio buttons:

- **Yes:** Choose this option to have the event action filters stop processing after actions that meet this filter's parameters have been removed. Any remaining filters will not be processed, and no additional actions can be removed from this event.

- **No:** Choose this option to continue processing additional filters.

Step 15. In the Comments field, provide any comments that need to be stored with this filter, such as the purpose of the filter or why it is configured in a particular way.

Step 16. Click OK. The new event action filter now appears in the list on the Event Action Filters tab.

Step 17. Click Apply Changes to apply the new configuration to the router.

Verification

Verify the configuration of SEAP parameters using the CLI with the **show ip ips event-rules target-value-rating** command to see configured TVRs for IP address ranges in the network. Use the **show ip ips event-action-rules overrides** command to display all configured SEAP event action overrides and verify that they comply with the corporate policy. Additionally, use the **show ip ips event-action-rules filters** command to display the configured SEAP event action filter information. Example 13-7 shows these verification commands in use.

Example 13-7   *Verify SEAP Parameters Using the CLI*

```
Router# show ip ips event-action-rules filters
Filters


Global Filters Status: Enabled
```

Implementation Guidelines

Consider the following implementation guidelines when tuning the Cisco IOS Software IPS sensor:

■ Use event action filters to tune false positives from specific traffic flows.

■ Consider using event action filters to subtract a specific action from all signatures. For example, after initial deployment and when the IPS sensor signatures are still being tuned, use an event action filter to subtract configured blocking actions for all signatures.

Deploying Cisco IOS Software IPS Signature Updates

Signatures packs on Cisco IOS Software IPS-enabled routers can be updated either manually, as shown in the second task in this topic, or can be updated automatically by configuring the router to download updates from repositories.

Cisco distributes signature updates as digitally signed files, which can be securely transferred over untrusted networks to ensure their authenticity and integrity. Note that the signature update process is bound to the license on the router. If a license on a router expires, it will no longer be able to apply any signatures created after the license expiration date, but it will continue to analyze traffic using the existing, preexpiration IPS signatures.

The router can be configured to update itself from Cisco.com, if the router has Internet connectivity or if a local staging server can be used. The local staging server must have the signature packs downloaded manually by an administrator for them to be available for the router to retrieve.

Configuration Tasks

Two tasks must be completed to configure automatic signature updates.

The following tasks detail the process in Cisco Configuration Professional:

Task 1: Install and verify the signature update license on the router.

Task 2: Configure the router to automatically update its signature database from Cisco.com or a local server.

Configuration Scenario

The scenario used for the following two tasks includes uploading a license file to the router and then enabling automatic updates from Cisco.com (at https://www.cisco.com/cgi-bin/front.x/ids/locator/locator.pl) or a local server at 10.1.1.1. The configuration steps in the following sections assume that the Cisco ISR is already configured for basic IPS functionality and full IP connectivity among the necessary networks.

Task 1: Install Signature Update License

The first task that must be completed is to install the appropriate signature update license on the router. The license is a file that can be obtained by providing the appropriate Product Authorization Key (PAK) to the Cisco licensing web application.

Note: The Cisco Product License Registration application can be found at www.cisco.com/go/license.

Use the **license install** command to download and install the license file to the router. Use the **show ip ips license** command to display license information, especially its validity and expiration date. Example 13-8 shows the usage of these two commands.

Example 13-8 *Install and Display Signature Update License Information*

```
Router# license install http://10.1.1.1/Router-sig-license-2010.lic
Router# show ip ips license


IPS License Status valid
    Expiration Date: 2010-12-31
    Signatures Loaded:    Not Available   S0.0
    Signature Package:    Not Available   S0.0
```

Task 2: Configure Automatic Signature Updates

The second task illustrates how to configure the router to attempt to retrieve automatic signature updates from Cisco.com or a local server.

To do this, first configure the update URL using the **ida-client server** *url* command. Use the https://www.cisco.com/cgi-bin/front.x/ids/locator/locator.pl URL. Next, create an auto-update profile using the **ip ips auto-update** command. Use the **cisco** command inside the profile to designate obtaining updates from Cisco.com. To control when the update attempts occur, use the **occur-at** command. Example 13-9 illustrates the setup of the configuration to retrieve automatic updates from the Cisco.com repository as well as to provide the Cisco.com credentials that will be used for authentication through using the **username** command. Example 13-10 illustrates the setup of the configuration to retrieve automatic updates from a local staging server.

The following specifics are used in the example:

■ **Days of the week:** 0-6 (Sunday–Saturday)

■ **Minutes:** Minutes from the top of the hour (0)

■ **Hour:** Hour of the day (3:00 a.m.)

Example 13-9   *Configure Automatic Signature Updates from Cisco.com*

```
Router(config)# ida-client server url https://www.cisco.com/cgi-bin/
front.x/ids/locator/locator.pl
Router(config)# ip ips auto-update cisco
Router(cnofig-ips-auto-update)# occur-at weekly 0-6 0 3
Router(config-ips-auto-update)# username CCOUSERNAME password CCOPASSWORD
Router(config-ips-auto-update)# exit
Router(config)# password encryption aes
Router(config)# key config-key password-encryption
```

Example 13-10   *Configure Automatic Signature Updates from a Local Server*

```
Router(config)# ip ips auto-update
Router(config-ips-auto-update)# occur-at weekly 0-6 0 3
Router(config-ips-auto-update)# url https://10.1.1.1/sigupdate/ios-sig-update.pkg
```

Verification

To verify automatic signature update operation, use the **show ip ips license** command. The output will show the current signature set release loaded and the dates of its release and application. Example 13-11 shows the command usage and output.

Example 13-11   *Verification of Signature Updates*

```
Router# show ip ips license



IPS License Status valid
```

```
Expiration Date: 2010-12-31
Signatures Loaded:  2010-03-24.S479
Signature Package:  2009-03-19.S479
```

Monitoring Cisco IOS Software IPS Events

A successful intrusion prevention system must include a review of the generated events. Although intrusion prevention by nature can be configured to automatically react to traffic patterns that match signatures, you must analyze log information as well.

Cisco IOS Software IPS Event Generation

Monitoring and managing IPS events fall into one of two categories:

- Real-time event monitoring and management

- Performing analysis on archived log information

Cisco IPS sensors produce several types of events, such as intrusion alerts and status events, that are communicated to client applications such as event management applications using the proprietary SDEE protocol. The Cisco IPS sensors can also be configured to forward intrusion events to its local syslog facility.

SDEE is a standardized IPS communication protocol developed by Cisco for the IDS Consortium at the International Computer Security Association (ICSA). Cisco IPS sensors use SDEE to provide an application programming interface (API) to the IPS that can integrate with third-party management and monitoring solutions. This gives users a choice of third-party solutions to use for monitoring and managing events generated by the Cisco IPS sensor.

SDEE uses a pull communication model for event messages. This allows management consoles to pull alerts from the Cisco IPS sensors over an HTTPS connection.

On a Cisco IOS Software IPS-enabled router, SDEE is always running, but it does not receive and process IPS events unless SDEE notification is specifically enabled. Characteristics of the SDEE protocol are as follows:

- When Cisco SDEE notification is enabled, by default, 200 events can be stored in the local event store. This number can be increased to hold a maximum of 1000. All stored events are lost if SDEE notifications are disabled, and a new local event store is allocated when the notification feature is enabled again.

- The local HTTP or HTTPS server must be enabled on the router when enabling SDEE. It is highly recommended to use HTTPS to secure the data as it travels across the network.

- The Cisco IOS IPS router can send IPS alerts through syslog and can have the SDEE notification feature enabled at the same time.

Cisco IME Features

Cisco IPS Manager Express (IME) is an IPS management application designed to meet the requirements of small- and medium-sized businesses. Cisco IME provides a comprehensive set of application functions but is very intuitive and easy to navigate. There is a high-level information display that integrates the functions of the application that enables quick assessment of network activity and decreases threat response times. There are many functions that can be customized to align with a particular environment, which allows users to adapt the application to their needs and preferences.

Cisco IME can manage both the dedicated Cisco IPS sensor appliances and modules as well as the Cisco IOS Software IPS sensors. The following features are provided for managing the Cisco IOS Software IPS sensors:

- **Monitor events:** IME provides the ability to monitor the IPS events generated by the sensor.

- **Generate reports:** Cisco IME comes with built-in reporting capabilities that allow reports to be generated quickly using predefined templates. The reports are based on current events and/or historical event data stored in the IME event database.

The Cisco IPS Manager Express supports up to ten simultaneous Cisco IPS sensors and has a limit of 100 events per second. The application is available free of charge and can be downloaded from Cisco.com.

Cisco IME Minimum System Requirements

Installing Cisco IPS Manager Express (IME) is a simple task. However, ensure that the system upon which Cisco IME will be installed meets the minimum installation requirements. IME has the following system requirements:

- IBM PC–compatible system with a 2-GHz or faster processor

- Color monitor with at least 1024 x 768 resolution and a video card capable of 16-bit colors

- 100 GB of hard drive space

- 2 GB of RAM

- Java Runtime Environment 1.5.0_07 or higher

- Operating systems:
  - Microsoft Windows Vista Business and Ultimate (32-bit only)

  - Microsoft Windows XP Professional (32-bit only)

  - Microsoft Windows 2003 server

Note: IME supports only the 32-bit U.S. English and Japanese versions of Windows. IME does not support Windows OS virtualization.

Configuration Tasks

Two tasks must be completed to integrate a Cisco IOS Software IPS router with the Cisco IME:

Task 1: Configure the SDEE event feed on the router.

Task 2: Add each Cisco IOS Software IPS router as a sensor to the Cisco IME device list.

Configuration Scenario

The scenario used for the following two tasks includes adding a Cisco IOS Software IPS sensor with an IP address of 10.1.1.1 into a preinstalled Cisco IME system. Additionally, adding the configuration to the router to enable the HTTPS server and the SDEE event store will be completed. For the Cisco IME to connect to the SDEE server on the router, appropriate credentials (username/password combination) must be generated on the router as well.

The steps in this configuration sequence assume that the Cisco ISR is already configured with basic IPS functionality and that full IP connectivity for required connectivity already exists.

Task 1: Configure SDEE and HTTPS Server on the Router

In the first task, the router is configured as the SDEE event server and also has the HTTPS server enabled. A username and password combination is also created with which the Cisco IME will authenticate to the router when retrieving Cisco IPS events from the SDEE event store.

First, enable authentication, authorization, and accounting (AAA) using the **aaa new-model** command and configure default login authentication and exec authorization methods that use the local database. The is accomplished using the **aaa authentication login default local** and the **aaa authorization exec default local** commands. This AAA functionality is needed to allow Cisco IME subscriptions to the local SDEE server using the router's HTTPS server.

Note: When configuring AAA methods, be careful to ensure that the configuration does not impact other access methods or adversely affect traffic flowing to and through the router.

The next step is to enable the router's HTTP server using the **ip http server** command, enable HTTPS with the **ip http secure-server** command, and configure AAA for HTTP connections by using the **ip http authentication aaa** command.

Note: A self-signed certificate will be generated when HTTPS is enabled. This certificate authenticates the HTTPS server to clients. Depending on your environment, it may be necessary to provision a PKI-based certificate for this authentication purpose.

After the HTTPS server is enabled, create a local user account that the Cisco IME will use by entering the **username** command. It is recommended that a long, random password be used because it will be stored in the Cisco IME device database.

Finally, enable SDEE on the router using the **ip ips notify sdee** command. This will create the local SDEE event store and allow authenticated remote systems to pull events from the event store.

Example 13-12 demonstrates putting the commands together to enable SDEE and HTTPS on the router.

Example 13-12 *Configure SDEE and HTTPS Server on the Cisco ISR*

```
Router# configure terminal
Router(config)# aaa new-model
Router(config)# aaa authentication default local
Router(config)# aaa authorization exec default local
Router(config)# ip http server
Router(config)# ip http secure-server
Router(config)# ip http authentication aaa
Router(config)# username viewer secret ghjWqwkAD2342525daa
Router(config)# ip ips notify sdee
Router(config)# end
Router # copy running-config startup-config
```

Task 2: Add the Cisco IOS Software IPS Sensor to Cisco IME

In the second task, the Cisco IOS Software IPS sensor is added to the Cisco IME device database by completing the following steps. Open Cisco IME and perform the following steps:

Step 1.   Navigate to Home > Device List and click Add, as shown in Figure 13-7.

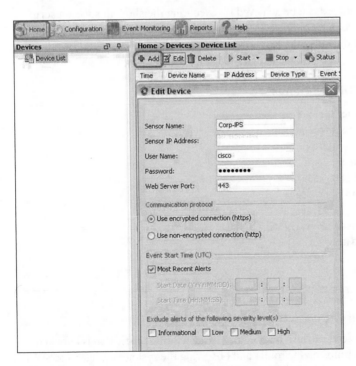

Figure 13-7 *Add Device to Cisco IPS Manager Express*

Step 2.   Enter the information in the required fields in the Add Device dialog box:

    a.   Enter the name and IP address of the router being added.

    b.   Enter the username and password configured for Cisco IME on the router.

    c.   Select the preferred communication protocol (HTTPS or HTTP).

    d.   Select the event start time by either selecting the Most Recent Alerts check box or by entering a start date and time in the Start Date and Start Time fields. To receive a continuous event feed from this moment on, choose the Most Recent Alerts option.

    e.   Under Exclude Alerts of the Following Severity Level(s), optionally select the check boxes of any levels that you want to exclude. The default is to have all levels configured. It is more appropriate to receive all event levels and then use event action filters to exclude specific events.

    f.   Click OK to add the sensor to the IMS system.

Step 3.   If you are connecting to the router of a trusted network, when asked to accept the certificate, click Yes. The IME will store the authorized router certificate locally for subsequent connections.

Note: If you click No to reject the certificate, Cisco IME will not be able to connect to the router.

Verification

Verification of the event feed can be achieved by executing the **show ip sdee subscriptions** command on the router. On Cisco IME, examine the Event Status field in the device list. The field should display the feed as Connected. The CLI output is shown in Example 13-13.

Example 13-13   *Verify SDEE Operation*

```
Router# show ip sdee subscriptions
Configured concurrent subscriptions: 1


SDEE open subscriptions: 1
Subscription ID Router_23452_45384
Client address 10.2.1.101 port 55044
  Subscription opened at 19:03:08 CDT Nov. 15, 2010
  Subscription lat accessed at 13:24:32 CDT Nov. 17, 2010
  Total GET requests: 1345
  Max number of events: 184
  Timeout: 5
```

Verification: Local Events

Verification of an event feed can also be obtained by generating traffic that is known to trigger specific IPS signatures on the router and observing the syslog messages and SDEE events. Routers will always generate syslog messages for every signature that is triggered.

The **show ip sdee alerts** command can be used to view the events that are written to the local SDEE event store. Example 13-14 shows sample output from this command.

Example 13-14   show ip sdee alerts *Command Output*

```
Router# show ip sdee alerts


Event storage:1000 events using 656000 bytes of memory
                           SDEE Alerts

SigID       SrcIP     DstIP     SrcPort   DstPort   Sev   Event ID          SigName
1:100 2004  10.0.0.2  10.0.0.1  8         0         2     10211478597901    ICMP
Echo Req
2:100 2004  10.0.0.2  10.0.0.1  8         0         2     10211478887902    ICMP
Echo Req
3:100 2004  10.0.0.2  10.0.0.1  8         0         2     10211479247903    ICMP
Echo Req
4:100 2004  10.0.0.2  10.0.0.1  8         0         2     10211479457904    ICMP
Echo Req
5:100 2004  10.0.0.2  10.0.0.1  8         0         2     10211479487905    ICMP
Echo Req
```

Verification: IME Events

In the Cisco IME, events pulled from the router's SDEE event store are displayed in the Event Monitoring pane. Double-click an individual event to examine event details for each signature event that triggered.

Cisco IOS Software IPS Sensor

Several Cisco IOS CLI commands can be used to troubleshoot IPS sensor issues. It is recommended to generate traffic that is known to cause one of the configured signatures to trigger and then use the following commands to troubleshoot:

- **show ip ips license**

- **show logging / show ip sdee events**

- **show ip ips signatures**

- **show ip ips event-action-rules filters**

- **debug ip ips** *engine*

- **debug ip ips auto-update**

The following steps represent the recommended process flow for troubleshooting signature triggering on a Cisco IOS Software IPS sensor-enabled router. This process is to troubleshoot a situation in which malicious traffic does not trigger IPS signatures:

Step 1.   Verify that signatures do not actually fire because of triggering events. Use the **show logging and show ip sdee events** commands. Events on the router, but not on the event-monitoring software, indicate an SDEE communication issue rather than a signature-triggering issue.

Step 2. Check that the desired IPS functionality is enabled on all required interfaces. The **show ip ips interfaces command** will display all interfaces on which IPS is enabled.

Step 3. Check to see whether the signatures that are expected to trigger are actually loaded on the router. Use the show logging command to determine whether there were any signature compilation errors. Verify that the IPS license is valid with the **show ip ips license** command. Use the **show ip ips signatures** command to find the signature with the problem and verify that it is enabled and not retired.

Step 4. Ensure that the signature is not being filtered by SEAP event action filters by using the **show ip ips event-action-rules filters** command.

Example 13-15 shows sample output from some of these commands.

Example 13-15 *Troubleshooting Commands*

```
Router# show ip ips license
IPS License Status Valid
Expiration Date: 2009-12-31
Signatures Loaded: 2009-06-25 S375
Signature Package: 2009-06-25 S375


Router# show ip ips signature count
Cisco SDF release version S310.0 ß signature package release version
Trend SDF release version V0.0
Signature Micro-Engine: multi-string: Total Signatures 8
multi-string enabled signatures: 8
multi-string retired signatures: 8
!
Router# show ip ips event-action-rules filters
Filters


Global Filters Status: Enabled


Router# show ip ips auto-update


IPS Auto Update Configuration
URL : tftp://192.168.0.2/jdoe/ips-auto-update/IOS_reqSeq-dw.xml
Username : not configured
Password : not configured
Auto Update Intervals
  minutes (0-59) : 0
  hours (0-23) : 0-23
  days of month (1-31) : 1-31
  days of week: (0-6) : 1-5
```

Troubleshooting Resource Use

One of the common issues found when deploying Cisco IOS Software IPS sensors is the lack of router memory to accommodate the signature database. Use the show logging command to search the logs for %SYS-3-MALLOCFAIL error messages, as demonstrated in Example 13-16. Another Cisco IOS IPS message to search for that would indicate that the compilation of the signature package failed is the %IPS-3-ENGINE_BUILD_FAILED error message.

Example 13-16 show logging *Command Output*

```
Router# show logging
000167: Jun 27 20:50:10.019 NewYork: %SYS-2-MALLOCFAIL: Memory allocation of 8
bytes failed from 0x619282D8, alignment 0
Pool: Processor  Free: 111022040  Cause: Interrupt level allocation
Alternate Pool: None  Free: 0  Cause: Interrupt level allocation
 -Process= "<interrupt level>", ipl= 1 -Traceback= 0x6299A28Cz 0x6377C2C0z
0x6191F720z 0x6034453Cz 0x60345290z
```

Additional Debug Commands

The debug ip ips auto-update command will debug the automatic update process. If all the previous troubleshooting steps have not solved the problem, the debug ip ips *engine-name* command can be used to debug the traffic inspection process used by a particular signature engine. This command should only be used in a test environment because its output is very verbose. Example 13-17 demonstrates output from the debug ip ips auto-update command.

Example 13-17 debug ip ips auto-update *Output*

```
Router# debug ip ips auto-update
Fail to connect to cisco.com
Nov 20 01:52:53.114: IPS Auto Update: ida_connect() failed.
Nov 20 01:52:53.114: IPS Auto-update: Request for download failed!
Nov 20 01:52:53.114: %IPS-4-IPS_AUTO_UPDATE_LOAD_FAILED: IPS Auto Update unable
to load IPS signature file from cisco
Nov 20 01:52:53.114: Timezone and summer-time offset in seconds = 3600
Nov 20 01:52:53.114: IPS Auto Update: setting update timer for next update: 1 hr
s 0 min
```

Exam Preparation

As mentioned in the section, "How to Use This Book," in the Introduction, you have several choices for exam preparation: the exercises here, the memory tables in Appendix C, the final exam preparation chapter, and the exam simulation questions on the CD-ROM. The following questions present a bigger challenge than the exam itself because they use an open-ended question format. By using this more difficult format, you exercise your memory better and prove your conceptual and factual knowledge of this chapter. You can find the answers to these questions in Appendix A, "Answers to the DIKTA Quizzes and Fill in the Blanks Questions."

Review All Key Topics

Review the most important topics in the chapter, noted with the Key Topics icon in the margin of the page. Table 13-5 lists a reference of these key topics and the page numbers on which each is found.

Table 13-5 *Key Topics*

Key Topic Element	Description	Page
Table 13-2	Advantages and limitations of signature-based IPS	338
Bulleted list	Sensor accuracy	339
Paragraph	Software versus hardware IPS platform	340
Table 13-4	Cisco IPS hardware modules	341
Bulleted list	Important deployment guidelines	342

Complete Tables and Lists from Memory

Print a copy of Appendix C, "Memory Tables" (found on the CD), or at least the section for this chapter, and complete the tables and lists from memory. Appendix D, "Memory Table Answers," also on the CD, includes completed tables and lists to check your work.

Define Key Terms

Define the following key terms from this chapter, and check your answers in the Glossary:

intrusion detection system (IDS), intrusion prevention system (IPS), Security Device Event Exchange (SDEE)

Fill in the Blanks

1. When a signature is matched, the Cisco IOS IPS sensors can _____, _____, or _____.

2. A _____ signature is present in router memory and can be enabled without recompiling the signature database.

3. SDEE uses a pull mechanism to pull alerts from IPS sensors over a/an _____ connection.

4. The signature update license is configured on the router using the _____ command.

5. When Cisco SDEE notification is enabled, by default, _____ events can be stored in the local event store. This number can be increased to hold a maximum of _____.

6. The _____ command can be used to view the events that are written to the local SDEE event store.

7. The _____ command displays all interfaces on which IPS is enabled.

8. The Cisco IOS IPS router can send IPS alerts through _____ and can have the _____ feature enabled at the same time.

References

For additional information, refer to these resources:

Cisco Systems, Inc. Cisco Intrusion Prevention System: Introduction, www.cisco.com/go/ips.

Cisco Systems, Inc. Cisco IOS Security Command Reference, Release 15.0M, www.cisco.com/en/US/partner/docs/ios/security/command/reference/sec_book.html.

Cisco Systems, Inc. Cisco Intrusion Detection System Event Viewer 3DES Cryptographic Software Download, www.cisco.com/cgi-bin/tablebuild.pl/ids-ev.

Cisco Systems, Inc. Cisco IOS Security Configuration Guide, Release 12.4: Configuring Cisco IOS Intrusion Prevention System (IPS), www.cisco.com/en/US/docs/ios/security/configuration/guide/12_4/sec_12_4_book.html.

Wikipedia, Christmas Tree Packet, http://en.wikipedia.org/wiki/Christmas_tree_packet.

This chapter covers the following subjects:

- **Choose an appropriate VPN LAN topology:**
  Covers the four main LAN topologies that are appropriate for VPNs to help you choose the correct one for your environment.

- **Choose an appropriate VPN WAN technology:**
  Covers the main WAN technologies that are used in site-to-site VPNs.

- **Evaluate core features of IPsec VPN technology:**
  Covers the core features of IPsec VPN technologies.

- **Choose appropriate VPN cryptographic controls:** Covers the various cryptographic controls for VPNs along with criteria for choosing appropriate controls for your needs.

CHAPTER 14

Introduction to Cisco IOS Site-to-Site Security Solutions

This chapter introduces site-to-site VPN technologies offered by Cisco IOS Software. An IPsec Virtual Private Network (VPN) is a technology that is deployed, in some cases, as an alternative to or as an augmentation to a traditional WAN infrastructure. IPsec VPNs typically are used to provide connectivity between an organization's sites. For example, a branch office can be connected to enterprise headquarters using IPsec VPN technology. IPsec VPNs are also used in conjunction with traditional WAN technologies, such as Frame Relay and Asynchronous Transfer Mode (ATM) circuits. IPsec VPNs do not change WAN requirements; however, they support multiple WAN Layer 2 protocols and provide higher reliability and scalability while usually being more cost-effective. This chapter overviews the many topologies and technologies that are possible with IPsec VPNs.

"Do I Know This Already?" Quiz

The "Do I Know This Already?" quiz helps you decide whether you really need to read the entire chapter. If you already intend to read the entire chapter, you do not necessarily need to answer these questions now.

The ten-question quiz, derived from the major sections in the "Foundation Topics" portion of this chapter, helps you determine how to spend your limited study time.

Table 14-1 outlines the major topics discussed in this chapter and the "Do I Know This Already?" quiz questions that correspond to those topics.

Table 14-1 *"Do I Know This Already?" Foundation Topics Section-to-Question Mapping*

Foundation Topics Section	Questions Covered in This Section
Choose an Appropriate VPN LAN Topology	1–4
Choose an Appropriate VPN WAN Technology	5, 6
Evaluate Core Features of IPsec VPN Technology	7, 8
Choose Appropriate VPN Cryptographic Controls	9, 10

Caution: The goal of self-assessment is to gauge your mastery of the topics in this chapter. If you do not know the answer to a question or are only partially sure of the answer, you should mark this question wrong for purposes of the self-assessment. Giving yourself credit for an answer that you correctly guess skews your self-assessment results and might provide you with a false sense of security.

1. Which network topology is in use when two sites interconnect using a secure VPN using point-to-point connectivity?

   a. Hub-and-spoke network

   b. Partially meshed network

   c. Individual point-to-point VPN connection

   d. Fully meshed network

   e. Star topology network

2. Which network topology is in use when one central site is considered a hub and all other sites connect directly to the hub site? Most user traffic flows between their respective spoke networks and the hub, but when necessary, two spoke sites can communicate by the hub network acting as a relay between the spoke networks.

   a. Partially meshed network

   b. Star topology network

   c. Hub-and-spoke network

   d. Fully meshed network

   e. Individual point-to-point VPN connection

3. Which network topology is in use when multiple sites interconnect with each other dependent upon their communication needs? Each site can have multiple connections to other sites, but there is no one site that is more important than another. If connectivity is needed between two sites that does not exist, another direct VPN connection is added to the network topology.

   a. Hub-and-spoke network

   b. Individual point-to-point VPN connection

   c. Star topology network

   d. Fully meshed network

   e. Partially meshed network

4. Which network topology is in use when every network has a direct VPN connection to every other network? This topology provides any-to-any communication and provides the most optimal direct path for network traffic.

   a. Fully meshed network

   b. Star topology network

   c. Partially meshed network

   d. Individual point-to-point VPN connection

   e. Hub-and-spoke network

5. Which of the following VPN technologies uses nontunneled IPsec as its encapsulation mode?

   a. Individual IPsec tunnels

   b. Cisco Easy VPN

   c. Dynamic Multipoint VPN (DMVPN)

   d. Group Encrypted Transport (GET) VPN

6. Which VPN technology can dynamically and automatically build spoke-to-spoke IPsec tunnels?

  a. Individual IPsec tunnels

  b. Cisco Easy VPN

  c. Dynamic Multipoint VPN (DMVPN)

  d. Group Encrypted Transport (GET) VPN

  e. None of these answers are correct.

7. The Internet Key Exchange (IKE) protocol communicates over which port?

  a. UDP 500

  b. UDP 50

  c. TCP 500

  d. ESP 500

  e. TCP 443

8. Which encapsulation mode, when deployed in tunnel mode, provides confidentiality, authenticity, integrity, and antireplay by encapsulating and protecting the entire original IP packet?

  a. Authentication Headers (AH)

  b. Internet Security Association and Key Management Protocol (ISAKMP)

  c. Diffie-Hellman key exchange with Perfect Forward Secrecy (PFS)

  d. Encapsulating Security Payload (ESP)

9. What should be performed to determine that optimal VPN policies are chosen?

  a. Use default settings for everything.

  b. Use 802.1X as the encryption algorithm.

  c. Perform a formal or informal risk assessment.

  d. Install Cisco MARS.

10. Most cryptographic systems fail because of what reason?

  a. Cryptographic keys are too short

  b. Using pre-shared keys over certificate-based authentication

  c. Inadequate key management operational processes

  d. Weak encryption keys

The answers to the "Do I Know This Already?" quiz are found in Appendix A. The suggested choices for your next step are as follows:

- **8 or less overall score:** Read the entire chapter. This includes the "Foundation Topics" and the "Exam Preparation" section.

- **9 or 10 overall score:** If you want more review on these topics, skip to the "Exam Preparation" section. Otherwise, move on to Chapter 15, "Deploying VTI-Based Site-to-Site IPsec VPNs."

Foundation Topics

Site-to-site VPNs are a popular way to provide secure communication between sites. Secure communication is essential when transmitting over public networks, and IPsec provides protection to important data. There are several choices to be made when designing site-to-site VPN architectures, including the following:

- Choosing an appropriate VPN LAN topology

- Choosing an appropriate VPN WAN technology

- Choosing appropriate VPN cryptographic controls

Upon completion of this chapter, you will have adequate information to make these decisions.

Choose an Appropriate VPN LAN Topology

A network topology depicts the way in which nodes in a network interconnect to form a network. Network topologies for VPN technologies are typically logical in nature because of the fact that the physical connectivity does not affect the capability of the VPN to successfully establish. As long as the two end devices can reach each other, the underlying physical connectivity is insignificant.

The four typical VPN topologies used to create site-to-site VPNs are as follows:

- **Individual point-to-point (P2P) VPN connection:** Two sites connect to each other using secure VPN technologies. Each required connection between two sites requires manually creating a VPN connection.

- **Hub-and-spoke network:** There is a central site that is considered to be a hub and all other sites (the spokes) peer only with the hub. Most traffic patterns exist from spoke to hub, but connectivity between spokes can be relayed through the hub site.

- **Partially meshed network:** Multiple sites requiring connectivity with other sites. VPNs are built as the need arises so that each site will have multiple VPN connections to several other sites.

- **Fully meshed network:** Multiple sites that have a VPN connection to each and every other site. This topology provides the most optimal traffic flow.

Table 14-2 provides a summary of VPN topology details.

Table 14-2   *VPN Topology Comparison*

P2P Tunnels	Hub-and-Spoke	Partial Mesh	Full Mesh
Independent connections between sites	Used when there are a large number of sites that communicate with a central site	Used when a small number of sites need connectivity to many of the other sites but not necessarily all	Used for optimal any-to-any communications
Simple to configure	Provides scalable configuration at the hub	Requires scalable configuration of multiple peers	Requires scalable configuration at all peers

Input Parameters for Choosing the Best VPN LAN Topology

Information about a network must be gathered and analyzed to choose the best VPN topology for an environment. Traffic patterns must be identified so that connectivity requirements can be determined. These patterns can be learned by using Cisco NetFlow capabilities or other traffic analysis tools. In addition to normal traffic patterns, business application requirements should be reviewed to determine whether there are certain applications that have special connectivity requirements. This will have an impact on the topology that is chosen.

General Deployment Guidelines for Choosing the Best VPN LAN Topology

Consider the following general guidelines when determining which VPN topology provides the optimum path and performance for a network:

■ Using individual, manually configured site-to-site VPN connections if the number of required connections is low and managing them can be easily accomplished.

■ Converting an existing partially meshed network to either a fully meshed network or a hub-and-spoke network to facilitate deployment of VPN topologies.

■ Using the hub-and-spoke VPN topology if the physical network infrastructure is already a hub-and-spoke design. This will lend itself to easier deployment and management of the VPN topology.

■ Using the full-mesh VPN topology if there is a requirement for any-to-any connectivity with optimal traffic flow.

Choose an Appropriate VPN WAN Technology

Although IPsec provides standards for transmission protection and key management, there are several deployment choices that must be made. Proper analysis of network traffic patterns and business requirements is required to make these deployment decisions.

The main choices that must be made when deploying site-to-site VPN technologies are in the following areas:

- **User traffic encapsulation technology:** IPsec provides many different encapsulation methods (Authentication Header [AH] and Encapsulating Security Payload [ESP]) and several encapsulating modes (transport mode, tunnel, and a mixed hybrid mode used by Group Encrypted Transport [GET] VPN). Most implementations use IPsec tunnel mode or a combination of IPsec and generic routing encapsulation (GRE) as a method of transport. GET is a mixed encapsulation method that is usually considered as a nontunneling mode and therefore is not recommended for use over public networks.

- **Configuration scalability:** In an environment with a large number of required VPN peers or one that is expected to grow substantially, the network architect should choose a VPN technology that includes configuration scalability to make managing (adding and removing sites from VPNs) VPNs easier.

- **Authentication scalability:** As with configuration scalability, authentication of peers in an IPsec VPN architecture can become cumbersome. Each peer must authenticate a large number of other peers, especially if the partially or fully meshed topologies are deployed. Using a pre-shared key that must be manually shared between peers will not scale well. The number of passwords that need to be shared among peers is found with the formula $n*(n-1)/2$. A network that is fully meshed with 100 nodes would require manually sharing 4500 passwords. Using Public Key Infrastructure (PKI) to provide authentication using certificates provides a scalable solution but requires a properly deployed and maintained PKI and supporting infrastructure to already be in place.

Input Parameters for Choosing the Best VPN WAN Technology

Choosing the appropriate VPN technology for an environment requires analysis of the underlying network. If the VPN will be built across a public transport network, you must choose a tunneling VPN method. You must also consider configuration and authentication scalability when choosing a VPN technology because it will greatly affect network manageability. Table 14-3 summarizes the input parameters.

Table 14-3   *VPN Technology Input Requirement Parameters*

Input	Description
Transport network routing	Determines the choice between tunneling and nontunneling VPN technologies
Topology	Determines the choice between different configuration and authentication methods

Four main site-to-site VPN WAN technologies are available in the Cisco IOS Software:

- **Individual IPsec tunnels:** This technology is implemented using Virtual Tunnel Interfaces (VTI) or GRE over IPsec tunnels. A separate point-to-point tunnel must be provisioned for each and every tunnel peering, limiting this solution with very low configuration scalability. If pre-shared keys are used for authentication between the two peers, this solution is considered to have low authentication scalability. Individual IPsec tunnels are adequate for any transport and can therefore be used across the public Internet, but should be used only in environments where the number of tunnels is very small.

■ **Cisco Easy VPN:** Created to support hub-and-spoke networks, Easy VPN provides very high hub configuration scalability and authentication scalability using either pre-shared keys or PKI. Although this book does not cover Easy VPN configuration for site-to-site VPNs, it is very similar to Easy VPN remote access VPN deployment. Easy VPN does support IP tunneling; therefore, it is adequate for users over any transport network, including the Internet.

■ **Cisco Dynamic Multipoint VPN (DMVPN):** DMVPN is based on a hub-and-spoke configuration but allows spoke-to-spoke tunnels to be dynamically and automatically provisioned. Configuration scalability is high because only spoke-to-hub peering needs to be configured, and as long as PKI is used for authentication, authentication scalability is high as well. DMVPN can be used in hub-and-spoke, partial mesh, and full mesh environments. It is also adequate for connections that traverse public networks, such as the Internet, because it supports IP tunnels.

■ **Cisco GET VPN:** Cisco GET VPN uses a mixed encapsulation in which the IP addressing of the packets does not get changed as it is encapsulated. Because of this, it can only be deployed over networks that can route the internal addresses, such as Multiprotocol Label Switching (MPLS) or private WAN circuits. GET VPNs cannot be deployed over the Internet because of this. Cisco GET defaults to a full mesh topology with a small number of policy/authentication hubs called *key servers*. Because of this, Cisco GET provides high configuration and authentication scalability.

Table 14-4 summarizes the features of the four VPN technology choices.

Table 14-4 *VPN Technology Comparison*

Criterion	P2P IPsec	Easy VPN	DMVPN	GET VPN
Encapsulation	Tunneled IPsec	Tunneled IPsec	Tunneled IPsec	Nontunneled IPsec
Configuration scalability	Low	High for the hub	High for any device	High for any device
Authentication scalability	Low	High with PSK or PKI	High with PKI	High with PSK or PKI
Suitable topologies	P2P	Hub-and-spoke	Hub-and-spoke Partial mesh Full mesh	Full mesh
Suitable transport networks	Any, including the Internet	Any, including the Internet	Any, including the Internet	Private WAN or MPLS; no Internet

General Deployment Guidelines for Choosing the Best VPN WAN Technology

Consider the following general guidelines when determining which VPN technology provides the optimum site-to-site IPsec VPN protection:

- A VPN technology that supports tunneling must be chosen if the transport network does not route internal VPN address spaces. All Cisco IOS Software IPsec VPN technologies except GET VPN use IP tunneling.

- Fully meshed networks demand configuration and authentication on every device. This can be achieved by deploying PKI-based authentication.

- Hub-and-spoke implementations require high configuration and authentication scalability on the hub device. This makes a hub-and-spoke network much easier to deploy in some cases.

Core Features of IPsec VPN Technology

IPsec is a set of security protocols that work together to provide security to IP traffic while in transit. Defined in RFC 4301, "Security Architecture for the Internet Protocol," IPsec provides access control, integrity, authentication, and protection against replays and confidentiality. These services are implemented at the IP layer and therefore protect IP and upper-layer protocols.

IPsec enables a system that chooses various security protocols, determines the necessary algorithms to use for a chosen service, and implements the cryptographic keys needed for those services. IPsec can be used to protect paths between a pair of hosts, between a pair of security gateways (typically a router or firewall), and between a gateway and a host.

In addition to providing encryption at the IP network layer, IPsec also defines a new set of headers that are added to the IP datagram. This new header is inserted after the original IP header and before the Layer 4 protocol. Table 14-5 provides a list of the protocols that comprise IPsec and descriptions of each.

Table 14-5   *IPsec VPN Protocols*

Protocol	Description
Internet Key Exchange (IKE)	Provides a framework that provides policy negotiations and key management processes.
Authentication Headers (AH)	Encapsulation for authentication of user traffic, although this is hardly used anymore. Provides data integrity, data origin authentication, and protection against replay.
Encapsulating Security Protocol (ESP)	Encapsulation for encryption and authentication of user traffic. Provides data integrity, data origin authentication, protection against replay, and confidentiality to user traffic.

IPsec Security Associations

IPsec uses the concept of a Security Association (SA) as a means to describe fundamental security parameters, such as encryption algorithms, keys, traffic specifications, and others. SAs are used by AH and ESP, as well as by one of the major functions within the IKE protocol. SAs are created as a result of an IPsec VPN connection being established between two hosts or two gateways. When a protected connection is created, there will be two SAs that are created, one for each direction.

Internet Key Exchange (IKE)

IKE is a protocol defined by RFC 2408 that uses parts of several other protocols, such as Internet Security Association Key Management Protocol (ISAKMP), Oakley, and Secure Key Exchange Mechanism (SKEME), to dynamically create a shared security policy and authenticated keys for services that require keys, such as IPsec. IKE establishes a secure, authenticated connection that is defined by an IKE SA. This SA is completely distinct from the IPsec SA. The IKE SA is established between two entities and is used to negotiate IPsec SAs. This process calls for the two entities to authenticate themselves to each other and then establish shared session keys that IPsec encapsulations and algorithms use to convert clear-text messages into cipher text.

Reasons to implement IKE in an IPsec configuration include

- Scalability. Without IKE, all IPsec VPN negotiations must be performed manually, on all hosts.

- Manageable manual configuration.

- SA characteristics negotiation.

- Automatic key generation.

- Automatic key refresh.

IPsec Phases

IPsec has two phases:

- **Phase 1:** Two IKE peers establish a secure, authenticated channel and establish shared keying information using a Diffie-Hellman key exchange. This channel is known as the IKE (or ISAKMP) SA. Phase 1 can function in either main mode or aggressive mode.

- **Phase 2:** Additional SAs are established for use by services, such as IPsec or any other service that needs secure keying material or parameter negotiation, or both. IPsec session keys are derived from the initial keying material that was obtained during the Phase 1 Diffie-Hellman key exchange. The IPsec session keys can be optionally created using new, independent Diffie-Hellman key exchanges by enabling the Perfect Forward Secrecy (PFS) option. This Phase 2 exchange is called the IKE Quick Mode. IKE Quick Mode is one of two modes of IKE Phase 2, with the other being the Group Domain of Interpretation (GDOI) Mode used by GET VPN.

IKE Main and Aggressive Mode

IKE Phase 1 can operate in either main or aggressive mode:

- **Main mode:** Permits more flexible IKE policy negotiation and always protects peer identity. This means that an eavesdropper cannot discover the identity of either peer in the IKE exchange. IKE main mode does not support peers with dynamically assigned addresses when using pre-shared keys for authentication. It does support them when PKI-based authentication is in use.

- **Aggressive mode:** Does not provide very much IKE policy negotiation and does not protect peer identity, which could make your VPN susceptible to session hijacking. IKE aggressive mode does support pre-shared key authentication for dynamically addressed peers using names to authenticate. Aggressive mode is faster than main mode but clearly provides a lower level of security.

Encapsulating Security Payload

ESP encapsulation provides a mixture of security services for IPv4 and IPv6, such as confidentiality, authenticity, and integrity of IP data. ESP also provides protection from anti-replay by encrypting, sequencing, and authenticating data that is to be protected; placing it in the data portion of the IP ESP payload; and then sequencing and authenticating the ESP encapsulated packet. Figure 14-1 depicts the headers and trailers that are added to the IP packet as well as what portion of the packet is encrypted or authenticated by ESP.

IPV4 Packet Without ESP Encapsulation

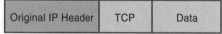

IPV4 Packet Without ESP Encapsulation

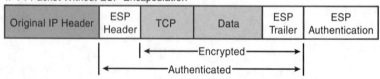

Figure 14-1 *ESP Packet Encapsulation*

Note: There is a performance cost associated with using ESP. This cost is primarily because of the encryption and decryption processes that take place on the data, but there is a packet size cost because of the additional overhead in bytes that ESP adds to an IP packet.

In tunnel mode, ESP encapsulates and protects the entire IP packet. Because the entire IP packet is encapsulated, including the original IP header, a new header is created so that the packet can be forwarded. The new header will have the IP addresses of the encrypting routers. The overhead added to a packet for the ESP encapsulation process is 20 bytes.

Choose Appropriate VPN Cryptographic Controls

As equally as important as choosing an appropriate VPN topology and VPN technology, choosing the proper cryptographic controls ensures that user data is adequately protected.

Choosing the right controls means analyzing risk assessments, the underlying network environment, and customer requirements. There are several cryptographic features about which the network designer must make decisions:

- Choosing IKE peer authentication and algorithms as well as credentials of adequate strength.

- Choosing a policy to protect the IKE key management session (IKE SA). This includes choosing an IKE session encryption algorithm, IKE packet authentication algorithm, and IKE packet integrity assurance algorithms.

- Choosing a policy to protect user traffic. This includes choosing traffic encryption, authentication, and integrity assurance algorithms.

- Choosing key management procedures and processes. This includes key creation, secure key exchange, key storage, key revocation, and key destruction.

IPsec Security Associations

Choosing adequate cryptographic controls means understanding the sensitivity of the data being protected and the trustworthiness of the underlying transport network. Highly sensitive data and an untrusted transport network (such as the Internet) would require stronger controls and longer key lengths.

Another factor that will affect choices about cryptographic controls is the hardware and software capability of existing network devices. IPsec mechanisms can require high-performance CPUs. Some VPN features might require a specific version of Cisco IOS Software that could require a memory upgrade. Table 14-6 summarizes the input parameters.

Table 14-6 *Cryptographic Control Input Parameters*

Input	Description
Sensitivity of data and trustworthiness of the transport network	Determines cryptographic algorithms, key length, and key management
Hardware and software capability	Determines support and usability of hardware and software to provide performance needed for chosen cryptographic controls and key lengths

Algorithm Choices

The two main factors to take into consideration when choosing an encryption algorithm are as follows:

- The views of the cryptographic community will indicate to you whether a particular algorithm is considered trustworthy. Most new algorithms are broken fairly easily, and the ones that have been in use for a long time protecting data are recommended.

- The algorithm under consideration must provide key lengths that meet the organization's data protection requirement. Typically, breaking an encryption algorithm is done through brute-force attacks, so key length is paramount to withstanding these attacks.

In addition to these basic security criteria, performance of an algorithm is another factor that affects which one is chosen. For example, Advanced Encryption Standard (AES) is typically much faster than Triple DES (3DES) on the same hardware.

The cryptographic controls that comprise an ISAKMP policy are discussed in the sections that follow. These are the choices you must make to ensure that your VPN meets the security requirements of your organization.

Encryption Algorithms

Both AES and 3DES are good, trusted choices, with 128-bit AES preferred over other key lengths of AES because of recently discovered noncritical weaknesses in 192-bit and 256-bit AES. 3DES is not recommended for use with Cisco GET VPNs because of possible reuse of its reinitialization vector when using the same group key for many peers.

HMAC Algorithms

Secure Hash Algorithm 1 (SHA-1) is recommended for the Hash-based Message Authentication Code (HMAC) integrity and authentication algorithm. It is the only recommended choice for Cisco IOS Software IKE/IPsec implementations, even though it does contain weaknesses.

Peer Authentication/Signature Algorithms

Rivest, Shamir, and Adelman (RSA) is recommended for asymmetric algorithms as long as an adequately long key is used and the private key is well protected.

Key Exchange Algorithms

For key exchange in IPsec, the Diffie-Hellman algorithm is recommended given that long enough keys are used.

Table 14-7 summarizes the algorithm choices you must make when deploying IPsec VPNs along with the recommended cryptographic control.

Key Topic

Table 14-7   *Algorithm Choices*

Algorithm Role	Recommendations
Peer authentication	Challenge-response - PSK or RSA-based
IKE session encryption	AES-128 or 3DES
IKE session packet authentication and integrity	SHA-1 or HMAC
User traffic encryption	AES-128 or 3DES
User traffic packet authentication and integrity	SHA-1 or HMAC
Key exchange	Diffie-Hellman

Key Length Recommendations

Key length can have a direct influence on the strength of protection provided by a particular algorithm. With most algorithms, the level of protection provided is directly dependent on the key length chosen. Choosing a key length should be done so that the key will protect data for an adequate period of time as long as the algorithm is a trusted algorithm.

Table 14-8 shows minimum recommended key lengths for asymmetric and symmetric encryption algorithms.

Table 14-8   *Key Length Recommendations*

Protection Period	Symmetric Method (3DES/AES) Minimum Key Length	Symmetric Method (HMAC) Minimum Key Length	Asymmetric Method (RSA/DH) Minimum Key Length
Short-term protection against medium organizations (until 2012)	80	160	1248
Medium-term protection (until 2020)	96	192	1776
Medium-term protection (until 2030)	112	224	2432
Long-term protection (until 2040)	128	256	3248

General Deployment Guidelines for Choosing Cryptographic Controls for a Site-to-Site VPN Implementation

Consider the following general guidelines when choosing appropriate cryptographic controls for a site-to-site VPN implementation:

- Always base cryptographic control choices on the result of either formal or informal risk assessment to ensure that the best protection is deployed across untrusted networks. If assessments are not available and cannot be performed, use the strongest protection controls available to reduce risk.

- Consider the dependencies between cryptographic controls so as to not introduce a weakness that actually increases risk to organizational data.

- Most attacks against cryptographic systems today are aimed at the key management system, which is vulnerable to attack because of human factor involvement. To mitigate this, ensure that very efficient key management processes and procedures exist (manually creating keys, revoking keys, storing keys, and so on).

Design and Implementation Resources

Cisco has provided several design and implementation guides that are available on Cisco.com. The Design Zone for WAN/MAN has an IPsec VPN design overview document. In addition, there are several, more specific design guides found on the site. The guides include the following:

■ Group Encrypted Transport VPN Design Guide

■ Infrastructure Protection and Security Service Integration Design for the Next Generation WAN Edge

■ Dynamic Multipoint VPN Design Guide

■ Point-to-Point GRE over IPsec Design Guide

■ Layer 3 MPLS VPN Enterprise Consumer Guide

■ V3PN: Redundancy and Load Sharing Design Guide

■ IPsec Direct Encapsulation VPN Design Guide

Exam Preparation

As mentioned in the section, "How to Use This Book," in the Introduction, you have several choices for exam preparation: the exercises here, the memory tables in Appendix C, the final exam preparation chapter, and the exam simulation questions on the CD-ROM. The following questions present a bigger challenge than the exam itself because they use an open-ended question format. By using this more difficult format, you exercise your memory better and prove your conceptual and factual knowledge of this chapter. You can find the answers to these questions in Appendix A, "Answers to the DIKTA Quizzes and Fill in the Blanks Questions."

Review All Key Topics

Review the most important topics in this chapter, noted with the Key Topics icon in the margin of the page. Table 14-9 lists a reference of these key topics and the page numbers on which each is found.

Table 14-9 *Key Topics*

Key Topic Element	Description	Page
Bulleted list	Four LAN topologies	372
Bulleted list	VPN WAN technology considerations	374
Bulleted list	Four VPN WAN technologies	374
Bulleted list	VPN WAN technologies general guidelines	376
Table 14-5	VPN IPsec protocols	376
Bulleted list	IPsec phases	377
Figure 14-1	Encapsulating Security Payload	378
Table 14-7	IPsec algorithm recommendations	380

Complete Tables and Lists from Memory

Print a copy of Appendix C, "Memory Tables" (found on the CD), or at least the section for this chapter, and complete the tables and lists from memory. Appendix D, "Memory Table Answers," also on the CD, includes completed tables and lists to check your work.

Define Key Terms

Define the following key terms from this chapter, and check your answers in the Glossary:

Internet Key Exchange (IKE), Authentication Headers (AH), Encapsulating Security Payload (ESP), site-to-site VPN, hub-and-spoke network, partially meshed network, fully meshed network, P2P tunnels, Group Encrypted Transport (GET) VPN, generic routing encapsulation (GRE), Public Key Infrastructure (PKI), Virtual Tunnel Interfaces (VTI), Cisco Easy VPN, Dynamic Multipoint VPN (DMVPN), Security Association (SA), AES, DES, HMAC algorithm

Fill in the Blanks

1. Use individual P2P VPN peering only when the number of VPN connections is _____.

2. When using any-to-any communications with direct communication paths with low latency and high throughput, a _____ topology is typically the only choice.

3. A VPN technology that starts with a hub-and-spoke topology but allows dynamically and automatically built VPNs between spoke sites is _____.

4. Cisco GET VPN is considered to be a _____ encapsulation mode and therefore cannot be used on transport networks that cannot route internal VPN addresses.

5. _____ provides a framework that provides policy negotiations and key management processes.

6. _____ is a set of security protocols that work together to provide security to IP traffic while in transit.

7. _____ provides a mixture of security services for IPv4 and IPv6, such as confidentiality, authenticity, and integrity of IP data.

8. A VPN technology that supports _____ must be chosen if the transport network does not route internal VPN address spaces.

References

BlueKrypt - Cryptographic Key Length Recommendation, www.keylength.com.

IPsec VPN WAN Design Overview, www.cisco.com/en/US/docs/solutions/Enterprise/WAN_and_MAN/IPSec_Over.html.

Group Encrypted Transport VPN Design Guide, www.cisco.com/en/US/prod/collateral/vpndeve/ps6525/ps9370/ps7180/GETVPN_DIG_version_1_0_External.pdf.

Infrastructure Protection and Security Service Integration Design for the Next Generation WAN Edge, www.cisco.com/en/US/docs/solutions/Enterprise/WAN_and_MAN/IPSNGWAN.html.

Dynamic Multipoint VPN Design Guide, www.cisco.com/en/US/docs/solutions/Enterprise/WAN_and_MAN/DMVPDG.html.

Point-to-Point GRE over IPsec Design Guide, www.cisco.com/en/US/docs/solutions/Enterprise/WAN_and_MAN/P2P_GRE_IPSec/P2P_GRE.html.

Layer 3 MPLS VPN Enterprise Consumer Guide, www.cisco.com/en/US/docs/solutions/Enterprise/WAN_and_MAN/L3VPNCon.html.

V3PN: Redundancy and Load Sharing Design Guide, www.cisco.com/en/US/docs/solutions/Enterprise/WAN_and_MAN/VPNLoad/VPN_Load.html.

IPsec Direct Encapsulation VPN Design Guide, www.cisco.com/en/US/docs/solutions/Enterprise/WAN_and_MAN/Dir_Encap.html.

This chapter covers the following subjects:

- **Plan a Cisco IOS Software VTI-based site-to-site VPN:** Introduces the virtual tunnel interface (VTI) and discusses pre-deployment tasks for VTI-based VPNs.

- **Configure basic IKE peering using pre-shared keys:** Presents the essential parameters to successfully configure Internet Key Exchange (IKE) between two peers.

- **Configure and verify static point-to-point IPsec VTI tunnels:** Learn how to configure static, point-to-point VPNs.

- **Configure and verify dynamic point-to-point IPsec VTI tunnels:** Learn how to configure dynamic, point-to-point VPNs.

CHAPTER 15

Deploying VTI-Based Site-to-Site IPsec VPNs

IP Security (IPsec) virtual tunnel interfaces (VTI) greatly simplify the configuration process that is required to create site-to-site VPN tunnels. One major benefit of using IPsec VTIs is that it is no longer required to apply an IPsec crypto map to a physical interface. IPsec VTIs function like any other real interface on the router so that many other Cisco IOS Software features can be applied to them. This chapter covers deployment of static and dynamic point-to-point VTI tunnels using Cisco IOS Software.

"Do I Know This Already?" Quiz

The "Do I Know This Already?" quiz helps you decide whether you really need to read the entire chapter. If you already intend to read the entire chapter, you do not necessarily need to answer these questions now.

The eight-question quiz, derived from the major sections in the "Foundation Topics" portion of this chapter, helps you determine how to spend your limited study time.

Table 15-1 outlines the major topics discussed in this chapter and the "Do I Know This Already?" quiz questions that correspond to those topics.

Table 15-1 *"Do I Know This Already?" Foundation Topics Section-to-Question Mapping*

Foundation Topics Section	Questions Covered in This Section
Plan a Cisco IOS Software VTI-Based IPsec VPN	1, 2
Configure Basic IKE Peering Using Pre-Shared Keys	3, 4
Configure Static Point-to-Point IPsec VTI Tunnels	5, 6
Configure Dynamic Point-to-Point IPsec VTI Tunnels	7, 8

Caution: The goal of self-assessment is to gauge your mastery of the topics in this chapter. If you do not know the answer to a question or are only partially sure of the answer, you should mark this question wrong for purposes of the self-assessment. Giving yourself credit for an answer that you correctly guess skews your self-assessment results and might provide you with a false sense of security.

1. The line protocol of a virtual tunnel interface depends on the state of which of the following?

   a. Physical interface

   b. Routing table

   c. VPN tunnel

   d. Peer's VPN tunnel

   e. Crypto map

2. The encapsulation on a virtual tunnel interface must be which of the following?

   a. Frame Relay

   b. ATM

   c. AH or ESP

   d. ISAKMP

   e. HDLC

3. The IKE policy on both peers must match on all parameters except for which of the following?

   a. Authentication

   b. Encryption algorithm

   c. Diffie-Hellman group

   d. Pre-shared key value

   e. ISAKMP lifetime

4. Industry best practices recommend that you use which hash algorithm and DH key length combination for IKE phase 1 policies?

   a. SHA-1 and DH group 5

   b. MD5 and DH group 1

   c. AES-128 and IPsec

   d. DES and RSA

   e. 3DES and ISAKMP

5. Why should static point-to-point virtual tunnel interfaces use IP unnumbered addresses?

   a. It makes static routing easier.

   b. VTIs cannot have their own IPs and must use IP unnumbered addresses.

   c. For a peer to find them.

   d. To conserve IP address space.

6. The line protocol on a virtual tunnel interface goes up and down based upon which of the following?

   a. Seeing its own Ethernet loopback packet return

   b. Successful Layer 2 connectivity

   c. The state of the IPsec SA negotiation

   d. The network administrator not shutting the interface

   e. None of these answers are correct.

7. Where are dynamic point-to-point VTI tunnels deployed?

   a. On the hub router

   b. On each spoke router

   c. On the hub router and on each spoke router

   d. On the VPN concentrator

   e. None of these answers are correct.

8. The IP address of a virtual tunnel interface must be configured using which interface command?

   a. ip address

   b. ip address dhcp

   c. ip address pppoe

   d. ip unnumbered

The answers to the "Do I Know This Already?" quiz are found in Appendix A. The suggested choices for your next step are as follows:

■ **6 or less overall score:** Read the entire chapter. This includes the "Foundation Topics" and the "Exam Preparation" sections.

■ **7 or 8 overall score:** If you want more review on these topics, skip to the "Exam Preparation" section. Otherwise, move on to Chapter 16, "Deploying Scalable Authentication in Site-to-Site IPsec VPNs."

Foundation Topics

VTI-based IPsec site-to-site VPNs are a much simpler way to protect user data while it is in transit between two sites. This chapter covers planning a VTI-based site-to-site IPsec VPN, configuring basic IKE peering with pre-shared keys (PSK), configuring static IPsec VTI tunnels, and configuring dynamic IPsec VTI tunnels using Cisco IOS Software.

Plan a Cisco IOS Software VTI-Based Site-to-Site VPN

IPsec VTIs make it much easier to provide protection to user data when configuring a site-to-site VPN tunnel. Using a virtual tunnel interface is much simpler than using generic routing encapsulation (GRE) or Layer 2 Tunneling Protocol (L2TP) tunnels for encapsulation and IPsec crypto maps. One aspect that is much simpler is that there is no longer a requirement to statically map an IPsec crypto map to a physical interface on the router. The IPsec tunnel endpoint is associated with a virtual interface. Because this virtual tunnel interface is a full-featured routable interface, many of the common interface options that can be applied to physical interfaces can now be applied to the IPsec virtual tunnel interface. Figure 15-1 shows a basic IPsec VTI diagram. User data between the Fast Ethernet 1/0 interface on R1 and the Fast Ethernet 1/0 interface on R3 is protected by the encapsulation and encryption of the IPsec VTI tunnel.

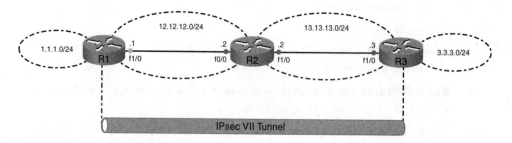

Figure 15-1 *Basic IPsec VTI Tunnel*

When using the VTI IPsec configuration, fewer configuration lines are required because after the virtual tunnel interface is created and an IPsec profile is applied to it, the crypto maps are automatically generated for each tunnel. This chapter covers VTI-based VPNs with static or dynamic peering and pre-shared keys for IKE authentication.

Virtual Tunnel Interfaces

An IPsec VTI is a feature in Cisco IOS Software that is used to support IPsec VPNs. VTIs support native IPsec tunneling, including interoperability with standards-based IPsec implementations of other vendors. The IPsec tunnel endpoint is associated with a routable virtual interface that allows many common interface features to be applied to the IPsec tunnel.

Several features of the VTI include

- VTIs act as regular tunnels, one for each remote side of the VPN.

- The encapsulation must be either IPsec Encapsulating Security Payload (ESP) or Authentication Header (AH).

- The line protocol depends on the state of the VPN tunnels (IPsec Security Associations [SA]).

Example 15-1 shows an IPv4 IPsec tunnel attached to interface GigabitEthernet0/0 on the local router and at the remote router's tunnel endpoint of 192.168.2.2. Traffic to be sent through the tunnel (interesting traffic) is specified in the IPsec profile named ENC-Profile.

Example 15-1 *IPsec VTI Configuration*

```
Router# configure terminal
Router(config)# interface Tunnel0
Router(config-if)# description VPN tunnel to branch office
Router(config-if)# ip unnumbered GigabitEthernet0/0
Router(config-if)# tunnel source GigabitEthernet0/0
Router(config-if)# tunnel destination 192.168.2.2
Router(config-if)# tunnel mode ipsec ipv4
Router(config-if)# tunnel protection ipsec profile ENC-Profile


Router# copy running-config startup-config
```

IPsec VTIs have many benefits:

- **Simplify configuration:** Configuring IPsec peering is much simpler when using virtual tunnel interfaces as compared to configuring IPsec peering with crypto maps or GRE/IPsec tunnels.

- **Flexible interface feature support:** An IPsec VTI is a Cisco IOS Software interface that offers the flexibility of accepting features that can be applied to physical interfaces (that operate on ciphertext traffic) or the IPsec VTI that operates on clear-text traffic.

- **Support for multicast:** IPsec VTIs support multicast traffic such as voice and video.

- **Better scalability:** IPsec VTIs require fewer SAs to support all types of traffic.

- **Routable interface:** Like GRE/IPsec, VTIs support all types of IP routing protocols, which provides scalability and redundancy.

The IPsec VTI has the following limitations:

- The IPsec VTI is limited to only IP unicast and multicast traffic, while the GRE/IPsec tunnels support a much wider range of protocols and applications.

- Cisco IOS Software IPsec stateful failover is not supported on VTIs, although other redundancy features, such as dynamic routing protocols, can be used as alternative failover methods.

Table 15-2 summarizes the benefits and limitations of using Cisco IOS Software IPsec VTIs.

Table 15-2   *VTI Benefits and Limitations*

Benefits	Limitations
Simplified configuration	No multiprotocol support—IP only
Flexible interface feature support	No Cisco IOS Software IPsec failover support
Multicast support	
Improved scalability	
Simple routing protocol capabilities	

Input Parameters

The following information must be accumulated when configuring VTI-based VPNs:

- **Existing hardware:** Need to determine whether existing hardware can provide the performance required to support VTI-based VPNs. Integrated Services Router (ISR)/ISR-Generation 2 (G2) routers can include an Advanced Integration Module (AIM) hardware accelerator, onboard encryption modules, or even software encryption.

- **Existing software:** Need to determine whether existing software can support strong cryptographic algorithms and support for VTI routers only.

- **Addressing and routing:** Need to determine current IP addressing scheme and routing paths to direct traffic through the virtual tunnel interface.

- **Cryptographic standards:** For a VPN link to establish, both endpoint devices must agree on a set of algorithms to be used for the connection.

Table 15-3 summarizes the information that must be gathered prior to deploying a VTI-based IPsec VPN.

Table 15-3   *Input Parameters*

Input	Description
Existing hardware and software	Required to determine feature support
IP addresses of VPN endpoint termination devices	Required to determine routing outside the VPN
IP addresses of internal networks	Required to determine routing inside the VPN
Cryptographic standards and security requirements	Required to choose the appropriate algorithms and key management inside IPsec VPNs

Deployment Tasks

Deploying VTI-based site-to-site tunnels requires that some of or all the following high-level tasks be performed:

Step 1.   Configure Internet Key Exchange (IKE) peering between VPN endpoints.

Step 2.   Configure an IPsec traffic protection policy on all peers.

Step 3.   Configure a static or dynamic VTI tunnel on each peer.

Step 4.   Configure static or dynamic routing over the VTI tunnels.

Deployment Choices

Some choices need to be made when deploying VTI-based site-to-site tunnels. Table 15-4 provides information about these choices.

Table 15-4   *IPsec VTI Deployment Choices*

Deployment Choice	Criteria
Static or dynamic VTI tunnels	Dynamic VTI tunnels should be for the hub in large hub-and-spoke implementations. Otherwise, static VTI tunnels are recommended.
Static or dynamic routing protocol over the VTI tunnels	Dynamic routing protocols should be used in large networks or to provide redundancy with multiple VTI tunnels. Otherwise, static routing over VTI tunnels is recommended.

General Deployment Guidelines

Consider the following guidelines when deploying VTI-based site-to-site IPsec VPNs:

- Use VTI-based site-to-site VPNs as the default IPsec technology for individual point-to-point VPN links and for hub-and-spoke VPNs.

- Consider deploying Dynamic Multipoint VPN (DMVPN) or Group Encrypted Transport (GET) VPN for larger environments with partial or fully meshed VPN requirements.

Configuring Basic IKE Peering

When configuring VTI-based site-to-site IPsec VPNs, the first step that must be completed is to configure IKE peering between VPN peers. Determine an appropriate IKE Internet Security Association and Key Management Protocol (ISAKMP) Phase 1 policy that meets the requirements of the organization and then configure these policies on all peers. Developing a well-planned IKE policy plan prior to deployment will enhance the chances of a successful deployment. The following list of parameters must be configured in an

ISAKMP policy. These parameters must match on the two peers for a successful Phase 1 negotiation:

- **Determine the peer authentication method:** Choose the authentication method based on credentials from all peers. Cisco IOS Software provides support for pre-shared keys; Rivest, Shamir, and Adleman (RSA)–encrypted nonces; and RSA signatures to authenticate IPsec peers.

- **Determine the protection policy for the IKE session:** Choose the encryption and hashing algorithms.

- **Determine the key length:** Choose the length of the Diffie-Hellman keys.

- **Determine the IKE session lifetime:** Choose an appropriate lifetime for the IKE session.

The choices made for the preceding parameters provide the data that will be needed later in the configuration steps.

Cisco IOS Software Default IKE PSK-Based Policies

Cisco IOS Software Release 12.4(20)T introduced default IKE policies. There are eight default policies with priorities ranging from 65507 to 65514, with 65507 having the highest priority and 65514 having the lowest priority. The highest-priority pre-shared key–based policy (65508) in Table 15-5 provides the highest protection of the default policies. It provides Advanced Encryption Standard (AES) for the encryption algorithm, Secure Hash Algorithm (SHA) for the hash algorithm, and Diffie-Hellman (DH) group 5.

Table 15-5 *Cisco IOS Software Default IKE PSK-Based Policies*

Priority	Authentication Algorithm	Encryption Algorithm	Hash Algorithm	DH Group
65508	PSK	AES	SHA	5
65510	PSK	AES	MD5	5
65512	PSK	3DES	SHA	2
65514	PSK	3DES	MD5	2

Policies that use message digest algorithm 5 (MD5) for the hash algorithm or DH group 2 as SHA-1 and DH5 are stronger.

Configuration Tasks

Perform the following steps to configure basic IKE peering:

Task 1.   (Optional) Configure an IKE (ISAKMP) policy on each peer.

Task 2.   Generate authentication credentials (PSKs) for each pair of peers.

Task 3.   Configure authentication credentials.

Configuration Choices

Several choices must be taken into consideration when configuring basic IKE peering. The default IKE policies provide adequate security, but certain environments might dictate requirements that necessitate choosing different IKE policy aspects. For example, choosing a stronger DH group to provide longer protection might satisfy requirements but will come at a cost to performance, because the stronger DH group will mean heavier computational load during the IKE exchange.

IKE lifetimes are configured by default to be conservative. If VPN peers will not agree on an IKE lifetime parameter, change it to an acceptable value. Note that Cisco IOS Software does not require that the IKE peers have matching IKE lifetime settings for a successful exchange. The IKE SA will establish by adjusting its IKE session lifetime to the shorter of the two settings.

Configuration Scenario

The configuration scenario used in the topic's configuration sequence that follows includes two IKE peers that have 172.17.1.1 and 172.17.2.4 configured on their untrusted interfaces. They will be configured using the following policy parameters:

- **IKE authentication:** Pre-shared keys

- **IKE hash algorithm:** SHA-1 Hash-based Message Authentication Code (HMAC)

- **IKE encryption:** 128-bit AES

- **IKE key exchange:** Diffie-Hellman Group 14 (2048-bit key length)

- **IKE session lifetime:** One hour (3600 seconds)

A strong pre-shared authentication key will also be generated and configured on both peers as part of the scenario. Assumptions are that connectivity between the two peers exists and that IKE sessions are permitted along the path between the two outside interfaces of each peer.

Task 1: (Optional) Configure an IKE Policy on Each Peer

The first configuration task for IKE peering is optional because of the default policies provided by Cisco IOS Software. To create a custom IKE policy that meets organizational requirements, create the policy with the crypto isakmp policy global configuration command. Inside this policy, set the necessary parameters with the commands shown in Example 15-2.

Example 15-2 *Configure IKE Policy*

Key
Topic

```
Router# configure terminal
Router(config)# crypto isakmp policy 10
Router(config-isakmp)# authentication pre-share
Router(config-isakmp)# hash sha
Router(config-isakmp)# encryption aes 128
Router(config-isakmp)# group 14
```

```
Router(config-isakmp)# lifetime 3600
Router(config-isakmp)# exit
Router(config)# crypto isakmp key !%@$^#@&%RRETWERsdf address 172.17.2.4
Router(config)# end
Router# copy running-config startup-config
```

Tasks 2 and 3: Generate and Configure Authentication Credentials on Each Peer

The second and third configuration tasks are the generation and configuration of authentication credentials (pre-shared keys). Be sure to create random, long pre-shared keys to provide strong protection. Bind the pre-shared key to the tunnel destination IP address of each peer using the **crypto isakmp key** command, as shown in Example 15-3.

Example 15-3   *Bind Pre-Shared Key to IKE Peer*

```
Router# configure terminal
Router(config)# crypto isakmp key !%@$^#@&%RRETWERsdf address 172.17.2.4
Router(config)# end
Router# copy running-config startup-config
```

Verify Local IKE Policies

Use the **show crypto isakmp policy** command to display the parameters configured for each local IKE policy. Unless you have added custom IKE policies with the **crypto isakmp policy** command or have removed the default IKE policies with the **no crypto isakmp default policy** command, the default IKE policies will be displayed as the output of the **show isakmp policy** command. Example 15-4 shows the parameters that are displayed after the command is issued.

Example 15-4   *Verify IKE Policy on Local Router*

```
Router# show crypto isakmp policy



Global IKE policy
Protection suite of policy 10
    Encryption algorithm:  AES - Advanced Encryption Standard (128 bit keys)
    Hash algorithm:          Secure Hash Algorithm
    Authentication method: Pre-shared Key
    Diffie-Hellman Group:  #14 (2048 bit)
    Lifetime:             3600 seconds, no volume limit
```

Verify Local IKE Sessions

Use the **show crypto isakmp sa** command to display the current IKE Security Associations (SA) on the local router. The QM_IDLE status indicates successful establishment of the IKE SA, meaning that the ISAKMP process is idle after having successfully negotiated and established SAs. Example 15-5 shows the output of the **show crypto isakmp sa** command.

Example 15-5   *Displaying the Current IKE SA on Local Router*

```
Router# show crypto isakmp sa
IPv4 Crypto ISAKMP SA
Dst              src              state         conn-id    status
172.17.2.4       172.17.1.1       QM_IDLE         1004      ACTIVE
```

Note: With the Cisco IOS Software crypto map based system, the IPsec subsystem will request SAs to be established upon seeing interesting traffic that matches the crypto map. In a VTI-based IPsec VPN, IPsec requests SA establishment as soon as the virtual tunnel interface (VTI)s are fully configured.

Verify a Successful Phase 1 Exchange

The **debug crypto isakmp** debugging command will display the "SA has been authenticated" debug message after the IKE Phase 1 peering is successful.

Implementation Guidelines

Consider the following implementation guidelines when configuring basic IKE peering:

- Each peer must have the same IKE policy. The lifetime parameter is the only one that is not required to match. Multiple policies can be configured to support several peers.

- If possible, it is recommended to use the same, strong IKE policy for all peers.

- Do not use the same key for all peers or groups of peers.

- If possible, use a utility to generate random pre-shared keys.

Troubleshooting IKE Peering

Several commands are provided by Cisco IOS Software to troubleshoot basic IKE peering. Use the **ping** command to first verify connectivity between the two peers. Use **the** traceroute command to troubleshoot connectivity issues if pings fail.

The **show crypto isakmp policy** command can be executed on both peers to compare IKE parameters and ensure that they match. The **debug crypto isakmp** debugging command will display debugging messages during IKE negotiation and session establishment. These debugging commands should be executed and analyzed on both peers.

Troubleshooting Flow

Follow these steps to proceed through the recommended flow for troubleshooting IKE peering:

Step 1.   Verify peer reachability using the **ping** and **traceroute** commands with the tunnel source and destination IP addresses on both peers. If connectivity is verified, proceed to Step 2; otherwise, check the path between the two peers for routing or access (firewall or access list) issues.

Step 2.   Verify the IKE policy on both peers using the **show crypto isakmp policy** command. Debug messages revealed by the **debug crypto isakmp** command will also point out IKE policy mismatches.

Step 3.   Verify IKE peer authentication. The **debug crypto isakmp** command will display unsuccessful authentication.

Step 4.   Upon successful completion of Steps 1–3, the IKE SA should be establishing. This can be verified with the **show crypto isakmp sa** command and looking for a state of QM_IDLE.

Configuring Static Point-to-Point IPsec VTI Tunnels

Static VTI VPN tunnels provide secure connectivity between two sites. Deploying static VTI tunnels involves configuring a Cisco IOS Software tunnel interface on both VPN peers. These tunnel interfaces uniquely identify the peering between the two sites. Static VTI tunnels are permanently established immediately after being configured and can be used to provision a limited number of site-to-site IPsec tunnels in either hub-and-spoke or meshed IPsec VPNs.

Default Cisco IOS Software IPsec Transform Sets

Transform sets are bundles of cryptographic algorithms that are used together to protect traffic flows as defined by a VPN policy. IPsec transform sets define the encapsulation (ESP or AH), the packet authentication/integrity algorithm (SHA-1 or MD5), and the IPsec mode (transport or tunnel) that is used with a VPN policy.

Cisco IOS Software Release 12.4(20)T introduced default IPsec transform sets, as summarized in Table 15-6. If custom transform sets are not configured, IKE negotiation results in the use of ESP encapsulation, 3DES encryption, and SHA-1 HMAC for authentication/integrity.

Table 15-6   *Cisco IOS Software Default IPsec Transform Sets*

Priority	Encapsulation	Encryption Algorithm	Hash Algorithm
Higher	ESP	3DES	SHA-1
Lower	ESP	AES-128	SHA-1

Configuration Tasks

Perform the following tasks to configure site-to-site VPN peering using a static point-to-point VTI tunnel on each peer:

Key Topic

Task 1.   Configure IKE peering between the two peers. The configuration steps were provided in the previous topic.

Task 2.   (Optional) Configure an IPsec transform set. This is optional because default transform sets are used if no custom transform sets are configured.

Task 3.   Configure an IPsec protection profile to specify a traffic protection policy for the VTI tunnel.

Task 4.   Configure a VTI and provide it with IP addressing.

Task 5.   Enable IPsec encapsulation on the VTI and apply the IPsec protection profile to the VTI.

Task 6.   Configure static or dynamic routing through the VTI tunnel.

Configuration Choices

The following configuration choices must be analyzed prior to configuring a VTI-based IPsec tunnel:

■   The optional, second step in the task list calls for configuring an IPsec transform set. The default transform set with higher priority uses Triple DES (3DES) as its encryption algorithm, which can cause lower performance on some platforms. The decision must be made to either use the default transform set or to create a custom one that uses AES-128.

■   Terminating the VTI tunnel on a loopback interface will provide redundancy as opposed to when a physical interface is used. The choice to use a loopback to route around a failed physical interface can provide resiliency to your VPN tunnel.

Configuration Scenario

The configuration scenario used in the topic's configuration sequence that follows includes two IKE peers that have untrusted interfaces using the IP addresses of 172.17.1.1 and 172.17.2.4. A static VTI tunnel between the IP addresses with static routing will be configured. Assumptions are that connectivity between the two peers exists and that IKE sessions are permitted along the path between the two outside interfaces of each peer. Also assumed is that basic IKE peering, as covered in the previous topic, is in place.

Task 1: (Optional) Configure an IKE Policy on Each Peer

Refer to the section, "Task 1: (Optional) Configure an IKE Policy on Each Peer," under the section "Configuring Basic IKE Peering," which documented how to configure IKE peering between the two peers.

Task 2: (Optional) Configure an IPsec Transform Set

The second configuration task is the optional task of creating a custom IPsec transform set. For example, to configure an IPsec transform set named AES128-SHA that uses ESP tunnel mode, with 128-bit AES encryption and SHA-1 HMAC integrity/authentication algorithms, you would enter the following:

```
Router(config)# crypto ipsec transform-set AES128-SHA esp-aes 128 esp-sha-hmac
```

Task 3: Configure an IPsec Protection Profile

Task 3 in the VTI-based VPN peering sequence is the configuration of an IPsec protection profile. The IPsec protection profile specifies the traffic protection policy for the VTI tunnel and includes the following basic parameters:

- **IPsec transform set used in the protection policy:** The default IPsec transform set will be used if a custom transform set has not been configured.

- **IPsec SA (session key) lifetimes:** The default lifetime of 1 hour will be used if not configured differently.

- **Perfect Forward Secrecy (PFS):** PFS will not be negotiated by default.

Example 15-6 shows the **crypto ipsec profile** global configuration command being used to create a named IPsec profile (MYIPsecProfile). Inside profile configuration mode, the administrator has specified a custom transform set using the **set transform-set** command and specifying the name of the custom transform set.

Example 15-6 *Configure IPsec Protection Profile*

```
Router(config)# crypto ipsec profile MYIPsecProfile
Router(ipsec-profile)# set transform-set AES128-SHA
Router(ipsec-profile)# end
Router# copy running-config startup-config
```

Task 4: Configure a Virtual Tunnel Interface (VTI)

The fourth configuration task for VTI-based VPN peering is the creation and basic configuration of the VTI:

Step 1.   Using a new, unused tunnel interface number, create a new tunnel interface using the **interface tunnel** configuration command and give it an IP address and subnet mask using the **ip address** interface configuration command. As an alternative, use IP unnumbered addressing as shown in Example 15-7 by issuing the **ip unnumbered** command.

Step 2.   Configure a tunnel source address by using the **tunnel source** interface configuration command.

Step 3.   With the **tunnel destination** interface configuration command, configure a tunnel destination address by specifying the remote peer's remote IP address.

Key
Topic

Example 15-7 *Configure a Virtual Tunnel Interface (VTI)*

```
Router(config)# interface Tunnel0
Router(config-if)# ip unnumbered GigabitEthernet0/0
Router(config-if)# tunnel source GigabitEthernet0/0
Router(config-if)# tunnel destination 172.17.2.4
Router(config-if)# end
Router# copy running-config startup-config
```

Task 5: Apply the Protection Profile to the Tunnel Interface

Task 5 is a required task that configures the IPsec encapsulation on the tunnel using the **tunnel mode ipsec ipv4** command and applies the traffic protection policy to the tunnel by using the **tunnel protection ipsec profile** command. Example 15-8 illustrates the usage of these commands.

Example 15-8 *Apply a Protection Profile to a Tunnel Interface*

```
Router(config)# interface Tunnel0
Router(config-if)# tunnel mode ipsec ipv4
Router(config-if)# tunnel protection ipsec profile MYIPsecProfile
Router(config-if)# end
Router# copy running-config startup-config
```

Task 6: Configure Routing into the VTI Tunnel

In the sixth and final configuration task, Example 15-9 shows a configuration that is routing to all reachable networks through the tunnel. The example shows a static route for the 10.1.2.0/24 network that is pointing to the Tunnel0 interface. The other VPN router will have a similar configuration that routes the 10.1.1.0/24 network (the local router's inside LAN) into the VTI VPN tunnel.

Example 15-9 *Configure Routes Pointing to the New Tunnel Interface*

```
Router(config)# ip route 10.1.2.0 255.255.255.0 Tunnel0
Router(config-if)# end
Router# copy running-config startup-config
```

Implementation Guidelines

Consider the following when configuring static point-to-point VTI tunnels:

- It is recommended that the VTI tunnel use unnumbered IP addressing to conserve IP address space.

- Using dynamic routing protocols instead of static routing statements will increase the scalability and manageability of a VTI-based VPN deployment.

- To prevent recursive routing lookups, make sure that the tunnel destination is learned over the physical interface and not the tunnel interface.

Verify Tunnel Status and Traffic

Verify the status of the local tunnel interface using the **show interface tunnel** command. The output of this command will provide information about the status of the line and the line protocol of the tunnel interface. Recall that line protocol on a virtual tunnel interface is dependent upon the IPsec SA bound to that interface. Line protocol will go up when an IPsec SA is successfully established. It also shows packet counts for input and output traffic statistics.

To verify the status of the IPsec SA for a particular peer, execute the **show crypto ipsec sa peer** command. This command provides statistical information such as the number of packets that have been successfully encapsulated/decapsulated, encrypted/decrypted, and hash-digested/verified by IPsec. Verify that the statistics have nonzero values and that the IPsec SAs are filled in with numbers, indicating that IPsec SAs have been negotiated.

The **show ip route | include Tunnel** command will display all routes pointing to the virtual tunnel interface. Routes for destination networks that are reachable through VPN peers should be pointing toward the appropriate VTI.

The **debug crypto isakmp** command displays messages about IKE events. After the IKE SA has been established, IKE moves to Quick Mode to negotiate IPsec SAs. During quick mode negotiations, the "IPsec policy invalidated proposal" message indicates a mismatch in IPsec (IKE Phase 2) policies on the two peers. Investigate the Phase 2 parameters on each peer to locate the one that does not match.

Look for the "sa created" debug message in the output of the **debug crypto ipsec** debugging command. This success message should also cause the tunnel interface line protocol to change its state to "up."

To summarize, you troubleshoot static point-to-point VTI tunnels by using several commands to verify that Phase 1 completed successfully. After ensuring that basic IKE peering has succeeded, follow with these troubleshooting commands to make sure that Phase 2 completed successfully and that you can route traffic through the tunnel. The following commands help troubleshoot Phase 2 negotiation and routing through the tunnel:

- **show interface tunnel** verifies the status of the virtual tunnel interface.

- **debug crypto isakmp** displays debugging messages about IKE events.

- **debug crypto ipsec** displays debugging messages about IPsec SA establishment.

- **show crypto ipsec sa** can directly verify the status of an IPsec SA.

- **show ip route | include Tunnel** displays all routes pointing to local tunnels interfaces.

Troubleshooting Flow

Perform the following steps to troubleshoot static VTI tunnels:

Step 1. If traffic is not flowing through the tunnel, first check to see that the IKE SAs are successfully established. If the SAs are in place, proceed to Step 2.

Step 2. Verify that the IPsec SAs are established. Use the **show crypto ipsec sa, debug crypto isakmp, debug crypto ipsec,** or **show interface tunnels** command to verify and troubleshoot IPsec SAs. After the IPsec SAs are established, proceed to Step 3.

Step 3. Verify the routing of user traffic. Use the **show ip route | include Tunnel** command to verify routing. Use static or dynamic routing to correct routing if necessary.

Configure Dynamic Point-to-Point IPsec VTI Tunnels

Dynamic VTIs (DVTI) provide scalable hub configurations in hub-and-spoke VPNs for site-to-site and remote-access connectivity. With DVTIs, there is no requirement to statically map IPsec sessions to physical interfaces. Instead, VTIs on the hub are created dynamically as tunnels to the hub are established. A virtual access interface is dynamically created based on a preconfigured virtual template that includes all the required IPsec configuration as well as any Cisco IOS Software features that are desired, such as quality of service (QoS), NetFlow, or access control lists (ACL).

Using dynamic VTIs requires minimal configuration on the hub router to support a VPN with a large numbers of VTIs. When a spoke peer initiates a tunnel, the tunnel and dynamic VTI are created. On the spoke peer, use a static VTI to establish a tunnel with the hub peer.

Virtual Templates and Virtual Access Interfaces

When a dynamic VTI is created as spoke peers attempt to create VPN connections with the hub peer, dynamic VTIs on the hub do not appear as a tunnel interface as they do with static VTIs. Instead, they appear as virtual access interfaces that are created from information configured in a virtual template interface. Virtual template interfaces are sets of common settings that contain the information needed to build the virtual access interfaces. The settings in the virtual template interface are for all dynamic interfaces and include the hub IP address inside the tunnel (unnumbered), the tunnel mode (IPsec), and the tunnel protection, and can optionally include other Cisco IOS Software services, such as NetFlow accounting or firewall policy settings. The router uses this information to create a virtual access interface (DVTI). Other information in the virtual template interface is added to the virtual access interface as the spoke completes IKE negotiations, such as the tunnel source and destination IP address.

Example 15-10 portrays a virtual template and the virtual access interface that is created as tunnels to the hub are established. A virtual access interface is dynamically created based on a preconfigured virtual template that includes all the required IPsec configuration as well as any Cisco IOS Software features that are desired, such as QoS, NetFlow, or ACLs.

Example 15-10 *Virtual Template and Virtual Access Interface Configuration*

```
Interface Virtual-template 1
  Ip unnumbered FastEthernet0/0
  Tunnel mode ipsec ipv4
  Tunnel protection ipsec profile Profile1
  Ip flow ingress
  Zone-member security B2BVPN-Zone

Interface Virtual-access 125
Ip unnumbered FastEthernet0/0
Tunnel source 10.1.1.1
Tunnel mode ipsec ipv4
```

```
Tunnel destination 10.1.1.2
Tunnel protection ipsec profile Profile1
No tunnel protection ipsec initiate
Ip flow ingress
Zone-member security B2BVPN-Zone
```

ISAKMP Profiles

Another feature of Cisco IOS Software, called an ISAKMP profile, is required to use DVTIs. ISAKMP profiles contain a set of **match** statements used to define a peer or set of peers. For example, with a basic pre-shared key VPN, peer identity is based upon IP address. However, the peer identity could also be based on a peer's fully qualified domain name (FQDN) or fields from a peer's certificate subject name. ISAKMP profiles can possibly match on a single peer, multiple peers, or even no peers based on the identity information received during the IKE negotiations.

ISAKMP profiles are used to find remote peers that can use virtual template interfaces and create DVTIs from it.

Configuration Tasks

Perform the following tasks to configure site-to-site VPN peering using a dynamic point-to-point VTI tunnel on a hub router:

Key Topic

Task 1.   Configure IKE peering using pre-shared key key rings instead of per-peer ISAKMP keys.

Task 2.   (Optional) Configure an IPsec transform set. This is optional because default transform sets are used if no custom transform sets are configured.

Task 3.   Configure an IPsec protection profile to be applied to the virtual template interface.

Task 4.   Configure a virtual template interface on which IPsec encapsulation will be enabled and the protection profile from Task 3 will be applied.

Task 5.   Configure an ISAKMP profile to map remote peers to the configured virtual template interface.

Configuration Scenario

The configuration scenario used in the topic's configuration sequence that follows includes two IKE peers that have untrusted interfaces using the IP addresses of 172.17.1.1 and 172.17.2.4. A static VTI tunnel between the IP addresses with static routing will be configured. Assumptions are that connectivity between the two peers exists and that IKE sessions are permitted along the path between the two outside interfaces of each peer. Also assumed is that basic IKE peering, as covered in the previous topic, is in place.

Figure 15-2 shows the configuration scenario for the configuration tasks that follow. The hub router will be configured to protect bidirectional traffic from both SiteA (10.1.2.0/24) and SiteB (10.1.3.0/24). These networks are connected directly to the central site (10.1.1.0/24). The hub will be configured for dynamic VTI by creating a VTI tunnel template that will accept tunnels from both peers and then dynamically create the point-to-point hub-and-spoke tunnels (DVTIs). Assumed for this scenario are the facts that full connectivity exists where required and that IKE peering is configured on all peers.

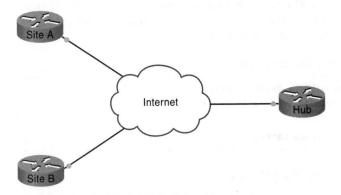

Figure 15-2 *Dynamic VTI Scenario*

Task 1: Configure IKE Peering

The first task in configuring a dynamic point-to-point VTI tunnel on the hub router is to create authentication pre-shared keys for remote peers and then group them into a named key ring using the **crypto keyring** global configuration command. Use the **pre-shared-key address** command inside the key ring to specify a pre-shared key for a specific peer IP address. The command usage is shown in Example 15-11.

Example 15-11 *IKE Peering with Pre-Shared Key Key Ring*

```
Crypto keyring NEWKEYRING
  Pre-shared-key address 172.17.2.4 key ier58ewrui90aEEQEd0erq9u2i3j5p
  Pre-shared-key address 172.17.2.7 key iqwur@#$7234898245@#3jk23jh244
```

Task 2: (Optional) Configure an IPsec Transform Set

The second configuration task is the optional task of creating a custom IPsec transform set on the hub router. To configure an IPsec transform set named AES128-SHA that uses ESP tunnel mode, with 128-bit AES encryption and SHA-1 HMAC integrity/authentication algorithms, you would enter the following:

```
Router(config)# crypto ipsec transform-set AES128-SHA esp-aes 128 esp-sha-hmac
```

Task 3: Configure an IPsec Protection Profile

Task 3 in the VTI-based VPN peering sequence is the configuration of an IPsec protection profile. The IPsec protection profile specifies the traffic protection policy for the VTI tunnel and includes the following basic parameters:

- **IPsec transform set used in the protection policy:** The default IPsec transform set will be used if a custom transform set has not been configured.

- **IPsec SA (session key) lifetimes:** The default lifetime of 1 hour will be used if not configured differently.

■ **Perfect Forward Secrecy (PFS):** Will not be negotiated by default.

Example 15-12 shows the **crypto ipsec profile** global configuration command being used to create a named IPsec profile (MYIPsecProfile). Inside profile configuration mode, the administrator has specified a custom transform set using the **set transform-set** command and specifying the name of the custom transform set.

Example 15-12 *Configure IPsec Protection Profile*

```
Router(config)# crypto ipsec profile MYIPsecProfile
Router(ipsec-profile)# set transform-set AES128-SHA
Router(ipsec-profile)# end
Router# copy running-config startup-config
```

Task 4: Configure a Virtual Template Interface

Task 4 in the DVTI VPN peering sequence is the configuration of a virtual template interface upon which common settings for dynamic VTIs will be defined as well. Example 15-13 shows the **interface Virtual-template1 type tunnel** global configuration command being used to create a virtual template interface.

Example 15-13 *Configure a Virtual Template Interface*

```
Interface Virtual-template1 type tunnel
Ip unnumbered GigabitEthernet0/0
Tunnel mode ipsec ipv4
Tunnel protection ipsec profile MYIPsecProfile
```

Note: The IP address of a virtual template interface must be configured using the **ip unnumbered** interface command.

Task 5: Map Remote Peer to a Virtual Template Interface

The final task involves configuring an ISAKMP profile that maps remote peers to the newly created virtual template interface. First, the ISAKMP profile is created using the **crypto isakmp profile** command and then references the key ring associated with the peer group using the **keyring** ISAKMP profile configuration command.

Next, use appropriate **match** statements to identify remote peers (IP addresses of spoke peers). This is accomplished with the **match identity address** command. Finally, specify the virtual template interface that the router will use to create a dynamic VTI for this peer. Example 15-14 shows the ISAKMP profile and remote peer mapping being executed.

Example 15-14 *Configure an ISAKMP Profile and Map Remote Peers*

```
Router# show crypto isakmp profile ISAKMPProfile
  Keyring NEWKEYRING
  Match identity address 172.17.2.4 255.255.255.255
  Match identity address 172.17.2.7 255.255.255.255
  Virtual-template 1
```

Verify Tunnel Status on the Hub

The tunnel status on the hub router can be displayed using **the show ip interfaces brief |
include Virtual-Access** command. The output should show a virtual access interface for
each dynamically created virtual tunnel interface (VTI) (each spoke peer). A special Vir-
tual-Access1 interface is used internally by Cisco IOS Software and is always present in
the output of this command.

The **show interfaces virtual-access** command can be used to ensure that the dynamic
VTI is operating properly. The virtual access interface is always in the "up" state. The line
protocol will be up when the IPsec SA negotiation is completed successfully.

The complete configuration for a dynamic VTI virtual access interface can be seen by using the **show running-config interface Virtual-access** command. Note that the configuration for the virtual access interface is created dynamically based in part on the
information contained in the virtual template interface and is not automatically saved to
the startup configuration, nor can it be saved manually.

Implementation Guidelines

Consider the following deployment guidelines when implementing dynamic VTI VPNs:

- Dynamic routing protocols must be used inside tunnels to provide intra-VPN routing.
  Static routes cannot be used on the hub router because of the unnumbered addressing on the VTIs, and therefore there are no specific next-hop addresses to route. Static routing can be used on the spoke, if required.

- Pre-shared keys for IKE peer authentication limits configuration scalability because
  authentication credentials must be configured on each spoke peer.

- Spoke peers must use a static IP address if IKE pre-shared authentication and IKE
  main mode are used. This is because of the IKE protocol, but it can be overcome by
  using either certificate-based authentication or by using IKE aggressive mode with
  pre-shared keys.

- Unnumbered IP addressing is mandatory with DVTI tunnels.

Exam Preparation

As mentioned in the section, "How to Use This Book," in the Introduction, you have several choices for exam preparation: the exercises here, the memory tables in Appendix C, the final exam preparation chapter, and the exam simulation questions on the CD-ROM. The following questions present a bigger challenge than the exam itself because they use an open-ended question format. By using this more difficult format, you exercise your memory better and prove your conceptual and factual knowledge of this chapter. You can find the answers to these questions in the appendix.

Review All Key Topics

Review the most important topics in this chapter, noted with the Key Topics icon in the margin of the page. Table 15-7 lists a reference of these key topics and the page numbers on which each is found.

Table 15-7 *Key Topics*

Key Topic Element	Description	Page
List	Features of the Virtual Tunnel Interface	391
Example 15-1	VTI configuration	391
Table 15-2	VTI benefits and limitations	392
Table 15-4	Deployment choices	393
List	Deployment guidelines	393
List	ISAKMP parameters	394
Example 15-2	Configure IKE policy	395
Example 15-5	**show crypto isakmp sa**	397
List	IKE implementation guidelines	397
Step list	Troubleshooting IKE	397
List	Static site-to-site VTI tunnels	398
Example 15-7	Configure VTI	400
Example 15-8	Apply a protection profile to a VTI	401
List	Static site-to-site VTI tunnel implementation guidelines	401
List	Troubleshoot static VTI tunnels	402
List	Dynamic site-to-site VTI tunnels	404
List	Dynamic site-to-site VTI tunnel implementation guidelines	407

Complete Tables and Lists from Memory

Print a copy of Appendix C, "Memory Tables" (found on the CD), or at least the section for this chapter, and complete the tables and lists from memory. Appendix D, "Memory Table Answers," also on the CD, includes completed tables and lists to check your work.

Define Key Terms

Define the following key terms from this chapter, and check your answers in the Glossary:

crypto map, virtual tunnel interface (VTI), Advanced Integration Module (AIM), transform set, Dynamic VTIs (DVTI), Internet Key Exchange (IKE), Authentication Headers (AH), Encapsulating Security Protocol (ESP)

Fill in the Blanks

1. One major benefit of using IPsec VTIs is that it is no longer required to apply a _____ to a physical interface.
2. VTIs support native IPsec tunneling, including _____ with standards-based IPsec implementations of other vendors.
3. IPsec VTIs support _____, such as voice and video.
4. IPsec _____ define the encapsulation (ESP or AH), the packet authentication/integrity algorithm (SHA-1 or MD5), and the IPsec mode (transport or tunnel) that is used with a VPN policy.
5. Many of the _____ interface options that can be applied to physical interfaces can be applied to the IPsec virtual tunnel interface.
6. Cisco IOS Software IPsec _____ is not supported on VTIs.
7. In a VTI-based IPsec VPN, IPsec requests SA establishment as soon as the virtual tunnel interfaces (VTI) are _____.
8. _____ IP addressing is mandatory with DVTI tunnels.

Reference

Cisco IOS Security Configuration Guide: Secure Connectivity, Release 12.4T, www.cisco.com/en/US/partner/docs/ios/sec_secure_connectivity/configuration/guide/12_4t/sec_secure_connectivity_12_4t_book.html.

This chapter covers the following subjects:

- **Describe the concept of a public key infrastructure:** Discusses the fundamentals of public key infrastructure.

- **Configure, verify, and troubleshoot a basic Cisco IOS Software Certificate Server:** Learn how to configure a Certificate Server on a Cisco IOS Software–based router.

- **Enroll a Cisco IOS Software VPN router into a PKI and troubleshoot the enrollment process:** Covers enrolling a VPN router into a public key infrastructure. It also covers troubleshooting problems with that process.

- **Configure and verify the integration of a Cisco IOS Software VPN router with supporting PKI entities:** Leads you through configuring a VPN router to authenticate ISAKMP peers using PKI.

CHAPTER 16

Deploying Scalable Authentication in Site-to-Site IPsec VPNs

IPsec Virtual Private Networks (VPN) can be implemented with several different authentication methods. Public key infrastructure (PKI) provides a highly scalable authentication solution for VPNs.

"Do I Know This Already?" Quiz

The "Do I Know This Already?" quiz helps you decide whether you really need to read the entire chapter. If you already intend to read the entire chapter, you do not necessarily need to answer these questions now.

The nine-question quiz, derived from the major sections in the "Foundation Topics" portion of this chapter, helps you determine how to spend your limited study time.

Table 16-1 outlines the major topics discussed in this chapter and the "Do I Know This Already?" quiz questions that correspond to those topics.

Table 16-1 *"Do I Know This Already?" Foundation Topics Section-to-Question Mapping*

Foundation Topics Section	Questions Covered in This Section
Describe the Concept of a Public Key Infrastructure	1, 2, 8
Configure, Verify, and Troubleshoot a Basic Cisco IOS Software Certificate Server	3, 4
Enroll a Cisco IOS Software VPN Router into a PKI and Troubleshoot the Enrollment Process	6, 7
Configure and Verify the Integration of a Cisco IOS Software VPN Router with Supporting PKI Entities	5, 9

Caution: The goal of self-assessment is to gauge your mastery of the topics in this chapter. If you do not know the answer to a question or are only partially sure of the answer, you should mark this question wrong for purposes of the self-assessment. Giving yourself credit for an answer that you correctly guess skews your self-assessment results and might provide you with a false sense of security.

1. What is the one central trusted introducer called?

   a. Identity certificate

   b. RSA algorithm

   c. Certificate authority

   d. X.500 distinguished name

   e. None of these answers are correct.

2. A list of all certificates that are no longer valid is called which of the following?

   a. Old certificate list

   b. Revoked Certificate List

   c. Certificate Revocation List (CRL)

   d. Invalid Certificate Authority List

   e. Expired Certificate List

3. Which of the following is something that can cause issues in a PKI system?

   a. Synchronized time

   b. Variable time

   c. Unsynchronized time

   d. Manually configured time

   e. None of these answers are correct.

4. The SCEP interface on a Cisco IOS Software Certificate Server is enabled with what command?

   a. **ip scep server**

   b. **set scep server enable**

   c. **ip http server**

   d. **crypto server scep**

   e. None of these answers are correct.

5. To integrate PKI-based authentication with site-to-site VPNs, which protocol must be configured to use PKI-based authentication?

   a. IKE

   b. GRE

   c. AAA

   d. RSA

   e. VPN

6. PKI clients can enroll to the Cisco IOS Software Certificate Server using which two types of enrollment?

    a. SCEP

    b. IKE

    c. TACACS

    d. Manual

7. Which storage method is considered the most secure for storing a Cisco IOS Software PKI client's private key?

    a. USB Smart Token

    b. NVRAM in clear text

    c. Encrypted on an external USB storage

    d. Encrypted on NVRAM

    e. Private section in NVRAM

8. What information does the client send to the CA during the enrollment process?

    a. IP address

    b. Client's private key

    c. Client's public key

    d. Name of device

9. By default, what will the IKE process on Cisco IOS Software routers accept if signed by its locally defined trustpoint CA?

    a. A client IP address

    b. Client's private key

    c. Any valid certificate

    d. A new CRL

The answers to the "Do I Know This Already?" quiz are found in Appendix A. The suggested choices for your next step are as follows:

- **7 or less overall score:** Read the entire chapter. This includes the "Foundation Topics" and the "Exam Preparation" sections.

- **8 or 9 overall score:** If you want more review on these topics, skip to the "Exam Preparation" section. Otherwise, move on to Chapter 17, "Deploying DMVPNs."

Foundation Topics

Using public key infrastructure (PKI) provides a scalable solution for site-to-site IPsec VPNs. This chapter provides a description of public key infrastructure and covers planning a PKI integration with Cisco IOS Software site-to-site IPsec VPNs. After this, implementing a basic Cisco IOS Software Certificate Server, enrolling a Cisco IOS Software VPN router into a PKI, and integrating a Cisco IOS Software VPN router with supporting PKI entities will be covered as well.

Describe the Concept of a Public Key Infrastructure

IPsec VPNs can use public key infrastructure to provide a scalable solution for peer authentication. Digital signatures are commonly used by many authentication protocols for traffic running over untrusted or public networks.

Public key cryptography, which usually uses the Rivest, Shamir, and Adelman (RSA) algorithm, uses pairs of keys called the public key and private key for its encryption and digital signature processes. Both of these activities call for an exchange of public keys between the two entities that want to communicate. For digital signature verification, the verifying party must securely obtain the public key of the party that signed traffic with its private key. Obtaining the public key must be done in a secure manner to maintain the authenticity and integrity of the public key.

Note: Public key exchanges must be performed between each pair of entities that need to communicate. This means that for n parties to communicate with each other, the number of public key exchanges is a function of n multiplied by n. This shows that manual public key exchanges are not scalable and should only be considered for the very smallest of implementations.

Manual Key Exchange with Verification

One way to ensure that the public key exchange is done securely is to exchange the public keys over the untrusted transport in the clear, but to verify them in another out-of-band channel that is considered secure. This could mean reading the public key and/or its fingerprint (hash digest) back over the telephone to the sending party for verification. This method is very tedious, prone to mistakes, and not scalable.

Trusted Introducing

Pretty Good Privacy (PGP), one of the best-known attempts to overcome the scaling problem, is an email and file encryption system based on public key cryptography. PGP uses a concept call *trusted introducing*, in which existing point-to-point key exchanges can be tied together to help with the public key distribution issue.

Figure 16-1 shows an example in which users A, B, and C all have their own public/private key pair and the *trusted introducer* is user B. (User B is not labeled in the diagram.) Also,

- Users A and B have securely exchanged their public keys using the previously mentioned manual method of out-of-band verification.
- Users B and C have also securely exchanged their public keys using manual verification.

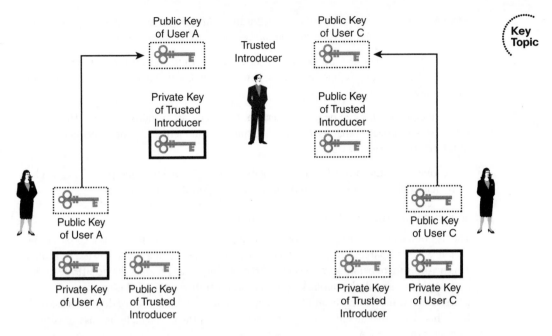

Figure 16-1 *Showing Where the Trusted Introducer Is (User B)*

With this setup, users A and B (and users B and C) can securely exchange messages in their respective point-to-point relationships. They have two ways to use PKI to secure messages. In one way, they can digitally sign the messages for authenticity and integrity with their own private key as the sender and verify the signature with the corresponding private key as the receiver. The other way is that they can encrypt the message with the public key of the other party, and the receiver will decrypt the message with its own private key.

This scenario provides two point-to-point secure channels. One channel is between users A and B and the other is between users B and C. The question is: Can this be used to connect users A and C in their own point-to-point trust relationship?

The answer is yes. User B will act as a trusted introducer because he has a secure channel with both user A and user C. When user A and user C need to exchange their public keys securely, they can do it with the assistance of user B, if that user is considered trustworthy to perform this introduction. The steps are as follows:

Step 1.   User B digitally signs the public key of user A (which it has locally) and sends it to user C.

Step 2.   User C can then verify the signature of user B (because it has the public key of user B) and can consider the public key of user A to be authentic.

Step 3.   User B digitally signs the public key of user C (which it has locally) and sends it to user A.

Step 4.   User A can then verify the signature of user B (because it has the public key of user B) and consider the public key of user C to be authentic.

This method involves RSA public keys being signed with RSA private keys to provide a method of exchanging public keys in a secure manner. Users A and C can now communicate securely.

This principle of trust can be used in certain topologies and is fairly scalable. The downside to this approach is that users can make mistakes and jeopardize other hosts because of the trusting nature of this approach.

The evolution of this procedure that has a much higher scalability and provides much better manageability is to use a *trusted third-party* cryptographic protocol.

Public Key Infrastructure: Certificate Authorities

The use of a trusted third-party protocol with public key cryptography is also based on digitally signing public keys, but extends the idea to the use of a single trusted introducer. This involves there being only one central trusted introducer (called the certificate authority [CA]) that signs all the public keys in its administrative domain (this means servers, users, routers, and so on). In addition, all entities in this administrative domain trust the CA. This means that all entities have the public key of the CA, which they use to verify messages from the CA.

Figure 16-2 depicts a situation in which each entity has its own pair of asymmetric cryptographic keys, a public and private key. User A and C want to communicate securely. The trusted introducer (the CA is the trusted third party) is trusted by all users.

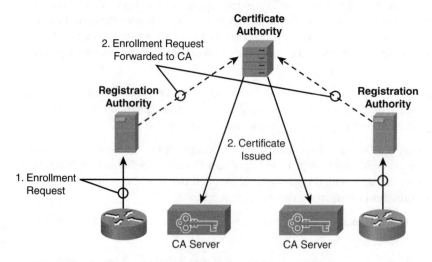

Figure 16-2   *Trusted Introducer: Certificate Authority*

All entities trust the CA by virtue of having obtained its public key in a secure manner. This process of obtaining the public key of the certificate authority in a secure manner (such as out-of-band or manually reading over the telephone) is called *authenticating the CA.*

To participate in the PKI system, all end users must enroll with the CA, which involves a process in which they submit their public key and their name to the CA. Figure 16-2 shows a trusted introducer (this time, the certificate authority) and the users that trust it.

After a user submits his public key and name to the CA, the CA verifies the identity and public key of the enrolling user. If it finds the user's information (public key and name) to be authentic, the CA then digitally signs the submitted information with its private key.

This creates an *identity certificate* for the submitter. An identity certificate is a piece of information that binds a PKI member's name to its public key and puts it into a standard format. The identity certificates are returned to the users bound together with the signature of the CA. The users then install them and can use them until they either retire or are revoked.

Now that each entity has the public key of the certificate authority along with its own identity certificate, which has been signed by the certificate authority, the identity can verify any data that is signed by the CA.

The entities can now act independently of the CA and establish point-to-point communications with each other by exchanging information about themselves by using the CA-authenticated identity certificate.

This means that end users can now mutually exchange certificates over untrusted public networks and use the digital signature of the certificate authority as the trust mechanism for the public key exchange. Note that this is possible because each entity can prove the authenticity and integrity of the CA's signature because each identity has the certificate authority's public key. Essentially, the user's identity certificate is trusted because it is bound to the Certificate Server's digital signature (private key). The Certificate Server's digital signature is trusted and can be verified because each entity obtained the CA's public key securely.

This exchange of identity certificates does not prove the identity of the sender. Certificates simply provide a level of assurance that a specific name is connected to a specific public key. Identity can be proven through the use of an authentication protocol that can use certificates (which contain public keys) in certain procedures that prove an entity's possession of the private key that corresponds to that public key.

Note: The public key of the CA is also distributed in the form of a certificate issued by the CA itself. This is also called a self-signed CA certificate, because the signer and holder of the certificate are the same entity.

X.509 Identity Certificate

The identity certificate is a document that binds together an entity's name and its public key and is signed by the certificate authority so that every other end-user entity will be able to verify it (by virtue of having the CA's public key already).

Note that certificates are not secret information and it is not required to encrypt them. They are protected by a digital signature that proves their authenticity and integrity.

The typical data found in an X.509 identity certificate is as follows:

- Name of the certificate holder

- Public key of the holder

- Digital signature of the CA

Other fields that might be included are as follows:

- Certificate serial number

- Certificate expiration data

- Algorithms used to generate the signature

X.509 is a well-known standard that defines the basic PKI data formats like the certificate itself and the Certificate Revocation List (CRL) formats to enable basic interoperability.

The format defined by the X.509 standard is used extensively in today's networks. It can be found in these locations:

- On secure web servers for website authentication with Secure Socket Layer (SSL)

- On web browsers for services that implement client certificates in the SSL and Transport Layer Security (TLS) protocols

- With user mail agents to support mail protection using the Secure Multipurpose Internet Mail Extension (S/MIME) protocol

- In IPsec VPNs, where certificates are used as a public key distribution mechanism for IKE RSA-based authentication

Certificate Revocation Checking

One problem with the manual key exchange process that was resolved by PKI was the issue of scalability. Another issue presented by the manual exchange process is the problem of key management. In the event that an entity's private key is compromised, every other entity would need to be signaled to no longer trust that key.

Certificate Revocation Lists

A PKI can offer a simple solution to the key management problem in the form of Certificate Revocation Lists (CRL). CRLs contain a list of all certificates that are no longer valid. The CRL is signed by the CA and marked with a time stamp. It is stored on an HTTP server, a Lightweight Directory Access Protocol (LDAP) server, or a Simple Certificate Enrollment Protocol (SCEP) server.

It is the responsibility of the PKI end user to obtain a fresh CRL after the old one has expired and to ensure that any of the certificates that it wants to use are not on the current CRL.

A certificate is placed on a CRL if it is no longer considered trusted. This can take place for the following reasons:

- Private key compromise

- Contract termination for a PKI user

- Loss of private keys because of memory loss

- Device replacement

A CRL can exist as a single list, which can become quite large, or be broken up into several smaller CRLs (multipart CRLs), accessible through different distribution points. The CRL Distribution Point (CDP) URL for a certificate is listed in the certificate itself.

Online Certificate Status Protocol

The problem with CRLs is that they can contain stale information. They are issued periodically, usually every few hours, and therefore can contain out-of-date information. If a key is compromised in the middle of an update period, there is a window of time in which a compromised key can be used by an attacker.

The Online Certificate Status Protocol (OCSP) provides real-time verification of certificates against a database of revoked certificates. When an entity receives a certificate from another user, the user queries the OCSP server in real time to verify whether the received certificate has been revoked. This eliminates the weakness of CRLs but requires a highly stable and highly available server from which users can obtain verifications.

Using Certificates in Network Applications

A public key infrastructure (PKI) is a system in which every entity has its own public key signed by the trusted CA. This provides an efficient public key distribution model that supports large-scale public key-based technologies.

PKI provides entities with a scalable, secure mechanism for distributing, managing, and revoking encryption and identity information.

Keep in mind that a PKI is only a way to securely share public keys between users and other entities. The application for which a public key is used is completely different. Applications that use PKI include

- Email clients look up recipient certificates in a directory, and after verifying them, extract the public key and use it to encrypt mail to that person.

- VPN routers can exchange their certificates over an untrusted network. The public key inside a certificate is used to challenge the other peer to provide proof of the corresponding private key, and therefore authenticate it.

- Web servers that have certificates that are issued by well-known certificate authorities. Web clients have the CA certificates of those CAs and can verify the identity of a web server by obtaining the certificate at the beginning of an HTTPS session, verify it using the CA certificate, and extract its public key; the clients can then use this information to challenge the server to provide proof of its private key. This is typically done by sending the web server a random piece of data encrypted with the public key from the certificate and verifying that the server can decrypt it. This process essentially authenticates the server.

- In the same process as the web servers, the Cisco Unified Communications Manager authenticates to the IP phone and the IP phone to the Cisco Unified Communications Manager when configured to use TLS-protected signaling.

- A trusted public key from a certificate can be used to securely transport a symmetric (session) key of a symmetric algorithm to the other party.

Deployment Choices

A choice that you must make when deploying a PKI-based VPN is whether to use a dedicated, limited, VPN-only PKI that enrolls only VPN devices as its end users or to use a larger, enterprise PKI, where VPN devices are just one type of entity that shares the same PKI with other entities such as web servers, users, and other network devices. Table 16-2 depicts the comparison of these two options.

Table 16-2 *VPN-Only PKI Compared with Enterprise PKI*

VPN-Only PKI	Enterprise PKI
Only "users" are VPN devices.	VPN devices are just one type of certificate holder.
Few interoperability concerns.	Can present interoperability issues.
Relatively simple authorization.	Can require complex authorization.
PKI management can be fully embedded in network devices.	PKI management is usually external.
Difficult or impossible to authenticate entities outside the PKI.	PKI entities can authenticate any device from the same PKI.

Deployment Steps

The major steps for implementing a PKI-enabled IPsec site-to-site VPN are as follows:

Step 1.   (Optional) Deploy the Cisco IOS Software Certificate Server if you are not using an existing PKI, such as an enterprise PKI or an outsourced PKI, for VPN authentication.

Step 2.   Enroll all VPN devices into the PKI. This mandatory task requires the generation of RSA key pairs on all VPN devices, CA authentication (the secure installation of the CA certificate on each VPN device), and enrollment of each VPN device into the PKI (each device sends its name and public key to the CA and receives its identity certificate in return).

Step 3.   Configure IKE to use PKI-enabled authentication and to use the local identity and CA certificates on each device. This is mandatory to obtain scalable authentication, particularly in a partial or full meshed VPN scenario.

Step 4.   (Optional) Configure advanced PKI integration to perform more than basic revocation checks using CRLs.

Input Parameters

The following input parameters are needed when building a PKI-enabled IPsec site-to-site VPN:

- Choose between a VPN-only **PKI or an enterprise-wide PKI and then determine the parameters used to access that PKI.**

- **Local security requirements:** This determines the choice of cryptographic algorithms (such as the hash functions when generating certificates), key lengths, and key lifetimes.

- **Local naming standards:** This determines the names that are used inside certificates of VPN devices. These can be X.509 distinguished names, fully qualified domain names, or both.

- **Device-provisioning process:** This process is used to set up new devices that will now need to include highly detailed procedures to prevent human error from jeopardizing the PKI.

Deployment Guidelines

When implementing a site-to-site VPN using PKI for peer authentication, consider the following deployment guidelines:

- Management procedures and organizational practices can reduce the trust levels that are introduced by implementing a PKI. Procedures for PKI enrollment, user registration, validating CA certificates, CA physical access and signing, and revocation need to be rigorous and strictly adhered to daily.

- Activities such as checking for certificate expiration and ensuring that CRLs are downloaded and kept up to date is very important. An accurate, trusted time source is required in VPNs for PKI implementations.

- Ensure that the provisioning of certificates is not the only activity that is considered critical. The entire certificate management lifecycle must be planned and managed properly. This includes key generation, enrollment, key/certificate renewal, revocation, and key destruction.

Configure, Verify, and Troubleshoot a Basic Cisco IOS Software Certificate Server

The Cisco IOS Software Certificate Server was introduced in Cisco IOS Software Release 12.3(4). The Certificate Server feature is supported on all platforms that run a security image. The supported hardware ranges from the Cisco 800 Series routers to the Cisco 7400 Series routers and also includes the Cisco ASR Series routers. The load experienced by running the Certificate Server is not typically a significant performance factor for IPsec network availability. Deploying the proper model of Cisco routers on which to run the

Certificate Server function can greatly optimize performance and reliability. The Cisco IOS Software Certificate Server includes the following notable features:

■ It provides a certificate authority function to devices that can enroll to it using SCEP or using a manual cut-and-paste enrollment process.

■ It can act as a root or a subordinate certificate authority. This chapter will cover implementing the Cisco IOS Software Certificate Server as a standalone root server.

■ It provides enhancements that can simplify the management of the certificate lifecycle such as supporting automatic reenrollment of clients to simplify certificate renewal.

■ It includes a backup function to create a backup of Cisco IOS Software Certificate Server keys and auxiliary files.

■ It provides support for redundancy, where the configuration and its functionality can be replicated to another Cisco IOS Software device. Full coverage of this redundancy feature is beyond the scope of this guide.

Several factors influence the selection of the appropriate router for the Certificate Server function:

■ **Key length:** CPU utilization of a router can be pushed to a greater level for long periods of time because of the computational requirements of processing large RSA cryptography keys. This can cause an enrollment queue to grow when there is a long key pair in use and the router receives another Cisco IOS Software VPN router enrollment request.

■ **Concurrent enrollments:** Large environments that could have constant and frequent certificate enrollments and reenrollments can suffer long wait times if low-performance routers are used as the Certificate Server.

■ **CRL location:** The Cisco IOS Software Certificate Server stores its database on the local flash memory of the router. High-volume environments can suffer long queue lengths because of the fact that the individual data files must be written to the file system before the next certificate enrollment in the queue can be serviced.

Configuration Tasks for a Root Certificate Server

Perform the following tasks to implement the Certificate Server on Cisco IOS Software:

Task 1: Create an RSA key pair to be used as the certificate authority key pair. The private key will be used to sign user certificates, and the public key will be distributed to all routers as the certificate authority self-signed certificate. Although this step is optional, a dedicated key pair will automatically be created of only minimally acceptable strength.

Task 2: Create a PKI trustpoint that designates the key pair that is intended to be used within the Certificate Server.

Task 3: Create the Certificate Server itself. A name for the CA is provided during this step.

Task 4: Configure the location of the CA's files. This can either be on the router itself or on external storage on a remote server.

Task 5: Configure an issuing policy in which the administrator can either manually grant all certificate requests or the server can automatically issue certificates. An additional enrollment password can also be configured to authenticate enrolling entities.

Task 6: Configure the revocation policy in which the specific CRL parameters used by the Certificate Server are created.

Task 7: Configure the SCEP interface on the Certificate Server router.

Task 8: Enable the Certificate Server after all the parameters have been configured.

Note: Prior to configuring a Cisco IOS CA server, you must conduct proper planning to determine the values that are needed to join the PKI (such as certificate lifetimes and CRL lifetimes). After some of the core settings have been configured and certificates have been granted, changing settings requires that the Certificate Server be reconfigured and the peers must reenroll.

Configuration Scenario

The configuration tasks that follow will be performed with these considerations:

- A dedicated 2048-bit key pair will be generated to be used exclusively by the Certificate Server.

- The CA will be configured to use the local file system to store and publish its files. The /myca folder will be created and designated as the Certificate Server database location.

- The following certificate policy will be configured and enforced:
  - The CA certificate lifetime will be set to 10 years.

  - End-user identity certificates will be issued with a 2-year lifetime.

  - Certificate Server will be set to manually grant identity certificate requests.

  - The CA's CRL will be published every 4 hours.

Task 1: Create an RSA Key Pair

The first task creates a dedicated RSA key pair. The key pair will be assigned a name (label) and created with an appropriate key length. The **exportable** keyword is used to designate the key as exportable so that it can be backed up. Example 16-1 contains the commands for Task 1.

Example 16-1 *Generate Dedicated RSA Key Pair*

```
Router# crypto key generate rsa label CS-KEYS modulus 2048 exportable


The name for the keys will be: CS-KEYS


%The key modulus size is 2048 bits
%Generating 2048 bit RSA keys, keys will be exportable....[OK]
```

Key
Topic

Note: A PKI trustpoint is used mainly on PKI clients (VPN routers) to define the location of the CA.

Task 2: Create a PKI Trustpoint

Task 2 creates a named PKI trustpoint on the Certificate Server router, and inside it, references the label of the dedicated key pair that was created previously in Task 1. A PKI trustpoint is only used to define the key pair of the Certificate Server. If Task 1 was not completed, the CA server will autogenerate a 1024-bit RSA key pair after the CA configuration is completed. Example 16-2 shows the configuration to create the trustpoint.

Example 16-2   *Create the PKI Trustpoint*

```
Router(config)# crypto pki trustpoint MY-CS
Router(ca-trustpoint)# rsakeypair CS-KEYS
```

Tasks 3 and 4: Create the CS and Configure the Database Location

Task 3 and 4 create the Certificate Server, assign its name, and specify storage locations. Follow these steps and refer to Example 16-3 for guidance:

Step 1.   Create a Certificate Server using the crypto pki server command, and assign the same name that was used in Task 2 to create the PKI trustpoint. This configures the Certificate Server to use the dedicated key pair.

Step 2.   Within the Certificate Server, specify an X.500 name for the Certificate Server using the issuer-name command. Following the X.500 distinguished name format, use organizational standards to create a locally meaningful name. There must be at least one canonical name (CN) configured.

Step 3.   Configure the location for the CA's files using the database url command. The location can either be the local file system or an external storage location that is reachable over a trusted network path.

Step 4.   Configure the database level using the database level command to specify how much information the CA will store in the database:

Minimum: Enough information is stored only to continue issuing new certificates without conflict. This is the default.

Names: In addition to the information stored at the minimum level, the serial number and subject name of each certificate can be stored as well.

Complete: In addition to minimum and names levels, each issued certificate is written to the database.

Note: Do not store the entire issued identity certificate if NVRAM or Flash is used for the database as it may quickly run out of space.

Example 16-3   *Create the Certificate Server and Configure the Database Location*

```
Router(config)# crypto pki server MY-CS
Router(cs-server)# Issuer-name CN=MY-CS,OU=VPN,O=Cisco,C=US
Router(cs-server)# Database url flash:/my-cs
Router(cs-server)# Database level complete
```

Task 5: Configure an Issuing Policy

Task 5 configures the certificate issuing policy on the CA. Follow these steps and refer to Example 16-4 for guidance:

Step 1.   Specify the hash algorithm to be used in the certificate-signing process. By default, Cisco IOS Software Certificate Server uses Message Digest 5 (MD5) for the cryptographic hash function. Because it is not recommended to use MD5, change the hash function to use Secure Hash Algorithm 1 (SHA-1).

Step 2.   Configure the lifetime of issued certificates. After the lifetime expires, clients must reenroll to obtain new certificates. This is usually in the range of one year to several years.

Step 3.   Configure the lifetime of the Cisco IOS Software Certificate Server signing (CA) certificate. After this lifetime expires, the CA will need to regenerate its self-signed certificate and possibly do so with new RSA keys. This will render all issued certificates invalid, forcing a reenrollment of all clients. This is usually done on the order of 5 to 20 years.

Step 4.   Designate the grant method. By default, the Certificate Server uses manual granting, by which the administrator must grant each request. Automatic granting can be configured, optionally, with an additional password to authenticate certificate requests.

Example 16-4   *Create the Issuing Policy*

```
Router(config)# crypto pki server MY-CS
Router(cs-server)#  hash sha1
Router(cs-server)#  lifetime certificate 730
Router(cs-server)#  lifetime ca-certificate 3650
Router(cs-server)#  no grant auto
```

Task 6: Configure the Revocation Policy

Task 6 configures the revocation policy. If SCEP, the default option, is used to distribute the CRL, there is nothing to configure. To tune the lifetime of the CRL, use the lifetime crl command inside the Certificate Server configuration. Example 16-5 shows the use of this command.

Example 16-5   *Change Revocation Policy Lifetime*

```
Router(config)# crypto pki server MY-CS
Router(cs-server)# lifetime crl 4
```

Task 7: Configure the SCEP Interface

In Task 7, the SCEP interface is configured on the Certificate Server. This is essentially enabling the Cisco IOS Software HTTP server that provides the SCEP server to PKI clients. The CA will automatically enable and disable SCEP services based on the state of the HTTP server. If the HTTP server is not enabled, only manual Public Key Cryptography Standards (PKCS) #10 enrollment is supported on the Cisco IOS Software Certificate Server. To enable the HTTP server, enter the following command:

```
Router(config)# ip http server
```

Task 8: Enable the Certificate Server

After all the parameters have been configured and adjusted, Task 8 enables the Certificate Server. Use the **no shutdown** command in certificate server configuration mode to enable the Certificate Server. The command and resulting output are shown in Example 16-6.

Example 16-6   *Enable the Certificate Server*

```
Router(cs-server)# no shutdown
% Some server settings cannot be changed after CA certificate generation.
% Please enter a passphrase to protect the private key
% or type Return to exit
Password:
Re-enter password:

% Certificate Server enabled.
Router(cs-server)#
```

Note: To make changes to the Certificate Server's configuration, the server must be shut down first. Do not forget to reenable the server after completing the changes.

Cisco Configuration Professional Support

Limited management of the Certificate Server can be performed by using Cisco Configuration Professional:

- Cisco Configuration Professional can create a Certificate Server using a default configuration.

- There are no user-selectable parameters.

- There are no GUI configuration options.

- The server can be started and stopped.

- Backups can be created Cisco IOS Software Certificate Server keys and auxiliary files.

- There is an interface to administer certificate requests, issue certificates, and revoke certificates.

Verify the Cisco IOS Software Certificate Server

The **show crypto pki server** command can be used to verify the Cisco IOS CA server status. The output, among other information, will show the status as enabled or disabled and shows the CA certificate fingerprint.

Feature Support

Table 16-3 shows the required Cisco IOS Software releases and the functionality supported in them.

Table 16-3   *Cisco IOS Software Certificate Server Feature Support*

Feature	Software Release
Cisco IOS Software Certificate Server	12.3(4)T
Automatic CA Certificate Rollover	12.4(2)T
Certificate Server Auto Archive	12.3(11)T
Cisco IOS Software CA Server Redundancy	15.0(1)M
Use of USB Smart Token for Certificate Server Private Key Storage	12.4(11)T
Certificate Server Split Database	12.4(4)T

CA Certificate Rollover

The Certificate Server supports CA certificate rollover to facilitate making key pair and certificate changes easier at expiration. This process happens in three stages:

- In stage one, there are only the active CA certificate and key pair.

- In stage two, the rollover certificate and key pair are generated and distributed. After the CA generates the rollover certificate and key pair and saves its configuration, it can respond to client requests for the rollover certificate and key pair. The CA responds with the rollover certificate and key pair to all new client requests. This causes the clients to store the rollover CA certificate and key pair.

- In stage three, the rollover CA certificate and key pair become the active CA certificate and key pair. All devices that have the valid rollover certificate rename the rollover certificate to the active certificate, and the previous active certificate and key pair are deleted.

Automatic Archiving

For Cisco IOS Release 12.3(8)T or earlier, you can create your Certificate Server key pair as exportable. During the initial setup of the Certificate Server, the CA certificate and CA keys are automatically archived to facilitate restoring them if the original copy or original configuration is lost. With Cisco IOS Release 12.4(11)T and later, it is recommended that you store your CA server keys on a USB token if your router has a USB token configured and available.

> **Note:** The CA backup file is extremely important and should be securely stored. In addition to this backup, it is recommended that the serial file (.ser) and the CRL file (.crl) also be backed up. Both are critical to restoring the server if needed.

Certificate Server Redundancy

The Cisco IOS Software Certificate Server Redundancy feature allows two routers to become a redundant cluster. This feature depends on the Cisco IOS Software Stateful Switchover (SSO) protocol to provide the synchronization of the CA server state across two routers running HSRP.

USB Smart Token for CA Private Key Storage

This feature allows administrators to store the private key of the Cisco IOS Software Certificate Server on a supported USB Smart Token. This provides better protection of the key as compared to storage on the router file system.

Certificate Server Split Database

This feature allows administrators to set storage locations and publish locations for specific server file types. This allows critical file types (such as the serial number files and the archive files [.p12 or .pem]) to be stored in one location and noncritical files, such as general certificates (.crt), to be stored either in the same location or in a different location.

Implementation Guidelines

Key Topic

The following guidelines should be considered when implementing the Cisco IOS Software Certificate Server to support VPN devices:

- Cisco IOS Software Certificate Server is a good choice of CA server and recommended as a CA to support VPN-only deployments.

- Establish good processes and procedures when granting certificates, and ensure the validity of requesting user and device identities.

- Consider using a remote server with fast, large, and reliable storage to hold the CA server files.

- Consider publishing the CRL on a highly available server so that it does not affect PKI authentication.

- The Cisco IOS Software Certificate Server can be used as a CA subordinate as a part of your enterprise PKI. This is beyond the scope of this guide.

Troubleshooting Flow

In the event of problems with the Cisco IOS Software Certificate Server not initially starting, or not operating after a configuration change or environment change, follow these
steps to troubleshoot the issue:

Step 1. Verify that the Certificate Server parameters have been configured to the appropriate values. Use the **show crypto pki server** and **show logging buffer**
commands to search for potential errors.

Step 2. Verify that the time on the Certificate Server is set properly. Use the **show clock**
or **show ntp associations** commands to determine the accuracy of the time.

Step 3. Verify the reachability and operation of remote storage if the CA is configured
to use it. The inability to reach critical and noncritical files can affect the operations of the Cisco IOS Software Certificate Server.

PKI and Time: Additional Guidelines

Having synchronized time is vital for PKI, but PKI does not require that the time be extremely accurate.

Time synchronization issues can cause certificate validation failures if the current time on
the VPN device is outside the validity range of the CA certificate.

Enroll a Cisco IOS Software VPN Router into a PKI and Troubleshoot the Enrollment Process

To take advantage of PKI authentication for your VPNs, you must enroll your router into a
PKI. In the following sections, the Cisco IOS Software provides the PKI client that will interact with the CA when authenticating for the VPN establishment.

PKI Client Features

Cisco IOS Software includes a PKI client that allows it to enroll into a PKI. The Cisco IOS
Software PKI client supports SCEP or manual enrollment, can automatically enroll and
reenroll to the PKI, supports several configuration options for certificate revocation and
authorization checks, and can integrate with authentication protocols that need its services, such as the IKE protocol in IPsec VPNs.

This topic covers how to configure enrollment using the Cisco IOS Software PKI client.
This is the process of adding a service to the PKI by authenticating to the CA and submit-
ting the device's name/public key to the CA to obtain a certificate.

Today, several protocols are in use for enrollment. Some of the common ones are as follows:

■ **File-based requests:** The end user formats an enrollment request in the form of a
Public Key Cryptography Standards (PKCS) #10 message in a file. The file is transferred to the CA, which signs the information and returns a PKCS #10 response file
with an embedded certificate.

■ **Web-based requests:** Used by web browsers and executed directly over the HTTP
protocol.

■ **Simple Certificate Enrollment Protocol (SCEP):** A lightweight, HTTP-based protocol for enrollment of network devices.

Enrollment for smart cards is another special method of note.

Note that none of these methods automatically solve the issue of operating over untrusted networks. Two-way authentication is always recommended for this reason.

Simple Certificate Enrollment Protocol

Simple Certificate Enrollment Protocol (SCEP) is a lightweight enrollment protocol that is mainly used by Cisco. SCEP enables network devices to communicate with a PKI server (the CA). It has become an industry standard for enrollment of VPN devices and is supported by most leading vendors of VPN and PKI systems.

Key Storage

One of the most critical concerns with public key cryptography is the security of the private key. Private keys must be protected because if a private key were to become compromised, every entity that holds the public key that is associated with that private key must obtain a new public key and possibly obtain new certificates as well.

Cisco IOS Software provides support for three possible private key storage methods:

- Storing the private key in private NVRAM on the router, which is a special hidden segment on the device NVRAM. The file is stored in clear text but is not accessible using Cisco IOS Software file manipulation commands.

- Storing the private key in either private NVRAM or some other storage device such as an external USB key in an encrypted form. Cisco IOS Software will encrypt the private key using symmetric encryption, and the decryption key (password) must be provided before the key can be used. This makes this operationally challenging in many environments.

- Storing the private key in an external USB Smart Token. This provides the strongest protection because the private key cannot be copied from the Smart Tokens, and all cryptographic operations are performed on the token itself.

Configuration Tasks

Perform the following tasks to configure the PKI client in Cisco IOS Software:

Task 1:   This task involves creating an RSA key pair to be used for the identity certificate. The step is optional because if there is an existing RSA key pair on the router, it can be used. It is recommended that a dedicated RSA key pair be used for each identity certificate.

Task 2:   On the enrolling router, create a PKI trustpoint to identify the CA. Creating the trustpoint also entails configuring the enrollment parameters, such as the enrollment method, the location of the CA (URL if SCEP is used), designating the RSA key pair, and configuring a list of device names.

Task 3:   Authenticate the certificate authority by installing an authentic copy of the CA certificate on the enrollment device.

Task 4: Create an enrollment request on the enrolling router and submit it to the CA.

Task 5: On the CA, issue the router's identity certificate and then install it on the enrolling router.

The enrollment procedure is the first task in the process of building trust between the CA and a user.

Configuration Scenario

Figure 16-3 and the list that follows depict the scenario to be used in the upcoming configuration sequence.

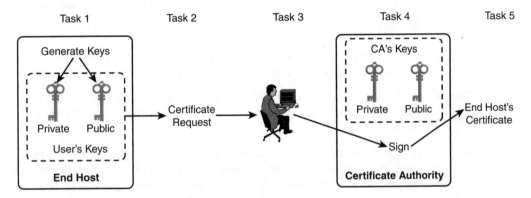

Figure 16-3 *Configuration Scenario*

- The router (end host) will generate and use a dedicated RSA key pair for the identity certificate.

- The CA (pictured in Task 4) is at IP address 10.1.1.1 and will be accessed by the router using SCEP.

- The router's subject name will be CN=R1, OU=VPN, O=Cisco, and C=US, and its FQDN is R1.vpn.cisco.com.

Task 1: Create an RSA Key Pair

The first task involves creating a dedicated RSA key pair. The key pair is assigned a name (label) and created with an appropriate key length. Use the **crypto key generate rsa** command to generate a 2048-bit RSA key pair labeled VPN-KEYS. Example 16-7 demonstrates the use of the **crypto key generate rsa** command for Task 1.

Example 16-7 *Generate a Dedicated RSA Key Pair*

```
Router# crypto key generate rsa label VPN-KEYS modulus 2048 exportable



The name for the keys will be: VPN-KEYS
```

```
%The key modulus size is 2048 bits
%Generating 2048 bit RSA keys, keys will be exportable....[OK]
```

Task 2: Create an RSA Key Pair

Task 2 creates the PKI trustpoint using the **crypto pki trustpoint** global configuration command. Now in trustpoint configuration mode, the entered details about the CA, enrollment parameters about the VPN router, and contents of the certificate will define the router's identity. This is the point at which organizational security policy requirements need to be identified to ensure that the parameters used in the certificate are adequate.

Complete the following steps and refer to Example 16-8 to configure the PKI trustpoint:

Step 1. Create a named trustpoint with the **crypto pki trustpoint** command. Issuing this command also places the VPN router in trustpoint configuration mode.

Step 2. If the PKI uses SCEP for enrollment, specify the enrollment URL. If the CA is the Cisco IOS Software Certificate Server, use a URL with an IP address of the CA.

Step 3. (Optional) Specify a custom X.500 and/or FQDN that will be included in the identity certificate. If this step is skipped, the VPN router automatically uses its FQDN name (determined by the host name and domain name). The example shows both name formats being specified.

Step 4. (Optional) Specify the revocation check procedure for the CA. By default, Cisco IOS CA configures a mandatory CRL revocation check for a new trustpoint.

Step 5. Specify the RSA key pair to be used for enrollment using the **rsakeypair** command.

Example 16-8 *Create a PKI Trustpoint*

```
Router(config)# crypto pki trustpoint MY-CS
Router(ca-trustpoint)#  enrollment url http://10.1.1.1:80
Router(ca-trustpoint)#  fqdn router.vpn.domain.com
Router(ca-trustpoint)#  subject-name CN=router,OU=VPN,O=Cisco,C=US
Router(ca-trustpoint)#  revocation-check crl
Router(ca-trustpoint)# rsakeypair VPN-KEYS
```

Task 3: Authenticate the PKI Certificate Authority

Task 3 of the enrollment process is to authenticate the CA by obtaining its self-signed certificate. If SCEP is in use, the PKI client will perform this action in clear text over HTTP, so some security precaution must be taken.

The received CA certificate must be verified by comparing the fingerprint of the received information with either an administrator over the phone or by another secure method (encrypted email, for example). If the information matches, a valid, authenticated CA certificate was received.

Complete the following steps and refer to Example 16-9 to authenticate the CA:

Step 1.   Enter configuration mode on the enrolling VPN router.

Step 2.   Request the CA certificate from the enrollment URL over SCEP with the **crypto pki authenticate** *trustpoint* command.

Step 3.   Verify the fingerprint of the received information against the known valid fingerprint that was received securely. The **show crypto pki server** command will show the fingerprint on a Cisco IOS Software Certificate Server.

Step 4.   Answer yes if the information matches.

Example 16-9   *Authenticate the PKI Certificate Authority*

```
Router(config)# crypto pki authenticate VPN-PKI
Certificate has the following attributes:
  Fingerprint MD5: 57684939 FE23980A 23498DB3 234DAF33
  Fingerprint: SHA1: 18438EE9 923FED1C CC132ADB BBDE234A

% Do you accept this certificate? [yes/no]: yes
Trustpoint CA certificate accepted.
```

Task 4: Create an Enrollment Request on the VPN Router

In Task 4, the **crypto pki enroll** global configuration command is used to submit the VPN router's name and public key to the CA. The CA will sign the information and return an identity certificate to the VPN router. Using the **no** form of this command can be used to delete an enrollment request.

Complete the following steps to create an enrollment request:

Step 1.   Enter configuration mode on the enrolling VPN router.

Step 2.   Request the identity certificate from the enrollment URL over SCEP with the **crypto pki enroll** *trustpoint* command as demonstrated here:
Router(config)# **crypto pki enroll MY-CS**

Step 3.   Optionally, enter a revocation password that might be required by the CA administrator to revoke this certificate in the future.

Step 4.   The results display local device names configured as part of the trustpoint. Answer yes to send the request to the CA.

Fingerprint Validation and Man-in-the-Middle Attacks

Failure to perform fingerprint validation steps could result in a potential attacker successfully executing a man-in-the-middle (MITM) attack against a session and then replacing legitimate data with fake data. The attacker potentially could

- Substitute a fake certificate for the real CA certificate. This results in the VPN router trusting the attacker's CA instead of the real CA.

- Substitute a fake public key for the real public key. This results in the CA issuing a certificate to the attacker instead of the legitimate VPN router.

Mitigating the possibility of interception and substitution requires two out-of-band authentication procedures:

- The PKI client (VPN router) must verify that it received the correct CA certificate.

- The CA must verify that it received the correct enrollment information from the PKI client.

Task 5: Issue the Client Certificate on the CA Server

The final task of the enrollment process involves having the information in the enrollment examined and then granting or rejecting the request if the Certificate Server is running in manually granting mode. Otherwise, the request will be automatically granted. The configuration sequence that follows is performed on a Cisco IOS Software Certificate Server.

Complete the following steps to grant or reject the client certificate:

Step 1. Examine pending requests by running the **show pki server** *name* **requests** command. All requests will be displayed. Each request will have a request identifier (ReqID), the fingerprint of the information submitted (to be compared to the locally calculated fingerprint), and the name of the requesting VPN router.

Step 2. Find the request being considered and validate its fingerprint against the client's fingerprint.

Step 3. To grant the request when in manual granting mode, execute the **crypto pki server** *name* **grant** *req-id* command. To reject the request, use the **crypto pki server** *name* **reject** *req-id* command.

Upon granting the certificate, it will automatically be downloaded through SCEP by the PKI client and installed on the VPN router.

Certificate Revocation on the Cisco IOS Software Certificate Server

If an issued certificate must be revoked, use the **crypto pki server** *name* **revoke** *serial-number* command. Serial numbers can be seen if the CA is configured to use complete database level and the certificates are stored on the Certificate Server. Otherwise, there should be another administrative procedure that is tracking issued certificates by serial number.

Cisco Configuration Professional Support

The Cisco Configuration Professional can be used to enroll to a PKI on a Cisco VPN router. From the home page, choose **Configure > Security > VPN Components > Public Key Infrastructure > Certificate Enrollment Wizards**. When prompted, select the correct type of enrollment that is desired.

Verify the CA and Identity Certificates

To verify that the CA certificate and identity certificate have been properly installed on the VPN router, use the **show crypto pki certificates** command. The output of this command shows the certificate availability and the time frames for which they are valid, as demonstrated in Example 16-10. If the identity certificate's status is Pending, the VPN router has not received the certificate back from the certificate authority.

Example 16-10   *Verify PKI Certificate Installation*

```
Router# show crypto pki certificates



Certificate
  Subject Name
    Name: myrouter.example.com
    IP Address: 10.0.0.1
  Status: Available
  Certificate Serial Number: 0123456789ABCDEF0123456789ABCDEF
  Key Usage: General Purpose
CA Certificate
  Status: Available
  Certificate Serial Number: 3051DF7123BEE31B8341DFE4B3A338E5F
  Key Usage: Not Set
```

Feature Support

Table 16-4 shows the required Cisco IOS Software releases and the functionality supported in them.

Table 16-4   *Cisco IOS Software PKI Client Feature Support*

Feature	Software Release
SCEP Support	11.3T
Auto-enrollment	12.2(8)T
Auto-reenrollment	12.3(7)T

Auto-Enrollment and Auto-Reenrollment

The **auto-enroll** command can be used to have a VPN router automatically request a router identity certificate from the CA using parameters in the configuration. If an RSA key does not exist that matches the requested key label, this command will cause a new key pair to be generated. Adding the **regenerate** argument will cause a new key pair to be generated as well upon reenrollment. Note that some CAs require new keys for reenrollment to succeed.

Implementation Guidelines

Consider the following when implementing the Cisco IOS Software PKI client on VPN devices:

- With external CAs, get enrollment and revocation information ahead of time and test interoperability prior to production implementation.

- Test the process of CA authentication prior to production implementation.

- Ensure that private keys are protected appropriately. USB Smart Tokens provide one of the highest levels of protection.

- Auto-enrollment requires planning. Do not just plan the CA into automatic granting mode because this has security and risk implications as well as can affect production availability.

Troubleshooting Flow

In the event of problems with the Cisco IOS Software PKI Client not enrolling, follow these steps to troubleshoot the issue:

Step 1.   Verify the reachability between the PKI client and the CA server using standard connectivity testing methods. Also, ensure that the SCEP server is functioning by running the **debug crypto pki transactions** command.

Step 2.   Verify that the time on the PKI client is set properly. Incorrect time can cause devices to reject certificates.

Configure and Verify the Integration of a Cisco IOS Software VPN Router with Supporting PKI Entities

Cisco IOS Software–based routers can use PKI and certificates to authenticate peers when establishing VPNs. The following sections cover IKE peer authentication for use with VPNs on Cisco IOS routers.

IKE Peer Authentication

Cisco IOS Software routers can use PKI and certificates for authentication of peers in an IPsec VPN. As an IPsec VPN is being negotiated between two devices, the peers will first authenticate each other using PKI certificates instead of pre-shared keys (passwords).

The PKI-based authentication for an IPsec VPN follows this process:

Step 1.   The peers send their identity certificates to each other at the beginning of the IKE session.

Step 2.   Each peer checks the CRL to validate the received identity certificate.

Step 3.   The peers challenge each other to sign a random value with each peer's private key.

Step 4.   The peers then validate the signature by using the public key in the identity certificate.

IKE Peer Certificate Authorization

By default, the IKE process on Cisco IOS Software routers will accept any valid certificate signed by any of its locally defined trustpoint CAs.

This can be risky for several reasons:

- Not all trustpoints can be VPN related.

- Not all VPN-related trustpoints contain only VPN routers.

- Not all VPN-related trustpoints can be the correct peer for a specific tunnel.

Certificates can be authorized to limit subjects that can be peered with.

Configuration Tasks

To configure PKI-enabled IKE authentication for IPsec VPNs, perform some of or all the following configuration tasks, depending on which are required for the environment:

Key Topic

Task 1:   Optionally, configure an IKE (ISAKMP) policy that uses PKI-based authentication of peers.

Task 2:   Optionally, create an ISAKMP profile and bind it to a VPN association. This is used if there is more than one trustpoint and there is a requirement to bind a particular remote VPN peer to a particular trustpoint (CA certificate).

Task 3:   Optionally, configure certificate-based authorization of remote peers so that they can only associate with particular VPNs. This is recommended in most scenarios.

Configuration Scenario

The upcoming set of configuration tasks involves configuring a Cisco IOS router (R1) to establish an IKE session with another router using the following settings:

- The IKE session will be authenticated using RSA signatures.

- The IKE session will user 128-bit AES encryption and DH group 14 for key exchange.

- The R1 peer will be configured to accept the remote peer only if it can be authenticated using PKI-based credentials and based on its identity. Only peers whose name contains the OU=VPN, O=Cisco, and C=US x.500 identifiers can connect to the VPN.

Assumptions are that both peers are currently enrolled into a common PKI and that they both have the CA's certificate. Additionally, the example assumes that both peers have a VTI-based IPsec configuration that will trigger the IKE process to obtain the necessary IPsec session keys.

Task 1: Configure an IKE Policy

Task 1 involves configuring the IKE policy that includes the RSA signatures (rsa-sig) authentication method. Example 16-11 shows the command usage.

Example 16-11   *Create IKE Policy to Use RSA Signatures for Authentication*

```
Router(config)# crypto isakmp policy 10
Router(config-isakmp)# authentication rsa-sig
Router(config-isakmp)# encr aes
Router(config-isakmp)# group 14
```

Task 2: Configure an ISAKMP Profile

Task 2 configures the ISAKMP profile that specifies that a specific trustpoint only will be used to verify the remote peer's identity certificate.

Complete the following steps and refer to Example 16-12 for the command usage:

Step 1.   Create a named ISAKMP profile using the **crypto isakmp profile** *name* command.

Step 2.   In ISAKMP profile configuration mode, set the local trustpoint that will be used to verify the peer's certificate with the **ca trust-point** *trustpoint_name* command.

Step 3.   Enter the IPsec profile configuration mode and apply the ISAKMP profile to the IPsec profile using the **set isakmp-profile** command.

Example 16-12   *Configure an ISAKMP Profile*

```
Router (config)# crypto isakmp profile MY-ISAKMP-PROFILE
Router (conf-isa-prof)# match certificate MYCERTMAP
Router (conf-isa-prof)# ca trust-point VPN-PKI
!
Router (config)# crypto ipsec profile MY-IPsec-PROFILE
Router (ipsec-profile)# set isakmp-profile MY-ISAKMP-PROFILE
!
Router (config)# interface Tunnel 0
Router (config-if)# tunnel protection ipsec profile MY-IPsec-PROFILE
```

Task 3: Configure Certificate-Based Authorization of Remote Peers

Task 3 limits peers with which the VPN router will establish IKE and IPsec sessions by using certificate maps to describe the allowed authenticated peers based upon fields in their identity certificates.

Complete the following steps and refer to Example 16-13 for the command usage.

Step 1.   Create a certificate map using the **crypto pki certificate map** command.

Step 2.   In the certificate map entry, provide the conditions for accepting a remote peer based on the contents of the peer's certificate. The example shows that the subject name must contain (co) appropriate OU, O, and C parameters in the X.500 name.

Step 3.   In the ISAKMP profile, add a condition to map the peer's certificate against the certificate map using the **match certificate** command.

Example 16-13   *Using Certificate Maps to Limit Allowed VPN Peers*

```
Router(config)# crypto pki certificate map MY-CERT-MAP 10
Router(ca-certificate-map)# subject-name co ou=VPN, o=Cisco, c=US
!
Router (config)# crypto isakmp profile MY-ISAKMP-PROFILE
Router (conf-isa-prof)# match certificate MY-CERT-MAP
```

Verify IKE SA Establishment

Use the **debug crypto isakmp** command to look for the ISAKMP policy using rsa-sig for authentication, successful certificate authorization when a peer matches the profile, and the successful establishment of the IKE SA. Example 16-14 shows what the output of this command looks like.

Example 16-14   debug crypto isakmp *Command Output*

```
Router# debug crypto isakmp


20:26:58: ISAKMP (8): beginning Main Mode exchange
20:26:58: ISAKMP (8): processing SA payload. message ID = 0
20:26:58: ISAKMP (8): Checking ISAKMP transform 1 against priority 10 policy
20:26:58: ISAKMP:       encryption DES-CBC
20:26:58: ISAKMP:       hash SHA
20:26:58: ISAKMP:       default group 1
20:26:58: ISAKMP:       auth pre-share
20:26:58: ISAKMP (8): atts are acceptable. Next payload is 0
```

Feature Support

Table 16-5 shows the required Cisco IOS Software releases and the functionality supported in them.

Table 16-5   *Cisco IOS Software IKE Peer Authentication Feature Support*

Feature	Software Release
IKE RSA authentication support and PKI integration	11.3T
ISAKMP profiles with multiple RSA key pairs	12.2(15)T
ISAKMP profiles with certificate authorization lists	12.2(15)T

Implementation Guidelines

Key Topic

Consider the following when implementing the Cisco IOS Software IKE peer authentication on Cisco VPN devices:

- Always use CRLs to access revocation information.

- It is highly recommended to authorize remote peer certificates when using non-VPN-only PKIs or with multiple trustpoints in the configuration.

- Consider using a general naming convention to include groups of valid routers as opposed to exact remote peer names because using specific names will not scale in meshed VPN environments.

Troubleshooting Flow

In the event of problems with the Cisco IOS Software PKI Client not enrolling, follow these steps to troubleshoot the issue:

Step 1. Verify that the certificates shared by the peers have not been revoked and are still valid.

Step 2. Verify that the peers authenticate using certificates.

Step 3. Verify that the certificate-based authorization does not inhibit the creation of IKE SAs. If the IKE SA authenticates but fails to negotiate IPsec SAs, this could be a sign of failed authorization.

Configuring Advanced PKI Integration

By default, Cisco IOS Software Certificate Server makes the CRL available using SCEP. Some instances might require that the CRL be published to an external server. In these cases, the Certificate Server can be configured to publish the CRL to a particular URL so that it will be available to clients. The CRL Distribution Point (CDP) URL inside the certificate can be used to provide the location to clients. Example 16-15 portrays a server exporting its CRL over FTP to a remote server using the **database url crl publish** command. It also includes a custom CDP URL using the **cdp-url** command that points to the CRL.

Example 16-15 *Publish CRL to External Server*

```
Router(config)# crypto pki server MY-CS
Router(cs-server)# database url crl publish ftp://crl.company.com username admin
password ****
Router(cs-server)# cdp-url http://crl.company.com/MY-CS.crl
```

Configuring CRL Handling on PKI Clients

By default, Cisco IOS Software PKI clients check the CRL for revocation information, and if the CRL is not reachable, all sessions will be rejected until the PKI client has a current CRL. This behavior can be modified so that PKI clients will accept peers even if the CRL is unavailable. A client can be configured to accept peers without CRL confirmation by using the **revocation-check crl none** command. Additionally, to request that the CRL be downloaded immediately, issue the **crypto pki crl request** *name* global configuration command. See Example 16-16 for the commands to allow this.

Example 16-16 *Configuring CRL Handling on PKI Clients*

```
Router (config)# crypto pki trustpoint VPN-PKI
Router(ca-trustpoint)# revocation-check crl none
Router(ca-trustpoint)# exit
Router(config)# crypto pki crl request MY-TRUSTPOINT
```

Using OCSP or AAA on PKI Clients

If using a CRL does not satisfy organization requirements for revocation, Cisco IOS Software Online Certificate Status Protocol (OCSP) client or an AAA client can be used to satisfy real-time revocation operation. These technologies are not covered in this course.

Exam Preparation

As mentioned in the section, "How to Use This Book," in the Introduction, you have several choices for exam preparation: the exercises here, the memory tables in Appendix C, the final exam preparation chapter, and the exam simulation questions on the CD-ROM. The following questions present a bigger challenge than the exam itself because they use an open-ended question format. By using this more difficult format, you exercise your memory better and prove your conceptual and factual knowledge of this chapter. You can find the answers to these questions in Appendix A, "Answers to the DIKTA Quizzes and Fill in the Blanks Questions."

Review All Key Topics

Review the most important topics in the chapter, noted with the Key Topics icon in the margin of the page. Table 16-6 lists a reference of these key topics and the page numbers on which each is found.

Table 16-6 *Key Topics*

Key Topic Element	Description	Page
Figure 16-1	Trusted introducer	415
List	Trusted introducer transactions	415
Table 16-2	Compare VPN-only and enterprise PKIs	420
List	Steps to deploy PKI-enabled site-to-site VPNs	420
List	Input parameters for PKI-enabled site-to-site VPNs	421
List	Deployment guidelines for PKI-enabled site-to-site VPNs	421
List	Cisco IOS Software Certificate Server features	422
List	Choose appropriate router for CA function	422
Task list	Implement a CA on a Cisco IOS router	422
List	CA certificate rollover stages	427
List	Implementation guidelines for the Cisco IOS Software Certificate Server	428
List	Troubleshooting the Cisco IOS Software Certificate Server	429
List	Cisco IOS Software private key storage methods	430

Table 16-6 *Key Topics*

Key Topic Element	Description	Page
List	Cisco IOS Software PKI client configuration tasks	430
List	Steps for authenticating the CA	433
List	Implementing the Cisco IOS Software PKI client on VPN devices	436
List	Troubleshooting the Cisco IOS Software PKI client	436
List	PKI-based VPN authentication steps	436
List	Task list for PKI-based IKE authentication	437
Example 16-11	Creating an IKE policy to use RSA signatures for authentication	438
List	Configuring an ISAKMP profile	438
List	Implementation guidelines for Cisco IOS Software IKE peer authentication	440

Complete Tables and Lists from Memory

Print a copy of Appendix C, "Memory Tables" (found on the CD), or at least the section for this chapter, and complete the tables and lists from memory. Appendix D, "Memory Table Answers," also on the CD, includes completed tables and lists to check your work. Although there are no memory tables in this chapter, you will find some memory tables for other chapters.

Define Key Terms

Define the following key terms from this chapter, and check your answers in the Glossary:

public key infrastructure (PKI), public key cryptography, Pretty Good Privacy (PGP), certificate authority (CA), X.509, Certificate Revocation List (CRL), Online Certificate Status Protocol (OCSP), Simple Certificate Enrollment Protocol (SCEP), man-in-the-middle (MITM) attack

Fill in the Blanks

1. _____ is where existing point-to-point key exchanges can be tied together to soften the public key distribution problem.

2. When enrolling to a PKI, clients submit their _____ and _____ to the CA.

3. When deploying PKI-enabled VPNs, one of the major choices is whether to use a _____ PKI or an _____ PKI.

4. _____ provides data integrity, data origin authentication, protection against replay, and confidentiality to user traffic.

5. Digital signatures are commonly used by many authentication protocols for traffic running over _____ networks.

6. To participate in the PKI system, all end users must _____ with the CA, which involves a process in which they submit their public key and their name to the CA.

7. An _____ is a piece of information that binds a PKI member's name to its public key and puts it into a standard format.

8. The Cisco IOS Software Certificate Server stores its database on the local _____ of the router.

References

Configuring and Managing a Cisco IOS Certificate Server for PKI Deployment, www.cisco.com/en/US/docs/ios/sec_secure_connectivity/configuration/guide/sec_cfg_mng_cert_serv.htm.

Configuring Authorization and Revocation of Certificates in a PKI, www.cisco.com/en/US/docs/ios/sec_secure_connectivity/configuration/guide/sec_cfg_auth_rev_cert.html.

This chapter covers the following subjects:

- **Understanding the Cisco IOS Software DMVPN architecture:** Covers the integration of several technologies to deploy DMVPNs to hub and spoke routers.

- **Plan the deployment of a Cisco IOS Software DMVPN:** Discusses the environmental information that you must analyze to successfully deploy a DMVPN.

- **Configure and verify Cisco IOS Software GRE tunnels:** Learn to configure GRE tunnels and integrate them with other Cisco technologies to create secure communication paths.

- **Configure and verify a Cisco IOS Software NHRP client and server:** Covers the deployment of NHRP on both the client (spoke router) and server (hub router).

- **Configure and verify a Cisco IOS Software DMVPN hub:** Discusses successfully deploying DMVPNs on the hub router.

- **Configure and verify a Cisco IOS Software DMVPN spoke:** Discusses successfully deploying DMVPNs on the spoke routers.

- **Configure and verify dynamic routing in a Cisco IOS Software DMVPN:** Covers adding dynamic routing to a DMVPN.

- **Troubleshoot a Cisco IOS Software DMVPN:** Discusses troubleshooting the configuration of a DMVPN.

CHAPTER 17

Deploying DMVPNs

Dynamic Multipoint Virtual Private Networks (DMVPN) are a feature of Cisco IOS Software that makes the deployment of large hub-and-spoke, partial mesh, and full mesh VPN topologies much easier.

"Do I Know This Already?" Quiz

The "Do I Know This Already?" quiz helps you decide whether you really need to read the entire chapter. If you already intend to read the entire chapter, you do not necessarily need to answer these questions now.

The ten-question quiz, derived from the major sections in the "Foundation Topics" portion of this chapter, helps you determine how to spend your limited study time.

Table 17-1 outlines the major topics discussed in this chapter and the "Do I Know This Already?" quiz questions that correspond to those topics.

Table 17-1   *"Do I Know This Already?" Foundation Topics Section-to-Question Mapping*

Foundation Topics Section	Questions Covered in This Section
Understanding the Cisco IOS Software DMVPN Architecture	1–4
Plan the Deployment of a Cisco IOS Software DMVPN	5
Configure and Verify Cisco IOS Software GRE Tunnels	6
Configure and Verify a Cisco IOS Software NHRP Client and Server	7
Configure and Verify a Cisco IOS Software DMVPN Hub	8
Configure and Verify a Cisco IOS Software DMVPN Spoke	9
Configure and Verify Dynamic Routing in a Cisco IOS Software DMVPN	10

Caution: The goal of self-assessment is to gauge your mastery of the topics in this chapter. If you do not know the answer to a question or are only partially sure of the answer, you should mark this question wrong for purposes of the self-assessment. Giving yourself credit for an answer that you correctly guess skews your self-assessment results and might provide you with a false sense of security.

1. Which mechanism provides a scalable multiprotocol tunneling framework with optional dynamic routing?

   a. NHRP

   b. IPsec

   c. GRE

   d. 802.1X

   e. None of these answers are correct.

2. Which mechanism provides dynamic mutual discovery of spoke devices?

   a. GRE

   b. IKE

   c. NHRP

   d. DHCP

   e. Expired Certificate List

3. Which mechanism provides key management and transmission protection?

   a. NHRP

   b. GRE

   c. mGRE

   d. IDS/IPS

   e. IKE + IPsec

4. To integrate PKI-based authentication with site-to-site VPNs, which protocol must be configured to use PKI-based authentication?

   a. IKE

   b. GRE

   c. AAA

   d. RSA

   e. VPN

5. DMVPNs can use pre-shared keys or PKI-based IKE authentication. Either choice is acceptable for a hub-and-spoke network, but which of the following is recommended for a fully meshed network?

   a. IPsec

   b. DH group 14

   c. Pre-shared keys

   d. PKI-based authentication

6. GRE uses which IP protocol in combination with IPsec VPNs to pass routing information between connected networks?

    a. 89

    b. 50

    c. 47

    d. 51

    e. None of these answers are correct.

7. When a spoke router initially connects to a DMVPN, it registers its inner (tunnel) and outer (physical interface) IP address with which of the following?

    a. NHRP server

    b. DHCP server

    c. Cisco ACS Server

    d. Cisco Security Manager

    e. None of these answers are correct.

8. What Cisco IOS Software command designates the tunnel interface as multipoint GRE mode?

    a. tunnel source

    b. tunnel destination

    c. tunnel mode gre multipoint

    d. interface gre 0/0 multipoint

9. If a DMVPN spoke router is configured with a point-to-point GRE interface, the spoke will only participate in which type of topology?

    a. Strict hub-and-spoke

    b. Partial mesh

    c. Full mesh

    d. Token ring

    e. None of these answers are correct.

10. On the hub, what is the main factor that determines whether the DMVPN will operate as strict hub-and-spoke or as partially/full mesh?

    a. Routing protocol functions

    b. Network administrator preference

    c. Bandwidth to the hub

    d. Cisco router hardware model

    e. Cisco IOS Software Release

The answers to the "Do I Know This Already?" quiz are found in Appendix A. The suggested choices for your next step are as follows:

- **8 or less overall score:** Read the entire chapter. This includes the "Foundation Topics" and the "Exam Preparation" sections.

- **9 or 10 overall score:** If you want more review on these topics, skip to the "Exam Preparation" section. Otherwise, move on to Chapter 18, "Deploying High Availability in Tunnel-Based IPsec VPNs."

Foundation Topics

This chapter covers the integration of multipoint Generic Routing Encapsulation (mGRE) with Next Hop Resolution Protocol (NHRP) and IPsec to deploy Dynamic Multipoint Virtual Private Networks (DMVPN) on hub-and-spoke devices. Verification and troubleshooting of DMVPN operation will also be covered. Upon completing this chapter, you will be able to configure and troubleshoot a Cisco IOS Software DMVPN.

Understanding the Cisco IOS Software DMVPN Architecture

The Cisco DMVPN feature allows administrators to deploy scalable IPsec VPNs for both small and large networks. The Cisco DMVPN feature combines the features and benefits of mGRE tunnels, IPsec encryption, and the Next Hop Resolution Protocol (NHRP) to provide a solution that easily provisions VPN peers. DMVPN also supports dynamically addressed spoke routers as long as appropriate peer authentication is used.

DMVPNs can be deployed using two models:

- **Hub-and-spoke:** A hub-and-spoke DMVPN requires that each branch (spoke) have a point-to-point GRE interface that is used to build a tunnel to the hub router. All traffic between spokes must flow through the hub router. This model provides a scalable configuration on the hub router but does not provide direct spoke-to-spoke communication.

- **Spoke-to-spoke:** A spoke-to-spoke DMVPN requires that each branch (spoke) have an mGRE interface through which dynamic spoke-to-spoke tunnels are used for spoke-to-spoke traffic. This model provides a scalable configuration for all involved devices and also provides direct spoke-to-spoke communication. Be aware that DMVPN does not immediately produce a mesh (partial or full) topology. It initially establishes a hub-and-spoke topology from which a partial or full mesh is generated dynamically as traffic patterns dictate.

The primary benefits of implementing a DMVPN are as follows:

- **Hub router configuration reduction:** Traditional IPsec VPNs involved configuring the crypto map characteristics, the crypto access control list (ACL), and the GRE tunnel interface on each spoke router. The DMVPN feature allows you to create a single mGRE tunnel interface and a single IPsec profile, and does not require crypto ACLs on the hub router. This makes the size of the configuration on the hub router relatively the same, even as spoke routers are added to the network.

- **Automatic IPsec initiation:** GRE relies on NHRP to configure and resolve peer destination addresses. This allows IPsec to immediately trigger to dynamically create point-to-point GRE tunnels and begin negotiation of IPsec sessions without traditional IPsec configuration.

- **Support for spoke routers configured with dynamic addressing:** Traditional IPsec hub-and-spoke VPNs required that all sites be configured with static IP addresses on spoke router interfaces because that information is required when configuring the GRE tunnel destination IP address and the IPsec peer address. DMVPNs allow spoke routers to have dynamic interface IP addresses and to use NHRP to register the spoke router's interface IP address with the hub router.

Building Blocks of DMVPNs

DMVPNs use the benefits of other Cisco features to provide the best of hub-and-spoke and full mesh VPN topologies. The Cisco features that DMVPNs combine are as follows:

- **mGRE:** mGRE allows a single Generic Routing Encapsulation (GRE) interface to support multiple GRE tunnels and makes the configuration much easier. Using GRE tunnels provides support for IP multicast and non-IP protocols to traverse the interface as well. Support for IP multicast enables the use of dynamic routing protocols such as Enhanced IGRP (EIGRP) or Open Shortest Path First (OSPF) to update routing tables and create redundant VPN paths if needed. All DMVPN members use either GRE or mGRE interfaces to build tunnels between other peer devices.

- **NHRP:** Next Hop Resolution Protocol (NHRP) is a client and server protocol where the hub acts as the NHRP server and the spokes are the NHRP clients. The NHRP database maintains mappings between the router (public, physical interface) and the tunnel (inside the tunnel interface) IP addresses of each spoke. Each spoke registers its public and internal tunnel addresses when it boots and queries the NHRP database for the addresses of other spokes. NHRP is used to make the configuration and management of a partial or full mesh environment less complex, like that found in a hub-and-spoke network.

- **IPsec:** IPsec provides transmission protection for GRE tunnels. DMVPNs form a permanent hub-and-spoke IPsec VPN that can dynamically reconfigure itself into a partial or full mesh configuration as needed.

Hub-and-Spoke Versus On-Demand Fully Meshed VPNs

The DMVPN cloud topology can support either a hub-and-spoke or a spoke-to-spoke deployment model. The hub-and-spoke deployment model requires that each hub router be configured with an mGRE interface and each branch router (spoke) be configured with a point-to-point GRE interface. The spoke-to-spoke deployment model requires that both the hub router and branch routers (spokes) are configured with mGRE interfaces to forward traffic to peers. A DMVPN cloud is a collection of routers that are configured with either an mGRE interface or a point-to-point GRE interface (or a combination of the two) and that share the same subnet.

Because the typical VPN is used to secure private or corporate traffic over a shared public infrastructure, like the Internet, there are two distinct IP address domains:

- The enterprise addressing space, which is sometimes referred to as the private or inside addresses. These are the addresses that are assigned to the (m)GRE interfaces and are registered with the NHRP server by each spoke.

- The infrastructure addressing space, which is sometimes referred to as the service provider, public, or outside addresses. These are the addresses on the router's physical interfaces and used as addresses in tunnel envelopes (the source and destination addresses in the GRE/IPsec packet headers).

DMVPN Initial State

Figure 17-1 illustrates a DMVPN where the top router (hub) and the other three spoke routers are configured to connect to the hub using NHRP, GRE, and IPsec. Initially, all spokes build a GRE/IPsec tunnel with the hub and register with NHRP on the hub.

3 Spoke 1 hub – DMVPN IPsec over GRE with NHRP

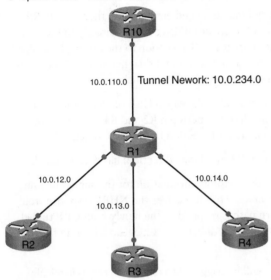

Figure 17-1 *DMPVN: Hub-and-Spoke Model*

In its initial state, the network is purely hub-and-spoke and can stay that way if desired. The initial network properties are

- The hub knows the outer and inner IP addresses of each spoke in its NHRP database.

- Three spoke-to-hub GRE/IPsec tunnels are created.

- Any traffic from a spoke (whether to a hub or another spoke) must travel through the hub.

DMVPN Spoke-to-Spoke Tunnel Creation

In a spoke-to-spoke DMVPN topology, spokes can locate each other and dynamically build tunnels directly to each other.

In Figure 17-1, consider a PC on R2's inside network sending traffic to a server on R4's internal network:

Step 1.   Dynamic routing (already configured over the permanent hub-to-spoke GRE/IPsec tunnels) populates each spoke's routing table so that each spoke knows about the subnets behind the other spokes.

Step 2.   R2 consults its routing table for a route to the subnet behind R4. The routing table provides a next-hop IP address of R4's tunnel IP.

Step 3.   R2 consults its local NHRP cache for R4's tunnel IP address and finds no entry. It sends an NHRP query to the NHRP server (the DMVPN hub router) to resolve the inner (tunnel) address to an external physical IP address on R4.

Step 4.   The NHRP server, which maintains inner (tunnel) and outer (physical) addresses for spoke routers, sends an NHRP reply to R2, which informs it that the inner tunnel IP on R4 is reachable through its outer (physical) IP address.

Step 5.   R2 receives the response from the server and enters it into the local NHRP cache. IPsec is triggered on R2 to create an IPsec tunnel directly to the outer (physical) address on R4. R2 initiates an IKE session to the outer (physical) address of R4 using its outer (physical) address and then negotiates IPsec security associations (SA) for a spoke-to-spoke GRE tunnel.

Step 6.   After the IPsec tunnel is created, R2 will create a GRE tunnel to the outer (physical) address on R4, and all traffic between R2 and R4 will now flow through this tunnel with no more participation by the hub router.

Step 7.   At this point, only traffic from R2 to R4 (one direction) has been enabled.

Step 8.   For two-way traffic, R4 needs next-hop information for the subnet behind R2. R4 queries the NHRP server. After it receives the NHRP response from the NHRP server, the return path is mapped to the newly built GRE tunnel and the response traffic is now sent directly to R2, encapsulated in the GRE/IPsec tunnel.

When the NHRP entries age out, IPsec will be triggered to tear down the dynamically built spoke-to-spoke tunnel. Timers can be tuned to have these tunnels tear down sooner.

DMVPN Benefits and Limitations

Table 17-2 outlines the benefits and limitations of DMVPNs.

Table 17-2   *DMVPN Benefits and Limitations*

Benefit	Limitation
It provides the creation of a very scalable fully meshed VPN topology, where tunnels are dynamically built and torn down according to traffic patterns.	It requires PKI-based authentication of peers to provide scalable spoke-to-spoke IKE authentication.
It requires little configuration efforts because the hub router configuration does not need to change as new peers are added.	It can be more complex to troubleshoot than classic IPsec tunnels because of the required understanding of NHRP and mGRE as well as GRE and IPsec.

Table 17-2 *DMVPN Benefits and Limitations*

Benefit	Limitation
It uses GRE tunnel interfaces and can therefore take advantage of other Cisco IOS Software features such as dynamic routing, QoS, and advanced security features.	
It can be used over public networks because the GRE/IPsec tunneling hides internal addressing.	

Plan the Deployment of a Cisco IOS Software DMVPN

A successful DMVPN deployment requires that you gather information about your current environment. The following sections discuss gathering and analyzing that information.

Input Parameters

Information to be gathered as input when deploying a DMVPN includes the following:

- **Hardware and software on existing routers:** This is needed to determine the performance of the routers and whether the Cisco IOS Software release supports DMVPN features.

- **Cryptographic standards and security requirements:** Information concerning local security requirements and security policies will dictate information such as cryptographic algorithms, key lengths, and tunneling protocols.

Deployment Tasks

Deploying a DMVPN requires completing the following configuration tasks:

Task 1. Configure Internet Key Exchange (IKE) sessions between each DMVPN spoke and the hub, including Internet Security Association and Key Management Protocol (ISAKMP) policies and authentication information.

Task 2. Configure NHRP sessions between each DMVPN spoke and the hub.

Task 3. Configure mGRE tunnels and IPsec profiles on the DMVPN hub.

Task 4. Configure GRE (for pure hub-and-spoke DMVPNs) or mGRE (for partial or full mesh DMVPNs) tunnels and IPsec profiles on DMVPN spokes.

Task 5. Configure dynamic routing over DMVPN tunnels.

Deployment Choices

The process of configuring DMVPNs comes with several deployment choices. The deployment choices and helpful information is provided next:

- **Pre-shared keys or PKI-based IKE authentication:** Either choice is acceptable for a hub-and-spoke, but public key infrastructure (PKI)–based authentication is recommended for scalability in an environment with fully meshed DMVPNs.

- **Single or multiple hubs:** This depends on redundancy requirements. Dual hubs and links can provide both device and path redundancy.

- **Hub-and-spoke or full mesh topology:** Use full mesh if there is a significant amount of spoke-to-spoke traffic; otherwise, consider a hub-and-spoke topology.

General Deployment Guidelines

Consider the following deployment guidelines for DMVPN implementations:

- Use DMVPNs to deploy large hub-and-spoke or full mesh VPN networks.

- Use dynamic routing protocols to route traffic across the DMVPNs.

- DMVPN is a suitable technology for providing secure paths over insecure networks such as the Internet because it hides internal IP addressing.

Configure and Verify Cisco IOS Software GRE Tunnels

Generic Routing Encapsulation (GRE) was designed to carry multiprotocol and IP multicast traffic between sites that might not have IP connectivity. Cisco developed GRE as a protocol that can encapsulate a wide variety of protocol packet types inside IP tunnels.

GRE uses IP protocol 47 and is used with IPsec VPNs to pass routing information between connected networks. A tunnel interface supports header types for each of the following:

- A passenger protocol or encapsulated protocol, such as IP, AppleTalk, DECnet, or IPX

- A carrier protocol (GRE in this case)

- A transport protocol (IP only in this case)

GRE Features and Limitations

GRE has many useful features and is supported by many vendors, so interoperability is usually not an issue for basic GRE point-to-point tunnels. GRE tunnels support multiple network protocols and IP multicast. One of the significant advantages of GRE tunneling over (non-VTI) IPsec tunnels is that GRE uses Cisco IOS Software interfaces that can utilize QoS features.

GRE does have some limitations:

- GRE provides no cryptographic protection for traffic and must be combined with IPsec to provide it.

- There is no standard way to determine the end-to-end state of a GRE tunnel. Cisco IOS Software provides proprietary GRE keepalives for this purpose.

- It can be CPU intensive on some platforms.

- Tunnels can sometimes cause maximum transmission unit (MTU) and IP fragmentation-related issues.

Most systems installed today leave the default MTU set to 1500 bytes and, in most cases, generate packets at this size limit. The tunneling adds a 24-bit GRE header to the packet, which then makes the packet larger than the MTU size. If an application sets the Don't Fragment (DF) bit, this causes a problem when the tunneling system causes the packet to be fragmented.

Point-to-Point Versus Point-to-Multipoint GRE Tunnels

GRE tunnels can be deployed as point-to-point tunnels or point-to-multipoint GRE tunnels. This section provides a comparison of the two deployment options.

The main characteristics of GRE point-to-point configurations are as follows:

- They are typically used as simple point-to-point tunnels that act like point-to-point WAN links or as the connections from spoke to hub router in hub-and-spoke VPNs.

- There is a separate GRE tunnel interface configured on each peer for each GRE peer.

- They do not require NHRP because other peers (their destination tunnel address) are statically configured.

- They provide support for unicast, multicast, and broadcast traffic.

The main characteristics of GRE point-to-multipoint configurations are as follows:

- Only one tunnel interface must be configured for a router to support multiple GRE peers. For a hub-and-spoke network, a single mGRE tunnel interface on the hub can be used for many spoke peers.

- Devices taking advantage of mGRE interfaces require the use of NHRP to build dynamic GRE tunnels. This also provides the option to have peers (usually spokes) that are dynamically addressed.

- mGRE interfaces also support unicast, multicast, and broadcast traffic.

Figure 17-2 shows a DMVPN with both types of GRE tunnels. The solid lines are point-to-point, hub-and-spoke GRE tunnels, and the dashed arrow shows how mGRE permits tunnels to be dynamically built between two spokes. Using mGRE on the spokes as well combined with NHRP provides a topology in which devices can dynamically create partial or full meshed VPN networks.

Point-to-Point Tunnel Configuration Example

Example 17-1 provides a sample configuration for a basic point-to-point GRE tunnel. Figure 17-3 shows the example.

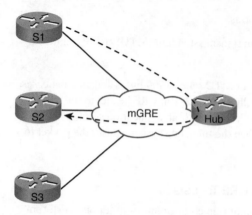

Figure 17-2 *GRE Point-to-Point and Point-to-Multipoint Tunnels*

Example 17-1 *Configure Basic Point-to-Point GRE Tunnel*

```
R1(config)# interface tunnel0
R1(config-if)# tunnel mode gre ip
R1(config-if)# tunnel source  192.168.0.1
R1(config-if)# tunnel destination 192.168.0.2
R1(config-if)# ip address 10.0.0.1 255.255.255.255

R2(config)# interface tunnel0
R2(config-if)# tunnel mode gre ip
R2(config-if)# tunnel source 192.168.0.2
R2(config-if)# tunnel destination 192.168.0.1
R2(config-if)# ip address 10.0.0.2 255.255.255.255
```

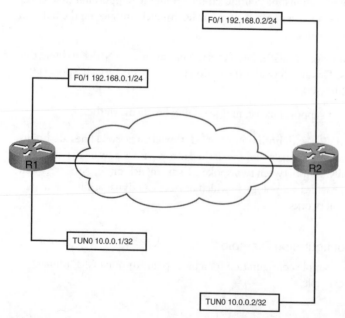

Figure 17-3 *Point-to-Point Tunnel Configuration Example*

Configuration Tasks for a Hub-and-Spoke Network

To configure GRE tunneling in hub-and-spoke GRE networks, complete the following tasks:

Task 1: Configure a multipoint GRE interface on the hub.

Task 2: Configure a point-to-point GRE interface on each spoke that connects to the hub mGRE interface.

Configuration Scenario

The configuration scenario involves creating a hub-and-spoke network with an mGRE interface on the hub and a point-to-point GRE interface on the spoke. The hub has an outer physical IP address of 172.17.0.1 and a tunnel IP address of 10.1.1.1. The spoke has an outer physical IP address of 172.17.2.4 and a tunnel IP address of 10.1.1.2.

Task 1: Configure an mGRE Interface on the Hub

Task 1 is to create a Cisco IOS Software tunnel interface using the **interface tunnel** global configuration command and make it an mGRE interface with the **tunnel mode gre multipoint** command. The task also includes enabling the IP process on the interface by giving it an IP address with the **ip address** command. Also, you need to specify the tunnel endpoints with the **tunnel source** and **tunnel destination** commands, as shown in Example 17-2.

Note: Using the multipoint interface requires a subnet large enough to handle all the spoke tunnels because the multipoint and the spoke tunnel interfaces will be a part of the same logical IP subnet.

Example 17-2   *[Hub] Configure an mGRE Interface*

```
Hub(config)# interface tunnel0
Hub(config-if)# tunnel mode gre multipoint
Hub(config-if)# tunnel source 172.17.0.1
Hub(config-if)# tunnel destination 172.17.2.4
Hub(config-if)# ip address 10.1.1.1 255.255.0.0
```

Task 2: Configure a GRE Interface on the Spoke

Task 2 is to create a Cisco IOS Software GRE tunnel interface as a partner to the hub's multipoint GRE interface using the **interface tunnel** global configuration command and the **tunnel mode gre ip** command. The task also includes enabling the IP process on the interface by giving it an IP address that is included in the hub's IP subnet with the **ip address** command. Also, you need to specify the tunnel endpoints with the **tunnel source** and **tunnel destination** commands. Example 17-3 shows the commands in use.

Example 17-3   *[Spoke] Configure a GRE Interface*

```
Spoke(config)# interface tunnel0
Spoke(config-if)# tunnel mode gre ip
Spoke(config-if)# tunnel source 172.17.2.4
Spoke(config-if)# tunnel source 172.17.0.1
Spoke(config-if)# tunnel destination 172.17.0.1
```

Verify the State of GRE Tunnels

After a hub-and-spoke GRE tunnel is configured, the **show interface tunnel** command can be used to verify its state. The line protocol of a GRE tunnel is up as long as there is a route to the tunnel destination. This is not the case if GRE keepalives are configured (not recommended if using dynamic routing protocols). The line protocol on mGRE tunnel interfaces is always up. Example 17-4 shows the output from a tunnel interface in the up/down state.

Example 17-4   show interface tunnel *Command Output*

```
Router# show interfaces tunnel 0



Tunnel4 is up, line protocol is down
  Hardware is Routing Tunnel
  MTU 1500 bytes, BW 9 Kbit, DLY 500000 usec, rely 255/255, load 1/255
  Encapsulation TUNNEL, loopback not set, keepalive set (10 sec)
  Tunnel source 0.0.0.0, destination 0.0.0.0
  Tunnel protocol/transport GRE/IP, key disabled, sequencing disabled
  Last input never, output never, output hang never
  Last clearing of "show interface" counters never
  Output queue 0/0, 0 drops; input queue 0/75, 0 drops
  Five minute input rate 0 bits/sec, 0 packets/sec
  Five minute output rate 0 bits/sec, 0 packets/sec
     0 packets input, 0 bytes, 0 no buffer
     Received 0 broadcasts, 0 runts, 0 giants
     0 input errors, 0 CRC, 0 frame, 0 overrun, 0 ignored, 0 abort
     0 packets output, 0 bytes, 0 underruns
     0 output errors, 0 collisions, 0 interface resets, 0 restarts
```

To quickly verify that a GRE tunnel is passing traffic, use the **ping** command and specify the tunnel IP address of the remote GRE peer. Also, observe routing protocol neighbor relationships. If they have established successfully, the tunnel must be passing traffic. Note that both methods require NHRP because mGRE is in use.

Configure and Verify a Cisco IOS Software NHRP Client and Server

NHRP is used by routers to determine the IP address of the next hop in IP tunneling networks. When a spoke router initially connects to a DMVPN, it registers its inner (tunnel) and outer (physical interface) IP address with the hub router (the NHRP server) whose IP address is configured on the spoke router (NHRP client).

The hub router places an entry in its NHRP cache and returns a registration reply. The spoke router now sees the hub router as a valid Next Hop Server (NHS) and queries it when trying to locate any other spokes and networks in the NHRP domain. The NHRP client registration enables the mGRE interface on the hub to build a dynamic GRE tunnel back to the spoke, which in turn creates a mapping between the tunnel IP and physical IP address for each spoke that registers with the hub.

(m)GRE and NHRP Integration

As stated, NHRP maps tunnel IP addresses to outer transport IP addresses. This means that in a hub-and-spoke DMVPN deployment, no GRE or IPsec information about the spoke is configured on the hub router. The spoke router is configured with information about the hub using NHRP commands. When the spoke router starts up, it automatically initiates an IPsec tunnel with the hub router. It then notifies the NHRP server (hub router) of its current physical interface IP address. This notification is beneficial because

- The hub router configuration is drastically shortened and simplified because it does not need to know any GRE or IPsec information about the spoke router. It is learned through NHRP.

- Adding a new spoke router to the DMVPN requires no configuration on the hub. The spoke is configured with the hub information and dynamically registers with the hub router. Dynamic routing protocols distribute information about the spoke to the hub, which in turn propagates the information to the other spokes.

Configuration Tasks

To configure NHRP, complete the following tasks on the hub and spokes in a DMVPN:

Task 1: Configure an NHRP server on the hub.

Task 2: Configure NHRP clients on the network spokes.

Configuration Scenario

The configuration scenario involves creating a basic hub-and-spoke network with an mGRE interface on the hub and a point-to-point GRE interface on the spoke. The hub has an outer physical IP address of 172.17.0.1 and a tunnel IP address of 10.1.1.1. The spoke has an outer physical IP address of 172.17.2.4 and a tunnel IP address of 10.1.1.2. The NHRP network ID is 1.

Task 1: Configure an NHRP Server

Task 1 is to create an NHRP server on the hub router. Create a new NHRP server on the tunnel interface using the **ip nhrp network-id** interface command. The NHRP network ID must be the same on the NHRP server and its NHRP clients. If NHRP is being used over an untrusted network, configure NHRP authentication with the **ip nhrp authentication** command.

To support dynamic routing protocols, enable support of IP multicast traffic with the **ip nhrp map multicast dynamic** interface command. This allows each spoke to register as a receiver of multicast traffic, causing the hub to replicate and forward multicast packets to the spoke routers. See Example 17-5 for the command usage.

Example 17-5   *[Hub] Configure an NHRP Server*

```
Hub(config)# interface tunnel0
Hub(config-if)# ip nhrp network-id 1
Hub(config-if)# ip nhrp authentication ADFqeqrDA
Hub(config-if)# ip nhrp map multicast dynamic
```

Task 2: Configure an NHRP Client

Task 2 is to create an NHRP client on each spoke router. As configured on the hub, configure the NHRP network ID and NHRP authentication string with the **ip nhrp network-id** and **ip nhrp authentication** commands. Then, specify the location of the NHRP NHS with the **ip nhrp nhs** interface command. To allow the spoke to register its multicast capability with the hub, use the **ip nhrp map multicast** command. Finally, specify a static NHRP map that enables the spoke to reach the NHRP server over its address. Example 17-6 displays the command sequence being used.

Example 17-6   *Configure NHRP Client*

```
Spoke(config)# interface tunnel0
Spoke(config-if)# ip nhrp network-id 1
Spoke(config-if)# ip nhrp authentication ADFqeqrDA
Spoke(config-if)# ip nhrp nhs 10.1.1.1
Spoke(config-if)# ip nhrp map multicast 172.17.0.1
Spoke(config-if)# ip nhrp map 10.1.1.1 172.17.0.1
```

Verify NHRP Mappings

The **show ip nhrp command** can be used to show NHRP mapping information for a device, as demonstrated in Example 17-7.

On the hub (NHRP server), this command displays NHRP mappings for all registered spokes.

On the spoke (NHRP clients), this command should show a static mapping for the hub router, a local mapping for the local spoke, and dynamic mappings for any spokes to which the local spoke is sending traffic.

Example 17-7   show ip nhrp *Command Output*

```
Router# show ip nhrp
10.0.0.2/32 via 10.0.0.2, Tunnel0 created 00:17:49, expire 00:01:30
  Type: dynamic, Flags: unique registered used
```

```
    NBMA address: 172.17.0.2
    Group: test-group-0
```

Debugging NHRP

The **show ip nhrp nhs** command displays the NHRP next-hop server information and can be used to show NHRP mapping information for a device, as demonstrated in Example 17-8. The **show ip nhrp nhs detail** command helps find issues with NHRP registrations. If the req-failed field shows a number greater than 0, there might be a network ID or authentication mismatch. It can also indicate a connectivity problem with the NHS.

Example 17-8 *Debugging NHRP*

```
Router# show ip nhrp nhs


Legend: E=Expecting replies, R=Responding, W=Waiting
Tunnel0:
192.0.2.1  W priority = 2 cluster = 0
192.0.2.2  RE priority = 0 cluster = 0
192.0.2.3  RE priority = 1 cluster = 0

Router# debug nhrp packet
NHRP activity debugging is on
Router#
NHRP: Send Purge Request via ATM3/0.1, packet size: 72
 src: 135.206.58.55, dst: 135.206.58.56
 (F) afn: NSAP(3), type: IP(800), hop: 255, ver: 1
     shtl: 20(NSAP), sstl: 0(NSAP)
 (M) flags: "reply required", reqid: 2
     src NBMA: 47.0091810000000002ba08e101.525354555355.01
     src protocol: 135.206.58.55, dst protocol: 135.206.58.56
 (C-1) code: no error(0)
       prefix: 0, mtu: 9180, hd_time: 0
       addr_len: 0(NSAP), subaddr_len: 0(NSAP), proto_len: 4, pref: 0
       client protocol: 135.206.58.130
NHRP: Receive Purge Reply via ATM3/0.1, packet size: 72
 (F) afn: NSAP(3), type: IP(800), hop: 254, ver: 1
     shtl: 20(NSAP), sstl: 0(NSAP)
 (M) flags: "reply required", reqid: 2
     src NBMA: 47.0091810000000002ba08e101.525354555355.01
     src protocol: 135.206.58.55, dst protocol: 135.206.58.56
 (C-1) code: no error(0)
       prefix: 0, mtu: 9180, hd_time: 0
       addr_len: 0(NSAP), subaddr_len: 0(NSAP), proto_len: 4, pref: 0
       client protocol: 135.206.58.130
```

To troubleshoot even deeper, use the **debug nhrp packet** command to see registration failures.

Configure and Verify a Cisco IOS Software DMVPN Hub

Dynamic Multipoint Virtual Private Networks (DMVPN) are a feature found in Cisco IOS Software that makes it much easier to deploy VPN tunnels. The following sections cover configuring the hub routers in a DMVPN.

Configuration Tasks

Perform the following configuration sequence to configure a DMVPN hub:

Task 1: (Optional) Configure an IKE policy. Recall that if one is not created, the hub router will use default IKE policies.

Task 2: Generate/configure spoke authentication credentials. This typically involves enrolling into a PKI to obtain a certificate for authentication purposes.

Task 3: Configure an IPsec profile with an optional transform set. If a transform set is not configured, the router will use default IPsec transform sets.

Task 4: Create an mGRE tunnel interface.

Task 5: Configure an NHRP server on the mGRE interface.

Task 6: Associate the IPsec profile with the mGRE interface to configure tunnel protection.

Task 7: Configure an IP address and IP fragmentation/segmentation parameters on the mGRE interface.

Configuration Scenario

The configuration scenario involves creating a basic hub-and-spoke network with an mGRE interface on the hub and a point-to-point GRE interface on the spoke. The hub has an outer physical IP address of 172.17.0.1 and a tunnel IP address of 10.1.1.1. The spoke has an outer physical IP address of 172.17.2.4 and a tunnel IP address of 10.1.1.2. The NHRP network ID is 1.

The assumption is that there is full IP connectivity among all physical interfaces.

Task 1: (Optional) Configure an IKE Policy

Task 1 is to optionally create an IKE policy with the **crypto isakmp policy** global configuration command. Example 17-9 shows an IKE policy specifying Rivest, Shamir, and Adelman (RSA) signatures for authentication and Diffie-Hellman group 14 to protect the key exchange command.

Example 17-9   *[Hub] Configure an Optional IKE Policy*

```
Hub(config)# crypto isakmp policy 10
Hub(config-isakmp)# auth rsa-sig
Hub(config-isakmp)# group 14
```

Task 2: Generate and/or Configure Authentication Credentials

Task 2 of this configuration sequence specifies that certificates be used for authentication. Refer to the configuration process covered in previous sections of this book and enroll the hub router into the PKI and configure other PKI-relevant items.

Task 3: Configure an IPsec Profile

Task 3 creates a named IPsec profile using the **crypto ipsec profile** command that allows the transform set and encapsulation mode to be specified. Example 17-10 shows an empty IPsec profile, which indicates that the default transform sets will be used to protect GRE traffic.

Example 17-10   *Configure an IPsec Profile*

```
Hub(config)# crypto ipsec profile IPsec-PROFILE
```

Task 4: Create an mGRE Tunnel Interface

Task 4 creates the mGRE tunnel interface. Enter the **interface tunnel** command and then configure basic GRE parameters. The **tunnel mode gre multipoint** command designates the tunnel interface as mGRE, and the **tunnel source** command specifies the physical interface to which the GRE tunnel is bound. The **tunnel key** command is required and must match the tunnel key configured on the spokes. This command allows network administrators to run more than one DMVPN at a time on the same router. The GRE tunnel key therefore uniquely identifies the DMVPN. Example 17-11 shows the sequence of commands.

Example 17-11   *Create an mGRE Tunnel Interface*

```
Hub(config)# interface tunnel0
Hub(config-if)# tunnel mode gre multipoint
Hub(config-if)# tunnel source GigabitEthernet0/0
Hub(config-if)# tunnel key 13579
```

Key Topic

Task 5: Configure the NHRP Server

Task 5 configures an NHRP server on the hub router inside the mGRE tunnel interface. The **ip nhrp network-id** command specifies the NHRP network ID, and the **ip nhrp authentication** command configures authentication for NHRP traffic. Finally, the **ip nhrp map multicast dynamic** command registers the multicast capabilities of the device. Example 17-12 shows the sequence of commands.

Example 17-12   *Configure the NHRP Server*

Key Topic

```
Hub(config-if)# ip nhrp network-id 1
Hub(config-if)# ip nhrp authentication WERQRQ$
Hub(config-if)# ip nhrp map multicast dynamic
```

Task 6: Associate the IPsec Profile with the mGRE Interface

Task 6 specifies the IPsec protection profile created in Step 3 as the tunnel protection mechanism with the **tunnel protection ipsec profile** command. Example 17-13 shows the profile being applied to the mGRE interface.

Example 17-13   *Apply the IPsec Profile to the mGRE Interface*

```
Hub(config)# interface tunnel0
Hub(config-if)# tunnel protection ipsec profile IPsec-PROFILE
```

Task 7: Configure IP Parameters on the mGRE Interface

Task 7 specifies the IP address for the mGRE tunnel interface. This must be a large enough subnet to accommodate all spoke routers. Optionally, to avoid problems with fragmentation of user packets, set the IP MTU side with the **ip mtu** command and set the TCP maximum segment size (MSS) value using the **ip tcp adjust-mss** interface command. Example 17-14 shows the profile being applied to the mGRE interface.

Example 17-14   *Configure IP Parameters on the mGRE Interface*

```
Hub(config)# interface tunnel0
Hub(config-if)# ip address 10.1.1.1 255.255.0.0
Hub(config-if)# ip mtu 1400
Hub(config-if)# ip tcp adjust-mss 1360
```

Cisco Configuration Professional Support

Cisco Configuration Professional (CCP) allows administrators to avoid the CLI configuration for the DMVPN hub and configure the hub and spoke by manually filling in the settings or by utilizing the DMVPN hub configuration wizard. Refer to the Cisco Configuration Professional User Guide, v2.4 for detailed information about using CCP to configure the DMVPN hub. This guide can be found at www.cisco.com/en/US/docs/net_mgmt/cisco_configuration_professional/v2_4/olh/ccp.pdf.

Verify Spoke Registration

One of the first troubleshooting steps should be to verify spoke registrations on the hub router. As demonstrated in Example 17-15, the **show dmvpn** command provides a snapshot view of the spoke registration state.

The output shows entries for all connected spokes and provides the following information:

- The spoke nonbroadcast multiaccess (NBMA) address. This is either the physical interface or a loopback to which the tunnel is attached.

- The spoke tunnel address as it is configured on the GRE or mGRE tunnel.

- The tunnel state.

- The tunnel uptime.

Example 17-15 show dmvpn *Command Output*

```
Router# show dmvpn


Legend: Attrb --> S - Static, D - Dynamic, I - Incomplete
        N - NATed, L - Local, X - No Socket
        # Ent --> Number of NHRP entries with same NBMA peer

! The line below indicates that the sessions are being displayed for Tunnel1.
! Tunnel1 is acting as a spoke and is a peer with three other NBMA peers.

Tunnel1, Type: Spoke, NBMA Peers: 3,

 # Ent   Peer NBMA Addr Peer Tunnel Add State   UpDn Tm Attrb
 ----- --------------- --------------- ----- -------- -----
     2     192.0.2.21       192.0.2.116   IKE     3w0d D
     1     192.0.2.102      192.0.2.11   NHRP 02:40:51 S
     1     192.0.2.225      192.0.2.10    UP     3w0d S
```

Verify Registered Spoke Details

The **show dmvpn detail** command reveals additional information about DMVPN peers, as demonstrated in Example 17-16. The detailed output shows IKE SA information and IPsec statistics, such as the number of packets the router has decrypted and encrypted on this tunnel and the target network.

Example 17-16 *show dmvpn detail Command Output*

```
Router# show dmvpn detail
Legend: Attrb --> S - Static, D - Dynamic, I - Incomplete
        N - NATed, L - Local, X - No Socket
        # Ent --> Number of NHRP entries with same NBMA peer
------------- Interface Tunnel1 info: -------------
Intf. is up, Line Protocol is up, Addr. is 192.0.2.5
   Source addr: 192.0.2.229, Dest addr: MGRE
  Protocol/Transport: "multi-GRE/IP", Protect "gre_prof",
Tunnel VRF "" ip vrf forwarding ""

NHRP Details: NHS: 192.0.2.10 RE 192.0.2.11   E

Type: Spoke, NBMA Peers: 4
 # Ent   Peer NBMA Addr Peer Tunnel Add State   UpDn Tm Attrb    Target Network
 ----- --------------- --------------- ----- -------- ----- ------------------
     2       192.0.2.21       192.0.2.116   UP 00:14:59 D      192.0.2.118/24
IKE SA: local 192.0.2.229/500 remote 192.0.2.21/500 Active
          Capabilities:(none) connid:1031 lifetime:23:45:00
  Crypto Session Status: UP-ACTIVE
```

```
fvrf: (none)
IPSEC FLOW: permit 47 host 192.0.2.229 host 192.0.2.21
       Active SAs: 2, origin: crypto map
       Inbound:  #pkts dec'ed 1 drop 0 life (KB/Sec) 4494994/2700
       Outbound: #pkts enc'ed 1 drop 0 life (KB/Sec) 4494994/2700
   Outbound SPI : 0xD1EA3C9B, transform : esp-3des esp-sha-hmac
    Socket State: Open
```

Implementation Guidelines

Consider the following DMVPN hub implementation guidelines when deploying the DMVPN hub:

- For IKE peering, each hub-to-spoke peering is the same as a classic IPsec VPN peering. However, if using dynamic spoke-to-spoke tunnels, these too need to be authenticated. This necessitates using a scalable authentication method, such as PKI.

- The hub and all spokes must be on the same IP subnet on the tunnel interface. This is required for the routing protocols to advertise the DMVPN as a single IP subnet. This is necessary so that all next-hop addresses appear to directly connect to the tunnel interface.

- If using redundant interfaces on the hub router, the DMVPN can be attached to a loopback interface. The loopback must be included in routing processes in this case.

Feature Support

DMVPN features have been released in phases by Cisco. Basic DMVPN is supported in Release 12.2(13)T and higher. In these releases, spoke-to-spoke traffic must be sent over the hub.

Cisco IOS Software Release 12.3(9)a added support for dynamic spoke-to-spoke tunnels. Reduced latency, hub redundancy, and hierarchical hub design was introduced with Release 12.4(6)T. Release 15.0(1)M provides support for DMVPN tunnel health monitoring and recovery.

Configure and Verify a Cisco IOS Software DMVPN Spoke

DMVPNs are a VPN solution for hub-and-spoke, partial mesh, and full mesh networks that involve much less configuration than traditional VPN implementations. The following sections cover configuring the DMVPN spoke routers.

Configuration Tasks

Perform the following configuration sequence to configure a DMVPN spoke:

Task 1:   (Optional) Configure an IKE policy. Recall that if one is not created, the hub router will use default IKE policies.

Task 2:   Generate/configure spoke authentication credentials. This typically involves enrolling into a PKI to obtain a certificate for authentication purposes.

Task 3:   As with configuring the hub, an IPsec profile with an optional transform set can be configured. If a transform set is not configured, the router will use default IPsec transform sets.

Task 4:   Create an mGRE tunnel interface (or a GRE interface for strict hub-and-spoke DMVPNs).

Task 5:   Configure NHRP client parameters on the mGRE interface.

Task 6:   Associate the IPsec profile with the mGRE interface to configure tunnel protection.

Task 7:   Configure an IP address and IP fragmentation/segmentation parameters on the mGRE interface.

Configuration Scenario

The configuration scenario involves creating a basic hub-and-spoke network with an mGRE interface on the hub and a point-to-point GRE interface on the spoke. The hub has an outer physical IP address of 172.17.0.1 and a tunnel IP address of 10.1.1.1. The spoke has an outer physical IP address of 172.17.2.4 and a tunnel IP address of 10.1.1.2. The NHRP network ID is 1.

The assumption is that there is full IP connectivity among all physical interfaces.

Task 1: (Optional) Configure an IKE Policy

Task 1 is to optionally create an IKE policy with the **crypto isakmp policy** global configuration command. Example 17-17 shows an IKE policy specifying RSA signatures for authentication and Diffie-Hellman group 14 to protect the key exchange command.

Example 17-17   *[Spoke] Configure an Optional IKE Policy*

```
Spoke(config)# crypto isakmp policy 10
Spoke(config-isakmp)# auth rsa-sig
Spoke(config-isakmp)# group 14
```

Task 2: Generate and/or Configure Authentication Credentials

Task 2 of this configuration sequence involves specifying that certificates be used for authentication. Refer to the configuration process covered in the section, "Enroll a Cisco IOS Software VPN Router into a PKI and Troubleshoot the Enrollment Process," in Chapter 16, "Deploying Scalable Authentication in Site-to-Site IPsec VPNs" and enroll the hub router into the PKI and configure other PKI-relevant items.

Task 3: Configure an IPsec Profile

Task 3 creates a named IPsec profile using the **crypto ipsec profile** command that allows the transform set and encapsulation mode to be specified. Example 17-18 shows an empty

IPsec profile, which indicates that the default transform sets will be used to protect GRE traffic.

Example 17-18 *Configure an IPsec Profile*

```
Spoke(config)# crypto ipsec profile IPsec-PROFILE
```

Task 4: Create an mGRE Tunnel Interface

Task 4 creates the mGRE tunnel interface. Enter the **interface tunnel** command and then configure basic GRE parameters. The **tunnel mode gre multipoint** command designates the tunnel interface as mGRE and the **tunnel source** command specifies the physical interface to which the GRE tunnel is bound. The **tunnel key** command is required and must match the tunnel key configured on the spokes. This command allows network administrators to run more than one DMVPN at a time on the same router. The GRE tunnel key therefore uniquely identifies the DMVPN. Example 17-19 shows the sequence of commands.

Example 17-19 *Create an mGRE Tunnel Interface*

```
Spoke(config)# interface tunnel0
Spoke(config-if)# tunnel mode gre multipoint
Spoke(config-if)# tunnel source GigabitEthernet0/0
Spoke(config-if)# tunnel key 13579
```

Task 5: Configure the NHRP Client

Task 5 configures an NHRP client on the spoke router inside the mGRE tunnel interface. The **ip nhrp network-id** command specifies the NHRP network ID, the **ip nhrp authentication** command configures authentication for NHRP traffic, and the **ip nhrp nhs** command specifies the hub as the NHRP server. Finally, the **ip nhrp map multicast dynamic** command registers the multicast capabilities of the device. Example 17-20 shows the sequence of commands.

Example 17-20 *Configure the NHRP Client*

```
Spoke(config-if)# ip nhrp network-id 1
Spoke(config-if)# ip nhrp authentication WERQRQ$
Spoke(config-if)# ip nhrp nhs 10.1.1.1
Spoke(config-if)# ip nhrp map multicast 172.17.0.1
Spoke(config-if)# ip nhrp map 10.1.1.1 172.17.0.1
```

Task 6: Associate the IPsec Profile with the mGRE Interface

Task 6 specifies the IPsec protection profile created in Step 3 as the tunnel protection mechanism with the **tunnel protection ipsec profile** command. Example 17-21 shows the profile being applied to the mGRE interface.

Example 17-21   *Apply the IPsec Profile to the mGRE Interface*

```
Spoke(config)# interface tunnel0
Spoke(config-if)# tunnel protection ipsec profile IPsec-PROFILE
```

Task 7: Configure IP Parameters on the mGRE Interface

Task 7 specifies the IP address for the mGRE tunnel interface. This must be an IP address in the same network as the hub's mGRE subnet. Optionally, to avoid problems with fragmentation of user packets, set the IP MTU side with the **ip mtu** command and set the TCP MSS value using the **ip tcp adjust-mss** interface command. Example 17-22 shows the profile being applied to the mGRE interface.

Example 17-22   *Configure IP Parameters on the mGRE Interface*

```
Spoke(config)# interface tunnel0
Spoke(config-if)# ip address 10.1.1.2 255.255.0.0
Spoke(config-if)# ip mtu 1400
Spoke(config-if)# ip tcp adjust-mss 1360
```

Verify Tunnel State and Traffic Statistics

The **show dmvpn detail** command provides a snapshot view of the state of the spoke's association with the hub.

The output displays entries for all connected spokes and provides the following information:

- Session information (NBMA address, tunnel address, state, uptime, and target network)

- State of IKE SAs

- Crypto session status

- Traffic counters to show that user traffic is being protected

Configure and Verify Dynamic Routing in a Cisco IOS Software DMVPN

Some factors must be taken into consideration when using dynamic routing protocols across a DMVPN. These considerations are even more important when implementing a spoke-to-spoke design because the DMVPN cloud is like an NBMA network.

Many routing protocols use IP multicast to discover other participating nodes. For this reason, NHRP multicast maps must be configured on the spoke routers to register their multicast capability with the hub. The hub router can be configured with a dynamic multicast map that will replicate multicast traffic to the spokes that have registered to receive IP multicast. This permits the hub and spoke routers to forward multicast and broadcast, but it does not permit spokes to receive broadcasts from other spokes.

In a DMVPN, routing neighbor relationships only happen between the hub and each spoke. There is never any spoke-to-spoke routing peering. Thus, the hub will propagate information from each spoke network to the other spokes.

Note that routing protocol functionality on the hub is the main factor in determining whether a DMVPN will remain as a strict hub-and-spoke network or expand to a partial or full mesh by propagation of routes between spokes. The other factor is whether spokes use a GRE interface (only allows a strict hub-and-spoke topology) or an mGRE interface, which permits mesh topologies.

EIGRP Hub Configuration

EIGRP can be used in either strict hub-and-spoke networks or in partial/full mesh networks.

Configuring EIGRP in a strict hub-and-spoke DMVPN deployment is fairly straightforward. Generally speaking, you should disable automatic summarization on the hub and disable EIGRP split horizon so that the hub will propagate information about spoke networks to other spokes. Disable split horizon with the **no ip split-horizon eigrp** *AS-number* interface configuration command.

Mesh DMVPNs cause a problem for route propagation because spoke routers cannot directly exchange information with one another, even though they are on the same logical subnet. This requires the hub router to advertise the subnets from the spokes on the same subnet, and the advertised route must contain the original next hop as it was learned by the hub router from the originating spoke. The **no ip next-hop-self eigrp** *AS-number* interface configuration command takes care of this requirement. Examples 17-23 and 17-24 show the configuration for the use of EIGRP with both DMVPN topologies.

Example 17-23 *EIGRP with Hub-and-Spoke*

```
router(config)# router eigrp 1
router(config-router)# no auto-summary
router(config-router)# exit
!
router(config)# interface tunnel 0
router(config-if)# no ip split-horizon eigrp 1
```

Example 17-24 *EIGRP with Full Mesh*

```
router(config)# router eigrp 1
router(config-router)# no auto-summary
router(config-router)# exit
!
router(config)# interface tunnel 0
router(config-if)# no ip next-hop-self eigrp
Routet(config-if)# no ip split-horizon eigrp 1
```

Note: Do not include the outside address space of the tunnel in a routing protocol running inside the tunnel.

OSPF Hub Configuration

Running OSPF in a DMVPN presents the same challenges as running OSPF over other networks. The hub should be configured as a designated router (DR) because it is in direct communication with all the spokes. Typically, there is no backup designated router (BDR).

In strict hub-and-spoke DMVPNs, this can be simplified by including the tunnel interface in the OSPF router process and configuring the tunnel interface on the hub as a point-to-multipoint OSPF network type and on the spokes as point-to-point network types. There is no need for a BDR, and this makes the branches consider the hub as the only path off the subnet. This will greatly simplify the Dijkstra algorithm process for the OSPF area.

For mesh DMVPNs, configure the mGRE tunnel on the hub as an OSPF broadcast network and each spoke router with an OSPF priority of 0 to prevent a spoke from becoming a DR. Examples 17-25 and 17-26 show OSPF configurations for DMVPN topologies.

Example 17-25 *OSPF with Hub-and-Spoke*

```
router(config)# interface tunnel 0
router(config-if)# ip ospf network point-to-multipoint
router(config-if)# ip ospf priority 10
```

Key Topic

Example 17-26 *OSPF with Full Mesh*

```
router(config)# interface tunnel 0
router(config-if)# ip ospf network broadcast
router(config-if)# ip ospf priority 10
```

Key Topic

Hub-and-Spoke Routing and IKE Peering on Spoke

Verifying routing in a strict hub-and-spoke DMVPN can be accomplished by running the **show ip route** command on a spoke router to ensure that all spoke networks are reachable through the hub, as demonstrated in Example 17-27. The next hop for each spoke prefix should be the hub tunnel IP address. In addition to verifying routes, verify that IKE SAs have established with the **show crypto isakmp sa** command and look for a state of QM_IDLE, as demonstrated in Example 17-28.

Example 17-27 **show ip route** *Command Output*

```
Router# show ip route


Codes: I - IGRP derived, R - RIP derived, O - OSPF derived,
       C - connected, S - static, E - EGP derived, B - BGP derived,
       * - candidate default route, IA - OSPF inter area route,
       i - IS-IS derived, ia - IS-IS, U - per-user static route,
       o - on-demand routing, M - mobile, P - periodic downloaded static route,
       D - EIGRP, EX - EIGRP external, E1 - OSPF external type 1 route,
```

```
          E2 - OSPF external type 2 route, N1 - OSPF NSSA external type 1 route,
          N2 - OSPF NSSA external type 2 route

Gateway of last resort is 10.119.254.240 to network 10.140.0.0

O E2 172.150.0.0 [160/5] via 10.119.254.6, 0:01:00, Ethernet2
E      172.17.10.0 [200/128] via 10.119.254.244, 0:02:22, Ethernet2
O E2 172.70.132.0 [160/5] via 10.119.254.6, 0:00:59, Ethernet2
O E2 10.130.0.0 [160/5] via 10.119.254.6, 0:00:59, Ethernet2
E      172.30.0.0 [200/128] via 10.119.254.244, 0:02:22, Ethernet2
E      10.129.0.0 [200/129] via 10.119.254.240, 0:02:22, Ethernet2
E      172.80.129.0 [200/128] via 10.119.254.244, 0:02:22, Ethernet2
```

Example 17-28   show crypto isakmp sa *Command Output*

```
Router# show crypto isakmp sa


f_vrf/i_vrf    dst             src           state         conn-id    slot
      /vpn2    172.21.114.123  10.1.1.1      QM_IDLE           13      0
```

Full Mesh Routing and IKE Peering on Spoke

Verifying routing in a full mesh DMVPN can be accomplished by running the **show ip route** command on a spoke router to ensure that all spoke networks are reachable directly through the spoke router that advertises the network.

Troubleshoot a Cisco IOS Software DMVPN

You must consider the hub and the spoke routers when troubleshooting connectivity issues between the hub and a spoke router in a DMVPN. For spoke-to-spoke issues between two spokes, you must troubleshoot on the hub as well as the two spoke routers.

Troubleshooting Flow

The following steps are a suggested troubleshooting sequence in the event that there is an issue with DMVPN deployments:

Step 1. Verify an IKE peering between the hub and spokes (or between spoke and spoke if that is where the issue is) by using the **show crypto isakmp sa** command. If it is not established, verify connectivity between the two hosts using **ping** and verifying routes for connectivity issues.

Step 2. Verify the operation of NHRP, GRE, and IPsec. Use the **debug dmvpn detail all** command to see helpful output.

Step 3. Verify routing over the DMVPN. Check to see whether the routing protocol has established spoke-to-hub neighbor relationships inside the DMVPN using the **show ip route** command. Ensure that all spoke networks are reachable from the hub and at the correct next hops by pinging the hub from the spoke routers or pinging the hub router from each spoke. If there is a problem, check the NHRP multicast mapping.

Exam Preparation

As mentioned in the section, "How to Use This Book," in the Introduction, you have several choices for exam preparation: the exercises here, the memory tables in Appendix C, the final exam preparation chapter, and the exam simulation questions on the CD-ROM. The following questions present a bigger challenge than the exam itself because they use an open-ended question format. By using this more difficult format, you exercise your memory better and prove your conceptual and factual knowledge of this chapter. You can find the answers to these questions in Appendix A, "Answers to the DIKTA Quizzes and Fill in the Blanks Questions."

Review All Key Topics

Review the most important topics in the chapter, noted with the Key Topics icon in the margin of the page. Table 17-3 lists a reference of these key topics and the page numbers on which each is found.

Table 17-3   *Key Topics*

Key Topic Element	Description	Page
List	DMVPN deployment models	451
List	Benefits of DMVPNs	451
List	Hub and spoke initial properties	453
List	DMVPN spoke-to-spoke tunnel creation	453
Table 17-2	DMVPN benefits and limitations	454
List	DMVPN deployment choices	456
List	DMVPN deployment guidelines	456
Section	GRE features and limitations	456
Section	Point-to-point and point-to-multipoint GRE comparison	457
Task list	Tasks for configuring GRE tunneling in a hub-and-spoke topology	459
Example 17-2	Configuring an mGRE interface	459
Example 17-3	Configuring a GRE interface	460
Task list	Configuring NHRP on the hub and spokes in a DMVPN	461
Example 17-5	Configuring an NHRP server	462
Example 17-6	Configuring an NHRP client	462
Task list	Configuring a DMVPN hub	464

Table 17-3 *Key Topics*

Key Topic Element	Description	Page
Example 17-9	Configuring an optional IKE policy	464
Example 17-11	Creating an mGRE tunnel interface	465
Example 17-12	Configuring an NHRP server	465
Example 17-13	Applying an IPsec profile to the mGRE interface	466
Example 17-14	Configuring IP parameters on the mGRE interface	466
List	Implementation guidelines for a DMVPN hub	468
Task list	Configuring a DMVPN spoke	468
Example 17-18	Configuring an IPsec profile	470
Example 17-19	Creating an mGRE tunnel interface	470
Example 17-20	Configuring an NHRP client	470
Example 17-21	Applying an IPsec profile to an interface	471
Example 17-22	Configuring IP parameters on an mGRE interface	471
Example 17-25	Configuring OSPF on a hub-and-spoke DMVPN topology	473
Example 17-26	Configuring OSPF on a full mesh DMVPN topology	473
Step list	Troubleshooting sequence for DMVPN deployments	475

Complete Tables and Lists from Memory

Print a copy of Appendix C, "Memory Tables" (found on the CD), or at least the section for this chapter, and complete the tables and lists from memory. Appendix D, "Memory Table Answers," also on the CD, includes completed tables and lists to check your work. Although there are no memory tables in this chapter, you will find some memory tables for other chapters.

Define Key Terms

Define the following key terms from this chapter, and check your answers in the Glossary:

Internet Key Exchange (IKE), Authenticating Headers (AH), Encapsulating Security Protocol, multipoint Generic Routing Encapsulation (mGRE), Next Hop Resolution Protocol (NHRP)

Fill in the Blanks

1. A _____ cloud is a collection of routers that are configured with either an mGRE interface or a point-to-point GRE interface (or a combination of the two) and that share the same subnet.

2. The _____ created on the mGRE interface on the hub must be large enough to accommodate all the spoke routers' GRE interfaces.

3. The NHRP network ID must be the same on the NHRP _____ and its NHRP _____.

4. The Cisco DMVPN solution integrates NHRP, _____, and _____.

5. DMVPN greatly simplifies the configuration requirements on the _____ router.

6. NHRP on the hub provides DMVPN spokes with the ability to locate other _____ routers.

7. _____ populates each spoke's routing table so that each spoke knows about the subnets behind the other spokes.

8. In a hub-and-spoke deployment, all traffic between spokes must flow through the _____.

Reference

Cisco Design Zone for WAN/MAN, IPsec VPN WAN Design Overview, www.cisco.com/application/pdf/en/us/guest/netsol/ns171/c649/ccmigration_09186a008074f22f.pdf.

This chapter covers the following subjects:

- **Plan the deployment of Cisco IOS Software site-to-site IPsec VPN high-availability features:** Covers methods for providing redundancy to site-to-site VPNs.

- **Use routing protocols for VPN failover:** Covers deploying routing protocols to provide path redundancy.

- **Choose the most optimal method of mitigating failure in a VTI-based VPN:** Covers path and device redundancy in single- and multiple-transport networks.

- **Choose the most optimal method of mitigating failure in a DMVPN:** Covers providing redundancy in a DMVPN.

CHAPTER 18

Deploying High Availability in Tunnel-Based IPsec VPNs

IPsec Virtual Private Networks (VPN) have become a method of providing primary connections between sites. In the recent past, IPsec site-to-site VPNs were used as a backup path between sites that was enabled when a traditional WAN circuit went down. The IPsec VPN, in this case, was the secondary, backup means of communication. With the IPsec VPN becoming the primary communication path, network designers must understand the different types of failures that can occur and put in place a high-availability solution that will protect an organization from outages.

"Do I Know This Already?" Quiz

The "Do I Know This Already?" helps you decide whether you really need to read the entire chapter. If you already intend to read the entire chapter, you do not necessarily need to answer these questions now.

The eight-question quiz, derived from the major sections in the "Foundation Topics" portion of this chapter, helps you determine how to spend your limited study time.

Table 18-1 outlines the major topics discussed in this chapter and the "Do I Know This Already?" quiz questions that correspond to those topics.

Table 18-1 *"Do I Know This Already?" Foundation Topics Section-to-Question Mapping*

Foundation Topics Section	Questions Covered in This Section
Plan the Deployment of Cisco IOS Software Site-to-Site IPsec VPN High-Availability Features	1, 2
Use Routing Protocols for VPN Failover	3, 4
Choose the Most Optimal Method of Mitigating Failure in a VTI-Based VPN	5, 6
Choose the Most Optimal Method of Mitigating Failure in a DMVPN	7, 8

Caution: The goal of self-assessment is to gauge your mastery of the topics in this chapter. If you do not know the answer to a question or are only partially sure of the answer, you should mark this question wrong for purposes of the self-assessment. Giving yourself credit for an answer that you correctly guess skews your self-assessment results and might provide you with a false sense of security.

1. What can be used to mitigate device failure?

    a. Single ISP transport networks

    b. Multiple ISP transport networks

    c. Multiple devices at a site

    d. Redundant interfaces on a VPN device

2. What can be done to provide high availability when the cost of redundant devices cannot be justified?

    a. Use single ISP transport networks

    b. Use multiple ISP transport networks

    c. Use redundant interfaces

    d. Use multiple devices at a site

3. When a transport network is not under organizational control, it might be necessary to choose which of the following?

    a. A different VPN technology

    b. Traditional WAN circuits

    c. Point-to-multipoint topology

    d. Redundant routers

    e. Multiple independent transport networks

4. Which interface command can be used to choose the best path when deploying the dynamic routing protocol OSPF?

    a. ip ospf cost

    b. ip ospf tuning

    c. ip ospf path

    d. ip ospf router

    e. None of these answers are correct.

5. In a VTI-based IPsec VPN, traffic that should be protected by the VPN tunnel should be routed how?

    a. Carefully

    b. Redundantly

    c. Dynamically

    d. Statically

6. What should be used to provide a virtual gateway for clients at the spoke site?

    a. IPsec

    b. DHCP

    c. HSRP

    d. AAA

    e. None of these answers are correct.

7. IPsec shared SAs are enabled with what command?

    a. **tunnel protection ipsec profile shared**

    b. **ipsec dual SA**

    c. **ip split sa**

    d. **crypto ipsec sa redundant**

    e. None of these answers are correct.

8. Which high-availability scenario provides the highest level of redundancy because it mitigates failures of devices, interfaces, access links, and transport networks?

    a. Static VTI-based VPN

    b. Single DMVPN

    c. Dual DMVPN

    d. Dual ISPs

The answers to the "Do I Know This Already?" quiz are found in Appendix A. The suggested choices for your next step are as follows:

■ **6 or less overall score:** Read the entire chapter. This includes the "Foundation Topics" and the "Exam Preparation" sections.

■ **7 or 8 overall score:** If you want more review on these topics, skip to the "Exam Preparation" section. Otherwise, move on to Chapter 19, "Deploying GET VPNs."

Foundation Topics

Providing high availability in a VPN network means protecting it from expected failures and enabling mechanisms that allow it to heal itself. This chapter provides information necessary for choosing recommended high-availability architectures and configuring a highly available IPsec VPN tunnel solution.

Plan the Deployment of Cisco IOS Software Site-to-Site IPsec VPN High-Availability Features

VPN Failure Modes

Site-to-site IPsec VPNs are becoming increasingly more popular solutions for connecting sites. Compared to the traditional WAN connections, they are more cost-effective. In fact, the IPsec VPN was, in some environments, the backup path that was used in the event that the primary WAN connection went down.

Now that the IPsec VPN is the primary connection, it needs to be highly available and be able to "heal" itself in the event of a failure. The network designer must be aware of the types of possible failures and the ways to recover from them.

The VPN has the following failure modes:

- **Failure of the path between the VPN peers:** This path can fail without affecting the status of a local interface, which makes it difficult to recognize. For VPNs that traverse the public Internet, this could be a failure at an Internet service provider (ISP), link congestion, or anything else that would prevent the two VPN peers from communicating with one another. This kind of failure is typically overcome by using redundant paths and/or devices and having dynamic routing protocols that route around the failed device or network segment.

- **Failure of a device:** Traditionally, redundant devices in combination with routing protocols and/or Hot Standby Router Protocol (HSRP) to provide high availability are used to provide high availability in the event of this type of failure.

- **Failure of a network interface of the link adjacent to one of the VPN devices that prevents one VPN peer from reaching the other:** This is similar to the failure of a physical WAN interface in traditional WAN networks. This can be resolved with redundant interfaces or redundant devices with a secondary circuit.

Partial Failure of the Transport Network

The first type of outage occurs when a VPN fails that traverses a transport network that is under control of the local network administrator (not an ISP connection). In this scenario, the VPN tunnel will fail to establish when a segment or device in the path between the two VPN peers fails. Mitigating this type of failure involves using a mechanism that detects failures in the transport network and automatically reroutes around the failure. This type of solution requires no high-availability features on the VPN devices themselves.

Partial or Total Failure of the Service Provider (SP) Transport Network

This type of outage occurs when the ISP transport network that provides connectivity between the two VPN peers fails. In this scenario, the local network administrator has no control over the routing protocols in the ISP network and cannot have any knowledge of how much, if any, redundancy exists in the ISP transport network. A possible solution to this type of failure would be to have two VPN tunnels that used different ISP transport networks. This provides a complete redundant solution to the failure of an ISP; however, it requires a mechanism to detect path failures (one ISP fails) and to automatically reroute traffic to the other ISP. This solution has the downside of high costs because of using multiple service providers.

Partial or Total Failure of a VPN Device

The last of the three general types of failures is where the failure occurs on or close to the VPN device. This would include the total failure of the VPN device, failure of the access link directly connected to the VPN device, or failure of the VPN device's network interface.

A reliable option for mitigating this kind of failure is to have a second VPN device at a VPN site where there are two VPN devices connected to the transport network. Failure of the VPN device could automatically fail over to the secondary VPN device if using HSRP or a similar protocol. Another option would be to have a redundant network interface in the same VPN device. This would protect against network interface failure, but not total device failure.

Note: Cisco IOS Software supports the use of HSRP on untrusted interfaces facing the transport network and terminating the VPN tunnel on the HSRP virtual address. This feature also provides stateful IPsec failover, but it only works with classic IPsec configuration using crypto maps. It does not work with Virtual Tunnel Interface (VTI) or Dynamic Multipoint VPN (DMVPN) tunnels.

Deployment Guidelines

When implementing high-availability mechanisms to overcome failures in a tunnel-based VPN, consider the following general guidelines:

Key Topic

- Design the VPN to meet an organization's requirements for availability. The design should provide a level of high availability that is commensurate with the cost of meeting availability needs.

- For locations that have continuous operation requirements, use redundant VPN devices to mitigate the risk of device failure.

- On sites that have a likelihood of an access link failure and where the cost of redundant devices cannot be justified, use redundant interfaces on the same device to provide connectivity to either a secondary access link or as a standby interface for the primary access link.

- If complete redundant paths are needed, either deploy a completely redundant network path that is under the control of local administration or use multiple-transport networks (two ISPs) and connect them to either redundant interfaces or redundant VPN devices.

- Remember that not all VPN sites require the same level of high availability. A hub-and-spoke network would have high-availability features for the hub routers and for the most critical spoke sites.

Use Routing Protocols for VPN Failover

When using site-to-site VPNs as an alternative to traditional WAN connectivity, it is important to use dynamic routing protocols to provide automatic failover. The following sections provide detailed information about using dynamic routing with VPN tunnels.

Routing to VPN Tunnel Endpoints

Dynamic routing protocols are one of the best ways to provide high availability to site-to-site IPsec VPNs. Because tunnel-based IPsec VPNs use Cisco IOS Software tunnel interfaces, configuring the high-availability features is similar to when they are configured on classic routed WAN interfaces.

Dynamic routing protocols will *automatically detect peer failures and path failures* and then *automatically reroute* around the failure if redundant paths and devices are in place.

One of the most common uses of routing protocols to ensure VPN high availability is where dynamic routing protocols are used in the transport network between two VPN peers. The tunnel endpoints should be included in the routing process so that, in the event of a device or path failure in the transport network, the routing protocol will automatically route around the failure and the connectivity between the two VPN peers will not be lost.

Routing Protocol Inside the VPN Tunnel

When the transport network is not under the network administrator's control, choosing to use multiple independent transport networks (two ISPs) at each VPN location can provide high availability to site-to-site IPsec VPN tunnels.

In this situation, each VPN device (one at each site) connects to both transport networks and two VPN tunnels, one over each transport network. With direct peering between the VPN devices, the interior gateway protocols (IGP) will see each of them as a single-hop point-to-point link, and keepalive packets can be exchanged directly between the two VPN devices over the tunnels. This setup will provide detection of both path and remote device failures because both instances will cause the loss of keepalive packets. This setup will be able to reroute around a path failure by sending traffic over the working path (VPN tunnel), but it will not mitigate a VPN device failure because each VPN site has a single VPN device.

Recursive Routing Hazard

You must take precautions when configuring dynamic routing protocols to ensure that there is a device that participates in the same routing protocol both outside the VPN tunnel (the transport network) and inside the tunnel (directly with VPN peers).

This could be a possibility if an organization is in control of the transport network and wants to provide high availability through dynamic routing, both inside the transport network and inside the VPN to ensure continuous connectivity.

This kind of routing requires that VPN devices be prevented from learning the paths to their remote peer tunnel destination IP addresses over the VPN tunnel itself. The single-hop path over the VPN will always be a better route than the path over the transport network. This situation will break the tunnel because it causes the VPN-encapsulated packet to be routed into its own tunnel interface instead of being routed out the correct physical interface that is used to reach the remote VPN peer. Cisco IOS Software will react to this behavior by flapping the tunnel interface.

Use either route filtering or a different routing protocol for the transport network and the VPN network to avoid this recursive routing issue.

Routing Protocol VPN Topologies

Routing protocols are ideal technologies to use with tunnel-based IPsec VPNs because the IPsec tunnels are routable interfaces to Cisco IOS Software. Two of the prominent technologies that support this functionality are IPsec Virtual Tunnel Interfaces (VTI) and the Dynamic Multipoint VPN (DMVPN) architecture.

In a VTI-based IPsec VPN topology, an interior routing protocol will see the VTI-based VPN tunnel as a point-to-point link, similar to a point-to-point leased WAN link. This means that redundant primary/secondary or load-balanced VTI tunnels can be deployed over two transport networks between two sites to provide path redundancy. These two tunnels can be terminated on two VPN devices to provide device redundancy as well. The configuration of this kind of high availability is exactly the same as it would be for a classic point-to-point WAN.

A DMVPN can look like either a point-to-multipoint (for strict hub-and-spoke DMVPNs) or a broadcast network (partial or full mesh DMVPNs). Routing protocol adjacencies are always established between spoke routers and the hub router. There is no spoke-to-spoke routing protocol peering. The hub will replicate all received route information to all other spokes. Configuring redundancy is similar to a classic nonbroadcast multiaccess (NBMA) network, and hub redundancy is especially important to maintaining routing propagation among the spokes.

Routing Tuning for Path Selection

Whichever tunneling IPsec VPN technology or topology is deployed, tuning the dynamic routing protocol to control best-path selection might be necessary.

Tuning routing protocols for path selection usually means choosing between two options:

- **Two site-to-site VPN tunnels, with one being the primary data path and the second tunnel being the secondary path:** In this option, the secondary path is used only if the primary fails. This option is configured simply by tuning the routing protocol cost so that the primary tunnel always appears as the best path.

- **Two site-to-site VPN tunnels, with load sharing between the two tunnels to increase available bandwidth:** This option is configured by setting equal costs on the two tunnels.

Routing Tuning for Faster Convergence

To improve convergence time, tune the timers used by routing protocols to check for peer availability. By tuning (shortening) these timers, peer and path failures can be detected (and routed around) much quicker.

Key Topic

Default timers depend on the dynamic routing protocol in use:

- **Open Shortest Path First (OSPF):** The default hello interval is 10 seconds, and the hold time is 40 seconds. Use the **ip ospf hello-interval** interface command to modify the hello timer and the **ip ospf dead-interval** interface command to modify the hold time. OSPF fast hellos can be used but only after adequate performance testing. This is configured by using the **ip ospf dead-interval minimal hello-multiplier** command.

- **Enhanced IGRP (EIGRP):** The default hello interval is 5 seconds, and the hold time is 15 seconds or higher on low-speed links (hello timer of 60 seconds and hold timer of 180 seconds). Use the **ip hello-interval eigrp** *AS interval* interface command to change the hello timer and the **ip hold-time eigrp** *AS holdtime* interface command to modify the hold timer.

- **Routing Information Protocol version 2 (RIPv2):** The default update timer is 30 seconds, and the default holddown timer is 180 seconds. Use **the timers basic** router configuration command to modify the RIP timers.

An additional amount of time is added to the overall convergence that is due to the specifics of each routing protocol that can prevent immediate recalculations of the best-path algorithm:

- **OSPF:** SPF (shortest path first) timer is 5 seconds. Use the **timers spf** OSPF router command to modify the SPF timer.

- **EIGRP:** A route could become active that can last for several seconds. If the backup route is reachable through a feasible successor, the recalculation is immediate.

Choose the Most Optimal Method of Mitigating Failure in a VTI-Based VPN

There are several methods that you can use to provide continuity in the event of a failure. The following sections describe the different types of mitigation techniques that are available for Cisco IOS Software VTI-based VPNs.

Path Redundancy Using a Single-Transport Network

For a VTI-based site-to-site IPsec VPN running over a single-transport network that is under the organization's control where only path redundancy is required, the following redundancy architecture is recommended:

- Include only the physical interfaces that terminate VPN tunnels in the dynamic routing protocol. Do not include the inside VTIs in the routing process. Instead, use static routing to protect anything that requires IPsec protection.

- Make sure to include all interfaces of devices in the transit network that the VPN tunnel will traverse in the routing protocol. This will allow automatic rerouting around failures in the transit network should one occur.

Path Redundancy Using Two Transport Networks

For a VTI-based site-to-site IPsec VPN running over two transport networks that are not under the organization's control (typically two ISPs) with only path redundancy required, the following redundancy architecture is recommended:

- On the VPN routers, use one routed network interface to connect to the first ISP and another routed network interface to connect to the second ISP.

- On the VPN routers, configure two permanent VTI tunnels, one over the first ISP network and one over the second ISP network. Configure static routes that point to the remote peer's tunnel destination IP addresses.

- On the VPN routers, configure that same dynamic routing protocol over both VTI tunnels and tune the cost of the tunnel interfaces to route over the preferred path.

Path and Device Redundancy in Single-Transport Networks

For a VTI-based site-to-site IPsec VPN with a single ISP, device redundancy and path protection are required. The solution to meeting this requirement is to add an additional VPN device (router) at each location. In this case, all routers are running HSRP and running the same OSPF process with tuning configured to set up a primary and secondary tunnel.

Path and Device Redundancy with Multiple-Transport Networks

To increase the high availability of this scenario by adding device redundancy, there are two options:

- Add a redundant device to critical sites and configure one VTI tunnel per device (one for each different ISP transport network). HSRP is used on the LAN side of the spoke routers to ensure that clients have a seamless failover to the redundant router.

- Use redundant interfaces in branch offices that do not have the redundant devices mentioned in the previous option. The single router still will have two tunnels (again, one over each ISP network). HSRP will be used on the LAN to provide a virtual gateway to the users. If one of the ISP transport networks fails, OSPF will route traffic over the secondary tunnel.

Choose the Most Optimal Method of Mitigating Failure in a DMVPN

The following sections present the mitigation techniques that you can use to provide redundancy in a DMVPN.

Recommended Architecture

To provide redundancy for a DMVPN topology, it is recommended to create two separate DMVPNs by using two hub routers and one or two spoke routers at remote sites.

Remote sites with a single spoke router on-site will become a member of both DMVPNs by registering with both hub routers. Remote sites with two spoke routers will have one spoke router registered with one hub router, and the other spoke router will register with the other hub router. HSRP will be configured on the two spoke routers to provide the virtual gateway for LAN users. Both scenarios will have a dynamic routing protocol running over both DMVPNs that will provide path and device redundancy. Tuning the routing protocol provides the capability to engineer traffic to take desired paths.

Configuring redundant DMVPNs is the same as configuring two independent DMVPNs with different tunnel keys and Next Hop Resolution Protocol (NHRP) network IDs. Figure 18-1 depicts a dual DMVPN topology and shows primary and secondary paths. Keep the following points in mind:

- The configuration of the dynamic routing protocol determines traffic patterns over the redundant tunnels (primary/secondary versus load sharing).

- Shared IPsec security associations (SA) must be configured on the spoke routers because dynamic spoke-to-spoke tunnels are being used in the DMVPN (meaning partial or full mesh DMVPN).

Shared IPsec SAs

In environments running a redundant solution using two DMVPNs with dynamic spoke-to-spoke tunnels, it is possible to have two or more generic routing encapsulation (GRE) tunnel sessions between the same two spokes. In this case, there are multiple tunnels between the same two endpoints, but they have different tunnel keys.

This situation requires that the two GRE tunnels be secured using a single IPsec SA because the IPsec Quick Mode request comprises two tunnels with the same tunnel source.

The **tunnel protection ipsec profile shared** command creates a single IPsec Security Association Database (SADB) for all tunnel interfaces that use the same profile and tunnel source interface. This allows the same IPsec SA to secure all GRE tunnels (same source and destination but different tunnel key).

Configuring a DMVPN with a Single-Transport Network

In this situation, configuring dual DMVPN environments to provide path and device redundancy means creating two separate DMVPNs on the spoke router that use different NHRP network IDs and tunnel keys. The primary DMVPN uses a lower cost for its tunnel by configuring the **ip ospf cost** interface command under the tunnel interface. The secondary DMVPN will have a higher cost configured with the **ip ospf cost** interface command. This should be configured on the tunnel interfaces on both the hub and spoke routers. Ensure that the **shared** command option is included in the **tunnel protection ipsec profile** command to allow IPsec SA negotiation to work properly. Examples 18-1 through 18-3 show the similarities and differences in the configurations. Note that the DMVPN configurations on the hubs create two DMVPNs with different NHRP network IDs and tunnel keys, and the spoke router is configured for both of these independent DMVPNs.

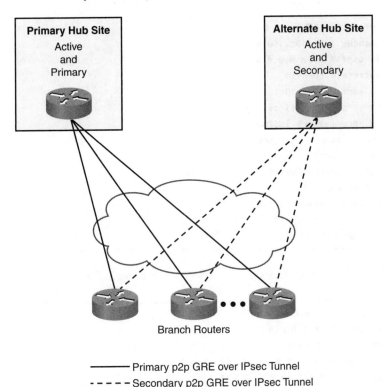

Primary p2p GRE over IPsec Tunnel
Secondary p2p GRE over IPsec Tunnel

Figure 18-1 *Redundancy with Dual DMVPNs*

Example 18-1 *Primary Hub Router Configuration for a DMVPN with a Single-Transport Network*

```
router(config)# interface FastEthernet 0/0
router(config-if)# standby 1 ip 192.168.0.1
router(config-if)# ip ospf 1 area 0.0.0.0
router(config-if)# interface tunnel0
router(config-if)# ip address 172.16.0.1 255.255.255.0
router(config-if)# ip nhrp map multicast dynamic
router(config-if)# ip nhrp network-id 100
router(config-if)# tunnel source FastEthernet 1/0
router(config-if)# yunnel mode gre multipoint
```

```
router(config-if)# tunnel protection ipsec profile VPN1
router(config-if)# tunnel key 100
router(config-if)# ip ospf 1 area 0.0.0.0
router(config-if)# ip ospf priority 10
router(config-if)# ip ospf cost 10
```

Example 18-2 *Secondary Hub Router Configuration for a DMVPN with a Single-Transport Network*

```
router(config)# interface FastEthernet 0/0
router(config-if)# standby 1 ip 192.168.0.1
router(config-if)# ip ospf 1 area 0.0.0.0
router(config-if)# interface tunnel0
router(config-if)# ip address 172.16.1.1 255.255.255.0
router(config-if)# ip nhrp map multicast dynamic
router(config-if)# ip nhrp network-id 200
router(config-if)# tunnel source FastEthernet 1/0
router(config-if)# tunnel mode gre multipoint
router(config-if)# tunnel protection ipsec profile VPN1
router(config-if)# tunnel key 100
router(config-if)# ip ospf 1 area 0.0.0.0
router(config-if)# ip ospf priority 10
router(config-if)# ip ospf cost 20
```

Example 18-3 *Spoke Router Configuration for a DMVPN with a Single-Transport Network*

```
router(config)# interface FastEthernet 0/0
router(config-if)# ip ospf 1 area 0.0.0.0
router(config-if)# interface tunnel0
router(config-if)# ip address 172.16.0.10 255.255.255.0
router(config-if)# ip nhrp map 172.16.0.1 172.17.0.1
router(config-if)# ip nhrp network-id 100
router(config-if)# ip nhrp nhs 172.16.0.1
router(config-if)# tunnel source FastEthernet1/0
router(config-if)# tunnel mode gre multipoint
router(config-if)# tunnel protection ipsec profile VPN1 shared
router(config-if)# tunnel key 100
router(config-if)# ip ospf network broadcast
router(config-if)# ip ospf priority 0
router(config-if)# ip ospf 1 area 0.0.0.0
router(config-if)# ip ospf cost 10
!
router(config)# interface tunnel1
router(config-if)# ip address 172.16.1.10 255.255.255.0
router(config-if)# ip nhrp map 172.16.1.1 172.17.0.2
```

```
router(config-if)# ip nhrp network-id 200
router(config-if)# ip nhrp nhs 172.16.1.1
router(config-if)# tunnel source FastEthernet1/0
router(config-if)# tunnel mode gre multipoint
router(config-if)# tunnel protection ipsec profile VPN1 shared
router(config-if)# tunnel key 200
router(config-if)# ip ospf network broadcast
router(config-if)# ip ospf priority 0
router(config-if)# ip ospf 1 area 0.0.0.0
router(config-if)# ip ospf cost 20
```

Configuring a DMVPN over Multiple-Transport Networks

Two independent DMVPNs can also be configured to use two ISP transport networks. The primary DMVPN will use one ISP transport network, and the secondary DMVPN will use the other ISP transport network. This provides the highest level of redundancy in that it mitigates failures of devices, interfaces, and the transport network. Refer to Examples 18-4 through 18-6. As with the case of a DMVPN over a single-transport network, the hub routers are configured with two distinct DMVPNs that have different NHRP IDs and tunnel keys. The spoke router is configured to peer with both of these DMVPNs and uses **ip ospf cost** to dictate which is the primary and which is the backup DMVPN.

Example 18-4 *Primary Hub Router Configuration for a DMVPN over Multiple-Transport Networks*

Key
Topic

```
router(config)# interface FastEthernet 0/0
router(config-if)# standby 1 ip 192.168.0.1
router(config-if)# ip ospf 1 area 0.0.0.0
router(config-if)# interface tunnel0
router(config-if)# ip address 172.16.0.1 255.255.255.0
router(config-if)# ip nhrp map multicast dynamic
router(config-if)# ip nhrp network-id 100
router(config-if)# tunnel source FastEthernet 1/0
router(config-if)# tunnel mode gre multipoint
router(config-if)# tunnel protection ipsec profile VPN1
router(config-if)# tunnel key 100
router(config-if)# ip ospf 1 area 0.0.0.0
router(config-if)# ip ospf priority 10
router(config-if)# ip ospf cost 10
```

Example 18-5 *Secondary Hub Router Configuration for a DMVPN over Multiple-Transport Networks*

Key
Topic

```
router(config)# interface FastEthernet 0/0
router(config-if)# standby 1 ip 192.168.0.1
router(config-if)# ip ospf 1 area 0.0.0.0
router(config-if)# interface tunnel0
```

```
router(config-if)# ip address 172.16.1.1 255.255.255.0
router(config-if)# ip nhrp map multicast dynamic
router(config-if)# ip nhrp network-id 200
router(config-if)# tunnel source FastEthernet 1/0
router(config-if)# tunnel mode gre multipoint
router(config-if)# tunnel protection ipsec profile VPN1
router(config-if)# tunnel key 100
router(config-if)# ip ospf 1 area 0.0.0.0
router(config-if)# ip ospf priority 10
router(config-if)# ip ospf cost 20
```

Example 18-6 *Spoke Router Configuration for a DMVPN over Multiple-Transport Networks*

```
router(config)# interface FastEthernet 0/0
router(config-if)# ip ospf 1 area 0.0.0.0
router(config)# interface tunnel0
router(config-if)# ip address 172.16.0.10 255.255.255.0
router(config-if)# ip nhrp map 172.16.0.1 172.17.0.1
router(config-if)# ip nhrp network-id 100
router(config-if)# ip nhrp nhs 172.16.0.1
router(config-if)# tunnel source FastEthernet1/0
router(config-if)# tunnel mode gre multipoint
router(config-if)# tunnel protection ipsec profile VPN1 shared
router(config-if)# tunnel key 100
router(config-if)# ip ospf network broadcast
router(config-if)# ip ospf priority 0
router(config-if)# ip ospf 1 area 0.0.0.0
router(config-if)# ip ospf cost 10
!
router(config)# interface tunnel1
router(config-if)# ip address 172.16.1.10 255.255.255.0
router(config-if)# ip nhrp map 172.16.1.1 172.17.0.2
router(config-if)# ip nhrp network-id 200
router(config-if)# ip nhrp nhs 172.16.1.1
router(config-if)# tunnel source FastEthernet1/0
router(config-if)# tunnel mode gre multipoint
router(config-if)# tunnel protection ipsec profile VPN1 shared
router(config-if)# tunnel key 200
router(config-if)# ip ospf network broadcast
router(config-if)# ip ospf priority 0
router(config-if)# ip ospf 1 area 0.0.0.0
router(config-if)# ip ospf cost 20
```

Exam Preparation

As mentioned in the section, "How to Use This Book," in the Introduction, you have several choices for exam preparation: the exercises here, the memory tables in Appendix C, the final exam preparation chapter, and the exam simulation questions on the CD-ROM. The following questions present a bigger challenge than the exam itself because they use an open-ended question format. By using this more difficult format, you exercise your memory better and prove your conceptual and factual knowledge of this chapter. You can find the answers to these questions in Appendix A, "Answers to the DIKTA Quizzes and Fill in the Blanks Questions."

Review All Key Topics

Review the most important topics in the chapter, noted with the Key Topics icon in the margin of the page. Table 18-2 lists a reference of these key topics and the page numbers on which each is found.

Table 18-2   *Key Topics*

Key Topic Element	Description	Page
List	VPN failure modes	484
List	High-availability deployment guidelines	485
List	Routing protocol timers	488
List	Path redundancy in a single-transport network	489
List	Path redundancy in a two-transport network	489
List	Path and device redundancy in a single-transport network	489
List	Path and device redundancy in a multiple-transport network	489
List	Important information for deploying redundant DMVPNs	490
Figure 18-1	Redundant DMVPNs	491
Example 18-1	Configuration of a primary hub in a single-transport network	491
Example 18-2	Configuration of a secondary hub in a single-transport network	492
Example 18-3	Configuration of a spoke in a single-transport network	492
Example 18-4	Configuration of a primary hub in a multiple-transport network	493
Example 18-5	Configuration of a secondary hub in a multiple-transport network	493
Example 18-6	Configuration of a spoke in a multiple-transport network	494

Complete Tables and Lists from Memory

Print a copy of Appendix C, "Memory Tables" (found on the CD), or at least the section for this chapter, and complete the tables and lists from memory. Appendix D, "Memory Table Answers," also on the CD, includes completed tables and lists to check your work. Although there are no memory tables in this chapter, you will find some memory tables for other chapters.

Define Key Terms

Define the following key terms from this chapter, and check your answers in the Glossary:

recursive routing, Security Association Database (SADB)

Fill in the Blanks

1. In the case of redundant DMVPNs with multiple GRE tunnels establishing between the same spokes, it is necessary to use _____ for IPsec SAs to establish properly.

2. The routing protocol detects both device and path failures using its _____.

3. You should design the VPN to meet an organization's requirements for availability. The design should provide a level of high availability that is commensurate with the _____ of meeting availability needs.

4. If _____ are needed, you should either deploy a completely redundant network path that is under the control of local administration or use multiple-transport networks (two ISPs) and connect them to either redundant interfaces or redundant VPN devices.

5. _____ will *automatically detect peer failures and path failures* and then *automatically reroute* around the failure if redundant paths and devices are in place.

6. In a VTI-based IPsec VPN topology, an interior routing protocol will see the VTI-based VPN tunnel as a _____ link.

7. An interior routing protocol will view a _____ as either point-to-multipoint (for strict hub-and-spoke DMVPNs) or as a broadcast network (partial or full mesh DMVPNs).

8. To provide redundancy for a DMVPN topology, it is recommended to create two separate DMVPN networks by using _____ and one or two spoke routers at remote sites.

9. Routing protocols can detect both _____ and _____.

Reference

Sharing IPsec with Tunnel Protection, www.cisco.com/en/US/docs/ios/sec_secure_connectivity/configuration/guide/share_ipsec_w_tun_protect.html.

This chapter covers the following subjects:

- **Describe the operation of a Cisco IOS Software GET VPN:** Covers a new category of VPNs that does not require a tunnel GET VPN and provides large-scale, connectionless, tunnel-free transmission protection that takes advantage of an existing routing infrastructure.

- **Plan the deployment of Cisco IOS Software GET VPN:** Covers gathering input information and making deployment decisions about your environment.

- **Configure and verify a Cisco IOS Software GET VPN key server:** Covers the functionality of the GET VPN key server and its configuration.

- **Configure and verify Cisco IOS Software GET VPN group member:** Covers the deployment of GET VPN group members.

- **Configure and verify high-availability mechanisms in a GET VPN:** Covers configuring high-availability mechanisms in a GET VPN topology.

CHAPTER 19

Deploying GET VPNs

The Cisco Group Encrypted Transport Virtual Private Network (GET VPN) technology is a solution that allows easy deployment of a complex, redundant, fully meshed VPN.

"Do I Know This Already?" Quiz

The "Do I Know This Already?" quiz helps you decide whether you really need to read the entire chapter. If you already intend to read the entire chapter, you do not necessarily need to answer these questions now.

The eight-question quiz, derived from the major sections in the "Foundation Topics" portion of this chapter, helps you determine how to spend your limited study time.

Table 19-1 outlines the major topics discussed in this chapter and the "Do I Know This Already?" quiz questions that correspond to those topics.

Table 19-1 *"Do I Know This Already?" Foundation Topics Section-to-Question Mapping*

Foundation Topics Section	Questions Covered in This Section
Describe the Operation of a Cisco IOS Software GET VPN	1, 2, 4
Plan the Deployment of a Cisco IOS Software GET VPN	3
Configure and Verify a Cisco IOS Software GET VPN Key Server	5
Configure and Verify a Cisco IOS Software GET VPN Group Member	6
Configure and Verify High-Availability Mechanisms in a GET VPN	7, 8

Caution: The goal of self-assessment is to gauge your mastery of the topics in this chapter. If you do not know the answer to a question or are only partially sure of the answer, you should mark this question wrong for purposes of the self-assessment. Giving yourself credit for an answer that you correctly guess skews your self-assessment results and might provide you with a false sense of security.

1. GET VPNs use which feature to provide large-scale transmission protection that uses the existing routing infrastructure? (Select all that apply.)

   a. Tunnel-free

   b. X.500

   c. Connectionless

   d. ISAKMP

   e. Encrypted

2. GET VPNs use a concept of which of the following to provide transmission protection? (Select all that apply.)

   a. Certificates

   b. IPsec

   c. Key servers

   d. Group members

   e. None of these answers are correct.

3. To implement a GET VPN over the Internet, which type of IP addresses must be used on all networks?

   a. Private

   b. Class A

   c. NAT

   d. Routable

   e. None of these answers are correct.

4. GET VPNs maintain which aspect of the data packet?

   a. Original IP header

   b. Size

   c. MAC address

   d. Don't Fragment bit setting

   e. None of these answers are correct.

5. Which of the following are the two choices of rekeying used by key servers?

   a. Unicast

   b. Symmetric

   c. Asymmetric

   d. Multicast

6. Which of the following do you configure to prevent traffic from traversing an un-trusted interface unless the group member is registered into a GET VPN?

    a. ACL

    b. Policy map

    c. Fail-closed policy

    d. GET VPN key server

    e. None of these answers are correct.

7. What event might lead to several independent groups of key servers rekeying group members with different session keys?

    a. Network split

    b. Route reconvergence

    c. Network merge

    d. None of these answers are correct.

8. There can be up to how many key servers on a network?

    a. Six

    b. Seven

    c. Eight

    d. Ten

The answers to the "Do I Know This Already?" quiz are found in Appendix A. The suggested choices for your next step are as follows:

- **6 or less overall score:** Read the entire chapter. This includes the "Foundation Topics" and the "Exam Preparation" sections.

- **7 or 8 overall score:** If you want more review on these topics, skip to the "Exam Preparation" section. Otherwise, move on to Chapter 20, "Deploying Remote Access Solutions Using SSL VPNs."

Foundation Topics

Fully meshed VPNs are typically challenging from a scalability and manageability standpoint. These kinds of deployments with a large number of sites are typically avoided because of their complexity. This chapter will cover the fundamentals of the Cisco IOS Software GET VPN technology, how to plan its deployment, how to configure and verify GET VPN key servers and members, and how to implement high availability for GET VPNs.

Describe the Operation of a Cisco IOS Software GET VPN

Beginning with Cisco IOS Software Release 12.4(11)T, GET VPNs provide large-scale, connectionless, tunnel-free transmission protection that takes advantage of an existing routing infrastructure. Even though it can be used with Multiprotocol Label Switching (MPLS), IP, Frame Relay, and ATM networks, it is an ideal cryptographic solution for MPLS VPNs that need site-to-site encryption.

With the introduction of GET VPNs, Cisco makes available a new category of VPN that does not require a tunnel. By removing the need to establish point-to-point tunnels, branch networks can scale larger and still maintain the network intelligence features that are necessary for voice and video quality, such as quality of service (QoS), routing, and multicast. GET VPNs provide a new standards-based IPsec security model that uses the concept of "trusted" group members. Trusted member routers use a common security methodology that is independent of requiring any point-to-point IPsec tunnel relationship.

GET VPNs can be deployed in a variety of WAN topologies, including IP and MPLS. MPLS VPNs that use GET achieve high availability, manageability, and cost-effectiveness while meeting transmission protection requirements. GET VPNs provide a flexibility that enables enterprises to manage their own security over a service provider WAN or to off-load the encryption services to the provider. GET VPNs simplify large Layer 2 or MPLS networks that need partial or full meshed connectivity.

Note: When deploying IPsec, it is recommended that hardware acceleration for IPsec be included in the chosen router platform to avoid performance degradation.

IPsec acceleration and the GET feature set are supported on the onboard cryptographic capabilities of the Cisco Integrated Services Routers (ISR), the Cisco 7200 Series routers, and the Cisco 7301 router with VPN modules. Refer to Cisco.com for support offered by other Cisco platforms.

Peer Authentication and Policy Provisioning

Group controller/key servers (GCKS), also known as key servers (KS), and group members are the two key components that comprise the GET VPN architecture. The key server authenticates all group members, performs admission control to the GET VPN domain, and creates and supplies group authentication key as security associations (SA) to group members. Group members provide transmission protection to sensitive site-to-site (member-to-member) traffic. Figure 19-1 illustrates the relationship between a key server and group members.

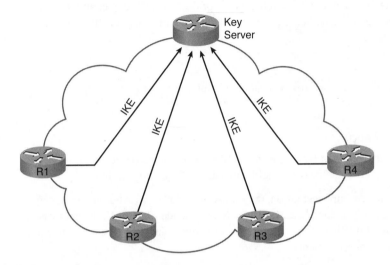

Figure 19-1 *GET VPN Key Server and Group Member Routers*

Key servers distribute keys and policies to all registered and authenticated group member routers. Key distribution and management are made easier because of the centralized distribution of keys and policies.

All communication between a key server and group members is encrypted and secured using the Internet Key Exchange (IKE) Group Domain of Interpretation (GDOI) protocol. IKE GDOI is a standards-based Internet Security Association and Key Management Protocol (ISAKMP) group key management protocol that provides secure group communications. GET VPNs use IKE GDOI as the group keying mechanism.

IKE GDOI supports the use of two keys: Traffic Encrypting Key (TEK) and Key Encrypting Key (KEK):

Key Topic

■ **TEK:** A key that is used to protect traffic between group members

■ **KEK:** A key this is used to protect rekeys (during a key refresh) between key servers and group members

The TEK is distributed to all group members by the key server, and they use the TEK to communicate to members of the group and to create and verify IPsec packets. The KEK is also distributed to group members who in turn use it to decrypt incoming rekey messages from the key server.

When a registration message is received, the key server generates information that contains the rekey policy (one KEK) and the new IPsec SAs (multiple TEK attributes, traffic encryption policy, lifetime, source and destination information about the traffic that needs to be protected, and the security parameter index (SPI)-ID that is associated with each TEK). The newly created IPsec SAs are then sent to the group members. The key server maintains a table that contains the IP address of each group member and its group association. When a group member registers, the key server adds the new IP address to its associated group table.

Note: Key servers and group members can simultaneously support multiple groups.

GET VPN Traffic Exchange

GET VPN group members that have valid group IPsec SAs assume that traffic they encrypt can be decrypted by some other legitimate GET VPN group member.

In a traditional multicast implementation, the sender does not know who potential recipients are. Using Protocol Independent Multicast - Sparse-Mode (PIM-SM), the multicast router sends multicast traffic to the configured rendezvous point (RP). The RP maintains a list of the multicast group recipients.

With GET VPNs, the sender assumes that the legitimate group members obtain a TEK from the group key server. The group member encrypts the multicast data, with header preservation, and the packet is switched out of the router. The replication of the multicast packet is performed in the core based on the source and multicast group IP address that is retained in the multicast data packet.

The secure data plane unicast packet is similar to the multicast example. In the secure data plane, the receiver does not know who potential encryption sources might be. The receiver assumes that the legitimate group members obtained a TEK from the group key server. The receiver authenticates the group membership when it is able to decrypt the data packet.

Packet Security Services

GET VPNs provide the same security benefits that IPsec provides. These security parameters include packet confidentiality (using cryptographic encryption algorithms such as AES [Advanced Encryption Standard] or 3DES [Triple Data Encryption Standard]), packet integrity and authenticity (using cryptographic HMAC [Hash Message Authentication Code] algorithms such as SHA-1 [Secure Hash Algorithm-1] HMAC or MD5 [Message Digest 5] HMAC), and a Cisco-proprietary time-based (instead of sequence number–based) antireplay protection mechanism. The standard sequence number method cannot be used in VPNs because synchronizing sequence number counters across many members is not feasible.

AES encryption is the recommended algorithm to use in GET VPNs. Because of the possibility of having large numbers of VPN group members using the same (group) session keys, and a fairly short initialization vector (IV) of 3DES, the use of 3DES in GET VPNs is not recommended.

Note that Network Time Protocol (NTP) is not required in GET VPNs (unless certificate-based authentication is used), because group members use proprietary pseudotime instead of standard time to create and verify timestamps.

Key Management Architecture

The GDOI, Group Domain of Interpretation, is the underlying standard for GET VPN as defined in RFC 3547. GDOI defines a key management protocol that is based on IKE/ISAKMP. It uses the same principles as IKE/ISAKMP to generate symmetric encryption keys but uses two keys, KEK and TEK. This key management protocol is an extension of IKE/ISAKMP and uses UDP port 848. One significant difference is that GDOI IKE SAs do not need to linger between members after initial establishment, but they can be quickly expired after a group member has authenticated to the key server and obtained the group policy. The second major difference is that GDOI IKE sessions do not get established between all peers in a VPN, only between each group member and the key server (or multiple key servers for redundancy).

One other notable difference is that all group members use the same set of session keys to protect network traffic. This is more efficient when compared to traditional IPsec VPNs in which each pair of peers has a private set of IPsec SAs that are shared only between those two peers.

Rekeying Methods

GET VPNs use rekey messages to refresh their IPsec SAs (session keys) outside of IKE sessions. When the group IPsec SAs are about to expire, one single rekey message for a particular group is generated on the key server. Distribution of the rekey message does not require that new IKE sessions be created. GET supports rekeying for unicast and multicast.

If any part of the enterprise network is not multicast capable, the unicast transport mechanism should be used to distribute the rekey message for all group members. The key server will send a separate rekey for every group member, and the group member must respond to the key server with an acknowledgment message. The key server will retransmit rekeys if it fails to receive the acknowledgment from the group member. If it fails to get a response from the group member after three rekeys, it removes the group member.

The key server maintains a list of the registered group members in the database and tracks the number of rekeys that have been sent and the acknowledgments received per group member. This database of information is extremely helpful in troubleshooting issues with a specific group member.

If the enterprise network is multicast capable, using multicast rekeying is recommended because it is more scalable.

The following are some general guidelines to consider regarding rekeying:

Key Topic

■   If most of the group members are only unicast capable, use unicast rekeying.

■   If most of the group members are capable of multicast and the entire enterprise network is capable of multicast, use multicast rekeying.

Table 19-2 provides some information that should be considered when deciding between using unicast or multicast rekeying.

Table 19-2   *Unicast Versus Multicast Rekeying Methods*

Unicast	Multicast
Use if infrastructure is only unicast capable	Must have multicast-capable infrastructure
Requires rekey acknowledgment	Retransmits the key several times without acknowledgments
Might require adjustment of router buffers and queues if there are a large number of peers	Fastest and most scalable method

When the key server sends out multicast rekeys to the group members, it sends a single multicast rekey packet to the core and the core replicates the packet for each multicast group member. Because multicast rekeying does not require acknowledgment, the rekeys will be retransmitted two or three times during the rekey period. Multicast rekeying for very large environments is more efficient and scalable because it makes use of the multicast replication provided by the core; therefore, it is the recommended rekeying method. Multicast rekeying also reduces key server load by drastically reducing the number of rekeying messages it must process.

Note: To use multicast transport for rekeying, the entire network must be multicastcapable, including the MPLS/IP core. That means Multicast VPN (MVPN) is required on the MPLS core.

When the key server uses unicast rekeying, the key server generates rekey messages for only a few group members at a time and makes sure that all group members receive the rekey message for the new SA before the old SA expires. This helps reduce the possibility of latency issues. Also, when the group members receive the rekey message from the key server, the group member sends an encrypted acknowledgment to the key server using the key received as part of the rekey message. This process keeps the list of active group members up to date and ensures that rekey messages are sent only to active group members.

Note: In a large network, unicast rekeying creates a large load on the key server because it must send unicast rekey messages and process all the acknowledgments received from every group member.

The number of retransmit attempts and the retransmit interval are configurable. As stated previously, the key server will remove a group member from which the key server fails to receive acknowledgment three times. The group member must fully reregister with the key server after its current IPsec SA expires to receive rekey messages. If the group member does not receive a rekey before the TEK expires, it reregisters with the key server before the current IPsec SA expires.

Note: In a large network, if there is a small part of the network that does not support multicast, the multicast transport mechanism can still be used for rekeying. This method of rekeying causes the small set of unicast group members to reregister, but it places a lower load on the key server than if the key server had to use the unicast transport with every group member. Each unicast member that is reregistering will do so before the current group key expires, which avoids any loss of data.

It is imperative for group members to synchronize the removal of old SAs and the installation of new SAs. As new SAs are received through rekey messages, outgoing data packets are still encrypted using the old SAs, but incoming packets are decrypted using both the old and the new SAs for a period of time. After a specified amount of time (T1), outgoing packets are encrypted using new SAs while incoming packets are still decrypted using both old and new SAs for a period of time. At the next interval (T2), old SAs are removed and new SAs encrypt and decrypt the traffic. T1 and T2 are set internally to 30 seconds.

Traffic Encapsulation

The benefit of GET VPNs is that they use the existing routing infrastructure rather than adding a tunnel-based overlay like traditional IPsec. Figure 19-2 shows how GET VPN data packets maintain their original IP source and destination addresses. This enables organizations to use existing Layer 3 routing information, which can address multicast replication inefficiencies and improve network performance. Encrypting multicast packets with IP address preservation is necessary to preserve the (S,G) (source, multicast group) information so that replication of multicast packets in the cores can be based on the original (S,G) information.

Benefits and Limitations

GET VPNs have the following benefits:

- Very scalable in that the configuration does not grow significantly when adding group members in a full mesh

- Provides scalable support for multicast traffic

GET VPNs also have the following limitations:

- VPN addresses must be routable in the transport network. This is because of the use of the original IP header, and in most cases, it prevents GET VPNs from being used over the Internet.

- The compromise of one peer has a larger effect because the group shares session keys.

- Key servers must be available during rekeys and registration for the entire network to operate.

Original IP Packet

IP Sec site-to-site IP Packet

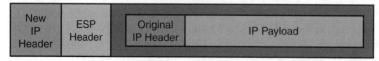

GET VPN IP Packet

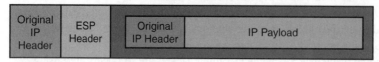

Figure 19-2 *GET Packet Structure*

Plan the Deployment of a Cisco IOS Software GET VPN

A successful GET VPN deployment requires that you gather information about your environment and then make deployment decisions about your environment. The following sections cover these activities.

Input Parameters

The following input parameters need to be determined and analyzed when deploying GET VPNs:

■ If using existing devices, ensure that hardware and software on the routers can adequately handle the cryptographic performance that is required and that the current software release supports GET VPNs on the existing platform.

■ Determine security requirements to deploy the correct data protection (algorithms, key lengths, and key lifetimes).

■ Carefully define traffic flows that require protection by the GET VPNs. Some traffic flows will need to be forwarded in the clear.

■ Determine whether high availability is needed, and ensure that the proper transport network and redundant equipment exist.

Deployment Tasks

The basic deployment tasks for implementing GET VPNs are as follows:

Task 1: Configure IKE sessions between each GET member and key server.

Task 2: Configure an IPsec traffic protection policy on the GET VPN key server.

Task 3: Configure GET VPN members to register into a GET VPN group.

Task 4: Optionally, tune local policies on members to override policies received from the key server.

Deployment Choices

GET VPN deployments require that decisions be made based on network requirements and capabilities. For IKE peer authentication, choose to use either pre-shared keys (PSK) or public key infrastructure (PKI). Pre-shared keys are easier to deploy, but pre-shared key–based main mode in IPsec does not provide support for dynamically addressed group members. High availability can be achieved by using multiple key servers. This simply adds configuration overhead. Local policies should be tuned when using dynamic routing protocols or in-band management protocols.

Deployment Guidelines

Three main guidelines to keep in mind when implementing a GET VPN are as follows:

- Use GET VPNs for scalable, site-to-site, full-mesh connectivity for a large number of sites.

- To implement GET VPNs over the Internet, routable IP addresses on all networks must be used.

- There is no scalability issue with deploying using pre-shared keys because only a limited number of IKE sessions are required (each group member to each key server). Other criteria, such as security requirements, must be taken into account when deciding between PSK and PKI.

Configure and Verify a Cisco IOS Software GET VPN Key Server

The GET VPN key server is a critical part of the GET VPN architecture. Most of the GET VPN configuration is done on the key server. Some of the configuration items are

- Group member authentication and admission control

- Traffic protection policy (definition of IPsec SA parameters)

- Rekeying policy (unicast or multicast, key lifetimes, retransmissions)

These configuration items are used by all group members unless they are overridden by a local policy configured on a specific group member.

Configuration Tasks

Perform the following configuration sequence to configure a GET VPN key server:

Task 1: (Optional) Configure an IKE policy. The default IKE policy can be used.

Task 2: Generate/configure authentication credentials for all group members.

Task 3: Generate or choose existing RSA keys on the key server to authenticate rekeys.

Task 4: Configure a traffic protection policy.

Task 5: Enable and configure the GET VPN key server function itself.

Task 6: (Optional) Tune the rekeying policy.

Task 7: Create a GET VPN crypto map and apply it on a key server interface. This enables the key server to listen for group member registration requests and distribute the configured traffic protection policy.

Configuration Choices

Two of the configuration tasks are optional:

■ Configure a nondefault IKE policy. You might want to configure an IKE policy that has higher security settings than those in the default policy.

■ Tune the rekeying policy to use unicast rekeying because multicast is the default. This is required if the transport network does not support multicast.

Configuration Scenario

Figure 19-3 illustrates the configuration scenario used for the configuration sequence that follows.

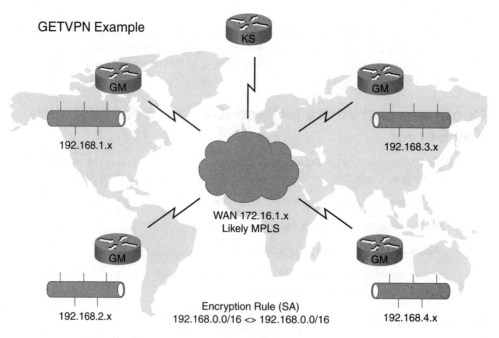

Figure 19-3   *GET VPN Configuration of Key Server*

The configuration sequence involves a full key server router configuration with the following policy:

■ IKE policy that uses pre-shared key authentication of peers and uses DH group 14 for the initial key exchange. All other IKE parameters will be left at their defaults.

■ The key server traffic protection policy should require protection for all traffic with source or destination addresses of 10.0.0.0/8 and also require AES 128-bit encryption and SHA-1 HMAC algorithms.

■ The GET VPN should use unicast rekeying that is authenticated with an RSA key pair that should be generated on the key server for that explicit purpose.

Task 1: (Optional) Configure an IKE Policy

Task 1 is to optionally create an IKE policy with the **crypto isakmp policy** global configuration command. Example 19-1 shows an IKE policy specifying RSA signatures for authentication and Diffie-Hellman group 14 to protect the key exchange.

Example 19-1 *Configure an Optional IKE Policy*

```
Router(config)# crypto isakmp policy 10
Router(config-isakmp)# authentication pre-share
Router(config-isakmp)# group 14
```

Note: IKE peering takes place only between each group member and the key server.

There must be an IKE policy on each group member that matches that of the key server.

Task 2: Generate and/or Configure Authentication Credentials

The second task of configuring the key server involves configuring authentication credentials. Pre-shared keys will be used as the authentication method. IKE main mode uses a unique PSK for each peer that is tied to a specific IP address. Example 19-2 shows the commands.

Example 19-2 *Generate and Configure Authentication Credentials*

```
Router(config)# crypto isakmp key ad73asmdkfl902380amadfjkasdjf 172.17.2.4
Router(config)# crypto isakmp key akjsdfljfdasdfu2389872jh3241u 172.17.0.1
```

Task 3: Generate RSA keys for Rekey Authentication

Task 3 creates the keys that will be used for rekeying authentication. To use redundant key servers, the generated keys must be exportable so that they can be imported on all other key servers. Example 19-3 shows a key being generated. Note that GET VPNs must have the same rekey RSA key pair on all key servers.

Example 19-3 *Generate RSA Keys*

```
Router(config)# crypto key generate rsa modulus 2048 label MYRSAKEYS exportable
```

Task 4: Configure a Traffic Protection Policy on the Key Server

Task 4 involves the configuration of the IPsec profile, an IPsec transform set, and a traffic flow specification.

The IPsec profile defines the encapsulation and cryptographic settings that will be distributed to the group members by the key server as part of the SA. The IPsec profile usually defines the transform set, session key lifetimes, and the requirements for Perfect Forward Secrecy (PFS).

The IPsec transform set defines a combination of security protocols, algorithms, and other settings to apply to IPsec-protected traffic. During the SA negotiation, peers agree to use a particular transform set for certain data flows. The transform set specifies one of two IPsec security protocols (Authentication Header [AH], Encapsulating Security Payload [ESP], or both) and specifies which algorithms to use with the chosen security protocol. Example 19-4 shows the configuration of the IPsec profile and transform set parameters.

Also in Task 4, traffic that is to be protected by the GET VPN IPsec profile must be defined. To do so, define an access control list (ACL) on the key server to define the traffic that must be protected. This information is pushed to the group members by the key server during their registration process. This allows the key server to choose or change the group policy dynamically as needed. The ACL can use both deny and permit ACL lines on the key server, which allows more granular control over the traffic that must be cryptographically protected. A deny entry in the ACL signifies traffic that is to be forwarded in the clear.

An ACL that is configured on the group member takes precedence over what is downloaded from the key server. The local ACL entries will be used at the top of the GET VPN ACL and then followed by the entries that are downloaded for the key server.

Example 19-4 *Configure Traffic Protection Policy on the Key Server*

```
Router(config)# crypto ipsec tranform-set MYSET esp-aes esp-sha-hmac
Router(config)# crypto ipsec profile MYIPsecPROFILE
 Set transform-set MYSET
Router(config)# ip access-list extended MYGETVPNACL
Router(config-acl)# permit ip 10.0.0.0 0.255.255.255 10.0.0.0 0.255.255.255
```

Task 5: Enable and Configure the GET VPN Key Server Function

Task 5 defines key server parameters and creates a policy that group members will use upon registration. Initially, use the **crypto gdoi** command to create a crypto GDOI group (a logical GET VPN). Use the **identity** command in GDOI group configuration mode to set the identity of the group to either an IP address or a number. The identity distinguishes the specific group configuration, because there can be multiple GET VPN groups on each key server or member.

The GDOI **server** group configuration command identifies that the group key server is defined locally on this router. Example 19-5 shows the configuration example.

The IPsec profile defines the encapsulation and cryptographic settings that will be distributed to the group members by the key server as part of the SA. The IPsec profile usually defines the transform set, session key lifetimes, and the requirements for Perfect Forward Secrecy (PFS).

Example 19-5   *Enable the GET VPN Key Server Function*

```
Router(config)# crypto gdoi group MYGETVPNGROUP
Router(config-gdoi)# identity number 1324
Router(config-gdoi)# server local
Router(config-gdoi)# address ipv4 172.17.0.1
Router(config-gdoi)# sa ipsec 10
Router(config-gdoi-sa)# profile MYIPsecPROFILE
Router(config-gdoi-sa)# match address ipv4 MYGETVPNACL
```

Task 6: (Optional) Tune the Rekeying Policy

Task 6 of key server configuration involves tuning the rekey options. Options that are available are rekey authentication, rekey transmit option, and a source address for rekeys. Configuring rekey options as part of the registration policy on the key server replaces the need to do it on all group member routers. Multicast is the default transport type for rekey messages.

The following options cover when to use multicast or unicast rekey transport:

- If all members of a group are multicast capable, use **no rekey transport unicast** (this means that multicast rekeying will be used).

- If all the members of a group are only unicast capable, use **rekey transport unicast**.

- If there is a mix of members in a group, and the majority of the members are multicast capable and only a few are unicast capable, use **no rekey transport unicast**.

In the last case, all unicast members must reregister because they do not receive the multicast rekeys, but this is less of a load on the key servers. Refer to Example 19-6 for the configuration commands.

Example 19-6   *Tuning the Rekey Policy*

```
Router(config-gdoi)# rekey transport unicast
Router(config-gdoi)# rekey authentication mypubkey rsa MYRSAKEYS
```

Task 7: Create and Apply the GET VPN Crypto Map

The last task of key server configuration creates a GDOI crypto map and applies that map to the interface. The crypto map entry must be of the type **gdoi** and reference the GDOI group created in Task 5 in this sequence. The crypto map must be applied to the interface to which group members will register. Example 19-7 shows the commands.

Example 19-7 *Create and Apply the GET VPN Crypto Map*

```
Router(config)# crypto map MYCRYPTOMAP 10 gdoi
Router(config)# set group MYGETVPNGROUP
Router(config)# interface GigabitEthernet0/0
Router(config-if)# crypto map MYCRYPTOMAP
```

Cisco Configuration Professional Support

Cisco Configuration Professional 2.0 supports the creation of GET VPN key servers on a managed device. It allows the key server to be configured either through a configuration wizard or by manually entering all the options.

Verify Basic Key Server Settings

The **show crypto gdoi** command displays information about the local GET VPN configuration. As demonstrated in Example 19-8, the output shows the GET VPN key server settings and the number of registered group members.

Example 19-8 show crypto gdoi *Command*

```
Router# show crypto gdoi
GROUP INFORMATION
Group Name                        : MYGETVPNGROUP (unicast)
Group Identity                    : 1234
Group Members                     : 34
IPSec SA Direction                : Both
Group Rekey Lifetime              : 86400 secs
Rekey Retransmit Period           : 10 secs
Rekey Retransmit  Attempts        : 2
        IPSec SA Number           : 8
        IPSec SA Rekey Lifetime   : 3600 secs
        Profile Name              : MYIPSECPROFILE
        Replay Method             : Count Based
        Replay Window Size        : 64
        ACL Configured            : access-list MYGETACL
     Group Server List            : Local
```

Verify the Rekey Policy

The **show crypto gdoi ks rekey** command displays detailed rekey settings that are active for a GET VPN group, as demonstrated in Example 19-9.

Example 19-9 show crypto gdoi ks rekey *Command*

```
Router# show crypto gdoi ks rekey
Group MYGETVPNGROUP (Unicast)
        Number of rekeys sent             : 23843
        Number of rekeys retransmitted    : 56
```

```
    KEK rekey lifetime (sec)        : 86400
    Number of retransmissions       : 2
    IPSec SA 10 lifetime (sec)      : 3600
```

List All Registered Members

On the key server router, the **show crypto gdoi ks members** command displays information about registered group members, as demonstrated in Example 19-10.

Example 19-10   show crypto gdoi ks members *Command*

```
Router# show crypto gdoi ks members
Group Member Information:
Number of rekeys sent for group getvpn : 10
Group member ID : 172.17.2.24
Group ID : 1234
Group Name : MYGETVPNGROUP
```

Implementation Guidelines

Consider the following implementation guidelines when configuring a GET VPN key server:

Key Topic

- Configure IKE peering between each group member and the key servers as in a traditional IPsec VPN, using pre-shared keys or PKI for authentication.

- Identify traffic that does not require IPsec protection and use deny statements on the ACL on the key server to exclude that traffic from the GET VPN protection.

- On the key server, make the ACL length as short as possible to minimize the number of SAs on the peers. Also, ensure that the ACL is symmetric and matches flows in both directions.

- If interface redundancy is required, bind the key server to a loopback interface. Ensure that the loopback is included in the crypto map definition.

Configure and Verify Cisco IOS Software GET VPN Group Members

GET VPN group members require very little effort because GET VPN key servers distribute most of the VPN settings to the group members. On the group member, the following must be configured:

- **Key server IP address:** Configure a list of all available key servers for a GET VPN group.

- **Key server IKE authentication details:** Specify the key server authentication credentials (pre-shared keys or PKI).

■ **Local policy overrides:** Optionally, configure local policy overrides that provide exceptions to the policy that is downloaded from the key server.

Configuration Tasks

Perform the following configuration sequence to configure a GET VPN group member:

Task 1: (Optional) Configure an IKE policy. The default IKE policy can be used.

Task 2: Generate/configure authentication credentials for all group members. These credentials must match the IPsec configuration on the key server.

Task 3: Enable and configure the GET VPN group member function.

Task 4: Create a GET VPN crypto map, and apply it on an untrusted group member network interface.

Task 5: (Optional) Configure a fail-closed policy. This is dependent upon the local security policy.

Configuration Choices

Two of the configuration tasks are optional:

■ **Configure a nondefault IKE policy:** You might want to configure an IKE policy that has higher security settings than those in the default policy. Also, consider configuring shorter SA lifetimes to reduce the load on the key server because IKE SAs do not need to remain after registration and policy download.

■ **Consider using a fail-closed policy:** This enhances the security posture and prevent packets from traversing the untrusted network while IPsec SAs are not yet established. There should still be exceptions to this to allow routing protocols and management traffic.

Configuration Scenario

Figure 19-4 illustrates the configuration scenario used for the configuration sequence that follows.

The configuration sequence involves configuring a GET VPN group member with the following policy parameters:

■ IKE policy that uses pre-shared key authentication of peers and uses DH group 14 for the initial key exchange. All other IKE parameters will be left at their defaults.

■ The untrusted network interface will not permit any user traffic through unless the group member has successfully registered in to the GET VPN.

■ The fail-closed policy should permit Secure Shell (SSH) to all group member loopback IP addresses (10.x.255.1 where x is unique for each member).

Task 1: Configure an IKE Policy

Task 1 is to optionally create an IKE policy with the **crypto isakmp policy** global configuration command. Example 19-8 shows an IKE policy specifying pre-shared keys for authentication, Diffie-Hellman group 14 to protect the key exchange, and setting the IKE lifetime to 300 seconds.

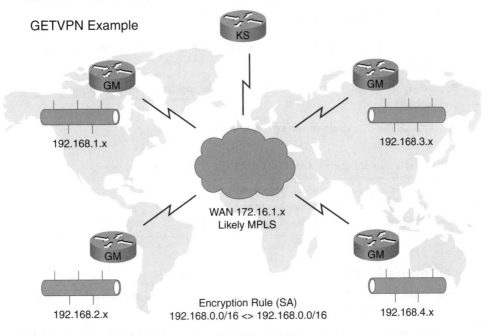

Figure 19-4 *GET VPN Configuration of Group Member Routers*

Example 19-11 *Configure an Optional IKE Policy and Authentication Credentials*

```
Router(config)# crypto isakmp policy 10
Router(config-isakmp)# authentication pre-share
Router(config-isakmp)# group 14
```

Key Topic

Note: The IKE configuration on the group member must match that of the key server, except for the IKE lifetime, which will negotiate down to the shortest configured time.

There must be an IKE policy on each group member that matches that of the key server.

Task 2: Generate and/or Configure Authentication Credentials

The second task of configuring the key server involves configuring authentication credentials. Pre-shared keys (PSK) will be used as the authentication method. Example 19-12 shows the commands.

Example 19-12 *Generate and Configure Authentication Credentials*

```
Router(config)# crypto isakmp key ad73asmdkf1902380amadfjkasdjf 172.17.2.4
Router(config)# crypto isakmp key akjsdfljfdasdfu2389872jh3241u 172.17.0.1
```

Key Topic

Task 3: Enable the GET VPN Group Member Function

Task 3 enables and configures the GET VPN group member function on the router. The subtasks that follow are needed and configured in Example 19-13:

- Create a GDOI group and assign a locally significant name. Use the **crypto gdoi group** command.

- Set up the group identity number to match the identity number configured on the key server.

- Provide the IP address of the key server.

Example 19-13 *Enable and Configure GET VPN Group Member*

```
Router(config)# crypto gdoi group MYGETVPNGROUP
Router(config-gdoi)# identity number 1324
Router(config-gdoi)# server address ipv4 172.17.0.1
```

Task 4: Create and Apply the GET VPN Crypto Map

Task 4 creates the GET VPN crypto map and then applies it to the untrusted network interface on the group member router.

The **set group** command in crypto map configuration mode maps the configured GDOI group to the crypto map. Finally, the **crypto map** interface configuration command applies the crypto map to the interface. See Example 19-14 for the configuration usage.

Example 19-14 *Create and Apply Crypto Map*

```
Router(config)# crypto map MYCRYPTOMAP 10 gdoi
Router(config-map)# set group MYGETVPNGROUP
Router(config)# interface GigabitEthernet0/0
Router(config-if)# crypto map MYCRYPTOMAP
```

Task 5: (Optional) Configure a Fail-Closed Policy

Task 5, the last and optional task of configuring a GET VPN group member router, is completely dependent upon an organization's security policy. Configuring a fail-closed policy means that no traffic can traverse through the untrusted network interface unless the member has successfully registered with the key server. Adding the **fail-close** option to the **crypto map MYCRYPTOMAP gdoi** command along with the **activate** command in crypto map configuration mode will enable the fail-closed feature. You should configure an ACL that excludes management traffic such as SSH. Deny statements in the ACL will allow specified traffic to traverse the interface in clear text. After the ACL is defined, use the **match address** command in crypto map configuration mode. Example 19-15 shows the configuration example.

Example 19-15 *Configure a Fail-Closed Policy*

```
Router(config)# crypto map MYCRYPTOMAP gdoi fail-close
Router(config-map)# match address MYFAILCLOSEACL
Router(config-map)# activate
```

Cisco Configuration Professional Support

As with the configuration of the GET VPN key server, Cisco Configuration Professional 2.0 supports the creation of GET VPN group members and can also be done either through a configuration wizard or by manually entering all the options.

Verify Registration of the Group Member

The **show crypto gdoi** command displays information about the status of the group member's registration. It also displays the key server that is defined in the configuration.

Implementation Guidelines

Consider the following implementation guidelines when configuring a GET VPN group member router:

- Lowering IKE lifetimes on group members is recommended to reduce the load on the key server.

- In most cases, it is highly recommended to use the fail-closed feature. Management traffic and other overhead traffic that do not require IPsec protection should be excluded by using deny statements in an ACL to exclude that traffic.

- Performance on the group member will be approximately 5 percent lower for ciphertext when compared to normal IPsec VPN throughput. The more complex time-based antireplay feature of GET takes longer than the typical IPsec sequence-based antireplay.

Troubleshooting Flow

Perform the following steps for troubleshooting GET VPN group members if the GET VPN IPsec SA does not establish:

Step 1. If the GET VPN IPsec SA does not establish, first test and verify connectivity for each peer. Use **ping** and **traceroute** commands between the key server and the group member to assist with verifying reachability.

Step 2. Ensure that the IKE policies on both peers (key server and group member) match. The **debug crypto isakmp** command can reveal mismatches in IKE policies. The only parameter in an IKE policy that does not have to match is the IKE lifetime parameter.

Step 3. Verify that the IKE SA is authenticated. Verify that pre-shared keys match if this is the authentication method being used.

Step 4. The IKE SA should be established. The **show crypto isakmp sa** command can show the status. The state of the SA should be GDOI_IDLE and registration should be successful.

Step 5.   Verify that the IPsec SA has established. Several commands, such as **show crypto gdoi**, **debug crypto gdoi events**, **debug crypto gdoi ks**, and others can reveal problems with the key server policy being pushed to the group members.

Configure and Verify High-Availability Mechanisms in a GET VPN

GET VPNs can have multiple key servers configured. These key servers (called cooperative servers) work together to deliver keys and policies to group members. One of the key servers will be elected as the primary server through the use of a proprietary protocol, Cooperative Key Server Protocol (COOP). The primary key server creates IPsec session keys and pushes them to its peer key servers. The peer key servers then distribute session keys to their registered group members. Each group member registers with one of the key servers, which allows them to exchange encrypted data as part of the same VPN. Note that the primary key server distributes the rekey to all group members.

In some cases, there might be several policies and keys being distributed by several cooperating key servers. There can be up to eight key servers on a network. One of the key servers will be elected the primary key server, and the others will synchronize with the aforementioned keys and policies. Key servers can be placed anywhere in the network, as long as they are reachable by the other key servers and the group member routers.

There are two reasons to have multiple key servers:

■   Allows a group member router to register with the key server router that is closest for performance reasons

■   Allows key server redundancy

Note: Rekey configuration, defined policies, and antireplay settings must be identical on all key servers.

It is recommended to bring up all cooperative key servers first, allow them to synchronize policies and keys, and then configure group members with primary and secondary key servers for registrations.

Cooperative key servers exchange one-way announcement messages, process and store the data content of protocol messages, and update their view of the group state. These announcement messages can contain the following components to help maintain state information:

■   **Sender priority (identity of a key server):** Describes the priority of the sender, which is configurable. The key server with the highest priority becomes the primary key server. If the priority values are the same, the key server with the highest IP address becomes the primary key server.

■   **Maintaining the sender role:** During the synchronization period, geographically disparate key servers might suffer from network latency and more than one key server will become the primary key server. After the latency is gone, the key servers will find each other, exchange role information, and revert to their proper role.

- **Request for a return packet flag:** All messages are defined as one-way messages. A key server can request state information from a peer to find out its role or request the current state of the group.

- **Group state:** This is the current IPsec SA and keys that are current for the group. If messages have not been heard from the primary key server for a certain period of time, the Primary Periodic Timer is activated. This causes a secondary key server to send an announcement to the primary key server requesting a return packet. If the secondary key server does not receive a response, the Dead Primary Timer begins. At this point, a reevaluation role time is set when a key server is moving to the primary key server state.

Network Splits and Network Merges

A possible negative aspect to deploying multiple key servers is when connectivity between key servers is down for a long period of time. If this *network split* occurs, it can lead to several independent groups of key servers, rekeying group members with different session keys. This will lead to connectivity issues between group members, because they will not be able to decrypt traffic from other GET VPN members. After the connectivity is restored, the GET VPN will automatically *merge* and unify session keys across all members. It is critical that communication among key servers not be interrupted.

Configuration Tasks

Perform the following configuration sequence to configure redundancy for GET VPNs:

Task 1: Key servers in the cluster must have the same RSA key pair. Export the main RSA key pair and import it to the other key servers.

Task 2: Configure a full mesh of IKE sessions between all key servers, which enables the key servers to mutually authenticate.

Task 3: Configure COOP between the key servers. The COOP runs over the IKE sessions between key servers.

Task 4: Configure the same traffic protection policy on all key servers.

Task 5: Configure all group members with multiple key servers for redundancy.

Configuration Scenario

Figure 19-5 illustrates the configuration scenario used for the configuration sequence that follows.

The configuration sequence involves configuring redundancy by creating a cluster between two GET VPN key servers with the following policy parameters:

- The key servers will use pre-shared keys for authentication and will use a lifetime of 86400 seconds for their IKE session. All other IKE parameters will be left at their defaults.

■ One key server will have a cluster (COOP) priority of 5, and the other router's priority will be set to 10.

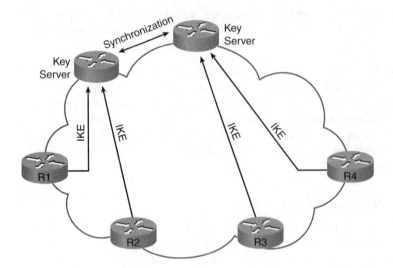

Figure 19-5   *GET VPN Redundant Key Servers*

Task 1: Distribute the Rekey RSA Key Pair

Task 1 is to export the RSA key pair of the key server that was configured first and then import it to all other key servers. Use the **crypto key export** command to export the key, and then use the **crypto key import** command to import the key to all other key servers.

Task 2: Configure a Full Mesh of Key Server IKE Peering

The second task of configuring redundancy is to configure IKE peering between all key servers. The IKE lifetime will be set to 86400 seconds because this is between key servers. Also, because of their criticality, issue the **crypto isakmp keepalive** command to verify mutual reachability of key servers. Example 19-16 shows the command breakdown.

Example 19-16   *Configure IKE Peering Between All Key Servers*

```
Router(config)# crypto isakmp policy 10
Router(config-isakmp)# lifetime 86400
Router(config)# crypto isakmp keepalive 10 periodic
```

Task 3: Configure COOP

Using the **crypto gdoi group** global configuration command, and then the **server local** command to enter local server configuration mode, key server redundancy must be enabled with the **redundancy** command. This will put you in COOP subconfiguration mode. In this mode, set the local key server priority (higher is better) by using the **local priority** command. Example 19-17 shows the commands in use.

Example 19-17 *Configure COOP*

```
router(config)# crypto gdoi group MYGETVPNGROUP
router(config-gdoi-group)# server local
router(config-local-server)# redundancy
router(gdoi-coop-ks-config)# local priority 10
router(gdoi-coop-ks-config)# peer address ipv4 172.17.0.2
```

All key server peers in the COOP cluster must be listed in this subconfiguration mode. Peers are specified with the **peer address ipv4** command.

Tasks 4 and 5: Configure Traffic Protection Policy and Multiple Key Servers on Group Members

Task 4 involves configuring the same policy on all GET VPN key servers. This means repeating Steps 1–3 on all the remaining GET VPN key servers.

Task 5 specifies multiple key servers on the group member using the **server** crypto gdoi group configuration command, as shown in Example 19-18.

Example 19-18 *Configure GET VPN Key Servers*

```
router(config-gdoi)# server address ipv4 172.17.0.1
router(config-gdoi)# server address ipv4 172.17.0.2
```

Verify IKE Peering

To verify IKE peering, verify connectivity between the peers and make sure that the IKE policies match.

Verify COOP Peering

The next troubleshooting process is to verify mutual COOP peering. For the local key server role, check the **Local KS Role:** line in the output of the **show crypto gdoi group** *group_ID* **ks coop** command, as shown in Example 19-19. It should display **Primary** for the primary key server or **Secondary** for all others. For each key server peers, the **IKE status:** should read **Established**.

Example 19-19 *Verify COOP Peering*

```
router# show crypto gdoi ks coop
Crypto Gdoi Group Name :group1
        Group handle: 2147483650, Local Key Server handle: 2147483650

        Local Address: 1.1.1.1
        Local Priority: 100
        Local KS Role: Primary   , Local KS Status: Alive
        Primary Timers:
                Primary Refresh Policy Time: 20
                Remaining Time: 17
                Antireplay Sequence Number: 313
```

```
Peer Sessions:
Session 1:
            Server handle: 2147483651
            Peer Address: 2.2.2.2
            Peer Priority: 99
            Peer KS Role: Secondary , Peer KS
```

Implementation Guidelines

Consider the following implementation guidelines when configuring a GET VPN COOP cluster and key server redundancy:

- IKE and IPsec SAs must be manually synchronized on all key servers that are in the COOP cluster.

- Place key servers at strategic positions in the network to gain as much efficiency with group member registrations while maintaining connectivity between key servers.

- By distributing group members across multiple key servers and controlling the order of the key servers in the configurations, some load balancing can be achieved.

Troubleshooting Flow

Perform the following recommended flow for troubleshooting redundant key servers:

Step 1.   If the COOP cluster fails to establish, check the key server IKE mesh using the **show crypto isakmp sa** command.

Step 2.   Verify the key server COOP mesh using the **show crypto gdoi ks coop, show logging | include COOP**, and **debug crypto gdoi coop** commands.

Exam Preparation

As mentioned in the section, "How to Use This Book," in the Introduction, you have several choices for exam preparation: the exercises here, the memory tables in Appendix C, the final exam preparation chapter, and the exam simulation questions on the CD-ROM. The following questions present a bigger challenge than the exam itself because they use an open-ended question format. By using this more difficult format, you exercise your memory better and prove your conceptual and factual knowledge of this chapter. You can find the answers to these questions in Appendix A, "Answers to the DIKTA Quizzes and Fill in the Blanks Questions."

Review All Key Topics

Review the most important topics in the chapter, noted with the Key Topics icon in the margin of the page. Table 19-3 lists a reference of these key topics and the page numbers on which each is found.

Table 19-3   *Key Topics*

Key Topic Element	Description	Page
List	Keys supported in IKE GDOI	503
List	GET VPN rekeying guidelines	505
Table 19-2	Unicast/multicast rekeying comparison	506
Figure 19-2	GET VPN packet structure	508
List	Input parameters for GET VPN deployment	508
List	GET VPN deployment tasks	508
List	GET VPN deployment choices	509
List	GET VPN key server configuration tasks	509
Example 19-1	Configuring an IKE policy	511
Example 19-2	Configuring authentication credentials	511
Example 19-3	Generating RSA keys	511
Example 19-4	Configuring traffic protection policy	512
Section	Enabling and configuring the GET VPN key server function	512
List	Choosing between multicast and unicast rekeying	513
Example 19-6	Tuning the rekeying policy	513
Example 19-7	Creating and applying the GET VPN crypto map	514
List	Key server implementation guidelines	515

Table 19-3 *Key Topics*

Key Topic Element	Description	Page
List	GET VPN group member configuration task list	516
Example 19-11	Configuring IKE policy and authentication credentials on group members	517
Example 19-12	Configuring authentication credentials on group members	517
Example 19-13	Enabling and configuring group members	518
Example 19-14	Creating and applying a crypto map	518
Example 19-15	Configuring a fail-closed policy	519
List	Configuring group member implementation guidelines	519
List	Configuring group member troubleshooting flow	519
List	Configuring redundancy for GET VPNs	521
List	GET VPN COOP implementation guidelines	524
List	GET VPN COOP troubleshooting flow	524

Complete Tables and Lists from Memory

Print a copy of Appendix C, "Memory Tables" (found on the CD), or at least the section for this chapter, and complete the tables and lists from memory. Appendix D, "Memory Table Answers," also on the CD, includes completed tables and lists to check your work.

Define Key Terms

Define the following key terms from this chapter, and check your answers in the Glossary:

GET VPN, key server, group members, Internet Key Exchange (IKE) Group Domain of Interpretation (GDOI) protocol, Traffic Encrypting Key (TEK), Key Encrypting Key (KEK)

Fill in the Blanks

1. Reducing _____ on group members is recommended to reduce the load on the key server.

2. If the key server fails to get a _____ to a rekey message from the group member after three rekeys, it removes the group member.

3. By distributing _____ across multiple key servers and controlling the order of the key servers in the configurations, some load balancing can be achieved.

4. The _____ defines the encapsulation and cryptographic settings that will be distributed to the group members by the key server as part of the SA.

5. GET VPNs use _____ as the group keying mechanism.

6. GET VPNs provide connectionless, tunnel-free encryption that leverages the existing _____ infrastructure.

7. GET VPNs are based on GDOI, which is defined in RFC _____.

8. GDOI is a standards-based ISAKMP group key management protocol meant to provide secure communication within a _____.

Reference

Group Encrypted Transport VPN (GET VPN) Design and Implementation Guide, www.cisco.com/en/US/prod/collateral/vpndevc/ps6525/ps9370/ps7180/GETVPN_DIG_version_1_0_External.pdf.

This chapter covers the following subjects:

- **Choose an appropriate remote access VPN technology:** Covers the decisions and considerations you need to make to select the appropriate remote access VPN technology for your environment.

- **Choose appropriate remote access VPN cryptographic controls:** Covers choosing the proper cryptographic controls to meet the security requirements for your organization.

- **Plan the deployment of a Cisco IOS Software SSL VPN gateway:** Covers gathering input and making decisions that are necessary for a successful SSL VPN gateway deployment.

- **Configure and verify common SSL VPN parameters:** In this section, you configure and verify the most common SSL VPN parameters.

- **Configure and verify client authentication and policies on the SSL VPN gateway:** For clients to connect to your gateway, it must be configured with parameters that can be matched by the clients. This section covers configuration and verification of client authentication and policies.

- **Configure and verify full tunneling connectivity on the Cisco IOS SSL VPN gateway:** Covers configuring the SSL VPN gateway to allow full tunneling for your clients.

- **Install and configure the Cisco AnyConnect client:** Covers configuring the Cisco AnyConnect client. There are many parameters that must match the policies on the SSL VPN gateway.

- **Configure and verify clientless access on the Cisco IOS SSL VPN gateway:** The SSL VPN gateway can also be configured to allow clientless access. This section covers the configuration of the necessary parameters to allow this type of connectivity.

- **Troubleshoot the basic SSL VPN operation:** Now that you have configured several different methods of VPN connectivity on the Cisco IOS SSL VPN gateway, you learn how to perform basic troubleshooting steps.

CHAPTER 20

Deploying Remote Access Solutions Using SSL VPNs

Remote access Virtual Private Network (VPN) technologies allow mobile workers to access internal resources over untrusted networks. The access is provided using transmission protection and access authentication and authorization technologies. Cisco IOS Software provides a set of remote access VPN features from which to choose. This chapter will discuss a comparison of remote access VPN technologies and then cover configuring, verifying, and troubleshooting a basic client-based and clientless SSL VPN solution on a Cisco Integrated Services Router (ISR).

"Do I Know This Already?" Quiz

The "Do I Know This Already?" quiz helps you decide whether you really need to read the entire chapter. If you already intend to read the entire chapter, you do not necessarily need to answer these questions now.

The 13-question quiz, derived from the major sections in the "Foundation Topics" portion of this chapter, helps you determine how to spend your limited study time.

Table 20-1 outlines the major topics discussed in this chapter and the "Do I Know This Already?" quiz questions that correspond to those topics.

Table 20-1 *"Do I Know This Already?" Foundation Topics Section-to-Question Mapping*

Foundation Topics Section	Questions Covered in This Section
Choose an Appropriate Remote Access VPN Technology	1, 2
Choose Appropriate Remote Access VPN Cryptographic Controls	3, 4
Plan the Deployment of a Cisco IOS Software SSL VPN Gateway	5, 6
Configure and Verify Common SSL VPN Parameters	7, 8
Configure and Verify Client Authentication and Policies on the SSL VPN Gateway	9
Configure and Verify Full Tunneling Connectivity on the Cisco IOS SSL VPN Gateway	10

Table 20-1 *"Do I Know This Already?" Foundation Topics Section-to-Question Mapping*

Foundation Topics Section	Questions Covered in This Section
Install and Configure the Cisco AnyConnect Client	11
Configure and Verify Clientless Access on the Cisco IOS SSL VPN Gateway	12
Troubleshoot the Basic SSL VPN Operation	13

Caution: The goal of self-assessment is to gauge your mastery of the topics in this chapter. If you do not know the answer to a question or are only partially sure of the answer, you should mark this question wrong for purposes of the self-assessment. Giving yourself credit for an answer that you correctly guess skews your self-assessment results and might provide you with a false sense of security.

1. Which type of SSL VPN architecture supports any IP application without application modification?

   a. Full tunneling

   b. Split tunneling

   c. Clientless tunneling

   d. None of these answers are correct.

2. Which type of VPN architecture allows remote users URL and CIFS file access to internal resources through a web browser?

   a. Split tunneling

   b. Full tunneling

   c. Clientless

   d. Terminal services

   e. None of these answers are correct.

3. What provides endpoint authentication for both the client and the server?

   a. Web browser

   b. SHA-1

   c. TCP traffic

   d. SSL/TLS

   e. None of these answers are correct.

4. What can directly influence the strength of protection provided by algorithms such as 3DES or AES?

   a. Key length

   b. Firewall rules

   c. IPS inspection engine

   d. Certificate expiration date

   e. None of these answers are correct.

5. What are the two choices of SSL VPNs?

   a. Clientless with a web browser

   b. Cisco AnyConnect VPN client

   c. Proxy mode

   d. None of these answers are correct.

6. After authentication, what does the Cisco ISR apply a set of to the user session?

   a. Static routes

   b. Split tunneling routes

   c. Authorization rules

   d. None of these answers are correct.

7. The SSL VPN gateway is enabled on the Cisco ISR with which command?

   a. inservice

   b. ssl vpn enable

   c. gateway

   d. vpn enable

   e. None of these answers are correct.

8. For proper authentication, what must be provisioned to the Cisco ISR?

   a. Memory upgrade

   b. IOS upgrade

   c. Identity certificate

   d. CA ROOT certificate

9. By default, which kind of certificate does the ISR create upon each reboot that will cause client warnings when attempting SSL VPN access because the certificate cannot be verified?

   a. Certificate authority

   b. Certificate CA

   c. Self-signed X.509 certificate

   d. ROOT certificate

10. What is assigned to the client as it connects in full tunnel mode?

    a. A unique client ID number

    b. A list of software to install

    c. IP address

    d. ROOT certificate

11. What is required for the initial installation of the Cisco AnyConnect client?

    a. On-site technician

    b. Terminal services session

    c. Administrative privilege

    d. Memory upgrade

12. What can users use to access internal resources with the ISR performing as a proxy to provide internal content on its SSL VPN portal?

    a. SSH

    b. Telnet

    c. Web browser

    d. Terminal session

13. What should be alleviated first as a factor for troubleshooting?

    a. Authentication problems

    b. Verify that the service is running

    c. Connectivity issues

    d. Proper authorization

The answers to the "Do I Know This Already?" quiz are found in Appendix A. The suggested choices for your next step are as follows:

- **10 or less overall score:** Read the entire chapter. This includes the "Foundation Topics" and the "Exam Preparation" sections.

- **11 or more overall score:** If you want more review on these topics, skip to the "Exam Preparation" section. Otherwise, move on to Chapter 21, "Deploying Remote Access Solutions Using EZVPN."

Foundation Topics

This chapter covers making appropriate choices of VPN technologies and cryptographic controls on a Cisco Integrated Services Router (ISR) for remote access. This chapter also covers basic SSL VPN implementation in detail.

Choose an Appropriate Remote Access VPN Technology

Remote access VPNs connect individual remote users to a set of resources on an organization's internal network. In some cases, it might connect them to a perimeter, extranet, or other exterior buffer type of network. Remote access (RA) VPNs typically use very strong client authentication, which requires users to prove their identity and encryption to protect transmissions across an untrusted network, typically the Internet.

Many RA VPNs employ various security controls above and beyond authentication and transmission protection, such as strictly limiting access to resources or assessing the security posture of remote clients prior to permitting access to the internal network.

Cisco IOS Software Remote Access VPN Options

Cisco IOS Software running on the Integrated Services Router (ISR) provides a wide array of remote access VPN technologies. These technologies differ in how they encapsulate user traffic and in the transmission protection (encryption) they provide.

The two primary encapsulation methods for deploying VPNs are SSL/TLS and IPsec cryptographic encapsulation protocols. Both offer authentication and transmission security features. There are two major modes for encapsulating user traffic:

- **Full tunneling VPNs:** Require VPN client software to be installed on the remote computer or dedicated VPN devices (hardware clients) to enable full routed IP access to internal resources. Cisco IOS Software provides support for SSL VPNs and IPsec (Easy VPN, or EZVPN) full tunneling software clients. The Cisco ISR acts as the remote access VPN gateway to which the remote user VPN sessions terminate. An ISR can also perform as an EZVPN IPsec hardware client, which would provide access to the VPN for an entire remote network.

- **Clientless VPN:** Access to corporate resources can be provided to remote users even when the remote device is not managed nor is there any VPN client software. Clientless deployments require that the user open a web browser, which acts as the VPN client, and the VPN gateway acts as a proxy device to the internal resources. This solution also allows organizations to provide a web portal interface to remote users from which they can launch applications to which they have been granted access. Clientless VPNs are easier to deploy than a full tunneling remote access VPN, but they typically provide limited access to resources when compared to the full tunnel.

Full Tunneling Remote Access SSL VPN: Features

In the full tunneling VPN architecture, remote users use the Cisco AnyConnect VPN client to establish a Secure Socket Layer/Transport Layer Security (SSL/TLS) tunnel with the Cisco ISR. After successful mutual authentication, the Cisco ISR will apply a set of authorization and accounting rules to the user's session. Next, after the Cisco ISR establishes a VPN environment for the remote user, the remote user can forward IP traffic into the SSL/TLS tunnel. This is done by the Cisco AnyConnect client creating a virtual network interface on the client through which all protected traffic is forwarded. The client can use any application to access any resource behind the Cisco ISR VPN gateway that is within the user's authorization rules.

Full Tunneling Remote Access SSL VPN: Benefits and Limitations

Table 20-2 lists the benefits and limitations of the full tunneling SSL VPN architecture.

Table 20-2   *Benefits and Limitations of Full Tunneling SSL VPN Architecture*

Benefits	Limitations
It supports any IP application without changing the application. It creates a transparency that creates an environment in which it is like being inside the protected network and having access to any corporate resource to which the user has access.	It requires that users install an SSL VPN client on their systems.
It does not require any user training except for initiating and terminating the VPN connection.	It requires administrative privileges to install the VPN client because the client needs to modify network interfaces and the IP stack to operate successfully.
It can traverse most firewalls and Network Address Translation (NAT) devices because the SSL VPN encapsulation uses the HTTPS port (TCP port 443) and looks just like any other HTTPS session.	
Because it is limited to users having the AnyConnect VPN client on their machines, it is mostly used on managed devices that are typically more trusted than unmanaged devices.	

Clientless Remote Access SSL VPN: Features

In the clientless remote access VPN architecture, remote users use their web browser to establish an SSL/TLS session with the Cisco ISR. After successful mutual authentication, the Cisco ISR will apply a set of authorization and accounting rules to the user's session and the user is presented with a web portal. The Cisco ISR can also deploy advanced security controls, such as a virtual desktop or a posture assessment to the VPN session.

Clientless SSL VPNs do not provide full network access like the full tunneling VPNs. To allow clientless remote access users to access corporate applications, the security appliance (ISR) acts as a proxy. It converts web and even some nonweb applications so that they can be protected by SSL. The Cisco ISR offers the following techniques to provide resource and application access:

- **URL and Common Internet File System (CIFS) file access:** When the client browser establishes the SSL session and the user is authenticated, the gateway can present a page with resource bookmarks. These allow the user to access preconfigured web pages or file shares. The user can also enter an address of a resource and access it that way if it is within the user's permission.

- **Port forwarding:** Provides access to TCP-based applications by mapping application-specific ports on the remote computer to application-specific ports on the internal servers. Port forwarding requires that a Java applet be downloaded to the client. This applet listens on ports on the client machine and forwards the connection to the gateway.

Clientless SSL VPN: Benefits and Limitations

Table 20-3 lists the benefits and limitations of the clientless SSL VPN architecture.

Table 20-3   *Benefits and Limitations of Clientless SSL VPN Architecture*

Benefits	Limitations
It can traverse most firewalls and NAT devices because the SSL VPN encapsulation uses the familiar HTTPS port (TCP 443) and looks like any other HTTPS connection.	It does not support all IP applications, although most web-based client-server applications are supported.
It does not require that users install a VPN client on their systems.	It might require user training because the way users access resources can change relative to what they are accustomed to doing.
It has no need for the user to have administrative privileges because there is no software to install.	It can potentially allow access from untrusted systems because any system with a web browser can attempt a connection. A layered security approach should be deployed to provide additional security controls.

Software Client Remote Access IPsec VPN (EZVPN): Features

The third remote access VPN architecture support on the Cisco ISR is the full tunneling client-based IPsec VPN architecture. With this option, remote users use the Cisco VPN client to build an IPsec tunnel with the Cisco ISR. Just as with the full tunneling remote access SSL VPN, after mutual authentication has taken place, the Cisco ISR will apply a set of authorization and accounting rules to the user's session. After the Cisco ISR establishes the appropriate VPN policy for the remote user, the user can transmit IP traffic into the IPsec tunnel. The client can use any application to access any resource to which he has authorization to access.

Hardware Client Remote Access IPsec VPN (EZVPN): Features

Another variation of the full tunneling IPsec VPN architecture is one in which the remote VPN endpoint is a hardware client device, such as another Cisco ISR. The hardware client device can provide remote access for an entire remote network and uses the same policies and configuration as software VPN clients.

Remote Access IPsec VPN: Benefits and Limitations

Table 20-4 lists the benefits and limitations of the full tunneling IPsec architecture.

Table 20-4 *Benefits and Limitations of Full Tunneling IPsec Architecture*

Benefits	Limitations
It supports any IP application without changing the application.	It requires that users install an IPsec VPN client on their systems.
It does not require any user training except for initiating and terminating the VPN connection.	It requires administrative privileges to install the VPN client on their systems.
It supports low-latency forwarding and enables the use of real-time applications such as IP voice or real-time video streams.	It has issues traversing firewalls, because IPsec and Internet Key Exchange (IKE) might not be allowed through enterprise firewalls as part of the organization's security policy.
Because it is limited to users having the IPsec VPN client, it is mostly used on managed devices.	

VPN Access Methods: Use Cases

Table 20-5 provides information to assist in choosing an appropriate VPN architecture.

Table 20-5 *VPN Access Methods: Use Cases*

Use Case	Full Tunneling SSL VPN	Clientless SSL VPN	Full Tunneling IPsec VPN
Mobile workers using managed devices requiring transparent network access	Yes	No	Yes
Mobile workers using unmanaged devices from public locations	No	Yes	No
Partners requiring controlled transparent access	Yes	No	Yes
Partners requiring controlled access without a client	No	Yes	No

Choose Appropriate Remote Access VPN Cryptographic Controls

Choosing the appropriate cryptographic controls for traffic that will traverse your remote access VPN is just as important as choosing the remote access VPN technology. The level of protection required by your organizational security policy should dictate the cryptographic controls that are implemented in your remote access VPN solution.

SSL/TLS Refresher

Transport Layer Security (TLS) and its predecessor, Secure Socket Layer (SSL), are cryptographic protocols that provide security for transmissions of public transports such as the Internet. These protocols are most often found in applications such as web browsing, electronic mail, and Voice over IP (VoIP).

The SSL protocol was developed by Netscape in 1994 to protect web transactions. Netscape developed SSL until version 3.0. In 1999, the IETF adopted SSL and called it Transport Layer Security (TLS). TLS is also known as SSL version 3.1.

Note: TLS version 1.0 is not compatible with SSL version 3.0 because TLS uses Diffie-Hellman and DSS (Data Security Standard) while SSL uses RSA (Rivest, Shamir, and Adelman). See RFC 2246 for further details.

Most web browsers have implemented SSL version 3.0 or 3.1 (TLS 1.0). Many other applications, such as SSL VPN clients, also use SSL/TLS for transmission protection.

SSL/TLS provides endpoint authentication for the client and the server, data encryption to ensure confidentiality, and data integrity/authentication to ensure data integrity. This protects traffic as it flows over public networks such as the Internet.

SSL/TLS is designed to do the following:

- Authenticate the server to the client

- Authenticate the client to the server (optional)

- Select joint cryptographic algorithms

- Generate shared secrets

- Build a protected connection (SSL/TLS tunnel) to secure TCP and UDP connections

Session and Key Management

Both the SSL and TLS protocols work in two phases:

- **Session establishment phase:** When the negotiation of parameters and peer authentication takes place.

- **Data transfer phase:** User data is exchanged securely between encapsulating endpoints.

Both phases take place inside the SSL/TLS Record Protocol.

Three subphases comprise the session establishment phase:

- In subphase 1, hello messages are exchanged to negotiate parameters including authentication and encryption algorithms.

- In subphase 2, one-way or two-way authentication between the client and server is performed. Unlike most authentication solutions where server authentication is optional, with HTTP and SSL, it is client authentication that is optional. A master key is also sent by the client using the public key of the server to start protecting the session.

- In subphase 3, the session key is calculated and the cipher suite is activated. Data integrity is provided by Hash-based Message Authentication Code (HMAC) using either Secure Hash Algorithm 1 (SHA-1) or Message Digest 5 (MD5). Confidentiality will be DES-40, DES-CBC, 3DEC-EDE, 3DES-CBC, RC4-40, or RC4-128.

Session keys are created using one of the following:

- RSA, where a shared secret is encrypted using the public key of the other peer.

- A fixed Diffie-Hellman (DH) key exchange, which uses a fixed DH value contained in a certificate.

- An ephemeral DH key exchange, which is based on the actual DH value signed with the private key of the sender. This provides the best protection because each session will have a different set of keys.

- An anonymous DH key exchange with no certificates or signatures. This should be avoided because it cannot prevent a man-in-the-middle attack because of the anonymity.

After the session keys are exchanged, SSL and TLS transmit data that is encapsulated inside an SSL- or TLS-encrypted envelope. This is the data transfer phase of the SSL/TLS protocols.

Each SSL session has a session ID that is exchanged during the authentication process. It differentiates between new and old sessions because sometimes old session IDs might be cached.

SSL can resume a session even if the TCP communication is interrupted. The client can request that the server resume an existing SSL session. The server will resume the SSL session if the server still has the session ID in its cache.

Transmission Protection

The SSL/TLS Record Protocol provides cryptographic envelopes to data being protected between the client and server. Application data is split into chunks (records) that are cryptographically protected (encrypted), and then a header and trailer are added. A series of these SSL records is then forwarded down to TCP or UDP for transmission.

Four record types are defined for signaling and secure data exchange. One record can contain up to 16,384 data bytes. The other three types are special records that exist for handshakes, signaling cipher change, and alert messages. Each record has a header, and data has an HMAC. Both the data and the HMAC are encrypted. There is also an option to compress the data portion.

Algorithm Choices in Cisco SSL Remote Access VPNs

Choosing the correct cryptographic control depends on the criticality of the data and the transport over which it is being sent. Table 20-6 provides a breakdown with recommendations.

Table 20-6   *Algorithm Choices for Cisco SSL VPNs*

Algorithm Role	Recommendations
User authentication	Static/one-time passwords or certificates
Server authentication	RSA-based (certificates)
Protocol versions	SSL 3.0, TLS 1.x
SSL/TLS session packet authentication and integrity	SHA-1 HMAC
SSL/TLS user traffic encryption	RC4, AES-128, or 3DES

It is recommended to use SSL 3.0 and TLS 1.x. Avoid version 2.0 of the SSL protocol because of known vulnerabilities in that version.

For encryption, Ron's Code 4 (RC4), Advanced Encryption Standard (AES), and Triple DES (3DES) are good choices typically trusted by the industry. AES 128-bit is preferred over the other key lengths of AES because of noncritical weaknesses in the 192-bit and 256-bit versions of AES.

For HMAC integrity and authentication, SHA-1 is recommended over MD5.

IKE Remote Access VPN Extensions

In IPsec remote access VPNs, the IKE protocol has built-in extensions for user authentication and remote system configuration. These properties are

- **IKE extended authentication (XAUTH):** XAUTH provides an additional user authentication step after IPsec peers have mutually authenticated each other. XAUTH supports user authentication using static and one-time passwords.

- **IKE mode configuration:** This allows the gateway to configure network parameters on the client. This feature can configure parameters such as assigning a client a tunnel IP address and configuring the client DNS servers, WINS servers, and split tunneling routes.

Both extensions take place after IKE peer authentication (IKE phase 1) and before IPsec policy negotiation (IKE phase 2).

Algorithm Choices in Cisco IPsec Remote Access VPNs

For IPsec remote access, use the guidelines as summarized in Table 20-7, which provides a breakdown with recommendations.

Table 20-7 *Algorithm Choices for Cisco IPsec VPNs*

Algorithm Role	Recommendations
Peer authentication	Pre-shared keys or certificates
IKE session encryption	AES-128 or 3DES
IKE session packet authentication and integrity	SHA-1 HMAC
User traffic encryption	AES-128 or 3DES
User traffic packet authentication and integrity	SHA-1 HMAC
Key exchange	Diffie-Hellman

For encryption, both AES and 3DES are good, trusted choices, with AES-128 being the preferred one.

For HMAC integrity and authentication, SHA-1 is recommended over MD5.

With asymmetric algorithms, RSA is recommended, provided that long-enough keys are used and the private key is adequately protected. Pre-shared keys can be used, but RSA is recommended.

For key exchange in IPsec, the Diffie-Hellman algorithm is trusted, provided that long-enough keys are used.

With many algorithms, the key length used directly affects the effectiveness of that algorithm. Table 20-8 provides recommended minimum key lengths for different uses.

Table 20-8 *Key Length Recommendations*

Protection Period	Symmetric Method (3DES, AES, RC4) Minimum Key Length	Symmetric Method (HMAC) Minimum Key Length	Asymmetric Method (RSA, DH) Minimum Key Length
Short-term protection for medium-size organizations or medium-term protection for small organizations (until 2012)	80	160	1248

Table 20-8   *Key Length Recommendations*

Protection Period	Symmetric Method (3DES, AES, RC4) Minimum Key Length	Symmetric Method (HMAC) Minimum Key Length	Asymmetric Method (RSA, DH) Minimum Key Length
Medium-term protection (until 2020)	96	192	1776
Medium-term protection (until 2030)	112	224	2432
Long-term protection (until 2040)	128	256	3248

Deploying Remote Access Solutions Using SSL VPNs

The Cisco IOS Software SSL VPN solution provides a choice to users by allowing either a client-based or clientless connection to a remote access VPN gateway that is implemented on a Cisco Integrated Services Router (ISR). A basic SSL VPN uses user authentication using usernames and static passwords and a single access control policy that applies to all users. This chapter describes how to configure, verify, and troubleshoot a basic client-based or clientless SSL VPN on the Cisco ISR.

Solution Components

The basic Cisco IOS Software SSL VPN solution entails remote users using either the Cisco AnyConnect VPN client or a web browser to create an SSL/TLS connection with the SSL VPN gateway running on the Cisco IOS Software–based ISR.

The basic SSL VPN uses bidirectional authentication, in which the client authenticates the ISR with a certificate-based authentication method and the ISR authenticates the user based on a username and password against its local user database. Upon successful authentication, the Cisco ISR will apply authorization and accounting rules to the user's session. After the ISR has established a secure VPN with the remote user, the user will be able to either securely transmit IP traffic into the SSL/TLS tunnel created by the AnyConnect client or use a web browser to request resources that are behind the Cisco ISR.

Deployment Tasks

The basic deployment tasks for creating a basic Cisco IOS Software SSL VPN with either the client-based or clientless solution are as follows:

Task 1: Configure the ISR with basic SSL VPN gateway features to include provisioning a certificate to enable SSL/TLS server authentication. This task is covered in detail in the section, "Configure and Verify Common SSL VPN Parameters."

Key Topic

Task 2: Configure basic user authentication by adding user accounts with passwords and creating an access policy for all remote users. This task is covered in detail in the section, "Configure and Verify Client Authentication and Policies on the SSL VPN Gateway."

Task 3: (Optional) Configure full tunneling VPN access to internal resources if the connection requires access that is like being connected to the internal network directly. This task is covered in further detail in the section, "Configure and Verify Full Tunneling Connectivity on the Cisco IOS SSL VPN Gateway."

Task 4: (Optional) Deploy the Cisco AnyConnect VPN client if full tunneling is required. This task is covered in further detail in the section, "Install and Configure the Cisco AnyConnect Client."

Task 5: (Optional) Configure clientless VPN access to internal resources if the connection only requires browser-based access. This task is covered in further detail in the section, "Configure and Verify Clientless Access on the Cisco IOS SSL VPN Gateway."

Input Parameters

Prior to implementing the basic Cisco IOS Software SSL VPN solution, you must gather and analyze several pieces of information about the network and system environments. These input parameters include the following:

■ The IP addressing plan will determine the VPN gateway addressing, and the network-naming convention will determine the name of the VPN gateway. This is needed to assign an IP address to the VPN terminating interface on the ISR and to assign an appropriate name to the VPN gateway's SSL/TLS identity certificate.

■ The corporate certificate policy and certificate settings to enroll the ISR into a Public Key Infrastructure (PKI) and include all required fields in an identity certificate that was received from the certificate authority (CA).

■ The enterprise policy for usernames and passwords to create the local user on the ISR.

■ The enterprise cryptographic policy to choose the appropriate SSL/TLS protocol versions and algorithm combinations.

■ The IP addressing plan for remote clients. This applies only when using full tunneling SSL VPNs because the ISR must assign IP addresses to remote clients.

■ Access policies that control resources that can be accessed by remote VPN users.

■ A list of remote users' client platforms to properly install the Cisco AnyConnect software images on the users' machines and the ISR.

Configure and Verify Common SSL VPN Parameters

The first deployment step for configuring a full tunnel SSL VPN is to configure basic SSL/TLS server parameters on the ISR. This includes installing a server identity certificate that the ISR will send to remote clients so that they can authenticate to the ISR, enabling the SSL/TLS server functionality on an interface, and optionally tuning the parameters to match local cryptographic policy.

By default, the ISR will create a self-signed X.509 certificate on each reboot that will cause client warnings when attempting SSL VPN access because the certificate cannot be verified because it is self-signed. This can be addressed in two ways:

■ Create a permanent self-signed certificate that is persistent across reboots. This certificate can be saved on clients and used if they access the ISR initially over a trusted network. This is usually not true and therefore not recommended.

■ Enroll the ISR into an existing PKI, with the clients authenticating the ISR identity certificate on each access by validating it using a valid CA certificate that was used to sign the ISR's identity certificate. This CA certificate would need to be provisioned on all clients for this authentication to work properly.

Configuration Tasks

Perform the following sequence to configure basic ISR SSL VPN gateway features:

Task 1: (Optional) Verify the SSL VPN license on the ISR that is intended to be used as the SSL VPN gateway.

Task 2: Provision an identity server SSL/TLS certificate to the ISR. This certificate will be used to identify the ISR to remote clients, and based on this certificate, remote clients will be able to authenticate to it.

Task 3: On the ISR, enable the SSL VPN gateway feature and configure the necessary parameters.

Task 4: Configure and optionally tune SSL/TLS settings on the ISR.

Task 5: (Optional) Configure stateless gateway high availability if gateway failover using two ISRs is required.

Configuration Choices

Some configuration choices must be made based on locally significant policies.

The first decision is whether to use self-signed or PKI-provisioned certificates. Self-signed certificates are usually only recommended for test purposes and not to be used in production because the clients can never validate the certificate. It is highly recommended to provision a certificate for a certificate authority that is trusted by the remote clients.

The second choice is whether to tune SSL/TLS settings regarding protocol modes and cryptographic algorithms. Typically, the default ISR SSL/TLS settings are adequate.

Configuration Scenario

A Cisco ISR is acting as an SSL VPN gateway and is connected to an untrustworthy external network and an internal enterprise network.

It is assumed that the ISR has already been configured with an identity certificate from a PKI trustpoint using the procedures learned in previous chapters.

Task 1: (Optional) Verify SSL VPN Licensing

Beginning with Cisco IOS Release 15.0(1)M, the SSL VPN gateway is a seat-licensed feature on the Cisco 880, Cisco 890, Cisco 1900, Cisco 2900, and Cisco 3900 platforms running the Cisco IOS Advanced Security feature set.

The first task of this sequence is to verify that the platform is properly licensed to support SSL VPN access. Use the **show webvpn license** command to see the number of licensed concurrent users. Example 20-1 shows the output from this command.

Example 20-1   *Displaying Supported SSL Licenses*

```
Router# show webvpn license



Available license count : 100
Reserved license count  : 100
In-use count : 0
```

Task 2: Provision an Identity Server SSL/TLS Certificate to the ISR

Task 2 is to provision an identity certificate by creating a PKI trustpoint in the router's configuration. This procedure can be performed by following the steps described in previous chapters.

Task 3: Enable the SSL VPN Gateway and Context

Task 3 involves creating an *SSL VPN gateway object* and an *SSL VPN context object* on the ISR. The gateway object defines the network parameters of the SSL VPN gateway server process, such as interface and the port that it will bind to and the SSL/TLS protocol parameters supported by the SSL VPN server. The SSL VPN context defines user authentication, authorization, and accounting (AAA) and configuration parameters applied to the users using the SSL VPN gateway.

As depicted in Example 20-2, first create an SSL VPN gateway object using the **webvpn gateway** command and give the gateway a name. Inside the gateway configuration, specify a local IP address configured on the router, along with the port number, using the **ip address** command to bind the SSL VPN gateway server to the IP address and port. Use the **logging enable** command to enable syslog messaging of SSL VPN–related messages. Activate the gateway using the **inservice** command.

Next, create an SSL VPN context using the **webvpn context** command and give it a name. The context defines the VPN-related properties of the SSL VPN gateway such as authentication methods and the user interface. Inside the context, associate it with the configured SSL VPN gateway using the **gateway** command and then activate the context with the **inservice** command.

Example 20-2 *Enable the SSL VPN Gateway and Context Parameters*

```
router(config)# webvpn gateway MY-GATEWAY
router (config-webvpn-gateway)#? ip address 172.16.1.1 port 443
router (config-webvpn-gateway)# ssl trustpoint MY-TRUSTPOINT
router (config-webvpn-gateway)# logging enable
router (config-webvpn-gateway)# inservice
!
```

Task 4: Configure and Tune SSL/TLS Settings

Task 4 involves creating and tuning SSL/TLS protocol settings of the SSL VPN gateway inside its webvpn gateway object. Specify the PKI trustpoint that will provide the SSL VPN server with an identity certificate. Optionally, enable specific SSL/TLS algorithm bundles (cipher suites) to be active on the gateway.

Enter SSL VPN gateway object configuration mode using the **webvpn gateway** command and use the **ssl trustpoint** command to specify a local named trustpoint to the SSL VPN gateway. In this mode also, optionally configure specific cipher suites using the **ssl encryption** command. See Example 20-3 for the configuration command usage.

Example 20-3 *Configure and Tune SSL/TLS Settings*

```
router (config)# webvpn gateway MY-GATEWAY
router (config-webvpn-gateway)# ssl trustpoint MY-TRUSTPOINT
router (config-webvpn-gateway)# ssl encryption 3des-sha1 aes-sha1
```

Task 5: (Optional) Configure Gateway High Availability

Task 5 is an optional task for integrating the SSL VPN server with the Cisco IOS Software Hot Standby Router Protocol (HSRP) feature to yield stateless redundancy using two ISR devices. HSRP will fail over to the other peer in the HSRP group if an interface fails. HSRP can also track interfaces in the router to trigger a switchover. Example 20-4 shows what the commands should look like.

Example 20-4 *Configure Gateway High Availability*

```
router (config)# interface GigabitEthernet0/0
router (config-if)# standby 1 ip 172.16.1.1
router (config-if)# standby 1 name SSLVPN-HSRP
router (config)# webvpn gateway MY-GATEWAY
router (config-webvpn-gateway)#  ip address 172.16.1.1 port 443 standby SSLVPN-HSRP
```

Gateway Verification

Use the **show webvpn gateway** command to confirm successful configuration of the gateway. The output should show the gateway in an up/up state, as shown in Example 20-5. The administrative status of the gateway will always be up or down. This status is configured with the **inservice** command. The operational status will always be up or down as well. This status is only in the up state if the gateway is in service and configured with a valid IP address.

Navigating to the URL of the SSL VPN gateway should present a default SSL VPN portal login page. If the identity certificate has been configured properly, there should be no certificate warnings.

Example 20-5 show webvpn gateway *Command Output*

```
router# show webvpn gateway


Gateway Name    Admin    Operation
------------    -----    ---------
MY-GATEWAY      up       up
```

Implementation Guidelines

Consider the following implementation guidelines when configuring Cisco IOS Software SSL VPN gateway features:

Key Topic

- Self-signed certificates should not be used if they can be avoided. In cases where the clients initially access the ISR over a trusted network, they can be considered, but it is generally not recommended to use them.

- Ensure that the name on the gateway is configured correctly in the identity certificate to avoid certificate issues.

Configure and Verify Client Authentication and Policies on the SSL VPN Gateway

When client-based or clientless users that authenticate with passwords connect to the ISR gateway, the ISR will initially assign them to the configured SSL VPN context attached to the gateway (MY-CONTEXT context that was configured in the previous topic). This context will define a default policy (MY-POLICY) that will be assigned to all users connecting to the gateway and will enforce a common set of clientless and client-based access settings to authenticate, authorize, and enable accounting for all RA VPN sessions.

Gateway, Contexts, and Policy Groups

Figure 20-1 shows the interaction between the SSL VPN gateway, context, and policy group objects. The gateway defines the basic network and cryptographic settings of the SSL VPN server used by the SSL VPN gateway. The SSL VPN context defines common building blocks used in user policies and the authentication methods used to authenticate remote users. Policy groups define sets of configuration and AAA settings that are applied to users. One policy group is dedicated as the default policy group for a context.

Basic User Authentication Overview

The simplest form of user authentication is to use the router's local user database and static passwords. The SSL VPN gateway can also use a remote AAA authentication method such as a RADIUS or TACACS+ server, client certificate-based authentication, or a combination of client certificates and local or remote passwords.

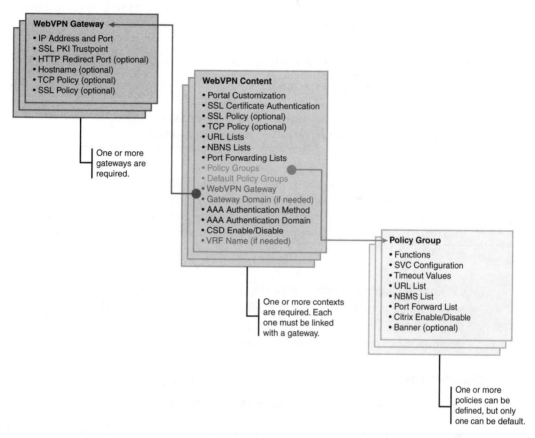

Figure 20-1   *Gateway, Contexts, and Policy Groups*

Configuration Tasks

Perform the following configuration sequence to configure basic authentication and a common policy for all users on the Cisco IOS Software SSL VPN gateway:

Task 1: Create a default policy and apply it to a context.

Task 2: Add users and their passwords to the ISR local user database and enable AAA authentication in the SSL VPN context.

Configuration Scenario

On the ISR, inside the MY-CONTEXT SSL VPN context, a new policy named MY-POLICY will be configured, and it will be assigned as the default policy for the context. Additionally, a new user named vpnuser with a static password and limited privileges will be created.

Task 1: Create and Apply a Default Policy

Task 1 is to enter SSL VPN context configuration mode by issuing the **webvpn context** command and creating a new policy named MY-POLICY using the **policy group** command. The new policy will also be made the default policy for the SSL VPN context by issuing the **default-group-policy** command. Example 20-6 shows this configuration.

Example 20-6   *Create and Apply a Default Policy*

```
router(config)# webvpn context MY-CONTEXT
router(config-webvpn-context)# policy group MY-POLICY
router(config-webvpn-context)# banner "Welcome to SSL VPN"
router(config-webvpn-context)# default-group-policy MY-POLICY
```

Given that there can be only one default policy group, a way to dynamically assign a user to any group policy is needed. RADIUS attributes can be used for this purpose. During authentication, the RADIUS server can push down the webvpn:user-vpn-group attribute. This Cisco AV-pair can designate the policy group to which the authenticating user will be assigned.

Task 2: Enable User Authentication Using Local AAA

In Task 2, a local AAA authentication method will be configured. In addition, as shown in Example 20-7, a local user account will be created, and the new AAA authentication method will be applied to the SSL VPN context.

Example 20-7   *Enable User Authentication Using Local AAA*

```
router(config)# aaa authentication login LOCAL-AUTHEN local
!
router(config)# username vpnuser privilege 0 secret 5
$25$05ikadSDAjaksfdjDw32PDij34214$4213
!
router(config)# webvpn context MY-CONTEXT
router(config-webvpn-context)# aaa authentication list LOCAL-AUTHEN
```

Implementation Guidelines

Consider the following implementation guidelines when implementing basic user authentication and common policy in an SSL VPN solution:

- Only use static passwords in small, single-device, low-risk environments.

- In a multidevice environment, migrate to a centralized AAA server.

- For stronger authentication, consider using certificates or one-time passwords.

- Ensure that the privileges (authorization) of local VPN user accounts are limited.

Configure and Verify Full Tunneling Connectivity on the Cisco IOS SSL VPN Gateway

Today's business trends toward saving costs and doing more with less are causing the use of remote connectivity to grow. Deploying full tunneling capability on the SSL VPN gateway provides a method of connectivity for your remote users that closely mimics working from the office.

Configuration Tasks

To configure basic AnyConnect full tunnel access using the Cisco IOS Software SSL VPN gateway, perform the following tasks:

Task 1: Enable full tunnel access in the SSL VPN policy group.

Task 2: Configure an IP address pool and assign the configured address pool to the SSL VPN policy group.

Task 3: (Optional) Configure client configuration parameters and assign them to the SSL VPN policy group.

Task 4: (Optional) Configure split tunneling to allow remote clients to directly access networks not located beyond the ISR VPN gateway and assign it to the SSL VPN policy group.

Task 5: (Optional) Configure an access control list (ACL) to implement access control to internal resources.

Configuration Scenario

Figure 20-2 depicts the network for this configuration scenario. The ISR will use an IP address from the 192.168.1.0/24 network for client IP addresses. Split tunneling will be allowed to access only the 10.0.0.0/8 network through the SSL VPN tunnel. Clients will be configured with an internal Domain Name System (DNS) server for host name resolution, and split DNS will be configured to forward queries for mydomain.com to the internal DNS server.

An ACL will allow only DNS resolution to the internal DNS server and HTTP access to an internal web server at 10.10.1.1. Assumptions are that the basic SSL VPN gateway settings for the SSL VPN gateway and contexts are previously configured on the Cisco ISR.

Task 1: Enable Full Tunneling Access

Task 1 in this configuration sequence involves downloading the Cisco AnyConnect client from Cisco.com and transferring it to the ISR flash memory. Transfer the Cisco AnyConnect software image to the ISR for all client operating systems that are required.

On the ISR, use the **webvpn install svc** command, as shown in Example 20-8, to install the image into the SSL VPN gateway, which will allow the gateway to install this image to users that connect through the SSL VPN portal.

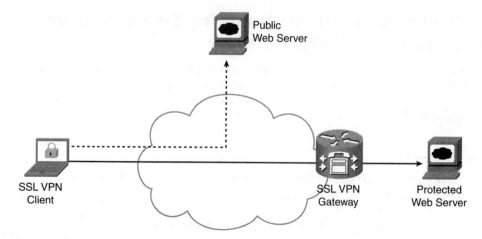

Figure 20-2 *Full Tunneling Scenario*

Example 20-8 *Enable Full Tunneling Access*

```
router(config)# webvpn install svc flash://anyconnect-win-2.4.0202-k9.bin
SSLVPN Package SSL-VPN-Client (seq:1): installed successfully
!
router(config)# webvpn context MY-CONTEXT
router(config-webvpn-context)# policy group MY-POLICY
router(config-vpn-policy)# functions svc-enabled
router(config-vpn-policy)# svc keep-client-installed
```

Next, enter the default policy group and enable full tunneling with the **functions svc-enabled** command and ensure that the gateway will not uninstall the AnyConnect client from the remote user's computer by issuing the **keep-client-installed** command.

Task 2: Configure Local IP Address Assignment

When clients connect with the full tunnel mode, the ISR assigns them an IP address that will be used by the clients to source their traffic. Private addresses can be used, but they must be able to be routed properly by the gateway in the internal network so that internal users know how to respond to them.

For Task 2, Example 20-9 shows the pool of IP addresses being created with the **ip local pool** command and then being configured as part of the default policy group with the **svc address-pool** command.

Example 20-9 *Configure and Assign Local IP Address*

```
router(config)# ip local pool MY-POOL 192.168.1.2 192.168.1.150
router(config)# webvpn context MY-CONTEXT
router(config-webvpn-context)#policy group MY-POLICY
router(config-vpn-policy)#svc address-pool MY-POOL
```

Task 3: (Optional) Configure Client Configuration

Task 3 involves configuring the ISR to push optional network configuration items such as the domain suffix and the IP address of internal DNS servers to the remote users.

Example 20-10 displays the configuration necessary to specify the domain suffix by using the **svc default-domain** command. The first DNS server that remote clients will use can be pushed to them using the **svc dns-server primary** command. An additional DNS server can also be pushed using the **svc dns-server secondary** command.

Example 20-10   *(Optional) Configure Client Configuration*

```
Router(config)# webvpn context MY-CONTEXT
Router(config-webvpn-context)# policy group MY-POLICY
Router(config-vpn-policy)# svc default-domain mydomain.com
Router(config-vpn-policy)# svc dns-server primary 10.1.1.1
```

Task 4: (Optional) Configure Split Tunneling

Task 4 involves configuring split tunneling to allow direct access to certain networks without using the VPN tunnel (bypassing it). This does increase risk by allowing remote users to have access to internal resources and other untrusted networks at the same time. Additional security controls should be considered if using this option.

Example 20-11 displays how to configure split DNS using the **svc split include** command. To have remote users use their non-VPN DNS servers to provide name resolution for the alternate non-VPN network, use the **svc split dns** command.

Example 20-11   *(Optional) Configure Split Tunneling*

```
Router(config)# webvpn context MY-CONTEXT
Router(config-webvpn-context)# policy group MY-POLICY
Router(config-vpn-policy)# svc split dns mydomain.com
Router(config-vpn-policy)# svc split include 10.0.0.0 255.0.0.0
```

Task 5: (Optional) Configure Access Control

The fifth task is to optionally configure an ACL that restricts remote users access to internal resources. Example 20-12 shows an ACL that permits access to UDP port 53 for access to a DNS server at 10.1.1.1 and TCP port 80 for access to HTTP services on the same server. This task is accomplished by first configuring a Cisco IOS Software stateless ACL and then applying it to the policy group using the **filter tunnel** command.

Example 20-12   *(Optional) Configure Split Tunneling*

```
Router(config)# ip access-list extended MY-ACL
Router(config-ext-acl)# permit udp any host 10.1.1.1 eq domain
Router(config-ext-acl)# permit tcp any host 10.1.1.1 eq www
!
```

```
Router(config)# webvpn context MY-CONTEXT
Router(config-webvpn-context)# policy group MY-POLICY
Router(config-vpn-policy)# filter tunnel MY-ACL
```

Cisco Configuration Professional Support

Cisco Configuration Professional 2.4 can be used to initially configure and tune the SSL VPN gateway on Cisco ISR devices. There is a configuration wizard or manual mode option that can be used for the configuration requirements. Navigate to **Configure > Security > VPN > SSL VPN > SSL VPN Manager** to begin the configuration steps.

Note: Documentation for Cisco Configuration Professional can be found at www.cisco.com/en/US/docs/net_mgmt/cisco_configuration_professional/v2_4/olh/ccp.pdf.

Install and Configure the Cisco AnyConnect Client

The Cisco AnyConnect SSL VPN client provides users with secure VPN connections to either the Cisco ISR SSL VPN gateway or the Cisco ASA 5500 Series Adaptive Security Appliances.

Network administrators must configure the AnyConnect client features on the ISR. After this is complete, the client software must be loaded on the ISR so that it will be automatically downloaded to remote users when they log in, or it can be manually installed as an application on the remote users' systems. The client has support for user profiles that are displayed in the user interface. The network administrator can assign features that are specific to individual users or groups through these profiles.

Note: The Cisco AnyConnect client requires administrative privileges for the initial installation.

The AnyConnect SSL VPN client packages must be downloaded from Cisco.com and uploaded to the Cisco ISR so that it can be downloaded in an on-demand fashion by clients from the SSL VPN portal.

The web launch installation method requires that the client connect to the ISR with a compliant web browser using HTTPS. The user must log on and successfully authenticate, and the ISR will redirect the user to the SSL VPN client through an ActiveX or Java applet. After the AnyConnect SSL VPN client has been successfully installed, the ISR will automatically log the user on to the network using the credentials provided during the original clientless connection.

The manual installation process involves obtaining the installer package (MSI for Windows) and installing the Cisco AnyConnect SSL VPN client. The configuration sequence in this topic covers this method of installation.

AnyConnect 2.4–Supported Platforms

The Cisco AnyConnect SSL VPN client supports the following operating systems:

■   Microsoft Windows 7, Windows Vista, and Windows XP

■   Apple Mac OS X (version 10.5 or later) on either Intel or PowerPC architectures

■   Red Hat Linux (version 9 or later)

■   Ubuntu 9 or later

See the Release Notes at Cisco.com for more information about full requirements and supported versions.

Configuration Tasks

To install and configure the AnyConnect client in a basic AnyConnect full tunnel implementation, perform the following tasks:

Task 1: Install the AnyConnect client.

Task 2: Verify that the client has valid root CA certificates installed. Each client should have a local, authentic copy of the root CA certificate that was used to issue the ISR identity certificate.

Task 3: Configure basic AnyConnect profile settings (fully qualified domain name [FQDN] of the ISR).

Task 4: Establish the SSL VPN full tunnel connection.

Configuration Scenario

The AnyConnect client will be installed and configured on Microsoft Windows XP, and the ISR will use an identity certificate issued by a global PKI. The name vpn.mydomain.com will resolve to the IP address of the untrusted ISR interface. This name will also be the canonical name of the ISR in the identity certificate.

Task 1: Enable Full Tunneling Access

The first task is to install the predeployed version of the AnyConnect client. Perform the following steps on the client:

Step 1.   Obtain the MSI installation package from Cisco.com and transfer it to the client system.

Step 2.   Double-click the MSI installation package to start the installation process.

Step 3.   Click Next to start the installation dialog process.

Step 4.   Examine the license agreement, select the I Accept the Terms of the License Agreement check box, and click Next.

Step 5.   Click Install to start the installation process.

Step 6.   Click Finish to close the installer.

Task 2: Verify Server Certificate Authentication Chain

On the client, look at the installed root CA certificates to make sure that the CA that issued the ISR identity certificate is in the list. This keeps the client from issuing certificate warnings when it attempts to create an SSL VPN connection.

Task 3: Configure Basic AnyConnect Profile Settings

Task 3 involves configuring profile settings on the client. Start the AnyConnect client and configure it with the ISR SSL VPN gateway information. Enter the FQDN, vpn.mydomain.com, in the Connect To field. This name must match exactly what is in the canonical name (CN) field on the ISR's identity certificate to avoid certificate warnings. Click Select to make the client connect to the ISR.

Task 4: Establish the SSL VPN Connection

After the connection is established, the ISR pushes instructions for the next step of establishing the connection. After being prompted for user authentication, enter the login credentials and click Connect.

Note: Alternatively, the WebLaunch feature can be used to start the VPN connection using a browser. If clientless SSL VPN is not enabled on the ISR untrusted interface, the ISR automatically starts the AnyConnect client after the user logs in to the main page. This is an alternative to Tasks 3 and 4.

Client-Side Verification

The AnyConnect SSL VPN client GUI will automatically minimize after a successful connection establishment. Click the AnyConnect icon in the Windows system tray to restore the GUI. In the Statistics pane, observe the state of the connection, the client's assigned IP address, the bytes sent and received, and the connection time. More detailed features can be displayed by clicking the Route Details tab, as illustrated in Figure 20-3.

Figure 20-3 *Cisco AnyConnect Route Details Tab*

To verify split tunneling and routing on the client, navigate to the Route Details tab of the Details window.

The network that is displayed in the Secured Routes pane shows the network segments that are being protected by the client. For example, a network of 130.39.0/16 in the Secured Routes pane indicates that this client traffic is being sent through the tunnel, while all other traffic would bypass the VPN client altogether.

Gateway-Side Verification

On the ISR, use the **show webvpn session context** command to see the list of connected clients. The **show webvpn session user** command can also be used to show detailed information about a particular user's VPN session. Example 20-13 demonstrates some sample output from both commands.

Example 20-13 *Verifying Operation on the SSL VPN Gateway*

```
Router# show webvpn session context SSL VPN



WebVPN context name: SSL VPN
Client_Login_Name  Client_IP_Address  No_of_Connections  Created   Last_Used
user1                  10.2.1.220                2         04:47:16  00:01:26
user2                  10.2.1.221                2         04:48:36  00:01:56


Router# show webvpn session user user1 context all

WebVPN user name = user1 ; IP address = 10.2.1.220; context = SSL VPN
     No of connections: 0
     Created 00:00:19, Last-used 00:00:18
     CSD enabled
     CSD Session Policy
        CSD Web Browsing Allowed
        CSD Port Forwarding Allowed
        CSD Full Tunneling Disabled
        CSD FILE Access Allowed
     User Policy Parameters
        Group name = ONE
     Group Policy Parameters
        url list name = "Cisco"
        idle timeout = 2100 sec
        session timeout = 43200 sec
        port forward name = "EMAIL"
        tunnel mode = disabled
        citrix disabled
        dpd client timeout = 300 sec
        dpd gateway timeout = 300 sec
```

```
keep stc installed = disabled
rekey interval = 3600 sec
rekey method = ssl
lease duration = 3600 sec
```

Cisco Configuration Professional

Navigate to the **Monitor > Security > VPN Status > SSL VPN (All Contexts)** pane to verify the client connections on the ISR. CCP provides aggregate monitoring statistics as well as individual user session monitoring.

Configure and Verify Clientless Access on the Cisco IOS SSL VPN Gateway

In situations in which your remote users do not require full connectivity or your security policy does not permit it, you can configure clientless access on the SSL VPN gateway and give them access to a smaller list of applications. The following sections cover configuring clientless access on the Cisco IOS SSL VPN gateway.

Basic Portal Features

Users can access internal resources by using a web browser with the ISR performing as a proxy to provide internal content on its SSL VPN portal. This type of connection is referred to as the clientless SSL VPN. Figure 20-4 shows the Bookmarks pane in which links to internal resources can be found. The Application Access pane displays a link to a Thin Client Application.

Figure 20-4   *SSL VPN Web Portal*

The portal will provide a free URL field in which users can enter a URL manually as well. By default, the Cisco ISR SSL VPN web portal does not restrict users and allows authenticated users to access all internal resources. Basic portal tuning can be configured so that the portal appearance is altered to either enable or disable some of the user's interface functionality.

Cisco Secure Desktop for Clientless Access

Cisco Secure Desktop (CSD) was developed to minimize the risk posed by allowing access to internal resources by remote devices using either the Cisco Clientless SSL VPN or the Cisco AnyConnect Client.

Prior to permitting a Cisco clientless or client-based connection, the remote machine will scan for a large set of antivirus and antispyware applications, firewalls, operating systems, and process names.

It also scans for any registry entries, filenames, and process names, collectively called the basic host scan. With an Advanced Endpoint Assessment License, Cisco Secure Desktop can use optional criteria as conditions for granting rights.

Inspections performed by the Cisco Secure Desktop inspectors can detect antivirus, personal firewall, and antispyware software and learn the version, product, and revision information about them to make policy decisions on the WebVPN gateway. The CSD inspectors will gather the "defined" information on the endpoint and send it to the WebVPN gateway. The gateway uses the user's login credentials, the computer scan results, and profile matching to assign a Dynamic Access Policy (DAP).

Cisco Secure Desktop encrypts data and files associated with, or downloaded during, the SSL VPN session. The session information is stored in the secure vault desktop partition.

When the session closes, Cisco Secure Desktop tries to minimize the risk posed by having information remaining on a client after a Cisco clientless SSL VPN or a Cisco AnyConnect session terminates. The goal is to reduce the possibility that cookies, browser history, temporary files, and downloaded content will remain on a system after a remote user logs out or an SSL VPN session times out. CSD overwrites and attempts to remove session data by using a U.S. Department of Defense (DoD) sanitation algorithm to provide endpoint security protection.

Port Forwarding Overview

The default web portal permits users to access web (HTTP or HTTPS) or file (CIFS) resources that are behind the gateway by translating the resources into the user's browser. To enable the use of native applications such as email clients or terminal programs over the clientless SSL VPN connection, the gateway implementation supports a feature called port forwarding.

Port forwarding uses a Java helper applet that is downloaded to remote users to provide access to certain applications that are not supported by the clientless SSL VPN by default. The Java helper needs the application to make a connection to the local host to provide port-forwarding functionality. This requires some modification of application settings:

Step 1.   After logging in to the SSL VPN portal, the Java applet that is downloaded from the SSL VPN portal dynamically modifies the local host's file. The Java applet then listens on the remote host's loopback address at port 3001 and forwards any incoming connections over the SSL VPN session.

Step 2.   The user opens a Telnet client and attempts to connect to an internal server on port 3001.

Step 3. The local host's file will be analyzed by the applet. It has an entry for the internal server that points to the loopback address (127.0.0.1) of the remote client. The Telnet client connects to the local host on port 3001, and the Java applet forwards this connection to the SSL VPN gateway through the tunnel.

Step 4. The gateway extracts the TCP session from the SSL VPN session, establishes a TCP connection with the internal target host on the standard Telnet port, and acts as a data relay between the two TCP sessions.

Port Forwarding Benefits and Limitations

The benefit of using the port forwarding feature is that it supports the use of fully featured, native applications that already exist on the remote machine.

The limitations of using the port forwarding feature are as follows:

- Port forwarding supports only simple, static-port TCP applications.

- Port forwarding requires preinstalled native applications on the remote systems.

- Users must change application settings such as the destination port of the server.

- Port forwarding requires administrative privileges because it changes the local host's file.

As you can see, port forwarding is appropriate for only limited access to applications. It is not appropriate for full access to the remote site. To access more applications at the remote end, you should consider using the full tunnel connection.

Portal ACLs

Normal access controls, such as the ISR interface ACL or the Zone-Based Policy Firewall access control model, are not used by the ISR clientless SSL VPN feature. Instead, it provides its own access control through the use of web-type ACLs. These ACLs are applied on a per-user or per-group basis and permit or deny access to URLs that are reachable through the SSL VPN portal. URL patterns can be used to specify allowed or denied URLs or even use multiple rules inside a web-type ACL. They use the same logic as a classic Cisco IOS Software ACL in that the first rule matched dictates the action, and there is an implicit deny all statement at the end of the ACL.

Note: Enabling or disabling portal features such as the free URL entry does not prevent a user from accessing particular internal resources. It only removes the user interface option. If a user enters a properly constructed URL into the browser address field, he can still access the resource behind the URL if properly authenticated. Web-type ACLs must be used to control access to internal resources with any reliability.

Configuration Tasks

To configure basic clientless access to a Cisco IOS Software SSL VPN gateway (ISR), perform the following tasks:

Key Topic

Task 1: Configure the SSL VPN portal features that are to be available to remote clientless users.

Task 2: (Optional) Configure port forwarding to allow native application access over the clientless session.

Task 3: (Optional) Configure the Cisco Secure Desktop to mitigate the risk associated with sensitive data being left on remote systems.

Task 4: (Optional) Configure web-type ACLs to limit access to internal resources.

Configuration Scenario

Figure 20-5 illustrates the scenario for the following configuration sequence. Remote users can only access a single web server at http://intranet.mydomain.com in the protected network and a file server share at cifs://W2K3S/share. Predefined bookmarks to access the web server home page and the file share name "share" will be created. To browse the W2K3S server and the rest of the Windows domain, the ISR will also be configured to query an internal WINS server at 172.16.1.137 for CIFS host name resolution.

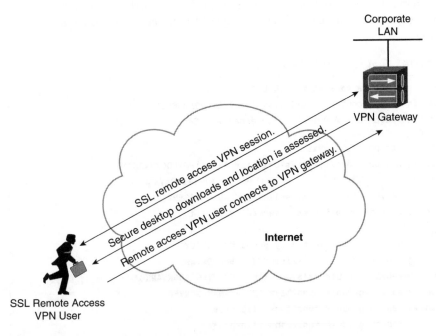

Figure 20-5 *Cisco Secure Desktop Operational Sequence*

The ISR will also be configured to download and enable the Java port-forwarding applet to the client. The client will listen on the local host's loopback on TCP 3001 and forward incoming connections to the internal terminal server 10.10.1.1.

The last configuration task is to load and enable the Cisco Secure Desktop on the Cisco ISR and use CSD to provide a protected environment from within which remote users can access internal resources.

Task 1: Enable Full Tunneling Access

The first task is to configure the SSL VPN portal features that are available to the remote clientless users.

Note: By default, the SSL VPN portal allows access to all features to be used but does not provide any bookmarks or predefined port-forwarding links to assist users.

First, configure an optional web bookmark list that defines an internal web server for users of a policy group. In the SSL VPN context object, use the **url-list** command to define new bookmarks, and then, inside the web bookmark's configuration mode, use the **url-text** and **url-value** commands to add one or more bookmarks. When you are done adding bookmarks, enter the policy group configuration mode and assign the web bookmarks list to the policy group using the **url-list** command.

Continue by adding optional CIFS bookmarks in the same fashion. Use the **cifs-url-list** command to define new bookmarks and then assign them using the **cifs-url-list** policy group configuration command. Examine Example 20-14 to see the commands for this first task.

Example 20-14 *Configure Split Tunneling*

```
router(config)# webvpn context MY-CONTEXT
router(config-webvpn-context)# url-list "MY-WEB-BOOKMARKS"
router(config-webvpn-url)# url-text "Internal Web Server" url-value
http://intranet.mydomain.com
router(config-webvpn-url)# exit
router(config-webvpn-context)# cifs-url-list "MY-CIFS-BOOKMARKS"
 url-text "Internal File Server" url-value "cifs://w2k3s/share"
router(config-webvpn-context)# nbns-list "MY-AD-NAMESERVERS"
router(config-webvpn-context)# nbns-server 10.10.1.1
!
router(config-webvpn-context)# policy-group MY-POLICY
router(config-webvpn-group)# url-list "MY-WEB-BOOKMARKS"
router(config-webvpn-group)# cifs-url-list "MY-CIFS-BOOKMARKS"
router(config-webvpn-group)# nbns-list "MY-AD-NAMESERVERS"
router(config-webvpn-group)# functions file-access
router(config-webvpn-group)# functions file-browse
router(config-webvpn-group)# functions file-entry
```

Task 2: (Optional) Configure Port Forwarding

Task 2 involves configuring an optional port-forwarding list of applications that are available to the remote clientless user through port forwarding.

Use the **port-forward** context object command to create a named list of ports to be forwarded by the Java applet. As shown in Example 20-15, inside the port forward object's configuration mode, use the **local-port** command to specify the local port on which the Java applet will listen, the **remote-server** and **remote-port** commands to enter the server to which the connection is to be relayed, and the *description* argument to provide a friendly name for remote users.

To apply this port-forwarding rule, enter the policy group configuration mode and assign the port-forwarding list using the **port-forward** command.

There can be multiple port forward rules in a port forward object, and you can also assign the same list to multiple policy groups, if required.

Example 20-15 *(Optional) Configure Port Forwarding*

```
router(config)# webvpn context MY-CONTEXT
router(config-webvpn-context)# port-forward "MY-PORT-FORWARD"
router(config-webvpn-port-fwd)# local-port 3001 remote-server "10.10.1.1" remote-
port 3389 description "Terminal Services"
router(config-webvpn-port-fwd)# exit

router(config-webvpn-context)# policy-group MY-POLICY
router(config-webvpn-group)# port-forward "MY-PORT-FORWARD" auto-download
```

Task 3: (Optional) Configure Cisco Secure Desktop

In Task 3, Cisco Secure Desktop is deployed to remote users if required. First, the Cisco Secure Desktop software must be downloaded from Cisco.com and then transferred to the ISR flash memory. On the Cisco ISR, use the **webvpn install csd** command to install the image into the SSL VPN gateway, which will enable the gateway to push the package to clientless remote users. See Example 20-16 for the correct commands.

To enable CSD for remote clientless users, use the **csd enable** command inside the SSL VPN context object. This applies to all clientless users regardless of their policy group.

Example 20-16 *(Optional) Configure Cisco Secure Desktop*

```
Router(config)# webvpn install csd flash://csd_3.5.841-k9.pkg
SSLVPN Package Cisco-Secure-Desktop : installed successfully

Router(config)# webvpn context MY-CONTEXT
Router(config-context)#csd enable
```

By default, CSD is not configured with any default policies, and there must be at least one Cisco Secure Desktop "location" and an associated policy in which to enable Cisco Secure Desktop features. Configure CSD by connecting to the ISR with a browser using HTTPS and requesting the csd_admin.html page. Authenticate to the page using the username "admin" and the enable secret of your ISR as the password.

Task 4: (Optional) Configure Access Control

Task 4 involves configuring optional access control to be applied to clientless users. Because clientless remote access users operate in a proxy-based mode or port forwarding, their access is not affected by traditional Cisco IOS Software ACLs or other rules or zones applied to interfaces. The SSL VPN uses web-type ACLs to control access for clientless users.

First, configure a named ACL in the SSL VPN context object that permits or denies access to particular URLs for portal-based access, and configure access to IP or TCP services for port-forwarding services. You cannot specify destination ports for port forwarding, but ports are already specified as part of the port-forwarding list. When this is done, apply the web-type ACL to the policy group with the **acl** command. Complete these commands as shown in Example 20-17.

Example 20-17 *(Optional) Configure Access Control*

```
router(config)# webvpn context MY-CONTEXT
router(config-webvpn-context)# acl "MY-PORTAL-ACL"
router(config-webvpn-acl)# permit url http://intranet.mydomain.com
router(config-webvpn-acl)# permit url "cifs://w2k3s/share"
router(config-webvpn-acl)# permit tcp any 10.10.1.1 255.255.255.255
router(config-webvpn-acl)# exit
!
router(config-webvpn-context)# policy-group MY-POLICY
router(config-webvpn-group)# acl "MY-PORTAL-ACL"
```

Basic Portal Verification

Portal feature configuration verification is achieved by successfully creating an SSL VPN session and logging in to the portal. Successfully accessing resources defined in the predefined bookmarks is an indication that the portal is configured correctly.

Web Application Access

The browser will display a floating toolbar with application-specific navigation icons that are to be used to return to the home page, open a URL over the clientless SSL VPN session, create user-specific bookmarks, move the toolbar to the other side of the window, or close the SSL VPN session.

File Server Access

To verify that access to file shares is working, browse to an internal resource using a browser interface, click a CIFS bookmark, or enter a URL in the free URL entry box.

Port Forwarding Access

To confirm the port-forwarding operation, log on to the SSL VPN portal and click the appropriate link that will cause the Java applet to forward a connection to the SSL VPN gateway. Most browsers require authentication to successfully connect.

Cisco Secure Desktop Verification

The Cisco Secure Desktop functionality can by tested by visiting the SSL VPN portal URL. The Cisco Secure Desktop applet should download and then analyze the remote user's computer. If CSD is configured to provide a secure desktop, the secure desktop should launch and a browser will open inside it.

Gateway-Side Verification

Confirmation of configuration can also be attained on the Cisco ISR by using the **show webvpn session context** command to see the list of connected remote clients. The **show webvpn session user** command will provide detailed information such as the configured portal features and user interface elements, such as bookmarks.

Troubleshoot the Basic SSL VPN Operation

Troubleshooting basic SSL VPN configuration includes performing troubleshooting actions on the SSL VPN gateway and on the client. The following sections cover the process of troubleshooting SSL VPN connectivity.

Port Forwarding Access

Troubleshooting SSL VPN session establishment can possibly call for troubleshooting on the client and on the ISR. First, discover and alleviate any connectivity issues using commands such as **ping** and **traceroute**, and use tools such as **nslookup** and **dig** to verify successful name resolution.

Troubleshooting Flow (VPN Establishment)

When having problems successfully establishing a VPN session, follow these steps to troubleshoot:

Step 1. Verify that the SSL session initially succeeds and that no negotiation problems exist. The **debug ssl openssl errors** command will show issues such as incompatible protocol versions or cipher suites.

Step 2. Make sure that there are no user authentication issues. Use the **debug aaa authentication** command to verify user authentication.

Step 3. Check to see whether the policy group allows SSL VPN tunnels by looking at the policy group configuration for the **function svc-enabled** command.

Step 4. Verify that the ISR is able to assign an IP address to the client. The **debug webvpn tunnel** command can assist with this.

Troubleshooting Flow (Data Flow)

When having problems connecting to resources over the tunnel, after the SSL VPN session establishes, use the following suggestions to troubleshoot:

Step 1. Verify that the correct routes are being protected (routed into the tunnel).

Step 2. Verify that the ISR is not denying traffic from the VPN tunnel. Check syslog messages on the Cisco ISR to look for these denies.

Step 3. Verify that the protected network has a route to the client-assigned IP addresses by looking at the routing tables of internal routers. Verify SSL VPN tunnels by looking at the policy group configuration for the **function svc-enabled** command.

Gateway-Side Issue

To troubleshoot on the Cisco ISR side, the **debug ssl openssl errors** and the **debug web-vpn tunnel** commands will show items such as incompatible cipher suites or failed address assignments because of missing local IP pools on the router.

Client-Side Issues: Certificates

One of the most common issues on the client are the certificate warning messages that are received during the VPN establishment. Three main reasons exist for this:

- If the ISR identity certificate cannot be verified because of a missing CA certificate on the client, install an authentic copy of the CA certificate to the client.

- A name mismatch between the name specified in the AnyConnect profile (the Connect To field) or the browser URL and the canonical name (CN) field in the ISR identity certificate. Fix these values so that they match to resolve this issue.

- An expired ISR identity certificate. Renew the identity certificate.

These types of issues should never occur in a production network. If users get accustomed to "accepting" invalid certificates upon receiving the warning messages, the VPN connection will be susceptible to man-in-the-middle attacks.

Exam Preparation

As mentioned in the section, "How to Use This Book," in the Introduction, you have several choices for exam preparation: the exercises here, the memory tables in Appendix C, the final exam preparation chapter, and the exam simulation questions on the CD-ROM. The following questions present a bigger challenge than the exam itself because they use an open-ended question format. By using this more difficult format, you exercise your memory better and prove your conceptual and factual knowledge of this chapter. You can find the answers to these questions in Appendix A, "Answers to the DIKTA Quizzes and Fill in the Blanks Questions."

Review All Key Topics

Review the most important topics in the chapter, noted with the Key Topics icon in the margin of the page. Table 20-9 lists a reference of these key topics and the page numbers on which each is found.

Table 20-9   *Key Topics*

Key Topic Element	Description	Page
Table 20-6	SSL VPN algorithm choices	539
Table 20-7	IPsec VPN algorithm choices	540
Table 20-8	Cryptographic key length recommendations	540
List	SSL VPN deployment tasks	541
List	SSL VPN parameter configuration tasks	543
List	Configuring basic ISR SSL VPN gateway features	546
List	Configuring basic authentication on the SSL VPN gateway	547
List	Implementing basic user authentication and common policy in an SSL VPN solution	548
List	Configuration tasks for configuring full tunneling	549
List	AnyConnect client configuration tasks	553
List	Clientless access configuration tasks	558
List	Troubleshooting VPN establishment	563
List	Troubleshooting VPN data flow	563

Complete Tables and Lists from Memory

Print a copy of Appendix C, "Memory Tables" (found on the CD), or at least the section for this chapter, and complete the tables and lists from memory. Appendix D, "Memory Table Answers," also on the CD, includes completed tables and lists to check your work.

Define Key Terms

Define the following key terms from this chapter, and check your answers in the Glossary:

full tunneling VPNs, Transport Layer Security (TLS), Secure Socket Layer (SSL), port forwarding, client-based remote user, clientless remote user

Fill in the Blanks

1. The ISR uses the identity certificate to _____ itself to remote clients.
2. _____ can increase the risk to remote clients and internal resources because the clients can potentially act as a relay between untrusted and trusted networks.
3. When terminating a clientless VPN, the ISR acts as a _____ to provide access to internal resources to remote users.
4. _____ VPNs require VPN client software to be installed on the remote computer or dedicated VPN devices (hardware clients) to enable full routed IP access to internal resources.
5. _____ VPNs are easier to deploy than a full tunneling remote access VPN, but they typically provide limited access to resources when compared to the full tunnel.
6. Clientless deployments require that the user open a web browser, which acts as the VPN client, and the VPN gateway acts as a _____ device to the internal resources.
7. The recommended algorithms for IKE session encryption are _____ and _____.
8. The recommended hash algorithm to provide message authentication and integrity is _____.
9. The recommended algorithms for encryption of user traffic are _____ and _____.
10. _____ requires administrative privileges because it changes the local host's file.

References

Cisco IOS SSL VPN Policy Groups, www.cisco.com/en/US/prod/collateral/iosswrel/ps6537/ps6586/ps6657/prod_white_paper0900aecd8051ac3a.html.

Cisco Secure Desktop (CSD) on IOS Configuration Example Using SDM, www.cisco.com/en/US/products/ps6496/products_configuration_example09186a008072aa7b.shtml.

This chapter covers the following subjects:

- **Plan the deployment of a Cisco IOS Software EZVPN:** Discusses the decision-making process that helps plan an EZVPN deployment. You must make choices about encryption algorithms, key management, and authentication among others to properly plan the deployment.

- **Configure and verify a basic Cisco IOS Software VTI-based EZVPN server:** Covers configuring and verifying operations on the EZVPN server on a Cisco IOS Software device.

- **Configure the Cisco VPN client:** Covers how to configure the Cisco VPN client parameters.

- **Configure and verify VTI-based EZVPN remote client functionality on the Cisco ISR:** Explains how to configure a Cisco ISR as an EZVPN remote hardware client. You also learn how to verify the operation of the hardware client.

- **Configure and verify EZVPN server and VPN client PKI features:** Covers how to configure and verify the use of PKI for authentication on the EZVPN server and the VPN client.

- **Troubleshoot basic EZVPN operation:** Covers the process to follow when troubleshooting EZVPN operation to ensure successful implementations.

CHAPTER 21

Deploying Remote Access Solutions Using EZVPNs

The Cisco Easy VPN (EZVPN) solution provides access to internal resources across an untrusted network transport to a remote access Virtual Private Network (VPN) gateway that is running on the Cisco Integrated Services Router (ISR).

"Do I Know This Already?" Quiz

The "Do I Know This Already?" quiz helps you decide whether you really need to read the entire chapter. If you already intend to read the entire chapter, you do not necessarily need to answer these questions now.

The ten-question quiz, derived from the major sections in the "Foundation Topics" portion of this chapter, helps you determine how to spend your limited study time.

Table 21-1 outlines the major topics discussed in this chapter and the "Do I Know This Already?" quiz questions that correspond to those topics.

Table 21-1 *"Do I Know This Already?" Foundation Topics Section-to-Question Mapping*

Foundation Topics Section	Questions Covered in This Section
Plan the Deployment of a Cisco IOS Software EZVPN	1, 2
Configure and Verify a Basic Cisco IOS Software VTI-Based EZVPN Server	3, 4
Configure the Cisco VPN Client	5, 6
Configure and Verify VTI-Based EZVPN Remote Client Functionality on the Cisco ISR	7, 8
Configure and Verify EZVPN Server and VPN Client PKI Features	9
Troubleshoot Basic EZVPN Operation	10

Caution: The goal of self-assessment is to gauge your mastery of the topics in this chapter. If you do not know the answer to a question or are only partially sure of the answer, you should mark this question wrong for purposes of the self-assessment. Giving yourself credit for an answer that you correctly guess skews your self-assessment results and might provide you with a false sense of security.

1. What enables Cisco Integrated Services Routers to act as VPN gateways?

   a. Cisco EZVPN Remote

   b. PKI

   c. Cisco EZVPN Server

   d. None of these answers are correct.

2. What can the EZVPN server use to create cryptographic tunnel contexts? (Select all that apply.)

   a. VTI

   b. IPsec

   c. Crypto map

   d. B and C

   e. None of these answers are correct.

3. Which of the following is preferred to EZVPN for deploying full tunneling?

   a. IPsec tunnels

   b. Traditional WAN circuits

   c. Client-based tunneling

   d. SSL VPNs

   e. None of these answers are correct.

4. Which is an additional authentication mechanism that can be used in addition to group passwords?

   a. XAUTH

   b. RADIUS

   c. TACACS+

   d. IPsec

   e. None of these answers are correct.

5. Recommended practice dictates limiting the size of which of the following to mitigate the fallout if a group password is compromised?

   a. Networks

   b. VPNs

   c. User databases

   d. Groups

6. Which type of authentication should you use to make the implementation resistant to a man-in-the-middle attack?

   a. One-way

   b. Two-way

    c. PKI-based

    d. Group password–based

    e. None of these answers are correct.

7. Which of the following is authenticated when using XAUTH with the EZVPN remote hardware device?

    a. Rrouter

    b. User

    c. Network

    d. None of these answers are correct.

8. Which of the following are modes of operation of the EZVPN Remote feature on hardware clients? (Select all that apply.)

    a. Client mode

    b. Network extension

    c. Network extension plus

    d. Client plus

9. What issue is mitigated by using certificate-based, rather than group password–based, EZVPN implementations?

    a. Man-in-the-middle attack

    b. DoS attacks

    c. Ping sweep

    d. Reconnaissance attack

10. What are the two areas to investigate when troubleshooting VPNs?

    a. Session establishment

    b. Data flow

    c. Your ISP

    d. None of the answers are correct.

The answers to the "Do I Know This Already?" quiz are found in Appendix A. The suggested choices for your next step are as follows:

■ **8 or less overall score:** Read the entire chapter. This includes the "Foundation Topics" and the "Exam Preparation" sections.

■ **9 or 10 overall score:** If you want more review on these topics, skip to the "Exam Preparation" section. Otherwise, move on to Chapter 22, "Final Preparation."

Foundation Topics

The basic EZVPN solution uses basic user authentication with usernames and passwords, client configuration, and IP address assignments, with a single access control policy. Configuring and verifying a basic EZVPN solution is covered in this chapter.

Plan the Deployment of a Cisco IOS Software EZVPN

With broadband access providing high-speed connections to the Internet, users have a new way to access sensitive enterprise resources at a remote location. This ease of access brings with it the need to secure the connection between the remote user and the enterprise. The need to provide authentication and encryption to ensure the protection of the data is required, but building a VPN between two routers can be complicated.

The Cisco EZVPN Remote feature implements the Cisco VPN client protocol, which allows most VPN parameters to be defined at the Cisco EZVPN Server. This server is typically a dedicated VPN device such as the Cisco ASA 5500 Series Adaptive Security Appliance or a Cisco IOS router that supports the Cisco VPN client protocol.

After the Cisco EZVPN Server has been configured, a VPN connection can be created with minimal configuration on a Cisco EZVPN Remote client, such as a Cisco Integrated Services Router (ISR). As the Cisco EZVPN Remote initiates a VPN tunnel, the Cisco EZVPN Server pushes the IP Security (IPsec) policies to the Cisco EZVPN Remote client and creates the corresponding VPN tunnel connection.

Internet Key Exchange (IKE) mode configuration allows a Cisco EZVPN Server to download an IP address and other network parameters to the Cisco EZVPN Remote as part of an IKE negotiation. In this exchange, the Cisco EZVPN Server assigns IP addresses to the Cisco EZVPN Remote to use as the "inner" IP address encapsulated under IPsec. This results in a known IP address from the client that will match against the IPsec policy.

To use IPsec VPNs between Cisco EZVPN Remotes with dynamic IP addresses and a Cisco EZVPN Server, an IPsec policy must be dynamically administered on the Cisco EZVPN Server after each client is authenticated. With IKE mode configuration, the Cisco EZVPN Server can set up the scalable policy for a very large number of clients, regardless of the IP addresses of those clients.

The Cisco EZVPN Remote feature provides automatic management of the following:

- Negotiation of tunnel parameters, such as addresses, algorithms, and lifetimes

- Building tunnels based on the parameters that were set

- Automatically create the Network Address Translation (NAT) or Port Address Translation (PAT) configuration and associated access control lists (ACL) that are needed

- Authenticate users by usernames, groups names, and passwords

- Managing security keys for encryption and decryption

- Authenticating, encrypting, and decrypting data through the tunnel

Cisco EZVPN Server enables Cisco Integrated Services Routers and Cisco ASA 5500 Series Adaptive Security Appliances to act as VPN gateways in site-to-site or remote access VPNs when the remote office device is using the Cisco EZVPN Remote feature. This feature allows security policies to be managed at the gateways and pushed to the remote VPN device. This ensures that the connections always have up-to-date policies before connections are established.

The Cisco EZVPN Server can also terminate IPsec tunnels that are initiated by remote users running VPN client software on their systems. This provides an ideal solution for mobile and remote workers to continue to be able to access enterprise resources while traveling.

Cisco EZVPN Remote allows the Cisco ISRs and the Cisco ASA 5500 Adaptive Security Appliances or Cisco VPN Software Clients to act as the remote VPN clients. The devices receive security policies from the Cisco EZVPN Server, which drastically minimizes the configuration and management requirements at the remote location. This is ideal for remote offices with little or no IT support.

Solution Components

A basic Cisco EZVPN solution is comprised of remote users with the Cisco VPN client software that is used to create an IPsec tunnel to a Cisco ISR EZVPN Server.

This basic solution typically uses bidirectional authentication, where the client authenticates the ISR with a group password for the authentication method and the ISR authenticates the user based on the group password and can optionally use a username and password method in addition to the group password. The Cisco ISR will apply a set of authorization and accounting rules to the user's VPN session after successful authentication. Following this, the ISR will establish an acceptable VPN environment with the remote user. After the VPN environment is built, the client sends IP traffic into the IPsec tunnel using a virtual network interface that is created on the client by the Cisco VPN client. The client can now use an application to access any resource behind the ISR VPN gateway for which he has authorization.

The EZVPN Server can use either crypto maps or Virtual Tunnel Interfaces (VTI) to create the cryptographic tunnel contexts for remote users. This chapter covers the VTI-based EZVPN Server.

Deployment Tasks

Deploying a basic Cisco EZVPN on a Cisco ISR requires that the following deployment tasks be completed:

> **Task 1:** Configure basic VTI-based EZVPN Server features. This includes configuring correct policies and profiles for IKE and IPsec. In this task, you configure groups that will contain client configuration settings as well as Internet Security Association and Key Management Protocol (ISAKMP) profiles for identifying multiple groups of remote users. The client configuration settings include network settings (DNS server, WINS server, domain suffix) and IP address assignment methods.

Key
Topic

Task 2: (Optional) Configure the EZVPN Server and VPN client to use Public Key Infrastructure (PKI)–based authentication using certificates, instead of group pre-shared keys.

Task 3: Install the Cisco VPN client and configure it to connect to the ISR EZVPN Server.

Task 4: (Optional) Configure the Cisco ISR to run as a hardware VPN client.

Input Parameters

Prior to implementing the basic Cisco EZVPN Server, you must gather and analyze several pieces of information. These input parameters include the following:

- The IP addressing plan that will determine the VPN gateway addressing and the network-naming convention that will determine the name of the VPN gateway. This is needed to assign an IP address to the VPN-terminating interface on the ISR and to assign an appropriate name to the VPN gateway's Secure Socket Layer/Transport Layer Security (SSL/TLS) identity certificate.

- The enterprise policy of user naming and the enterprise password to create a local user database on the ISR.

- The enterprise cryptographic policy to choose IKE and IPsec protocols that meet enterprise requirements.

- The IP addressing plan for remote clients. The ISR acting as an EZVPN Server must assign IP addresses to remote clients.

- Access policies that dictate the resources to which remote users have permission to access.

- A list of remote client platforms to be able to correctly provision the Cisco VPN client software image to clients.

Deployment Guidelines

When deploying the basic Cisco EZVPN solution using a Cisco IOS Software EZVPN Server, consider the following deployment guidelines:

- In general, the Cisco AnyConnect SSL VPN solution should be preferred over the EZVPN solution because it has much fewer issues with firewall traversal.

- Only use the basic EZVPN solution in low-risk environments where the risk associated with using static passwords for remote access is acceptable. Environments with higher risk levels should migrate to a solution that uses stronger forms of authentication such as certificates or one-time passwords.

- Consider using the basic EZVPN solution in environments that have little or no access control between the client and the ISR.

Configure and Verify a Basic Cisco IOS Software VTI-Based EZVPN Server

In the following sections, you configure the Cisco IOS Software EZVPN server. This includes configuring groups to which policy and profile settings will be applied as well as defining authentication mechanisms.

Group Pre-Shared Key Authentication

The basic EZVPN supports several levels of user and peer authentication. Peer authentication refers to the basic mutual authentication of two parties, such as the client and the ISR. With basic EZVPN, peer authentication uses group passwords that are configured on the ISR and on a group of VPN clients that typically share a common security policy. Extended Authentication (XAUTH) is an optional, one-way user authentication that can be added on top of the group passwords. XAUTH can support passwords or one-time passwords (OTP) and increases the security around remote access solutions in case the group password is compromised.

Group passwords are very vulnerable to compromise simply because of their shared nature. For example, if one laptop is stolen, the attacker will most likely be able to retrieve the group password from the system. If using XAUTH, this attacker would not have immediate access to internal resources because he would still need to provide valid user authentication credentials. However, having the group password would allow the attacker to launch a man-in-the-middle (MITM) attack and intercept the initial negotiation between the client and the ISR. The attacker would then be able to spoof the ISR's identity (using the group password). The client would not be able to tell that it was communicating with the attacker and would send XAUTH credentials over the IKE session to the attacker, who could then use these credentials to log in to the VPN.

Extended Authentication (XAUTH) Overview

Extended Authentication is a feature that can be enabled during the IKE negotiation that provides one-way user authentication that is used in addition to the group peer authentication. XAUTH takes place after IKE phase 1 completes and before the IKE phase 2 (IPsec SA) negotiations begin. This process uses the encrypted IKE security association (SA) to send credentials from the client to the ISR.

XAUTH should be used to provide additional authentication for remote access users. It can also be used to provide per-user services such as per-user IP addresses or access rules.

The following sections provide configuration guidance for implementing XAUTH using the local user account configured on the EZVPN Server. However, it can very easily be configured to use authentication, authorization, and accounting (AAA) authentication methods to leverage the centralized nature of using RADIUS, TACACS+, or other authentication protocols.

Configuration Groups and ISAKMP Profiles

To enable group authentication and client configuration features, two configuration objects must be added to the configuration for each group of users:

- **Client configuration groups:** Client configuration groups are configuration objects in Cisco IOS Software that provide authentication credentials and network configuration parameters that are to be applied to all clients in the group. These parameters can include the IP addresses assigned to clients, Domain Name System (DNS) servers, domain suffix, and the optional split tunneling parameter.

- **ISAKMP profiles:** EZVPN Server uses ISAKMP profiles to bind an identity to a virtual tunnel interface and client configuration policy. In the EZVPN Server, the VPN gateway uses ISAKMP profiles to associate a particular user group identity to a VTI template interface and the client configuration group.

Configuration Tasks

The first deployment step for configuring the Cisco EZVPN solution is to configure basic EZVPN Server on the ISR. The following configuration tasks should be completed to accomplish this:

Task 1: (Optional) Configure an IKE policy for a key management session between the remote VPN client and the EZVPN Server. This permits the IKE policy on the ISR to be tuned to provide stronger cryptographic algorithms than what is provided for in the default IKE policies.

Task 2: Tune the ISR IPsec transform sets if there is a requirement for stronger cryptographic algorithms than what is provided for in the default IPsec transform sets.

Task 3: Configure a dynamic VTI template interface that the ISR will use to create tunnel interfaces for each remote user.

Task 4: Configure a client configuration group in which the group authentication credentials will be configured, along with the address assignment policy and, if needed, any optional client network parameters.

Task 5: Configure an ISAKMP profile that will bind the remote user group to the client configuration group.

Task 6: Configure a local AAA authentication method and add user accounts to the ISR local user database.

Task 7: Configure an existing ISAKMP profile to also use Extended Authentication (XAUTH) prior to permitting access.

Configuration Scenario

In the configuration sequence, basic EZVPN Server functionality will be enabled along with tuning IKE and IPsec policies on the ISR. A dynamic VTI template will be configured. The ISR will use its GigabitEthernet0/0 interface for its untrusted connection and the GigabitEthernet0/1 interface for its trusted connection.

Next, a client configuration group named MY-GROUP and an ISAKMP profile named MY-ISA-PROFILE will be created. The group name MY-GROUP, with a long, random group password, will be configured inside the client configuration group.

All clients will be assigned IP addresses in the 10.255.0.0/24 network, be given the IP address of an internal DNS server at 172.16.200.53, and enable split tunneling to only protect traffic to 10.0.0.0/8.

Finally, a user named vpnuser will be created in the local user database, and XAUTH will be required for the group MY-GROUP.

Task 1: (Optional) Verify an IKE Policy

The first configuration step is to configure a custom IKE (ISAKMP) policy on the EZVPN Server using the **crypto isakmp policy** command, as depicted in Example 21-1. If one is not configured, the EZVPN Server will use the default IKE policies.

Example 21-1 *Configure an IKE Policy*

```
router(config)# crypto isakmkp policy 10
router(config-isakmp)# authentication pre-share
router(config-isakmp)# lifetime 3600
```

Task 2: Configure an IPsec Transform Set and Profile

Task 2 involves configuring a specific transform set and binds it to a new IPsec profile, using the **crypto ipsec transform-set** and **crypto ipsec profile** commands, as shown in Example 21-2.

Example 21-2 *Configure IPsec Transform Set and Profile*

```
router(config)# crypto ipsec transform-set MY-TSET esp-aes esp-sha-hmac
router(cfg-crypto-trans)# exit
router(config)# crypto ipsec profile MY-PROFILE
router(ipsec-profile)# set transform set MY-TSET
```

Task 3: Configure a Dynamic VTI Template

In Task 3, you configure a virtual template interface of the type "tunnel" from which the common settings for all dynamic VTIs are defined. The VTI in Example 21-3 is configured with IP unnumbered to interface GigabitEthernet0/0, configured with an IPsec tunnel encapsulation, and given the IPsec profile called MY-PROFILE.

Example 21-3 *Configure a Dynamic VTI Template*

Key Topic

```
Router(config)# interface virtual-template 1 type tunnel
Router(config-if)# ip unnumbered GigabitEthernet0/0
Router(config-if)# tunnel mode ipsec ipv4
Router(config-if)# tunnel protection ipsec profile MY-PROFILE
```

Task 4: Create a Client Configuration Group

Task 4 involves configuring a client configuration group and all the necessary parameters for properly configuring remote clients. The associated commands are given in Example 21-4.

Example 21-4 *Create a Client Configuration Group*

```
Router(config)# ip local pool MY-POOL 10.255.0.1 10.255.0.100
!
Router(config)# ip access-list extended MY-SPLIT-TUNNEL
Router(config-ext-acl)# permit ip 10.0.0.0 0.255.255.255 any
!
Router(config) # crypto isakmp client configuration group MY-GROUP
Router(config-isakmp-group)# key Adjkj232902sdjiaf934892u@@akdlfj
Router(config-isakmp-group)# domain mydomain.com
Router(config-isakmp-group)# dns 172.16.200.53
Router(config-isakmp-group)# pool MY-POOL
Router(config-isakmp-group)# acl MY-SPLIT-TUNNEL
```

Configure a local pool of IP addresses using the **ip local pool** command. The address range needs to be large enough to support the expected number of remote users. Add an extended access list that defines the traffic that must be forwarded through the tunnel. This access list works in conjunction with the split tunneling feature that is enabled in the client configuration group parameters by using the **acl** command. Finally, create a named client configuration group using the **crypto isakmp client configuration group** command to create one called MY-GROUP in which client network parameters will be configured as well.

Task 5: Create an ISAKMP Profile

Task 5 creates an ISAKMP profile that will match the identity of remote users and enable client configuration and VTI interfaces for the group. The associated commands are given in Example 21-5.

Example 21-5 *Create an ISAKMP Profile*

```
Router(config)# aaa authorization network LOCAL-AUTHOR local
!
Router(conf-isa-prof)# crypto isakmp profile MY-ISA-PROFILE
Router(conf-isa-prof)# match identity group MY-GROUP
Router(conf-isa-prof)# isakmp authorization list LOCAL-AUTHOR
Router(conf-isa-prof)# client configuration address respond
Router(conf-isa-prof)# client configuration group MY-GROUP
Router(conf-isa-prof)# virtual-template 1
!
Router(config)# crypto ipsec profile MY-PROFILE
Router(ipsec-profile)# set isakmp-profile MY-ISA-PROFILE
```

Begin by configuring the local network AAA authorization list with the **aaa authorization network** command. This will tell the router to use only the locally configured user database on the router for its authorization resource. Then, create the named ISAKMP profile using the **crypto isakmp profile** command. Example 21-5 uses the MY-ISA-PROFILE ISAKMP profile with the following additional parameters:

- Use the **match identity group** command to identify the group name that this ISAKMP profile will use.

- Use the **isakmp authorization list** command to point to an existing AAA authorization list.

- Use the **client configuration address respond** command to tell the EZVPN Server to respond to client requests for IP addresses.

- Use the **client configuration group** command to specify the configuration group that is to be associated with this ISAKMP profile.

- Use the **virtual-template** command to bind this ISAKMP profile (group of users) to a specific local dynamic VTI interface.

Tasks 6 and 7: Configure and Enable User Authentication

If there is a requirement for an additional level of authentication, configure the EZVPN Server to require XAUTH. Begin by creating a new local AAA authentication method using the **aaa authentication login** command. Then, create local user accounts in the local user database. Finally, configure the requirement for Extended Authentication (XAUTH) inside the existing MY-ISA-PROFILE ISAKMP profile using the **client authentication list** command. Perform these commands as shown in Example 21-6.

Example 21-6 *Configure and Enable User Authentication*

Key
Topic

```
Router(config)# aaa authorization login LOCAL-AUTHEN local
!
Router(config)# username vpnuser privilege 0 secret 438ajdkjGT980u1
!
Router(config)# crypto isakmp profile MY-ISA-PROFILE
Router(conf-isa-prof)# client authentication list LOCAL-AUTHEN
```

Cisco Configuration Professional Support

Cisco Configuration Professional (CCP) can be used to configure the Cisco EZVPN Server on a Cisco Integrated Services Router running Cisco IOS Software. The tool includes a wizard through which the administrator will be taken to create a new EZVPN Server function on the router. For authentication, CCP supports both using group keys and also extended user authentication. In addition, advanced deployments using certificate-based authentication are supported by Cisco Configuration Professional.

Manual configuration of the EZVPN Server feature can be performed in CCP as well. The network administrator can manually configure a new instance of EZVPN Server or discover an existing configuration by downloading it from a reachable router.

> **Note:**   Documentation for Cisco Configuration Professional can be found at www.cisco.com/en/US/docs/net_mgmt/cisco_configuration_professional/v2_4/olh/ccp.pdf.

Implementation Guidelines

When implementing a basic EZVPN solution, take the following implementation guidelines into consideration:

■ If possible in the environment, create groups of users that are relatively limited in size. This way, if a group password is compromised, the numbers of connections that are vulnerable to attack are limited. This makes it easier to reconfigure the clients with a new group password.

■ If the risk of a group password being compromised is too high, consider deploying PKI-based authentication. This will provide a stronger level of authentication and makes the peer authentication process resistant to a man-in-the-middle attack.

Configure the Cisco VPN Client

The second piece of the EZVPN solution is the Cisco VPN client. The following sections cover installing the client software.

Configuration Tasks

To deploy Cisco VPN clients in a basic Cisco EZVPN solution, the following configuration tasks should be completed:

Task 1: Install the Cisco VPN client on the systems.

Task 2: Configure the Cisco VPN client connection entry settings. These settings are the IP address of the EZVPN Server, the group name, and group password.

Task 3: Establish the EZVPN connection using the Cisco VPN client.

Configuration Scenario

In the configuration sequence, the Cisco VPN client will be configured on a Microsoft Windows XP system and configured to connect to an ISR at 172.16.1.1. The VPN client will use the MY-GROUP group name with a strong password. The remote user will use the vpnuser account to satisfy the XAUTH requirement.

Task 1: Install the Cisco VPN Client Software

You can find guidance for this task on Cisco.com.

Task 2: Configure the VPN Client Connection Entry

After the Cisco VPN client is installed, configure the connection entry that will provide the parameters to successfully establish a connection to the Cisco EZVPN Server. Perform the following steps to accomplish this:

Step 1.   Start the Cisco VPN client.

Step 2.   In the main window, click the New button to create a new connection entry.

Step 3. In the Connection Entry field, specify a name that describes the connection and optionally add a description.

Step 4. In the Host field, specify the IP address of the ISR untrusted interface (172.16.1.1).

Step 5. On the Authentication tab, select the group authentication method and enter the group name and password.

Step 6. Click Save to save the profile.

Task 3: Establish the EZVPN Connection

To test and verity the connection, select the configuration profile created in Task 2 and click the Connect button. When connected successfully, the Cisco VPN client will minimize itself by default.

Client-Side Verification

After the client is successfully connected, the ISR will push network configuration items to the client and provide the client with its IP address. Right-click the Cisco VPN Client system tray icon and choose to view Statistics. This will display connection details, including the assigned IP address, the negotiated cryptographic algorithms, and some statistical information on packets received and transmitted.

Navigate to the Route Details tab of the Statistics window and observe the network listed in the Secured Routes pane. The default of 0.0.0.0/0 indicates that all traffic is being protected by the tunnel, while an entry of 10.0.0.0/8 indicates that only 10.0.0.0/8 is being protected and any other traffic is simply forwarded out the system's normal network interface.

Gateway-Side Verification

Use the **show crypto session** username command on the ISR to verify the client's connection, as demonstrated in Example 21-7.

Example 21-7   show crypto session username *Command Output*

```
Router# show crypto session cisco


Crypto session current status
Interface: Virtual-Access2
Username: cisco
Profile: prof
Group: easy
Assigned address: 10.3.3.4
Session status: UP-ACTIVE
Peer: 10.1.1.2 port 500
```

```
IKE SA: local 10.1.1.1/500 remote 10.1.1.2/500 Active
IKE SA: local 10.1.1.1/500 remote 10.1.1.2/500 Inactive
IPSEC FLOW: permit ip 0.0.0.0/0.0.0.0 host 3.3.3.4
    Active SAs: 2, origin: crypto map
```

Configure and Verify VTI-Based EZVPN Remote Client Functionality on the Cisco ISR

Cisco EZVPN Remote allows a Cisco ISR or Cisco ASA to also act as a remote hardware VPN client with minimal configuration to connect to the VPN gateway.

The remote device is configured with authentication credentials and the IP address of the EZVPN Server and then receives the rest of its network configuration from the server client configuration object. To the EZVPN Server, there is no difference between a software VPN client and the EZVPN Remote hardware devices.

The Cisco EZVPN Remote feature supports a two-part process for authenticating the remote router to the central Cisco EZVPN Server:

- **Group-level authentication:** The first step is group-level authentication. This is part of the creation of the control channel and can use two types of authentication credentials:

- **PSKs:** Pre-shared keys mean that each peer has the key of the other peer.

- **Digital certificates:** This provides support for using RSA signatures for EZVPN Remote devices, which is much more secure than PSKs.

- **Extended Authentication (XAUTH):** This is an optional, additional level of authentication that can be used in addition to the group authentication. The remote client (the Cisco EZVPN Remote hardware device) sends a username and password to the EZVPN Server just as it is done with the Cisco VPN Software Client. The difference is that when using the router, the router itself is being authenticated as opposed to a user. After the XAUTH is successful, all PCs behind the Cisco EZVPN Remote router have access to the VPN tunnel.

If XAUTH is being used, it must be decided where to store the authentication credentials:

- **Store the XAUTH username and password in the configuration file on the router:** This option is typically used if the router is shared between many PCs and the goal is to have the VPN tunnel up all the time.

- **Do not store the XAUTH username and password on the router:** If this option is used, a PC user who is connected to the router is presented with a web page that allows the username and password to be manually entered.

EZVPN Remote Modes

The Cisco EZVPN Remote feature on hardware clients supports three modes of operation:

- **Client mode:** NAT and PAT are used to allow PCs and other hosts on the client side of the VPN to form a private network that does not use any IP addresses in the IP address space of the destination server. This mode automatically configures NAT or PAT translation and the ACLs needed to implement the VPN connection. These are temporary and automatically deleted from the configuration when the tunnel is torn down. The disadvantage of this mode is that the PCs on the client side are not reachable for sessions initiated from the central site.

- **Network Extension mode:** In this mode, PCs and hosts on the client side are given routable IP addresses that are fully reachable over the tunneled connection. PAT is not used in this option.

- **Network Extension plus mode:** This mode is identical to network extension mode with the additional capability of being able to request an IP address through IKE mode configuration and automatically assign it to an available loopback interface. The IPsec SAs for this IP address are automatically created by Cisco EZVPN Remote.

All three modes support split tunneling if there is a need for it. This allows traffic to corporate resources to be protected by the tunnel while Internet access is allowed to flow straight out of the service provider's connection to the Internet.

Configuration Tasks

To configure a Cisco ISR running Cisco IOS Software as an EZVPN Remote hardware client, perform the following tasks:

Task 1: Configure the EZVPN Remote connection profile on the EZVPN Remote hardware client.

Task 2: Designate the EZVPN interface roles on the EZVPN Remote hardware client.

Key Topic

Configuration Scenario

The Cisco EZVPN Remote feature will be configured on a Cisco ISR router. It will be configured to connect to a central Cisco ISR EZVPN Server and while operating in client mode that will use a group name and user name for identification and passwords for authentication.

Task 1: Configure EZVPN Remote Profile

Task 1 involves configuring the EZVPN Remote hardware feature by creating a local VTI template and configuring a connection profile that identifies the EZVPN Server, determines the hardware client's mode, and provides authentication credentials.

Begin with creating a VTI template of type "tunnel" using the **virtual-template** command, specify that it should use IPsec tunnel mode. Next, create a named EZVPN Remote connection profile using the **crypto ipsec client ezvpn** command. Example 21-8 shows the configuration with the profile settings:

- Use the **group** command to specify the group name and group password to authenticate to the EZVPN Server as a part of a group.

- Use the **username** command to specify the stored username and password used to provide additional authentication using XAUTH.

- Use the **virtual-interface** command to specify the local VTI template that will be used to create a tunnel interface for this connection.

- Use the **peer** command to identify the EZVPN Server to connect to.

- Use the **mode** client command to specify that the client will use client mode when establishing a connection to the VPN.

Example 21-8 *Configure an IKE Policy*

```
Router(config)# interface virtual-template1 type tunnel
Router(config-if)# tunnel mode ipsec ipv4
Router(config-if)# crypto ipsec client ezvpn MY-EXVPN-CLIENT
Router(config-crypto-ezvpn)# group MY-GROUP key AkjAFert32892Aaf2323AADF
Router(config-crypto-ezvpn)# virtual-interface 1
Router(config-crypto-ezvpn)#  peer 172.16.1.1
Router(config-crypto-ezvpn)#  mode client
Router(config-crypto-ezvpn)#  username vpnuser password 48u34ERW5325
```

Task 2: Designate EZVPN Interface Roles

Task 2 designates local interfaces as either inside (trusted) or outside (untrusted) to inform the EZVPN Remote function so that it can properly apply NAT (in client mode) or identify the protected network (in network extension mode).

Designate local interfaces in interface configuration mode using the **crypto ipsec client ezvpn** command with either the **inside** or **outside** arguments, as displayed in Example 21-9.

Example 21-9 *Configure IPsec Transform Set and Profile*

```
Router(config)# interface FastEthernet0/0
Router(config-if)# crypto ipsec client ezvpn MY-EZVPN-CLIENT outside
Router(config-if)# exit
Router(config)# Interface FastEthernet0/1
Router(config-if)# crypto ipsec client exvpn MY-EXVPN-CLIENT inside
```

Implementation Guidelines

When implementing EZVPN Remote, consider the following guidelines:

- EZVPN Remote hardware clients are most appropriately implemented in a strict hub-and-spoke environment. The major advantage of using EZVPN is that it supports dynamically addressed spokes.

- If the remote network requires only outbound connectivity, use EZVPN Remote in client mode. If the remote network requires two-way connectivity, use the EZVPN Remote solution in network extension mode.

Configure and Verify EZVPN Server and VPN Client PKI Features

EZVPN solutions can be deployed using certificates instead of group passwords to provide bidirectional authentication between remote clients and the EZVPN Server. This method of authentication will require all EZVPN devices to have an identity certificate that was provisioned by a trusted PKI and the CA certificate to verify the peer's certificate in the IKE peer authentication process.

Certificate-based EZVPN implementations can mitigate the MITM issue that is created by using group passwords.

Head-End PKI Configuration

To enable EZVPN Server to use certificates instead of group passwords for authentication, and to authenticate itself to a group of users, perform the following steps, as portrayed in Example 21-10:

Step 1. Enroll the EZVPN Server router into the PKI by creating a trustpoint, authenticating a CA, and obtaining an identity certificate.

Step 2. Specify the local identity of the router in the ISAKMP profile using the **self-identify fqdn** command and reference the identity specified in the PKI trustpoint.

Step 3. Inside the ISAKMP profile, specify the local trustpoint with the **ca trustpoint** command.

Step 4. Use the **match identity group** command to specify the identity of remote clients. Enroll remote clients so that the Organizational Unit (OU) field in their identity certificate contains their group name.

Example 21-10 *Head-End PKI Configuration*

```
Router(config)# crypto pki trustpoint MY-TP
Router(ca-trustpoint)# fqdn vpn.mydomain.com
Router(ca-trustpoint)# subject-name cn=vpn.mydomain.com
Router(ca-trustpoint)# exit
Router(config)# crypto isakmp profile MY-ISA-PROFILE
Router(conf-isa-prof)# self-identity fqdn vpn.mydomain.com
Router(conf-isa-prof)# ca trust-poitn MY-TP
 Match identity group MY-GROUP
```

VPN Client Configuration: SCEP Enrollment

To enroll the Cisco VPN client into a PKI, use the Simple Certificate Enrollment Protocol (SCEP) client that is a part of the Cisco VPN client to retrieve the CA certificate and to enroll into a PKI. Perform the following steps:

Step 1. In the Cisco VPN client interface, navigate to the Certificate tab and click the Enroll button.

Step 2. Choose Online in the Certificate Enrollment window. Specify the CA URL and the local domain in the CA Domain field. Click Next to continue.

Step 3. In the next window, enter the parameters that will determine the client's name inside the certificate. The VPN group name should be used as the OU field of the certificate. Click Enroll to complete the enrollment request.

VPN Client Enrollment Verification

The Cisco VPN client will now retrieve the CA certificate from the SCEP server and periodically poll the SCEP server to retrieve its identity certificate. The validity of the issued certificate can be verified by clicking the Verify button. The fields of the certificate will be displayed in a new window, allowing the information in the certificate (especially the OU that must match the group name) and the validity dates of the certificate.

VPN Client Configuration: Profile

To configure a connection profile that will use certificate-based authentication, perform the following steps on the Cisco VPN client:

Step 1. Start the Cisco VPN client.

Step 2. In the Cisco VPN client main window, click the New button to create a new connection entry.

Step 3. In the Connection Entry field, enter a locally significant name and an optional description.

Step 4. In the Host field, enter the IP address of the ISR untrusted interface (172.16.1.1).

Step 5. On the Authentication tab, select the certificate authentication method and select the proper identity certificate from the drop-down list.

Step 6. Click Save to save the profile.

Troubleshoot Basic EZVPN Operation

To provide the same stability with a VPN connection that is achieved with traditional circuits, you must be able to troubleshoot and restore the connectivity.

Troubleshooting Flow: VPN Session Establishment

To troubleshoot issues with session establishment, perform the following steps:

Step 1.   Check that IKE and IPsec protocols successfully negotiated based on matching IKE and IPsec policies on the client on the ISR. The **debug crypto isakmp** and **debug crypto ipsec** commands display information helpful to identifying mismatched parameters.

Step 2.   Verify that user authentication works. Use the **debug aaa authentication** command to display the AAA functions and output.

Step 3.   Verify that the router is able to assign IP addresses to the client. The ISR will indicate failures to assign an IP address in the output of the **debug crypto isakmp** command.

Troubleshooting Flow: VPN Data Flow

If the EZVPN session establishes successfully but connectivity over the tunnel fails, perform the following troubleshooting steps:

Step 1.   If using split tunneling, check that the correct routes are being protected and that they are present in the routing table.

Step 2.   Verify that the ISR is not denying traffic from the VPN tunnel.

Step 3.   Verify that the protected network has a route to the client-assigned addresses by examining the routing tables of routers on the internal network.

Exam Preparation

As mentioned in the section, "How to Use This Book," in the Introduction, you have several choices for exam preparation: the exercises here, the memory tables in Appendix C, the final exam preparation chapter, and the exam simulation questions on the CD-ROM. The following questions present a bigger challenge than the exam itself because they use an open-ended question format. By using this more difficult format, you exercise your memory better and prove your conceptual and factual knowledge of this chapter. You can find the answers to these questions in Appendix A, "Answers to the DIKTA Quizzes and Fill in the Blanks Questions."

Review All Key Topics

Review the most important topics in the chapter, noted with the Key Topics icon in the margin of the page. Table 21-2 lists a reference of these key topics and the page numbers on which each is found.

Table 21-2   *Key Topics*

Key Topic Element	Description	Page
List	Tasks that become automated by using EZVPN	572
List	EZVPN server deployment tasks	573
List	EZVPN server deployment guidelines	574
List	EZVPN server configuration tasks	576
Example 21-3	Configure a dynamic VTI template	577
Example 21-4	Configure a client configuration group	578
Example 21-5	Configure an ISAKMP profile	578
Example 21-6	Enable and configure client authentication	579
List	Cisco VPN client configuration tasks	580
List	EZVPN remote modes	582
List	EZVPN hardware client configuration tasks	583
Example 21-8	Configure EZVPN remote profile	584
Example 21-9	Configure the IPsec transform set and profile	584
List	EZVPN hardware client implementation guidelines	584
Step list	Steps to configure the EZVPN PKI head end	585
Example 21-10	Head-end PKI configuration	585
Step list	SCEP steps to enroll the Cisco VPN client into a PKI	585

Complete Tables and Lists from Memory

Print a copy of Appendix C, "Memory Tables" (found on the CD), or at least the section for this chapter, and complete the tables and lists from memory. Appendix D, "Memory Table Answers," also on the CD, includes completed tables and lists to check your work. Although this chapter doesn't have any memory tables, you will find some that are applicable in other chapters.

Define Key Terms

Define the following key terms from this chapter, and check your answers in the Glossary:

Cisco Easy VPN Server, Cisco Easy VPN Remote. Extended Authentication (XAUTH), Client configuration groups, EZVPN Client mode, EZVPN Network Extension mode, EZVPN Network Extension plus mode

Fill in the Blanks

1. Hosts behind the remote VPN router are not reachable for a session initiated from the central site in _____ mode.

2. The Easy VPN client can be the Cisco VPN client or an Easy VPN Remote hardware device such as the _____.

3. The Cisco Easy VPN Server can _____ IPsec tunnels that are initiated by remote users running VPN client software on their systems.

4. As the Cisco Easy VPN Remote initiates a VPN tunnel, the Cisco Easy VPN _____ pushes the IP Security (IPsec) policies to the Cisco Easy VPN Remote _____ and creates the corresponding VPN tunnel connection.

5. XAUTH takes place _____ IKE phase 1 completes and _____ the IKE phase 2 (IPsec SA) negotiations begin.

6. Group passwords are very vulnerable to compromise simply because of their _____ nature.

7. Configuring a basic Cisco ISR Easy VPN _____ consists of basic gateway configuration, group authentication, client configuration, and user authentication configuration.

8. The Cisco ISR can be used as an Easy VPN Remote _____.

9. You can enhance authentication by using _____ on remote clients and the Easy VPN Server.

Reference

Cisco IOS Security Command Reference, www.cisco.com/en/US/docs/ios/security/command/reference/sec_book.html.

This chapter covers the following subjects:

- **Tools for final preparation:** Outlines the tools that are available for exam preparation.

- **Suggested plan for final review/study:** Outlines a suggested plan for successfully studying for the 642-637 SECURE exam.

CHAPTER 22

Final Preparation

The first 21 chapters of this book cover the technologies, protocols, commands, and features required to pass the 642-637 SECURE exam. Although these chapters supply detailed information, most people need more preparation than simply reading the first 21 chapters of this book. This chapter details a set of tools and a study plan to help you complete your preparation for the exams.

This short chapter has two main sections. The first section lists the exam preparation tools that are useful at this point in the study process. The second section lists a suggested study plan now that you have completed all the earlier chapters in this book.

Note: Appendixes C and D exist as soft-copy appendixes on the CD included in the back of this book.

Tools for Final Preparation

The following sections list some information about the available tools and describe how to access those tools.

Pearson Cert Practice Test Engine and Questions on the CD

The CD in the back of the book includes the Pearson Cert Practice Test engine—software that displays and grades a set of exam-realistic multiple-choice questions. Using the Pearson Cert Practice Test engine, you can either study by going through the questions in Study mode or take a simulated (timed) SECURE exam.

The installation process requires two major steps. This book's CD has a recent copy of the Pearson Cert Practice Test engine. The practice exam—the database of SECURE exam questions—is not on the CD.

Note: The cardboard CD case in the back of this book includes the CD and a piece of paper. The paper lists the activation key for the practice exam associated with this book. *Do not lose the activation key*. On the opposite side of the paper from the activation code is a unique, one-time-use coupon code for the purchase of the *CCNP Security SECURE 642-637 Official Certification Guide*, Premium Edition.

Install the Software from the CD

The software installation process is routine compared with other software installation processes. To be complete, the following steps outline the installation process:

Step 1.   Insert the CD into your PC.

Step 2.   The software that automatically runs is the Cisco Press software to access and use all CD-based features, including the exam engine and viewing the CD-only appendixes. From the main menu, click the Install the Exam Engine option.

Step 3.   Respond to the window prompts as with any typical software installation process.

The installation process gives you the option to activate your exam with the activation code supplied on the paper in the CD sleeve. This process requires that you establish a Pearson website login. You need this login to activate the exam, so register when prompted. If you already have a Pearson website login, there is no need to register again. Just use your existing login.

Activate and Download the Practice Exam

After the exam engine is installed, activate the exam associated with this book (if you did not do so during the installation process) as follows:

Step 1.   Start the Pearson Cert Practice Test (PCPT) software from the Windows Start menu or from your desktop shortcut icon.

Step 2.   To activate and download the exam associated with this book, from the **My Products** or **Tools** tab, click the **Activate** button.

Step 3.   At the next screen, enter the Activation Key from the paper inside the cardboard CD holder in the back of the book. After you enter this, click the **Activate** button.

Step 4.   The activation process downloads the practice exam. Click **Next** and then click **Finish**.

After the activation process is completed, the My Products tab should list your new exam. If you do not see the exam, make sure that you have selected the **My Products** tab on the menu. At this point, the software and practice exam are ready to use. Simply select the exam and click the **Use** button.

To update a particular exam that you have already activated and downloaded, simply select the **Tools** tab and click the **Update Products** button. Updating your exams ensures that you have the latest changes and updates to the exam data.

If you want to check for updates to the Pearson Cert Practice Test exam engine software, simply select the **Tools** tab and click the **Update Application** button. This ensures that you are running the latest version of the software engine.

Activating Other Exams

The exam software installation process, and the registration process, only has to happen once. Then, for each new exam, only a few steps are required. For example, if you buy another new Cisco Press Official Cert Guide or Pearson IT Certification Cert Guide, extract the activation code from the CD sleeve in the back of that book (you don't even need the CD at this point). From there, just start the exam engine (if it is not still up and running) and perform Steps 2 through 4 from the previous list.

Premium Edition

In addition to the free practice exam provided on the CD-ROM, you can purchase additional exams with expanded functionality directly from Pearson IT Certification. The Premium Edition of this title contains an additional two full practice exams as well as an eBook (in both PDF and ePub format). In addition, the Premium Edition title also has remediation for each question to the specific part of the eBook that relates to that question.

Because you have purchased the print version of this title, you can purchase the Premium Edition at a deep discount. A coupon code in the CD sleeve contains a one-time-use code as well as instructions for where you can purchase the Premium Edition.

To view the Premium Edition product page, go to http://www.pearsonitcertification.com/store/product.aspx?isbn=1587142805.

Cisco Learning Network

Cisco provides a wide variety of CCNP Security preparation tools at a Cisco Systems website called the Cisco Learning Network. This site includes a large variety of exam preparation tools, including sample questions, forums on each Cisco exam, learning video games, and information about each exam.

To reach the Cisco Learning Network, go to www.cisco.com/go/learnnetspace, or just search for "Cisco Learning Network." You need to use the login that you created at www.cisco.com. If you don't have such a login, you can register for free. To register, simply go to www.cisco.com, click **Register** at the top of the page, and supply some information.

Memory Tables

Like most Official Cert Guides from Cisco Press, this book purposefully organizes information into tables and lists for easier study and review. Rereading these tables can be very useful before the exam. However, it is easy to skim over the tables without paying attention to every detail, especially when you remember having seen the table's contents when reading the chapter.

Instead of simply reading the tables in the various chapters, this book's Appendixes C and D give you another review tool. Appendix C, "Memory Tables," lists partially completed versions of many of the tables from the book. You can open Appendix C (a PDF file on the

CD that comes with this book) and print the appendix. For review, you can attempt to complete the tables. This exercise can help you focus on the review. It also exercises the memory connectors in your brain, which forces a little more contemplation about the facts.

Appendix D, "Memory Table Answers," also a PDF file located on the CD, lists the completed tables to check yourself. You can also just refer to the tables as printed in the book.

Chapter-Ending Review Tools

Chapters 1–21 have several features in the "Exam Preparation" section at the end of each chapter. Many of you have probably reviewed each chapter using these tools. You may have used some or all of these tools. It can also be helpful to use these tools again as you make your final preparations for the exam.

Suggested Plan for Final Review/Study

This section lists a suggested study plan from the point at which you finish reading Chapter 21 until you take the 642-637 SECURE exam. Certainly, you can ignore this plan, use it as is, or just take suggestions from it.

The plan uses five steps. If you are following the plan verbatim, proceed by part through the steps as listed. That is, starting with Part I (Network Security Technologies Overview), do the following six steps. Then, for Part II (Cisco IOS Foundation Security Solutions), do the following six steps, and so on. The steps are as follows:

Step 1. Review the key topics, the Do I Know This Already? (DIKTA) questions, and the Fill in the Blanks questions: You can use the table that lists the key topics in each chapter, or just flip the pages looking for key topics. Also, reviewing the DIKTA questions from the beginning of the chapter and the Fill in the Blanks questions at the end of the chapter can be helpful for review.

Step 2. Complete the memory tables: Open Appendix C on the CD and print the entire appendix, or print the tables by major part. Then, complete the tables.

Step 3. Do hands-on practice: Most people practice configuration and verification before the exam. Whether you use real gear, a simulator, or an emulator, practice the configuration and verification commands.

Step 4. Build configuration checklists: Glance through the Table of Contents, looking for major configuration tasks. Then, from memory, create your own configuration checklists for the various configuration commands.

Step 5. Use the Pearson Cert Practice Test engine to practice: The Pearson Cert Practice Test engine on the CD can be used to study using a bank of 210 unique exam-realistic, multiple-choice questions available only with this book.

The following sections describe some of the steps for which a little more explanation may be helpful.

Step 1: Review the Key Topics, the DIKTA Questions, and the Fill in the Blanks Questions

This review step focuses on the core facts related to the 642-637 SECURE exam. The exam will certainly cover other topics as well, but the DIKTA questions, the Fill in the Blanks questions, and the Key Topics items attempt to focus attention on the more important topics in each chapter.

As a reminder, if you follow this plan after reading the first 21 chapters, working a major part at a time helps you pull each major topic together.

Step 2: Complete the Memory Tables

The memory tables are an additional tool that can be used for exam preparation. An incomplete version of these tables is designed to be printed out and completed to test the topic knowledge. The complete version of these tables can also be used as a crib sheet for important facts from each chapter.

Step 3: Do Hands-On Practice

Although this book shows you many different configuration commands and specific configuration examples, there is no substitute for hands-on practice. This short section provides a couple of suggestions regarding your efforts at practice from the CLI.

Most people use one or more of the following options for hands-on skills:

- **Real gear:** Either purchased (often used), borrowed, or rented
- **Simulators:** Software that acts like real gear
- **Emulators:** Software that acts like router hardware, with IOS running inside that environment

For real gear, this book makes no attempt at suggesting how to go about getting, borrowing, or renting gear. There are a number of different available outlets for used Cisco equipment that can be used to obtain a reasonably priced lab for practice.

As of this writing, there are no comprehensive CCNP Security simulators. While Cisco IOS simulators exist that simulate many basic functionalities at the associate level, they come up short on more advanced configurations.

The last option is to use an emulator, of which there are two noteworthy options. For the general public, a group of two free software offerings cooperate to allow you to run multiple instances of IOS: Dynagen (see www.dynagen.org) for the CLI interface and GNS3 (see www.gns3.net) for the graphical interface. All these tools rely on another tool called *dynamips*, which emulates the Cisco hardware. The Dynagen and GNS3 software provides different configuration methods for utilizing this functionality (GNS3 actually uses Dynagen as a back end). There are legal questions about utilizing these emulators with

Cisco IOS Software, and they are simply mentioned in this book as available options without condoning or recommending their use.

Step 4: Build Configuration Checklists

This book contains a number of different configuration commands and configuration examples. Review those commands that are the least well known and practice them. After this is complete, write down these configuration checklists from memory to ensure your understanding.

Step 5: Use the Exam Engine

The Pearson Cert Practice Test engine on the CD includes a database of questions created specifically for this book. The Pearson Cert Practice Test engine can be used in either study mode or practice exam mode, as follows:

- **Study mode:** Study mode is most useful when you want to use the questions for learning and practicing. In Study mode, you can select options such as whether you want to randomize the order of the questions, automatically view answers to the questions as you go, test on specific topics, refer to specific sections of the text that resides on the CD, and so on.

- **Practice Exam mode:** This mode presents questions in a timed environment, providing you with a more exam-realistic experience. It also restricts your ability to see your score as you progress through the exam, view answers to questions as you are taking the exam, and refer to sections of the text. These timed exams not only allow you to study for the actual 642-637 SECURE exam, but they also help you to simulate the time pressure that can occur on the actual exam.

When doing your final preparation, you can use study mode, practice exam mode, or both. However, after you have seen each question a couple of times, you will likely start to remember the questions, and the usefulness of the exam database may be reduced. So, consider the following options when using the exam engine:

- Use this question database for review. Use Study mode, and study the questions by major book part, just as with the other final review steps listed in this chapter. Plan on getting another exam (possibly from the Premium Edition) if you want to take additional simulated exams.

- Save the question database, not using it for review during your review of each book part. Save it until the end so that you will not have seen the questions before. Then, use practice exam mode to simulate the exam.

Choosing the correct mode from the exam engine's user interface is pretty obvious. The following steps show how to move to the screen from which to select study or practice exam mode:

Step 1.   Click the **My Products** tab if you are not already in that screen.

Step 2.   Select the exam you want to use from the list of available exams.

Step 3.   Click the **Use** button.

By taking these actions, the engine should display a window from which you can choose **Study** Mode or **Practice Exam** Mode. When in Study mode, you can further choose the book chapters, limiting the questions to those explained in the specified chapters of the book.

Summary

The tools and suggestions listed in this chapter have been designed with one goal in mind: to help you develop the skills required to pass the 642-637 SECURE exam. This book has been developed from the beginning to not just teach the technologies but also to understand the reason for their specific uses and the configuration steps to be taken when implementing them. Regardless of your experience level leading up to taking the exams, it is our hope that the broad range of preparation tools, and even the structure of the books, will help you pass the exams with ease. We hope you do well on the exam.

Answers to Chapter DIKTA Quizzes and Fill in the Blanks Questions

Chapter 1 "Do I Know This Already?" Quiz Answers

1. B
2. A, C, and D
3. D
4. A and D
5. A, B, and E
6. A, C, and E
7. A, D, and E
8. B
9. A, C, and D
10. E

Chapter 1 Fill in the Blanks Answers

1. The integrity security aspect protects network data from being altered in transit.
2. The Security Control Framework (SCF) ensures network and service availability.
3. The SCF model defines the harden, isolate, and enforce actions to obtain complete control.
4. To provide total visibility, the SCF defines the identify, monitor, and correlate actions.
5. The Network Time Protocol (NTP) is typically used with the correlation SCF action.
6. The design blueprints have been designed around various PINs in a network; PIN stands for Places in the Network.
7. The SAFE design principle Regulatory Compliance and Industry Standards was developed to make sure that designs were easily capable of meeting industry benchmarks.

8. The security focuses of service availability, DoS/DDoS protection, data confidentiality/integrity, and server protection are used most in the `intranet data center` design blueprint.

9. The part of the network that typically connects to end users which all exist within similar geographic areas is defined in the `Enterprise Campus` design blueprint.

10. The management design blueprint is defined to increase security through the use of the `Network Access Control, data confidentiality,` and `integrity` security focuses.

Chapter 2 "Do I Know This Already?" Quiz Answers

1. A

2. A, C, and D

3. B and E

4. A, B, and E

5. E

6. B

7. A, C, and D

8. A, C, and E

Chapter 2 Fill in the Blanks Answers

1. Politics within an organization can cause a lack of `consistency` within the security policies.

2. A good disaster recovery plan must included contingencies for both `physical` and `virtual` security breaches.

3. Unauthorized network access is made easier when `poorly designed access controls` are implemented on the network.

4. `Phreakers` are individuals who have extensive knowledge of telephone networks and switching equipment.

5. Hackers with malicious intend are referred to as `black hats`.

6. `Vertical` scans scan the service ports of a single host and request different services at each port.

7. The most effective way to protect your sensitive data is to save it in an `encrypted` format or to send it through an `encrypted` connection.

8. The five core reasons for intruding on a system or network are `curiosity, fun and pride, revenge, profit,` and `political` purposes.

Chapter 3 "Do I Know This Already?" Quiz Answers

1. C

2. A

3. C

4. A, B, and D

5. C and D

6. A, B, and D

7. A

8. D

9. C

10. D

Chapter 3 Fill in the Blanks Answers

1. Cisco Integrated Services Routers (ISR) differ from the Catalyst switches in that the security features are handled by the `main CPU` in the router as opposed to specialized ASICs.

2. The Cisco Configuration Professional (CPP) is a graphical user interface (GUI) device management application for `Cisco Integrated Services Routers`.

3. `Cisco Security Manager` is an application from Cisco that can be used to deploy and manage security features on Cisco devices.

4. `Authentication` is the process of determining that a user is who he says he is.

5. Ensuring that a user can only execute commands for which he has the proper privilege level is called `authorization`.

6. `Vertical` scans scan the service ports of a single host and request different services at each port.

7. `Cisco IPS Manager Express` is a free event-monitoring solution for Cisco IPS events, including the IPS functionality provided by Cisco IOS Software running on a Cisco ISR.

8. Availability of security features on the Cisco IOS Software Catalyst switch is very `platform` dependent.

Chapter 4 "Do I Know This Already?" Quiz Answers

1. B
2. A
3. D
4. C
5. B
6. A
7. A and B
8. B
9. C
10. D

Chapter 4 Fill in the Blanks Answers

1. The trunking mode on a switchport can be sensed using Dynamic Trunking Protocol (DTP).
2. The Content Addressable Memory (CAM) table in a switch stores information, such as MAC addresses, switchport, and associated VLAN parameters.
3. The default CAM aging timer on the Cisco Catalyst switch is 5 minutes.
4. STP prevents bridging loops in a redundant switched network environment.
5. A DHCP server dynamically assigns IP addresses to hosts on a network.
6. ARP also has another method of identifying host IP-to-MAC associations, which is called Gratuitous ARP (GARP).
7. The switchport mode that actively attempts to make a switchport a trunk is dynamic desirable.
8. The sticky secure switchport security classification includes dynamically learned addresses that are automatically added to the running configuration.
9. The DHCP snooping binding table includes the client MAC address, IP address, lease time, binding type, VLAN number, and interface information.
10. The three different private VLAN classifications include promiscuous, community, and isolated.

Chapter 5 "Do I Know This Already?" Quiz Answers

1. C
2. A, C, and D
3. A, C, and F
4. A, B, and E
5. B, C, and E
6. A, C, and E
7. C
8. A
9. B
10. A, C, and D

Chapter 5 Fill in the Blanks Answers

1. The `Low-Impact` deployment mode reduces known issues with other protocols' time-outs and networked services.
2. The `MAC Authentication Bypass (MAB)` feature provides the ability for a host without 802.1x support to gain full network access.
3. The `Restricted VLAN` feature provides the ability for a host to gain some network access even after failing authentication.
4. When implementing 802.1x, the `authentication server` is the entity that validates the identity of the requesting host.
5. The `PAP` and `CHAP` protocols are not supported by 802.1x natively without external tunneling support.
6. In a LAN environment, the `EAPOL` protocol is used to transport EAP traffic.
7. When the supplicant initiates the 802.1x connection, it sends an `EAPOL-Start` frame to start the connection.
8. When using EAP-MD5, a `hash` is sent in lieu of a password on the network.
9. The `Protected Access Credential (PAC)` is relied on by EAP-FAST to help establish tunneling.
10. When using EAPOL, the PAE group address is always set to `01:80:C2:00:00:03`.

Chapter 6 "Do I Know This Already?" Quiz Answers

1. A, B, and C

2. C

3. A

4. B

5. D

6. B

7. A

8. D

9. C

10. C

Chapter 6 Fill in the Blanks Answers

1. `802.1X` is an IEEE standard that provides a framework for authenticating and authorizing network devices connected to LAN ports and for preventing access in the event that the authentication fails.

2. Configuring `reauthentication` will cause a period verification to take place, thus ensuring that the client is still connected and the port should remain in the authenticated state.

3. Enable 802.1X globally on the switch with the **dot1x system-auth-control** global command.

4. Verify the operational status of the 802.1X configuration on your device by using the **show dot1x** command.

5. `Network Access Restrictions (NAR)` can be used to restrict 802.1X users to only access the network from a certain network address space.

6. The Cisco IOS Software **dot1x test eapol-capable** command can be used to verify that the 802.1X authentication is functioning properly.

Chapter 7 "Do I Know This Already?" Quiz Answers

1. A and C

2. C

3. E

4. B and D

5. B

6. A and C

7. C

8. A and C

9. A, B, and C

Chapter 7 Fill in the Blanks Answers

1. The `machine` and `user` do not both authenticate to the network at the same time. `Machine` authentication is only needed when the user logs off.

2. With the **`enable fast reconnect`** optional EAP-TLS parameter, the TLS session keys are essentially cached, thus allowing faster reauthentication by not having to perform a full TLS handshake.

3. The **`authentication priority`** command can be used to choose a preferred authentication method over another.

4. When the user sends an `HTTP` request to the web server, the switch intercepts the user's HTTP session request and presents the user with a pop-up dialog box that has a username and password field.

5. Beginning with `Release 12.2(33) SXI` of Cisco IOS Software, the **dot1x host-mode** command was replaced with the **`authentication host-mode`** command.

6. When configuring fail-open policies, label an interface as critical by using the **`authentication event server dead action authorize vlan`** interface configuration command.

7. To handle Wake-on-LAN devices in an 802.1X environment, configure the interface as `unidirectionally controlled` by using the **`authentication control-direction in`** interface command.

8. Use the `multidomain authentication` with `MAB` to authenticate non-802.1X IP phones based on their MAC addresses.

Chapter 8 "Do I Know This Already?" Quiz Answers

1. B and D

2. C and D

3. C

4. A and D

5. B

6. A and B

7. C and D

8. A and D

9. C and D

10. B

Chapter 8 Fill in the Blanks Answers

1. There is a(n) `implicit` deny at the end of each access list.

2. An extended access list can use the number ranges of `100-199` and `2000-2699`.

3. The wildcard mask that would be used with a subnet mask of 255.255.255.192 would be `0.0.0.63`.

4. When assigning reflexive access lists to an interface, they are typically placed `outbound` on an interface facing away from the internal network or `inbound` on an interface facing toward the internal network.

5. Both PHDF and TCDF are formatted using `XML`.

6. When using FPM, traffic can be classified using `TCDF` files or using the `CLI`.

7. FPM is only able to inspect `IPv4` unicast packets.

8. `Key` fields are used by NetFlow to identify specific flows.

9. Unicast RPF can operate in `strict` or `loose` mode.

10. When configuring Unicast RPF, the first thing that must be configured is `CEF`.

Chapter 9 "Do I Know This Already?" Quiz Answers

1. A

2. C and D

3. B

4. A and D

5. B and C

6. B

7. A and B

8. D

9. C

10. B

Chapter 9 Fill in the Blanks Answers

1. The control plane includes the group of processes that are run at the `process` level and control most high-level control IOS functions.

2. The `central switch engine` is responsible for the high-speed routing of packets that typically come from nondistributed interfaces.

3. `Distributed` control plane services are considered first, and then the conditioned traffic is passed through to `aggregated` control plane services.

4. Output control plane services are applied after the packet exits the control plane and are only available with `aggregate` control plane services.

5. `Control Plane Policing` allows the control plane to be considered like a separate entity with its own input and output interface.

6. With Control Plane Protection, the control plane interface is split into four pieces, an aggregate and `three subinterfaces`.

7. The `control plane host subinterface` receives all control plane IP traffic that is directed at one of the device's interfaces.

8. The `queue-thresholding` feature enhances Control Plane Protection by providing a mechanism for limiting the number of matched protocol packets allowed at the process level.

9. `MD5` works by creating a one-way hash out of a shared secret and sending this hash between source and destination.

10. A `key chain` is essentially an electronic repository of keys and their respective shared secret and validity schedules.

Chapter 10 "Do I Know This Already?" Quiz Answers

1. B
2. A
3. C
4. D
5. B
6. B
7. A and D
8. C and D
9. A and C
10. A and D

Chapter 10 Fill in the Blanks Answers

1. The highest available configuration mode is `global configuration mode`, which is used to configure feature options for the entire device.

2. When using the **enable secret** command, the password is secured using the MD5 algorithm.

3. Role-based CLI access provides the ability to set up as many as 15 CLI views, which are configured to run commands that are configured for different job functions.

4. The configuration of SSH without the use of labels requires that the `host name` and `domain name` be configured first.

5. The `Management Information Base (MIB)` is a virtual information storage location that contains collections of managed objects.

6. The `version 1` and `version 2` versions of SNMP utilize community name-based security.

7. The `authPriv` SNMP security model supports both authentication and encryption.

8. MPP gives you the ability to limit the source of management traffic to a specific interface on a device.

9. Cisco recommends that the `AutoSecure` feature not be used in production environments.

10. A `rising` threshold is triggered when the CPU utilization exceeds a configured threshold.

Chapter 11 "Do I Know This Already?" Quiz Answers

1. A and C
2. A and C
3. D
4. B
5. A
6. D
7. C
8. B
9. A

Chapter 11 Fill in the Blanks Answers

1. A typical NAT implementation includes a single `internal` stub host that requires translation to an `external` network.

2. There are three different types of NAT that can be configured: `static`, `dynamic`, and `overloaded`.

3. `Overloaded NAT (PAT)` has a many-to-one relationship with traffic conversations being differentiated by port number.

4. The configuration of `static NAT` requires a local address that will be translated and an external address that will be used in place of this local address on the external network.

5. With dynamic NAT, the source address(es) is/are identified through the use of a `standard IP ACL`.

6. By default, the translation entry timeout is `24 hours` with dynamic NAT.

7. In a typical NAT configuration, the internal network hosts see the external host address `unaltered`.

Chapter 12 "Do I Know This Already?" Quiz Answers

1. A and C

2. D

3. A

4. C

5. D

6. A and C

7. A and C

8. B

9. A and D

10. C

Chapter 12 Fill in the Blanks Answers

1. A firewall is used to enforce an access policy between `security domains`.

2. In IOS versions before 15.0.1M, intrazone traffic was `permitted` by default.

3. Traffic policy is applied `unidirectionally` between zones using zone pairs.

4. Zone pairs can be set up to protect the control and management planes by using the `system-defined self zone`.

5. The PAM feature is used to map `nonstandard ports` onto `common services`.

6. With Layer 3/4 traffic, the class map type is always the `inspect type`.

7. When using the inspect type policy map, the creation of a parameter map is `optional`.

8. If no zone pair is defined, traffic will `not flow` between zones.

9. The URL filter feature provides the ability to `pass`, `drop`, or `log` the traffic whose URL matches the configured characteristics.

Chapter 13 "Do I Know This Already?" Quiz Answers

1. C
2. C
3. D
4. C
5. B
6. A
7. A
8. A

Chapter 13 Fill in the Blanks Answers

1. When a signature is matched, the Cisco IOS IPS sensors can send an alarm, drop the packet, or reset the connection.

2. A disabled signature is present in router memory and can be enabled without recompiling the signature database.

3. SDEE uses a pull mechanism to pull alerts from IPS sensors over a/an HTTPS connection.

4. The signature update license is configured on the router using the **license install** command.

5. When Cisco SDEE notification is enabled, by default, 200 events can be stored in the local event store. This number can be increased to hold a maximum of 1000.

6. The `show ip sdee alerts` command can be used to view the events that are written to the local SDEE event store.

7. The `show ip ips interfaces` command will display all interfaces on which IPS is enabled.

8. The Cisco IOS IPS router can send IPS alerts through `syslog` and can have the `SDEE notification` feature enabled at the same time.

Chapter 14 "Do I Know This Already?" Quiz Answers

1. C
2. C
3. E
4. A
5. D
6. C
7. A
8. D
9. C
10. C

Chapter 14 Fill in the Blanks Answers

1. Use individual P2P VPN peering only when the number of VPN connections is `very low`.

2. When using any-to-any communications with direct communication paths with low latency and high throughput, a `fully meshed` topology is typically the only choice.

3. A VPN technology that starts with a hub-and-spoke topology but allows dynamically and automatically built VPNs between spoke sites is `DMVPN`.

4. Cisco GET VPN is considered to be a `nontunneled` encapsulation mode and therefore cannot be used on transport networks that cannot route internal VPN addresses.

5. `Internet Key Exchange (IKE)` provides a framework that provides policy negotiations and key management processes.

6. `IPsec` is a set of security protocols that work together to provide security to IP traffic while in transit.

7. `ESP encapsulation` provides a mixture of security services for IPv4 and IPv6, such as confidentiality, authenticity, and integrity of IP data.

8. A VPN technology that supports `tunneling` must be chosen if the transport network does not route internal VPN address spaces.

Chapter 15 "Do I Know This Already?" Quiz Answers

1. C

2. C

3. E?

4. A

5. D

6. C

7. S

8. D

Chapter 15 Fill in the Blanks Answers

1. One major benefit of using IPsec VTIs is that it is no longer required to apply a `crypto map` to a physical interface.

2. VTIs support native IPsec tunneling, including `interoperability` with standards-based IPsec implementations of other vendors.

3. IPsec VTIs support `multicast traffic` such as voice and video.

4. IPsec `transform sets` define the encapsulation (ESP or AH), the packet authentication/integrity algorithm (SHA-1 or MD5), and the IPsec mode (transport or tunnel) that is used with a VPN policy.

5. Many of the `common` interface options that can be applied to physical interfaces can be applied to the IPsec virtual tunnel interface.

6. Cisco IOS Software IPsec `stateful failover` is not supported on VTIs.

7. In a VTI-based IPsec VPN, IPsec requests SA establishment as soon as the Virtual tunnel interface (VTI)s are `fully configured`.

8. Unnumbered IP addressing is mandatory with DVTI tunnels.

Chapter 16 "Do I Know This Already?" Quiz Answers

1. C
2. C
3. C
4. C
5. A
6. A and D
7. A
8. C and D
9. C

Chapter 16 Fill in the Blanks Answers

1. `Trusted introducing` is where existing point-to-point key exchanges can be tied together to soften the public key distribution problem.
2. When enrolling to a PKI, clients submit their `public key` and `name` to the CA.
3. When deploying PKI-enabled VPNs, one of the major choices is whether to use a `VPN-only` PKI or an `enterprise` PKI.
4. `Encapsulating Security Payload (ESP)` provides data integrity, data origin authentication, protection against replay, and confidentiality to user traffic.
5. Digital signatures are commonly used by many authentication protocols for traffic running over `untrusted or public` networks.
6. To participate in the PKI system, all end users must `enroll` with the CA, which involves a process in which they submit their public key and their name to the CA.
7. An `identity certificate` is a piece of information that binds a PKI member's name to its public key and puts it into a standard format.
8. The Cisco IOS Software Certificate Server stores its database on the local `flash` memory of the router.

Chapter 17 "Do I Know This Already?" Quiz Answers

1. C
2. C
3. E
4. A

5. D

6. C

7. A

8. C

9. A

10. A

Chapter 17 Fill in the Blanks Answers

1. A `DMVPN` cloud is a collection of routers that are configured with either an mGRE interface or a point-to-point GRE interface (or a combination of the two) and that share the same subnet.

2. The `subnet size` created on the mGRE interface on the hub must be large enough to accommodate all the spoke routers' GRE interfaces.

3. The NHRP network ID must be the same on the NHRP `server` and its NHRP `clients`.

4. The Cisco DMVPN solution integrates NHRP, `GRE`, and `IPsec`.

5. DMVPN greatly simplifies the configuration requirements on the `hub` router.

6. NHRP on the hub provides DMVPN spokes with the ability to locate other `spoke` routers.

7. `Dynamic routing` populates each spoke's routing table so that each spoke knows about the subnets behind the other spokes.

8. In a hub-and-spoke deployment, all traffic between spokes must flow through the `hub router`.

Chapter 18 "Do I Know This Already?" Quiz Answers

1. C

2. C

3. E

4. A

5. D

6. C

7. A

8. C

Chapter 18 Fill in the Blanks Answers

1. In the case of redundant DMVPNs with multiple GRE tunnels establishing between the same spokes, it is necessary to use `shared IPsec SAs` for IPsec SAs to establish properly.

2. The routing protocol detects both device and path failures using its `keepalives`.

3. You should design the VPN to meet an organization's requirements for availability. The design should provide a level of high availability that is commensurate with the `cost` of meeting availability needs.

4. If `complete redundant paths` are needed, you should either deploy a completely redundant network path that is under the control of local administration or use multiple-transport networks (two ISPs) and connect them to either redundant interfaces or redundant VPN devices.

5. `Dynamic routing protocols` will *automatically detect peer failures and path failures* and then *automatically reroute* around the failure if redundant paths and devices are in place.

6. In a VTI-based IPsec VPN topology, an interior routing protocol will see the VTI-based VPN tunnel as a `point-to-point` link.

7. An interior routing protocol will view a `DMVPN` as either point-to-multipoint (for strict hub-and-spoke DMVPNs) or as a broadcast network (partial or full mesh DMVPNs).

8. To provide redundancy for a DMVPN topology, it is recommended to create two separate DMVPN networks by using `two hub routers` and one or two spoke routers at remote sites.

9. Routing protocols can detect both `path failures` and `VPN device failures`.

Chapter 19 "Do I Know This Already?" Quiz Answers

1. A and C
2. C and D
3. D
4. A
5. A and D
6. C
7. A
8. C

Chapter 19 Fill in the Blanks Answers

1. Reducing IKE lifetimes on group members is recommended to reduce the load on the key server.

2. If the key server fails to get a response to a rekey message from the group member after three rekeys, it removes the group member.

3. By distributing group members across multiple key servers and controlling the order of the key servers in the configurations, some load balancing can be achieved.

4. The IPsec profile defines the encapsulation and cryptographic settings that will be distributed to the group members by the key server as part of the SA.

5. GET VPNs use IKE GDOI as the group keying mechanism.

6. GET VPNs provide connectionless, tunnel-free encryption that leverages the existing routing infrastructure.

7. GET VPNs are based on GDOI, which is defined in RFC 3547.

8. GDOI is a standards-based ISAKMP group key management protocol meant to provide secure communication within a group.

Chapter 20 "Do I Know This Already?" Quiz Answers

1. A
2. C
3. D
4. A
5. A and B
6. C
7. A
8. C
9. C
10. C
11. C
12. C
13. C

Chapter 20 Fill in the Blanks Answers

1. The ISR will use the identity certificate to `identify` itself to remote clients.

2. `Split tunneling` can increase the risk to remote clients and internal resources because the clients can potentially act as a relay between untrusted and trusted networks.

3. When terminating a clientless VPN, the ISR acts as a `proxy` to provide access to internal resources to remote users.

4. `Full tunneling` VPNs require VPN client software to be installed on the remote computer or dedicated VPN devices (hardware clients) to enable full routed IP access to internal resources.

5. `Clientless` VPNs are easier to deploy than a full tunneling remote access VPN, but they typically provide limited access to resources when compared to the full tunnel.

6. Clientless deployments require that the user open a web browser, which acts as the VPN client, and the VPN gateway acts as a `proxy` device to the internal resources.

7. The recommended algorithms for IKE session encryption are `AES-128` and `3DES`.

8. The recommended hash algorithm to provide message authentication and integrity is `SHA-1 HMAC`.

9. The recommended algorithms for encryption of user traffic are `AES-128` and `3DES`.

10. `Port forwarding` requires administrative privileges because it changes the local host's file.

Chapter 21 "Do I Know This Already?" Quiz Answers

1. C
2. A and C
3. D
4. A
5. D
6. C
7. A
8. A, B, and C
9. A
10. A and B

Chapter 21 Fill in the Blanks Answers

1. Hosts behind the remote VPN router are not reachable for a session initiated from the central site in `client` mode.

2. The Easy VPN client can be the Cisco VPN client or an Easy VPN Remote hardware device such as the `Cisco ISR`.

3. The Cisco Easy VPN Server can `terminate` IPsec tunnels that are initiated by remote users running VPN client software on their systems.

4. As the Cisco Easy VPN Remote initiates a VPN tunnel, the Cisco Easy VPN `Server` pushes the IP Security (IPsec) policies to the Cisco Easy VPN Remote client and creates the corresponding VPN tunnel connection.

5. XAUTH takes place `after` IKE phase 1 completes and `before` the IKE phase 2 (IPsec SA) negotiations begin.

6. Group passwords are very vulnerable to compromise simply because of their `shared` nature.

7. Configuring a basic Cisco ISR Easy VPN `Server` consists of basic gateway configuration, group authentication, client configuration, and user authentication configuration.

8. The Cisco ISR can be used as an Easy VPN Remote `hardware client`.

9. You can enhance authentication by using `certificates` on remote clients and the Easy VPN Server.

Over time, reader feedback allows Cisco Press to gauge which topics give our readers the most problems when taking the exams. To assist readers with those topics, authors can create new materials that clarify and expand upon those troublesome exam topics. As mentioned in the Introduction, this additional content about the exam will be posted as a PDF document on this book's companion website: www.ciscopress.com/title/9781587142802.

This appendix provides you with updated information if Cisco makes minor modifications to the exam upon which this book is based. When Cisco releases an entirely new exam, the changes are usually too extensive to provide in a simple updated appendix. In those cases, you need to consult the new edition of the book for the updated content.

This appendix attempts to fill the void that occurs with any print book. In particular, this appendix does the following:

- Mentions technical items that might not have been mentioned elsewhere in the book

- Covers new topics if Cisco adds new content to the exam over time

- Provides a way to get up-to-the-minute current information about content for the exam

CCNP Security 642-637 SECURE Exam Updates, Version 1.0

Always Get the Latest at the Companion Website

You are reading the version of this appendix that was available when your book was printed. However, given that the main purpose of this appendix is to be a living, changing document, it is important that you look for the latest version online at the book's companion website. To do so, follow these steps:

Step 1.   Browse to www.ciscopress.com/title/9781587142802.

Step 2.   Select the Updates option under the More Information box.

Step 3.   Download the latest "Appendix B" document.

Note: The downloaded document has a version number. Comparing the version of this print Appendix B (version 1.0) with the latest online version of this appendix, you should do the following:

- **Same version:** Ignore the PDF file that you downloaded from the companion website.

- **Website has a later version:** Ignore this Appendix B in your book and read only the latest version that you downloaded from the companion website.

If no appendix is posted on the book's website, that simply means that there have been no updates to post and that version 1.0 is still the latest version.

Technical Content

The current version of this appendix does not contain any additional technical coverage.

Index

Numerics

802.1x. See IEEE 802.1x

A

access attacks, 33-35

access mode (switchports), 68

accuracy of IPS sensors, 339-340

ACLs (access control lists), 187-196

  dynamic assignments, configuring, 159-165

  extended ACLs, 192

  management ACLs, 253-254

  reflexive ACLs, 193-194

  standard ACLs, 189-192

  time-based ACLs, 194-196

  verifying, 196

adjusting EAPOL timers, 119-120

advanced IEEE 802.1x deployment, planning, 143-144

applications, security weaknesses, 28

applying

  FPM traffic policies, 202

  traffic policy, 225-226

architecture, SCF, 12-13

ARP spoofing, 67

ASR (attack severity rating), 348

attacks

  access attacks, 33-35

  control plane

    mitigating, 43

    routing protocol spoofing, 222

    slow-path DoS attacks, 222

  data plane attacks, mitigating, 44

  DoS attacks, 35

  management plane, 248

    mitigating, 45

  motivations for, 29-31

  reconnaissance attacks, 31-33

  routed data plane

    slow-path DoS attacks, 186

    traffic flooding, 187

  routed data plane, IP spoofing, 186

  switched data plane attacks, 60-67

    ARP spoofing, 67

    CAM flooding attacks, 61-63

    DHCP starvation attacks, 66

    IP spoofing, 67

    MAC address spoofing, 63

    STP spoofing attacks, 63-65

    VLAN hopping attacks, 60-61

authentication

  guest authentication, configuring IEEE 802.1x, 119-120

  IBNS, 94-96

    IEEE 802.1x enhancements, 94-96

J-K

L

Q-R

T

technology weaknesses as network security vulnerability, 27-28

threats to network security, 29

time-based ACLs, 194-196

timers

EAPOL, adjusting, 119-120

PAT, configuring, 286-287

traffic class, defining, 197-200

traffic exchange, GET VPNs, 504

traffic flooding, 187

traffic policies, defining, 200-202, 224-225

transform sets, 398

transparent firewall support (ZBPFW), 300

Trojan horses, 35

troubleshooting

Cisco DMVPN, 474-475

Cisco EZVPN, 587

Cisco IOS IPS sensors, 363-365

Cisco IOS Software Certificate Server, 429

IEEE 802.1x, 134-135

IKE peering, 397-398

NHRP, 463-464

SSL VPNs, 563-564

static point-to-point VTI tunnels, 402

trunk mode (switchports), 68

tuning Cisco IOS IPS signatures, 347-353

TVR (Target Value Rating), 348-349

U

Unicast RPF, 209-211

unresponsive supplicants, troubleshooting, 135

unstructured threats, 29

updating signatures, 355-358

usage, Cisco SAFE, 15-16

user EXEC mode, 248

V

verifying

ACLs, 196

Cisco IOS IPS signature policies, 346-347

Cisco IOS Software Certificate Server, 421-426

dynamic VLAN/ACL assignments, 164-165

Flexible NetFlow, 209

FPM, 203

IEEE 802.1x functionality, 121, 134-135

IKE policies, 396

static point-to-point VTI tunnels, 401

Unicast RPF, 211

web authentication, 172

views, configuring, 252

viruses, 34

VLAN hopping attacks, 60-61

mitigating, 70-71

VLANs, dynamic assignments

configuring, 159-165

verifying, 164-165

W

X-Y-Z

CISCO

ciscopress.com: Your Cisco Certification and Networking Learning Resource

Subscribe to the monthly Cisco Press newsletter to be the first to learn about new releases and special promotions.

Visit **ciscopress.com/newsletters**.

While you are visiting, check out the offerings available at your finger tips.

– Free Podcasts from experts:
- • OnNetworking
- • OnCertification
- • OnSecurity

Podcasts

View them at **ciscopress.com/podcasts**.

– Read the latest author **articles** and **sample chapters** at ciscopress.com/articles.

– Bookmark the Certification Reference Guide available through our partner site at **informit.com/certguide**.

Connect with Cisco Press authors and editors via Facebook and Twitter, visit **informit.com/socialconnect**.

FREE Online Edition

Your purchase of **CCNP Security Secure 642-637 Official Cert Guide** includes access to a free online edition for 45 days through the Safari Books Online subscription service. Nearly every Cisco Press book is available online through Safari Books Online, along with more than 5,000 other technical books and videos from publishers such as Addison-Wesley Professional, Exam Cram, IBM Press, O'Reilly, Prentice Hall, Que, and Sams.

SAFARI BOOKS ONLINE allows you to search for a specific answer, cut and paste code, download chapters, and stay current with emerging technologies.

Activate your FREE Online Edition at www.informit.com/safarifree

> **STEP 1:** Enter the coupon code: CSPQFDB.

> **STEP 2:** New Safari users, complete the brief registration form.
> Safari subscribers, just log in.

If you have difficulty registering on Safari or accessing the online edition, please e-mail customer-service@safaribooksonline.com